THE CORRESPONDENCE OF

Alexander Pope

ALEXANDER POPE
From the drawing by William Hoare

THE

CORRESPONDENCE

OF

Alexander Pope

EDITED BY

GEORGE SHERBURN

VOLUME IV

1736–1744

OXFORD

AT THE CLARENDON PRESS

1956

Oxford University Press, Amen House, London E.C.4
GLASGOW NEW YORK TORONTO MELBOURNE WELLINGTON
BOMBAY CALCUTTA MADRAS KARACHI CAPE TOWN IBADAN

PRINTED IN GREAT BRITAIN

CONTENTS

VOLUME IV

PORTRAIT OF ALEXANDER POPE DRAWN BY WILLIAM HOARE — *Frontispiece*

LETTERS 1736–1744 — *p.* 1

POSTSCRIPT — 525

1736

This year was unusually peaceful. Apart from two journeys to Bevis Mount (Lady Peterborow) and another presumably brief unidentified journey, Pope oscillated quietly between London and Twickenham. What he was chiefly working on would seem to be the preparation of the 'authentic' edition of his *Letters*. The texts for this volume were very likely established early in the year, but Pope was desirous—though not too hopeful—of raising a subscription for the volume that would enable him to avoid excessive indebtedness to his new admirer and 'angel', Ralph Allen. His endeavours to persuade Swift to return his letters were from this time more energetic, partly due, no doubt, to Lord Orrery's alarmist accounts of Swift's failing health together with Swift's equally melancholy reports on his condition. Except for the amusing epistle from *Bounce to Fop*, printed as 'by Dr. S—t', Pope published no new poems this year. While at Southampton he worked on another imitation of Horace—doubtless that addressed to 'Augustus'.

Of the 49 letters printed here for 1736 no less than 19 are new to collections of Pope's letters.

*POPE *to* THE COUNTESS OF BURLINGTON[1]

Chatsworth

Madam,—This Paper is not even, & this Ink is not good, yet I venture both to tell your Ladiship how much I am obliged to you. and to desire a most material Insertion may be made in your Copy, which came into my head in your Coach, (which, by moonlight, is very Inspiring)

after the words.—I was eased of the greatest pain that ever such an Offender could give me.

be pleasd to add these.

Nor was I displeased, when I saw nothing worse was added, at the circumstance of finding that the most abusive of all mortals was become in some measure, (contrary to his intention) the Instrument of

[1] This letter must postdate the middle of July 1735 when (on the 14th) Curll published in his second volume of *Mr. Pope's Literary Correspondence* the 'Initial Anecdotes of the Life and Family' of the poet, here mentioned. At this time Pope announced (*The London Gazette*, 15 July) that Curll's publication compelled him to prepare an authentic edition of his letters. This was certainly undertaken first in an octavo format, and under the influence of Ralph Allen promoted to quarto and folio status. The 'Booksellers' in this octavo edition (1737 a) indicate that in its original form Pope's Preface was couched in the first person, and the passage here sent to Lady Burlington (as amanuensis) is designed for insertion in a first-personal form of the Preface. That places the letter in 1735 or 1736, but where in that period it is impossible to say. The letter stops abruptly, and is probably incomplete.

my Justification, and had published, in these Letters, enough to obviate the Scurrilities he himself was preparing.

However, I could not escape the Tail of the Shower, which fell upon me in Anecdotes of my Life & Family. &c.

Address: To the Rt Hon. the Lady Burlington.
Endorsement: Mr. Pope. [in Lady Burlington's hand]

*POPE *to* FORTESCUE [*January* 1735/6]

Harvard University

Knowing your constant kind desire to know my state of health, I send to acquaint you of it. I am much better tho not yet so well as to go out, & therfore wish to see you once more at Mr Cheselden's to day or to morrow. I am very sollicitous & impatient to be assured of what I hope for so much as the Promotion that's spoken of for you.[1] No man living would be gladder to have it confirmed, as soon as you can tell it me. | Dear Sir | Ever yours | faithfully. | A. Pope.

Address: To | Wm Fortescue Esq. | in Bellyard
Endorsement: Mr. Pope. | Jan. 1735/6.

POPE *to* BROOME 12 *January* [1735/6]

Elwin–Courthope, viii. 181

Jan. 12, [1736].

You may wonder at my long omission to answer yours, though indeed I am grown a very unpunctual correspondent to all my friends, and have wholly desisted from corresponding in general but upon absolute necessity, after so severe an experiment, how much more dangerous it is to me than to any other honest man to tell his private thoughts to his friends. I could not propose to Lintot what you desired all this while, he having been in the country and ill of an asthma, but I will in a short time.[2] Though I have had no correspondence or conference with him these ten years, yet, in your cause, I will try; but I fear I can have no influence with him. I may truly say I approve greatly your verses on Death, and doubt not I shall do the same of your other corrections.

I had also a mind not to write to you till I could perform my promise of altering the line in the Dunciad.[3] I have prevailed with much

[1] The newspapers were suggesting various 'places' for Fortescue at this time. Early in February he was made one of the Barons of the Exchequer.

[2] Pope, answering Broome's letter of 1 Dec., has not yet been able to see Lintot about reprinting Broome's poems.

[3] The cancelled leaf omitted all mention of Broome in the text of, and note to, Bk. III, l. 328 (of earlier editions). The cancel first appears in the edition called by Sutherland 1736 a and by Griffith 405. The indication that the edition ran to 1,000 books is interesting.

ado to cancel an impression of a thousand leaves to insert that alteration, which I have seen done, and I will in a week send you the small edition of my works, where you will find it done, by your carrier, when I find the direction whither to direct the books, which I have mislaid. In the meantime, I enclose the leaf. You will observe I have omitted the note as well as the verse, and again told them I translated but half the Odyssey.

Pray, if you find any letters of mine, send them. The sooner I had them the better for the design I mentioned to you.[1] In a word, dear Broome, be assured I love you; and having overleaped the vacancy of our friendship, am as truly as ever yours.

†SWIFT *to* POPE *7 February* 1735/6

1740

Feb. 7, 1735–6.

It is some time since I dined at the bishop of Derry's, where Mr. Secretary Cary[2] told me with great concern, that you were taken very ill. I have heard nothing since, only I have continued in great pain of mind, yet for my own sake and the world's more than for yours; because I well know how little you value life both as a Philosopher and a Christian, particularly the latter, wherein hardly one in a million of us hereticks can equal you. If you are well recovered, you ought to be reproached for not putting me especially out of pain, who could not bear the loss of you; although we must be for ever distant as much as if I were in the grave, for which my years and continual indisposition are preparing me every season. I have staid too long from pressing you to give me some ease by an account of your health; pray do not use me so ill any more. I look upon you as an estate from which I receive my best annual rents, although I am never to see it. Mr. Tickel[3] was at the same meeting under the same real concern; and so were a hundred others of this town who had never seen you.

I read to the Bishop of Derry the paragraph in your letter which concerned him, and his Lordship exprest his thankfulness in a manner that became him. He is esteemed here as a person of learning and conversation and humanity, but he is beloved by all people⌜: He is a most excessive Whig, but without any appearing rancor; and his Idol is K. William; besides, 3000 *l.* a year is an invincible sweetner⌝.[4]

[1] The design must be that of an authorized edition of the correspondence. Broome seems to have returned no letters. See Pope to Broome, 18 Nov. 1735.

[2] Walter Carey, Esq., secretary to the Duke of Dorset (the Lord-Lieutenant). Carey is supposed to have been the 'Umbra' satirized by Pope in the poem of that name (*Miscellanies*, i (1727). The Bishop of Derry was Dr. Rundle.

[3] Tickell, the translator of *Iliad* i (1715), had long been reconciled to Pope.

[4] This passage in half-brackets appears only in 1740 and 1741 Dab.

I have no body now left but you: Pray be so kind to out-live me, and then die as soon as you please, but without pain, and let us meet in a better place, if my Religion will permit, but rather my Virtue, although much unequal to yours. Pray let my Lord Bathurst know how much I love him; I still insist on his remembring me, although he is too much in the world to honour an absent friend with his letters. My state of health is not to boast of; my giddiness is more or less too constant: ⌜I have not an ounce of flesh between the skin and bone; yet I walk often four or five miles, and ride ten or a dozen. But⌝[1] I sleep ill, and have a poor appetite. I can as easily write a poem in the Chinese-language as my own. I am as fit for Matrimony as invention; and yet I have daily schemes for innumerable Essays in prose, and proceed sometimes to no less than half a dozen lines, which the next morning become wast paper. What vexes me most is, that my female friends who could bear me very well a dozen years ago, have now forsaken me, although I am not so old in proportion to them, as I formerly was: which I can prove by Arithmetick, for then I was double their age, which now I am not. Pray put me out of fear as soon as you can, about that ugly report of your illness: and let me know who this Cheselden is, that hath so lately sprung up in your favour? Give me also some account of your neighbour[2] who writ to me from the Bath. I hear he resolves to be strenuous for taking off the Test; which grieves me extremely, from all the unprejudiced Reasons I ever was able to form, and against the Maxims of all wise christian governments, which always had some establish'd Religion, leaving at best a toleration to others.

Farewel my dearest friend! ever, and upon every account that can create friendship and esteem.

POPE *to* BROOME — 25 *March* 1736

Elwin–Courthope, viii. 182

Twitenham, March 25, 1736.

I have been a good while a little surprised, and somewhat in pain, at not having heard from you, after I had sent you what I thought you could not but take kindly, a sacrifice of that leaf in a whole edition of the Dunciad, which alone you could be displeased with. I had discharged at the same time your commission to Lintot, but you know, I suppose, he died the next week after he came to town.[3] I had also expressed my desire to you to enter some fresh memorial of the revival of our old friendship in inserting a letter or two into my collection out

[1] This passage in half-brackets appears only in 1740 and 1741 Dab.

[2] The Dublin editions (1741 Dab) identify the neighbour as Bolingbroke, but it is more likely to be William Pulteney, who is elsewhere spoken of as Pope's neighbour and who had written Swift from Bath, 22 Nov. 1735. See Ball, v. 279.

[3] Lintot died 3 Feb. 1736.

of those which you may have chanced to keep of mine, and which you told me you would send up to that end. I hope you received my two volumes octavo before the first[1] of which I caused your kind verses to me to be placed, with the rest of those I esteemed. I directed them all to Mr. Smith, as you ordered, by the carrier from the Saracen's Head, near two months ago. I chiefly fear you may be ill, for I truly wish you health and long life, and shall upon all occasions be glad to show you my disposition is friendly to all mankind, and sorry at any time, whether through mistakes or too tender resentments, or too warm passions—which are often nearer akin than undiscerning people imagine—to have wounded another. I beg to hear from you, and am sincerely yours.

†POPE *to* SWIFT 25 *March* 1736

1740

March 25, 1736.

If ever I write more Epistles in Verse, one of them shall be address'd to you. I have long concerted it, and begun it, but I would make what bears your name as finished as my last work ought to be, that is to say, more finished than any of the rest. The subject is large, and will divide into four Epistles, which naturally follow the Essay on Man,[2] *viz.* 1. Of the Extent and Limits of Human Reason, and Science, 2. A view of the useful and therefore attainable, and of the un-useful and therefore un-attainable, Arts. 3. Of the nature, ends, application, and the use of different Capacities. 4. Of the use of *Learning*, of the *Science* of the *World*, and of *Wit*. It will conclude with a Satire against the misapplication of all these, exemplify'd by pictures, characters, and examples.

But alas! the task is great, and *non sum qualis eram*! My understanding indeed, such as it is, is extended rather than diminish'd: I see things more in the whole, more consistent, and more clearly deduced from, and related to, each other. But what I gain on the side of philosophy, I lose on the side of poetry: the flowers are gone, when the fruits begin to ripen, and the fruits perhaps will never ripen perfectly. The climate (under our Heaven of a Court) is but cold and uncertain: the winds rise, and the winter comes on. I find myself but little disposed to build a new house; I have nothing left but to gather up the reliques of a wreck, and look about me to see what friends I have![3] Pray whose esteem or admiration should I desire now to procure

[1] The octavo *Works* (i and ii) were published by Lintot in January.

[2] On this project, never realized, see Spence, p. 315, and *Essays . . . presented to David Nichol Smith* (1945), pp. 57–58.

[3] The clandestine text of 1740 is here corrupt: it reads 'how friends I have'. Swift edited this (1741 Dab) to read 'what friends I have'; and the London texts of 1741 and 1742 read 'how few friends I have left.'

by my writings? whose friendship or conversation to obtain by 'em? I am a man of desperate fortunes, that is a man whose friends are dead: for I never aimed at any other fortune than in friends. As soon as I had sent my last letter, I received a most kind one from you, expressing great pain for my late illness at Mr. Cheselden's. I conclude you was eased of that friendly apprehension in a few days after you had dispatch'd yours, for mine must have reached you then. I wondered a little at your quære, who Cheselden was? it shews that the truest merit does not travel so far any way as on the wings of poetry; he is the most noted, and most deserving man, in the whole profession of Chirurgery; and has sav'd the lives of thousands by his manner of cutting for the stone.—I am now well, or what I must call so.

I have lately seen some writings of Lord B's,[1] since he went to France.[2] Nothing can depress his Genius: Whatever befals him, he will still be the greatest man in the world, either in his own time, or with posterity.

Every man you know or care for here, enquires of you, and pays you the only devoir he can, that of drinking your health. ⌜Here are a race sprung up of young Patriots, who would animate you.⌝[3] I wish you had any motive to see this kingdom. I could keep you, for I am rich, that is, I have more than I want. I can afford you room for your self and two servants; I have indeed room enough, nothing but myself at home! the kind and hearty house-wife is dead! the agreeable and instructive neighbour is gone! yet my house is inlarg'd, and the gardens extend and flourish, as knowing nothing of the guests they have lost. I have more fruit-trees and kitchen-garden than you have any thought of; nay I have good Melons and Pine-apples of my own growth. I am as much a better Gardiner, as I'm a worse Poet, than when you saw me: But gardening is near a-kin to Philosophy, for Tully says *Agricultura proxima sapientiae.* For God's sake, why should not you, (that are a step higher than a Philosopher, a Divine, yet have too much grace and wit than to be a Bishop) e'en give all you have to the Poor of Ireland (for whom you have already done every thing else) so quit the place, and live and die with me? And let *Tales Animae Concordes* be our Motto and our Epitaph.

POPE *to* FORTESCUE — 26 *March* 1736

1817 (Warner, p. 53)

March 26, 1736.

Your very kind letter was not more kind than entertaining, in the agreeable description of Monmouth and its situation. And what you

[1] B's] Bolingbroke's *1741 Dab.*

[2] It is not clear just which of Bolingbroke's writings have been forwarded to Pope.

[3] The sentence is omitted in the London texts of 1741–2.

tell me of your own temper of mind, in the present discharge of your office,[1] I feel very livelily with and for you. It is a dreadful duty, yet a noble one; and the hero you thought so much of at Monmouth, had, or ought to have had, his glory overcast and saddened, with the same reflection: how many of his own species he sentenced to death, in every battle he gave. I am not so clear in his character, as in that of Edward the Third. There seems a little too much of a turn to vanity, and knight (king errantry, I would say,) in his motives of quarrel with the Dauphine of France. And it appears by some of the Monkish historians, that he was much a bigot, and persecuted hotly for religion. After all, your office of a judge is more conscientious, and tends much more directly to public welfare. You may certainly, with a better title than any conqueror, sleep heartily, provided it be not upon the bench. You guessed rightly, (I should now say rather, you judged rightly,) when you supposed this weather was too fine to be sacrificed in London, where the sun shines on little else than vanity; but I have paid for taking my pleasure in it too exorbitantly. The sun at this season, and in this climate, is not to be too much depended on. *Miseri quibus intentata nites!*[2] may be applied to the favours and smiles of the English planet, as properly as to those of an Italian lady.

The matter of my complaint is, that it has given me a rheumatism in one arm to a violent degree, which lies useless and painful on one side of this paper, while the other is endeavouring to converse with you at this distance. God knows, if your family be across the water[3] just now, I shall not be able once to see them there. But it is not five days ago, that they were in London, at that filthy old place Bell-yard, which you know I want them and you to quit. I was to see them one of the only two days I have been in town this fortnight. Your too partial mention of the book of Letters, with all its faults and follies, which Curl printed and spared not, (nor yet will spare, for he has published a fourth sham volume yesterday,)[4] makes one think it may not be amiss to send you, what I know you will be much more pleased with than I can be, a proposal for a correct edition of them; which at last I find must be *offered*, since people have misunderstood an advertisement I printed some time ago, merely to put some stop to that rascal's books, as a promise that I would publish such a book. It is therefore *offered* in this manner; but I shall be just as well *satisfied*, (if the public will,) without performing the offer. I have nothing to add, but that Mrs. Blount, whose health you shew a kind regard to, is better, and

[1] In February Fortescue had been made a Baron of the Exchequer. As one of the presiding judges he held the Lent Assizes this year in Monmouth on 18 Mar., at which he must have written Pope a letter, not now known.

[2] Horace, *Carmina*, I. v. 12–13.

[3] At The Vineyard, Richmond.

[4] *Mr. Pope's Literary Correspondence*, vol. iv. This contained no new Pope letters, but offered new insults in its prefatory matter and its footnotes.

Lady S. well. May health attend you and quiet; and a good conscience will give you every other joy of life, how many rogues soever you sentence to death. 'Tis a hard task! but a harder to mankind, were they unpunished, and left in society. I pity you, and wish it may happen as seldom as possible. | Your's, sincerely, | A. Pope.

Address: To William Fortescue, Esq.

POPE *to* THE EARL OF ORRERY[1] 2 *April* [1736]

The Pierpont Morgan Library

Twit'nam, Apr. 2d.

My Lord,—*I write by the same Post that I receive your very obliging and humane Letter. The Consideration you show towards me, in the just appreciation that any News of the Dean's Condition might alarm me, is most kind and generous!* Yet allow me to joyn, even with that Tender Concern, my Sentiment of your own Illness, which I was so happy as not to have had any apprehension of. I heartily rejoice you are recover'd, and would fain owe the advancing Season the further blessing of perfecting that Recovery.

The very last post[2] *I writ to ~~the Dean~~ him a long Letter, little suspecting him in that dangerous Circumstance.* [The fear which has a good while been before my eyes, of any Ill use which may be made of My Letters, which he told me he had (too partially) kept by him, made me beg he would transmit them into Safe hands for me; I wish those hands, my Lord, were your own; in which I could trust any thing; even my Life: and (to be plain) I think few hands in Ireland safe. But][3] *I was so far from fearing his Health*, that I was proposing Schemes, and hoping Possibilities, for our Meeting once more in this World. I am weary of it; and shall have One reason more, and one of the strongest that Nature can give me (even when she is shaking my weak frame to pieces) ~~for~~ to be willing to leave this world, when Our dear Friend is on the Edge of the other. Yet I hope, I would fain hope, he may yet hover a while on the brink of it, to preserve to this wretched age a Relique, and Example, of the last.—I beg you (my Lord) as you have put me into the utmost pain by that information which you intended should give me ease, be so good as to continue to acquaint me how the Dean does?[4] I will not excuse to you my Omis-

[1] The year date has been cut away in the original, but 1736 is certainly right. The endorsement confirms it. The postmark suggests that the letter was misdated by one day.

[2] If 'the last post' means 25 Mar., one must note that as published the letter contains no appeal for the return of the letters. The letter may be lost, or Pope may have excised the appeal when printing the letter.

[3] The brackets here seem to have been inserted by an early editor.

[4] The whole tone of Orrery's account of Swift's health evidently was such as to increase Pope's fear for his letters—at the moment (when he was preparing his edition of 1737) a major preoccupation.

sion of writing so long; You seem to know, you prove that you know, my Heart, in overlooking it: and I must be, in the Sense of that, & many other of your Qualities, with great truth, | My Lord | Your most faithfull & | oblig'd, (let me add affectionate) | Servant, | A. Pope.

Address: To the Right Honble the | Earl of Orrery, | Dublin: | Ireland.
Postmark: 1/AP
Endorsement: Mr Pope. | April 2d 1736.

*POPE *to* ALLEN[1] 7 *April* [1736]

Egerton 1947

Twitenham. Apr. 7th

After thanking you for your very kind Visit, and yet more for the Extreme Zeal and Friendship you manifested to me on occasion of my Letters, in so warm a Desire that I should be justified even during my life, which truly is less my Concern than yours (a very uncommon Obligation) I must tell you a thing that has vexed me. Mr Leake[2] came after you, 2 or 3 hours after you went, & (I being gone out but for half an hour) was refused by my Servants to see the place, which I had myself invited him to: In general they never show the house (which you know is nothing) in my Absence; but the Garden I never hinder them to show, but when I have Company with me. Had I had the least Imagination of Mr Leake's meeting you, I had taken more Care, & had mentiond him, but I concluded him gone to Redding. We were talking of Wrong headed men: Mr Leake I know is none, but he may think this odd enough without being one: pray therfore tell him the truth. About five minutes after, they let in a Poet upon me at dinner, whom I never saw before, & who had nothing to say to me. It puts me in mind of what Mr Craggs used to say of his Porter, when he was Secretary of State, "This is a fellow I keep, to keep out every Man I wish to see, & let in every man I hate to see." For those people gave the Servant most mony, who had most to beg of the Master.

I hope your Journey proved both pleasant & healthy, & that the End of it will be yet more so; that you may injoy first your Schemes,

[1] This is the first of Pope's letters to Ralph Allen (1694–1764), famous for having devised for the Post Office a system of cross-posts (very lucrative to himself and advantageous to the nation); also for his stone quarries near Bath that were of great use in the rebuilding of that beautiful city, and also for his generous patronage of Pope and of Henry and Sarah Fielding. His friendship with Pope was occasioned by his delight in the letters published in 1735. He wished Pope to bring out an elaborate 'authentic' edition of his correspondence, and has evidently (cf. the first sentence of the letter) just visited the poet and offered financial aid towards the edition.

[2] James Leake (1686–1764), for years the leading bookseller at Bath. See *Notes & Queries*, 12 S. xi. 224–5.

& then the Execution, & then the Completion, of them; for those are three distinct pleasures: I know that in every one of these you make the Enjoyment they give your Friends a main part, and therfore they ought to rejoyce in the pleasure you take, since you only take it to Communicate. Adieu, & believe me sincerely | Sir | Your affectionate & faithful | Servant | A. Pope.

POPE *to* FORTESCUE[1] [13 *April* 1736]

Professor C. B. Tinker

Twit'nam. Tuesday

I need not tell you I am heartily glad of your return: my Rheumatism having left me, is not a greater joy. But I cannot leave this place at this Important Time, when Every Hour of my being here gives it a new Improvement, as you'l see when you come, (I hope on Saturday) I enquird, but did not find the Ladies were so early at Richmond as you writ me word. Indeed the Easterly Wind was enough to discourage them. I send you the Paper[2] which I see by what you said, you like better than I do. I hope the subscription will fail, so far at least as to excuse me from the thing I never liked, & have been over-persuaded to do. ⟨I⟩ am | Truly & always Yours. | A. Pope

If you take any Subscribers in, you must give them a receit in this form.

Received of — one guinea, being the Whole Payment for a Vol: of Mr Pope's Works in Prose which (if the Impression does not go on) I promise to Return on demand after Midsummer next.

W. F.

Address: To | The Honorable Mr Baron | Fortescue, in Bellyard | by Lincolns Inne | London.

Postmark: 14/AP

Endorsement: Mr Pope. | Apr. 1736.

POPE *to* THE EARL OF ORRERY 16 *April* 1736

The Pierpont Morgan Library

Twitenham Apr. 16. | 1736

My Lord,—I think it incumbent upon me to write your Lordship a Second Letter, after thanking you for the Particular account of the

[1] The date is inferred from the postmark and the endorsement. 13 Apr. fell on a Tuesday (as superscribed by Pope).

[2] Evidently a paper of printed Proposals for the *Letters*. Considering the difficulty in marketing his *Works* (1735) in quarto as well as Curll's threats to reprint any authentic letters, Pope very likely would have been contented to keep his *Letters* in the modest octavo format, which probably he had begun work on some months before the project of a quarto edition was formed.

Dean, whose Attack would have alarmed me excessively without your most friendly Care to tell the softest news. I beggd so earnestly a further account and have still so great ground of Fear for your own Welfare, that I dread the cause of your Silence. God preserve You my Lord, & all such few Men, & such fewer Noblemen, as yourself! Mr Stopford just now sent me a Letter concerning our dear Friend the Dean, which still leaves me in pain. I beg you, my Lord, put me out of that I feel for you both. I ought not to suffer any thing relating to me (in whom your Goodness takes, on all occasions, so much Interest) to be published without transmitting it to your hands: therfore you see, to what my Friends & my Enemies have reduced me! They both conspired first to preserve, & then to publish my Letters; & now they both resolve to accept, what I advertised merely to put a stop to a rascally Editor, as a Promise from myself of Publication. The inclosed is meant either to acquit that seeming promise, or (which I should better like) to free me from it: if the Number of Subscriptions fall short, as I heartily wish & think it will. But this is a Secret to your self. Believe me, my Lord, with the sincerest sense of your Virtues, & the most true Gratitude for those which you manifest particularly in my regard, | Your Lordships faithfull | obliged & obedient Servant | A. Pope.

I wish excessively a line from the Dean: it is 3 months since I had one, & I've written thrice to him; twice by private hands, once by Post. He will be glad. to know (& so will Mr Stopford whose Letter I gave to Mr Pulteney) that Mr P. is better, & going to Bath.

Endorsement: Mr Pope. April 16th 1736.

†SWIFT *to* POPE — 22 *April* 1736

1740

Dublin, April 22, 1736

My common illness is of that kind which utterly disqualifies me for all conversation; I mean my Deafness; and indeed it is that only which quite discourageth[1] me from all thoughts of coming to England; because I am never sure that it may not return in a week. If it were a good honest Gout, I could catch an interval, to take a voyage, and in a warm lodging get an easy chair, and be able to hear, and roar among my friends. "As to what you say of your Letters, since you have many years of life more than I, my resolution is to direct my Executors to send you all your letters, well sealed and pacqueted, along with some legacies mentioned in my Will, and leave them entirely to your disposal: those things are all tied up, endors'd and locked in a cabinet, and

[1] which quite discourageth] which discourageth *1741 L; 1742 L.*

I have not one servant who can properly be said to write or read. No mortal shall copy them, but you shall surely have them when I am no more."[1] I have a little repined at my being hitherto slipped by you in some Epistle,[2] not from any other ambition than that Title[3] of a Friend, and in that sense I expect you shall perform your promise, if your health and leisure and inclination will permit. I deny your losing on the side of Poetry; I could reason against you a little from experience; you are, and will be some years to come, at the age where[4] Invention still keeps its ground, and Judgment is at full maturity: but your subjects are much more difficult when confin'd to Verse. I am amazed to see you exhaust the whole science of Morality in so masterly a manner. Sir W. Temple said that the loss of friends was a Tax upon long life: It need not be very long, since you have had so great a share, but I have not above one left: and in this Country I have only a few general companions of good nature and middling understandings. How should I know Cheselden? on your side men of fame start up and dye before we here (at least I) know any thing of the matter. I am a little comforted with what you say of Lord B's[5] Genius still keeping up, and preparing to appear by effects worthy of the author, and useful to the world.—Common reports have made me very uneasy about your neighbour, Mr. Pultney.[6] It is affirmed that he hath been very near death: I love him for being a Patriot in most corrupted times, and highly esteem his excellent Understanding. Nothing but the perverse nature of my disorders, as I have above described them, and which are absolute disqualifications for converse, could hinder me from waiting on you at Twitenham, and nursing you to Paris. In short my Ailments amount to a prohibition, although I am as you describe your self, what *I must call well*, yet I have not spirits left to ride out, which (excepting walking) was my only diversion. And I must expect to decline every month, like one who lives upon his principal sum which must lessen every day; and indeed I am likewise literally almost in the same case, while every body owes me, and no body pays me. Instead of a young race of Patriots on your side which gives me some glympse of joy, here we have the direct contrary, a race of young wicked

[1] The quotation marks, lacking in 1740 and 1741 Dab, were added in the London editions (1741–2) to advertise the relation of the passage to the Dublin origin of the texts. Curll in 1741 Lc adds a footnote: '*Faulkner's* Press is a quicker Conveyance, and so they came *safe* to Mr. Curll. The *Irish Editor* of them is well known.' Curll pretended to reprint his edition from that of Dublin, which had no copyright in London. Actually he reprinted Pope's quarto text.

[2] in some Epistle] in your Epistles *1741 L; 1742 L.*

[3] that Title] the Title *1741 L; 1742 L.*

[4] where] when *1741 L; 1742 L.*

[5] B's] Bolingbroke's *1741 Dab.*

[6] *The Lond. Daily Post*, 8 May 1736, reported 'William Pulteney, Esq; is so well recovered from his Nervous Fever, that he has rode out twice or thrice this week, and continues at Petersham for the Benefit of the Air.' In *The Lond. Eve. Post* of 22 May he was reported as leaving for Gravesend and the German Spa.

Dunces[1] and Atheists, or old Villains and Monsters, whereof four-fifths are more wicked and stupid than Chartres. Your wants are so few, that you need not be rich to supply them; and my wants are so many, that a King's seven millions of guineas would not support me.

POPE *to* ALLEN[2] 30 *April* [1736]

Egerton 1947

Twitnam. Apr. 30th

Sir,—I saw Mr Morice[3] yesterday who has readily allowed Mr Vandiest[4] to copy the Picture. I have enquired for the best Originals of those two Subjects which I found were Favorite ones with you, & well deserve to be so, the Discovery of Joseph to his Bretheren, and the Resignation of the Captive by Scipio. Of the latter my Lord Burlington has a fine one done by Ricci, & I am promis'd ye other in a Good Print from One of the chief Italian Painters. That of Scipio is of the exact Size one would wish for a Basso Relievo, in which manner in my opinion you would best ornament your Hall, done in Chiaro oscuro.

A Man not only shews his Taste but his Virtue, in the Choice of such Ornaments: And whatever Example most strikes us, we may reasonably imagine may have an influence upon others, so that the History itself (if wellchosen) upon a Rich-mans Walls, is very often a better lesson than any he could teach by his Conversation. In this sense, the Stones may be said to speak, when Men cannot, or will not. I can't help thinking (& I know you'l joyn with me, you who have been making an Altar-piece) that the Zeal of the first Reformers was ill placed, in removing *Pictures* (that is to say Examples) out of Churches, and yet suffering *Epitaphs* (that is to say, Flatteries and False History) to be the Burden of Church-walls, & the Shame, as well as Derision, of all honest men. I have run out my leaf, & will only add my sincere Wishes for your happiness of all kinds. I am, with Esteem & affection, | Dear Sir | Yours, | A. Pope

P.S. I have heard little yet of the Subscriptions[5]—I intend to make a Visit for a fortnight from home to Lady Peterborow at Southampton,[6] about the middle of May. After my return I'll inquire what has been done, & I really believe what I told you will prove true & I shall be honorably acquitted of a task I am not fond of.

[1] young wicked Dunces] young Dunces *1741 L*; *1742 L*.

[2] Printed by Warburton in Pope's *Works*, ix (1751), 310.

[3] The son-in-law of Bishop Atterbury.

[4] Johan Van Diest, chiefly a portrait-painter, was the son of Adriæn Van Diest (1656–1704), a Dutch landscape-painter resident in England after about 1673.

[5] For his own edition of the first volume of his letters; undertaken at Mr. Allen's request. —Warburton, 1751.

[6] Pope wrote to Allen from Southampton, 5 June 1736.

Talking of Epitaphs, puts me in mind of sending you my Sense of them which I threw into an Epigram. as it was never printed, I give it you.

To one who wrote Epitaphs

Friend! in your Epitaphs I'm griev'd
So very much is said,
One half will never be believd,
The other never read.

Address: To | Ralph Allen, Esqr at | Bath.
Postmark: /MA

*THE EARL OF BURLINGTON *to* POPE[1] 3 *May* [1736]

Chatsworth

London May 3

I should be unworthy of the friendship you honor me with, if I coud defer the pleasure of being with you, one minute, without an absolute occasion for it. my case is this, Lord Bruce comes from his Country house in Wiltshire, on particular business with me, and intends to dine with me on wednesday, and to go back in two days, I hope Thursday may be the same thing to you, when I will certainly waite on you. I shou'd not have been so circumstantial, if it had not been to convince you, that what I say is real, I hope you are persuaded that my affection for you is so. ever yours | Burlington

*POPE *to* THE EARL OF BURLINGTON[2] [4 *May* 1736]

Chatsworth

Tuesday.

My Lord,—Next to the First day that gives me hopes of seeing you, I shall always count happy the Second. Thursday therefore will make me so, & I will expect you.

I should be a worse man than even Libellers can represent me, if I did not think real what ever you are pleas'd to profess, tho it be so much above my desert, as that long Friendship with which you have honour'd me. It cannot be greater than that Gratitude with which I have as long, & shall for ever receive it. I am | Your Lordships most faithfull Servant. | A. Pope.

I beg Lady Bs acceptance of my real services.

[1] The year seems probable from the fact that Lord Bruce wrote to the Earl of Cardigan, 2 May 1736, from Wiltshire, 'I intend being at London tomorrow night' (Hist. MSS. Comm., *Montagu House MSS.* [Buccleuch], i. 389). May 3 was a Monday. See the following letter for Pope's reply.

[2] The date is determined through the fact that this is a reply to the preceding letter.

POPE *to* FORTESCUE[1] [5?] *May* 1736

1797 (Polwhele, i. 324–5)

Wednesday, May, 1736.

My days are become so uncertain, that I find I shall not have *to-morrow* in my power. This moral sentence is too true in my regard, for I see my proposal of Mr. Crank's dining here will not be. I therefore beg to lay hold of the present day, and that you'l all come and dine here directly; for after this day I must be held down to two successive parties for morning, noon, and night. The prince's marriage influencing others, has this effect on me, to reverse what was before promised. Pray, if you can't dine here to day, come in the afternoon and sup, or come on Friday evening. Adieu! I am ever sincerely, your most faithful servant, A. Pope.

I have put pickled pork and pease in readiness for dinner.

POPE *to* THE EARL OF ORRERY 10 *May* 1736

The Pierpont Morgan Library

Twickenham. May 10. 1736.

My Lord,—I give you sincere thanks for knowing so well of how much Concern your Lordships Health is to me: and for increasing my Satisfaction at the Dean's Recovery, by adding to it an account of your own. Sint tales animae concordes! is the Wish every good man must make, when Two such as you are together; yet it is a Vexation to me to reflect, that I cannot obtain you, but by his loss of you. Were not my own Carcase (very little suited to my Soul) my worst Enemy, were it not for the *Body of this Death*, (as St Paul calls it) I would not be seperated from you, nor suffer the Dean to be Wholly yours. Nevertheless while I am complaining of my Infirm Frame, I must own it does not make me quite miserable, in any thing but This Impediment. I linger on, without direct Sickness, & it seems to tell me I may outlive every Man & every thing I love or esteem. A wretched Consolation! I begin almost to wish for *Young* Friends (which is yet inconsistent with the dislike of *New* ones) whom I may not be every month trembling for, at this rate. When I cast my eye lately, over that volume which they have stolen of my Letters, One Reflection arose to me at every page, so strongly, that it would be the most proper & the most Melancholy Motto for 'em in the world. It was that which Catullus has exprest in these lines,

Cum Desiderio veteres revocamus Amores,
Atque olim missas flemus Amicitias![2]

[1] The Prince of Wales was married on 27 Apr., and so one may presume the earliest Wednesday in May is the probable date. Pope is dining with the Burlingtons tomorrow, and hence urges Fortescue to come today.

[2] Catullus, xcvi. 3. See also To Swift, 30 Dec. 1736.

I am tempted to say a great deal more to your Lordship, but so severe a fate, & such an Exposal of my private Thoughts as has befallen me in the publication of my freest Letters, has given me a check that will last for life. So much Candour & Good nature as I know are in your mind, would draw out one's most naked Sentiments, without any Care about the cloathing them. And I am heartily sorry I can't expose myself to you alone. The same Excess of Humanity which sees all in the best light prompts to an Indulgence for whatever is well-meant; and that, joind to the great Partiality I find your Lordship has for me, would move you to keep my Trash, as our Friend Swift has done. So that for the future I must be for the most part content to reserve the Expressions of my heart for my Friends in Conversation, except in the Dean's regard, whom alone it is my Misery not to hope to Converse with! And whenever I catch myself a-thinking upon paper, I must stop short, with | I am | My Lord | Your truly obliged & faithful | Servant, | A. Pope.

I shall write to the Dean in a post or two by the Common post, which conveys my Letters soonest tho not safest, & I am ashamd of nothing I say of, or to Him. The other ways are too tedious.

Pray tell him, Mr Pulteney never had any thing apoplectic, he is better, rides out every day, & is going to France. Lord Bolingbroke will pass this Summer in a studious Retirement near Fontainbleau, which I am very glad of for the sake of the Learned World.

Endorsement: Mr Pope. May 10th 1736.

*MATHER BYLES *to* POPE[1] [1736?]

The New England Historical and Genealogical Society.

Sir,—It is now several years since I boldly introduced my self to your notice; since which Time I have written several replies to the only Answer I ever recieved from You, till at last I concluded your Silence forbid my pressing the Matter any further. I was, however, somewhat amazed, by receiving a present of the *Odyssey*, directed, I think, by Your own Hand, without a letter to accompany it.

But As I have not been able to explain these matters to my self, I take the Liberty once more to write to you. I have sometimes doubted your Letters might be taken up, in order to fill the volumes of Curl. The many Publick Abuses you have met with, will never Lessen Your Character. The Sun looks bigger thro' a Fog: And most of the Letters,

[1] The Rev. Mr. Byles here makes a last attempt to cultivate an epistolary friendship with Pope. His letter was carefully composed with many blots and rewritings in the letterbook. Written presumably in 1736 after the arrival of the spring fleet in Boston.

which were published without your Consent, and the Last Year Collected into one Volume, (with the promise of another) by *T. Cooper*, I read with a particular pleasure, as they lead me into the First thoughts, and Domestick Character of so great a man.[1]

One Favour I must exceedingly beg of you, unless you have a Mind to be haunted by more letters.[2] . . . And that is a Collection of Your Works compleat, in Twelves.[3] Yet I would not be just like him neither of whom you speak, as only in great modesty, asking,

My Friendship, and a prologue, & ten pounds[4]

But I will honestly pay the Bookseller whom you shall order to send them. And tho' this will make many Duplicates in my Library, yet it will keep me from being imposed upon by Spurious writtings, which come out in Your Name.

The little Things inclosed I am far from thinking will have any thing to Recommend them to you, except only as they intend Respect, and come from a far Countrey. I am | Sir | Your very humble Servant.

Heading in the letterbook: To Allexander Pope, Esqr | Twickenham.

POPE *to* MRS. KNIGHT[5] 17 *May* [1736]

Elwin–Courthope, ix. 455

Twickenham, May 17.

Madam,—Though I forget all the town at this season, I would not have you think I forget your commissions; but (to put it upon a truer foot) I can't forget a person I so really loved and esteemed as the subject of the enclosed inscription. It is now as I think it ought to be, and the sooner it is engraved the better. As soon as I can leave this place I shall wait upon you, and try if I can persuade you to take any country-seat beside Godsfield,[6] though but for a day. I am sincerely your most faithful servant.

[1] The edition of the letters that Mr. Byles had seen was apparently that issued in June 1735 with the name of T. Cooper on the title-page. (Here called 1735e; in Griffith 384.) The title-page is for 'Vol. I' and there is no title-page for vol. ii, which is bound with vol. i. It is this fact that leads Mr. Byles to say 'with the promise of another': he thought the volume incomplete.

[2] At this point in tiny script between the lines is a line that is undeciphered.

[3] There was no authorized edition in twelves, but in the summer of 1735 Gilliver brought out a small octavo edition such as became the normal trade size. The folio and quarto editions were continued chiefly for subscribers to the *Iliad* and *Odyssey*.

[4] *Epistle to Dr. Arbuthnot*, l. 48.

[5] The year is assumed from the fact that Pope apparently encloses the lines intended for the tomb of John Knight, Esq., who died in 1733. The lines are printed in EC, ix. 435. According to *The Lond. Eve. Post*, 17 July 1736, the monument had been erected 'yesterday'. The *Post* gives the Latin inscription followed by an epitaph in five English couplets. Both Latin and English may be assumed from this letter to be by Pope. See Ault, *New Light*, p. 334.

[6] Normally *Gosfield*.

POPE *to* FORTESCUE [11 *or* 18] *May* 1736

1797 (Polwhele, i. 324)

Twicknham, Tuesday night, May, 1736.

It is very long that I have not heard any thing of you. The illness you left me under at Chiswick continued violently five whole days, two of which I was in London, and returned as ill hither. Upon the whole, I've had head aches most of the time I have past since. I inquired, and find you've been but one night at Richmond. Where are you? and how are you? I fancy you've been in Essex, or on some excursion. I think to be in London for two days at the end of this week, and then at home all the next. Pray let me know at which place I may see you most to your conveniency; who, while I live, shall be always, truly, dear Sir, yours, | A. Pope.

Address: To the Hon. Mr. Baron Fortescue, in Bell-yard, Lincoln's Inn, London.

POPE *to* FORTESCUE[1] [30] *May* 1736

1797 (Polwhele, i. 324)

Sunday, May, 1736.

I am gone (before this can reach you) to Southampton, where my stay will be a fortnight. I was sorry to have no opportunity of passing a day with you and yours; but I propose it often after my return. In the mean time the purpose of this letter is to desire you and them to make what use you will of my house and gardens, which are large enough to lodge you all, and to try if they bear a country life, any where but in Devonshire. Dear Sir, believe me ever, sincerely, your most affectionate faithful friend and servant, | A. Pope.

Address: To the Hon. Mr. Baron Fortescue, in Bell-yard, by Lincoln's Inn, London.

POPE *to* ALLEN[2] 5 *June* [1736]

Egerton 1947

Southampton. June 5th

Sir,—I need not say I thank you for a letter which proves so much Friendship for me; I have much more to say upon it, than I can, till we meet. But, in a word, I think your Notion of the Value of those

[1] Pope wrote to Allen from Lady Peterborow's (Southampton) on 5 June. On 16 June he wrote to Bethel from Twickenham, after spending a fortnight (as here planned) at Bevis Mount. Hence this letter must have been written on the 30th, the only possible Sunday.

[2] Printed by Warburton in 1751. Parts of the letter here placed in half-brackets were omitted from his text.

Things[1] is greatly too high, as to any Service they can do the *Publick*; and as to any advantage they may do to *my own character* I ought to be content with what they have done alredy. I assure you I do not think it the least of those advantages, that they have occasion'd me the Good will (in so great a degree) of so worthy a Man.[2] I fear, (as I must rather retrench than add to their number, unless I would publish my own Commendations) that the Common Run of Subscribers would think themselves injur'd by not having every thing, which Discretion must Suppress; & this, they (without any other Consideration than as Buyers of a Book) would call *giving them an Imperfect Collection*: Whereas the Only Use to my own Character *as an author*, of such a publication, would be the Suppression of many things: And as to my Character *as a Man*, it would be but just where it is; unless I could be so *Vain* (for it could not be *Virtuous*) to add more & more honest Sentiments; which when done *to be printed*, would surely be wrong, & weak also.

I do grant, it would be some pleasure to me, to Expunge several idle passages, which will otherwise, if not go down to the next age, pass at least in this, for mine; altho' many of them are not, and God knows none of 'em my Present Sentiments, but on the contrary, wholly dis-approvd by me.

And I do not flatter you when I say, that pleasure would be increased to me, in knowing I should do what would please *You*. But I cannot persuade myself to let the whole burden, even tho' it were a Publick Good, lye upon you; much less to serve my Private Fame, entirely at another's expence.[3]

But understand me rightly: Did I believe half so well of them as you do, I would not scruple your assistance; because I am sure that to occasion you to contribute to a Real Good, would be the greatest Benefit I could oblige you in. And I hereby promise you, if ever I am so happy as to find any just Occasion where your Generosity & Goodness may unite for such a worthy End, I will not scruple to draw upon you, for any Sum, to effect it.

As to the present affair; that you may be convinced what Weight your Opinion & your Desires have with me, I will do what I have not yet done: I will tell my Friends I am as willing to publish this book, as to let it alone. And ⌜I will give out ten more Papers of Proposals to ten more; As for the determining the Time to this Midsummer, since the Proposals have never been otherwise made publick, & never advertised in the Papers, & as no Mony has been taken, &

[1] Pope's letters.

[2] Mr. Allen's friendship with the Author was contracted on the sight of his Letters, which gave the former the highest opinion of the other's general benevolence and goodness of heart.—Warburton, 1751.

[3] Mr. A. offered to print the Letters at his own expense.—Warburton, 1751.

no Engagement made; I will let my friends try a little longer; & I make no doubt, (upon their being satisfyd that I have no dislike to it, & upon their acting in it instead of being Passive) the Number will rise higher. I think I can see, without any Sollicitation, as far as 200 Quarto. If there were 400 certain, I would begin to print; and,⌝ rather than suffer You to be taxed at your own rate, publish in the News next winter the Proposals, ⌜which probably would raise 100 more for the Quarto, which is the Number requisite to complete the Sets of my Verse Volume: In which Scheme I would print no smaller size by *Subscription*, but for common Sale only. But the mischief is, this would retard the Impression all this year.⌝

I tell you all these particulars, to show you how willing I am to follow your advice, nay to accept your assistance in any Moderate degree, but I think you should reserve so great a Proof of your Benevolence to a better occasion.

Since I wrote last, I have found on further Enquiry that there is another fine Picture on the Subject of Scipio & the Captive by Pietro da Cortona, which Sir Paul Methuen has a Sketch of: & I believe is more expressive than that of Ricci, as Pietro is famous for Expression: I have also met with a fine Print of the Discovery of Joseph to his Bretheren a design which I fancy is of La Sueur, a noble painter, & will do perfectly well.[1] ⌜For your two others, that of Jonathan with the Circumstance of shooting his Arrow, may easily be done (tho I do not know that it has been done except in a Print in Blome's History of the Bible)[2] And I could wish you pitchd on that admirable piece for Expression, the Death of Germanicus by Poussin, for the 4th since the Action of Scipio's drawing his Sword &c. will be very difficult to get well done, & has not (I am afraid) ever been attempted by any good hand. You will thus have two of sacred, & two of prophane History.⌝

⌜Dear Sir, It is I who should make an Excuse for a very tedious, & very careless Letter: but as I hope you don't intend I should print it, I am pretty easy. I can trust you with my freedoms, & with my Errors too, But pray have the mercy on me to burn them; since, by a peculiar hardship, I must not be allowed even to Think in private. One Period however there shall be in this Letter, which I am not asham'd if all the world saw, that I really Esteem you as a Friend to all Virtue & an Impartial Christian, qualities that make me (equally justly and sincerely) Dear Sir Yours.⌝ | A. Pope

[1] As printed by Warburton the letter ends at this point.

[2] Nicolas Fontaine, *History of the Old and New Testaments*, published (in English translation) by Richard Blome in 1700, 1711, &c.

*POPE *to* HUGH BETHEL 16 *June* [1736]

Egerton 1948

Twitnam, June 16.

I send you these in great hurry, lest Mr Draper[1] should be gone. I must give you one trouble more to let me know in a fortnight or 3 weeks the names of those you & your Brother have procurd to the Subscription, for in that time I ought to resolve the thing.

The Letter so odly directed I had yesterday from Sir Clement Cottrel. I came just now from Lady Peterborow's at Southampton where I spent a fortnight, & we often drank your health & wishd you there. Mrs Blount I've not seen but sent her your kind letter, she has had her Rash again, tho not very violently. Mrs Pratt is going with the Duchess[2] to Spaw, this week.

I heartily thank you for your repeated offer in relation to my Sister. I have furnished her with [150]pd & she has Lost it, being cast in the Law suit, (or rather I believe *I* have lost it) But I shall be able to make a shift till more of my Rents come in; It is right sometimes to Love our Neighbor, not only as well, but better than one'self, and to retrench from our own Extravagances to assist them in theirs. For it was meer Folly of not making proper articles, that subjected her to this loss.[3] As soon as I hear again from you, pray acquaint me how to direct to you for the rest of the Season, that I may sometimes tell you, more at large, how truly I am | Dear Sir | Ever | Yours, | A. Pope.

Address: To Hugh Bethel Esq; to be | left with Mr Draper, at the | Lady Strickland's in | Gro'venor Square.

POPE *to* FORTESCUE[4] [*Post* 16 *June* 1736]

1797 (Polwhele, i. 322)

I have just received a note from Mrs. Blount, that she and lady Gerard will dine here to-day, which puts off my intention on lord Ilay. I wish you would dine with them, and we may go to lord Ilay's in the evening. But this you see hinders my being wholly at your

[1] Mr. Draper (cf. the address of the letter) was evidently a friend of Lady Strickland (widow of Sir William, 4th Baronet), and would carry letters to Bethel. The Stricklands were Yorkshire neighbours of Bethel.

[2] Mrs. Pratt, widow of John Pratt, Esq., of Ireland, was companion and friend to the Duchess of Buckingham and useful in the care of the invalid Duke Edmund. The party is reported in *The Lond. Eve. Post*, 17 June 1736, as leaving for France on the 15th. Mrs. Pratt remained with the young duke until he died in Rome. For a detailed obituary of her see *Gent. Mag.* xxxix (1769), 461–2.

[3] The paragraph to this point was quoted by Ruffhead, p. 502, who supplies the bracketed digits, no longer visible. In 1734 Pope had lent Mrs. Racket £300.

[4] The date is altogether hypothetical. Polwhele prints *Hay* instead of *Ilay*; but this is almost certainly an error. In such letters as mention this lord and are preserved in Pope's holograph the name is clearly Ilay, but it is easily mistaken for Hay.

service 'till to-morrow, when I will certainly be so at any place or time. Yours affectionately, ever, | A. Pope.

Address: To Wm. Fortescue, esq.

POPE *to* FORTESCUE[1] [*June* 1736]

Professor C. B. Tinker

I have been detained by 2 or 3 accidents from dining with you, one of which is, the Rebuilding of the Temple, which I hope will in Glory equal the First.[2] I wish the Ladies & You would come this afternoon & give your assistance. If you go to Marble hill you'l easily come on, & sup with me on Westphaly Ham &c. or drink Tea at least. I will if you please go with you to morrow to Lord Ilay's & afterwards dine with you, if it suit your other Engagements.

Adieu, but I hope not for many hours. | Yours Entirely, | A. Pope.

2 a clock.

Address: To the Honble | Mr Baron Fortescue. | at the Vineyard in Richmond.

Endorsement: Mr Pope | June. 1736.

*POPE *to* THE EARL OF BURLINGTON[3] [? *June* 1736]

Chatsworth

I am extremely unlucky, having been un-ingaged these five days, & on this only incapable to wait on you. I am ingaged to Mrs Knight & her sister, (two Widows of 10000 pd apiece) who dine here & whom afterwards I promisd to show Chiswick, which I'm afraid will not now be so Convenient for My Amours, since you'l have not only Company there, but (for all I know) powerful Rivals, in Sir Clement & the General. But to morrow you shall have what you will of me in Town, & any other day in Town or Country: for no man, believe me my Lord, is with more truth & warmth | Your most obliged obedient Servant | A. Pope.

Address: Earl of Burlington

[1] Fortescue's endorsement indicates that this letter was written after Pope's return from Southampton; i.e. the latter half of June.

[2] The shell temple in his garden had collapsed in 1735.

[3] This letter was evidently written within the period from 2 Oct. 1733 to 23 Mar. 1736/7 in which Mrs. Knight was a widow. The letter was written, also, at a time when several people were in or near London; i.e. Mrs. Knight, Mrs. Elliott, Sir Clement Cottrell, General Dormer, Pope, and Lord Burlington.

*POPE *to* ALLEN 18 *July* [1736]

Egerton 1947

Sir,—It is with sincere Concern I apprehend your Indispositions are still heavy upon you, for (besides your Journey which you say your Physicians advised) Mr Leake left word you had been ill, and Mr Vandiest (whom I saw in town together with that picture, in which I made a small Alteration) told me the same thing: I observd too that the short Letter you writ to Him was not in your own hand, which increas'd my fears. You will really oblige me in giving me an account of yourself; and that I may oblige you in return, I will allow you to remit the 45 guineas which you say some of your Friends & Leake have *really subscribed.*[1] And to content you as far as I can, I will put the book to the press in 3 weeks time, & determine to leave out Every syllable to the best of my judgment that can give the least ill Example to an Age too apt to take it, or the least Offence to any Good or Serious Man. This being the Sole Point for which I have any sort of desire to publish the Letters at all, is, I am persuaded, the chief point which makes You, in friendship to My character, so zealous about 'em. And therefore how small soever be the Number so printed, provided I do not lose too much (for a man of more Prudence than Fortune) I conclude *that work* will be done, & *that End* answer'd, were there but one or two hundred books in all.

I could wish, if your health receive any benefit from one Journey, that you would take another hither, and look over some Letters which I would ask your opinion whether to insert or not? I am sure, if you thought they could be of any Service to Virtue, or answer any One good purpose; whether (considerd as writings) they brought me any Credit or not, they should be given to the world, and let them make me a worse Writer, provided they could make but one better man.

I wish you Life, & Peace, & Contentment. For myself, if I live, I desire nothing so much as to live in the good opinion of reasonable men: I would prefer that Condition of life even to Health itself: but

[1] The italicized words indicate a desire by Pope (Elwin would call it *pretense*) to be independent of charity in the publication of the quarto *Letters.* Warburton (not an unbiased witness) is our authority for believing that Allen subsidized the edition. Evidently he used influence and perhaps paid to get Leake of Bath to underwrite the book by taking fifty copies. On the last page of this letter (left blank by Pope) Allen wrote the following: 'Mem. | July 25th remited to Mr Pope a Bill for £52 : 10 : 0 upon Mr J Norse 3 Days after Sight with money. Mr Jea Leake of Bath is to repay me. | R Allen.' Presumably Leake was to repay as he sold copies of the guinea book. Pope's receipt, preserved as Egerton 1947, f. 10, is as follows: 'July the 29th 1736. | Receivd of Ralph Allen Esq. fifty guineas, for which I promise to deliver Him fifty Books of the Prose Volume of my Works in Quarto by Midsummer next, or to return the said fifty guineas. | A. Pope.' The bastard title of the quarto *Letters* was *The Works of Mr. Alexander Pope, in Prose.*

next that, Health; & after health, Length of days. May these last be your portion; the first you will secure to yourself.

I am | Dear Sir | Sincerely Yours. | A. Pope.

July the 18th

*POPE *to* ALLEN — 30 *July* [1736]

Egerton 1947

July 30.

The desire I have to acquaint you punctually of my Receipt of the Note,[1] makes me content to say so little, rather than to defer my answer a post longer. For I remember, & like, the Saying of a Friend of mine (no Poet) that Punctuality is a Branch of Moral Honesty, & that an unpunctual Man is a Thief of his Neighbor's *Time*, which he can never repay. Yet I will add one word more, which is to thank you heartily for the good account you give of your health, & to thank you again for your promise to pass a few days here. I wish it could be *before* the Middle of next Month August, for I have an Engagement which must be punctual, on the 15, 16, 17, & 18, in Windsor forest. You'l be pleasd to hear that I shall have put the first Sheet of the Book to the Press next Week. I'm in some doubt whether to print 300, or 500 Quarto? the first number being all I see certain; tho' there were 500 of the former volumes, of which above 100 remain on my hands. Be it as it will, I may truly own to your satisfaction, that You have determined me to this; & the Book if of any Authority or value, will be really owing to You. Adieu in haste, & let me hear when we may meet? I am Sincerely | Yours. | A. Pope

Address: To | Ralph Allen, Esqr | at | Bath.
Postmark: 31/IY

LORD BATHURST *to* POPE — 14 *August* 1736

Elwin–Courthope, viii. 353

Cirencester, Aug. 14, 1736.

I think myself much obliged to you, dear sir, for your obliging letter, and to show you that I would not trespass too far upon your goodness, I will not insist upon your coming if it will be too fatiguing to you, but at the same time if you do intend to go this year to Lord Cobham's, one day's journey further will make but little odds. You will rest a day or two at Rousham, and then if my coach meets you half-way you may come hither to dinner. I cannot promise to meet you there myself,

[1] The note for fifty guineas received from Allen and in this letter receipted. See the note to the preceding letter.

because I have a great deal of business upon my hands at this time, and am uncertain whether I may not be unavoidably detained at the time you appoint. But if you will appoint your day when my coach shall meet you at Burford, I am sure it is not very far from Mr. Dormer's to that place, and if you can persuade them[1] to come with you it will be a great pleasure to me. The general did make me a promise of a visit this last winter in town for some time this summer. Now to show you that I have a most manifest want of you at this present juncture I send you the enclosed plans. That marked (a) was drawn first. Afterwards I had a mind to have a cupola on purpose to try the effect of the Cornish slate, which we can have from Bristol at a pretty easy rate. In the plan marked (b) the building is described and the ground plot. It must be of that shape because it is to answer three walks, and the materials must be the same as those with which the seat was built, because they are already brought to the place, and because I think that rough stone exceedingly pretty, and am ready to stand all the jokes of *Rusticus expectat*,[2] etc. N.B. This building will be backed with wood, so that nothing more can be seen but the three sides. I design the ribs of the cupola shall be done with lead, which I will gild or paint of gold colour, which being set off by the blue slate will look admirably well. I will certainly make the three arches like that in the plan marked (a), but I am in doubt how to settle the fascias and the cornice, etc. Now I leave it entirely to you either to come and settle this affair yourself or send the directions. Another building is to be erected afterwards to answer the other diagonal which will also overlook the lake, no contemptible body of water I can assure you. It will be at least as big as the canal at Riskins. Besides this you will see that I have brought a great quantity of very good hewn stone from the old house at Saperton[3] to the great centre in Oakley wood. Nothing is wanting but your direction to set the work forward. I have also begun to level the hill before the house, and an obelisk shall rise upon your orders to terminate the view. I am sure you will not now make any feigned excuse, and I hope you will have no real one to prevent your coming. If you can go to Lord Cobham's you can certainly come here, and I will go back with you thither, for I have promised him to make him a visit this summer. If you are hindered from that expedition by any indisposition then I must lament my misfortune, and

1 The brothers Robert and (General) James Dormer.

2 An allusion to the joke in Horace, Epistle I, ii. 42. Rough stone used architecturally is called 'rustic'.

3 Lord Bathurst had purchased the Sapperton estate in 1711 in order to enlarge his park, and had demolished the house. Pictures of Cirencester Park, with commentary by Mr. Christopher Hussey, can be found in the issues of *Country Life* for 16 and 23 June 1950. It is not clear which of the numerous architectural trifles that adorn the park was at this time under construction.

be content with your directions at a distance. Pray let me hear from you by next post, for I shall wait with great impatience. The foundation of the building, described in the enclosed plan, will be laid by that time, and one arch up; but I will do no more before you come, if by the next you tell me that you will be so good to your faithful servant.

*POPE *to* FORTESCUE — 16 *August* 1736

The Pierpont Morgan Library

I thank you for your account of your Reception on the Humber, & at Lanesboro'.[1] Which I shewd to Lord Burlington, with your Compliments, & had them properly returned to you. I had written to you the post before, & told you my Abdication of Twitnam for the Shepherds Hutt, where I lay safely conceald 2 days. I've been there last week once, for the last time this month, being to set out for Lord Bathursts in a Week more. I conclude you will be pleased to have your Bed occupied by a Lady in my absence,[2] tho I could better like it were so while I was present: But her Modesty has hitherto not permitted her to use you or me so freely; for she is yet in London, much to her sorrow. Indeed I could be glad of any Occasion to contribute to her better Health & greater Quiet, than she ever enjoys in her own strange Family: and any thing that weans her from it, & could teach her to live by her self, would be the best Service that could be done her. I fancy, if she once felt the Sweets of Independency, & Peace, she could not return to noise & oppression; And never was any Place so proper to prove *in how very Little Compass* these Enjoyments may lie, than your House of five foot. But I've much ado to persuade her to try it for a week or two during my journey, without your Express Permission: Much less can I move her to go with me to a place her Physician prescribes, the Bath, 3 parts in 4 of the Way to which, I am going alone in a Coach. What a Prude is a Woman, that manages her reputation with a Judge, & an old Poet? (or rather Philosopher)? If we cannot persuade her, it will be a Shame both to Poetry & Oratory; & Mr Bethel, with all his Plainness, must be allowed to have more Rhetoric, who could prevail on One Lady to travel with him in a Chaise all over Italy, & another to live & dye under his Tuition in France. I envy you the pleasure of meeting so honest a Man[3] as scarce any Circuit can afford; and one that I wish were a Judge too, that you might travel together, seeing all the Evil and doing all the Good under the Sun. I dare say the Reflection of doing Right to the Injurd must

[1] Fortescue had presided in the Summer Assizes at Kingston-upon-Hull 29 July, and at York during the week of 2 Aug. He had visited Bethel at Beverley and had seen Lanesboro, Lord Burlington's Yorkshire estate.

[2] Martha Blount.

[3] i.e. as Hugh Bethel.

counterbalance the pain one of your soft nature may find in punishing the Guilty. For the most part, in doing the latter, you do both, whereas in the former you do but one of these: I've often thought, Good nature, properly felt, would make a rigorous Judge, & give a sort of Joy in passing the Sentence, both as it is *Justice*, and as it is *Example*; tho it might make him weep for it afterwards, & draw the more pity, not only to consider it is a *Man* that suffers, but that a *Man* can be capable of the *Vice* which deserves it.

I have nothing to tell you from this Side of the world from whence all that is particularly dear to you is now gone, unless it be the Memory of some friends, & the Good will you bear us. Be assurd, no one of them is more constantly mindful of you or of the many proofs of your friendship, than | Dear Sir | Your ever faithful | & affect: Servant | A. Pope

Twit'nam | Aug. 16. 1736

†POPE *to* SWIFT 17 *August* 1736

1740

Aug. 17, 1736.

I find, tho' I have less experience than you, the truth of what you told me sometime ago, that increase of years makes men more talkative but less writative: to that degree, that I now write no letters but of plain business, or plain how-d'ye's, to those few I am forced to correspond with, either out of necessity, or love: And I grow Laconic even beyond Laconicisme; for sometimes I return only Yes, or No, to questionary or petitionary Epistles half a yard long. You and Lord Bolingbroke are the only men to whom I write, and always in folio. You are indeed almost the only men I know, who either can write in this age, or whose writings will reach the next: Others are mere mortals. Whatever failings such men may have, a respect is due to them, as Luminaries whose exaltation renders their motion a little irregular, (or rather causes it to seem so to others). I am afraid to censure any thing I hear of Dean Swift, because I hear it only from mortals, blind and dull: And you shou'd be cautious of censuring any action or motion of Lord B.[1] because you can hear[2] it only from shallow, envious, or malicious reporters. What you writ to me about him I find to my great scandal repeated in one of yours to —[3] whatever you might hint to me; was this for the prophane? the thing, if true, should be conceal'd; but it is I assure you absolutely untrue, in every circumstance. He has

[1] B.] Bolingbroke *1741 Dab.*

[2] you can hear] you hear *1741 L*; *1742 L.*

[3] The blank is difficult to fill. Elwin thought a remark to Sir William Wyndham caused Pope's comment. Ball suggested Ford as the name; but Ford was a friend of Bolingbroke's, not among the 'profane'. If suggestions are still in order, why not Oxford?

fixed in a very agreeable retirement near Fontainbleau, and makes it his whole business *vacare literis.* But tell me the truth, were you not angry at his omitting to write to you so long? I may, for I hear from him seldomer than from you, that is twice a year[1] at most. Can you possibly think he can neglect you, or disregard you? if you catch yourself at thinking such nonsense, your parts are decay'd. For believe me, great genius's must and do esteem one another, and I question if any others can esteem or comprehend uncommon merit. Others only guess at that merit, or see glimmerings of their minds: A genius has the intuitive faculty: Therefore imagine what you will, you cannot be so sure of any man's esteem as of his. If I can think that neither he nor you despise me, it is a greater honour to me by far, and will be thought so by posterity, than if all the House of Lords writ Commendatory Verses upon me, the Commons order'd me to print my Works, the Universities gave me publick thanks, and the King, Queen and Prince crown'd me with Laurel. You are a very ignorant man; you don't know the figure his name and yours will make hereafter: I do, and will preserve all the memorials I can, that I was of your intimacy; *longo, sed proximus, intervallo.*[2] I will not quarrel with the present Age; it has done enough for me, in making and keeping you two my friends. Do not you be too angry at it, and let not him be too angry at it; it has done and can do neither of you any manner of harm, as long as it has not and[3] cannot burn your works: while those subsist, you'll both appear the greatest men of the time, in spite of Princes,[4] and Ministers; and the wisest, in spite of all the little Errors you may please to commit.

Adieu. May better health attend you, than I fear you possess; may but as good health attend you always as mine is at present; tolerable, when an easy mind is join'd with it.

*POPE *and* MARTHA BLOUNT *to* FORTESCUE

26 *August* [1736]

The Pierpont Morgan Library

Twitnam: Aug. 26.

The same post I writ to you, I received yours from Durham, & made one more visit to your Hermitage; from which I am now to fly over Mountains & Plains to places remote,[5] there being no Peace at

[1] twice a year] twice or thrice a year *1741 L; 1742 L.*

[2] *Aeneid*, v. 320.

[3] and] nor *1741 Dab.*

[4] spite of Princes] spite Princes *1741 Db.*

[5] Fortescue is still on the Northern Circuit, and Pope is preparing to go to Cirencester. It was perhaps about this time that an episode, unmentioned in Pope's letters, was reported to Swift in a letter from Mrs. Pendarves (i.e. Delany), 2 Sept. 1736. Pope 'was leading a young lady into a boat, from his own stairs, her foot missed the side of the boat, she fell into the water, and pulled Mr. Pope after her; the boat slipped away, and they were immediately out of their depth, and it was with some difficulty they were saved. The young lady's name is Talbot.'—Ball, v. 377. Pope did not go to Cirencester. See iv. 39.

Twitnam. And in the conclusion, the Shepherds Tabernacle will be inhabited by a proper person for Innocence & Simplicity, to abide for ever in such Tabernacles, Mrs Blount, who comes thither directly. I expect her here to day, & keep my Letter open, that she may under her own hand tell you, what a life she means to lead there: I hope twill be such as may not derogate from the Character of a Judge of this Land, nor bring any Scandal upon you. She is resolved to obey your Injunctions & rise early, which she has practisd by way of Preparation at Lady Gerards before, and literally gets up by six every morning. The weather here is inviting beyond expression; I hope you find the Consolation of it in your Journies. I am a very poor Traveller, & shall think of you every jolt I feel. Pray make my Services memorable and respectable (that is a properer phrase than acceptable, when a person of your Dignity is the bearer of them) to Mr Murray: He is one of the few people whom no man that knows, can forget, or not esteem. I shall make your Compliments where I go: I hope to be back again before Michaelmass, & pray tell Mr M. so, who gave me some hopes I might see him about that time. Lord Burlington sends you his Services: his Lady has been very ill of a Fever. I hope you will let me hear often from you; where-ever I am, they send yours after me. News I have none; I think the Court itself is as idle as I am; the Great World sleeps, & I am glad on't, for then the Little World sleeps too. I love my Superiors so well, that I rejoice when they partake My own happiness.—As to my health, I think it, upon the whole, better: but I hope yours is better still, or it is worse than I wish you. I have nothing to add, but that assurance which can never vary, that I am Ever Yours.

[*From here in Miss Blount's hand*]

Sir,—I can't enough thank you, for the pleasure & convenience you'l afford me in your house; which Mr Pope assures me you will your self be pleased with. I do really think it will contribute to my health. I shall be here (if I wanted other memorandums of you) put daily in mind of my obligations to you; and daily wish you the same quiet & satisfaction which I shall receive thro your means. All health attend you! I am Faithfully Yours M; Blount

Address: To the Honble Mr | Baron Fortescue: | in | Bell Yard | by | Lincolns Inne | London.

Endorsement: Mr Pope | Augst 26. 1736.

POPE *to* MRS. KNIGHT[1] *6 September* 1736

Bowles (1806), x. 117–19

Sept. 6, 1736.

Madam,—I take your rebuke in Mrs. Blount's letter kindly; but indeed I know nothing so fruitless as letter-writing. It can amount only to this, to be certified that our friends live, and that we live mindful of them; the first of which one may generally know otherwise, and the latter no friend can or ought to doubt. I have often heard of you; and, without hearing particulars, am satisfied, that while you are alive, you are doing some good, and remembering those of whom you have the same opinion. Indeed, I know but one circumstance in which it is very pleasing (if not very reasonable) on both sides, to demand, and to tell, all particulars of, and to one another: it is, when two people are in love. Now you see, Madam, that whenever I write to you often, it will amount to a direct declaration, which I fear would immediately make you yourself put a stop to it. Therefore, not to be impertinent at my age, I'll be content with putting you in mind (though I think myself happy enough not to believe it necessary) that I wish to be your servant in any thing. But it would be downright impudence to imagine your regard for me extended to a desire of knowing a thousand things about a person so little significant to your real service or welfare.

I like better the Christian language, of saying *I pray* for yours here and hereafter; which is true, and which is, in reality, all we can do for one another, for the most part: and I think Mrs. Elliot will be on my side. If we both join in these prayers, I hope more good may accrue to your soul, than I dare name, or than the Rev. Mr. Harte may allow of.

In the mean time, I will only pray that you may be delivered from all evil, and particularly, in the first place, from all evil workers, or workmen, who are as dirty and as noisy as devils, in your house. But you may wish me joy of workmen in my garden; which I think as delightful, as the others are dreadful. You may as much expect to see a new garden, when you come to Twitnam, as I to see a new house when I go to Gosfield. I hope they will drive you out to London, since I shall be kept hereabouts all the autumn. I guess Mr. Harte is in his element, among builders and bookcases: I wish him happy sincerely in every thing.

I foresee Mr. Newsham's return is approaching.[2] I doubt not he will bring you back the completion of your happiness; and if he does, I must say you will owe something to Mr. Mallet, in not only restoring you a son as good as he carried him out (which few tutors do), but

[1] Bowles printed this letter (lacking an address presumably) as to 'Mrs. Nugent'; but Mrs. Knight did not marry Nugent until March of 1736/7.

[2] Mallet, as tutor, had been guiding young Newsham about Europe for some months.

in a great degree making and building up, as well as strengthening and improving, what is the greatest work man or woman ought to be proud of, a worthy mind and sound body. May the just occasion of so much pride and pleasure to you, ever continue! Nothing on earth better than this can be wished you by | A. P.

*POPE *to* ALLEN 8 *September* [1736]

University of Chicago

Sept. 8.

I hope you are returned in perfect health: Providence I believe will guard you, for good purposes. I think it fortunate that I was well while I had your Company to injoy; the very day you left me, Health left me; & I've had Headakes almost constantly. I will try your Remedy, & travel, in a week or two, to Southampton,[1] if I find I can be of any Use there: If not, I'll go on Gardening here; Tis an innocent Employment, & the same that God appointed for his First Man. I've sent you the Hymn, a little alterd, & enlargd in one necessary point of doctrine, viz: the third Stanza, which I think reconciles Freedom & Necessity; & is at least a Comment on some Verses in my Essay on Man, which have been mis-construed. Mr. Hooke transcribed this Copy, without having one himself; as I believe no man has, since I gave it twenty years ago, in its first State, to the Duke of Shrewsbury.[2]—I have sifted into the Affair of that Gentleman,[3] & find he has no other scruple of receiving Subscriptions, but the fear his health may retard the Impression so long, as to render the Subscribers uneasy. Therfore I will do the thing you proposed, & add more of any of my friends, or myself. Adieu dear Sir; let me know Sometimes that you live, & are pretty well: All other happiness a Right Mind will give itself. I am truly | Yours. | A. Pope

Address: To | Ralph Allen Esq: at | Bath. | Way of London.

A
Prayer to God
1715.

Father of All, in ev'ry Age,
In ev'ry Clime ador'd,
By saint, by savage, and by Sage
Jehovah, Jove, or Lord!

[1] Pope went to Southampton (to Lady Peterborow) for the second time this year in October, to aid in perfecting the gardens at Bevis Mount, of which place he was very fond.

[2] Charles Talbot, Duke of Shrewsbury (1660–1718).

[3] Nathaniel Hooke. The subscriptions were for his *Roman History*, of which vol. i (dedicated to Pope) was advertised in *The Daily Gazetteer*, 28 Feb. 1737/8, as to be 'deliver'd to the subscribers by G. Hawkins only'. It was printed by James Bettenham and others.

Thou Great First Cause, least understood,
Who hast my Sense confin'd,
To know but this, that Thou art Good,
And that myself am blind.

Yet gav'st us in this dark Estate
To know the Good from Ill;
And, binding Nature fast in Fate,
Left'st Conscience free, and Will.

What Conscience dictates to be done,
Or warns me not to do,
This, teach me more than Hell to shun,
That, more than Heav'n pursue.

What Blessings thy free Bounty gives,
Let me not cast away,
For God is paid when man receives,
T'enjoy, is to obey.

But not to Earth's contracted span
Thy Goodness let me bound,
Nor think Thee Lord alone of Man,
When thousand Worlds are round.

Let not this weak unknowing hand
Presume Thy Bolts to throw,
Or deal Damnation round the land,
On each I judge Thy Foe.

Save me alike from foolish Pride,
Or impious Discontent,
At ought thy Wisdom has deny'd
Or ought thy Goodness lent.

Teach me to feel another's woe,
To hide the fault I see;
As I to others mercy show,
That mercy show to me.

If I am right, Thy Grace impart
Still in the right to stay,
If I am wrong, oh teach my heart
To find that better way.

Mean as I am, not wholly so,
Since quicken'd by Thy Breath,
Oh lead me wheresoe're I go
Thro' this day's Life or Death.

This day be bread and peace my Lot,
All else beneath the Sun,
Thou knowst if best bestow'd or not,
And let Thy Will be done.

POPE *to* SLINGSBY BETHEL 14 *September* 1736

Elwin–Courthope, ix. 156

Twickenham, 14 Sept., 1736.

I lately received a very good account from your brother of his health. I should be glad to have as good an one of your own, of which I have not heard, since you told me you wanted it. I am sorry your affairs would not permit you to have tried to improve it here; and I fear they will rarely suffer you to call this way. I write this to give you a trouble, in case you can help me to some good dry Madeira, fit for present use, which I would be glad to have half a hogshead of, or in the mean-time a few dozen: your brother's telling me it often fell in your way made me presume so far on your good nature. If any subscribers to my Prose works have fallen in your way (of which Mr. Bethel lately sent me his list) be pleased to tell me, and whether for the guinea or half guinea books?[1] The number will be sufficient without the names, for which I must speedily issue out receits. I am, sir, your most obliged and affectionate humble servant.

*POPE *to* FORTESCUE 21 *September* [1736]

Arthur A. Houghton, Jr.

Sept. 21. [1736]

I am as you guess'd, returned from one Journey,[2] & now I must add I am going on another: But to the quietest place I can go to, where I never yet pass'd a fortnight, but by a fatality, I think, I fall to writing verses. I wrote there my last Epistle; & began an Imitation of the finest in Horace this spring; which I propose to finish there this autumn.[3] I mean Lord Peterborow's at Southampton, where I am to

[1] When published in May 1737, Pope's *Letters* were advertised to sell for a guinea in large folio or quarto. The small folio sold for a half-guinea.

[2] The place from which he has returned is unknown. His journey is anticipated in his letter to Fortescue, 26 Aug., and might have been directed to Cirencester, but see iv. 39.

[3] He wrote there (or at least finished) his *Epistle to Dr. Arbuthnot* and very likely the *Sober Advice* (which he does not own). The poem now in process must be *The First Epistle of the Second Book of Horace* (to Augustus), published in May 1737.

put the last hand too to the Garden he begun, & lived not to finish. It is a place that always made me Contemplative, & now Melancholy; but tis a Melancholy of that sort which becomes a Rational Creature, & an Immortal Soul. I propose to go next week & stay till the middle or toward the End of October, when I hope to find you in London, as well or better than you set out. It gives me pleasure to reflect that you are now at your own Home,[1] and in a Condition of Life which may encourage you to beautify and improve that which may be the Receptacle of your Age, & the End of all your Labors. You can cast a Glympse at Posterity, in your Daughter, & please yourself in the thought of Childrens Children enjoying it: I see nothing but Mrs Vernon, or [a] Sugar-baker, to succeed to my Plantations. However they will have abundantly recompensed my Care, if they serve to receive, amuse, & shelter a few such friends as you, at your Intervals of leisure, while I live: relieve a laborious Lawyer between the Terms; inspire a Political Acquaintance between a Saturday Evening & Munday, with Schemes for public Good in Parliament; or receive with hospitality a discarded Courtier. *Mihi & Amicis*, would be the proper Motto over my Gate; & indeed, Plus Amicis quam Meipsi.—Mrs Bl. is still very happy in your house, all alone! It is a sort of agreabler kind of *Hospital* to her, where she recovers health, & has an old Nurse to tend her in Mrs Shepherd.[2] As she has the House for nothing, it may be properly calld her *almshouse*, and is of a Size extremely well adapted for one. I suppose she prays, as good Papists in those cases do & ought, for her Benefactor.

Lady Suffolk I am told is returned;[3] b[ut I] have lived wholly out of town, & have seen none of the Travellers yet, nor probably shall for some weeks, having no business in London but when some Particular Friends are there, and I think there are but few Particular Friends. The rest of this paper will only serve to give my best wishes to all your family, & to desire to hear still from you. Whereever I am, I am Most affectionatly Yours. [unsigned]

Address: To the Hon: Mr Baron Fortes-|cue. in | Bellyard, by | Lincolns Inne | London.

Endorsement: Mr Pope | Septr. 21. 1736.

Postmark: 22/SE

[1] In Devonshire, to which this letter will be forwarded by Fortescue's servants in London.

[2] This good woman probably gives The Vineyard its privately used nickname of 'Shepherd's Hut'.

[3] *The Lond. Daily Post*, 12 May 1736, had reported: 'The Hon. George Berkeley, Esq; and his Lady the Countess of Suffolk arrived last Saturday at Calais, on their way to the Duke of Richmond's House at Aubigny in France, to visit the Earl of Berkeley.' Pope reports their return.

*POPE *to* SLINGSBY BETHEL 30 *September* 1736

Sotheby's Catalogue for Sale of 23 November 1900, lot 284

I am going on Monday to Southampton for a Fortnight, after which I shall be found at any time, if you have the leisure to come hither. Mrs. Blount sends you her faithful services, who is here at Richmond, I send you as you was pleased to order, some of the half guinea Receits, for which your signing will do as well as mine, & I have as yet signed none. But I would have everybody told that, *unless they have a mind for the Larger Print*, which cannot be pyrated, tho' in a smaller I doubt not it will.

*POPE *to* THE EARL OF ORKNEY[1] 4 *October* 1736

Craster Tower

Twick'nham: Octr 4. 1736.

My Lord,—Give me leave to tell you *honestly*, which is better than *with Respect*, (tho I truly bear you a great deal, and no more than is due to so long and approved a worth, conspicuous both in publick & private Life) that I am something more than honour'd & obliged; I take your Letter *most kindly*. And let me (my Lord) use these phrases to you in my acknowledgments for it, rather than those which are more common, & less sincere. The great Goodness you are pleas'd to express in your concern for my health of Body & the great Partiality in regard to my better Part, my mind, which would be very little worth if it were no better than my body; Both these I am highly obliged by. I thank God my Illness is gone well over, & I am capable of performing a Promise I made to visit a Friend, just at this time, whose Gardens I have ingaged to finish. So that I must not hope to injoy the pleasure your Lordship so kindly would afford me at Bath; and can only wish to claim a share of the Honour & Friendship you offer me, at your return. I shall be a good part of the winter in London, & there I can have the pleasure of planning & drawing Schemes, as well as of seeing & consulting yours, against the next Planting Season. We may so far enjoy Cliveden, in spite of bad weather;[2] and I may have some merit, in Sacrificing to the Place before I enjoy it.

I hope then to find you My Lord, in as good Vigour as is reputable for an Old Soldier; who (I dare say) would be sorry, not to have born

[1] The text is from a transcript kindly made by Sir Edmund Craster, who found at Craster Tower, Northumberland, an early transcript made by John Craster, Esq. (d. 1764), who was an executor of Lord Orkney's will. The (first) Earl of Orkney, one of Marlborough's generals, died in 1737. Note the 'character' of Marlborough in the second paragraph.

[2] One assumes that his lordship wishes Pope's advice on 'improving' the gardens at Cliveden, where he lived at this time. Since his lordship died in Jan. 1736/7, doubtless 'the pleasure of planning & drawing schemes' came to naught.

any one Fatigue, or not to have had any one Wound, which contributed any way to the Good, or Glory of his Country. I am indeed afraid, the Great General you mention was not acted entirely by so good a spirit, but had meaner mixture with his great Qualities: But I lament with you his negligence, in not procuring what real Merit he had, & what shining Virtues as a Public man, to be better transmitted to Posterity.

I have nothing (my Lord) to add, but my Thanks, and my wishes to deserve the distinction & good will you shew me. I have truly one merit, which is, that I honour Worth in all Professions & in all Parties: and I cannot help being particularly, not only in justice, but by Inclination, My Lord, your most obedient, most faithfull, and humble Servant | A. Pope

Endorsement: A letter of Mr Popes to Ld. Orkney

*POPE *to* ALLEN — 7 *October* [1736]

Egerton 1947

Southampton Oct. 7.

I was prevented from my Intention of enquiring concerning your Health & giving you something a better account of mine than I did in my last, by my Journey to Southampton. However it shall no longer delay the pleasure I unfeignedly take in putting you in mind of me, as one who is truly your Servant & Friend. This place is very pleasing to me, both from the memory of what it has been in my Lords time, & what it is now: Here I live very much in my own way; Nor is the Ease & Enjoyment of it lessened, but advanced, by the Employment of planting & improving many Parts of it: To be *at Ease* is the greatest of happiness (at Ease, I mean, both of Mind & Body) but to be *Idle* is the greatest of unhappiness, both to the one & the other.

I gave Mr Hook what you sent me,[1] in Money, not telling him from whom it came, tho there could be no harm, or Shame, in telling him his Benefactor, Yet as you did not Explicitely say so, I would not without your leave. He has given me a Receit for as many Books as subscribed for: it seems they will be Two large Quarto's at 15s. each. I went no farther than to assure him the Subscription was not my own.

I have the headake while I write this, but not so violently as at some other times. My Lord & Lady Burlington, ever since you & I were there,[2] have been ill by turns, till their intention of going to

[1] Allen evidently is 'doing good by stealth' in aiding the subscription for Hooke's *Roman History* (4 vols., 1738–71).

[2] Evidently when Allen visited Pope in August he was taken to Chiswick to meet the Burlingtons.

Yorkshire is intirely frustrated, and they both will be at the Bath this Season. He has had a dangerous Fever & Relapse. I should be more inclined than ever I yet was, to pass a few weeks there, (you may guess the reason) and in the Planting Season; but the Care, & dispatch, necessary for my Book, will not allow it. You may truly impute the Merit however, of a friendly Intention, which whenever I can execute it will be a Real Contentment to Sir Your faithful Servant | A. Pope

I propose God willing to be at home again by the 20th. I say God willing, on all accounts; but particularly now, when I fear the bad weather, & very bad way which I am informed is about Basingstoke, may be difficult to me. And I must go the worst way, by that place, because I hope there to serve a Friend.[1] adieu. These Letters will never come into our Collection, therfore let us Commend ourselves honestly, when we do or suffer any thing in a Good Cause.

The Lady of this place designs to be at Bath a month or 2 in the Winter: I know you'l be glad to do her any Service if she wants it, as I know the Value you set on a deserving person, even tho' a Person of Quality.—once more Adieu.

I am imploying much of your Stone in the Ornaments of this place. pray tell me if it will do for Paving in a room very little frequented? I know it is rather too soft for any other paving.

Address: To | Ralph Allen Esq; at | Bath.
Endorsement: Southton

*POPE *to* RICHARD SAVAGE[2] 17 *October* 1736

Add. 4478c

I answer Yours by the first Post, since I find they are in so much Hast about Mr Gay's Life. It is not possible for me to do his Memory the Justice I wish in so much Hurry. Therefore I would by no means have my Name made use of, where I cannot have the Account such as it ought. I only recommend to your Friendship, that nothing be said of any particular Obligations that worthy & ingenious Man had to me, further than a sincere Esteem & the Natural Effe[ct] of it. I am sure they will do him Injustice, if they say more on that Article.[3]

[1] Pope's only friend at Basingstoke, so far as is known, was Thomas Warton the elder, who was vicar there. In 1717 he had given Pope a copy of *Gorboduc* (see Pope to Digby, 2 June 1717—a letter printed in 1735—and Warton the younger's *Hist. of Eng. Poetry*, iii [1781], 356–7), from which, at Pope's instance, Joseph Spence had in March of 1736 published a modern edition of that little known classic. Whether Pope's return via Basingstoke had anything to do with any of these facts is doubtful.

[2] This letter, discovered by Mr. Edward Ruhe as transcribed in the diary of Thomas Birch (Add. MS. 4478c, ff. 17–18), has been edited with comment by Mr. Ruhe in *RES*, v (1954), 171–4. For this present edition also Mr. Ruhe kindly transcribed the letter. It concerns the life of Gay to be printed in *The General Dictionary*, 2 Dec. 1736.

[3] Critics had more than once attributed to Pope an undue share in Gay's successes.

And as to that of his being apprenticed to one *Willet*, &c.[1] what are such things to the public? Authors are to be remember'd by the Works & Merits, not Accidents of their Lives. But if they will speak of his Condition of Life, let them remember to say *he was born of an ancient Family*, & *Secretary*, not *Servant*, *to the Duchess of Monmouth.* As to that, which would be most material, his true Character, it was every way amiable; & none of his Schoolfellows could draw that, which was manifested in the future Course of his Life to those of the Nobility & first Genius's of his time, who loved him, & with whom he convers'd intirely.[2] I take Mr. Hill's Zeal very kindly, & it is agreeable to that spirit & Warmth which he always shews for Virtue & Learning. I am only afraid of his exceeding in what he says concerning me. I do own, I wish, since I cannot now contribute (upon the foot the Work stands) any *Additions*, that I might have the power of some Expunctions, & could see the Proofs to that End. Otherwise it will be better I should not be privy to the least of the matter. I shall be in London, & will be heard of at Mr. Dodsley's in five or six days.[3] Adieu, Dear Sir, & believe me, without forms, affectionately Yours | A. Pope.

Southampton *Oct.* 17th, 1736.

POPE *to* MRS. KNIGHT — 30 *October* 1736

Bowles (1806), x. 119–20.

Saturday, Oct. 30, 1736.

Dear Madam,—After hoping to be able to dine with you this day, my very uneasy indisposition of cholic and headach rendered it impracticable: and it has continued in such a manner all this day too, that I find I must never attempt to dine so late as a fashionable hour. I really dread the consequence of doing it at Marble-Hill; when you

[1] In 1706 Gay had been released from his apprenticeship to a London silk mercer, whose name seems to occur here.

[2] The implication is that Aaron Hill and perhaps Gay's other well-known schoolfellow, William Fortescue, lacked the sense of Gay's amiability that people such as Swift and the Duchess of Queensberry had loved.

[3] Further information from Mr. Ruhe communicates an entry Birch made in his diary for 1 Nov. 1736 (f. 18v): 'Recd the Proof sheet of the Article on Mr. Gay from Mr. Pope, who alter'd the first line in his Epitaph of that Poet.' In Add. 4475, f. 27, appear loose notes for a life of Gay, among which are some of the details to which Pope objected; but none of the objectionable details occurs in the printed life, which concludes with the remark: 'For several particulars in this Article we are obliged to two very ingenious Gentlemen, *Aaron Hill* Esq; and *Richard Savage* Esq; the latter of whom procured this article to be revised by Alexander Pope Esq.' [*General Dictionary*, v (1737), 408.] Mr. Ruhe has found a mutilated letter dated [ ]t 19, 1736, from Savage to Birch, which indicates that letters, now unknown, passed between Pope and Savage on this subject. It is not certain that the initial T, with which the printed life is signed, means (as Professor Griffith has suggested in his *Bibliography*, p. 374) that Theobald was the author of it. If he was, Pope's unwillingness at first to be privy to its details is understandable. The fascicle of the *Dictionary* was announced as published on 2 Dec. 1736.—*The Craftsman.*

set out thence after twelve, it will be three before you can be there, and four before they'll dine. I can, therefore, upon serious consideration, no more propose any enjoyment in waiting on you on Monday; but rather will meet you at Lady Suffolk's that day or the next, and go home in the mean time as I can, dreading a fresh cold. You see what an unable man you have to do with! Well may he call himself an humble, very humble servant.

*POPE *to* HUGH BETHEL — 2 *November* 1736

Egerton 1948

Novr. 2d 1736.

It was a very great Pleasure to me to hear from you, after a long Intermission (for so I thought it) which partly my Rambles & intended Rambles occasioned. I put them off with almost as much difficulty as I might have made them, & at the Expence of writing Letters in folio to Lord Bathurst about his Plans. I went only to Southampton, where the Roads are good, the accomodation good, Friends all the way, & a most agreable Retreat at the End, with a very valuable Person to crown all the Satisfaction of it. With her I often drank your health, but with Temperance. My health was advantaged evidently by the Quiet I there enjoy'd, & the little Exercise it obliged me to. Since my return, which has been but a fortnight, I have been taken up with my book,[1] which is above half printed & will be deliverd by Ladyday next, ⌜I have not taken any care more than I think decent, about saving myself harmless in the expence; nor do I see much taken; by none so much as yourself, I assure you hitherto, considering the Sphære you move in. I have many awkwardnesses in it, & hate to speak of it; tis really to no purpose I do it, but to *Serve Myself*, which Is a Motive I am not us'd to make my *Sole* one.⌝[2] For all it can do is to shew, I disapprove many things I formerly thought & wrote, by my omitting them in this Edition. And that no other value is to be set upon the rest; but as they are the markes of a plain mind, & undesigning heart, is a serious truth: For considerd as a *Book*, it is nothing.

I have seen your good Brother, who is your Brother, in the great readiness he shews, to do another any good turn. He has helpd me to some unpay'd-for Madera, & is zealous in pursuing your directions. He hopes you will hasten your coming hither on account that Sir Will. Codringtons family come early. He has long had an Intermitting Fever about him, for which he still takes the bark.

I have so much, & so little, to say of Mrs Patty Bl[oun]t that I wish you'd come, & join with me in forcing her to do herself right. I

[1] The *Letters*.

[2] This passage was quoted by Ruffhead, p. 499.

am tired with good Wishes for her, they are so ineffectual: her Virtues & her Weaknesss go hand in hand; I don't know which are greater: but every one who is her friend on account of the first must frett at the latter, since nothing can do her good for want of her own Cooperation. She is very sensible of any true Friendship, at the same time that she dissappoints any true Friend. And her constant Memory & Regard of You in particular, is greater than [I can] express.

I beg you will remember me among your friends, Mr Moyzer, Col. Gee, &c. No Yorkshire Hearts can bear you more good wishes, than ours here do. You will give us equal pleasure whenever you come among us; for sincerely Mrs P.[1] & I always think you come too late, & go away too soon.

Adieu dear Sir. | Your ever faithfull, ever | affectionate Servant | A. Pope

Mr Baron Fortescue sends you his most sincere Service Mr Kent enquires always of you I've seen Mr Cleland very little of late, but I gave him your Services the other day.

Address: To | Hugh Bethel Esqr at | Beswick, near Beverley | Yorkshire
Postmark: 2/NO

POPE *to* ALLEN[2] — 6 *November* 1736

Egerton 1947

Nov. 6. 1736.

I do not write too often to you for many reasons, but one which I think a good one is, that Friends should be left to think of one another for certain Intervals without too frequent Memorandums it is an Exercise of their Friendship, & a Tryal of their memory: and moreover to be perpetually repeating assurances is both a needless & a suspicious kind of Treatment, with such as are sincere. Not to add the Tautology one must be guilty of, who can make out so many Idle words as to fill pages with saying One thing. For All is said in this word, I am truly Yours.

I am now as busy in Planting for myself as I was lately in planting for another.[3] And I thank God for every Wet day & for every Fog, that gives me the headake, but prospers my works. They will indeed out-live me (if they do not die in their Travels from place to place, for my Garden like my Life, seems to me every *Year* to want Correction & require alteration, I hope at least, for the better.) But I am pleasd to think my Trees will afford Shade & Fruit to Others, when

[1] Mrs. P[atty Blount].

[2] Printed almost entire by Warburton in 1751. He omitted the parts towards the end of the letter here placed in half-brackets, and later editors have contentedly reprinted his abbreviated text.

[3] The Countess of Peterborow at Southampton.

I shall want them no more. And it is no sort of grief to me, that those others will not be Things of my own poor Body, but it is enough they are Creatures of the same Species, and made by the same hand that made me. I wish, (if a Wish would transport me) to see You in the same Employment, and it is no partiality even to You, to say it would be as pleasing to the full to me, if I could improve your Works, as my own.

Talking of works, mine in prose are above 3 quarters printed, & will be a book of 50 & more sheets in 4°. As I find what I imagin'd, the slowness of subscribers, I will do all I can to disappoint *You* in particular, & intend to publish in January, when the Town fills, an Advertisement that the book will be deliverd by Lady-day,[1] to oblige all that will subscribe, to do it; In the meantime I've printed Receits, which put an End to any persons delaying upon pretence of *Doubt*, by determining that Time. I send you a few that you may see I am in earnest Endeavoring all I can to save your money, at the same time that nothing can lessen the Obligation to me. ⌜If Leake think it (as I believe he will) more Satisfactory to those he has taken in, to give them these receits instead of his own, I will send you what number you please. Only I would have him write his own name at the top of each Receit, to distinguish thro' what hands they past.⌝

⌜Mr Hook gave me no Separate receits but only one general Memorandum, which I can therfore throw away. I wait to let him know his benefactor when you like I should.⌝

I thank God for your health, & for my own which is better than usual. ⌜I have some Commissions from Lady Peterborow to you about Bath-Stone, but the Designs are not yet quite setled, & if she speak of it, tell her so. I am sincerely Ever Yours. | A. Pope⌝

[1] *The London Gazette*, 8–12 Feb. 1736/7, printed the following advertisement:

'Speedily to be published, | In Quarto, large Folio, and small Folio, | The WORKS of Mr. POPE in PROSE; *And first, an* Authentic Edition of his *LETTERS*, with large Additions of several never before printed, between Him, the late Bishop Atterbury, and other Eminent Persons. |

'All this Author's Genuine Works in Verse having been publish'd in Quarto, large Folio, and small Folio; those he has written in Prose are intended to be publish'd in the same Manner, to accommodate such Persons as are desirous to complete those Setts. No more will be printed than *Five Hundred*, the Reason for which is, that when a larger Number were printed of the former *Poetical* Volumes, the Proprietors were considerably Losers, by their being immediately Pyrated in an incorrect and scandalous Manner.

'Subscriptions for the LETTERS, at One Guinea the whole Payment for the Quarto or large Folio, and half a Guinea the small Folio, are taken in by J. & P. Knapton, at the Crown in Ludgate-street; L. Gilliver, at Homer's Head over against St. Dunstan's Church in Fleet-street; J. Brindley, in New Bond-street; and Rob. Dodsley, at Tully's Head in Pall Mall.

'N.B. Whatever Persons have the former Volumes and would complete their Setts, are desired to pay their Subscriptions by or before the Fifteenth of next Month at farthest; the Number being so small, and the Books to be delivered as soon as the Subscription is full.

'Whoever wants the former Volumes may have them at the same Places.'

POPE *to* THE EARL OF ORRERY *7 November* 1736

The Pierpont Morgan Library

Twit'nam. Nov. 7th 1736.

My Lord,—I know Your Humanity, and I know your Friendship: therfore I can say nothing unworthy of them, as it would be, did I pretend to talk of either. I use you well, in giving You opportunities of exerting them; for that, I am sure, obliges you most.

I wrote about six weeks since, a long letter to the Dean,[1] whom we so justly value & love: In that, I said what I thought would come to you better recommended, & strengthen'd, my opinion of, & my obligation to, Your Lordship. I find you have not seen him, nor probably that Letter, which was as much to You as to Him. I imagin'd you had been both in Dublin. The subject you are so Considerately kind as to mention, was a part of it; It is certain, it is of the highest Importance to me, that what Letters I have written to him (you may be sure very free and unreserv'd ones) may not fall into bad hands. I mentiond to him my desire to put them into Your Lordship's, where I knew they would be safe, nor is there Any Secret of my Heart I wish hidden from you. But his answer was, *he had kept Every Scrap I ever writ, & would take care of them.* I earnestly beg your Lordship (should that happen which may God Almighty prevent!) that you will take all possible methods to get them into your Custody. This Letter will be a Warrant for your so doing, to any person he may leave them to. But God forbid we should live (at least that I should live) to feel this Stroke![2] Multis Fortunae vulneribus perculsus, huic uni me Imparem Sentio.

When you get to Dublin (whither I direct this, supposing you will see our dear Friend as soon as possible) pray put the Dean in mind of me, & tell him I hope he receivd my last. Tell him how dearly I love, how greatly I honour him; how gratefully I reflect on every Testimony of his Friendship; how much I resolve to give the Best I can of my Esteem for him, to Posterity: and assure him the World has nothing in it I admire so much; nothing, the Loss of which I should regret so much, as His Genius, and His Virtue.[3]

Why (my Lord) do you not tell me how you enjoy your own health? no man is more sincerely desirous to hear of the Encrease of it, than |

[1] The last preceding letter extant is dated 17 Aug.—rather more than six weeks. The letter to which Pope refers seems to be lacking.

[2] Doubtless Swift's health was bad, but there was surely no need to take seriously his reiterated expectations of an immediate death. Orrery seems so to have taken them, and to have been consistently alarmist to Pope about the Dean's health. The anxiety evoked naturally increased Pope's desire to have his letters back.

[3] At the beginning and end of this paragraph Pope or another placed editorial brackets, to indicate that (*a*) the paragraph might be printed or (*b*) that it should be omitted in printing. Elwin–Courthope first printed it. See Orrery's *Remarks*, p. 230.

My Lord, Your Ever obliged, most | obedient humble Servant, | A. Pope.

Be pleas'd to direct to me at Twit'nam near Hampton Court.

Upon folding this letter, I find the hurry in which I wrote, in the concern your News[1] affected me with, has made me write it on the wrong side. pray pardon my inattention, on this occasion.

My Book is above half printed, & will come out by Lady-day next. It makes too large a Quarto.

Endorsement: Mr. Pope, Novbr: 7th 1736. No. 6.

*POPE *to* THE EARL OF BURLINGTON

27 *November* [1736]

Chatsworth

Nov. 27th.

My Lord,—I was very watchful in my Enquiries of yours and my Lady Burlington's state of health from any quarter that I could hear of it. To have written, to know from yourself, was but to force you to do what you knew I wishd. It is with sincere Concern that I am interested in your Welfare, & that I learn from Mr Kent that my Lady continues so disorderd, as not to have begun the Waters till lately. It would be a real Satisfaction to me to know she mends, of all her Complaints, or of any. I hope the account I hear of your self, my Lord, is true, that you are perfectly well. Mr Lyttleton[2] acquaints me how happy he is in your Favour; I can promise you a great many pleasures in the further knowledge of each other: The minds of worthy men, like all true merit, open by degrees; & a man that glares at first sight is like a Picture that glares at first sight, (I don't say so of a Woman)

The greatest news I have to tell you is, that the Signior[3] is in perfect tranquillity, enjoying his own Being, & is become a happy but plumper copy of General Dormer. In sweetness of manners, he is allowed on all hands to be a meer Ludovico Dolce. We dined together upon Pictures, Mademoiselle du Parc,[4] and a Mummy. I go frequently to him, not only thro' the affection I bear him, & the Respect I pay to

[1] The news of Swift's ill health. Swift himself, writing to William Richardson, 23 Oct. 1736, speaks of his 'ill state of health' and laments that he 'cannot ride above a dozen miles in a day'.—Ball, v. 384–5.

[2] Both Lyttelton and Lord Burlington were at Bath now. See Lyttelton to Pope, 4 Dec. 1736.

[3] The common nickname of the Italianate Yorkshireman, William Kent.

[4] Mlle du Parc was a name made famous by a lovely actress of the plays of Corneille, and other dramatists. She died in 1668, and the reference here may be to a later beauty, adored by Kent.

his Genius, but in good earnest to learn what I can, & as often as I can, of yourself & my Lady; to whom I would write, if I could say a thing that would please her; the best I could say, for my self, would be but a Repetition of the many wishes I make for her recovery.

I am | My Lord, | Your most obliged faithfull | humble Servant | A. Pope.

||SWIFT *to* POPE 2 *December* 1736

Longleat Portland Papers, xiii (Harleian transcripts)[1]

I think you ow me a Letter, but whether yo do or not I have not been in a condition to write. years and Infirmatyes have quite broke me. I mean that odious continual disorder in my Head. I neither reed, nor write; nor remember, nor converse All I have left is to walk, and ride. The first I can do tolerably; but the latter for want of good weather at this Season is Seldom in my Power; and haveing not an ounce of Flesh about me; my Skin comes off in ten miles riding because my Skin and bone[2] cannot agree together. But I am angry, because you will not Suppose me as Sick as I am, and write to me out of perfect Charity, although I should not be able to answer. I have too many vexations by my Station and the Impertinence of People, to be able to beare the Mortification of not hearing from a very few distant Friends that are left; and, considering how Time and Fortune hath ordered[3] matters, I have hardly one friend left but your Self. What Horace Says, Singula de nobis anni precedantues[4] I feel every Month, at farthest; and by this computation, if I hold out two years, I Shall think it a Miracle. My Comfort is you begin[5] to distinguish So confounded early, that your Acquaintance with great men of all Kinds was allmost as antient as mine, I mean Witcherly, Row, Prior, Congreve, Addison, Parnel, &c. and in Spight of your Hart, you have owned me a Cotemporary, not to mention Lord Oxford, Bulingbroke, Harcourt, Peterborow. In Short, I was t'other day recollecting twenty Seven great Ministers or men of Wit and Learning, who are all dead, and all of my Acquaintance within twenty years past neither have I the Grace to be Sorry, that the present times are drawn to the Dregs as well as my own Life—may my friends, be happy in this and a better life, but I value not what becomes of Posterity when I consider

[1] A new scribe here transcribes Swift's difficult hand, and some of his more absurd errors are silently corrected from the text printed in 1740. Pope in printing omitted passages here placed in half-brackets.

[2] me; . . . my Skin and bone] me, my skin and bone cannot agree *1742 La.*

[3] hath ordered] have ordered *1740–2.*

[4] The scribe's hash made from *praedantur*. Correct in the printed texts. See Horace, *Epistles*, II. ii. 55.

[5] begin] begun *1740; 1741 L; 1742 L*: began *1741 Dab.*

from what monstors they are to Spring—My Lord Orrery writes to you toMorrow, and you See I Send this under his Cover or at least franck'd by him. He has 3000 a year about Cork, and the Neighborhood, and has more than three years rent unpayd This is our condition in these blessed Times, I writ to your Neighbor[1] about a month ago, and Subscribed my name: I fear he hath not received my Letter, and wish you would ask him; but perhaps he is Still a rambling; for we hear of him at Newmarket, and that Borehave hath restored his health—Can you put me out of pain concerning Lord Bol[2]—I mean partly as to his Health, but chiefly as to his fortune for he hath been so long a Squanderer of both, that I lament him more than I do my Self, who never enjoy a healthy hour. ⌜I hope you Sometimes See my Lord and Lady Oxford, I love them dearly, but we Seldom correspond of late because we have nothing to say to each other; and it is enough when I desire you to present my humble Service and all good Wishes to them, and the Dutchess their Daughter.⌝ How my Services[3] are lessened of late with the number of my friends on your Sides! yet my Lord Bathurst and Masham[4] and Mr Lewis remain, and being your acquaintance I desire when you See them to deliver my Compliments but chiefly to Mrs Patty Blunt[5] and let me know whether she be as young and agreeable as when I Saw her last. Have you got a Supply of new friends to make up for those who are gone? and are they equall to the first? I am afraid it is with Friends as with Times; and that the Laudator temporis acti se puero[6] is equally applicable to both. I am less grieved for living here, because it is a perfect Retirement, and consequently fittest for those who are grown good for nothing; For this Town and Kingdom are as much out of the World as North Wales—My head is so ill, that I cannot write a Paper full as I used to do; and yet I will not forgive a blank of half an Inch from you—I had reason to expect from some of your Letters that we were to hope for more Epistles of Morality, and I assure you, my Acquaintance resent that they have not Seen my name at the head of one. The Subjects of Such Epistles are more[7] usefull to the Publick, by your manner of handling them than any of all your Writings, and although in so profligate a world as ours they may possibly not much mend our manners, yet Posterity will enjoy the Benefit whenever a Court happens to have the least relish for Virtue and Religion.[8] ⌜Pray God

[1] Pulteney.

[2] *Lord Bol—* is only a dash in 1740 and 1741 Dab; in 1741–2 L all is omitted from *Can you put me* down to *Daughter*. All eds. 1741–2 omit the passage in half-brackets.

[3] i.e. the number of friends to whom I send 'services' in my letters.

[4] Bathurst and Masham] Bathurst and Lord Masham *1740–2*.

[5] Mrs. Patty Blunt] Mrs. P.B. *1741 L*; *1742 L*.

[6] Horace, *Ars poetica*, l. 173.

[7] more] the most *Longleat*.

[8] As printed by Pope the letter ends here just before the last sentence, which, in the transcript, has the Latin phrase inserted in the hand of Lord Oxford himself.

long preserve my dearest Friend in Life and health, and Happyness or rather you may say with Horace, Det Vitam, det opes, animam mihi ipse parabo.[1] I am ever entierly yours. &c.⌝

⌜Dublin Dec. 2. 1736.⌝

LYTTELTON *to* POPE[2] — 4 *December* [1736]

Hagley

Decr 4

You judged very right that I shoud suffer a great deal of Uneasiness from your letter coming to me in Another hand,[3] and the reason given for it by Lord Cornbury; but Lord Burlington very soon relievd me by telling me he had reciev'd the following post, a very long and chearfull one in your own. I was just sitting down to return you thanks, when your second Letter came and made me happy by giving me a further Assurance of your health, & of that friendship, which, though I never doubt, I can't recieve a New Mark of without delight.

I am so vastly recoverd by these Waters that I can now enjoy the kindness of my friends without fearing they shoud suffer by their concerns for me: I can hardly think of being ever ill again after drinking down Health another Month; and must desire you for the future to consider me as being, next to the Royal family, the most incapable of Sickness, Pain, or any bodily infirmity, of all the Men you ever knew excepting only the Immortal Doctor Cheyney, who desires his compliments to you, and bids me tell you that he shall live at least two centuries by being a Real and practical Philosopher, while such Gluttonous Pretenders[4] to Philosophy as You, Dr Swift and My Lord Bolingbroke die of Eating and Drinking at fourscore. The Doctor is the greatest Singularity,[5] and the most Delightfull I ever met with. I am not his Patient, but am to be his Disciple, and to see a Manuscript of his which comprehends all that is necessary, salutary, or usefull, either for the Body or the Soul.

Lord Burlington has left Bath a great deal sooner than I hoped, or he intended, for fear of my Lady's catching the Small pox, which is very much here, and a bad sort. I refer you to him for all the News this place affords which he will give you much more agreably than I

[1] *Epistles*, I. xviii. 112.

[2] For some years Pope had been acquainted with Lyttelton's father, Sir Thomas, and doubtless with George Lyttelton himself. This, however, seems to be the earliest of their letters to be preserved. It was first printed under the wrong date of 1739, but Elwin rightly places it in 1736.

[3] A headache or other slight ailment at times led Pope to use an amanuensis.

[4] The description is additional evidence of Pope's reputation for overeating!

[5] Dr. George Cheyne (1671–1743), now residing at Bath, was a distinguished physician, whose character Lyttelton admirably sketches in this letter.

can, and must beg you to make my compliments to Lady Suffolk, Mr Murray and Mrs Blunt, the last of whom I am particularly oblig'd to, and wou'd always have her see me with your eyes, that she may not only be very partial to me, but perceive, notwithstanding all her Modesty, that there is none of her Sex upon whose friendship I set a greater, or perhaps an equal Value.

George Grinville[1] is in a fair way of Recovery; the Waters agree with him, and he mends in all respects. Cheyney says he is a Gyant, a son of Anack, made like Gilbert the late Lord Bishop of Sarum,[2] and may therefore if he pleases live for ever; this present Sickness being nothing but a fillup which Providence gave him for his Good to make him temperate, and putt him under the care of Doctor Cheyney. When we tell the Doctor, that He always has been temperate, a Water Drinker, and Eater of Whitemeats, he Roars like a Bull, and says we are all Liars; for had he been so, he cou'd not have had an Inflamation, which he is ready to prove by all the Rules of Philosophy, Mathematicks, and Religion. Lord Orkney may just keep life enough to be in pain a year or two longer.[3] I am sorry for him with all my Soul, for he is a Man of great Merit to the Publick, and . . .[4] who has been little Rewarded in proportion to the Services he has done.

Adieu My Dear Mr Pope, take care of yourself that we may have some Eminent Merit left among us, and to make a great part of the happiness of your most faithfull and oblig'd humble servant | G Lyttelton

Bath December the 4th

MARTHA BLOUNT *and* POPE *to* MRS. KNIGHT

10 *December* [1736]

Stowe 755

I resolve to write to you once before you come to town, tho you make ever so much hast; as I think both by inclination & necessity you will. & tho I have nothing to say to you but to Mrs Elliot, & nothing to say to her but about Horsses. Mr Noell hears she no long'r hires horsses of the Man she employd last year, therfore begs me to desire he may have her Custome again. I hope this petition will operate soon, as I hope her devotion this Christmass will bring her hither, and that you'l not be able to stay behind her. Lady Suffolk & Mr Berkeley are well, & in town, the King is expected on Sunday. tho there is so

[1] George Grenville (1712–70), nephew of Lord Cobham and cousin of Lyttelton, was at this time a 'Boy Patriot' at the beginning of a long and influential career in politics.

[2] Cheyney was a relative of the bishop's.

[3] Lord Orkney died within two months after this was written.

[4] At this point in the letter two lines have been illegibly overscored.

little in this letter, you will take it not the less kindly since it contains so great a truth as the assurance of being to you both a Faithfull & | ever Mindfull Servant | M Blount

Decer the 10

I have hinderd Mrs B. from making her letter longer, and now I find I have as little to say myself. But about Christmass time there is great plenty of Good wishes sent about the kingdome, and I should be ashamed if Gosfield had not mine. It is a place I have been very happy in,[1] and abounds with Plenty, Peace, and chearful Countenances. I doubt not at this season all people *round it* are happy. God forbid any one *in it* should not! when it is considerd, that nothing has been done but by His ordination.

I am naturally led, from a Christian Sentence, to think of Mrs Elliot for whose Welfare of body & Mind I sincerely wish, not to say, pray. I hope as Mrs B. does, that the Motive she mentions can not fail to bring her to Town, & then you can not stay long if at all, behind. Believe, among all those who desire this, none does it more than | Your most faithfull & most | obliged Servant | A Pope

Address: To | Mrs Knight, at Gosfield, | near Braintree, in | Essex.
Postmark: 11/DC
Endorsement: Mrs Blunt & | Mr Pope Decbr | the 10 1736

LYTTELTON *to* POPE[2] — 22 *December* [1736]

Hagley

Bath Decem: the 22d

My Cold is gone, and I am now so much recoverd that I grow very impatient to get away from Bath; You need not be told that the Desire of seeing you is one great cause of that impatience, but to shew you how much I am Master of my passions, I will be quiet here for a week or ten days longer, and then come to you in most outrageous Spirits, and Overset you like Bounce when you let her loose after a regimen of Physick, and Confinement.

I am very glad that His R. H. has receiv'd two such honourable Presents at a time, as a whelp of *her's*[3] and the Freedom of the City. Poor Lord Orkney is gone away from hence so weak and ill that I scarce think he can reach London. I made your compliments to him

[1] Pope visited Gosfield in 1731 and perhaps at other times.

[2] Most of the personal references in this letter were explained in Lyttelton's last (4 Dec. 1736).

[3] In May had been published *Bounce to Fop, an Heroick Epistle* 'by Dr. S—t'. Mr. Ault rightly assigns the poem to Pope (*New Light*, pp. 340–50). In ll. 69–80 the poet offers a whelp to the Prince of Wales—an offer which his royal highness seems now to have accepted.

which he receiv'd with all the pleasure which One in his condition feels from the praise of a Wise and Virtuous Man; with more I dare say than he wou'd have receiv'd as kind a message from a Minister of State:

Nam veræ voces tum demum pectore ab imo ducuntur.[1]

I am sorry Mrs Blunt has any complaint; and that Lady Suffolk can't get rid of her's; but your continuing well and in good spirits is such good news that it makes amends for all the rest: it even comforts me for the loss of that Sweet Fœtus, which, had it liv'd, might have been a Princess[2] Royal. Mr Grinville, who is very much recoverd, and Mr Hammond, who is the joy and dread of Bath,[3] join in compliments to you with your most Affec': | G Lyttelton

†POPE *to* SWIFT 30 *December* 1736

1740

Decemb. 30, 1736.

Your very kind letter has made me more melancholy, than almost any thing in this world now can do. For I can bear every thing in it, bad as it is, better than the complaints of my friends. Tho' others tell me you are in pretty good health, and in good spirits, I find the contrary when you open your mind to me: And indeed it is but a prudent part, to seem not so concern'd about others, nor so crazy ourselves as we really are: for we shall neither be beloved or esteem'd the more, by our common acquaintance, for any affliction or any infirmity. But to our true friend we may, we must complain, of what ('tis a thousand to one) he complains with us; for if we have known him long, he is old, and if he has known the world long, he is out of humour at it. If you have but as much more health than others at your age, as you have more wit and good temper, you shall not have much of my Pity: But if you ever live to have less, you shall not have less of my Affection. A whole People will rejoyce at every year that shall be added to you, of which you have had a late instance in the publick rejoycings on your birth-day. I can assure you, something better and greater than high birth and quality, must go toward acquiring those demonstrations of publick esteem and love. I have seen a royal birth-day uncelebrated, but by one vile Ode, and one hired bonfire. Whatever years may take away from you, they will not take away the general esteem, for your Sense, Virtue, and Charity.

The most melancholy effect of years is that you mention, the catalogue of those we lov'd and have lost, perpetually increasing. How

[1] Lucretius, iii. 57.

[2] *Of Orange* is crossed out.

[3] James Hammond was a protégé of Lord Chesterfield; as a poet he is far from terrifying.

much that Reflection struck me, you'll see from the Motto I have prefix'd to my Book of Letters, which so much against my inclination has been drawn from me. It is from Catullus,

Quo desiderio veteres revocamus Amores,
Atque olim amissas flemus Amicitias![1]

I detain this letter till I can find some safe conveyance; innocent as it is, and as all letters of mine must be, of any thing to offend my superiors, except the reverence I bear to true merit and virtue. But I have much reason to fear, those which you have too partially kept in your hands will get out in some very disagreeable shape, in case of our mortality: and the more reason to fear it, since this last month Curl has obtain'd from Ireland two letters, (one of Lord Bolingbroke and one of mine, to you) which we wrote in the year 1723, and he has printed them,[2] to the best of my memory, rightly, except one passage concerning Dawley which must have been since inserted, since my Lord had not that place at that time: Your answer to that letter he has not got; it has never been out of my custody; for whatever is lent is lost, (Wit as well as Mony) to these needy poetical Readers.[3]

The world will certainly be the better for this change of life. He seems, in the whole turn of his letters, to be a settled and principled Philosopher, thanking Fortune for the Tranquility he has been led into by her aversion, like a man driven by a violent wind, from the sea into a calm harbour. You ask me if I have got any supply of new Friends to make up for those that are gone? I think that impossible, for not our friends only, but so much of our selves is gone by the mere flux and course of years, that were the same Friends to be restored to us, we could not be restored to our selves, to enjoy them. But as when the continual washing of a river takes away our flowers and plants, it throws weeds and sedges in their room; so the course of time brings us something, as it deprives us of a great deal; and instead of leaving us what we cultivated, and expected to flourish and adorn us, gives us only what is of some little use, by accident. Thus I have acquired,

[1] Pope used this same quotation from Catullus in his letter to Orrery, 10 May 1736.

[2] In *The Lond. Eve. Post*, 11 Nov., Curll had advertised: 'This Day is published (from the Original Manuscripts, transmitted from Ireland) with a curious Print of Lord Bolingbroke, *Letters written by Mr. Pope and Lord Bolingbroke, to Dean Swift, in the Year 1723*.' The two letters (they are probably a single joint letter) were issued also under the title *New Letters of Mr Alexander Pope, and several of his Friends*, and they were at once included in vol. v of *Mr. Pope's Literary Correspondence* (see here iv. 60). When reprinting in 1741 Lc Curll changed his story about the letters coming from Ireland and on p. 217 added a note: 'These two Letters were given to Mr. *Curll* by a Gentleman of Essex.' Somehow, one guesses, Pope fed these letters to Curll so that he might have further reason to urge on Swift (as he here does) the return of his letters. For texts of the two letters, see ii. 183–9.

[3] In Pope's London editions of 1741–2 he quoted most of this paragraph, beginning with 'But I have much reason . . .' to emphasize its relation to the publication of the Swift–Pope correspondence. The shifted reference of 'He' in the next line suggests an excision.

without my seeking, a few chance-acquaintance, of young men,[1] who look rather to the past age than the present, and therefore the future may have some hopes of them. If I love them, it is because they honour some of those whom I, and the world, have lost, or are losing. Two or three of them have distinguish'd themselves in Parliament, and you will own in a very uncommon manner, when I tell you it is by their asserting of Independency, and contempt of Corruption. One or two are link'd to me by their love of the same studies and the same authors: but I will own to you, my moral capacity has got so much the better of my poetical, that I have few acquaintance on the latter score, and none without a casting weight on the former. But I find my heart harden'd and blunt to new impressions, it will scarce receive or retain affections of yesterday; and those friends who have been dead these twenty years, are more present to me now, than these I see daily. You, dear Sir, are one of the former sort to me in all respects, but that we can, yet, correspond together. I don't know whether 'tis not more vexatious, to know we are both in one world, without any further intercourse. Adieu. I can say no more, I feel so much: Let me drop into common things—Lord Masham has just married his son.[2] Mr. Lewis has just buried his wife.[3] Lord Oxford wept over your letter in pure kindness.[4] Mrs. B.[5] sighs more for you, than for the loss of youth. She says she will be agreeable many years hence, for she has learn'd that secret from some receipts of your writing.—Adieu. If you have lost a vol. of Rymer's *Foedera*, Mr. Arbuthnot will restore it you.[6]

[1] The 'Boy Patriots', when in 1741 they could read this account, must have raised their eyebrows. Warton (Pope's *Works* [1797], ix. 291) says: 'Some of these new friends were, I know, displeased at the manner in which they are mentioned in this Letter.' See Swift to Pope, 9 Feb. 1736/7 and notes.

[2] To Henrietta, daughter of Salway Winnington, Esq., of Stanford Court, on 16 Oct. 1736.

[3] She died 21 Nov. in London.

[4] Over the melancholy expressed in the letter of 2 Dec.

[5] B.] Blount *1741 Dab.*

[6] The London editions of 1741–2 omitted this last sentence. One assumes that George Arbuthnot going over his father's books had come upon a stray volume lent long ago to the Doctor by Swift. The sentence is not in Elwin–Courthope.

1737

Pope's correspondence in this year is focused on the publication of the 'authentic' edition of his letters and the tedious process of persuading Swift to return the letters Pope had written to him. Once these two things are achieved, correspondence for the year wanes. A long series of rambles gets very little attention in letters. One would like further letters covering the friendship of Pope with Lord Cornbury, which seems especially notable in this year.

POPE *to* THE EARL OF ORRERY[1] 14 *January* [1736/7]

The Pierpont Morgan Library

Twitn'am Jan. 14. | 1736/37.

My Lord,—Your Lordships great Good nature, and constant Memory, in whatever regards those you favor, appears to me very strongly in your late letters. I had answerd the first of them but for the promise you made me of a second, to which I therfore thought some new Reply might be needful. But I find Every thing you do demands fresh Acknowledgment, as every day of your life, I believe, you are thinking how to serve or oblige. I mentiond Your Lordship in my first letter to the Dean, as the Person I could wish trusted with the Copyes or Originals of those Letters. On his silence, I writ another, about a week ago, pressing the necessity of that Care, but without naming You again. He wrote to me (in that Letter you franked) without any reply, as if he had not receivd my first, & asked me some Questions relating to Lord Bo: which I had fully before acquainted him of. I hope you find no remarkable defect in his Memory, tho it is what he complains of to me. Indeed his Whole Letter was very melancholy, and with so warm Expressions of Tenderness towards me, that it doubled my Concern. Within this month, the same Villain that publishd my other Letters, has printed two to the dean: one from Lord Bo: the other from me: the Copies whereof (he says in his advertisements) came from Ireland,[2] as indeed they must, for I had none: It could have come about only by the Deans lending them out of his hands. The Dean's answer to those Letters I have by me, very safe. No doubt this fate will befall every Scrap he has, & he tells me he has ev'ry Scrap I ever writ to him.—But I am tiresome to your Lordship on this head: Yet as It concerns your Friends, & is Matter

[1] In the date the year has been added by Lord Orrery.
[2] See Pope to Swift, 30 Dec. 1736.

of Honour, I know you make it your own case.—My present Book might have been much the better, had my other Friends kept *All* I wrote, or kept *nothing*. As it is, it can be but of One Use, & that is only to myself; to prove I never thought my Letters fit for the World, by keeping Copies; there not being any sort of Series to be recover'd, or any Letters left of the most Material Subjects that have past in my time. It will only show, that such & such Men were my friends, & give me an opportunity to manifest my own disapprobation of many things I writ, by omitting them. I acknowledge with gratitude your Lordships Zeal in taking care that This should not be done too much at my own expence, or cost me more in Mony than it can be worth in Fame. As to the Mony you receive, be pleasd to return it to Brindley,[1] but favor me at the same time with notice of it. He paid me the 7 guineas. The books I will send (I think by April at farthest) as you shall direct. I am overruled by my friends here, as to the Miscellaneous Prose pieces,[2] which they would omit, & make the Volume consist wholly of Letters; with a view of enlarging it hereafter with Other Letters, which may come in order, rather than to break the order by inserting things between of so different a nature. This will make the present Volume less, than I threatend you with: Both are actually printed, & are too great a bulk together. Would the Dean send me those Letters, & mark over every sentence he would leave out, I would copy, & return them to him: That point, if you have any opportunity, I wish you could bring him to: Indeed it is a mortifying prospect, to have one's most secret opinions, deliverd under the Sacredness of Friendship, betrayed to the whole World, by the unhappy Partiality of one's own best Friends in preserving them.

Excuse my Lord, all this, from a Man Sick of writing, sick of publishing, tired of the Vanity of Fame, as much as of any other of the Vanitys of his Youth; Only pleas'd & proud, of the good opinion, & Indulgence of Worthy Men; & in particular of yours, shewn so eminently to | My Lord | Your most obliged & faithful | humble Servant, | A. Pope.

Endorsement: Mr Pope. | Janry 14th 1736–7.

[1] James Brindley of New Bond Street first appears as one of Pope's publishers with the quarto *Letters*.

[2] 'Thoughts on Various Subjects' had been printed to conclude the volume. The sheets were cancelled, and four letters were added—two of which are the 'new' letters published by Curll, letters from Pope and Bolingbroke to Swift. The cancelled sheets were saved and used in the quarto edition of Swift–Pope letters, *Works in Prose*, vol. ii (1741). See Griffith, pp. 358 and 430.

*POPE *to* JONATHAN RICHARDSON[1] [*February* 1736/7]

Professor F. W. Hilles

The business of this, next to the Assurances of my true affections, is to desire you to send me inclosd to my Lord Cornburys near Oxford Chappel the Exact size of the Plate for the title page of my book. Which is wanted so far as to stop the printing the Title. I am with sincere regard | Your most affect: hum-|ble Servant, | A. Pope

Munday | night.

Address: To Mr Richardson in | Queens Square | Bloomsbury. | Giles

THE EARL OF ORRERY *to* POPE[2] 5 *February* 1736/7

Harvard University

Dublin: February 5th: 1736–37.

Contrary Winds kept away Yours of the 14th of January from me till last Monday. You seem as sick of Fame, as I am of Ireland. The Time was when You courted Her: She now courts You: pray don't be coy, but have that Regard to Prince Posterity, which his Highness will certainly have for You. My Wishes to serve You are boundless my Power is close limited, and my Opportunities are very few: be assur'd I am happy in the Thoughts of doing any Thing acceptable to You: Command me therefore freely, and without Reserve.

Your Apprehensions of the Dean's Memory are too well grounded: I think it decays apace: and I own I am shock'd when I see any new Instance of it's Failure. Designing People, who swarm about him will make their advantage of This.[3] I watch as closely as is possible, but I can seldom see him alone—I will endeavour to gain the Point you mention, but I have found him lately very Shy upon the Subject.[4]—pray contrive to lett me have those two Letters (printed by Curle) to Him. I possibly may make some Use of Them towards securing the other Papers.—Whatever Progress I make in this Affair, if any, You shall have the earliest Notice of It.

[1] This letter is to be related to that of 3 Mar., also to Richardson. How long before that letter this should date it is impossible to say. Mondays for this February were 7, 14, 21, 28. The plate in question was a line engraving of Pope's head in profile, done by Richardson and inscribed in the engraving *Amicitiæ causa*. In some states the plate bears the date 1736.

[2] The text is from Orrery's autograph transcript in Orrery Papers, vol. vii.

[3] Orrery must include Mrs. Whiteway in this designing group, and yet letters from his lordship to her indicate a most cordial and friendly relationship.

[4] The shyness may be due to his desire to prevent publication of Pope's letters to him or to a desire to publish them himself. One recalls Faulkner's statement (Swift's *Works*, Dublin, 1772, xiv, pp. v–vi) that about this time Swift offered his letters to Faulkner to publish. Certainly Swift is shy in the letters preserved to us when it comes to replying to Pope's solicitations concerning the letters.

Be so good to send me over thirty of your Quarto and Thirty of your small Folio Books; for tho' there is not that Number subscrib'd for, yet it is not impossible but when they come over I can dispose of Them. When People see the Book in the hands of Others, they'l be desirous to have it Themselves, especially the Ladies who never cast their Eyes upon a fine Thing without wishing for it. at worst, I can but bring Them back again: I trouble You with this Request because in my late Correspondence with *Brindley*, I perceive, whatever His Heart may be, his Head is but a bad One. If there is no Ship coming from London to Dublin, pray, forward Them to Me by the Chester Waggon, Lett the Box be directed to Mrs *Kenna* at Chester to be forwarded to the E. of *Orrery* at Dublin.—If I thought Brindley could comprehend This, You should not have heard a word of It.—All, All, your other Commands shall be obey'd.

There is handing about this Town, with the Secrecy usual on such Occasions, a Letter of the Bishop of *Rochester's* concerning *Iapis*.[1] Is it to appear amongst your Letters? The Judicious, and People of deep Penetration, who are innumerable, swear it was wrote to You. But hitherto It has escap'd Print: & remains a valuable universal Manuscript.

I am much pleas'd with the Design of making two Volumes of your Prose Works—I hope They will not stop there. The Dean has a large Collection of Papers, which I heartily wish safe in your Hands. His Health is excellent at present, but his Giddiness returns so often & so suddenly that I dread the Consequence.—I have lately had a great Loss in my good Freind & Father the Earl of *Orkney*: We were prepar'd for the Blow by his long illness: and It was some alleviation to find him reliev'd from an Excess of Pain. My Correspondence is much enlarg'd on this melancholy Occasion, but I will always find time to Assure You that I am, Sir, | Your very affectionate faithfull Servant. | Orrery.

Heading: To Alexander Pope, Esq.

†SWIFT *to* POPE[2] 9 *February* [1736/7]

1740

Feb. 9, 1735–6.

I cannot properly call you my best friend, because I have not another

[1] Atterbury's dissertation, *Antonius Musa's Character, represented by Virgil, in the Character of Iapis*, first published in 1741, is to be found in his *Epistolary Correspondence* (ed. J. Nichols), i (1783), 329–71. It was addressed to Dr. John Friend.

[2] In the editions of 1740–2 this letter was both misplaced (before that of 7 Feb. 1735/6) and misdated, 1735/6. Ball (v. 414–16) placed it in 1736/7, and that is probably its proper place. It clearly answers Pope's letter of 30 Dec. In his letter to Pope, 2 Dec. 1736, Swift had mentioned Horace's *singula de annis*, and Pope probably enclosed in his letter of the 30th

left who deserves the name, such a havock have Time, Death, Exile and Oblivion made. Perhaps you would have fewer complaints of my ill health and lowness of spirits, if they were not some excuse for my delay of writing even to you. It is perfectly right what you say of the indifference in common friends, whether we are sick or well, happy or miserable. The very maid-servants in a family have the same notion: I have heard them often say, Oh, I'm very sick, if any body cared for it! I am vexed when my visitors come with the compliment usual here, Mr. Dean I hope you are very well. My popularity that you mention is wholly confined to the common people, who are more constant than those we mis-cal their betters. I walk the streets, and so do my lower friends, from whom and from whom alone, I have a thousand hats and blessings upon old scores, which those we call the gentry have forgot. But I have not the love, or hardly the civility, of any one man in power or station: and I can boast that I neither visit or am acquainted with any Lord Temporal or Spiritual in the whole kingdom; nor am able to do the least good office to the most deserving man, except what I can dispose of in my own Cathedral upon a vacancy. What hath sunk my spirits more than even years and sickness, is reflecting on the most execrable Corruptions that run through every branch of publick management.

I heartily thank you for those lines translated, *Singula de nobis anni, &c.* You have put them in a strong and admirable light;[1] but however I am so partial, as to be more delighted with those which are to do me the greatest honour I shall ever receive from posterity, and will outweigh the malignity of ten thousand enemies.[2] I never saw them before, by which it is plain that the letter you sent me miscarry'd.—I do not doubt that you have choice of new acquaintance,[3] and some of them may be deserving: For Youth is the season of virtue: Corruptions

the translation, for which Swift thanks him. The entire imitation of Horace, Epistle II, ii, was not published until Apr. 1737, and Pope probably sent over only the one passage from that Epistle together with the compliment to Swift in the Epistle to Augustus. One can hardly assume that he risked sending complete texts of poems to Ireland before they had appeared in London, but he may have done so.

Certain editors have seen in this letter signs of Swift's mental decay through melancholy. To counter such an unwarranted interpretation one may quote Lord Orrery (*Orrery Papers*, i [1903], 183, 192), who in Dec. 1736 reports: 'The Dean enjoys more Health than he has felt for some Years past . . . [he] grows younger as his Years increase.' And in Jan. 1737 he records his presence when 'The Dean feasted his Clergy last week with Ladies, Music, Meat, and Wine'. At times the Dean was lonely and gloomy, but in reading letters passing between long-separated friends one must be aware that it was indecent not to be melancholy over absent friends.

[1] *The Second Epistle of the Second Book of Horace Imitated*, ll. 72–73. (Probably addressed to Col. Dormer of Rousham: published in Apr. 1737.)

[2] Lines 221–4 of *The First Epistle of the Second Book of Horace Imitated.* (Addressed to 'Augustus' and published in May.)

[3] Pope's new acquaintances would include the Boy Patriots, Lyttelton, West, and above these, Lord Cornbury; his friends would also include 'new' poets such as Thomson, Mallet, Harte, Dodsley, and others.

grow with years, and I believe the oldest rogue in England is the greatest. You have years enough before you to watch whether these new acquaintance will keep their Virtue, when they leave you and go into the world; how long will their spirit of independency last against the temptations of future Ministers, and future Kings.—As to the new Lord Lieutenant,[1] I never knew any of the family; so that I shall not be able to get any jobb done by him for any deserving friend.

*POPE *to* HUGH BETHEL 11 *February* [1736/7]

Yale University

Twitenham. Feb. 11.

I was in full hopes of what I had long wished for, the pleasure of seeing you, when I heard from Lady Codrington that your ill health detain'd you, and now again that you are still detain'd by a Return of your Asthma.[2] I cannot say how much I am uneasy, till I know from your own hand the true State of your health; and my apprehension is the greater, because Mrs Blount has since writ me word you have taken Quicksilver to no effect, which used to be your sure Remedy. I am now arrived, to that part of Life, when I cannot afford to bear the Hazard of a Friend; & every Attack which Sickness makes on such an one, shakes me to the very Heart. Many times I have wished, our Fortune might have been to have lived together; and tho' we cannot, I can but just endure to be Seperated from you all the Summer: The Winter lost a part of its Severity on my Constitution, when it restored You to me. But when it pleases God to debar me of that only-remaining Satisfaction, I shall give up the Only Joy left me in this Season, & keep out of Town obstinately all the Year. Every year that is added to me, diminishes the Amusements which London afforded, except in the Society of a few like you, but for whom, I would not live in Society. I therfore hope, and earnestly pray, that you may recover your health, enough to make a Journey hither desireable to You; which will restore me to that Tranquillity which I assure you I cannot have, till I see You again. Dear Sir, pray write one line to | Your Ever faithful | A. Pope.

Address: To Hugh Bethel Esq, at | Beswick, near | Beverley | Yorkshire
Postmark: [1]6/FE

1 Duke of Devonshire.—1741 Dab.
2 The asthma of 'blameless Bethel' slides into verse in the *Essay on Man*, iv. 126.

POPE *to* JONATHAN RICHARDSON[1] 3 *March* [1736/7]

The Historical Society of Pennsylvania

I hope your Friend has done justice to your Work, in rolling off that excellent Etching in My Titlepage which will be the most Valuable thing in the book. As soon as they, together with the Headpiece & Initial Letter to the Preface are done, & the Sheets quite dry, I must desire your Care again to cause them to be very cleanly packed up & sent to the Printer's Mr Wright on St Peter's hill, who should give his Receit for them & return him also the Copper Headpiece & Letter to the Preface. You know the *least Dirt* thrown on the best Work, or best character, will spoil the whole Grace of it. And pray acquaint Mr Knapton, that I will satisfy him in the amplest manner he pleases, as well as be obliged for his Care. I am at present ill, in the Country, & not able to be in town, I fear soon enough to have told you this in person, or have taken any part of the Trouble off your hands. But We know one another. Adieu. My Service to your son. | Your ever affectionate | A. Pope.

Twitenham March 3d.

Address: To Mr Richardson in | Queens Square. | Bloomsbury | London.
Frank: Free. | G. Berkeley

POPE *to* THE EARL OF ORRERY[2] 4 *March* 1736/7

The Pierpont Morgan Library

My Lord,—After having condoled several times with you on your own Illness & that of our Friends, I now claim some share myself, for I have been down with a Fever which yet confines me to my chamber. Just before, I wrote a Letter to the Dean, full of my Heart, & among other things press'd him (which I must acquaint your Lordship, I had done twice before for near a twelvemonth past) to secure me against that Rascal Printer by returning me My Letters; which (if he valued so much) I promist to send him Copies of, merely that the Originals might never fall into such ill hands, & therby a hundred Particulars be at his mercy which would expose me to the Misconstruction of many, the Malice of some, & the Censure perhaps of the

[1] The year was inserted by Elwin from Richardson's transcript. It is made certain by the reference to the engraving for the title-page of Pope's *Letters*, published 19 May 1737. Cf. the letter to Richardson here placed at the beginning of February of this year.

[2] Apparently here printed for the first time from the original letter. Hitherto it has been printed by Hawkesworth and succeeding editors from the transcript sent to the Dean by Orrery in a letter from Cork, 18 Mar. 1736/7. Orrery omitted from his transcript the last paragraph and a half, now first printed.

whole world.[1] A fresh Incident made me press this again; which I inclose to show you, & that you may show him. The Man's Declaration that he had these *two Letters of the Deans* from *Your Side the Water*, with *several others* yet lying by,[2] (which I cannot doubt the truth of because I never had a Copy of either) is surely a Just Cause for my Request. Yet the Dean, answering *Every other Point* of my Letter with the utmost Expressions of Kindness, is silent upon this, and the *third time* silent. I begin to fear he has alredy lent them out of his hands; and in whatever hands, while they are Irish hands, allow me My Lord to say they are in dangerous hands. Weak Admirers are as bad as malicious Enemies, & operate in these cases alike, to an authors disparagement or Uneasiness. I think this I made the Dean so just, so necessary a Request, that I beg your Lordship to second it by showing him what I write.—I told him, as soon as I found myself obligd to publish an Edition of Letters to my great sorrow, that I wish'd to make use of some of these, nor did I think Any Part of my Correspondencies would do me greater honour, & be a really a greater pleasure to me, than what might preserve the Memory how well we lovd one another. I find the Dean was not quite of the same Opinion, or he would not, I think, have denyd this. I wish, some of those sort of people always about a Great Man in Wit, as well as about a great Man in Power, have not an Eye to some little Interest in getting the Whole of these into their own possession. I'll venture however to say, They would not add more Credit to the Deans Memory by their Management of them, than I by Mine: And if, as I have a great deal of Affection for him, I have with it *Some Judgment* at least, I presume My Conduct herein might be better confided in.

Indeed his Silence is so remarkable, it surprizes me. I hope in God it is not to be attributed to what he complains of, a Want of Memory: I would rather suffer from any other cause than what would be so unhappy to him. My sincere Love for this most valuable, indeed Incomparable Man, will accompany him thro Life, & pursue his memory were I to live a hundred lives, as many as his Works will live, which are absolutely Original, unequald, unexampled. His Humanity, his Charity, his Condescention, his Candour, are equal to his Wit, &

[1] The possibility was that in some letters to Swift Pope may have dropped remarks of a political cast which worried him.

[2] In his prefatory 'To my Subscribers *encore*' in *Mr. Pope's Literary Correspondence*, vol. v, Curll says: 'Beside, what is here presented to You, I have Several other very valuable Originals in my Custody, which, with these, were Transmitted to me from Ireland.' Remarks like this, current as well in Curll's newspaper advertisements, naturally alarmed Pope. Curll was lying, but Pope could not be sure of that. This letter by Pope, barring some tactful flattery for the Dean, is a straightforward plea for the return of his letters so that he might publish them as a monument of friendship. Swift, to whom Orrery forwarded the letter, saw it as such, and agreed, finally, that Pope might have the letters. The letters of March to July that passed between Swift, Orrery, and Pope tell the story.

require as good and true a Taste to be equally valued. When all this must dye (this last I mean.) I would have gladly been the Recorder of so great a part of it, as shines in his Letters to me, & of which my own are but so many acknowledgments.—But perhaps before this reaches your hands My Cares may be over, & Mr Curl & evry body else may say & lye of me as they will; The Dean, old as he is, may have the task to defend me[1]—You'l pardon my Lord the very bad hand I write, when indeed my head is held up with difficulty Yet even in a fever I can't forget to answer anything you ask That Letter of the Bishop's was not writ to me[2]—

I was truly grievd for my Lord Orkney, he was always distinguishingly civil to me, but the last Summer came to see me, & wrote me a very friendly Invitation to accompany him to the Bath, in which Letter & Conversations he opend a great deal of his mind to me. Adieu my worthy Lord. I will obey your directions, If I do well; it will be April or May before the books can be sent. I can't write more, but my Mind is full of acknowledgments to you. Your concerning yourself so much about this Book of Letters has made me trouble you with this Remonstrance to our dear Friend the Dean; tho I am very unable to write so much. I am constantly | My Lord. | Your most faithfull | obliged humble Servant | A. Pope.

March 4. 1736

Endorsement: Mr Pope. March 4. 1736–7.

THE EARL OF ORRERY *to* SWIFT[3] 18 *March* 1736/7

Add. 4806

Corke. March 18 1736/37.

This is occasion'd by a Letter I have receiv'd from Mr Pope: of which I send You a Copy in my own Hand, not caring to trust the Original to the Accidents of the Post. I likewise send you part of a fifth Volume of Curl's Thefts,[4] in which you'l find two Letters to You (One from Mr Pope the Other from Lord Bolingbroke) just publish'd with an impudent Preface by Curl. You see, Curl like his Freind the Devil glides thro' all Key holes, and thrusts himself into the most private Cabinets.[5]

[1] The letter as hitherto printed ends at this point.

[2] The 'letter' concerning Antonius Musa as Iapis in Virgil by Atterbury. See Orrery's letter of 5 Feb. 1736/7.

[3] This is a covering letter enclosing to Swift Pope's letter to Orrery (or most of it) dated 4 Mar. The enclosure made Pope's desires as to their letters perfectly clear.

[4] This remark seems sure proof that Curll's vol. v (advertised in June 1737) was already in circulation. Pope in fact quotes from it in his letter of 4 Mar.

[5] In the transcript of this letter now preserved in the MS. Orrery Papers at Harvard, Orrery (who made the transcript himself) adds at the end of this paragraph: 'He boasts of

I am much concern'd to find that Mr Pope is still uneasy about his Letters: but I hope a Letter I sent him from Dublin (which he has not yett receiv'd) has remov'd all Anxiety of that Kind. In the last discourse I had with You on this Topic, I remember you told me, He should have his Letters, and I lost no Time in letting him know your Resolution. God forbid that any more Papers belonging to either of You especially such sacred Papers as your familiar Letters should fall into the Hands of Knaves & Fools, The profest Enemies of You both in particular, and of all honest and worthy Men in general. I have said so much on this Subject in the late happy hours You allow'd me to pass with You at the Deanery that there is little Occasion for adding more upon It at present: especially as you'l find in Mr Pope's Letter to Me a Strength of Argument that seems irresistible. As I have thoughts of going to England in June, You may depend upon a safe Carriage of any Papers You think fitt to send Him. I should look upon myself particularly fortunate to deliver to him those Letters he seems so justly desirous of. I entreat You, Give me that Pleasure. It will be a happy reflexion to me, in the latest Hours of my Life, which whether long or short, shall be constantly spent in endeavoring to do what may be acceptable to the virtuous & the wise.[1] I am, dear Sir, | Your very faithfull | & oblig'd humble Servant | Orrery.

Address: To | The Revd Doctor Swift Dean of St Patrick's | at the Deanery House | Dublin.

Frank: Free | Orrery

Endorsement (in Swift's hand): E. Orrery | Mar—21st 1736 | answered

THE EARL OF ORRERY *to* POPE 18 *March* 1736/7

Harvard University

Corke. March 18th: 1736-37.

The Account you give me of your Health strikes me with great Anxiety for You. The Honour you have done me in your Freindship and Correspondence, demands the utmost Gratitude of my Heart: and you have the highest Zeal, Affection, and Integrity that I am capable of Attendants upon your Commands. From your humanity I must insist upon an Answer to This as soon as possible: All I desire to know, is How You do? Three words will satisfye Me in that

more Letters from Ireland, but I hope his veracity in that Point is as little to be depended upon as in all Others.' Apart from this added sentence the letterbook transcript varies from the original in the British Museum only in very small or accidental slips.

[1] At the bottom of the page, where this letter ends, Orrery has written 'Turn over', and the two pages of the inside of the letter folder are occupied with his transcript of Pope's letter of 4 Mar. Probably the reason for not transcribing the last paragraph and a half for Swift, apart from its irrelevance, is that there was not convenient space on the paper.

Particular: but if you have the least Regard for your faithfull Servant, delay not a Moment to remove the Uneasiness I am in at present.

You had not receiv'd my last Letter when you wrote to me: I have forgott it's date. It was wrote amidst Lawyers and Agents in the hurry and Confusion of leaving Town: I either told you, or meant to tell you, that I had with some difficulty brought the Dean to say, that "You should have your Letters."—There are People as you observe about every Man of Witt that are full of selfish Views, and mean Designs. Their Buesness is to do Mischeif: to instil Doubts: to raise Phantoms, and to hurt as much as possible. They are Enemies to all generous Sentiments, and yet openly profess those Virtues, which they privately abhor. The Dean whose mind cannot stoop even to see low Artifice, and whose Soul is as far superiour to Baseness as to Stupidity, admitts such Wretches (with whom this Country abounds) too near his Heart. But I think I have now defeated their Malice, and carried the Point We have been so long labouring at.

I send You a copy of my Letter to the Dean, and I have sent to him a Copy of Yours to Me. I chose to be short that He might be more attentive to Yours. I dread Nothing so much as his Want of Memory, which indeed, I sigh to say it, seems to encrease every Day. His Affection to you is unlimited. He talks of You with a melancholy Pleasure, such as arises from almost a certainty of never meeting You in this world again. Would to God I could see the Dean remove himself and his Papers into your Custody. I wish his last Hours may glide away under your Roof. You & only You can do Justice to his Witt, his Virtues, and his Works. But instead of That We may live to see him mangled & dismember'd by Irish Butchers: with this Consolation only that we did all in our Power to hinder It. I have often urg'd his Going to England. Another Sessions here may make Dublin very uneasy to Him; at least I fear It will. But He is resolv'd not to stir. Heaven guard You both in perfect Health, & in as much Happiness as you can be asunder. I am, dear Sir, | Yours most faithfully. | Orrery.

Heading: To Alexander Pope Esq at | Twick'nam near Hampton Court | Middlesex.

†POPE *to* SWIFT 23 *March* 1736/7

1740

March 23, 1736–7.

Tho' you were never to write to me, yet what you desired in your last, that I would write often to you, would be a very easy task: For every day I talk with you, and of you, in my heart; and I need only set down what that is thinking of. The nearer I find myself verging to that period of life which is to be labour and sorrow, the more I prop myself upon those few supports that are left me. People in this state are like props indeed, they cannot stand alone, but two or more of them can stand, leaning and bearing upon one another. I wish you and I might pass this part of life together. My only necessary care is at an end. I am now my own master too much; my house is too large; my gardens furnish too much wood and provision for my use. My servants are sensible and tender of me; they have inter-married, and are become rather low friends than servants: and to all those that I see here with pleasure, they take a pleasure in being useful. I conclude this is your case too in your domestic life, and I sometimes think of your old house-keeper as my nurse; tho' I tremble at the sea, which only divides us. As your fears are not so great as mine, and I firmly hope your strength still much greater, is it utterly impossible, it might once more be some pleasure to you to see England? My sole motive in proposing France to meet in, was the narrowness of the passage by sea from hence, the Physicians having told me the weakness of my breast, &c. is such, as a sea-sickness might indanger my life. Tho' one or two of our friends are gone, since you saw your native country,[1] there remain a few more who will last so till death, and who I cannot but hope have an attractive power to draw you back to a Country, which cannot quite be sunk or enslaved, while such spirits remain. And let me tell you, there are a few more of the same spirit, who would awaken all your old Idæas, and revive your hopes of her future recovery and Virtue. These look up to you with reverence, and would be animated by the sight of him at whose soul they have taken fire, in his writings, and deriv'd from thence as much Love of their species as is consistent with a contempt for the knaves of it.

I could never be weary, except at the eyes, of writing to you; but my real reason (and a strong one it is) for doing it so seldom, is Fear; Fear of a very great and experienc'd evil, that of my letters being kept by the partiality of friends, and passing into the hands, and malice of enemies, who publish them with all their Imperfections on their head; so that I write not on the common terms of honest men.[2]

Would to God you would come over with Lord Orrery, whose care

[1] A footnote to this passage in 1741 Dab explains: 'The *Dean* was born in *Ireland*: This I mention because the Sentence marked may be understood in a double Sense.' Pope for some reason thought Swift born in England. He told Spence (*Anecdotes*, p. 161) that Swift said he was born 'in the town of Leicester'. Someone (Pope, Spence, or Swift) misunderstood his informant.

[2] Pope evidently has not yet had word from Orrery that he is to get his letters back from Swift. In this passage he recurs to his difficulties, and in all probability suppresses a passage begging again for the return of the letters. If he printed evidence of his desire to publish (evidence such as he gave to Orrery on 4 Mar. 1736/7) and, above all, evidence that the letters were returned, his own connexion with the publication in 1741 would be perfectly clear. Modest prudery forbade that it should be.

of you in the voyage I could so certainly depend on; and bring with you your old housekeeper and two or three servants. I have room for all, a heart for all, and (think what you will) a fortune for all. We could, were we together, contrive to make our last days easy, and leave some sort of Monument, what Friends two Wits could be in spite of all the fools of the world. Adieu.

POPE *to* THE EARL OF ORRERY 28 *March* [1737]

The Pierpont Morgan Library

My Lord,—As long as I can find in the World some Friendships which make it worth living in, and some Virtues which render it worthy living for, I cannot but thank God for my Recovery. Tho' as to one's Self, when Life is verging toward that Period, after which the Psalmist tells us it is Labor & Sorrow only, it would be a juster Motive to thank God for a Relapse. However while the Mind continues sound, the Temper not sower, tho the Constitution broken, the Head not wrong, nor the Heart weak & foolish, a Man ought neither to be uneasy himself at the Decline of Life, nor to make others so. I comply therfore with your Lordships Humane Desire, in acquainting you that I am here still, & that I have not only lost my Fever, but recover'd almost all the little Strength & Vigor I ever was Master of.

My Eyes suffer the most by my past ailment, and I write large, to give you less trouble in reading, than I have in writing. My letter will do little more than just what you bid me, tell you I am better; But I ought not to omit Expressing my hearty thanks for your good Offices, both to me & the Dean; particularly your assuring me that he, of his own accord (agreeably both to the Justice, the Kindness, & the good Judgment he ever shows) promised to send me my Letters (I hope by your own Hands when you return.) I have a Plot upon them,[1] by their means to take occasion to erect such a *Particular* & so *Minute* a Monument of His & my Friendship, as shall put to shame any of those Casual & cold Memorandums we see given by most ancient & Modern Authors, of their Regard for each other, & which yet Posterity have thought exemplary. I love him beyond all Forms of Wit & Art, & would show how much more the *Heart* of a sincere Esteemer & Honourer of Worth & Sense can do, than the Tongue or Pen of a ready Writer, in representing him to the world. Pray tell him this, and add, that As soon as I have those Letters, I will have them

[1] There is no *secret* plot (secret from Swift, that is); for Pope has repeatedly assured Swift that he wished to publish the letters as a monument of their friendship. After receiving this letter Orrery could hardly have doubted the source of the edition of 1741. He plays along, however, with Pope's pretences at that time.

transcribed, leaving out such parts as I think triffles or un-interesting, & return ~~them~~ back to him those Copies, or (if he prefers it) the Originals, blotting out those passages so as not to be read by others. I desire him to cross over before he sends them, such as He disapproves of, or at least would not have seen by others.

The Book of Letters now printed, is retarded in the hope of an Act of Parliament now depending, which may secure it from Pyracy.[1] I have receivd from Brindly the 12 guineas. If the Book come not out before June (the Commencement of the intended act being no sooner) pray acquaint me what to do as to your Lordship's subscribers? I'll send 'em if you will, tho it should indanger their pyracy in Ireland too early. Your great Good nature will excuse the very abrupt manner I write in, I am this very day wholly taken up in solliciting Lords to attend the Duchess of Buckingham's Cause, which comes on to morrow.[2] I wish her Success, if it be as just as undoubtedly she thinks it. I've lately seen some private Papers of the young Duke, by which I am satisfied he was a most worthily-disposed young man, & worthy that Good opinion & that Distinction your Lordship show'd him. Pardon me, My Lord, that I end as I begun, with nothing but the Declaration most in my favour that I am truly Yours with all Gratitude | A: Pope.

London March 28th 1737.[3]

Endorsement: Mr. Pope.

*POPE *to* [SLINGSBY BETHEL][4] [*Early* 1737?]

I am obliged to you much, for your Care and Punctuality in my affairs. In three days time my Waterman shall bring you Twenty small folio Receits.[5]

I must next desire you to send me a List of your Subscribers who have already paid, and when your Brother comes to Town, I will

[1] In the *Gazette*, 22 Mar., Pope had advertised that 'the First Part of the Works of Mr. Pope in Prose' (i.e. his Letters) was already printed and ready for distribution, 'But a *Bill* being now depending in *Parliament*, to secure the *Property of Books*, it is presumed the Subscribers will admit of a short Delay in the Delivery of the same, till the Fate of the said Bill is determined.' The Bill did not pass, and the *Letters* were finally put on sale on 19 May.

[2] The Journals of the House of Lords record that on 28 Mar. the petition of the Duchess against the execution of her husband's will (the executors including her friends Trevor, Orrery, and Bathurst) and for setting aside large conditional bequests to Duke John's natural son, Charles [Herbert] Sheffield, was heard, and that the final vote on the cause came, as Pope indicates, on the 29th. The Duchess lost. See *Journals*, xxiv. 675, 678–9, and xxv. 11, 24, 65, 66.

[3] The year is added in Lord Orrery's hand.

[4] The text is from a transcript of the original kindly made by Professor Geoffrey Tillotson.

[5] The matter of 'receits' places the letter during the period of subscribing to Pope's *Letters*. Since Hugh Bethel has not yet come to town, one may place it in the early spring of 1737. It can hardly be later. Pope advertised publicly for subscribers in the *Gazette*, 8–12 Feb. 1736/7.

desire his with your Company for one day at least (a Sunday, or any other that you can best spare) to settle both his & yours. For the Publication draws so nigh, that I must necessarily receive them, & take order for their being deliverd in what manner you best like. I am sincerely | Sir | Your faithfull humble | Servant | A. Pope.

When I am in London, I am | at my Lord Cornburys near | Oxford Chappel.

I shall return to Town about Wensday.

*POPE *to* BUCKLEY[1] 13 *April* [1737]

The New York Public Library (Berg)

Twickenham April 13.

It is so long since I heard from you or saw you, that I fear very much for your health. When last I was in Town I wrote to acquaint you; & the day I left the town, Mr Cheselden told me you had been ill, but hoped you recoverd since he saw you. I have been here a week, & intend to return to town the next; When if I find a line from you, I shall be glad to meet & dine with you any where, or concert a time to draw you hither for a day or two or to see you at Crouch-end.

In the meantime (that I may always put you upon doing what you like so well, as any Office for me) I'll be glad you desird Mr Knapton to send me word what number of Second Vols. of my Works, Quarto or folio, are in his hands? which I am to make some addition to, of New Works, & would print a number accordingly, in each Size: Thus I am fulfilling the act of Parliament before it commences. I wish you had spoken to Lord Carteret,[2] & then I think all that we could do, is done.—Liberavimus animas nostras—I heartily hope this may find you as well as I wish you, who am very truly & affectionately, | Dear Sir | Yours: | A. Pope.

As I was sealing this, I receive yours, & shall be glad to see you on Tuesday, at Lord C.s[3] I wish you had made me more assured of your health.

Address: To | Sam. Buckley Esq. in | Chartreux Square | London.
Postmark: 13/AP

[1] In 1735 Pope had published vol. ii of his (poetical) *Works*, and now he wishes to print copies of his later poems—imitations of the first and second Epistles of Book II of Horace and two of Horace's odes, &c. Some of these were not available in quarto. The Copyright Bill now being considered by Parliament was to go into effect on 1 June 1737: thus Pope is 'fulfilling the act . . . before it commences'. But the Bill was presently thrown out!

[2] Carteret had aided Buckley in getting subscribers to his Thuanus, and presumably Pope wishes him solicited for a vote on the copyright business. One cannot be sure.

[3] Probably Buckley *has* spoken to Lord Carteret, and arranged to meet Pope at his lordship's on Tuesday the 19th. But possibly Pope refers to Lord Cornbury's house, where he has often stayed recently.

*POPE *to* HUGH BETHEL[1] [? *May* 1737]

Egerton 1948

I am in pain for fear of missing you in Town, where I have nothing to call me but yourself, & Mrs Blount (who is here) tells me you may be at Guildford. I desire to know by the bearer when I may be sure of you a day, to go together to the Tower, & dine & lye with you? Why will you not return hither, & pass a day or 2 between Mrs Blount & me, who resolves not to let you go without seeing you again in Town, & visiting your Sisters with you. I desire a word by the Bearer, (or Post if he misses you) adieu dear Sir, | Yours Ever Sincerely | A. Pope.

Wensday night

Address: To Hugh Bethel Esq. at Sir | Wm Codrington's, Arlington-Street

*POPE *to* HUGH BETHEL [*May* 1737]

Egerton 1948

I will not fail to call at your house in Arlington st.[2] on Tuesday morning, as soon as I can get to town, & be ready to go with you to Tower-hill, either that day (if you are prest in Time) or the next, on which Mrs Blount says she would go too: (For it seems she cannot get to London so soon as she intended.) But if that be too late, or inconvenient to you, I will go on Tuesday, & be wholly at your devotion as long as you please. I am grieved that you cannot make a longer stay with me than these Short Views for a day or two at my own House, or interrupted by others every where else. I have no body here whom you would dislike, & seldome anybody, nay would have nobody, did you like to pass more Days with me. Be assured I sincerely love you, & esteem you: & wish more of our Lives were past together.

Your faithfull & ever | affectionate Servant | A. Pope.

Have you sent for your Books which Brindly[3] bound to Lord Cornbury's? You must allow me to tell you I have reckond with him for the Binding, that my poor Present may not be imperfect.

Address: To Hugh Bethel Esqr | at Sir Wm Codrington's in | Arlington Street

[1] The date of this letter must be uncertain, but it seems to precede that immediately following, and that can be placed shortly after the publication of the *Letters* on 19 May. Since the *Letters* had been printed some weeks before publication, binding need not require a later date, but a later date is possible.

[2] See the address on the preceding letter. Sir William Codrington is Bethel's brother-in-law.

[3] The safe assumption is that Pope's poor present, bound like Lord Cornbury's copy (or sent to his lordship's house?), is a copy of the quarto *Letters*.

*POPE *to* ALLEN[1] 14 *May* 1737

Egerton 1947

Twickenham May the 14. 1737.

A great deal of Law-business, not for Quarrels of my own, (for I thank God I never had any about Money or Possessions) has kept me in Perpetual Vexation; & the Ill health, which with one of my infirm Constitution, is the Consequence of any Vexation or Business, have hinderd me from saying more to you of what my Heart suggested, upon your Present happy situation;[2] in which (you may honestly believe) no Man bears a truer part than Myself. I am concerned to find by yours that any Allay could happen to it, as your late Indisposition was. I pray for the Removal of all Physical Evils from you, & I dare say You will contract no Artificial ones.

The Proposal I had made to myself, of publishing the Book by the tenth, was retarded by the Artifices of a Bookseller, who has some share in an Additional Part, viz. the *Tracts*[3] which I was willing should come out in the same size at the same time, to complete the Edition; with Every Fragment, If I may so say, of my writing: tho I could not join them with my Book as not being my own Property. I mean these things written by me *in conjunction with any others.* I have orderd Mr Knapton to send Mr Leake his Books; only of your last number, I chose to send *Ten* in *large folio* rather than in *Quarto*; it being very probable that some of your Subscribers may prefer them to the other, as indeed it is the more pompous book and better for such as have not Quarto's of the Former Volumes. If they do not chuse these, they shall be changed. I'l send you, for your own proper Use, besides these, One Sett, in the very fine Royal, (of which I printed a few, just to present to my Particular Friends) and One more, for Mrs Allen; If you will, a third for Gen. Wade:[4] with some Additional Poems not hitherto printed, but which I shall publish in a common way this week. But let me first know in what manner You chuse to have them stitchd or bound & in what Colour? &c, that you may see me, as an Author, as I hope you will do as a Man, in All Lights & Shapes. Dear Sir adieu: & know me, for Yours Ever faithfully, | A. Pope

[1] The postscript (only) was printed in Ruffhead (1769), pp. 482–3. Elwin also prints only the postscript.

[2] Allen's second marriage (to Elizabeth Holder of Bath) had taken place in London (St. Martin's-in-the-Fields) on 24 Mar. 1736/7.

[3] Pope, as Professor Griffith has pointed out, actually had reprinted his 'Thoughts on Various Subjects' from the *Miscellanies* (1727) for inclusion in the 1737 edition of his letters. Evidently the publisher of the *Miscellanies* (Motte) objected, and Pope had the sheets kept and used them in the volume of Swift letters (1741). It hardly seems possible that in 1737 Pope intended to include in his *Works in Prose* all the 'Tracts' that appear in the volume of 1741, but his statement here is explicit. The property in the 'Tracts' would perhaps have reverted from Motte to Pope by 1741.

[4] General George Wade, later Field-Marshal, was the father of the first Mrs. Allen. He was also (from 1722) M.P. for Bath.

P S.

The Bill,[1] about which some honest Men as well as I, took some pains, is thrown out, for this Sessions. I think I told you it was a Better Bill when it *went into* the H. of Commons, than when it *came out*. They had added Some Clauses that were prejudicial (as I think) to the True Intention of Encouraging Learning; and I was not Sorry the H. of Lords objected to them. But it Seem'd reasonable that if *Particulars* only were Objected to, they should be referr'd to a Committee, to *Amend* them, and not to *reject the Whole* for them. But Human Passions min[gle] with Public Points, too much, & Every mans Private Concerns are preferrd, by Himself, to the *Whole*. Tis the Case in almost everything. It really was not mine; in the part I had herein; and therfore I am not, in my own particular, the worse, for the Miscarriage of the Bill. and yet I am sorry for it. Tho, if the General Purport of it be again brought in, another Sessions, without those Clauses which were Added by the Commons to the Original Draught, I should be gladder, that it was now thrown out.

I've heard not a word from Ireland.[2]

Address: To | Ralph Allen, Esqr | at Bath. | Bath.
Postmark: 14/MA

THE EARL OF ORRERY *to* POPE — 17 *May* 1737

Harvard University

Dublin. May 17th: 1737.

As You complain'd of a weakness in your Eyes, I was resolv'd not to strain them by any Thing I should write till I could send you some Answer of Consequence to your last Letter. The Dean assures me, "You shall have every Line You ever wrote to him, return'd to You by my Hands." I am thus much nearer *England* than I was, and indulge myself in the Thoughts of seeing You, next Month or the beginning of July. You shall know the exact time of my being in London: and from the moment I have the Papers in my Possession You may depend upon their never being seen by any Eyes but your own, which, I hope, will then be strong enough to peruse them, without the least uneasiness.

The sooner your Prose Works are sent the better. They can scarce come now before the first of June.[3] I have remitted six Guineas more

[1] On this Bill see Pope to Orrery, 28 Mar. 1737, and to Buckley, 13 Apr. 1737, together with the notes to the letters.

[2] Concerning the return of his letters by Swift. Allen evidently knew of Pope's hopes.

[3] Orrery wishes to distribute the copies for which he has secured subscriptions before he leaves Ireland. If the books arrived on 1 June (the day on which the impending new copyright was to go into effect—if the Bill passed) there would be no possibility of piracy.

by a private Hand to Brindley which is the remainder of the money I have as yet receiv'd for Subscriptions.

I am sorry to tell You that all you have written, and all I have said to bring *the Dean* over to *England* is to no Purpose. He is immoveable, & resolv'd not to stir from *Dublin*. He complains of his Health, and indeed with too much Cause. He shuts himself up and lives retir'd. He wants a Freind whose Heart and Genius are fit companions for him. Who is That but yourself? It is now in vain to think or hope to see You together. I place that amongst a thousand fruitless Wishes of my Soul, which is fill'd with many melancholy Reflexions on his Account. I dare not committ any of Them to Paper, at least in a tender regard for your Health I will add no more at present than that I am | Your faithfull & obedient Servant. | Orrery.

Heading: To Alexander Pope Esq; | at Twick'nam in Middlesex .

POPE *to* THE EARL OF ORRERY — 21 *May* 1737

The Pierpont Morgan Library

May 21st 1737.

My Lord,—You, whose Goodness extends to all Circumstances, will excuse mine at this moment, who am in so extreme a Hurry in a room full of Lawyers, signing hearing, & witnessing Deeds, in some of which the best part of my Property is concernd,[1] & can only tell your Lordship, that this Day or to morrow a large Box will goe by the Chester Waggon to Mrs Kenna at Chester, to be forwarded to you at Dublin; No ship was now going, & tho the Bishop of Derry obligingly offerd to put it on board with his Goods which are to go in 3 weeks, I fear'd that Time would be too late for this Cargo to meet your Lordship at Dublin. I rather hope you will be leaving that place by that time, & hast'ning to this Country, which very much wants honest Men and True Lovers of it. Could you persuade the Dean to come with you! I have just now had an opportunity to praise his Name in Verse,[2] I doubt not I should have fresh occasion; were he here co-operating with you in some publick Good. I have sent that Poem to your Lordship with a Book of Letters in a fine paper, as

[1] These remarks about lawyers and property are intriguing. They probably are a more or ess facetious echo of a remark in the beginning of Orrery's letter to Pope, 18 Mar. 1736/7. The 'property' may be the edition of his *Letters*, which he is sending out to agents or subscribers. Possibly the lawyers are concerned in the publishing arrangements also; but the beginning of his letter to Allen (14 May) suggests that perhaps the troubles of his sister are now being settled by lawyers.

[2] Pope is sending presentation copies of the *Letters* and of the imitation of Horace, Epistle i of Book II to Lord Orrery and Dean Swift. Swift is praised in the poem, lines 221–4. In his letter of 30 Dec. 1736 Pope had sent these lines (but not the entire poem) to Swift, who acknowledged them in his reply of 9 Feb. 1736/7.

a poor Present; another I have for you here; & I've done the like to the Dean. These will come to you by a private hand. The others by the Waggon, contain Ten Quarto's, ten large Folios (which I think the best Impression) & thirty small folios, as you directed: with some of the former Vols which you writ for. I beg your Lordship to finish what you began with the Dean, in relation to those Letters he promisd to send me by your hands, in which I will punctually do as He would have me. But have the Originals I must; or great Misfortune will attend it.

I writ him a warm Letter, upon his having promised them to you; & another very long one to yourself. I hope they were Both receivd. My Lord adieu, & know you have not obliged an ungrateful, nor engaged an un-affectionate person. I am truly & lastingly, my Lord, | Yours most faithfully. | A. Pope.

I shall write to the Dean by next Post;[1] it is the third Letter I've sent, since I heard of him.

Endorsement: Mr Pope | May 21st: 1737.

†SWIFT *to* POPE 31 *May* 1737

1740

Dublin, May 31, 1737.

It is true, I owe you some letters,[2] but it has pleased God, that I have not been in a condition to pay you. When you shall be at my age, perhaps you may lie under the same disability to your present or future friends. But my age is not my disability, for I can walk six or seven miles, and ride a dozen. But I am deaf for two months together, this deafness unqualifies me for all company, except a few friends with counter-tenor voices, whom I can call names if they do not speak loud enough for my ears. It is this evil that hath hindred me from venturing to the Bath, and to Twitenham; for deafness being not a frequent disorder, hath no allowance given it; and the scurvy figure a man affected that way makes in company, is utterly insupportable.

It was I began with the petition to you of *Orna me*, and now you come like an unfair merchant, to charge me with being in your debt; which by your way of reckoning I must always be, for yours are always guineas, and mine farthings; and yet I have a pretence to quarrel

1 Promises like this are frequently well intended but not kept; but since the next letter from Pope to Swift preserved to us is that of 12 Oct. 1738, it is apparent that after returning Pope's earlier letters to Lord Orrery Swift was not careful to preserve all succeeding letters. If Pope speaks truly about three letters to Swift without reply, not all the early letters were returned *and printed*.

2 This bears out Pope's final statement in his letter to Orrery, 21 May.

with you, because I am not at the head of any one of your Epistles.[1] I am often wondring how you come to excel all mortals on the subject of Morality, even in the poetical way; and should have wondred more, if Nature and Education had not made you a professor of it from your infancy. "All the letters I can find of yours, I have fastned in a folio cover, and the rest in bundles endors'd; But, by reading their dates, I find a chasm of six years, of which I can find no copies; and yet I kept[2] them with all possible care: But, I have been forced, on three or four occasions to send all my papers to some friends, yet those papers were all sent sealed in bundles, to some faithful friends; however, what I have, are not much above sixty."[3] I found nothing in any of them to be left out: None of them have any thing to do with Party, of which you are the clearest of all men, by your Religion, and the whole Tenour of your life; while I am raging every moment against the Corruptions in both kingdoms, especially of this; such is my weakness.

I have read your Epistle of Horace to Augustus; it was sent me in the English Edition, as soon as it could come. They are printing it in a small octavo. The curious are looking out, some for flattery, some for ironies in it; the sour folks think they have found out some:[4] But your admirers here, I mean every man of taste, affect to be certain, that the Profession of friendship to Me in the same poem, will not suffer you to be thought a Flatterer. My happiness is that you are too far engaged, and in spight of you the ages to come will celebrate me, and know you were a friend who loved and esteemed me, although I dyed the object of Court and Party-hatred.

Pray who is that Mr. Glover, who writ the Epic Poem called Leonidas,[5] which is re-printing here, and hath great vogue. We have frequently good Poems of late from London. I have just read one upon

[1] These remarks, made elsewhere also by Swift, indicate that he preferred a poetical memorial to his friendship with Pope to such a memorial as their letters would make. That preference may be a reason for unwillingness to return the letters, which Pope frankly avowed his intention of publishing.

[2] kept] keep *1741 L; 1742 L.*

[3] If Swift returned anything like sixty letters from Pope to himself, Pope suppressed at least half of them. Ball (vi. 198–200) gives a table of the correspondence as published at various times. At least nine letters of Pope to Swift have been preserved which were not returned to Pope at this time. Eight of them antedate Orrery's departure from Dublin with the returned packet. The chasm here mentioned by Swift still exists for the years 1717–22, and but for the joint letter from Pope and Bolingbroke of 1723 might extend through 1724. This joint letter (published by Curll) evidently was not in Swift's hands in 1737.

The passage beginning 'All the letters' and ending here with 'sixty', was 'quoted' by Pope in the London texts, to call attention to its relation to the history of the correspondence.

[4] This seems not necessarily to imply that the Dublin edition was already published, but merely that Swift had shown his copy to the curious and admiring before he turned it over to a publisher.

[5] Richard Glover (1712–85) had published in April his 'patriotic' epic *Leonidas* (nine books of blank verse), to the great satisfaction of the anti-Walpole faction. It was highly praised by Lyttelton, Fielding, and others.

Conversation,[1] and two or three others. But the croud do not incumber you, who like the Orator or Preacher, stand aloft, and are seen above the rest, more than the whole assembly below.

I am able to write no more; and this is my third endeavour, which is too weak to finish the paper: I am, my dearest friend, yours entirely, as long as I can write, or speak, or think. | J. Swift.

THE EARL OF ORRERY *to* POPE — 2 *June* 1737

Harvard University

Dublin: June 2d: 1737.

I am this moment come from the Dean, who was writing to You, and will send me his Letter when finish'd to enclose.[2] He has told me what indeed is surprizing, that There is a Chasm of Letters, in your Correspondence, of six Years. A great length of Time, considering how constantly You wrote, and how carefully he kept your Letters. Two causes only can be assign'd for It. They are either stolen by People who have had Admission into his Closet, or else are not return'd by Those with whom he entrusted his Papers on some certain occasions. The latter is most probable. I will try to find out, if possible, where they are: tho' the Persons who were knavish enough not to restore Them, will I fear be cunning enough still to conceal Them.[3] however no method shall be left untried to discover the Truth of this Affair, upon which I must be more silent than I would: but if I have a proper Opportunity You shall hear more fully from me. at present I can only say that the Dean is guarded, not defended, by Dragons and[4] all the monstrous Animals of the Creation. His Health grows worse and worse: his Deafness and Giddiness encrease: and He is seldom chearful but when talking of You, It is a Topic, that He delights to speak on & I to hear.

You will find by my last, that I purposely deferr'd writing to You, till I had seen the Dean. Your Commands are always deeply imprinted in my Heart & Head. I am much oblig'd to You for the Presents that you intend me, & which I expect every Day. Excuse the hurry I write in, for I am now deep in buesness in hopes to reach England before this Month is out. I am, dear Sir, | Your | very faithfull, | humble Servant. | Orrery.

[1] *An Essay on Conversation* (1737) is a poem (anonymous) of 624 lines in couplets.

[2] Evidently the letter of 31 May.

[3] Unfortunately but perhaps unintentionally in more than one letter Orrery gives Pope grounds for suspicion of Swift's friends or servants. The probable truth is that Swift was not nearly so careful in keeping his letters as he thought. There were also the Pilkingtons in the background, and presently Mrs. Whiteway falls under suspicion.

[4] In the letterbook 'Dragons and' is crossed out. Very likely the words were in the letter as sent?

POPE *to* ALLEN[1] 8 *June* 1737

Egerton 1947

June 8th 1737

I was very sorry to hear how much Concern your Humanity & Friendship betrayed you into, upon the false report which occasiond your Grief. I am now so well, that I ought not to conceal it from you, as the just Reward of that Goodness which made you suffer for me. Perhaps when a Friend is really dead, (if he knows our Concern for him) he knows us to be *as much Mistaken* in our Sorrow, as You now were: so that what we think a Real Evil, is, to such Spirits as see things truly, no more of moment than a meer Imaginary one. It is equally as God pleases; let us think, or call it, Good or Evil.

⌜Mr Knapton has by this time Three Books of the Letters, in large Royal paper Quarto. If your Friend Gen. W.[2] or any other, prefer the Large folio, (which several do) I can make up one or 2 Whole Sets, with the first & second volumes of the Same. You must not refuse this further small Compliment, which is of no other value than as the Complete Sets are rare to be had. Mrs Allen obliges me in what you tell me, & has a great Right in me, because I am very much Yours: It is in Proportion to that Friendship, that her Claim is so strong.⌝ I wish the World would let me give myself more to such people in it as I like, & discharge me of half the Honours which persons of higher Rank bestow on me, & for which one generally pays a little too much of what they cannot bestow, Time & Life. Were I arrivd to that happier Circumstance, you would see me at Widcombe,[3] and not at Bath. But whether it will be as much in my power, as in my wish, God knows: I can only say I think of it, & think of it with the pleasure & Sincerity, becoming one who is Yours & Mrs Allen's true & faithfull Servant. | A. Pope

⌜You are not to forget (and if you do, I am not to forget) that fifty more books are due to you.

⌜If any of those large folios I sent, are not so well liked by your Subscribers, they may have Quarto's instead of them on your first intimation.⌝

Address: To | Ralph Allen Esq | at | Bath.
Postmark: 9/IV

[1] Printed by Warburton, 1751, with the omission of the second paragraph down to 'I wish the world', and the omission also of the postscript.

[2] General Wade.

[3] At Prior Park, that is, which was under construction, 1736–43. Pope had not yet visited it.

THE EARL OF ORRERY *to* SWIFT[1] 12 *June* 1737

Harvard University

June 12th 1737.

You mistook me, dear Sir, as to *Mr Pope's* Letters: The incomparable Author has sent Each of Us a Present of Them, and of his last Imitation of *Horace*, by a private Hand, from *London* but They are not yet arriv'd; when your Book comes, (which I fancy is entrusted to the Bishop of Derry,[2] and he will be here this week) you may send me back That which you have now.

I will certainly see you very often before I go. I will constantly write to you when I am gone, & will require no Answer, but at your utmost Leisure & in your best Health.

As my Journey depends upon Law Buesness, I mean References, Accounts &c. I am put off *de Die in Diem* & cannot positively say when It will be. But as my Children, my Freinds, & my Health call loudly for my Presence in England, I hope to obey their Summons either the last week in this month, or the first in the next.—I cannot bear the Thoughts of parting with you: Let us settle It by a Letter the last day wrote from each other. Do not say, Do not think We are to part forever. Had I no Buesness in Ireland The Sight of you would more than make amends for a Sea Sickness. As I draw nearer loosing you, my Affection, which lay close in my Heart, rises in Letters, in Sighs, in Tears, therefore you will excuse this Trouble from | your most affectionate oblig'd | & faithfull humble Servant. | Orrery.

Heading: To The Revd Dr Swift Dean | of St Patrick's.

THE EARL OF ORRERY *to* POPE[3] 14 *June* 1737

Harvard University

Dublin: June 14th: 1737

A great Part of my Time has been employ'd, since I wrote to You last, in searching after those Letters which are missing; I have visited all the Persons whom I thought likely to have Them in Possession, and have made use of many Arguments and of some Art to no Purpose. The Dean tells me, The Chasm begins in the year 1722 and I find that a Letter from You to the Dean in the year 25[4] was printed lately without your Knowledge. This alarms me and makes me apprehend that They are on your Side o' the Water and in very improper Hands.

[1] The text is from the Orrery Letterbooks, VII. It has been printed before, but is included here as showing that the Epistle to Augustus and Pope's *Letters* had not yet reached Dublin.

[2] Dr. Rundle.

[3] The text is from the Orrery Letterbooks, VII.

[4] Orrery seems to be writing in a hurry, and probably errs in writing dates here. The letter lately printed dates 1723, not '25; and the chasm pretty certainly is that following 1716.

Whatever can be done on my Part to recover Them, certainly shall: but hitherto my Endeavours have been in vain. Tell me, but tell me soon, any further Commands You may have for Me in Ireland.

I am impatient to be in my native Country, to embrace my Children and my Freinds, to improve and delight myself by your Conversation, & to gain a little Health and Quiet which I cannot hope for whilst I stay in this Town. Lawyers, like Surgeons, will not part with Us out of their Claws, till their Bill is rais'd to a great Height, and even then They leave many a Scar behind Them. To this villainous Tyranny, and to an unhappy Agreement I made with the greatest[1] Knave in Xtendom, I owe the uncertainty of my Return, but I still flatter myself with the hopes of Liberty the latter End of this Month. My Joy will be incompleat since I must leave the Dean behind me. He has not yet put the Letters into my Hands, They are reserv'd for the Dona extrema. Those from *Brindley* are come safe, but your kind present by a private Hand is not arriv'd.—Your Heart can better tell You than my Words express What I feel now I am approaching so near an eternal Farewell to the Dean. I have but one Alleviation to my Sorrow, which is the hopes of meeting with the same indulgence from You that I have ever found from Him, because I am most truly | Your faithfull & obedient | humble Servant. | Orrery.

†SWIFT *to* POPE[2] [*June*] 1737

1741 La

Dublin, July 23, 1737.

I sent a letter to you some weeks ago, which my Lord Orrery inclosed in one of his, to which I receiv'd as yet no answer, but it will be time enough when his Lordship goes over, which will be as he hopes in about ten days, and then he will take with him "all the letters I preserved of yours, which are not above twenty-five. I find there is a great chasm of some years, but the dates are more early than my two last journeys to England, which makes me imagine, that in one of those journeys I carry'd over another Cargo."[3] But I cannot trust my memory half an hour; and my disorders of deafness and giddiness

[1] Brettridge Badham, Esq;—Lord Orrery's marginal note in the Letterbooks.

[2] First printed in the London quarto of 1741, and reprinted in the 'Supplement' to the Dublin editions of the year. The July date is obviously wrong; for on 23 July Orrery wrote from England to Swift, and had already delivered to Pope the letters in question. Possibly, as Ball suggests, 23 July is the date on which Pope received the letter.

[3] Swift places the 'chasm' rightly before 1726: Orrery certainly miswrote or was misinformed in his statement to Pope (14 June 1737). But writing to Pope 31 May Swift had said he had not 'much above sixty' letters, and now he has only twenty-five. Possibly he meant he had only sixty of all the correspondences that he kept with Pope's letters. Twenty-five is about what he sent to Pope, apparently.

increase daily. So that I am declining as fast as it is easily possible for me, if I were a dozen years older.

We had your volume of Letters, which I am told are to be printed here:[1] Some of those who highly esteem you, and a few who know you personally, are grieved to find you make no distinction between the English Gentry of this Kingdom, and the savage old Irish, (who are only the vulgar, and some Gentlemen who live in the Irish parts of the Kingdom) but the English Colonies, who are three parts in four, are much more civilized than many Counties in England, and speak better English, and are much better bred. And they think it very hard, that an American who is of the fifth generation from England, should be allowed to preserve that title, only because we have been told by some of them that their names are entered in some parish in London. I have three or four Cousins here who were born in Portugal, whose Parents took the same care, and they are all of them Londoners. Dr. Delany, who as I take it, is of an Irish family, came to visit me three days ago, on purpose to complain of those passages in your Letters; he will not allow[2] such a difference between the two climates, but will assert that North-Wales, Northumberland, Yorkshire, and the other Northern Shires have a more cloudy ungenial air than any part of Ireland. In short, I am afraid your friends and admirers here will force you to make a Palinody.

As for the other parts of your volume of Letters, my opinion is, that there might be collected from them the best System that ever was wrote for the Conduct of human life, at least to shame all reasonable men out of their Follies and Vices.[3] It is some recommendation of this Kingdom, and of the taste of the people, that you are at least as highly celebrated here as you are at home. If you will blame us for Slavery, Corruption, Atheism, and such trifles, do it freely, but include England, only with an addition of every other Vice.—I wish you would give orders against the corruption of English by those Scribblers who send us over their trash in Prose and Verse, with abominable curtailings and quaint modernisms.[4]—I now am daily expecting an end of life: I have lost all spirit, and every scrap of health; I sometimes recover a little of my hearing, but my head is ever out of order. While I have

[1] The London quarto.

[2] Dr. Delany complains that Pope has printed opprobrious remarks, made by Swift, concerning the Irish climate. Swift, in turn, complains somewhat because Pope has inserted, for example, Swift's letter of 20 Sept. 1723 in his quarto of 1737 (taking it supposedly from Curll's *New Letters of Mr. Alexander Pope . . .* 1737; found in Curll's fifth volume of *Mr. Pope's Literary Correspondence*) without giving Swift a chance to delete the offensive remarks concerning the dullness of the air and the people of Ireland.

[3] Pope would be pleased by this: it states admirably one major avowed purpose in publishing his letters.

[4] Swift here again may be objecting mildly to Pope's own texts of his letters. The later Dublin editions are consistently more conservative in expanding *'em* to *them*, *till* to *until*, &c.

any ability to hold a commerce with you, I will never be silent, and this chancing to be a day that I can hold a pen, I will drag it as long as I am able. Pray let my Lord Orrery see you often; next to yourself I love no man so well; and tell him what I say, if he visits you. I have now done, for it is evening, and my head grows worse. May God always protect you, and preserve you long, for a pattern of Piety and Virtue.

Farewel my dearest and almost only constant friend. I am ever, at least in my esteem, honour, and affection to you, what I hope you expect me to be. | Yours, &c.

POPE *to* JONATHAN RICHARDSON[1] 17 *June* [1737]

The Pierpont Morgan Library

June 17.

Nothing is more true than what you observe, that a Friend is happy, in finding all Resemblances in himself to the other. This is just my case at this moment, for I was actually sate down to put you in mind of me, when I receivd your Letter to put me in mind of you. Be assured we think alike, & alike warmly. It was my very ill fortune that has never let me remain a Quiet Week in Town, or in the Country, this long time; Law, & Sickness, & Company, have conspired to Alienate me from my Friends, from my Pleasures, from my Studies, from my Self. I intend to be My own Master again & Your Servant, next week; If you can pass Sunday Sennight here (by which time I hope your good Companion & Son may be able to attend you) let it be so; if not, tell me any other Day, or take 2 days, when he may lye here, to fatigue him less.—It was by my Order that Book was sent you, as a small token only that I distinguish You from the Common Race of Men, as much as the best Royal Paper is distinguishd from Common Fool's Cap. I have a Particular Book for your Son of all my Works together, with large Margins, knowing how good an use he makes of them in all his books; & remembring how much a worse writer, far, than Milton, has been mark'd, collated, & studied by him.

Adieu. Even this I write in haste, but am never forgetful of you. Dear Sir | His, and | Your affectionate Friend | & Servant | A. Pope.

Address: To | Mr Richardson, at his | house in | Queens Square, | Bloomsbury. | London.

Postmark: 18/IV

[1] The year is highly uncertain. Pope seems to be sending Richardson a large folio copy of the *Letters*, in recognition of the engraving of Pope's head, *amicitiae causa*, placed on the title-page. The particular copy of 'all my Works together' suggests that thus surprisingly early the younger Richardson was collating variant editions of Pope's poems in the margins of quarto sheets. Some of these are preserved in the Huntington Library.

POPE *to* JONATHAN RICHARDSON[1] [29 *June* 1737]

Roscoe (1824) (facsimile to front i. 482)

If your Self & your Son can mount this day, & enjoy my Groves all to Ourselves all this day & as much of the night as the fine moon now allows, I am wholly yours for this day & till noon to morrow. This being the first Vacancy I've been able to obtain, I offer it you, before Courts, & Crowds, & Confusion come upon me.

Good morrow! | I am truly | Yours, | A. Pope.

Wensday | Five aclock | in the morning.
29 June 1737

Address: To | Mr Richardson in | Queens Square | Bloomsbury.

*POPE *to* JONATHAN RICHARDSON[2] [? *July* 1737]

Arthur A. Houghton, Jr.

Saturday.

I have not been in Town so long, or unable to reach to your End of the Town, that I desire to hear how you do, & how your Son does? I am really concerned in Both. I should invite you hither, but that to morrow I go from home, & toward the end of the week, hope to see you & Mr Cheselden in Town. pray let him know I have not forgot him, as I think he has not me, tho 'tis very long since we gave each other any proof to the contrary. I am, with all affection | Dear Sir | Your faithful Servant | A. Pope.

Address: To | Mr Richardson, in | Queens Square | Bloomsbury.

*POPE *to* — PIGOTT[3] [1737?]

Harvard University

Sir, This is the Inscription I would prefer to that I gave you upon

1 The date is added in Richardson's hand. If the preceding letter (17 June) belongs in 1737, one must assume that the Richardsons could not come to Pope 'Sunday sennight' (the 26th), and are now being asked for the earliest succeeding date possible for Pope.

2 Though impossible to date surely, this letter fits into a period about July 1737 when the younger Richardson was ill. But inquiries as to health are usually mere politeness in these letters.

3 This note, with the epitaph enclosed, was probably addressed to one of Pigott's sons shortly after the famous barrister's death in July of this year. The time of erecting a monument is of course doubtful. The letter has been bound into a copy of Pope's *Odyssey*, presented to the elder Pigott in 1726. Pigott lived at Whitton, near the river Crane into which Pope was plunged in his coach accident of Sept. 1726. Upon being rescued, Pope was taken to Pigott's house. The grandson of Pigott (also Nathaniel) sent to *The Gentleman's Magazine* for September and October of 1784 an account of his grandfather's career. Pope made three drafts (all preserved) of the epitaph.

further consideration. Pray let Mr Schemakers ingrave it as it here stands. The words underlined must be in small Capitals.

Your affect: Servant. A. Pope.

To the Memory of
NATHANIEL PIGOTT Barrister at Law:
Who Gave more Honour to his Profession,
than he Derived from it.
Possessed of the highest Character,
By his *Learning*, *Judgment*, *Experience*, *Integrity*,
Depriv'd of the highest Stations,
only by his *Conscience* & *Religion.*
Many he assisted in the Law,
More he preserved from it.
A
Friend to *Peace*, Guardian of *Property*, and Protector of the Poor.
A Servant of *God*, and Lover of his *Country.*
He died July 5. 1737. Aged 76 years.

POPE *to* JONATHAN RICHARDSON[1] 18 *July* [1737]

Add. 32567

Found in a Glass Window in the Village of Chalfont in Bucks.

Fair Mirror of foul times! whose fragile sheene
Shall, as it blazeth, break: while Providence
(Aye watching oer his Saints with eye unseene)
Spreads the red rod of angry Pestilence.
To sweep the Wicked & their Counsels thence.
Yea all to break the Pride of lustful kings
Who Heaven's Law reject for brutish Sense
As erst he Scourgd Jessides sin of yore
For the fair Hittite, when on Seraph's Wings
He sent him War, or Plague or famine Sore.

1 The text is from Mitford's transcript, not from the original. Essential comment on the letter is found in one from George Vertue to the Earl of Oxford printed in the *Hist. MSS. Comm.*, *Portland*, vi. 66: '1737–38, February 24.—Some time ago I related to your Lordship how some lines said to be writ by Milton on a glass window were sent to Mr. Richardson, and they are now printed in Milton's works now ready to be published. By a letter I saw last night in the hands of the Rev. Mr. Birch, the whole discovery is made that Mr. Pope and Lord Chesterfield (if I mistake not) had laid this bait for the Connoisseur, who swallowed it, and entertained his intimates with great pleasure many times concerning his knowledge of Milton's pen and style, which he pronounced he knew with the greatest certainty. I could wish your Honour had been in view of Richardson when this discovery was made a day or two ago only. In short, they are obliged to reprint the sheet in the book in a hurry, it being to be published next Monday.' Birch's edition of Milton's prose (with a life) is advertised in *Gent. Mag.* viii. 168 as published 3 Mar. 1738.

July 18.

I have been in Oxfordshire & Buckinghamshire these ten days, & return to Twitnam by Thursday,[1] when I hope to see you & fix a day after Sunday next, or on Friday, or Saturday, if you can send me word to Lord Cornburys by Oxford Chapel.

The above was given me by a Gentleman, as I travelld.—I copyd it for you. You will tell me more of it perhaps than I can. | Yours ever | A. Pope

Address: To Mr. Richardson in Queens Square Bloomsbury.

POPE *to* JONATHAN RICHARDSON[2] [*July* 1737?]

1833 (Thomas Thorpe)

[Pope tells Richardson he had picked up a very worthy clergyman, Dr. Green,[3] a parish priest, who gave Pope his company from Oxford to London—'Pray let me see you together, that I may see how well you can agree with orthodoxy? I believe you and I condemn no man; we are either so orthodox, or not so orthodox, quere which?']

THE EARL OF ORRERY *to* SWIFT 23 *July* 1737

1768 (Deane Swift)

July 23, 1737.

If I were to tell you who enquire for you, and what they say of you, it would take up more paper than I have in my lodgings, and more time than I stay in town. Yet *London* is empty: not dusty, for we have had rain: not dull, for Mr. *Pope* is in it: not noisy, for we have no cars: not troublesome, for a man may walk quietly about the streets: in short, 'tis just as I would have it till Monday,[4] and then I quit *St. Paul's*, for my little church at *Marston*.

Your commands are obeyed long ago. Dr. *King* has his cargo, Mrs. *Barber* her conversation, and Mr. *Pope* his letters.[5] To-morrow I pass with him at *Twickenham*: the *olim meminisse* will be our feast. Leave

[1] Pope was perhaps returning from Oxford on Thursday the 21st.

[2] An undated letter with this description was offered in Thorpe's *Catalogue of Autograph Correspondence* (1833) as a part of lot 809. It seems possibly to fit into Pope's ramble of this period.

[3] Dr. Green may be Dr. Samuel Green, rector of St. George the Martyr, London. If so, the letter must date in or after 1733 when he became Doctor. No other doctors of his name seem to qualify.

[4] Orrery writes on a Saturday, and is spending Sunday at Twickenham with Pope: the London Sabbath will hardly oppress him.

[5] Dr. King gets the manuscript of Swift's *Four Last Years of the Queen*, Mrs. Barber gets his *Polite Conversation* with permission to print it for her own benefit, and, finally, Pope gets his packet of letters returned from Swift. Orrery had left Dublin on the 5th, and Pope has returned from Oxford within the week to receive the letters.

Dublin and come to us. Methinks there are many stronger reasons for it than heretofore; at least I feel 'em: and I'll say with *Macbeth*, Would thou could'st![1]

My health is greatly mended; so, I hope, is yours: write to me when you can, in your best health, and utmost leisure; never break through that rule. Can friendship increase by absence? Sure it does; at least mine rises some degrees, or seems to rise: try if it will fall by coming nearer: no, certainly it cannot be higher. Yours most affectionately. | Orrery.

*POPE *to* THE EARL OF BURLINGTON[2]

Chatsworth [*July or August* 1737]

My Lord,—I am return'd home & long to see you, even more than to see Chiswick in this radiant weather. I thought of going thither this Day, but I hear you are to entertain the Committee of the Bridge: and this makes me (instead of waiting on you) send you a Petition, in favor of Mr Bowack, to be their Secretary or Clerk. I spoke of him to you once before, & at the same time Mr. Arundel promised me his Vote. He has been long Writing-master at Westminster School, is known to most of the Young Nobility & Gentry who can write & read, and is a very honest man. He has also been hitherto imployed, as Secretary or whatever it is called, by the former Undertakers, Gentlemen who managed for the Bridge. Your Vote & Interest will oblige me much—I shall take the first opportunity to assure your Lordship in person with how much truth I am | My Lord | Your most faithful & obligd | Servant | A. Pope.

Twit'nam: | Saturday morn:

Address: To the Rt. Hon. the Earl of Burlington.

*POPE *to* ALLEN 26 *July* [1737]

Egerton 1947

July 26.

When your Letter came to Twickenham [I was in][3] Buckinghamshire, & receivd it not till long after the date. As soon as I did receive it, I orderd the Books, the first & second vols. to Mr Knapton's for Gen. Wade. to be bound as you directed.[4] I am truly concerned that

[1] *Macbeth*, II. ii. 74.

[2] The date possible for the letter lies before 24 Aug. when (*Lond. Eve. Post*, 25 Aug. 1737) Mr. John Bowack (see *DNB*) was appointed assistant secretary to the Commissioners of the Bridge. It lies after Pope's return from Oxfordshire and Buckinghamshire. Since the newspapers record during August meetings of the Commissioners of Westminster Bridge as taking place in London, it is probable that the entertainment at Chiswick dates in July, probably either the 23rd or 30th—which were Saturdays.

[3] These words (except a part of *in*) are torn away in the original.

[4] Allen had evidently sent directions in answer to Pope's letter of 8 June.

your Headakes continue to molest you so frequently: your Pain afflicts me, tho your Resignation Edifyes me. The sentiments you express upon the Anniversary of your birthday shew you a Good Man, & therfore I have reason to be glad that you can account the Friendship I bear you one of the Satisfactions of your life: Otherwise, it might be but a disgrace to be rank'd among the things you like, if you liked such things & Men, as many do like, & make their Enjoyments. I trust in God such a friendship will out-last all those that are built upon Vanity, Interest, or Sensuality, the common grounds [upon] which people build them. I am in haste, & need not add more; 'tis the most material, as well as most comfortable Reflection I can make, Adieu. I have some hopes of going to Southampton, from whence I shall aim at getting to you; unless a Journey to Oxford upon an affair I cannot put off, interferes: If it should, I will endeavor to pass a week with you at the End of Autumn, & so to Cirencester. I desire Mrs Allen to believe me hers, as I am | Your true Friend | & Affectionate | Servant | A. Pope.

It will please you to know, I have receivd the packet of Letters from Ireland safe,[1] by the means of my Lord Orrery.

Address: To | Ralph Allen Esq. at | Widcomb, near | Bath.
Postmark: [illegible; as is another post-office stamp.]

*POPE *to* ROBERT DODSLEY[2] 20 *August* [1737]

1861 (Mrs. Delany)

Pray deliver to Mrs. Pendarves, or bearer, the book of letters, in quarto, or large folio, as she pleases. | A. Pope.

Address: To Mr. Dodsley, Bookseller in Pall Mall, | Augst 20th.

*POPE *to* ALLEN 28 *August* [1737]

Egerton 1947

Cirencester. Aug. 28.

I have delayed writing to you till I could give you some account of my Progress, having all along had some View & hopes of making you a Visit. I am at last after near a months ramble, arrived at Cirencester

[1] On 23 July 1737 Lord Orrery, who had brought over the packet of Pope–Swift letters, wrote to Swift, 'Mr. Pope has his letters.'

[2] The text (from the *Autobiography of Mrs. Delany* [Llanover, 1861]) is excerpted from a letter from the Duchess of Portland to Mrs. Ann Granville, 24 Aug. 1737. She there says, 'I spoke to Lady Peterborow, and she immediately sent me the . . . order'; i.e. as printed here. Either Lady Peterborow was in London and was returning to Bevis Mount with Pope or possibly they were both at Bevis Mount when Pope wrote the order. Mrs. Delany was at this time the widow of the unloved Pendarves. She became Mrs. Delany in 1743.

with Lord Bathurst. I hoped to have got hither a fortnight ago, and now find I must necessarily get home in a fortnight more; this is the first day of my arrival, and I cannot stay less than a week here, to set some Works of my Lords, and some Buildings forward, setling Plans, &c. Yet if I could contrive to be with you, tho but for 2 or 3 days, I would, could I be of any Service to you in your Wood, &c. notwithstanding in truth, my Infirmityes render Travelling (especially in rocky roads) very prejudicial to me. At Bath I have no sort of Call, or Business, and would only be at your House, & Command: But if you have thoughts of coming toward London in any short time or no great need of me, let the Will serve for the Deed. After all, I have a strong Inclination to come to you, and if you send me a Messenger hither, or a Line, telling me the *First day* you will send or meet me at Tedbury,[1] & the *hour*, I will meet you there. Adieu. No man is more Truly Yours: A. Pope.

Address: To | Ralph Allen, Esq: | at Widcomb, | near | Bath.
Stamped: CIREN|CESTER

POPE *to* FORTESCUE[2] — 3 *September* 1737

1797 (Polwhele, i. 325)

September 3d, 1737.

It is long that I have not writ to you; but want of materials is a good reason for not writing at any time; and that which I never want, friendship and affection, have not much to say, tho' they feel much. The knowledge you will not fail, from long experience, to have, of mine for you, tho' it has had few means to prove itself; and the opinion, which, I flatter myself, you have of my being no ungrateful man to those who have proved theirs to me, will sufficiently convince you I am always thinking of, and wishing well to you. I have this summer contrived to make a circuit, almost as long as yours, tho' less useful: from which I am not yet returned. I have been now a full month on the ramble, first to Southampton and Portsmouth, but the stormy weather prevented my design on the Isle of Wight: Thence to Oxford, and Cirencester, and Bath. It will be near Michaelmas before I shall see Richmond, or Mrs. Blount, who went thither (as I hear by the last post) but two days ago, to enjoy the palace you left her, being much rejoiced to be at repose after a ramble she has also made. I hope Mrs. Spooner[3] is now in perfect health, tho' she had been ailing when I last saw her before her journey. I hope you are all together by this

[1] Tedbury (or Tetbury) lies between Cirencester and Bath.

[2] The remark, towards the end of this letter, about Bathurst's 'plantations' indicates that Pope is writing from Cirencester.

[3] Fortescue's daughter, who more than once seems to be in bad health.

time, or will about the time this letter reaches you; which comes to congratulate you on the sabbath of your labours, and to exhort you to concert this Michaelmas some improvements of your wood, &c. at Buckland, factura nepotibus umbras. But cut out some walks for yourself, while you yet have legs, and make some plain and smooth under your trees to admit a chaise or chariot when you have none. I find myself already almost in the condition, tho' not the circumstances, of an aged judge, and am forced to be carried in that manner over lord Bathurst's plantations. Do not be discouraged from giving me once more at least an account of yourself. If directed to Twitenham it will find its way to me. Be assured, I am with old sincerity, and ever shall be, dear Sir, your most affectionate and obliged friend and servant,| A. Pope.

Address: To the Hon. Mr. Baron Fortescue, in Bell-yard, near Lincoln's Inn, London.

*POPE *to* HUGH BETHEL — 25 *September* 1737

Egerton 1948

Sept. 25th | 1737

I stayed to write to you till I had ended my Journies, & till I could give you an account of the Success of them, & of the Effect they had both upon mine & Mrs Bs health. I can now tell you we are both the better, and that She, by the Use of the Spa water here, with Exercise, is in a very good way, but I think still in the way of being in as bad an one as ever, next Winter; for it seems to little purpose, that she parts for the Summer months with what is the Bane of her Quiet, (which is the Health of the Soul, & upon which the health of the Body so much depends,) when she constantly returns in the Winter, to the same House, the same Company, and the same Uneasinesses. I have been first at Southampton, then at Portsmouth, then Oxford, then Cirencester, then Bath, then Oxford agen, & so home. At Bath I went to Lady Coxe's; the Hour I stay'd there I gave to Dr Cheney (missing her, who it seems was gone for some time) ⌜The Dr magnifyed the Scarborow waters, & indeed all Waters, but above all, Common Water. He was greatly edifyed with me for having left off Suppers, & upon my telling him that most of my Acquaintance had not only done so, but had not drunk out 3 dozen of wine in my house in a whole Twelvemonth, he blessed God, & said, my Conversation was with Angels!⌝[1]

I have not yet seen my Lord Burlington since my return: I shall in 2 or 3 days, & make him know all you say. I fancy he goes again to Yorkshire very speedily.

[1] The passage in half-brackets was quoted by Ruffhead, p. 501 n.

I am glad by my rambles, to have escaped much of the disagreable noise, & the impertinent chatter of this place, about the late Difference of the Courts.[1] To the other reasons I gave you in my last, of my Joy in the *Sex* of the Child,[2] I may add this one more, now, That we may have no prospect in the next Generation, of a Third Quarrel between a Father & a *Son*. I am always sorry for any such, publick or private. I beg you will continue to acquaint me of the State of your health, for which at all times I am truly sollicitous, & more especially at this, when the Autumn is extremely sickly, & great numbers die of sudden Fevers. I hope this Distemperature of the Air is dissipated on the bleaker Hills & Wolds of Yorkshire. We found nothing of it on those of Glocestershire, & when we read in Newspapers of the Epidemic Distemper, we could not guess what it was, unl[ess] it were Madness: of which, in my return, I found three Doctors lockd up at Oxford, three old sober Women at Reding, and many young & old in Town. You may be sure there can be no such thing at Hampton Court, but at Twitenham I see many Symptoms, & grievous ones of it, & all about my Neighborhood. Adieu.

Address: To | Hugh Bethel Esqr at | Beswick, near Beverley | Yorkshire
Postmark: 4/OC

*POPE *to* ALLEN — 11 *October* 1737

Egerton 1947

Twitenham Oct. 11th 1737.

I cannot help sending You a line only to inquire of your safety, & whether No Part of your Family sufferd any way by it? The weather mended, and gave me hopes: I did so too, & I know you will be glad to know I am perfectly recoverd. The same reason will operate, to make you tell me all your Concerns are prosperous, and I half believe I shall have a line from you, as soon as you arrive, if all be well, which may meet This on the road. Our Desires of each others happiness every way being (I am sure) mutual, and keeping Equal Pace. Adieu, with my sincere Services to Mrs A. I am Your faithfully affectionate Servant. | A. Pope

I just now discover I've writ on a half Sheet of paper.

Address: To | Ralph Allen Esq; | at Widcombe, near | Bath
Postmark: 11/OC

[1] This 'difference' became acute upon the disobedience of the Prince of Wales in causing the Princess (31 July) to lie in at St. James's instead of at Hampton Court, as the King and Queen wished. On 10 Sept. the Prince had been ordered to remove from the palace, and thereafter he maintained a separate court.

[2] Princess Augusta (b. 31 July), who in 1764 married the Duke of Brunswick. Prince George (later King George III) was born 4 June 1738.

POPE *to* SLINGSBY BETHEL 12 *November* [1737]

Harvard University

Twitenham Nov. 12

Sir,—I have been some months rambling in the Country, from whence I am but lately returned into these parts. I have not forgot my debts of some Claret & Madera you procured for me, and I desire you to help me to 5 dozen Madera when you think it perfectly good, and to one dozen more of L'Eglise's best Claret. But in the meantime let me know what I owe you for the last, that I may send or wait on you, with the mony. I have a Letter from your Brother last week who is pretty well: He speaks of Mrs Blounts Interest, but she gives her service to you, & says she is in no haste at all. If I was sure to find you any day by a line, I would come to your house. I shall be in Town the Most part of next week, and lye at Lord Cornburys by Oxford Chappel, but generally go out early, unless I expect any Friend, and that is too unreasonable a distance to expect you who have more business than I. Therfore I would meet you any where else where you appoint, and when you are most at leisure. Adieu, and believe me sincerely | Sir | Your obliged & | very affectionate | humble Servant | A. Pope.

POPE *to* NATHANIEL COLE[1] 18 *November* 1737

Add. 25382

Sir,—I am with Mr Murray, who advises me to file a bill against James Watson Printer, near Doctors Commons (Mr Knapton may I believe tell where he lives) who hath Pyrated an Edition of my Letters in Octavo Entitled the Works of Alex: Pope Volume fifth and sixth consisting of Letters &c Printed in the name of T Johnson this Watson hath Employd Jacob Robinson Bookseller in the Strand to transact for the whole Impression with Lawton Giliver and since the said Giliver on the 15th of this Month did personaly meet the said Robinson and Watson where Watson proposed to deliver up the said impression being about 1500 books to [the said] Giliver on payment of about 60 po[unds] being nine pence farthing a Book

and the said Jacob Robinson did tell R[obert] Dodsley he could help him to the said impr[ession] on certain Conditions and therefore M[urray] thinks that Robinson should be made a defendant to the Bill

1 The body of the letter is in the hand of a lawyer, who omits punctuation and capital letters. The signature, postscript, and address are in Pope's hand. Dodsley and others brought the suit against Watson, who later attempted to pirate *The Dunciad*. Cole, so Courthope notes (x. 236), was at this time solicitor to the Stationers' Company.

The Coppy right was by me assign'd to Robt Dodsley Bookseller in Pall Mall before My first Publication Enterd and the nine books deliverd this Mr Murray says was a sufficient entry and assignment which is ready to produce you are desired to prepare a draught of this bill and to wait on Mr Murray with it as soon as possible the speed in which will be taken for a particular obligation to your affectionate & most | Humble servant | A. Pope.

[Nov]r 18. 1737

A fit of the headake hinderd my writing this in my own hand. If you want further Instructions I am at my Lord Cornbury's by Oxford chappel.

Address: To Mr Cole, in | Basinghall street

NATHANIEL COLE *to* POPE[1] [1737?]

Elwin–Courthope, x. 237

Sir,—I last night received the draught of your Bill settled by Mr. Murray. There are two blanks which should be supplied; the first is for the date of your assignment to Dodsley. In the copy which I have, the date is 24 March, 1737; but this I take to be a mistake, the year not commencing till 25 March, so that I suppose the year is 1736. The other blank is for day of publication of the letters, which should be some time after the nine books were left at Stationers' Hall. I am, &c., &c.

POPE *to* BUCKLEY[2] [23 *November* 1737]

Yale University

From Lord Cornburys | Wensday night

It is so very long since we have mett, & it is so sincerely my desire that we may sometimes renew our old Correspondence (for I think it's near twenty years that I have had occasions to know you for my Friend) that I can no longer hold from trying at an Appointment. If Saturday next you & Mr Cole & Mr Knapton can dine together, at

[1] The letter was returned to Cole with Pope's marginal comments. Only one was thought worth transcribing—'As to the day of publication I can't be certain, only that it was after delivery of the books in May, 1737. I sent several books (I find by a memorandum) on the 18th, so it was then published.'—Elwin (from Dilke).

It is assumed that this letter was written shortly after that of 18 Nov. 1737.

[2] The date, taken from EC, is very plausible but obviously uncertain. The Wednesdays when at this time Pope was in town were the 16th and 23rd. But his letter to Cole on the 18th says nothing about a dinner for the next day; hence the 23rd is more plausible. Queen Caroline died on 20 Nov., and Pope was interested in that event. On 6 Dec. Lord Bathurst wrote to Swift, 'I met our friend Pope in town; he is as sure to be there in a bustle, as a porpoise in a storm' (Ball, vi. 55).

any place within my Verge, I will be with you. I will come to Mr Knapton's by ten in the morning that day, & desire there to find your Commands, to him who is truly & Sincerely | Yours. | A. Pope.

I shall lye at Cheseldens on Friday night.

POPE *to* ALLEN[1] [24 *November* 1737]

Egerton 1947

The Event of this week or Fortnight has filled every bodys mind, and mine, so much, that I could not get done what you desired as to Dr Pearce. But as soon as I can get home where my Books lye, I will send them to Mr Knapton. The Death of great Persons[2] is such a sort of Surprize to *All*, as every one's death is to *himself*, tho' both should equally be expected & Prepared for. We begin to *esteem*, & *commend* our Superiours, at the time that we *pity* them, because *then* they seem not above ourselves. The Queen shewd, by the Confession of all about her, the utmost firmness and Temper to her last moments, and thro the Course of great Torments. What Character Historians will allow her, I do not know, but all her domestic Servants, & those nearest her, give her the best Testimony, that of sincere Tears. But the *Public* is always hard; rigid at best, even when just, in its opinion of any one. The only pleasure which any one either of high or low rank must depend upon receiving, is in the Candour or Partiality of Friends and that Smaller Circle we are conversant in: And it is therefore the greatest Satisfaction to such as wish us well, to know We Enjoy that. I therfore thank you particularly for telling me of the Continuance, or rather Encrease of those Blessings which make your Domestic life happy. I have nothing so good to add, as to assure you I pray for it, and am always faithfully & affectionately | Dear Sir, | Yours.

Mr Arbuthnot is not yet returned from France

Address: To R. Allen Esq. at | Widcombe, near | Bath.
Postmark: 24/NO

*POPE *to* FORTESCUE[3] [*December* 1737]

1931 (T. J. Wise facsimile)

Thursday night | Twitnam

I left the Town with my Lord Burlington, in hopes from the Last

[1] Printed by Warburton, 1751. His date for the letter is that of the postmark.

[2] Here Pope does not allude to the scandals reported concerning the last hours of Queen Caroline—scandals clearly implied a year later in his *Epilogue to the Satires*, ll. 79–83.

[3] The text is taken from the facsimile opposite p. 95 of Mr. Wise's *Pope Library*. Presumably the date is from Fortescue's customary endorsement.

account my Messenger brought me, that Mrs Spooner was recover'd, or much better. Till this day I heard, you were in pain concerning her, last Sunday; I hope in God she is not worse: I need not say how sincerely I take part in what so nearly concerns you. I have been here near a week, & propose not to be in town till the next. God preserve You & Yours! is the prayer of | Dear Sir, Your faithful affectionate Friend | & Servant | A. Pope.

Endorsement (printed, not in facsimile): From Pope, December 1737.

POPE *to* EDWARD HOLDSWORTH[1] *Dec.* 1737

1797 (Warton)

Twitenham, Dec. 1737.

Sir,—As I am not so happy (though I have long desired it) to be known to you otherwise than in my poetical capacity, so you will see, it is in the merit of that only that I take the liberty of applying to you, in what I think the cause of poetry. I understand that the Poetry-Professorship in Oxford will be vacant, and that Mr. Harte, of St. Mary Hall,[2] is willing to succeed in it. I think it a condescension in one who practises the art of poetry so well, to stoop to be a critick, and hope the University will do itself the credit to accept of him. Your interest is what I would beg for him as a favour to myself. You, who have used the Muses so ill as to cast them off when they were so kind to you, ought some way to atone, by promoting such good and faithful servants to them in your stead. But if Mr. Harte were not as virtuous and as blameless, as he is capable and learned, I should recommend him with an ill grace to one whose morals only have hindered his fortune, and whose modesty only prevented his fame. If ever you visit these seats of corruption in and about London, I hope you would favour me with a day or two's retirement hither, where I might try to show you, with what regard I truly am, Sir, | Your, etc.

[1] Holdsworth, four years older than Pope, had achieved some repute for his Latin mock-heroic, *Muscipula* (1709). He resigned his post at Magdalen College, Oxford, in 1715, rather than take oaths of allegiance to George I. He was apparently a protégé of Lord Digby's.

[2] Pope and Mrs. Knight had both been eager to get preferments for Harte: he failed of election to the professorship at this time.

1738

In this year Pope's correspondents are less frequently his early friends. Death has taken some; Swift is writing much less often, and, from 1736 to 1739, there are no letters to or from Lord Oxford. Of the new correspondents Allen and Lord Orrery are the most notable. Aaron Hill, looking for influence in getting a new tragedy staged, reopens a lapsed correspondence with long, dull epistles. The event of the year was the return of Lord Bolingbroke from France, in the hope of selling Dawley. Much longer than he expected he remained at Twickenham as Pope's guest—from July 1738 to the middle of April 1739. His presence kept Pope at home somewhat more closely than usual, and it kept his good friend Fortescue (Walpole's faithful henchman) somewhat aloof. Meanwhile the Burlingtons were staying much longer than usual in Yorkshire (from August 1738 to February 1739). The chief publications of the year were the two poems that now form 'The Epilogue to the Satires', and these led to attacks from the writers for the Court party (chiefly in *The Daily Gazetteer*), who could not stomach the epithet 'all-accomplished' as applied to Lord Bolingbroke. Pope's idolatry of his lordship's abilities was increased rather than diminished by the long hospitality of the visit.

*POPE *to* JONATHAN RICHARDSON[1] [4 *January* 1737/8]

Add. 25612

Wensday. [4 Jan. 1737]

I keep my promise in acquainting You a day before, that I will come to you to morrow morning by eleven, to sit till one if you please, for the Drs Picture.[2] If you do not want my *Face*, you must be content to have my *Heart*, & Conversation till then: For I want to *see You* more than you can to *see Me*. Adieu. Yrs A. P.

Address: To Mr Richardson | in | Queens Square

[1] The date is inserted in a hand presumably Richardson's. Pope wrote 'Wensday', and the 4th was Wednesday.

[2] The doctor is unidentified, but presumably is Dr. Mead, for whom Richardson painted Pope. The portrait was sold in 1754 (W. T. Whitley, *Artists and their Friends in England*, i. 29). There is now at Petworth House a profile portrait, reproduced in Pope's *Works* as edited by Warton (1797), Bowles (1806), and Roscoe (1824); on the back of the portrait is the inscription, 'This portrait of Pope was taken from life by Richardson for Dr. Mead the Physician, and given by him to Mr. Chetwyn of King's College, who left it by Will to Dr. Cooke, then Provost of King's, my father. A. Way, July, 1825.' 'A. Way' was Dr. Cooke's daughter, Elizabeth Anne (*TLS*, 30 May 1952, p. 368). Details for this note are due to the kindness of Professor Wimsatt.

POPE *to* THE EARL OF ORRERY[1] 2 *April* 1738

1752 (Orrery's *Remarks*, p. 229)

EXCERPT

I write this by the same post that I received your very obliging and humane letter. The consideration you shew towards me, in the just apprehension that any news of the Dean's condition might alarm me, is most kind and generous. The very last post I writ him a long letter, little suspecting him in that dangerous circumstance. I was so far from fearing his health, that I was proposing schemes, and hoping possibilities for our meeting once more in this world. I am weary of it; and shall have one reason more, and one of the strongest that nature can give me (even when she is shaking my weak frame to pieces) to be willing to leave this world, when our dear friend is on the edge of the other. Yet I hope, I would fain hope, he may yet hover a while on the brink of it, to preserve to this wretched age a relique and example of the last.

POPE *to* ALLEN[2] 28 *April* [1738]

Egerton 1947

Twitenham April 28.

It is a Pain to me to hear, your old Complaint so troublesome to you, & the Share I have born & still bear too often in the same Complaint, gives me a very feeling Sense of it. I hope we agree in every other Sensation beside this; for your *Heart* is always right, whatever your Body may be. I will venture too to say, my Body is the worst part of me, or God have mercy on my Soul! I can't help telling you the Rapture you accidentally gave the poor Woman (for whom you left a Guinea on what I told you of my finding her at the End of my Garden.) I had no Notion of her Want being so great, as I then told you, when I gave her half an one; But I find I have a Pleasure to come, for I will allow her Something yearly, & that may be but One year, For I think by her Looks she is not less than eighty—I am determined to take this Charity out of your hands, which I know you'l think hard upon You—but so it shall be.

⌜I like Mrs Allen so extremely, for all you tell me from time to

[1] Here again Lord Orrery has been alarming (and misleading) Pope as to Swift's health. Apparently the newspapers had this time collaborated in reports of his dangerous condition. See Alderman Barber to Swift, 13 Mar. 1737/8 (Ball, vi. 71). Swift's reply to Barber (31 Mar.: Ball, vi. 75) contains complaints of giddiness and deafness, such as Swift had been suffering from for a decade or more. See v. 18 for additional excerpts from Orrery's *Remarks*.

[2] Printed by Warburton in 1751, with the omission of the second paragraph and the mysterious postscript.

time, that it is not fit you should ever tell her of it, but keep it to yourself. However you may give my Service to her.⌉

Pray tell me if you have any Objection to my putting Your Name into a Poem of mine, (incidentally, not at all going out of the way for it) provided I say something of you which most people would take ill, for example, that you are no Man of high birth or quality?[1] You must be perfectly free with me on this, as on any, nay on Every, other Occasion.

I have nothing to add but my Wishes for your health: Every other Enjoyment you will provide for yourself which becomes a reasonable Man. Adieu. | I am truly Yours, | A. Pope

If another Letter to *Arthur Archibald* comes inclosed to you, you will send it me.[2] It is a *dark* design, yet such an one as You would enter into, and (if you please) may open the Letter. Once more adieu.

Address: To Ralph Allen Esqr | at Widcomb, near | Bath.
Postmark: 29/AP

POPE *to* THE REV. ALEXANDER POPE[3] 28 *April* 1738

1857 (Carruthers, pp. 9–10)

Twickenham, April 28, 1738.

Sir,—I received yours, in which I think you pay me more than is due to me for the accidental advantage which it seems my name has brought you. Whatever that name be, it will prove of value and credit when an honest man bears it, and never else; and therefore I will rather imagine your own good conduct has made it fortunate to you. It is certain I think myself obliged to those persons who do you service in my name, and I am always willing to correspond with you when it can be in any way beneficial to you, as you see by my speedy answer to your last. I should think it an impertinence to write my Lady Sutherland, or I would do so to thank her for the great distinction you tell me she shows me, who have no other merit than loving it wherever I find it, be it in persons of quality or peasants. I am not any altered from what you saw me only by some years, which give me less solicitude

1 A reference to the couplet in *One Thousand Seven Hundred and Thirty-eight* (to be published within a month) that praises 'low-born' Allen for doing good 'by stealth', &c. The epithet (Dialogue i. l. 135) was changed in editions after the first to 'humble'. See Pope to Allen, 2 Nov. 1738.

2 Pope, one trusts, is here advising Allen of a method by which the poet is doing good by stealth.

3 Carruthers (loc. cit.) and Donald Mackay (*Memories of our Parish*, 1925) give us information concerning this Presbyterian minister who in 1732 rode his pony all the way from Caithness to visit his great namesake at Twickenham. EC misdate the letter 1728—probably a printer's error.

for myself (as I am going to want nothing ere it be long), than for others who are to live after me in a world which is none of the best. I am, sincerely, your well-wisher and affectionate servant | A. Pope.

Address: To Mr. Alexander Pope, at Thurso, in the | county of Caithness, North Britain.

*HILL *to* POPE[1] — 11 *May* 1738

1753 (Hill)

From Buxton Wells, Derbyshire
May 11, 1738.

Sir,—I have been, for some time, a solitary Rambler; and having, in a tour which I began with last summer, and am in hopes of putting an end to with this, visited some of our own, and our neighbour's sea coasts, I stole the delight of conversing, great part of a day, with some vegetable children of yours, in Lady *Peterborough's* gardens, at *Mount Bevis.* I was so pleased, with many things I saw there, that I could have worshipped, in her groves, like a Druid:—I forgot myself, for many hours, into an escape from that proportion of pain, which imbitters our most tender reflections, when they relate to our offspring of a less grateful and prunable kind,[2] into an enjoyment of that serener satisfaction, which you are intitled to receive, above most men; and more capable, perhaps, of receiving, *under* the increase of your flourishing green families.

For my own part, even when a boy, I was very apt to be out of conceit with a life of much rapture or bustle; but what was then mere *election*, being now become *nature*, I assign myself no further concern with the world, than to accommodate my *desires* to my *lot*; for, after having vainly aspired to be *active*, to some good ends, and good offices, which I am not allowed the prosperity, that was necessary, for effectually reaching, all I now find remaining, as a task for my future solitude, is, to learn to be *lazy*, without *spleen*, and submit to be *useless*, with *temper*.

However, to confess a plain truth, I don't know, whether I am not setting up for a pretender to virtue, from a moderation, wherein *Nature* has more share than *Grace*; there being one among our passions, which you have taught us to detect in its coverts, where it makes the least noise of them all,—like the *still*, *soft voice*, wherein

[1] In spite of its diffuse rhetoric this letter seems worth printing (though EC did not print it) both as an example of contemporary 'criticism' of Pope's phrasing and as an example of the difficulty involved in this type of criticism.

[2] Whether it is his genuine offspring—Minerva, Urania, Astraea, or even his son Julius Caesar—that the rhetorical parent wished to prune may be doubted. He probably wishes he could induce the York Buildings Company to bear more fruit by way of revenue.

God condescended to come, when he would neither be found in the thunder, nor whirlwind.

"One, oft more *strong* than all—the love of *ease*."[1]

But what imports it, whether a person of so little consequence as myself, owes his content in retirement to his natural taste, or his indolence. There is *one* thing, I am sure, which we all of us owe to the *public*; and that is, some account of the uses we make of our leisure.—If I might be allowed to commute, in a pennance enjoined me by fortune, I would attone, very willingly, for my *doing* too little, by *thinking* as much, and as well as I am able: I should only be afraid of supposing myself *busiest*, when, in truth, I was most idlely *employed*. And of this probability, I wish I may not, just now, be about to give you a specimen.

I have lately been looking back upon a design, which I had gone a good length in, and laid by, in the year 1730.[2]—An Essay on Propriety, in the Thought and Expression of Poetry; wherein both Heads are considered, with a Limitation to three distinct Requisites—*Adaption*, *Simplicity*, and *Closeness*. It will be ready for publishing against winter; but finding many reflections, in this tract, which relate to some parts of your writings; wherein, if you were not mistaken, by *accident*, I myself have been so, by deliberate error of judgment, I would rather be set right, by your *own*, than the *publick's* opinion; and it is, therefore, the business of this letter, to bring you, first, a short sketch of my general purpose; and, in the next place, to offer you not only a private examination, but even the absolute and final *decision* of every such censure, as concerns you.

To begin at the wrong end, like a true modern Critic, I have, under the head of Expression, particularly, kept in my view, a very *common*, yet, I think, little *noted* defect of good writers; most of whom I find apt to throw out their conceptions but in gross, by a too general representation of the idea, as it strikes in the whole; disregarding, as an unnecessary care, to appropriate the WORDS they make use of, to their distinct and particular tendency. And, from this hasty and comprehensive inaccuracy of *writers*, I conceive it to arise, that the generality of *readers* (now no longer exacting that *choice* which makes elegance) seem to have lost sight and taste of that *delectus verborum*, wherein *Caesar*[3] (I think it was *Caesar*) placed the strength and foundation of *eloquence*; and whence only can arise such exactness as will justify a very lively imagination of your own:

"Expression is the dress of thought."

[1] *Essay on Man*, ii. 170.
[2] See Hill to Pope, 28 Jan. 1730/1, and Pope's reply to this present letter, 9 June 1738.
[3] Crassus, in *De Oratore*, iii. 150, is the speaker who voices this opinion.

I call it your imagination, because, I believe, the idea must have been *shape* (not *dress*) of *thought*; dress, however, an ornament, being a *concealment*, or *covering*; whereas expression is manifestation and *exposure*.

> Expression is the *birth* of thought—*grows* round,
> Limbs the loose soul, and shapes it into sound.[1]

But this is a start, and digressive:—What I was going to say, and return to, is this:—If any man wants proof, how much of the air of good poetry may be lost by that loose *surtout* dress, now in fashion, let him instruct himself, from your opposite examples—Let him attempt but to substitute another word, of equal effect, in the place of that living monosyllable *shagg'd* in one of your, I had almost said, *inhabitable* landskapes.

> "Ye grots, and caverns, *shagg'd*, with horrid thorn!"[2]

And, if afterwards he would convince himself, what indispensible necessity there remains, that the minutest regard should be had to a chain of such powerful *verbal* propriety, even by those happy and masterly hands, which have been taught by it, to build mountains in verse, 'till they not only stand out to the *eye*, but are felt, as it were, and walked over, by the fancy; he need only examine with care, and he shall see some of the most celebrated of those wonderful artists, taking pains to obscure their own images as often as, abandoning the reins to a luxuriant vivacity of genius, they will not stoop to bind meanings to syllables.

He would, here and there, find a place, even in the strongest and most animated of our writers, where, despising, perhaps (as in painting) the too trim and cold stiffness of *finishing*, he has his descriptions struck *flat*, by a *word*; as if fancy fell into the palsy.

Give me leave to explain, what I have ventured to say, by an instance; one of the last that would be in danger of discovery, from the *confiding* sagacity of your courteous and gentle perusers; but, which you will, yourself, see the *weight* of, in a moment.

When such a writer as *you*, for example, took a resolution of describing the swiftness of *Camilla*,[3] under the most agile hyperbole of lightness; even to her treading upon *cornstalks*, without *bowing* them; nobody can doubt, but your meaning, in such a description, must have been, that she *skimm'd* the scarce-touch'd plain, she *flew over*;—yet, when, on the contrary, your expression says, that she *scours* it—that unwary mis-use of one word, checks the speed of your airy idea, and presents to the fancy, a quite opposite image of *pressure*, *attrition*, and

[1] Hill's rewriting of the *Essay on Criticism*, ll. 318, 319.
[2] *Eloisa to Abelard*, l. 20.
[3] *Essay on Criticism*, l. 372.

adherence: And thus, by admitting even a single monosyllable, that concurs not in the general idea, you was so warmly conveying to the *reader*, it arrests the velocity you had in your view, with as sure and as sudden effect, as the *leaden death* did your *larks* in the *forest*, when they so beautifully left their little lives, in air, to the never-dying applause of the marksman who shot them.

You may reply, (I mean, any body, but you might reply) that, by the metaphorical sense of the word *scours*, as applied, in this place to *Camilla*, we ought to understand nothing more, than her rushing violently over the surface: It is true; but in that very violence, you will have discovered, by this time, the disagreement between your intent and expression: Let us only imagine we see her charging, at the head of her squadrons, or pursuing the disarray of an enemy; and, in a moment, it becomes elegant to say, she is *scouring the plain*; because military rapidity, including ideas of insult and hostility, must be supposed to *lay waste*, while it passes; so that what, in one case, is *propriety*, becomes but *obstruction*, in the other, being mis-applied to velocity, independent of force; where it ought to have been simply considered as *swiftness*. A writer of *your* rank, will never be capable of condemning such instances as these, under the thin plausibility of their being trifling, and verbal remarks; for, since your only design, in the place this is drawn from, was to instruct, by an example, how to paint *things* in *words*; such a word as defaces the very idea, you proposed to imprint, was an error, in the actual foundation, and must, in consequence, throw down the building. Besides, as the chief point here in view, was the structure or *sound* of your verse, with purpose to make it, in your own fine expression, an *echo to the sense*; the minutest exactness of choice, in the words, seems to have been of double demand and necessity.

Be so good, therefore, to tell me (and believe I ask it sincerely, for the sake of instruction) whether I am mistaken or not, when I think you rather contented yourself with the general idea, than examined into the coherence of particular parts, in one of the liveliest poetical pictures that ever was drawn; yet, additional whereto, I am under an unlucky necessity of sending you some, still too faint and imperfect new colourings; because, without taking that extraordinary liberty (liable as it is, to the appearance of something the reverse of my modester meaning), I know not, how to explain to you, within any reasonable compass of a letter, in what parts of the piece I was of opinion, so much happier a hand as your own, should have given it a more heightened resemblance, than that glowing one, you bestowed on it.

Soft, breathes the whisp'ring verse—if zephir plays:
Flows the stream smooth?—still smoother glide the lays,

Where high-swoln surges sweep the sounding shore,
Roll the rough verse, hoarse, like the torrent's rore:
When *Ajax* strives some rock's vast weight to throw,
The line too lab'ring, each dragg'd word moves slow.
Livelier, the light *Camilla* skims the plain,
Shoots o'er th' unbending corn, nor *shakes* th' unconscious grain.[1]

It would be offering an indignity to a temper and genius, like yours, to apprehend (from a freedom I had but only the private curiosity to use) any danger of being mistaken for coxcomb enough, to have thought of so empty a vanity, as that of comparing my numbers. The simple truth is, I amused myself, at that time, for my own satisfaction; but I now recommend to your reconsideration, one of your most admired great master-pieces of poetical harmony, with the honest and friendly intention of convincing you, by an instance, derived from yourself, that there appears still too much room, for a more verbal exactness of propriety, even in the works of our first class of writers.

I am afraid of growing tedious, if I should particularise all my reasons for imagining, you could have carried much farther than you did, the above noble likeness, between your *verse* and your *images*: Such as, that the word *strain*,[2] in your first line, requiring a *stretch'd* and impressive pronunciation, suits not the *softness* of the epithet.—As also, that, both in sound and acceptation there arises, from your expression *blows*,[2] at the end of the verse, a kind of ruffling air of *windyness*, too discomposing for the breath of a *zephyr*.

Add to these, that as, in the fourth line, you seem to have designed, in the first four words, a gloomy picture of high billows, rising, rolling, and swelling, while they are yet in their approach to the strand, the *fifth* word (as it gives beginning to the cadence of that verse) ought to have brought on a *burst*, like the hoarseness of those billows in their breaking—The rushing of a watery sound—a kind of hollow, washy murmur, like the workings of a surfy tide, repulsed and struggling amongst pebbles. But, I hope, it may be enough, to acquit me of impertinence, if I only say something more largely, concerning any one verse of the eight; for, while I shall be busy in so doing, I am sure, your apprehension will preclude, and run before my justification, so as to make needless either reasonings or apology.

"The line too labours,—and the words move slow."

I have wondered very often, how it happened to be possible, to so cultivated an *ear* as your *own*, not to distinguish, in the second division of this verse, a certain declination to improper *quickness*, that runs down

[1] Hill's confident rewriting of *Essay on Criticism*, ll. 366–72.
[2] *Essay on Criticism*, l. 366: 'Soft is the strain when Zephyr gently blows.'

hill, too current, and unincumbered, for the labour and resistance of the image. According to my poor perception, three words, at least of the five (which, I am sure, you must have meant, should move most slowly, because they convey both the *rule* and the *example*) dance away upon the tongue, with a *tripping* and *lyrical* lightness. And if such, in reality, is the case, then, from a want of that unpliant *repugnance*, that *obtundity*, or *bluntness* of structure, which you thought, you had sufficiently given them, and which would have kept them stubbornly distinct and inflexible, they incorporate into a numerous *fluidity*, that expresses not the *idea* in your *precept*.

It being my interest, to induce a *belief*, that my *Essay* would have something worth *reading*, it was, at least, no bad *policy*, to be as busy as I could with *your* writings; but you must not expect, you can furnish me with many instances of this kind. The assistance *you* offered most naturally, was on the contrary side of the prospect: As soon as I have finished, and transcribed the Essay, I will send it to *Twittenham*, in manuscript; resolving it shall carry no example of yours to the *press*, in a manner, against which you have any just exception.[1]

I make the same resolution concerning any thing I have said on your *thoughts*, where I found the field larger a little; tho' it tempted me too far out of my way, from conceptions originally your own, to your *remarks* upon the sentiments of *others*, and especially some of those in the *Bathos*, with which, however, upon reflection, I find no necessity to trouble the *publick*. Nay, were you to bid me expunge them, I should do it, with very great pleasure; for that would give me some *right* to propose your reviewing your censures yourself;—a resolution, which I heartily wish you would take, because a serious and critical condemnation of particular persons, by such *popular* writers as *you are*, (supposing it, at the same time, *severe* and *unjust*) must descend to *posterity*, with one of these two bad consequences attending it: either it must be taken for *equitable*, upon the strength of the critic's *reputation*, to the *disgrace* of an innocent *sufferer*, which your heart is too *honest* to aim at; or, if the censure itself is exploded, and found to want *weight*, it must transfer the *reproach* to the *censurer*; who, in that case, receives his own *injury*.—So that it were really a pity, if in a treatise, abounding with *truth*, *fire*, and *satire*, any thing should be found, by impartial posterity, less derived from your *judgment* than *passion*. But it is so probable, that I am, myself, in the wrong, at such times, when I chance to think *you* so, that I will beg your *own* sentiments on what follows, before I trust *mine* with the *publick*.

[1] Under date of 13 Jan. 1741 Hill wrote Mallet (*Works*, ii [1753]), 217: 'I had finish'd in 1739, *An Essay on Propriety*. . . . But I burnt those papers in a long, and melancholy illness . . . and so I did at the same time *another* piece. . . . The first of these I sacrific'd, to a *suspicion*, which I apprehended I had *grounds for*—That my *design* (tho' really *modest*, and *benevolent*) would *disoblige*, where it intended *service*, and be thought *conceited* or *invidious*.'

"None, but *himself*, can be his *parallel*."

The *Bathos*[1] says, of this line; with a keen and ironical *cruelty*, that it is profundity itself, and may seem borrowed from the thought of a *show-man*, who writ under the picture of his beast—This is the greatest elephant in the world, *except himself*.

What a pity! when, from men, whose opinions will be partially adhered to hereafter, we are obliged to learn *sharpness*, in place of *deliberation*, and prefer the *sparklings* and *appearance* of *wit*, before *penetration* and *solidity* in the *judgment*. Or, pray, did I see wrong when in the place, whence you cited this line, I discerned the most manifest *difference*, between *corporal* magnitude, on one side, and *rational* greatness, on the other? What relates to the *elephant*, I could easily find was *ridiculous*, because it implied bodily distinction of number, where the beast was but one and the same: But, how was there any resemblance of that blunder, in distinguishing between a man and his virtues? When we are told by the historians, that *Alexander* was *unequal* to *himself*, what less must we understand, by this figure, than that his actions were unlike, or *not parallels*? Why, but from effect of our rightly conceiving this duplicity of character, in one single person, do we *detest* in the murderer of *Clitus*, *Philotas*, and *Calisthenes*, the same individual great conqueror, whom we can never be weary of *admiring*, in the tents of *Darius*, and *Porus*? I believe, if you had not been angry, when you censured *that* line, in the *double distress*, you would have found in it, this *delicate praise*:—He was a man, than whom none had been *greater*; nor who had ever been *inferior* to *himself*:—His virtues were not only *strong*—they were *steady*.

There is another very bold declaration of your judgment, upon a thought, where, I believe, Mr. *Theobald* might expect from your *justice*, that, on some future rehearing of the cause, you will give sentence against yourself, in his favour. At least, I own, I could never apprehend, upon what supposition of mistake, in *expression* or *figure*, you came to introduce among *ridiculous* images, what (to me) seems as *natural* a reply, as ever was or could possibly be given, from a *lover*, in defence of his *mistress*, against a reproach, that her *birth* was beneath him.

—"Th' obscureness of her *birth*
Cannot eclipse the lustre of her EYES,
Which make her ALL one light."[2]

When I first read your note on this passage, I found myself compelled into a short *hesitation*, by the regard, that was due to your *judgment*; but I immediately acquitted the *thought*, as not only a

[1] Chapter vii (EC, x. 364).

[2] Ibid. chapter xi (EC, x. 380).

just, but a *lively* one; and the *expression*, as one of the most *proper* and *passionate* I had ever met with. And, to this day, I can understand it in no sense but one—Why talk'st thou to me of her *birth*?—How can defects in her *fortune* be seen through such dazzling excess in her beauty?

Let such rash unweighed censures, as these, stand (in other men's works) as a justification of your *own* exclamations against *malicious* and *ungenerous* criticism—But let it never be told to posterity, that there were such *spots* in the *sun* of our poetry; neither believe, I select these two passages, out of any particular tenderness for their author. I have not, for many years, either seen or corresponded with Mr. *Theobald*; they arose to my eye, by mere accident, as I was looking for a short hint, that might give you some notion of my plan, under each of the heads, which it treats of; and I send them you, from yourself, because it will be a real *delight* to me, and, by no means, a *disappointment* at all, to be better instructed, if I am wrong in my judgment; and, that you may be sure I am telling you truth, without affectation, false modesty, or compliment, I will, after you have seen and examined the whole Essay, leave out every thing, that relates to yourself, which I but observe to have been crossed by your pencil: For I shall then think my notes of most consequence, when they are *before* you, under private inspection; and especially, could they incline you to a review of some of the *least weighed*, and *most sharp* of your censures.—Nay, if I know you right, you will rather *thank* than *condemn* me, for adding, that I look on you as under an obligation of *moral* necessity, to do this *christian* and generous duty; lest, where a *writer* of your high rank in wit, has, through haste, been deceived in his *judgment*, his *mistake* should run down, and be *multiplied* among ten thousand implicit reporters.

I have written you a letter, that I now find, too late, to be grown into an unmerciful long one; yet, if it were not for shame, could go on to write much more, and on many agreeabler subjects, find a great deal to say of yourself, concerning whom, when upon any, I speak more than enough, you should forgive me an excess, you have tempted me into. If I was hearing you talk, I could be pleased with *your* subjects; but, 'till I find one for my use, which I can dwell on, with more satisfaction, you must learn to give place to yourself, in civility to, | Sir, | Your most affectionate, | And faithful Servant, | A. Hill.

POPE *to* HILL *9 June 1738*

1751 (Hill)

June 9. 1738.

Sir,—The Favour of yours of *May* the 11th, had not been unacknowledged so long, but it reached me not till my Return from a Journey, which had carried me from Scene to Scene, *where Gods might wander with Delight.* I am sorry yours was attended with any Thoughts less pleasing, either from the Conduct towards you of the World in general, or of any one else, in particular. As to the Subject-matter of the Letter, I found what I have often done in receiving Letters from those I most esteemed, and most wished to be esteemed by; a great Pleasure in reading it, and a great Inability to answer it. I can only say, you oblige me, in seeming so well to know me again;[1] as one extremely willing that the free Exercise of Criticism should extend over my own Writings, as well as those of others, whenever the Public may receive the least Benefit from it; as I question not they will a great deal, when exerted by you. I am sensible of the Honour you do me, in proposing to send me your Work before it appears: If you do, I must insist, that no Use in my Favour be made of that Distinction, by the Alteration or softening of any Censure of yours on any Line of mine.

What you have observed in your Letter I think just; only I would acquit myself in one Point: I could not have the least *Pique* to Mr. *Th.* in what is cited in the Treatise of the *Bathos* from the Play which I never supposed to be his:[2] He gave it as *Shakespear's*, and I take it to be of that Age: And indeed the Collection of those, and many more of the Thoughts censured there, was not made by me, but Dr. *Arbuthnot.*—I have had two or three Occasions to lament, that you seem to know me much better as a *Poet*, than as a *Man.* You can hardly conceive how little either Pique or Contempt I bear to any Creature, unless for immoral or dirty Actions: Any Mortal is at full Liberty, unanswer'd, to write and print of me as a Poet, to praise me one Year, and blame me another; only I desire him to spare my Character as an honest Man, over which he can have no private, much less public, Right, without some personal Knowledge of my Heart, or the Motives of my Conduct: Nor is it a sufficient Excuse, to alledge he was *so* or *so informed*, which was the Case with those Men.

I am sincere in all I say to you, and have no Vanity in saying it. You really over-value me greatly in my Poetical Capacity; and I am sure your Work would do me infinitely too much Honour, even if it blamed me oftener than it commended: For the first you will do with Lenity, the last with Excess. But I could be glad to part with some Share of any good Man's Admiration, for some of his Affection, and his Belief that I am not wholly undeserving to be thought, what I am to you, | Sir, | A most faithful, affectionate Servant, | A. Pope.

[1] Their correspondence seems to have lapsed after 1733.
[2] Hill might have retorted, 'But you cite it in the *Bathos* as by Theobald!'

HILL *to* POPE 17 *June* 1738

1751 (Hill)

June 17. 1738.

Sir,—The Pleasure, I was sure to receive with your Letter, brought an unexpected Chagrin in its Company, from a Vein of civil Reproach, that runs thro' it; which I can better discern, than account for; since I must not suspect, without wronging my Ideas of your Equity, that you could be displeas'd at the Freedom I took in my Sentiments.[1] If I believ'd they had given you the smallest Offence, I would rather commit my Essay, in its present rough State, to the Flames, than transcribe it, either for yourself, or the Publick.

Indeed it was with a kind of foreboding Reluctance that I censur'd any Passage of *yours*; and to confess the Truth, frankly, I had only one Reason for doing it. After I had convinc'd myself, thoroughly, that *Propriety*, in some of the Lights I was considering it under, had been universally neglected, in Poetry, I foresaw, it would be impossible to establish the Belief of a Fact so unlikely, without citing the strongest *Examples*:—To do this, from the Works of our *dead* Authors only, carry'd the Face of a *Meanness*, I could not tell how to submit to.—To draw formal Citations from any Pieces that had appear'd of my own (tho' full enough, God knows, of Absurdities, to have furnish'd more Proofs than I wanted), would have look'd too assuming, and silly:—To borrow such Instances out of other, less faulty, Cotemporaries, not however reputed among the sparkling great Luminaries of Wit, would have induc'd a mistaken Conclusion, that, in the Works of more masterly Writers, there were no such *Examples* to be met with.—And now,—Is there a good Judge in *England* (except one) who will not see, and acknowledge, the Necessity that threw me, unavoidably, upon *your* Writings?

However, I am glad, at my Heart, it was Dr. *A—t*[2] who made that Collection you mention; for I am almost unwilling to be found in the *Right*, when I disapprove what *your* Name has been stamp'd on; yet your own honest Argument (that it is not enough to excuse a Reporter of Falshoods, that he was told, and believed, what he published) must defend me against its Advancer: For neither is it a sufficient Excuse, that a *Writer*, whose Name, in the Front of a Book, has given Weight to the Censures it propagates, was not *Author* of some of those Censures; since whatever a Man sets his *Hand* to, he ought, first, to examine the *Truth* of.

I am charm'd, while I hear you disclaim that Propensity to *Pique* and *Contempt*, which, to speak with the Soul of a Friend, seems, to me,

[1] Is Hill in this letter being obsequious or ironical? In any case he is unimaginative and tedious.

[2] Arbuthnot.

the only *Spot* on your Character.—We are, All of us, in some Lights, or other, the *Dupes* of our natural Frailties: And when Mr. *Pope*, with the Warmth that becomes a great Mind, tells me how far he is from despising Defects in Men's *Genius*,—never feeling any Contempt but for the Dirt of their *Actions*; I am sure he says nothing but what he firmly believes to be true. And yet there are Pieces, well known to be *his*, many Passages whereof no Man, less appris'd than himself of his Heart's secret Views and Intentions, can read, without being strongly convinc'd of a Scorn, that regards *Genius* only: Tho', if he loves you but half so sincerely as I do, you have no sooner disavow'd the Design, than he concludes, the Imputation was groundless.

In the mean Time, 'tis Pity that a Thinker, so humane and benevolent, should indulge an Ambiguity, in the Turn of his Expression, that scatters Gall, which his Heart never licens'd; since I believe it a general Truth, that Men, of the openest and honestest Natures, sooner catch Fire at *Contempt*, than *Oppression*.—And, as to any *Dirtiness* in Actions which take Birth from Effect of such Influence, we may conclude, from those irresistible little Sallies of *Fury*, whereby, even among undesigning and innocent Infants, we see *Brother* precipitated into Outrage against *Brother*, immediately upon any cold Provocation of *Scorn*, that there is nothing *immoral* in what may be done, or declar'd, too offensively, under Impressions so violent, so involuntary, and natural.

After all this grave Face of Apology, I am an absolute Stranger to the *Grounds* upon which those Men, you refer to, proceeded.—Nay, I am so, for the most part, even to the *Measures* by which they provok'd you: All the Reason, indeed, that I have for giving you any of *my* Thoughts on the Subject, is deriv'd from your own starting into it (a little digressively) immediately after hinting some Occasions you had to lament, that I knew you less justly, as a *Man*, than as a *Poet*.—I will appeal to impartial Posterity, whether I do not know you much better, in both Lights, than ten thousand of those pretending *Esteemers*, of whose Affection you think yourself surer. It will never be in my *Will*, nor my *Power*, to transmit such a *Picture*, as yours, without its best, and most beautiful *Likeness*: I shall leave to duller *Dutch* Painters in Criticism, their unenvied Delight, to draw *Monsters*. And know very well, for my own Part, that I should but *disgrace* the desir'd Reputation of my *Pencil*, if I miss'd the *Resemblance*, too widely, in a Piece which must expect to be compar'd with Originals of the same, by many different *Masters*.

Tho' I acquit you of any further Allusion to *me*, than by that retrospect Glance, *en passant*, I have, *affectionately*, caught the Occasion of pointing out, to one of the least intentionally guilty among Men, a seeming *Tartness* of Spirit in himself, which he will easily *find*, when he looks for; and which, whenever he does find, and guard against, by submitting his *Wit* to his *Philosophy*, he will become the most *unnatural* good Man in the World; for he will leave himself not a *Fault*, to be blam'd for!

As to myself, who was born to mix Sin with Repentance, I plead guilty to all such Indictments as you, in that Place, *present* to my Memory.—I was always too perceptibly quick, in my Apprehension of *Contempts*, or *Indignities*:—A Temper, which would have been as *unpardonable*, as I confess it to be *weak*, and *self-mortifying*; but that the Fault, tho' of too swelling a Nature, leaves no Voids for Admission of *Malice*.—It is an offensive, indeed, but reconcileable Imbecility of Mind: *Shakespear* felt, and understood it, very finely.

> "It carries *Anger*, as the Flint does *Fire*!
> Which, being struck, throws out a hasty *Spark*,
> And then, grows cold again.—"[1]

Yet I will endeavour to redress this wrong Bent in my Temper, and make Way for the Rectification you are so good as to shew me my WANT OF.—And thus, in the Commerce of *Friendship*, as in Traffick, less generous, there is offer'd a mutual Exchange of Advantages:—Something, always, to *give* and to *gain*: And this makes *both Sides* more rich, and more satisfy'd.—What a Loss, then, have unsocial and vain Dispositions, which, by a sullen Seclusion from these Rights of Reproof, and Plain-dealing, cut off all the kind Use of Correction!—*Human Nature*, let it be as susceptible of *Grace* as it can, never yet wanted *Pride* enough to make Mortifications, of this Kind, a *Requisite*. Far from hating our *Friends* for a little faithful, tho' unwelcome, *Asperity*, let us think *him*, of all Men, *unhappiest*, who has never been bless'd with an *Enemy*.

And now, let me ask you (with a Transition very fashionably abrupt and uncritical)—How is your good and great *Friend*, Lord B—, to be reach'd?—You will scarce think I mean,—to be *emulated!* Ours is an Age that exposes such an oldfashion'd Politician, as HE is, to any *Fear*, sooner than that of a *Rival*. I have a Packet to send him, a little too large for the *Post*. It is a manuscript Piece,[2] which I purpose to *dedicate* to him, when publish'd. But it would be Prudence, and Decency, as Affairs stand at present, to wait his Permission, after reading it: Not that there is any thing nice, or exceptionable, in the Subject; and, I am sure, I have no need to add, tho' I speak of a *Dedication*, that mine has no *Views* like a *modern* one. If you will be so

[1] *Julius Caesar*, IV. iii. 111–13. Hill's passion for the *delectus verborum* leads him to substitute, in the second line quoted, words more 'appropriated' than Shakespeare had used.

[2] Hill's tragedy *The Roman Revenge*, concerning which he is about to become persistently tedious.

kind as to think how it may reach my Lord's Hands, I shall, in a few Days, send it open, to yours; begging you, first, to peruse, and then give it a Seal, and a Forwarding. If you will have the Goodness to authorize such a Trouble, please to do it under a Direction, like your last, to | Sir, | Your most humble | and affectionate Servant, | A. Hill.

POPE *to* HILL[1] 2[o] *June* 1738

1751 (Hill)

June 2, 1738.

Sir,—I sent you as honest an Answer as I could, to the Letter you favour'd me with; and am sorry you imagine any *civil Reproach*, or *latent Meaning*, where I meant to express myself with the utmost Openness. I would assure you, if you please, by my Oath, as well as my Word, that I am in no Degree displeas'd at any Freedom you can take with me in a private Letter, or with my Writings in publick. I again insist, that you alter or soften no one Criticism of yours in my Favour; nor deprive yourself of the Liberty, nor the World of Profit, of your freest Remarks on my Errors.

In what I said, I gave you a true Picture of my own Heart, as far as I know it myself. It is true, I have shewn a *Scorn* of some *Writers*; but it proceeded from an Experience that they were bad Men, or bad Friends, or vile Hirelings; in which Case, their being Authors did not make them, to me, either more respectable, or more formidable. As for any other Pique, my Mind is not so susceptible of it as you have seem'd, on each Occasion, too much inclin'd (I think) to believe. What may have sometimes seem'd a *Neglect* of others, was rather a *Laziness* to cultivate or contract new Friends, when I was satisfied with those I had; or when I apprehended their Demands were too high for me to answer.

I thank you for the Confidence you shew you have in me, in telling me what you judge amiss in my *Nature*. If it be (as you too partially say) my own Fault, I might soon be a perfect Character: For I would endeavour to correct this Fault in myself, and intreat you to correct all those in my Writings; I see, by the Specimen you generously gave me in your late Letter, you are able to do it; and I would rather owe (and *own* I owe) that Correction to your Friendship, than to my own Industry.

For all the last Paragraph of yours, I shall be extremely ready to convey what you promise to send me, to my Lord *B.* I am in Hopes very speedily to see him myself,[2] and will, in that Case, be the Bearer;

[1] In printing, the 1751 editor evidently dropped a digit after the 2 of the day date. The letter is obviously an answer to Hill's of the 17th, and must fall between the 17th and the 25th, when Hill again expatiates. EC corrected the date to 20.

[2] Bolingbroke was expected soon from France.

if not, I shall send it, by the first safe Hand, to him. I am truly glad of any Occasion of proving myself, with all the Respect that is consistent with Sincerity, | Sir, | Your most obliged and | affectionate Servant | A. Pope.

HILL *to* POPE 25 *June* 1738

1751 (Hill)

June 25. 1738.

Sir,—It is Time to relieve you from Subjects, and Lengths, like my last; yet you will hardly suspect such a Blindness, in my bad Understanding, as to think, I distinguish not the true *Cast* of some Colours which you need not have held quite so near me.—Notwithstanding all which, if I had not more Cause to distrust it, on *your* Side, than my *own*, I should flatter myself, we were born to be Lovers; we are so often, and so unaccountably, mistaking one another into *Reserves*, and *Resentments*! Yet I am sorry, whenever this happens, because the most *lost* Time, in Mens Lives, is *that* which they waste in *Expostulation*. They, who are *Friends*, find it *selfish*, and *diffident*—and between *Enemies* 'tis *inflaming*, and *fruitless*.

Indeed there would be no End of such—what must I call 'em?—*Elaircissements* is an affected *French* Word, and I am heartily sorry I *want* it.—In plain *Truth*, and *English*, I always did, and I still do, most affectionately *esteem* you, both as *Man* and as *Poet*: And if now-and-then, for a Start, I have been put out of Humour with *either*, I would fain have you think, it was no less your *own* Fault, than *mine*: At least, I am sure, I believ'd so. And if, whenever you suppos'd me to have acted inconsistently with myself, on that Principle, you had only been so kind, as to have declar'd *why* you thought so, I would openly, and immediately, either have demonstrated the *Mistake* to be *yours*, or confess'd, and abhorred, my *own Error*.—I will always stand *bound* to give, if not a *rational*, yet a *moral*, Account of my *Actions*: Not alone, as they regard Mr. *Pope*, but *Men*, in the remotest Situation below him: And whoever (let him be accus'd, either by Misapprehension or Calumny) would *decline* such a *Test* of his *Conduct* in Life, is so far from being worthy your *Friendship*, that he is a *Stranger* to both *Spirit* and *Honesty*.

Here, then, let us *rest* this Debate; and either resolve to let *fall* an unconfiding, and cold Correspondence, or much rather agree (if you please) to understand one another *better*, for the future.—As to my own Part, I never *will*—I never *did*—disoblige you, *unprovok'd*. And if, how unkindly soever impell'd, I write or do any thing unbecoming the Occasion—Think of me, as I would of your Enemies.

In the mean time, let even the little Trouble, you have so kindly allow'd me to give you, in the Inclos'd, be receiv'd as some Proof that I know, and respect, at my Heart, your double Claim, both in *Morals* and *Genius*. For you know *me*, I am sure, much less justly, if you can imagine me capable of corresponding, with an Air of *Good-will*, where I wanted a *personal Attachment*; or of begging, as I now very earnestly do (upon *any* Inducement, but the high Sense I have of your *Skill*), your frank and friendly *Inspection of the Tragedy*.[1] It would charm me, to have the Benefit of your Hand, or your Hints, before it appears on the *Theatre*.

As to my *Essay on Propriety*, you have obligingly convinc'd me, I may lay it before you, without Pain; Indeed, if I had made it unfit for *your* Eye, the *World* would have been still less likely to see it: I shall punctually obey your Command, neither to *omit*, nor to *soften*, in the Transcript: It is an Injunction I may safely comply with, since, if I have any thing to value myself upon in this Tract, it is from the Proofs, you will find it abound in, that some of your most retir'd, and most delicate Touches, have been, chiefly, the *Search* and the *Subject* of, | Sir, | Your truly affectionate, and | most humble Servant, | A. Hill.

*POPE *to* ALLEN[2] [6 *July* 1738]

Egerton 1947

If the Memory I every day have of your Friendship were to be told you, it would be a more constant Address than most people offer to their Best Benefactor, and a thousand Times more Sincere than Any ever offerd to an Earthly Prince on the Throne. So much higher is my Respect for Virtue than for Title, that You might suffer as much from the Importunity & Assiduity of an honest Heart, as your Betters (in this world) do, from that of an Interested one. But you may thank God for my Laziness, which seldom lets me take the pains of telling you & Mr Hook, how well I think of you both: And I am quite ashamed to have to do in the Way of Compliment, with two such Modest People.

I will therfore only reply to your Six hearty Lines, in as plain a manner. I do really wish myself with you; I know not how to be so; I am afraid I cannot get so near you as within fourscore miles, this Summer; My Infirmities increase ev'ry year: Tho my Spirit be prompt; my Flesh is weak. I have two great Tasks on my hands: I am trying to benefit myself, and to benefit Posterity; not by Works of

[1] Hill's *Roman Revenge*. The play is spoken of under various titles. It was never performed. It concerned the death of Julius Caesar.

[2] The day and month come from the postmark. The year is hypothetical. Hooke was with Allen in the later summer of 1738. Lord Bolingbroke arrived in London on 8 July, and came presently to stay with Pope (and to sell Dawley). Because of Bolingbroke Pope could not expect to go to Bath—though it was considered a remote possibility in August.

my own God knows: I can but Skirmish, & maintain a flying Fight with Vice; its Forces augment, & will drive me off the Stage, before I shall see the Effects complete, either of Divine Providence or Vengeance: for sure we can be quite Saved only by the One, or punishd by the other: The Condition of Morality is so desperate, as to be above all Human Hands.

I hope your Guest proceeds with alacrity, & not without some pleasure, in his Work; which the Encouragement of a Friend at his elbow will render less a burden; I wish I could ease him of any that he bears.

Believe me a true Wellwisher of yours & Mrs Allen's joint happiness, & always | Dear Sir | Yours faithfully | A. Pope.

Address: To Mr Allen, at his house | at Widcombe | near | Bath.
Postmark: 6/IY

LYTTELTON *to* POPE 13 *July* 1738

Hagley

Stowe July the 13th 1738

I am sorry I was so unlucky to be gone from London before your packet came, and that His R. H. was thereby deprived of the pleasure of seeing it so soon as you intended.

You compliment me on my Sincerity where it deserves no Compliment: To tell Truth to an Indifferent Author is a mark of Sincerity, for he is sure to be Angry, and unable to mend the faults you find; but in Works so near Perfection to point out some accidental blemishes, is no more than telling a fine Woman you dislike some little part of her Dress, which, by altering a Pin or two, she can easily correct.[1] All here are well, and much your Friends. Last Night's Papers say Lord Bolingbroke is arrived from France;[2] if it be true, I wish you joy. I shall leave this place Sunday, or Monday. Beleive, that I am *the Sincerest Man alive* when I assure you nobody can Esteem, and Love you more than | Your most faithfull Humble Servant | G Lyttelton

Address: To Alexan: Pope Esqr at | Twickenham in | Middlesex | by London
Postmark: 14/IY
Frank: Free G Lyttelton.
Endorsement: Returned | at Mr Pope's | Death.

[1] Lyttelton has evidently been reading the MS. of a poem, presumably the second dialogue of *One Thousand Seven Hundred and Thirty-eight* (now called the 'Epilogue to the Satires').

[2] The *Lond. Eve. Post*, 11 July 1738, reported the arrival of Bolingbroke from Calais, as of 'Saturday night last' (the 8th). At Stowe the news would arrive more slowly.

*POPE *to* HILL 15 *July* [1738]

1760 (Hill)

Sir,—I have been ill since the receipt of your letter, and was moreover inclined to be able to tell you, when I answered it, that the Tragedy, &c. were safe in the hands you intended them for.[1] But, first, I read it twice over, to my great satisfaction. I will not tell you my opinion further, till I can give you, with it, what will be the best sanction of my own, my Lord Bolingbroke. After a suspence of near a fortnight, I deferred sending it cross the seas, in hopes of what has since been determined, his journey hither. He is at present in London, and will in a few days be at Twitenham. I will lay hold of the first occasion to tell you his sentiments, and be assured of my full belief of the kind assurances you give me in your letter. Be as satisfied of my real desire of your friendship, and of the certainty that I will never do any thing that can deserve to lose it. I am, with esteem and obligation, | Sir, your most affectionate humble servant, | A. Pope.

London, July 15.

POPE *to* HILL[2] 21 *July* 1738

1751 (Hill)

July 21, 1738

Sir,—I need not assure you in many Words, that I join my Suffrage intirely with Lord *B.*'s in general, after a fourth reading your Tragedy of *Cæsar*. I think no Characters were ever more nobly sustained than those of *Cæsar* and *Brutus* in particular: You excel throughout in the Greatness of Sentiment; and I add, that I never met with more striking Sentences, or lively short Reprizes. There is almost everywhere such a Dignity in the Scenes, that instead of pointing out any one Scene, I can scarce point out any that wants it, in any Degree (except you would a little raise that of the *Plebeians* in the last Act.) That Dignity is admirably reconciled with Softness, in the Scenes between *Cæsar* and *Calpurnia:* And all those between *Cæsar* and *Brutus* are a noble Strife between Greatness and Humanity. The Management of the Whole is as artful as it is noble. Whatever particular Remarks we have made further, will be rather the Subject of Conversation than a Letter, of which we shall both be glad of an

[1] The hands of Bolingbroke.

[2] Together with this letter from Pope went one written on the same day and subject from Twickenham by Lord Bolingbroke. It is possibly more moderate in its praise than Pope's letter, but it calls *The Enquiry into the Merit of Assassination, The Tragedy of Caesar* (as the play seems to have been christened in MS.) 'one of the noblest Dramas that our language, or any age, can boast'. The entire letter from his lordship is printed in Hill's *Works* (2nd ed., 1754), ii. 17–18.

Opportunity, either here at *Twickenham*, or in Town, as shall best suit your Conveniency. Pray, Sir, let this confirm you in the Opinion you kindly, and indeed justly, entertain of the Wish I feel (and ever felt, notwithstanding Mistakes) to be, and to be thought, | Sincerely your obliged, affectionate, | and faithful Servant, | A. Pope.

HILL *to* POPE 31 *July* 1738

1753 (Hill)

July 31, 1738.[1]

Sir,—It was yesterday, before I had the pleasure of receiving your kind and obliging letter; together with Lord B—'s, (for which I have sent him my thanks in the inclosed). The coach brought your packet, a week past, from *London*: But I had made a little start, from my disagreeable situation in the skirt of a country town, with a view to resolve on a fitter,[2] where I must content myself, for some time, with forty-seven miles distant from *Twickenham*, 'till, like the story they tell of a *beast* not worth naming, I have made myself *lighter*, as a means to be safer; that is (in plain *English*) 'till I have sold the best part of a too little *fortune*—very falsely so called, while it could not procure *ease* to its *owner*. As soon as this hard task is over, I shall be able, with the greatest delight, to assure you, in your own beautiful garden, what an impression you have made on me, by your goodness.

Never was I more pleas'd and surpriz'd, than at hearing you had Lord B—ke at Twickenham: I mean, that you had him, your guest there, in *person*; for I knew his *idea* dwelt with you. Yet, I fear, he is a blessing we are to hold, as we do *summer*;—just to feel, and owe *fruit* to—and lose him. *France* is glad to draw *strength* from her neighbours; and will take pains to out-charm a dull climate, where she would leave as little *spirit* as possible.

As to the Tragedy, you return me, of *Cæsar*, you will not easily imagine, how glad I am, you were pleased with it; and how much more so, that you tell it me, with such a warmth of goodwill and generosity. But I am still further, if possible, obliged by your judicious and elegant *corrections*, hinted to me in such a number of places. Nor have I enough of true *protestant zeal*, to lose any one of your blessings, because (like a *Papist* as you are) you have given them me with the *sign of the Cross*.—No—I remember the effect of that sign, in the banner of *Constantine*, and I *reverence* it, as a token of *victory*. As for that low scene of *Plebeians*, in the last act, I will strike it quite out. 'Tis the best way of mending a fault, which was committed without

[1] On this day Hill also wrote to Lord Bolingbroke about the tragedy. See Hill's *Works* (1753), i. 286–9.

[2] About this time Hill removed to Plaistow (Essex).

use, or temptation. What a deal of *dumb magic* may be lodged in the *path* of a *pencil*! *Yours*, like its sable representative on the face of a dial, *says* nothing; and yet *points out*, and measures, and regulates, with the utmost *exactness*, as it passes! so salutary, and so necessary is the *eye* of a *friend*! How many *improprieties* might your reprehension have taught me to *rectify*! How many obscurities to clear up and enlighten! And, lastly, how many of the *ambitiosa ornamenta* (a poet's most dangerous, because most flattering favourites) might not such wholesome *black liaes*, of our *Horace*, have given me resolution to cut off, without mercy!

And so much for this Tragedy—except that, as I design it for the *stage*, this next winter, it would be infinitely kind in you (while I am a *hermit* on the back side of *Parnassus*) to speak what you think, where it properly offers, for its service, as well *before* the acting season, as *in* it.

Though I talk of the back side of *Parnassus*, I sometimes see company here, you would hardly expect, from the prospect; for where, but at an old fashioned country gentleman's, who lives in a hole at the foot of a hill, and a wood, like the cave of some captain of Banditti, should I meet the other day, with Part the Second of *One thousand*, *seven hundred*, *thirty eight*.

Stor'd with beauties, as every thing must be, that you write, for the public, shall I dare to confess, that I did not use to consider your works, of *this* vein, as those, from which you were surest of the love and admiration of posterity; but I find, in this, satire, something inexpressibly daring and generous. It carries the acrimony of *Juvenal*, with the *Horatian* air of ease and serenity. It reaches *heights* the most elevated, without seeming to design any *soaring*. It is raised and familiar at once. It opposes just *praise* to just *censure*, and, thereby, doubles the *power* of either. It places the *Poet* in a light for which *nature* and *reason* designed him; and attones all the pitiful *sins* of the *trade*, for, to a *trade*, and a *vile* one, poetry is irrecoverably sunk, in this kingdom. What a pity, that our rottenness begins at the *core*! and is a corruption, not of *persons* alone, but of *things*! One would, else, strongly hope, from a ridicule so sharp, and so morally pointed, that wicked men might be laughed into something, like penitence. But, alas! they are only bit by *Tarantula's*, who can be cured by the power of *musick*.—Not even the harp of *Apollo* had a charm to expel *vipers*, that have crept into the *entrails*.

Go on, however, to make *war*, with a courage, that reproaches a *nation's*; and live (would you *could*) just as long as 'till the *virtues*, your spirit would propagate, become as general, as the esteem of your genius!—I am, with great obligation and truth, | Sir, | Your most obedient, | And most affectionate Servant, | A. Hill

*POPE *to* HUGH BETHEL 31 *July* [1738]

Egerton 1948

Twit'nam July 31st.

I was truly a Condoler with Mr Moyzer,[1] and with the whole Country, for the death of his Father, & I may almost say Their Father, his beneficence was so diffusive. I was concern'd to see no more Notice taken of the loss of a Good man, in the publick prints; than which there cannot be a greater to any Age, but to this above any age. I was unlucky in missing 3 or 4 times of seeing the Colonel his Son, both at his lodging & at mine. It happen'd that the very hour we met, my Lord Bolingbroke came to carry me hither, where he has been so kind as to pass some days, & I hope will pass more before he leaves this Country; which will be as soon as he parts with Dawley, or ingages in another Settlement of his affairs, either of which cannot take up above a month. he is in extreme good health, a blessing which makes amends for many other misfortunes, and in very good Spirits, & strength of Parts, which render a man superior to most Losses. As to my own health, it does not mend, nor impair, except that for five or six days past, I have had a violent cold. My Journies this year will be shortend by my staying to have as much as I can of Lord B. perhaps in September I may ramble for a fortnight, or so. Mrs Blount is at Kew & so is her Sister in the neighborhood: They have left their house in town, & taken another,[2] into which our friend has the Resolution to goe with them, the only Resolution she has being to go counter to her Friends advices—I remonstrated to her in vain, early enough—I see her less than usual, as she hath been constantly with Lady Gerard, in Town & at Kew, & as the distance from me thither exceeds my walking, & takes up 4 or 5 hours going & coming: But the main reason is, that I see there 's no good to be done her, & she fretts me too much, who am too seriously concern'd for it. My Lord Burlington goes to Yorkshire with his whole family in about ten days. I have often wishd I could see you there, where I fancy you are most happy; for in Town you generally seem to think yourself not at home; & I would see my Friend quite at ease, without which the Satisfaction to one that truly wishes him so, is imperfect. But That, & another Wish I have long had, to go to Rome, are not likely to be accomplishd in haste. I believe I shall live & dye in one Iland, & almost in one County, now: for I am every day less desirous of what I find myself less capable. But I hope not to die in your debt (I mean of 400ll) if I live till Christmass: but deeply in your debt for a hundred friendly offices, if I lived till Doomesday: For which yet I am thoroughly gratefull, & exact in

[1] Pope frequently calls officers in the army 'Mr.' Colonel Moyser's father, John Moyser, Esq., of Beverley, had recently died.

[2] They had removed from Bolton Street to Welbeck Street.

remembring, (one Virtue these times doe not abound in) & truly, very truly, Yours.

Address: To Hugh Bethel Esqr at | Beswick, near Beverley | in | Yorkshire
Postmark: 1/AV (Possibly 7/AV.)

POPE *to* FORTESCUE 31 *July* 1738

1817 (Warner, p. 56)

July 31, 1738.

It was my intention sooner to have told you, of what, I know, is the news a friend chiefly desires, my own state of health. But I waited these three weeks almost, to give you a better account than I can yet do; for I have suffered a good deal from many little ailments, that don't altogether amount to a great disease, and yet render life itself a sort of one.

I have never been in London but one day since I parted from you, when I saw Mr. Spooner[1] and the rest of yours; and this day I took it into my head they might be at the Vineyard. I went thither, but Mrs. Shepherd told me, in a voice truly lugubrious, that nobody had seen her walls since you were last there. I comforted her over a dish of tea, and recommended her to read Milton on all such occasions of worldly disappointments.

I went home, and drank Sir Robert's health with T. Gordon;[2] for that day I was left alone, my Lord Bolingbroke being sent for to London, who has stayed with me otherwise constantly since his arrival in England, and proposes (to my great satisfaction) to do so, while he remains on this side the water. It is great pleasure to me that I never saw him better, and that quiet and hunting, together, have repaired his health so well. Your friend Sir Robert has but one of these helps; but I remember when I saw him last, which was the last time he sent to desire me, he told me he owed his strength to it. You see I have made him a second compliment in print in my second Dialogue,[3] and he ought to take it for no small one, since in it I couple him with Lord Bol—. As he shews a right sense of this, I may make him a third, in my third Dialogue.[4]

[1] John Spooner, Esq., son-in-law of Fortescue.

[2] Possibly Thomas Gordon, author of *The Independent Whig*, &c., one of Walpole's hired writers, and not likely to be calling on Pope, especially with Bolingbroke possibly about. The picture of Gordon in the Fourth Book of *The Dunciad*, ll. 493–516, however, suggests that Pope had seen Gordon *en pantoufles*. Elwin says that a cancelled MS. couplet of *1738* (EC, iii. 459 n.) satirized Gordon as Tacitus (an author whom he translated).

[3] The second dialogue of *1738* (Epilogue to the Satires) appeared on or about 18 July. Lines 132–5 are what Pope has in mind.

[4] Of which only a fragment, not published by Pope, exists, under the title of *One Thousand Seven Hundred and Forty*. A compliment to Walpole appears, incomplete, ll. 43–48. (See Pope's *Poetical Works* [Twickenham ed.], iv. 334.)

I should be glad to hear of any place, or thing, that pleases you in your progress. Lord Burlington was very active in issuing orders to his gardener, to attend you with pine-apples: he goes into Yorkshire next week.

Pray remember me to Mr. Murray. You need not tell him I admire and esteem him, but pray assure him that I love him.

I am sincerely, dear Sir, your's, | A. Pope.

Address: To the Hon. William Fortescue.

SWIFT *to* POPE AND BOLINGBROKE[1]

8–24 *August* 1738

1741 La

Dublin, Aug. 8, 1738

My dear Friend,—I have yours of July 25, and first I desire you will look upon me as a man worn out with years, and sunk by publick as well as personal vexations. I have entirely lost my memory, uncapable of conversation by a cruel deafness, which has lasted almost a year, and I despair of any cure. I say not this to encrease your compassion (of which you have already too great a part) but as an excuse for my not being regular in my Letters to you, and some few other friends. I have an ill name in the Post-Office of both Kingdoms, which makes the Letters addressed to me not seldom miscarry, or be opened and read, and then sealed in a bungling manner before they come to my hands. Our friend Mrs B.[2] is very often in my thoughts, and high in my esteem; I desire you will be the messenger of my humble thanks and service to her. That superior universal Genius you describe,[3] whose hand-writing I know towards the end of your Letter, hath made me both proud and happy; but by what he writes I hear he will be too soon gone to his Forest abroad. He began in the Queen's time to be my Patron, and then descended to be my Friend.

It is a great favour of Heaven, that your health grows better by the addition of years. I have absolutely done with Poetry for several years past, and even at my best times I could produce nothing but trifles: I therefore reject your compliments on that score, and it is no compliment in me; for I take your second Dialogue that you lately sent me, to equal almost any thing you ever writ; although I live so much out of the world, that I am ignorant of the facts and persons, which I presume are very well known from Temple-Bar to St. James's; (I mean the Court exclusive.)

"I can faithfully assure you, that every letter you have favour'd me with these twenty years and more, are sealed up in bundles, and

[1] First printed in 1741 La, this is a reply to the (lost) joint letter of 25 July.
[2] Martha Blount. [3] Bolingbroke, soon to go back to his forest of Fontainebleau.

delivered to Mrs. W—,[1] a very worthy, rational, and judicious Cousin of mine, and the only relation whose visits I can suffer: All these Letters she is directed to send safely to you upon my decease."[2]

My Lord Orrery is gone with his Lady to a part of her estate in the North: She is a person of very good understanding as any I know of her sex. Give me leave to write here a short answer to my Lord B's letter in the last page of yours.

My dear Lord,—I am infinitely obliged to your Lordship for the honour of your letter, and kind remembrance of me. I do here confess, that I have more obligations to your Lordship than to all the world besides. You never deceived me, even when you were a great Minister of State: and yet I love you still more, for your condescending to write to me, when you had the honour to be an Exil. I can hardly hope to live till you publish your History, and am vain enough to wish that my name could be squeez'd in among the few Subalterns, *quorum pars parva fui*; If not, I will be revenged, and contrive some way to be known to futurity, that I had the honour to have your Lordship for my best Patron; and I will live and die, with the highest veneration and gratitude, your most obedient, &c.

P.S. I will here in a Postscript correct (if it be possible) the blunders I have made in my letter. I shewed my Cousin the above letter, and she assures me "that a great Collection of[3] your / my letters to me, / you are put up and sealed, and in some very safe hand."

I am, my most dear and honoured Friend, entirely yours, | J. Swift. | It is now Aug. 24, | 1738.

POPE *to* LYTTELTON — 15 *August* [1738]

Hagley

I hope this will find you in all those Pleasures which a Good Mind takes in its Duties and its Affections, which in such an one, go together. The satisfaction of a Father who loves you not more tenderly than you love him, and of such Brothers as you make glad, tho' their elder; & such Sisters, whom you count as Riches, not Taxes,

[1] Mrs. Whiteway.

[2] Pope's letters for twenty years past had been returned to him a year back. Has Swift forgotten? If fabricated, this paragraph and the postscript risked exposure by Swift or by Mrs. Whiteway. Possible hypotheses: Mrs. Whiteway did not read the entire letter, or she had sealed parcels of Swift's papers and was at this time unaware of the return of Pope's letters.

[3] Tis written just thus in the Original. The Book that is now printed seems to be part of the Collection here spoken of, as it contains not only the Letters of Mr. *Pope*, but of Dr. *Swift*, both to him and Mr. *Gay*, which were return'd him after Mr. *Gay*'s death: Tho' any mention made by Mr. *P.* of the *Return* or *Exchange* of Letters has been industriously suprest in the Publication, and only appears by some of the Answers.—1741–2.

upon your Estate. I wish you all joy of one another. I am truly sorry to want the joy I proposed, & had placed in my heart, of seeing this in person: You do me justice I doubt not, and know tis a concern to me not to be able to reach you before you are obliged to leave that agreeable Scene. What puts it past any Hope I had, is, that yesterday my Guest[1] here was seized with a sort of Fever, the Concomitant of a Bileous Distemper which has formerly attack'd him, and generally holds some weeks. He is unable to leave this place, & that will retard his business in Town a week or two longer than I imagined when we parted. I can have no prospect of seeing you sooner than at Stowe, if then: But I desire to know by a line, six or seven days before you go thither.

My Lord Burlington has not had a Pineapple to Spare, till my Lady's going to Yorkshire, one excepted, which I sent to your Lodging the night before you left London. You did not tell me where to direct to the Carrier who is to bring them to Hagley. When I can get 2 or 3 together to send to Sir Thomas, Will it do, to send them box'd up to the Admiralty? or to your lodgings? I have bid the Gardiner inquire at both places, and also what days the Carrier goes out? of which you forgot to leave me a Memorandum in paper: (in which case he should have sent them directly to you.) Send me any Instructions to Twitenham and I will do all I can.

Lord Cornbury yesterday set out for Spa, in a ticklish State of health & extreme low Spirits. If all honest Men die, there will be great Joy at —[2] and if all Ingenious men lose their mettle, the Gazetteer will be Inestimable. I have had but very bad health since you left me, but tis no matter, tis all in the Way to Immortality. However I advise you to live, for the sake of this pretty World, and the Prettiest things in it. Adieu I am Sir Thomas's most obliged Servant for getting such a Son as you, and Your most faithfull, & ever truly most Affectionate Friend, | A. Pope.

Twitenham. | August 15.

Address: To | George Lyttelton, Esq.

Endorsement: Mr Pope's Letters.

*POPE *to* THE EARL OF BURLINGTON[3] 17 *August* 1738

Chatsworth

My Lord,—I know it will be Satisfactory to you to know of my Lord

[1] Bolingbroke recovered more rapidly than Pope expected. See his letter to Burlington, 17 Aug.

[2] Peter Cunningham, who transcribed the letter for EC, thought the dash showed signs of replacing *St*—for St. James's. No such signs are clear, but the intention is doubtless grasped by imagining either 'Court' or 'St. James's' as understood.

[3] At the end Pope dated 'Thursday morning' and Lord Burlington wrote in the exact date.

Bolingbroke's Recovery. I had written you a line by Mr Terret, but for a very silly accident; which was that my Paper was in the Room where my Lord slept, & I had not a scrap to write on. He is now so well as to go down stairs tho not abroad, & you'l be sure both to find, & to please him, if you have any hour to spare before your Journey.[1]

I must beg the favour of your Lordship to let Mr Scot come to me for an hour to day, to assist me about a Stove I am building, & he shall not be detain'd. A line I sent him yesterday I fear miscarried. And I think I may ask for a little fruit for Ld B. who may venture to day or to morrow to eat it, at least I shall. If we don't see your Lordship here, I will make you one Evenings Visit on Sunday, unless you tell me it will be inconvenient. No man living is with greater Truth & affection | My Lord | Yours most faithfully | A. Pope

Thursday | morning | Aug 17 | 1738

POPE *to* HILL — 17 *August* 1738

1751 (Hill)

Twickenham, Aug. 17. 1738

Sir,—I am forced to say but little to you, tho' my Spirit has been warm'd by the kind (and let me add, the just) Manner, in which you took our last Letter. My Lord (who has not only resolved to make himself my Guest, but an Inhabitant of this Place during all his Stay in this Kingdom) is at this Time fixed to this Place too closely, by a Fever, which has confined him to his Bed and Chamber some Days. I am but just now satisfied that he is out of danger; and I am as sure, as that he *lives*, that he will be glad to see you *here*. And I think it certain (if you can get those Affairs over which you mention, as soon as I wish you at Ease), that you may find him here this Fortnight: That I shall take a warm Part in bringing you together, my own Heart knows: And let me tell you, when you know that Heart as well, as I hope Fortune will not long hinder you from doing (tho' many unlucky Strokes of her Influence have been too strong upon us both, who *must* else have naturally united, as we mutually love and hate the same Things), I believe, trust, and pray, we shall perfectly understand one another. Believe me till then, upon my bare Assurance, very faithfully, without superfluous Words, in one Word, | Dear Sir, | Yours, | A. Pope.

*POPE *to* JONATHAN RICHARDSON[2] — [? 17 *August* 1738]

Yale University

The Fear I have to miss of you, join'd to the Knowledge I have of

[1] To Yorkshire.

[2] It seems impossible to date this letter, since Bolingbroke sat to Richardson more than

your great Readiness to take any Hint I can give you, makes me send this to tell you 2 things: first, that my Lord B. is recovering, I hope, apace, and will probably be with You the begining of the week; and secondly, that I am obliged to go for four hours from hence this morning; The Waterman ingages to deliver you this soon after Sun-rise, for that is an Hour to find You & the Lark, awake & singing. That you may long preserve that Spring, in your Autumn of life! is the true Wish of Dear Sir | Your | A. Pope

Mr Richardson

Address: To | Mr Richardson, in | Queens Square | Bloomsbury.

*POPE *to* ALLEN — 19 *August* [1738]

Egerton 1947

Aug. 19th

I hope you had a line of mine, in which I exprest my pleasure, to find Mr Hooke & You together in such good Company. I know not whether he is still with you, but if he is, pray tell him I am at all times glad to have any testimony of his remembrance. My Lord Bolingbroke has been some time my Guest at this place, & I hope will be so while he stays in England unless he be obliged to visit the Bath: And in that case I shall have *Two* Temptations to go thither. But his business keeps him near the Town at present, where he is prescribed in the meantime to drink the Bath-Waters, lest he should not have time to go thither. I write this to desire, you will be at the trouble of directing Some to be sent, in bottles twice a week 4 at a time; or if they can't be sent but once a week, 8 bottles at a time, to Mr Ansell a ~~Surgeon's~~ Pothecary, in New Brantford. I give you this trouble, knowing the Concern you will have in the health of so particular a Friend of mine, & so great a Man as he is in himself.

You may assure Mr Hook, that he has tryed to serve his Son in France,[1] as to the Abbé, and had succeeded, but for the disgrace of Chauvelin. I hope dear Sir I need not tell you the pleasure it will always be to me to hear you are well & happy; those words only,

once. But in July 1738 he was staying with Pope, was slightly indisposed, &c. A letter from Kent to Lord Burlington of 28 Nov. 1738 (printed here, iv. 149) and a letter from Pope to Richardson in December seem to indicate that a new portrait of Bolingbroke was done this year. The year 1742 is also quite possible. As far back as 1833 this letter was offered as item 801 in a catalogue of autographs by the dealer Thomas Thorpe. The catalogue says the letter is endorsed by Richardson 'Wedn. Aug. 17, 1733'; but no such endorsement is now on the letter. In 1733, 17 Aug. was a Friday, and Bolingbroke was at that time on a long visit at Orchard Wyndham (Sir William Wyndham's place). Possibly Thorpe read a vanished endorsement as 1733 when it should have been 1738.

[1] Mr. Hooke's younger son, Luke Joseph, had been granted his D.D. at the Sorbonne about 1736, and became a professor of theology there in 1742.—*DNB*. His father evidently thought Bolingbroke might aid the young man in his career.

without form, without ornament, without all affected Circumstance & Complement, are Sufficient to make an honest Man's letter to an honest Man, agreable, & worth a thousand of the Prettiest things that can be said by all the Courtiers, & Wits of the world. My own health is much as usual, enough to thank God for my Being, not enough to squander away in Excesses, which they mis-call Pleasures. If either you or Mr Hook would edify Dr Cheney, pray shew him this one period, & add my Services to him. I heard he was in London, after he had left it, & wished I had seen him at Twitnam, where he should have eat Sallads & Yams & Torja's, a Sort of Potato or Chesnut from the Isle of St. Christophers. Tell him, if ever I change my Religion it Shall be to his, or to the Quakers, I am not determind to which.—My hearty Services to Mrs Allen. Yours Ever.

Address: To | Ralph Allen Esq. at | Widcomb, near | Bath.
Postmark: 19/AV

HILL *to* POPE — 29 *August* 1738

1753 (Hill)

August 29, 1738.

I am sensibly touch'd, by the kindness of your last; and sorry at my heart, that I am unable to bring you my thanks for it, to *Twickenham.* It would have been a delight, of the warmest, and most desirable kind, to have seen my Lord, there, before he left *England.* But, (accustom'd to disappointment, and ill fortune) I am encumber'd with difficulties, which retard all my views; nor dare I determine how soon I can hope to be easier. Since I must not, therefore, be so happy, as your truly great friend has the goodness to wish me, only tell him, in my name, that he has a faithful servant, unknown, who always lov'd him from motives, which he deserves: and desires to be lov'd, from one, who has long weigh'd his spirit, and reflected on, and measur'd his *actions.* One who, less for my Lord's sake, than his country's, laments to observe it administer'd into a necessity of *fearing* his virtues. I cannot forbear to add, that I wish him great length of days; yet, am afraid, I include great happiness in the wish; since he will never be able to see, and hear, without misery, the *desolation* of a country, he was born for!

I ought to be asham'd, after thinking and speaking of Lord *B—ke*, to descend to such a theme as my Tragedy: But you have, *both*, been its friends, and benefactors, and it would be doing injustice to your good nature, if I forbore to inform you, that from a wholesome severity, which I was inflam'd into against myself, under influence of your saving black *Crosses*, I have effac'd, chang'd, and heighten'd it, (in two hundred places, and more) till, if now it fails on acting, to meet with a reception, a little extraordinary, I shall be mortify'd into a *conviction*, that it is time for me to have done writing!

I was about to have it sent you, again; that you might have seen the good effects of your censure: But, when I remember'd you had read it *four* times, I found not enough of the *Poet*, within me, to presume the unconscionable *fifth*, from an attention, that can be employ'd so much better.

God knows, when the season comes on, how far I may be master of opportunity, to attend it in its way to the Theatre, (where the managers are for *Farce*, and not *Tragedy*.) In the interim, I shall apply most of my leisure, to the finishing, and transcribing my Essay, that it may be legible, and come and beg your perusal: To whom sending every good wish, in my stead, I remain, | Dear Sir, | Your most obliged | And affectionate Servant, | A. Hill.

POPE *to* HILL[1] 30 *August* [1738]

1751 (Hill)

August 30. 1731.

The very Moment I receive yours, I dispatch this, to tell you with Sincerity both my Guest's and my own Concern to have no Hopes of seeing you; as well as, what is unfeignedly a yet greater Concern, our Sorrow at what you express to be the Occasion of it. He wishes, now, for Power, for no other Reason, than to be able to elevate Merit above that Fortune it commonly finds, from Power. And I can truly add, for my own Part, who never tasted Power, that I never felt any Uneasiness in a low Fortune, but that which it causes when I find it cannot prove the Regard and Love I bear to true Worth in any afflictive Circumstance.[2]

Excuse my pretending to say a Word on that Subject; all I meant to say (but the Overflowings of my Heart vented thus much) was, to beg you to think too favourably of us both, to imagine we should not be unhappy as much as dissatisfy'd, if we did not read once or twice more your Tragedy, after what you tell us of your having alter'd it on our Suggestions. We have a conscientious Fear, that you may have comply'd too implicitly with those *Marks*, rather of our scrupulous Sincerity, than of any certain Judgment; and have quench'd sometimes a Flame we admire, tho' we may fear; or sometimes heighten'd what may be natural, tho' we might think it low. Pray ease us, by favouring us with a second View of it.

And whenever you send me that Essay, you may be assur'd of my

[1] The edition of 1751 misplaces the letter and gives it the date of 1731. There can be no doubt that 1738 is correct.

[2] Afflictive circumstances were illness and a long-drawn suit in Chancery.

sincere Answer; tho' upon that Head I could rather wish it were given you personally. I hope a little Time will bring us together. Know me, most affectionately, dear Sir, | Yours, | A. Pope.

HILL *to* POPE 1 *September* 1738

1753 (Hill)

Sept. 1, 1738.

Sir,—You have oblig'd me, dear Sir, (in a manner that can never be forgot) by that sincere, and kind sense, you express, of the difficulties, which encumber my affairs. But, I assure you, were they greater, and more than they are, I should rather *enjoy*, than *lament* 'em, while they procur'd me the distinction of a generous wish, from such minds as your *own* and Lord *Bolingbroke*'s.

Another way, too, you are both of you, infinitely good: For you encourage me to the repetition of a trouble, I should never have had confidence, to think pardonable. After so many times reading the Tragedy, to be desirous of going over it again, is an honour, which, if it is found to deserve, it must be by improvements, deriv'd from your pencils. I am really at a loss, how to thank you enough, for those marks, both of your judgment and kindness, and you will see, how sincere I have been, in this sentiment, from its effect on the pages, I send you. But one thing I found strange in the benefit, is, that as soon as I consider'd your *crosses*, with the passages, against which they were plac'd, they explain'd what they meant, so convincingly, that I saw both the *defect* and the *remedy*; and yet I had often, and severely, before, taken those very places to task, without any such conviction of their wants! nay, this could not, in my case, arise from an *author*'s partiality to himself, because I know, I examin'd with rigour. I must, therefore, conclude, that familiarity with our own thoughts, and conceptions, *dulls* and *deadens* in us, our sense of their qualities,—as men are gradually *benumb'd* in sensations, that relate to their *wives*. By the way, that's a vile (modish) *simile*; for men, in *my* case, are *dull'd*, but in sense of *defects*: In the *other*, of *beauties*, and *virtues*.

After all, what a *profit* are we robb'd of by pride, when we decline this advantage of *censure*! I don't mean such kind censure, as *yours*, only—(*friends* touch every thing with the finger of *Midas*) but I speak it with regard even to the malice of *petulant* criticism. Even this is what *Poets*, methinks, have still cause to be fond of; since wherever an *error* is clear, the *instruction* is equally manifest: And, tho' it should happen, that the Critic *mistakes*, the Writer, however, reaps benefit; For while he can't, without impartial reflection, be convinc'd, whether injustice is done him—he acquires patience in search of that truth, and is but forced into a habit of judging.

I took as much care, as I could, to strike out, and insert with such plainness, as to preserve the old copy still legible; yet you will find it blotted, and scarified, all over; like a lady, to whom I have the pleasure of being a neighbour: She was once, I am told, very fair of complexion, and was then, full of faults, and of vanities; but being now become hard-fac'd, and pimply, she is grown amiable, and candid *within*; and pleasing no more, as a *belle*, gives delight, like a rational creature, I am, | Dear Sir, | Your most truly | Affectionate Servant, | A. Hill.

*POPE *to* JONATHAN RICHARDSON[1] [? *September* 1738?]

Arthur A. Houghton, Jr.

I have, literally, not been Master of two hours since I saw you, & I would not allott less to enjoy your Conversation. Pray if you can, let me have it this Evening after six at Mr Allen's, whither I will come on purpose to meet you, nearer you at that End of the Town which I most frequent, & must from this day be confined to. Your Son will accompany you. And if you please to bring with you the Plate of Lord Bolingbroke, with which you have obliged me, & Posterity, do: I am truly Ever | Yours. | A. Pope.

Thursday.

Address: To Mr Richardson, at | his house in | Queens Square | Bloomsbury
Endorsement (in a later hand?): 1738

POPE *to* THE EARL OF ORRERY 6 *September* [1738]

Maggs Bros. (1937)

My Lord,—I am at all times obliged to acknowledge Your Lordships Memory of me, and I hope you think it impossible I should not be constantly sensible of it; & constantly Happy in Your Happiness, tho perhaps the last man who has written to tell you so.[2] But I was Ashamed of your Message, to say you would have been here but for the accident that befell in your Journey,[3] (from which I hope your Lordship & my Lady Orrery are quite unharm'd.) It is my duty to wait on you, as I had done to day, but that it is the day of my Lord Bolingbrokes Return, after a short journey he made into the Country. He assures you of his Compliments, & we both propose to be at your

1 The date is uncertain, but at about this time Allen was in town and there was concern over the likeness of Bolingbroke done by Richardson.

2 That is, to congratulate him on his (second) marriage (30 June 1738) to Margaret Hamilton of Caledon.

3 His journey back from Ireland, where he had been this summer. The accident happened between Coventry and Creeke, and Lord Orrery's arm was sprained.

Lordships door the moment he can go to Town, for his stay in England will probably be short, his resolution being to go as soon as he has sold Dawley, for which there have been two or three Treaties on foot some time. The Dean's Letter made me melancholy, & I apprehend your account of him will not relieve me from it. Be assured, my Lord, I honour your Worth, & love your Humanity, both which Considerations will ever strongly bind me to be | My Lord | Your ever obliged | and faithfull Servant, | A. Pope.

Twitenham. | Sept. 6.

*POPE *to* THE COUNTESS OF BURLINGTON[1]

Chatsworth

[*c.* 8 *September* 1738]

Madam,—I lately received two Papers, one in Prose, the other in Verse, printed under the Title of the Gazeteer,[2] a News-letter so called, of which I have heard mention in Mr Pope's late Dialogue of 1738. Why the said Papers were sent to me, directed in a hand, which upon recollection I take to be the same which was used to convey the said Mr P's Poetry to the press;[3] and franked by a Noble Earl, his avowed Friend & Patron; I cannot conceive: Unless it were a Modest Intimation that the aforesaid Gazetteers were the Work of a Lady who is well known to bear much malice to me, & much Friendship to mine Enemies, at, & about Court. If I could prove this Upon her, she might be sure to be Immortalized in the next Piece of that Implacable Poet.[4] Indeed I think no Persons in the world but the authors of those Gazetteers, are Impudent enough to Expect any one will read them: & consequently it is the same thing to *Send* such a paper, as to own they *write* it. Upon my word Madam, your Verse and your prose are so like each other, that I do not know which is which? & I cannot say one is worse than the other. But if your Presumption runs so high as to imagine I will answer Either, God forgive you for it! I vow to God I would not, if Lord Harvey owned them; nay if Sir Robert, & his Brother, & Mr Paxton, & Ch. Churchill, & Mr Ripley, & Tom Walker,[5] all begged me on their knees to take notice of them so far.

[1] Written to Yorkshire, where the Burlingtons remained from late Aug. 1738 to Feb. 1739.

[2] Lady Burlington has sent Pope *The Daily Gazetteer* for 24 Aug. (containing a prose attack on Pope) and 26 Aug. (the verse attack).

[3] Lady Burlington had more than once served as Pope's amanuensis.

[4] These remarks are, of course, facetiously ironical.

[5] The names (satirized by Pope) are arranged in descending scale: Sir Robert Walpole and his brother Horatio, Nicholas Paxton (Solicitor to the Treasury), Charles Churchill (natural son of Mrs. Oldfield, later married to Lady Mary Walpole), Thomas Ripley (builder of Sir Robert Walpole's palace at Houghton), and Tom Walker (possibly the playwright and actor).

I do not care to name Names, but if I can guess at the Style of any of these great Writers, they have no hand in them, And consequently, Madam, all your Endeavours to work mischief out of this, are in vain. And it is ill and treacherously done, of That Court Lady I before Mention'd, to make Epigrams on those Persons, meerly (I doubt not) to have them pass for mine.[1] I know her Hand writing, tho she has disguised it a little; & so I believe you will, when you see them. Kent is clear in that opinion; but thinks there is an Allegory in one of the Epigrams, & doubts if it is not a reflection upon him at the bottom? He is very Umbrageous in his Drink, & says Lord H. writ the Gazetteer, tho Sir Archer owns it. I have nothing more to add, but that *The Suff'ring Triumvirate*[2] are all your Servants, & drink your health in Dorsetshire Ale with true devotion: Two of us have such Bad names, that Mr Kent's must be content to stand alone, lest the ingenious owner should *fall.* We therfore shall not sign 'em, but only assure your Ladyship & my Lord, we are as much yours & his Servants as the Signior himself.

Endorsement (by Lady Burlington): recd & | answer'd | Sept. 8 | 1738

*POPE *to* FORTESCUE[3] — 8 *September* 1738

The Pierpont Morgan Library

Sept. 8th 1738

I know it is a good while since I ought to have writ to you: I know I also intended it daily, & that is half an Excuse for my Omission, as Intentions are next a-kin to Actions. My own Conscience is clear, in bearing daily testimony that I love & remember you. A Friend of so many years, has a Title too good, to stand in need of New Deeds & Writings at every turn. And certain it is, that my old Affections are Sweetest to my Taste, as they observe it is, in the Fruit of Old Trees. I have been very happy these 3 weeks & more, in the Company of one of the oldest & first of my Friends, my Lord Bolingbroke: he has instructed me most, & in many instances proved he loved me the best, of any of a Rank so far above me. But what adds to the obligation is, his being of a Rank in Understanding & Learning more above Others,

[1] Two epigrams exist at Chatsworth (MS. 143. 76) which may be the ones sent to Pope in the letter he is here answering. In MS. 143. 76 they appear on the verso of a cover to a letter addressed to Lady Burlington at 'Lansborough'. She, like Pope, may have used letters as paper on which to compose.

Mr. H. A. Tipping, *Architectural Review*, lxiii (May 1928), 180–3, published four letters from William Kent to Lord Burlington. In one (dated 12 Sept. 1738), Kent writes: 'I forgot to tell you in my way to Esher on Sunday [the 10th] I call'd upon Mr Pope, he's going upon new works in his garden that I design'd there—he told me of a letter he had wrote to her [the countess?] of some witt that he had me a party of—'

[2] 'The suff'ring triumvirate' were Bolingbroke, Kent, and Pope.

[3] Pope's day date is badly formed, but pretty surely an 8. In endorsing the letter Fortescue read it as a 6.

than any Rank else can make a Man; and That Superiority too he has set aside in my favour.—It is with a *longo Intervallo*, that I name Another Old friend at this time, who gives me some Emotion, poor Jervas, whose *Last Breathings* are to be transferrd to Italy, for he sets sail to day, in hopes of some reprieve from his Asthma—Let me put you in mind, that we have known each other long enough to be old in friendship, tho not yet quite so in Years. However, I for my part am willing to be old in Disposition, so far as to seek Retreat & Peace: And You, as in the Character of a Judge, are also *Vir tristis & gravis.* I am as content to quit the clamorous Part of a Poet, Satire, as you could be to quit that of a Pleading Lawyer, Et in Otia tuta concedere —I no sooner heard of the death of the Master of the Rolls, but I wished in his room, the most Pacific, Patient Man I know, of that Profession.[1] More *Quiet* cannot be in any Law-Station; & *Quiet* is the Life of Innocence & Good nature: More Honour & more Title may; but which is best? Honour, Title, or Quiet? If my Wishes are the same with yours; may yours succeed! if not, still may yours (whatever they be) succeed! Adieu. I hope soon to see you, and remain as I always was, | Your true Friend & | faithful Servant | A. Pope.

Address: To the Honble Wm Fortescue | Esqr; in Bell-yard: | To be sent forwards.

Endorsement (by Fortescue): Mr Pope | Sept 6. 1738

POPE *to* HILL — 12 *September* 1738

1751 (Hill)

Sept. 12. 1738.

Sir,—I have now little to say of your Tragedy, which I return with my Thanks for your Indulgence to my Opinion, which I see so absolutely defer'd to, that I wish I had cross'd less frequently. I cannot find another Thing I think a Fault in you.

But my Lord thinks, three Things may yet be reconsider'd. *Brutus*, on Sight of the Warrant sign'd for his Death, takes at once the Resolution of murdering *Caesar*, as none of his Father. Quere, Whether in the Scene that follows between him and *Caesar*, all Tenderness on the Side of *Brutus*, and all beyond the Point of Honour that Friendship exacted, should not rather be avoided than heightened?

Another Quere is, Whether it would not beget more Indignation in the Audience against *Cassius*, and more Compassion for *Caesar*, to shew that *Cassius* suspected *Brutus* to be *Caesar's* son, and therefore exacted from *Brutus* the Oath of sparing neither *Father*, Relation, *&c.*

The Third Thing is, Whether the Efforts made by *Caesar* to pre-

[1] In July Fortescue had been transferred to the Court of Common Pleas. He did not become Master of the Rolls until 1741.

vent the Civil War, not only by the equal Offer he made, while the Matter was under Debate in the Senate (and which the Consuls *Lentulus* and *Marcellus* refused to report to the Senate), but by the Message he sent to *Pompey*, when he was at *Brundusium*, to desire a Meeting, to settle the Matter, and avoid the Civil War.—*Vid. Caes. Comm. de bell. Civili, lib.* 1. The Mention of these somewhere in the Play might help to remove the Prepossession against *Caesar*.

After our little Cavils (for so we will rather call minute and verbal Points of Criticism) we owe you the Justice to extol highly, what we highly approve, and you need not desire us to speak as we think: 'Tis what we have (in different Ways) done all our Lives, where it was to our Prejudice, and cannot but do here, where it is to our Honour. I only wish you a Stage, Actors, and an Audience worthy of you, and It.—I have often wished to live to see the Day when Prologues and Epilogues should be no more. I wish a great Genius would break thro' the silly, useless, Formality. But at least I would have one try, to leave the Audience *full* of the *Effects* of a good Tragedy, without an Epilogue. Let me add another Hint, concerning the Apparatus and Circumstantials of your Play (since I have nothing left more to wish in the Play itself); that you would intitle it barely, *The Tragedy of Caesar*, and give no Intimation of his being a *Patriot*; for I fear, instead of preparing the Audience, it might revolt them, and put all the little Criticks upon carping previously at the very Design and Character; which would appear by Degrees, and with the proper Preparations, in the Piece on the Stage. Another thing was a Thought of my Lord's, that it should be printed before acting, a Day or two; for the Sentiments are so thick-sown, and the Sense so deep sometimes, that they require more Attention and Thought than the Hearer may be apt to give on the first Representation. I am not positive, either as to his, or my Thought, but submit them to your Consideration.

I have nothing to add, but to lament our Unhappiness, that we cannot see you personally to confirm what these Letters tell you, of our real Opinion of your Work, Esteem of its Author, and Wishes for your Success, in this, and every thing. I am, | Sir, | Your most faithful and obliged Servant, | A. Pope.

*POPE *to* JONATHAN RICHARDSON[1] 20 *September* [1738]

The St. James's Chronicle, 25–27 July 1776

Sept. 20.

You may be certain of two Things, that I am ever the same to you, and that I see you whenever I can. I have never been in London but one Hour since we met. I have been ill for about a Fortnight.

[1] The year is most uncertain, but the letter seems to refer to the portrait of Lord Bolingbroke, made this year.

If I can leave this Place soon, I will come and take the Picture from your Hands, (to which originally) and from your Heart, (to which finally I owe it) and esteem it therefore more than if given me only by the noblest Friend I have.—The Case I send in the Interim.

Adieu. My hearty Service to your Son; and let the Father believe me (next to his Son) the most affectionate of his Servants. | A. P.

HILL *to* POPE — 23 *September* 1738

1753 (Hill)

Sept. 23, 1738.

You would sooner, dear Sir, have been troubled with my thanks, for your favour of the 12th, but that it came not to my hands, till the 20th: Mr. *Richardson*[1] being from home, and his people not entrusted with the direction, to forward my letters.

As soon as I had read, I perceiv'd the weight of your reason, for not hinting the *patriotism* of *Caesar*, too rashly; and therefore, tho' I had chang'd, before you saw it, and upon the same apprehension, a *title*, I design'd for the Tragedy, now found that caution too little; and immediately cross'd out those lines in the Prologue, which insinuated something of like purpose.

I find too, upon reflection, that the concern will be so visibly increased, by that finely judg'd hint, of my Lord's, for contriving to make *Cassius* appriz'd of the true birth of *Brutus* (and therefore including *fathers*, in the horrible abjuration, he dictates) that, in order to make way for such a scene, as I send you, wherein I account for the probability of that circumstance, and open the Play with its discovery, I have cut off as many lines in other places, where they could be spar'd, without weakening the scenes:—and among 'em, I have struck out those, which my Lord finds too *tender* in *Brutus* to *Caesar*, after sight of his *warrant*: For tho' I imagin'd there was something (tragically at least) allowable for certain involuntary motions of horror, certain powerful sensations of reluctance, and tenderness in *children*, about to do violence to *parents*, tho' they know 'em not, as such; yet I make it a maxim to give up opinion, implicitely, (in pieces of my own) to the judgment of men, of *great genius*. And I ground the resignation upon this principle (which I think is a just one) that even granting, I could clear up the point in dispute, to my own sense of the question; yet where the apprehension of *such* men but *hesitates*—the *meaning* must, to the bulk of mankind, be quite *dark* and *imperceptible*. And whatever is not *obvious*, is *error* in dramatical writings. I have also, thrown something into the scene, from my Lord's third kind hint, as a help toward

[1] Not Pope's friend the painter, but Hill's friend the printer—soon to become famous as the author of *Pamela*.

removing the popular prejudice against *Caesar's* inclination to *peace*. But, in this, I was too much confin'd by the plan; for the deaths of *Pompey* and *Cato* having happen'd, before, left particular transactions, between them and *Caesar*, remote from the present disposition of things; which, turning upon precipitate *passion*, must come on, with rapidity, and violence; and therefore, I was afraid, lest expostulatory deductions, while they concern'd matters, out of the current, might have given to good reasoning, the appearance of coldness.

What you say, against *Prologues* and, *Epilogues*, is a truth, which I heartily feel, and come into; But he ought to be very well *mounted*, who is for leaping the hedges of custom. As my affairs stand, at present, I should find it imprudent, to give away the third nights, (which till now, I have always left to the house) And, I doubt those disorderly heats, which must throw the *first* night into uproar, upon retrenching a popular folly, might have effects (for the above reason, *alone*,) to be apprehended.

It was, from the same *little* reason, (too narrow a one, I confess) that I took the liberty of desiring you in a former to *declare* your very generous, and good-natur'd thoughts of the *play* where you judg'd 'em most likely to be of service, toward the expectation, and report, that should fore-run a Tragedy. It was *impossible* (and I hope, you are sure of it) that I could desire you to *speak*, *what you think*, in any signification unworthy your *spirit*. *You*, who speak what you think, with more boldness, than most others dare *think* what you speak!

After all, I am asham'd, that I took such a freedom; and amaz'd, how I came to imagine it reasonable, I should charge your attention so heavily! I believe, I had doubts, when I sent you that letter, (as, indeed, I still have) from the too light, or too gay disposition, both in masters of Theatres, and Audiences. And, in truth, I am apprehensive, I have no great *Success* to expect, from the *Tragedy*.

No matter I am sure:—it *can* never have any, that will be either more great, or more priz'd, by its author, that *that*, which, by my *Lord Bolingbroke*'s goodness, and *yours*, it has already receiv'd in *your* judgments. Believe me, dear Sir, with an unchangeable affection, | Your oblig'd, | Humble Servant, | A. Hill.

POPE *to* THE EARL OF ORRERY[1] 25 *September* [1738]

The Pierpont Morgan Library

Twit'nam Sept. 25.

My Lord,—As soon as I returned to London, I was to wait on your

[1] This is Pope's commentary on Swift's strange letter of 8 Aug. 1738. Two things are to be remembered: (1) That apart from Swift's letter we have as yet no signs of the senility that was to overtake him in 1742. (2) That in various letters of 1737 (18 Mar., 2 and 14

Lordship with Mr Lewis, & tho disappointed was glad to find you abroad, in the hope your Arm is well recover'd after so much Suffering. I had with me the Dean's letter, but by some accident have lost it since, & only recollect what he said of the Letters was, that *Every letter* I had writ to him *these 20 years was found*, & *deliverd to* Mrs Wh. & that she was *directed* to *send them me after his decease*. The purport of the whole letter was a Complaint of the great decay of his Memory, & at the End, he writes a Postscript telling me that Mrs Wh. had just told him he was under a mistake, that the Letters were *not deliverd to her*, but in *some other safe hand*, *in Ireland*. If Mrs Wh. told your Lordship she *knew nothing* of them, her Whole Drift is too manifest, especially when she would print the History,[1] *every word as it stood*, notwithstanding all the Remonstrances of his Friends, & his own Submission to them.

I will not answer the Dean, till I have the honour to wait on your Lordship again, tho I think it will be to no purpose to say any more on that Subject.

I return the Verses you favord me with,[2] the latter part of which is inferior to the beginning, the Character too dry, as well as too Vain in some respects, & in one or two particulars, not true.

I beg my most humble respects to my Lady Orrery, and to be always known for one, who with the highest Esteem is | My Lord | Your most obliged & | most obedient Servant, | A. Pope.

Lord Bolingbroke sends your self & my Lady his Compliments.

Address: To the Rt Hon. the | Earl of Orrery, | Duke street | Westminster.
Endorsement: Mr Pope. | Sepr 25th 1738.

*POPE *to* GEORGE SELWYN[3] — 29 *September* [1738]

Yale University

Sir,—I should be wanting in that Quality with which you suppose me indu'd, Candour, if I were not sincere in my answer to your letter.

June) Lord Orrery had, probably unintentionally, aroused Pope's suspicions of Mrs. Whiteway and other friends of Swift so far as the disposal of the Pope letters was concerned. Swift's last letter (which alone of those here considered may have been 'edited' by Pope) was the final, natural cause of more than suspicion. Pope had apparent grounds for thinking that not all of his letters had been returned. He most unscrupulously used these grounds to deceive the public into thinking in 1741 that his letters had not been returned to him, but had been printed first in Ireland.

[1] *The Four Last Years of the Queen.*

[2] Supposedly *Verses on the Death of Dr. Swift*, published in London (Jan. 1738/9), in an abbreviated form devised by Dr. William King of St. Mary Hall, Oxford, and by Pope—possibly also Orrery had a hand. Swift, whose mind was not so far gone that he did not know the difference, had the full text printed thereafter in Dublin.

[3] The year is guess-work. George Augustus Selwyn (1719–91), celebrated later for his wit, was evidently at the time this was written very young. He matriculated at Hart Hall, Oxford, early in 1739, and by July of that year was on the Continent. (See Horace Walpole's

I cannot enough approve of so laudable an Employment of your Youthful Studies, as the Translation of Tully's Epistles; I think it will be as Reputable, if you take Sufficient Time in the Work; and shall be very ready to *joyn* myself to the number of your Friends, whose Opinion you may take in the prosecution of it.

As a proof of my Sincerity, I have remarkd an Errour at the Beginning; (to which however tis not improbable some Commentatour may have led you.) All I can advise in general is, that you will not be too hasty in complying with any man's Request, in proceeding in the Translation, without being fully acquainted with the General History of the Roman Affairs, & of Tully in particular, first: which will make many passages Clearer to you, than they can be, considerd singly, & un-relatively to others. I am | Sir, | Your most obedient | humble Servant, | A. Pope.

Twitnam, | Sept. 29.

Address: To Mr G. Selwyn, to be | left at Mr Dodsley's.

POPE *to* HILL[1] — 29 *September* [1738]

1751 (Hill)

Sept. 29. 1731

I return you the Inclos'd the Day after I receiv'd it, lest it should retard your finishing the Copy now the Year draws toward Winter: And tho' I am in a great Hurry, which allows me to say little, only to tell you, in my Lord's Name and my own, that we think you shew even more Friendship and Confidence in us, than we have hitherto been justly intitled to, from any Use our Opinion could be of, to a Judgment so good as your own. We are fully satisfy'd; and 'tis but at a Word or two, that I *can* carp, with the utmost and most extended Severity of a Friend. It will be with infinitely greater Promptitude, and Pleasure, that I shall speak (every-where) my real Approbation and Esteem of the Performance, in which I shall do no more than discharge my Conscience. I wish sincerely, I could as well serve you in promoting its Success, as I can testify it deserves all Success. You will, I am sure, be so candid, and so reasonable, as to conclude, I would not decline writing your Epilogue on any but a just Reason, and indeed

Correspondence (ed. Toynbee), i. 35–36.) The Selwyns lived in Cleveland Court, and thus were neighbours of Jervas. Either as a neighbourly acquaintance or as a proved master of letter-writing (? in 1737) Pope was asked to advise the young man on his projected translation.

[1] Dr. Brewster, *Aaron Hill*, p. 206 n., is evidently right in correcting the year of this letter. In 1751 and thereafter it has been printed as 1731, and the tragedy thought to be *Athelwold*. But the mention of *my lord* [Bolingbroke] and the talk of an epilogue fit the letter into the series of 1738.

(to me) an invariable Maxim, which I have held these Twenty Years. Every poetical Friend I have, has had my Word, I never would; and my Leave to take the same Refusals I made him, ill, if ever I wrote one for another: And this very Winter, Mr. *Thomson* and Mr. *Mallet* excuse me, whose Tragedies either are to appear this Season, or the next. I fansy the latter, as I have seen or heard of no more but a *first* Act, yet, of each.

I have lately had an address of *another Kind* from a Man of Letters, which gives me more Embarrass, and in the Conduct whereof I could wish I had your Advice, tho' I hardly know how to ask it. I hope soon to see the Critical Work you promis'd me, in which I hope to have some further Occasion of proving to you the real Deference I have to your Sentiments, and Esteem for your Person. I am, dear Sir, | Your faithful and affectionate, | obliged Servant, | A. Pope.

HILL *to* POPE — 4 *October* 1738

1753 (Hill)

Oct. 4, 1738.

I make haste, to accuse you of a little unkindness, in telling me, that having an affair, that embarrasses you, and wishing my advice in the conduct of it, you *hardly know how to ask it*.

When you know me, so well, as I will take care you shall, you will feel your own right to command me. As you want not, I am sure, either my *pen*, or my *judgment*, I am impatient to learn, in what sense my *advice* can be serviceable. If it were MORE than advice, you should have it more willingly, which however, I beg, that you would not believe, but make *trial*. If your concerns, in any light, may be serv'd, by my coming to London, no matter, whether seasonable, or not—It would *please* me, to despise every hazard, that can shew you the truth of my friendship. Therefore (all regard to my own cares or interests, *apart*) I am—by head, heart, or hand now, and always, in the most absolute manner, at your service.

As to the little affair of the Epilogue, I am *satisfied*, as I ought to be, with the very good reason you give me. And, even with regard to the Tragedy itself, after what you tell me, that Mr. *Mallet*, and Mr. *Thompson*, have Plays in a forwardness, rather than I will so much as think of suffering any interest of mine, to clash with that of either of those valuable men, I would forget, I had *written* a Tragedy. Indeed, the first intimation I had of Mr. *Mallet*'s being return'd from abroad, was by the above piece of news, in your letter. As soon as you can be so good to inform me, whether, where, and in what part of this winter, those gentlemen propose to bring on their Tragedies, I will regulate my own conduct accordingly.

Again, dear Sir, let me beg you to *prove*, whether, in whatever you may command me to think, or to *do*, for your service, you do not, in *that*, most engage and oblige, | Your affectionate, | And sincere humble Servant, | A. Hill.

†THE EARL OF ORRERY *to* POPE[1] 4 *October* 1738

1741 La

Marston, Oct. 4, 1738

Sir,—I am more and more convinc'd that your letters are neither lost nor burnt: but who the Dean means by a *safe hand* in Ireland is beyond my power of guessing, tho' I am particularly acquainted with most, if not all, of his friends. As I knew you had the recovery of those Letters at heart, I took more than ordinary pains to find out where they were, but my enquiries were to no purpose; and I fear whoever has them is too tenacious of them to discover where they lie. "Mrs. W— did assure me she had not one of them, and seem'd to be under great uneasiness that you shou'd imagine they were left with her. She likewise told me she had stopt the Dean's letter which gave you that information; but believ'd he would write such another; and therefore desir'd me to assure you, from her, that she was totally ignorant where they were."[2]

You may make what use you please, either to the Dean or any other person, of what I have told you. I am ready to testify it; and I think it ought to be known, "That the Dean says they are deliver'd into a safe hand, and Mrs.[3] W—declares she has them not. The Consequence of their being hereafter publish'd may give uneasiness to some of your Friends, and of course to you: so I would do all in my power to make you entirely easy in that point."

This is the first time I have put pen to paper since my late misfortune, and I shou'd say (as an excuse for this letter) that it has cost me some pain, did it not allow me an opportunity to assure you, that I am, dear Sir, with the truest esteem, | Your very faithful and | obedient Servant, | Orrery.

[1] Pope, in his 1741 quarto, printed this letter at the end of the Swift–Pope correspondence. No letterbook from Marston for this period is known, and so the text rests solely on Pope's printing. In tone and matter it fits in with other letters from Orrery, and there seems no reason to suspect its authenticity. Clearly, the idea of Pope and Orrery was that although some of Pope's letters were sent over to him in 1737, others still remained in Ireland.

[2] The quotation marks, again, are Pope's device for calling attention to the passage and its historical relevance.

[3] This *Lady* since gave Mr. *Pope* the strongest Assurances that she had used her utmost Endeavours to prevent the Publication; nay, went so far as to *secrete* the Book, till it was commanded from her, and delivered to the *Dublin* Printer: Whereupon her Son in law, *D. Swift*, Esq; insisted upon writing a Preface, to justify Mr. *P.* from having any Knowledge of it, and to lay it upon the corrupt Practices of the Printers in *London*; but this he would not agree to, as not knowing the Truth of the Fact.—1741 La.

In 1741 Dab the name *D. Swift*, Esq; in this note was abbreviated to 'D. S.,

*POPE *to* ALLEN 10 *October* [1738]

Egerton 1947

Oct. 10.

I thank you for the Account of your safe Arrival at home; there is the *End* of all your Wishes; than which there can be no greater happiness on this side of the Grave. Unhappy is the Man, who must ramble in search of it! I can pray for no greater blessing for a friend, than that he may Love his own Home, his own Family, & next his Neighbour; yet be resigned to leave his Present Residence, whenever Providence ordains; & Love his own Family, yet consider the Whole World as his Relations, tho' more distant.

My Lord B.[1] is leaving this place, so that no more Bathwaters need be sent; he desires you would be pleas'd to let me know, what he is indebted to the Person who sent them, and I shall repay him.

You will let Mr Hooke know my constant affection, and hearty wishes for him. I hope to hear of him as soon as he comes this way. I have a great inclination to pass a Month with you this Winter, but Any Court drives me away; it has been thrice my fate to be dispossest of my own House, when there was one at Hampton Ct. But when the Bath grows a private place, such as it was in the Court of King Bladud,[2] I will come and live with you. Adieu. Let Mrs Allen depend on my Sincere Esteem & Services. I am truly | Dear Sir | Your faithfull | & affect. Servant | A. Pope.

Address: To Ralph Allen, Esqr | at Widcomb, near | Bath.
Postmark: 10/OC

POPE *to* SWIFT 12 *October* 1738

1765 (Deane Swift)

Twitnam, Oct. 12, 1738.

My Dear Friend,—I could gladly tell you every week the many things that pass in my heart, and revive the memory of all your friendship to me; but I am not so willing to put you to the trouble of shewing it (though I know you have it as warm as ever) upon little or trivial occasions. Yet, this once, I am unable to refuse the request of a very particular and very deserving friend; one of those whom his own merit has forced me to contract an intimacy with, after I had sworn never to love a man more, since the sorrow it cost me to have loved so many, now dead, banished, or unfortunate. I mean Mr. *Lyttelton*, one of the worthiest of the rising generation. His nurse has a son, whom I would beg you to promote to the next vacancy in your

[1] Bolingbroke.

[2] For a modern account of this legendary king, supposedly the discoverer of the Baths, see Edith Sitwell, *Bath* (1932), pp. 23–29.

choir. I loved my own nurse, and so does *Lyttelton*: he loves, and is loved, through the whole chain of relations, dependents, and acquaintance. He is one who would apply to any person to please me, or to serve mine: I owe it to him to apply to you for this man, whose name is *William Lamb*,[1] and he is the bearer of this letter. I presume he is qualified for that which he desires; and I doubt not, if it be consistent with justice, you will gratify me in him.

Let this, however, be an opportunity of telling you—What?—what I cannot tell, the kindness I bear you, the affection I feel for you, the hearty wishes I form for you, my prayers for your health of body and mind; or, the best softenings of the want of either, quiet and resignation. You lose little by *not hearing* such things as this idle and base generation has to tell you: you lose not much by *forgetting* most of what *now* passes in it. Perhaps, to have a memory that retains the past scenes of our country and forgets the present, is the means to be happier and better contented. But, if the *evil* of *the day* be not intolerable (though sufficient, God knows, at any period of life) we *may*, at least we *should*, nay we *must* (whether patiently or impatiently) bear it, and make the best of what we cannot make better, but may make worse. To hear that this is your situation and your temper, and that peace attends you at home, and one or two true friends who are tender about you, would be a great ease to me to know, and know from yourself. Tell me who those are whom you now love or esteem, that I may love and esteem them too; and, if ever they come into *England*, let them be my friends. If, by any thing I can here do, I can serve you, or please you, be certain it will mend my happiness; and that no satisfaction any thing gives me here will be superior, if equal to it.

My dear Dean, whom I never will forget, or think of with coolness, many are yet living here who frequently mention you with affection and respect. Lord *Orrery*, lord *Bathurst*, lord *Bolingbroke*, lord *Oxford*, lord *Masham*, *Lewis*, Mrs. *P. Blount* (allow one woman to the list, for she is as constant to old friendships as any man); and many young men there are, nay all that are any credit to this age, who love you unknown, who kindle at your fire, and learn by your genius. Nothing of you can die, nothing of you can decay, nothing of you can suffer, nothing of you can be obscured, or locked up from esteem and admiration, except what is at the Deanry; just as much of you only as God made mortal. May the rest of you (which is all) be as happy hereafter as honest men may expect and need not doubt; while (knowing nothing more) they know, that their Maker is merciful. Adieu. | Your's ever, | A. Pope.

[1] Writing to Alderman Barber, 19 Apr. 1739, Swift desires Barber to tell Pope: 'I have provided for Mr. Lamb, whom he recommended to me, with a full vicar-choralship in my choir' (Ball, vi. 123).

POPE *to* THE EARL OF ORRERY 19 *October* [1738][1]

The Pierpont Morgan Library

Oct. 19th | 1738.

My Lord,—The Honour & Kindness you bestow on me, shall be always rememberd with real Gratitude: Nothing can more prove your great Sense of the One, or your warm Sense of the other, than so obliging so amicable an offer as that of interesting your self yet further, in endeavoring to prevent the dishonorable Treatment I apprehend with so much reason from the ill Use to be made of my Letters in Ireland. But I am convinced no more can be done in it; after what both the Dean & Your Lordship have written to me: And I shall commit it to Chance or Providence, with as much Temper as I can. The greatest kindness your Lordship can do me, will be to preserve your own Health, & your own Happiness, which I shall hereafter consider as a part of myne, since you are & will be, a Blessing to me in your Friendship, on all occasions. I hope in God your Arm is recoverd, & I intreat when you are well, to know it. I am sorry 'tis at so great a distance,[2] & can't help wishing Your future life were past nearer this Part of England. The Loss of my Lord Bolingbroke from this Neighborhood could be recompenc'd by nothing so well, & it has vext me at heart to think, no Man of *this Sort* was likely to succeed to the very best & most commodious House in England, as well as the cheapest. It cost him not twelve years ago near 25 thousand pound & will be sold for 5000; The Furniture, (perhaps the compleatest any where in a private house) for which an Upholsterer in my hearing offerd 3000, to take down & make money of, he will part with at that price where it is ready put up; And the Land by measurement, at the Rent it is now let at & Tenanted. There is an Advowson of 300 a year & a Royalty, which last is not to be valued nor the Timber. I am thus particular to your Lordship because after I mention'd the Thing in general at your house, I heard you had some thoughts of buying a large one, & had even your eye on this. I wish I had known as much then, & I think verily I could have brought You to agree, had it been my good fortune to have seen you together. I knew then & do now, that Such a Successor to his Labors would have been in some degree a Pleasure to Him, at least it would be more a Comfort to see any English Nobleman of any worth there, than some Child of Dirt, or Corruption; at best, some Money-headed & Mony-hearted Citizen: Such an one as Van Eck has prov'd himself to be,[3] who has gone off, (after the most open & Gentlemanly Usage in the world on my Lords

[1] The year is added by Lord Orrery.

[2] At Marston, Somersetshire.

[3] Joshua Vanneck (d. 1777) was, so Elwin tells us, a very rich merchant of Dutch origin. His failure to close the bargain for Dawley was annoying.

side,) in the most paltry manner imaginable. He suffered his Wife & him to live a fortnight in the place, to Examine the Wholsomness & Dryness of the House, take opinions of the Soil, & converse with the Farmers, &c. The Upshot proves 'twas a mere Contest between *Vanity* & *Avarice*, & the Mean hope my Lord was so prest as to sell for little or nothing.

Excuse my saying all this, for I say it for an End; I wish I could move your Lordship to think of it, & my Lady to see it. You can't conceive the Joy it would give to a Man so truly yours, as My Lord your Ever obligd, ever affectionate Servant | A. Pope.

Endorsement: Mr Pope. | October 19 : 1738.

*POPE *to* FORD[1] 22 *October* [1738]

Princeton University

Oct. 22d.

This is what I think may be decently & truly sayd of the Honest Man whose Inscription you desired. I could not deny it to your friendship; but you need not be told I ought not to be mentioned in it, for many reasons. The Latin Verse of Horace is so Very Patt to him, & at the same time so Great a Character & puts him in so fine a Light, that I think nothing can be Luckier. As to the Rest, either the Latin or the English may be used as you judge best. Pray take it as a Testimony of the Regard I have to your Request, for there is nothing I so much avoid as Prologues & Epitaphs: no mortal knows what to say, well, in either of these Compositions, they are so Threadbare. Believe me with Truth & affection, | Dear Sir Your most obedient faith|ful Servant | A. Pope

Address: To | Charles Ford Esqr in | Park-Place

*POPE *to* THE DUKE OF [ARGYLE][2] 25 *October* [? 1738]

Alnwick Castle

Twickenham | Oct. 25

My Lord Duke,—I think it a particular unhappiness, that by my

[1] The text is taken from *The Princeton University Library Chronicle*, vi (1944), 38–39, where the letter was first printed. The year, impossible to determine, probably postdates 1737, when Ford had to move to St. James's Place (Little Cleveland Court), which Pope might have confused with Park Place near by (see Ball, vi. 50–51). That the letter is late one may infer from Pope's increasing reluctance to be known as a writer of prologues or epitaphs. Connexion with the monumental inscriptions for the Duke of Buckingham, John Gay, and (1741) Shakespeare gave Pope some undesired repute in this type of composition.

[2] Printed from a transcript made at Alnwick by Professor F. M. Salter. The letter in 1950 was loosely laid into vol. 25, Percy Family Papers, 1730–6.

The year of the letter is obscure. It is tempting to place it in 1739, when Pope had visited His Grace at Adderbury, but there is some probability that the 'commands' that Pope did not

Absence for some days, I have had the Pleasure delayd of receiving your Grace's commands; I wish I could say of performing them; but I told Sir William Wyndham my Fears, that the only thing in which I could be of any Service in this, would rather be the best Judgment I could give of what Others had done, than any Ability of doing it myself. Indeed, the real desire I have to Snatch the first occasion I have ever been happy in, of doing the least thing agreable to your Grace, does make me very much wish I were capable to do, what I apprehend no man ever did; that is, to succeed in a thing I never thought my Talent, or made my Business: for even to Obey, (tho one were not able to gratify) Persons of your Grace's and the Duchesse's Distinction, is temptation enough to me to expose my self to the Censure of the world besides, | I am, with the sincerest respect, | Your Grace's | most obedient, most humble | servant, | A. Pope

LYTTELTON *to* POPE[1] 25 *October* [1738]

Hagley

I thank you for your letter to the Dean.[2] It is a sensible pleasure to me to receive any mark of your affection, and This is one, which you have made kinder by your manner of Giving it me. If the person I recommended be not the better for it, as I hope he will, yet I shall be the happier.

We are just returnd from My Lord Bathurst's where His R. H. gave and recievd much Satisfaction. I wish you had been of the Party, because I know He Wishes it, and because he can not be too often in your company. Don't complain of your being Useless to him; a Friend is never so, especially to a Prince. When the power of Pleasing in conversation is directed to the purpose of Instructing, and a right understanding joind to a good heart, One *in his Station* may draw the greatest services, as well as the greatest delight from One *in Your's*. Be therefore as much with him as you can, Animate him to Virtue, to the Virtue least known to Princes, though most necessary for them, Love of the Publick; and think that the Morals, the Liberty, the whole Happiness of this Country depends on your Success. If that Sacred Fire, which by You and other Honest Men has been kindled in his

receive were (since related to Wyndham) political in nature, and that Pope had been asked by His Grace to celebrate in some way the arrival of the Prince of Wales at Cirencester. Note the beginning of Pope's letter to Lyttelton on the subject. The arrival was 'too quick' for a letter Pope had intended, he says.

[1] Lyttelton did not give a year in dating this letter. Another has superscribed the date 'oct 25 | 1739', but that is wrong, since the Prince of Wales visited Cirencester Park 21–24 Oct. 1738. See *Gent. Mag.* viii (1738), 545, and *LEP*, 26 Oct. 1738. Hitherto the letter has been printed as of 1739.

[2] The letter of 12 Oct. 1738, recommending Lyttelton's protégé, William Lamb.

Mind, can be Preserv'd, we may yet be safe; But if it go out, it is a Presage of Ruin, and we must be Lost. For the Age is too far corrupted to Reform itself; it must be done by Those upon, or near the Throne, or not at all: They must Restore what we ourselves have Given up. They must save us from our own Vices, and Follies, they must bring back the taste of Honesty, and the Sense of Honour, which the *Fashion of Knavery* has almost Destroy'd. In doing this they will pursue their real Interest, and therefore though it is a great deal to Expect, it is not too much to Desire; and where Dispositions to it appear they ought to be cultivated with as much application as if Success were certain; nor is it Wise or Honest to Despair too soon. Why shou'd the Industry of Knaves to Corrupt exceed the Diligence of Honest Men to Guard from Corruption? Why shou'd the Flatterers of a Prince be more Alert, and indefatigable than his Friends? I say this to you, my Dear Pope. because I know how difficult it is to draw you to a Court, even to a Court without Guards, and under persecution. You may remember that I was almost forced to compell You to go and dine at Kue the last time you was there. And yet there never was a morning better spent by you, no, not in conversing with Lord Bolingbroke. In short if you had any Spirit in you, you wou'd come to Bath, and let the Prince hear every day from the Man of this Age, who is the Greatest Dispenser of Fame, and will be best heard by Posterity, that if he wou'd Immortalize himself, the only way he can take, is to deserve a place by his conduct in *some writings*, where he will never be admitted only for his Rank.

Lord Chesterfield is well, and much Your's, and so is Pitt. If Lord Bolingbroke be returnd to you, I beg my compliments. I am most affectionately Your's &c. | G Lyttelton

Bath October the 25th

Direct for me at Mrs Bassett's near the Cross bath.

*POPE *to* THE COUNTESS OF BURLINGTON[1]

29 *October* [1738]

Chatsworth

Twickenham Oct. 29th | [1738]

Madam,—Having done the Ecclesiastical Duty of the Day, equally filled with good things, viz: with a Sermon, a Dinner, & strong Beer, I write in the Spirit thereof, a Letter truly Ecclesiastical; consisting of

[1] The date offers complications. The day is either 29 or 28, and is a Sunday. The second day-digit might be either 8 or 9. The absence of the Burlingtons in Yorkshire, the visit (desired) of Kent to Twickenham, the drunkenness of 'my worthy lord' (Bolingbroke), and the mention of Lady Betty Murray all tend to place the letter in 1738. In 1738, 29 Oct. was Sunday.

an Early Application for a Living, which I understand will speedily fall in your Ladiships Gift, (& which of the many Great & valuable Gifts, with which God hath blessed your Ladiship, seemeth not to be the least and least valuable) I mean, *The Presentation of Eyam.*[1] Three Reasons there are, which I would offer to induce you to bestow it: The first, that my Noble Lord your excellent Consort hath promised me a Boon of this nature many years; and as it is written, that Man & Wife are One, may it not seem that your Ladyship stands hereby bound in some measure? The second reason is yet more cogent, that this Living is better worth than any of his Lordship's: And the third, to wit that the Person I reccommend is greatly meritorious, is a reason I cast at your feet, to weigh as much or as little as you think fit. Yet I will say, He is endowed with more *Edifying Qualities*, than Any below the *Pontifical* Dignity. He Should be *Pontifical*, he well deserves it, but is not allowd it under this Ministry, which he may truly call, *A Nest of Foxes.* He is as Learned, tho not so courteous as Bishop W—x; as Eloquent tho not so Courtly, as G—t; as wellbred, tho not so Bookish, as H—re, and (to sum up all) has as good a taste as R—le, & as good a Stomach as all the Clergy put together. I cannot say he is quite as accomplishd as Sh—ck,[2] but he is more Independent; being one who hath born Testimony to the Truth, in the face of Kings, Queens, & Potentates: One who hath ever Resisted New Doctrines & Opinions, holding fast by the Pillars of sound Antiquity; by no means a Respecter of Persons, but using Sharp Speeches to the Greatest: In a word, One under whom may be expected, more than from any Prelate living, the Restoration of Churches, the ReEstablishment of Ancient Colleges, and Increase of New Foundations: till the Walls of Jerusalem shall be built up, Holocausts and Whole Burnt Offerings shall be revived, and *Calves* (to fulfill the prophecy) shall be brought unto the Altar.

I think your Ladyship begins to find the Excellent Person at whom I point, (or rather to *Smoke* him, for he is very hot, & very fat)

Of Size that may a Pulpit fill,
Tho more inclining to Sit still.

And (with the leave of the Otherways-Excellent the Vicar of Barrow-

[1] This luscious living (£1,500) was too good to go out of the family: the death of a kinsman of Lady B. in 1737 had left it vacant. It had been given to another presumable kinsman named Bruce, whose health evidently kept him on the Continent, where he died in 1739. But all the talk of Eyam is a joke.

[2] At this distance it is invidious to supply names for these blanks, but conceivably Pope means Joseph Wilcocks (Dean of Westminster and Bishop of Rochester), John Gilbert (later Archbishop of York), Francis Hare, Bishop of Chichester (complimented also in *Dunciad*, iii. 204), Thomas Rundle (Bishop of Derry), and Thomas Sherlock (Master of the Temple). On the Vicar of Barrowby see iii. 329 and iv. 237.

by) I presume to name him, & defy any Objections, viz. Mr William Kent.

I protest it is my Zeal for Merit entirely (and a most disinterested one, for he will not so much as thank me for my pains) that moves me to propose him. He is totally ignorant of this Address, nor do I know any Motive he could have to accept of the Living, save to get into a Soft Pulpit, where is a Soft Cushion, to lay his Soft Head, & rest his tender Tail, from the Fatigues of a Horse, that now afflicts his Soul, moves his very Entrails (especially after dinner,) & troubles all the Bones within him; while not only the Spirit is wearyd, but the Flesh that should cleave to those bones, cleaves to the Saddle. I have sent two or three pressing Letters & Messages, to beg him to ride but one mile out of his way to Windsor,[1] to speak to me of a Matter that nearly concerns him. He has imagind it concern'd *me* & not *him*, I suppose, & therefore will not stir. In truth it is a Matter whereby he will get some hundred pounds, & do nothing for it; but this I will not tell him, till I drag him hither: When he comes, I will very gravely acquaint him how to put a good Sum into his pocket, & after holding him in suspense, propose the Benefice of Eyam, & that several of his Friends seriously advise him to enter into Orders. It is the only revenge I can think of for his Refusal to come to me, and he will be abundantly consolated by the Money at last.

Pray be so good as to write to Lady Betty Murray,[2] & tell her how many thousand fine things I said of her, before I guess'd Mr Murray could find them out. Because it is very necessary I should be well with her, to keep so good an Interest with Him, as I would fain do. See what an honest Reason this is, for my Civility to Other men's Wives!

Pray Madam continue to honour me with as many proofs of your Goodness as possible, but send us no more *Ale*, for my worthy Lord here[3] is drunk, & as a mark that he is deprivd at present of his Reason, bids me to write in his stead, to assure yourself & my Lord Burlington of his sincerest Services. I durst not sign my Name so near him, but that I have prudently omitted His. However I am my Lord's, & Madam Your most Obliged Servant

[1] Writing to Lady Burlington, 10 Nov. 1738, Kent remarks: 'I am going to Windsor to morrow, I hope the last time this year.' And in a letter to Lord Burlington of 10 Nov. he writes: 'In my way to Windsor a fortnight agoe, I call'd on Pope he had write me word twice he had great besnese with me, but when I came I found it was for some drawings . . . & that he wanted to know if my Lord Bruce is friend that had the great liveing was dead or dying, and if my Lady Burlington had it not in her guift to all this I was Ignorant.'—*Architectural Review*, lxiii (1928), 182. The earlier letter quoted is Chatsworth MS. 206.4.

[2] The future Lord Mansfield had, on 20 Sept. 1738, married Lady Betty Finch, daughter of the Earl of Nottingham.

[3] Doubtless Bolingbroke.

POPE *to* LYTTELTON[1] [*c.* 1 *November* 1738]

Hagley

Of all the kind Opinions you entertain of me, there is One which I deserve, the opinion that I am sincerely yours; & that I love Virtue, for I love You & such as you: Such are listed under her Banners, they fight for her; Poets are but like Heralds, they can only proclaim her, and the best you can make of me, is, that I am her poor Trumpeter.

The Prince's Visit to Lord Bathurst was too quick for a Letter which I intended him[2] on that occasion: It was a Letter of Instructions, in what manner a Great Man should treat a Prince, when Fortune gives him the Leading of one: Especially if the Prince happens to be a little Short sighted: *What* things one should make him see, and *how far*? What kind of Notions to give him, of the Extent, Nature & Situation of the *Land* about him? Above all, the Two great Arts so successfully practis'd by my Lord on other people, and so much more useful to be practis'd on a Prince; that of making him imagine, What is Highway or Common field to all his Subjects, to be His own Walks & Royalties; And that of imposing upon him What was the Work of our own hands but yesterday, for the Venerable Structure of our Ancestours.

But I have something at present to tell you which is more material; the Result of the Conference with Sir W. W.[3] and the Disposition in which it left him.

He seem'd strongly touch'd with a Sence of the Indignity, the Folly, and the Danger, that attend the present State & Conduct of the Opposition. He feels, (tho a little unwilling to own it) that these are ow'd to a Neglect of harkening five or six years ago to the Warning a Friend then gave him; who apprehended then what is now evident; viz: That the Opposition would be drawn off from the Original Principle on which it was founded, by two Persons;[4] one of whom never meant, & the other meant only by fits & starts The Publick Good: and to that end a Change of Measures as well as of Men: That these two persons would, by their own Overbearing & the Indolence of others, get a sort of prescriptive Right to a Negative, in all proceedings; and the Opposition by consequence would become nothing more than a Bubble-Scheme, wherein multitudes who intended the publick

[1] This letter, like that from Lyttelton of 25 Oct. (to which this is in part an answer), has been misdated as to the year—sometimes it is placed in 1741, sometimes in 1739. The visit of the Prince to Lord Bathurst, as well as the pervasive doctrine of Bolingbroke, places the letter in 1738. How long after the Prince's visit to Cirencester it is written cannot be determined. It marks the revulsion of 'patriots' from Carteret and Pulteney.

[2] Lord Bathurst.

[3] Sir William Wyndham.

[4] Lord Carteret and Wm. Pulteney.

Service, would be employ'd to no other purpose than to serve private Ambition.

He is fully persuaded, that the Part taken by his R. H. opens an Opportunity of rectifying these Errors, & retrieving & preventing these Mischiefs: But thinks his R. H. shou'd exert his Whole Influence, first to Prepare, & then to back the New Measure: who, the moment it takes place, will be the Head of the Party, and Those two Persons cease so to be that instant.

That it is proper to continue to live with Them, however, in all the same terms of friendly Intercourse, & with the same appearance of Intimacy; nay to strengthen the Plea to it, by shewing, how extremely they have been Trusted, deferrd to, & comply'd with.

That all such persons (many of which there certainly are) as may be determined to join in the pursuit of the *Original Measures* of the Opposition, should be so determin'd by All Sorts of private Application, (whether Whigs or Torys) But by no means applyd to in the *Collective Body*, or too generally, but in seperate Conversations & Arguments.

That upon every important occasion, the Things resolvd upon should be pushd by the Persons in this Secret, how much soever the others may hang off; which will reduce them to the Dilemma, of joyning with the Court, or of following their friends with no good grace.

Sir W. declared he had no difficulty of proceeding in this manner, nay thought on the contrary that if Sir Tho. San,[1] himself, & any 2 or 3 old Members more, with the Phalanx of Young Members, led on such an Opposition in a Debate, they would be followed by *Numbers, even at first*, that these Numbers would increase *every day* that a New Opposition would be thus created, (or rather the old one reviv'd) and in a word, That this must be done, or Nothing can be done, by any man of Sense or Virtue.

This, you may depend, is the present Disposition of Sir W. in which you & Lord Ch.[2] may certainly Confirm him, if you throw Oil, not Water, on it. That such a Spirit should be raised in him, was the Hint given me by the Person in whose room[3] you & I parted last. I see no harm if you told him *Who* has done thus much? but surely he must strongly be told, *Who* only can corroborate & render practicable the Effects of it?

Pray assure your Master of my Duty & Service: They tell me he has every body's Love already. I wish him Popular, but not Familiar, and the Glory of being beloved, not the Vanity of endeavouring it too much. I wish him at the Head of the Only Good Party in the King-

[1] Sir Thomas Lyttelton, Samuel Sandys, are intended. [2] Lord Chesterfield.
[3] Bolingbroke?

dome, that of Honest Men; I wish him Head of no other Party. And I think it a Nobler Situation, to be at the head of the Best Men of a Kingdom than at the Head of any Kingdom upon earth. For one is only a proof of his Birth, the other of his Merit. And God Knows *Meerly* to be Popular, that is to be at the head of a Mob, (for Partyes are but higher & more Interested Mobs) is as much below a Prince as keeping low Company is below a Gentleman, tho the First of the Club. And our People of England admire a King but as a Clown does a Squire, They are enough to spoil a Gude King as the Scotsman said of them when they followed James the first. (This Quotation Lord Bathurst sent me in a letter tother day, & it is a good one) Adieu. Make my Services to Lord Chesterfield, & take them yourself from | Your Sincere Servant[1]

Address: To | Mr Lyttelton, Secretary | to his Royal Highness. | at Bath.[2]

POPE *to* ALLEN[3] — 2 *November* [1738]

Bath Municipal Reference Library

I trouble you with my Answer to the Inclosed, which I beg you to give to Mr Lyttelton as I would Do him all the Good I can, which the Virtues I know Him possest of, deserve; & therfore I would Present him with so honest a Man as You, and You with so honest a Man as He. The Matter concerning Urns. I would gladly leave in your Care, and I desire four small ones, with their Pedestals, may be made, and Two of a Size larger. I'l send those Sizes to you, and send a Draught of the two Sorts, 4 of one, 2 of the other.

I am going to insert in the Body of my Works, my 2 last Poems, in Quarto. I always profit myself of the opinion of the Publick, to Correct my self on such occasions. And sometimes the Merits of particular Men, whose Names I have made free with for Examples, either of Good or of Bad, determine me to Alterations. I have found a Virtue in You more, than I certainly knew before, till I had made Experi-

[1] Pope did not sign the letter, but his name has been written in by a later hand. The letter itself is in Pope's hand throughout.

[2] In the address Pope added 'Secretary to his Royal Highness'. The rest of the address is in another and unknown hand. It is not Bolingbroke's hand, and Sir William's has not been available for comparison. The use of Pope and Lyttelton (the Prince's secretary) in this intrigue is interesting as technique.

[3] In EC, ix. 194 the second paragraph of this letter is printed by itself as from Warburton's edition of 1751. The present editor has not found it there. In connexion with this letter there is in Egerton MS. 1947, ff. 153–4, a text in Warburton's hand, apparently prepared for publication (but not published!), that embodies an 'amalgam' of three letters that are to be found in Egerton 1947 in Pope's hand. The three letters thus combined are the second paragraph of this present letter and sections from letters here placed in Apr. 1742 and on 18 July [1741]. This method of Warburton's may also be seen in a letter that he did publish as from Pope to himself, 28 Dec. 1742. The text here printed is from the original letter, preserved at Bath and not in Egerton 1947.

ment of it: I mean *Humility*: I must therfore in justice to my own Conscience of it, bear Testimony to it, and change the Epithet I first gave you, of *Low-born*, to *Humble*.[1] I shall take care to do you the justice to tell every body, this Change was not made at yours, or at any Friends Request for you: but my own Knowledge you merited it.

I receive daily fresh proofs of your kind remembrance of me, the Bristol waters, the Guinea Hens, the Oyl & wine (two Scripture Benedictions) all came safe, except the wine, which was turned on one side, & spilt at the Corks. however tis no loss to *me*, for that sort I dare not drink on account of the Bile: but my Friends may, and that is the same thing as if I did. adieu. Is Mr Hook with you? I wish I were, for a Month at least; for less I would not come. Pray advise him not to be so modest: I hope he sees Mr Lyttelton. I must Expect Your Good Offices with Mrs Allen, to let her know I honour a Good Woman much, but a Good Wife more. | I am ever | Yours faithfully, | A. Pope.

Twitnam: | Novr 2.

You will seal the Inclosed.

Address: To | Ralph Allen, Esqr at | Widcombe, near | Bath.

POPE *to* HILL 5 *November* 1738

1751 (Hill)

Nov. 5. 1738.

This is quite a Letter of Business, and therefore excuse it; I will not mix in it a Word of Affection, which I have not a Moment's time to express, and will not prejudice the sacred Idea of Friendship.

It is near a Month ago that I try'd to see Mr. *Thomson*, to know the Time of his Tragedy:[2] He was not within my Reach; and therefore at last I wrote to him, and also to Mr. *M*—,[3] to let them both know the Deference you paid them, and the heroic (I will not call it less) Disinterestedness you express'd in regard to them. I have not yet been able to hear where they are, or any way to have an Answer further, than I have learn'd it will be impossible for either of them to bring on their Plays early (a Friend of theirs telling me they are in no Forwardness) till the Middle or End of the Winter; therefore you may have

[1] The quarto edition of the poems now called 'Epilogue to the Satires' (in which this change in I. 135 was made) appeared 11 Jan. 1738/9. The epithet 'low-born' had appeared in the first edition (13 May 1738), and was evidently in no way applicable to Allen.

[2] James Thomson's *Edward and Eleonora*, now being written, was in Mar. 1739 denied the necessary permission under the new Licensing Act, and was not performed. Mallet's *Mustapha* was performed at Drury Lane, 13 Feb. 1738/9 and thereafter. Hill's play was not accepted by the managers.

[3] Mallet.

room. I wish from my Soul you may get yours first, as well acted as it deserves. A better, that may eclipse it, or even worthily follow it, I hardly expect to see.—But upon this Notice, I believe you may safely advance it, the sooner the better.

My Lord *B.* is yet with me, more properly I yet belong to him, Body as well as Mind (for my Mind is every-where his). I would to God you had any Opportunity of seeing us before we part; my House should be yours, as much of it as is not his. I believe I shall soon go with him on a little Journey before he quits *England.* You'll forgive the abrupt Conclusion of this; yet it may tell you all the longest and best-written Letter could tell you, that I am very sincerely, | Sir, | Your much obliged, and | really affectionate Servant, | A. Pope.

*HILL *to* POPE[1] — 8 *November* 1738

1753 (Hill)

Nov, 8, 1738.

You have been very obliging, in your endeavours, to inform me of the time, for Mr. *Thompson*'s, and Mr. *Mallet*'s new Tragedies; I have now sent my own to Mr. *Fletewood*, and desired it may be brought on about the beginning of *January*, in which case, it may have a fair chance to be *dead* and *forgotten*, before the best of the season is over.

Since I find Mr. *Thompson* not so forward, as I apprehended he was, in his *new* Play, I will acquaint you with something, that I *long* to say to him, concerning his *old* one; and, if you think I am right, in my opinion, I beg the favour of you to *say* it in my stead; 'Twill be said, I am sure, with more *weight*; and, from the *deference* I know he always had for your *judgment*, I believe, 'twill be said, with more *consequence*. . . .

POPE *to* HUGH BETHEL[2] — 19 *November* 1738

Egerton 1948

Nov. 19, 1738.

I often think of you, & am quite vex'd at the distance we live at. It frets me to think I must be writing, to tell you how much I esteem & love you, from time to time, when all the common proofs, the little offices, & Attentions of Friendship are intercepted between us, which

[1] The first two paragraphs of this letter seem worth reprinting as concerned with Pope's friendships. Pope in his reply (8 Dec.) tactfully declines to pass on as his own Hill's suggestions for remaking Thomson's *Agamemnon*. These suggestions run to almost nine pages of print, and are not here reproduced. They can be found in Hill's *Works* (1753), i. 308–19.

[2] Mr. Ault informed the editor that this letter was published in *The English Lyceum*, ii (1787), 199–201. It was reprinted in *The European Magazine* for Jan. 1788. It is here printed from the original. The last paragraph was quoted (cf. half-brackets) by Ruffhead, p. 500.

so much better express, & so much better reward, & Continue, real Affection. Half the Life of my Heart (if I may so call it) feels numb'd. I'm like one who has receivd a Paralytic Stroke & is dead on one Side, when half the Friends that warm'd me are absent. I would fain have *You* see how happy I am in the Acquireing my Lord Bolingbroke, tho but for a few months. Tis almost like recovering One from the Grave whom we gave for gone; however one can't expect to keep him long, one rejoyces in the present moments.

It seems hard, that when two Friends are in the same Sentiments, & wish the same things, they should not be happy together: But *Habit* is the Mistress of the World; & whatever is generally said, has more Sway than *Opinion*. Yours confines you to the Wolds of Yorkshire, mine to the Banks of the Thames. And yet I think I have less Dependance on others, & others less on me than most men I have ever known; so that I *Should be* Free. So should a Female Friend of ours; but *Habit* is her *Goddess*, I wish I could not say worse, her *Tyrant*: She not only *Obeys* but *Suffers* under her: And Reason & Friendship plead in vain. Out of Hell, and out of Habit, there is no Redemption.

I hope the Season is now coming that drives Friends together, as it does Birds, into warm Coverts & close Corners. That we may meet over a Fire, & tell the Stories of the Year. Indeed the Town Hours of the Day suit as ill with my Stomach, as the Wintery & dark Nights do with my Carcase, which I must either expose abroad, or sit & blind my Eyes with reading at home. I wish your Eyes may grow no worse; mine do, & make me more concern'd for you.

⌜Take care of your Health; follow not the Feasts (as I have done) of Lords, nor the Frolicks of Ladies: but be composed, yet chearful: Complaisant, yet not a Slave:⌝ I am, with all Truth—and all Affection, | Dear Sir, | Yours Ever, | A. Pope.

You will not forget me to Mr Moyser.

Address: To | Hugh Bethel at | Beswick, near | Beverley | Yorkshire.
Postmark: 21 / NO

*POPE *to* JONATHAN RICHARDSON[1] 19 *November* [1738]

1833 (Thomas Thorpe)

FRAGMENT

Twitnam, Nov. 19.

I hear the enamel picture is done. I beg you to take back into your

[1] The fragment, as lot 812, comes from the catalogue issued by Thorpe in 1833. Thc catalogue says the letter is franked by Lord Bathurst, and addressed to Richardson in Queen Square. Its year is uncertain, but in November of 1738 Richardson had a stock of Pope portraits (see Kent to Lord Burlington, here iv. 150), and Bolingbroke was in England at this

custody the two originals, which I think, and know to be of so great value, that I would have them in no hands but your own, till my Lord [Bolingbroke] takes his, and I mine. I desire you will cause mine of him, to be framed in the manner you best approve, for which I'll be in your debt. But what am I not in your debt for? I can pay you with nothing, but (literally) Your's, A. Pope.

POPE *to* LORD BATHURST[1] — 23 *November* 1738

Elwin–Courthope, viii. 355

Nov. 23, 1738.

My Lord,—I had epistolized you sooner but that knowing you were yet in your worldly pilgrimage (I will not say your carnal one, though you have seen Madam la Touche[2]) I did not know how to write *at* you; and even the post, all post haste as it is, cannot shoot you flying. Another reason was, my desire to satisfy your question about the affair of Dawley, which after many offers, is at last quite broke off, I think rather on the part of my lord than of Vanneck,[3] for he has been piqued so much at their dirty way of dabbling, rather than dealing, about it, that though the last offer came within 2000*l.* he will hear no more of them. The total was, that Vanneck expected the lands for 4*s.* per acre less than the tenants actually pay, the house for as little as the materials pulled down will bring, the furniture for 1000*l.* less than is offered by an upholsterer, the gardens and timber for nothing. My Lord has sent for Burward to set the rents of what is yet unlet, and I believe will find a difference of near 2000*l.* value in the whole, above what he himself first computed, provided he will have patience to sell part of the lands separately, and improve the rest, and let the house stand awhile the chance of a separate bargain.

I have deferred writing these ten days, in hopes he would have joined in this letter, but he laughs at me for imagining any body can tell where you are, or send it after you. If your lordship has been only over England, I think there is a chance you are returned by this time to Cirencester, unless you have been in Scotland, or in the Prince's mines in Cornwall. I am told his estate there is miserably neglected, to the annual loss of about 20,000*l.* You see, my lord, I acquaint myself a little with the value of estates; and it is no compliment to

time. But the frank calls 1738 in question, for Pope and Lord Bathurst had not recently met (see Pope to Bathurst, 23 Nov.). Franks, however, were sometimes accumulated for use when no lord was near! The other year most plausible is 1742, when, also, Pope and Bolingbroke had (on 12 July) sat to Richardson; but in 1742 Pope was at Bath, and if he dated from 'Twitnam' it would be because he was to return thither almost immediately.

[1] The original of this letter has not been found, though Elwin had it to print from.

[2] Having seen this lady, Lord Bathurst wrote to Swift, 6 Dec. 1737, 'I want no foreign commodities; my neighbour the Duke of Kingston has imported one, but I do not think it worth the carriage.' The duke had 'imported' this mistress under circumstances that caused her friends in France to charge abduction.

[3] See Pope to Lord Orrery, 18 Oct. [1738].

you to tell you, I am grieved extremely, when any friend of mine, or any good and beneficent man, even though he be a prince, loses too lightly his just rights and advantages, whereby the bounty of the greatest, and the quiet and independency of the meanest members of a community, is checked, if not destroyed; lessened, if not lost. So though I wish with you, my lord, that your labour and trouble were over, I do not wish your care so. Besides, as you are my financier, when you enrich yourself, you enrich and secure me,[1] who consider myself as one of your children, and I hope the poorest of them, but, however, one whom you have taken very good care of, these very many years.

The town has not been the less a desert, at least to me, for his majesty's return.[2] I have lived here and at Dawley. Just now came Lord Cornbury from abroad, to-morrow comes the duchess,[3] in a day or two more Lyttelton and Lord Chesterfield. Here is now all the good company I can wish, if you will but join it. Sure, you may and will before Lord B[olingbroke] goes, which cannot be till Christmas, your usual time. You would have a vast deal of health and a great flow of spirits did but a small proportion of the wine and punch we have drunk to your health, run into your veins. But a better proof of my sincere wishes for your welfare and prosperity I feel in my heart, which really longs to enjoy more of you than I can pretend to deserve or than is my share among so many as love and esteem you. But allow me, my dear lord, what you can, forgive me what you can, and love me as much as you can. It will be sufficient to make a very happy man of, my lord, your faithful, affectionate, ever obliged servant.

WILLIAM KENT *to* THE EARL OF BURLINGTON[4]

28 *November* 1738

Althorp

London Novr 28, 1738

My Lord,—I received yours, am sorry to here you had so bad a cold, io spero che la purgatzioni has carryd all of before this time—Jack campbell[5] and I have been to see how the mighty works go on at Euston, whe came back last sunday seven night with Mr Pelham as for news I believe you have more in the countery then I find here—

[1] Among Pope's bonds after his death was one for £2,000 lent to Lord Bathurst 25 March 1738, on which his lordship had repaid £1,500—Carruthers (1857), p. 456.

[2] From Hanover.

[3] Lord Cornbury and the Queensberrys had been at the Spa. The returning duchess is very likely Cornbury's sister, Duchess of Queensberry. Normally 'the duchess' would to Bathurst and Pope mean Katherine, Duchess of Buckingham.

[4] The original at Althorp has kindly been collated by Earl Spencer with the text printed by H. Avray Tipping in *The Architectural Review*, lxiii (1928), 209.

[5] Later to become 4th Duke of Argyle. His wife (d. 1736) had been Pope's friend Madge Bellenden, one of the Maids of Honour. Campbell's daughter became in 1739 the third wife of Burlington's relative, Lord Bruce.

whe have begun a weekly meeting at Whisk, there is Bryan & nando mark & mr Mills & my self,[1] next Thursday its to be at Marks (who dont Drink) Bryan and I dine at Thuanasis to prepare us for company at night—the Gen[2] has been very much out of order, but last night I was there and much better but he has three skreens & a blanket at the door he say'd as I have not had a regalo he would give me a medal of Milton pray my servise to her[3] & Lady Francess has had her letter[4]—I had not seen Pope but once this two months before last sunday morning & he came to town the night before the next morning he came before I was up it had raind all night & rain'd when he came I would not get up & sent him away to disturb some body else—he came back and sayd could meet with nobody, I got drest & went with him to Richarsons & had great diversion he shew'd three picturs of Lord Baulingbrok one for himself for Pope, another Pope in a mourning gown with a strange view of the garden to shew the obelisk as in memory to his mothers Death, the alligory seem'd odde to me,[5] but after I found, its to be in the next letters as I suppose some of the witt that was write to Londesbrough will be in print—the son of Richardson & Pope agree'd that popes head was Titziannesco, the old long Glow worm sayd whe have done our best

the Genll gives his service to you & has now got a regarlar fitt of the Goute he is still bronzo mad, & they have bought him the Quattro Shiavi of Gio: di Bolongia at Leghorn—Sir Clement desires his humble service to you, I have sup'd with his sister thats a good woman & talks very low'd—my service to mr Bethell and tell him his friend Pope is the greatest Glutton I know, he now talk of the many good things he can make, he told me of a soupe that must be seven hours a making he dine'd with mr Murry & Lady betty & was very drunk last sunday night he says if he comes to town[6] he'll teach him how to live & leave of his rosted apples & water—I forgot to tell you that Richerson give me all the prints he has grav'd, he has given me so many miltons, & three different popes, the last he has done is write behind his head in greek letters the English—thats the man, or this is the man, I cannot just tell—

I hope you'll keep CristX at chiswick after so many years I have not mis'd that I shall be so fancefull as to think it will be the last I shall ever be there—

I am | My Lord | Your Lordships most | humble servant | Wm Kent

[1] The whist-players were Bryan and Ferdinando Fairfax, Sir Mark Pleydell of Coleshill, and 'Mr. Mills'. See Kent's will as printed (pp. 89–91) in Margaret Jourdain's *Work of William Kent* (1948).

[2] General Dormer.

[3] To Lady Burlington.

[4] Lady Frances Arundell is mentioned in Kent's will.

[5] This portrait is not readily identified.

[6] That is, if Bethel comes to town, Pope will teach him. Bethel was the Ofellus of Pope's Imitation of Horace's Satire, II, ii.

Isaace Ware[1] desirs his Duty to you & is now ready with his plates & wants the writeing to print the rest of the Book Stephen tells me he has had a letter from you so I suppose will set out soon.

*POPE *to* J. RICHARDSON[2] *December* 1738

Trinity College, Cambridge

Be pleased to tell the Bearer what day to come for the Case and the Frame. Pray keep the Blue Picture by you, till my Lord comes, who sends you his heartiest Services. In haste | Yours | Ever | A. Pope.

Dec: 1738.

Address: For Mr Richardson.

POPE *to* HILL 8 *December* 1738

1751 (Hill)

Dec. 8. 1738.

I have been confirmed by Mr. *Thomson* as to the Retardment of his Play, of which he has written but two Acts. I have since seen Mr. *M*—, who has finished his, but is very willing yours should be first brought on, in *January* as you propose, or after his in *February*, whichsoever may be most agreeable to you. He farther offers any Assistance he can give you, in case of your own Absence, as to treating with Mr. *F*—[3] (with whom he thinks you can not be too careful or explicit), or attending the Rehearsals for you, which he promises to undertake with all Diligence, if you are not provided with another Friend in that Case. He has heard of some Impertinence which may be apprehended from one Person's Refusal or Unwillingness to act, and believes he can employ some proper Influence to bring him to a right Behaviour. These, with any other Services in which you may please to employ him, he bids me assure you, it will be a high Satisfaction to him to engage in.

I must express, on my own Part, a real Regret to be so little useful to you. I can do no more than join with Lord *B.* in paying due Praises to so meritorious a Work; our Suffrage is an airy Tribute, from whence no solid Good redounds to you; and I find myself still more inclined to the *Man*, than the *Author*, if I could be any way instrumental to the Happiness or Ease of so generous an one. I could almost wish

[1] Isaac Ware published his translation of Palladio in folio, dated 1739.

[2] Kindly transcribed from the Cullum Collection in the Trinity College Library by Professor John C. Hodges.

[3] Fleetwood, manager of Drury Lane Theatre, was so careless and inexplicit to Thomson that the poet presently took *Edward and Eleonora* to the rival house in Covent Garden.

myself a Minister to patronize such a Genius, and I could almost wish my Lord one again, for no other Reason; even tho' his Country wants such an one, as well as his Friends.

I have never once been able to see Mr. *Thomson* in Person; when I do (and it shall be soon) he shall know how much he is obliged to you for that Plan of an Alteration of his Tragedy, which is too good for me, with any Honesty, to put upon him as my own. Believe me, Sir, with great Truth, and the warmest Disposition to do you Justice (before Men and Angels), | Yours faithfully, | A. Pope.

HILL *to* POPE — 9 *December* 1738

1753 (Hill)

Dec. 9, 1738.

Give me leave by the enclos'd, to reply to the first part of yours, that which concerns Mr. *Mallet*'s kind offer; and after having the goodness to close it with one of your seals, please to send it him, as soon as convenient.

For the rest, that relates to yourself—Be it known by these presents, that I cannot allow you to call Mr. *Pope*'s and Lord *Bolingbroke*'s praises, *an airy tribute* in any sense but one—the superiority of their value, to the *earthiness* of less noble distinctions. I shall learn to regard my own thoughts, when they are able to procure me such praises: for how indeed, were vanity to be reckon'd a fault, could it have the sanction of wisdom and virtue?

As to the coming on of my Tragedy, I begin to suspect, that the Manager's hearts, at the Theatres, are more narrowly *piqu'd*, than their Player's—Few men have force in their minds, to love truth, that has serv'd 'em, unpleasingly: They forget the good *use*, in a disgust, they think due to the *censure*: But there is an odd, and unfortunate dilemma in the way of our childish desire to be *fondled*: When we are flatter'd by that beast call'd a *liar*, he has the skill to *lick* soft like a *Calf*; but then he crushes not so much as a *Fly*, for our benefit: Honest fact, on the other side, has a tongue, that is rough like a *Lyon*'s, able enough to deliver from insects, but it grates, like a *file*, where it passes; and endangers the skin, it would purify.

Let it go—no matter what Mr. *Fleetwood* designs or resolves: were his acting of *Cæsar*, capable of ten times the good, it can do me, I should myself, be incapable of quickening his phlegm any farther: There is a reluctance (I am afraid, it is a *pride*) in my nature, against soliciting any thing, that regards my own interest:—and especially, from the dull and unworthy: The cause I would fain *place* (for I love to be *near* you) in

"*The strong antipathy of good to bad!*"

where I hope, and believe, I may find it. For, I am sure, that I hate myself heartily, and with the malice and pain of an enemy, whenever I am fool enough, *not to be able* to hate, as I ought, either a *low* soul, or a *false* one. You will see through all this, that Mr. *Mallet*'s friendly offer was not only kind, but a very seasonable interposition.

What shall I now say, that can thank you enough, in return for your generous wishes? I would submit to be any thing, above a bad minister, for the power of rewarding your partiality: But I am about to plant myself among corn fields, and vineyards, where *video meliora proboq*;—and fortune will take care to prevent me from any danger of being tempted by the *Deteriora*, behind, in the close of it. I have been hastening, at the desire of a friend, a long discourse, that will be lost on the stage, or should have been able, by this time, to have made another essay, legible enough to wait on you, at *Twickenham*; where, that never more any evil thing may enter, is the sincere and affectionate prayer of, | Dear Sir, | Your most obliged, | And obedient Servant, | A. Hill.

*POPE *to* THE EARL OF BURLINGTON 19 *December* 1738

Chatsworth

Decr. 19th 1738.

My Lord,—If my writing to you could make you know, one tittle the more, that I am every day in the same degree I have been these twenty years, Yours; I would have written once a week. But all I could say is Tautology: Yours I am, & yours I will be. Your Lordship may judge how true this way of Thinking is, by examining your own breast, and I verily believe you will find there, that you are good enough to be to me all that you have long been, notwithstanding your Lordship has never thought of writing to me or of me. Mr Kent could tell you how often I talk'd of you, & wished for you; even at a time when I wish for few or none, when I am almost constantly with the Greatest Man I know, ever knew, or shall know.[1] He too is your faithful Servant; & we daily, when we meet, remember You. Our constant Toast is, *Libertati & Amicitiae*: & we do your Lordship (tho we think it of Few Lordships) the justice to allow you Equally Sensible of Both. He has not finished his Affairs, in which the same Face of Fortune that has been turned towards him many years, has been continued. He has found, that a Great House in this Nation is like a Great Genius, too good for the Folks about it; They are as little worthy of the one, as the other. You will therfore find him still here, & you will find him very much distinguishing Such as you, from Such as he found (& expected to find) your most noble & ignoble

[1] Bolingbroke.

Cotemporaries. I have been little in Town, as he never has once been there since you went but 2 days: whenever I have, I have seen Kent, & endeavourd to comfort him, under all his Calumniators & afflictions,[1] with the Representation, That *All* Great *Genius's have, & do suffer the Like.* Pray just tell my Lady Burlington that it is in the same manner I comfort myself against the Dreadful Papers She has Sent me:[2] and that I am still so little mortified at them, that I have the Impudence to think, my Services & true Respects are not the more unworthy her acceptance for all those people say of me. I hope soon to see your Lordship & Her, so rusticated & so ignorant, as to take my word when you return, that the Whole Court & Town has not a creature deserving more Credit than myself, when I declare I am, to you both, a | Most Obliged & most faith|full Servant. | A. Pope

POPE *to* THE EARL OF ORRERY — 20 *December* 1738

The Pierpont Morgan Library

Decr. 20. 1738.

My Lord,—You have Goodness & Candour in so great a degree, that I am in the less pain for an Omission, which your own Consciousness of your Obliging Conduct on every account towards me will make you certain cannot proceed, from Want, either of Sensibility, or Esteem. I owe your Lordship both, in an eminent degree: and it is chiefly from a Sense how little I am worth, to pay them, that I am silent in expressing them. If I felt less, I could write more: But All great Sensations dwell in silence. However, I would once or twice a year put in my claim to You: & pretend to be entituld to it no other way, than by the sincerest Desire to be yours, & the truest Wishes for yours & your whole Family's prosperity and felicity, These my Lord, you may be sure are Constant in me, & Uniform; and that I often recall, & feast my self upon, the Memory of your Benevolence & Virtue, when I do not by writing, and durst not by speaking (were you present) say a Syllable of it. The Dean's Letter was no small additional pleasure to your Lordship's.[3] I find him full of Old Friendships, & the same good

[1] Kent was always under attack as a painter (though in 1739 he was appointed to succeed Jervas as principal painter to the King); but it is possible that his work at Windsor, of which he speaks with some weariness in his letters, had evoked attack. In a letter to her ladyship (14 Dec.) Kent had said nothing of his sufferings as a genius. He remarks, 'I dined yesterday with Dr Mead with Lord Oxford Bryan St Audrey Pope &c.' The rest of the letter also (Chatsworth MS. 206.5) is personal gossip.

[2] See Pope's letter to her ladyship [8 Sept. 1738], for reference to these papers. Attacks on Pope and Bolingbroke, with frequent harping on the epithet 'all-accomplish'd' applied by Pope to his idol in the 'Epilogue to the Satires', II. 139, continued throughout the latter part of the year. See *The Daily Gazetteer* for 9 and 21 Nov. and 19 and 30 Dec.—and doubtless other issues.

[3] Swift had enclosed a letter to Pope in one to Lord Orrery, 21 Nov. 1738. Orrery evidently forwarded it, but Pope did not print or preserve it, so far as we know.

Heart & Head, whatever damages he may have sustain'd by Age & Decay otherwise. It contains, among other Testimonies, a high one of your Lordships Merit, & another which would not be unpleasing to my Lady Orrery. He says that "Two such Excellent persons, with abundance of good Sense, & amiable in every particular have half broke his heart by leaving him desolate." Shall I, my Lord, not profit by your Visit to England? When shall I meet you? You certainly guest right, when you imagind I would hasten to Town as soon as I heard you were there. Why would you conceal it from me? I hope the Publick will draw you within my reach speedily. You cannot bilk your Country, tho you can your Friends. I am with all respect & sincerity, | My Lord | Your most obliged & | most obedient Servant | A. Pope.

Endorsement: Mr Pope. | Decembr: 20th: 1738.

*POPE *to* FORTESCUE 25 *December* 1738

The Pierpont Morgan Library

It is with great Concern I hear of the Continuance of your Disorder which I well hoped had been only accidental: and more so, that you are obliged to go to Bath at this unpleasant Season. I wish you had less Confinement from that Circumstance of your Situation, which is in other respects so honourable and so desireable. The Attention to Business which it demands, (& which every worthy Man will be willing to give, to his Duty, & to the Good of his Fellow creatures, in any station) I fear has brought upon you this Disorder, the common Effect of too Sedentary a Life. I wish as you have sate for other Judges, others may sit for you, long enough to allow you the Competent Time to make the Bath beneficial to you. I am vexd at My Disappointments of late, in missing so often the opportunities I used to have of seeing you: They have been chiefly occasioned by my Willingness to show a just regard to another Friend to whom perhaps I may never have another occasion of showing it; and now you are ill, I grieve I could not show You the same regard by attending you to Bath, which I would infallibly have done.

I should be glad to hear first, that your journey was well & safely perform'd, & the Effect of the Waters after, as you can give me that satisfaction. Your Compliments to the Two Ladies I have made, the Evening I receivd your kind letter, & I made my best efforts to have got just to see you that Evening, but it was too Cold, & too late, for my sad infirm Carcase, which ill corresponds with the Motions of my Heart.

As you are at Bath, I hope you are acquainted with the Best Man there, and indeed one of the Best Men any where, Mr Allen: If you do not know him *Well*, you will not know him *Enough*; and pray let me lay one Obligation upon you as you have layd many on me, in making you know him better. Shew him this paragraph in my Letter, & it will answer a Letter I lately had from him, inviting me to Bath, whither I need no Inviting while Either of you are there, could I supersede what I think a duty. If ever you draw my affections nearer Devonshire than the Bath, you will have cause to think your self very Powerfull; for there's no Journey I dread like it, not even to Rome, tho both the Pope & Pretender are there. The last ten miles of Rock, between Malborow & Bath almost killed me once, & I really believe the Alps are more passable than from thence to Exeter. Jervas has written his Wife a most Poetical Letter of his Travels over them,[1] upon which I intend to ground my letter to him. If you send me yours, in folio, I'll fill it up, or add another Sheet to it. Your chimney piece I'll take care of; but God knows I little expect ever to sit by its side. I must be content to see the Light of your Countenance by a London or Twitnam Fire, at which places I have set up my Rest. I smile at you when you talk to me of our *mutually* renouncing the *Pomps* of the world. pray when was I a Partaker of them? what Ribans, what Titles, what Furs, yea what Coifs, did I ever wear, or attempt to wear? Mine are *poor* Vanities, a few of the *worse sort* of Laurels. I began my Life without any Views, & hope to end it without any Regretts. I have raised no Estate, nor aimd at it, tho I inherited none. I have liv'd decently, & not servilely, that's enough for me: I shall dye poor, but not dishonourd; and if no body weeps for me, nobody will curse my Memory. Let Greater Men say this, if they can, & let them be *good*, if they dare; but alas! they hardly dare to be *Quiet*, Their Trust is in other mens Meanness & Vices, or they would not be what we call Great. Your situation is a happy one as it makes your Honour & your Ease, your Reputation & your Conscience, Compatible. It is a fine Composition with Fortune, in this age of Corruption, if a man can possess his Place and his Soul in quiet at the same time. I sincerely rejoiced in your Elevation to this Rank; but I thank almighty God that I remain upon the same Level I was born. And I'd desire no greater bliss on Earth than to go out of the world as Innocent, and almost as naked, as I came into it. Believe me sincerely Dear Sir | Your Affectionate, & | Faithfull Friend & | humble Servant. | A. Pope.

Decr 25. 1738

Endorsement (by Fortescue): Mr Pope | Jan. 1738/9

[1] A description of his crossing of the Alps by a painter would be interesting indeed. Normally the roads were so bad that the frightful dangers rather than the poetic prospects were what impressed the traveller.

1739

The year 1739 follows the general pattern that Pope had evolved since the death of his mother. The early winter months were spent at home or in brief excursions to London, and a month-long ramble in July marked the summer. Late in the autumn, however, a variation in the pattern developed when Pope's health (and his new friendship with Ralph Allen) took him to Bristol and Bath. The winter of 1739–40 was unusually cold, and Pope was kept at Bath until February of 1740, longer perhaps than he wished.

Pope's own publications during the year were unimportant. He was evidently preparing the volume of Swift letters for the press. The major publication of the year, so far as Pope was concerned, was Warburton's *Vindication of the Essay on Man*. The increasing ascendancy of Warburton over Pope's mind was aided by the withdrawal in April of the rival mentor, Bolingbroke, to France—where he then intended to remain. A less distinguished friend, Richard Savage, was finally prevailed upon to retire in July, supposedly to Wales, actually to Bristol, where in the autumn Pope made no attempt to see him.

---

*POPE *to* ALLEN — 9 *January* [1738/9]

Egerton 1947

London. Jan 9.

I have accused my Self of Neglect, in not writing you a line before tho (as I've often Covenanted at the very first with many of my Friends, before I became a Correspondent) I told you how frequently I may be guilty of *Omissions*, for indeed I wrong my own heart in calling them *Neglects*. Your constant Memory of me needs no such proofs, as your Kindness perpetually gives me. Nor is there any Occasion of your sending Winged Messengers (whether Pigeons or Guinea Fowl) to prove I am not deserted by you. I had a great inclination to pass a month at Bath this Winter, & One Chance of doing it, this month, but that chance is now over. I must depend on your Journey in February, & hope you may make a few days stay at Twitnam as you come to town or as you return.[1] It is in much dissipation and Company that I snatch a few moments just to tell you my sincere Affection for you, and my true Wishes for yours & Mrs Allen's constant happiness and health. once more adieu. Mr Lyttelton, Dr

[1] Pope wrote again about the prospective visit (6 Feb.). On 17 Apr. it is past, and the Allens have returned home.

Broxholme & I drink your health, & the Post calls this Letter off the Table, & me to my Bed. | Yours Ever. | A. Pope.

Address: To | Mr Allen, at | Widcombe. | Bath
Postmark: /IA [digits illegible]

HILL *to* POPE — 15 *January* 1738/9

1753 (Hill)

Jan. 15, 1738–9.

If you happen to have an idle shelf in your study, that can make room for the inclosed,[1] it will take up but little. In its first old edition, it had a great many more faults, than at present; and its worst, a *rash Preface*; which has never appeared in the following. I repented, as I ought, of the sin—yet, could scarce say, I was sorry I committed it, since I owed to it a discovery of some virtues, which have *made*, and will *continue* me your friend, and your servant.

If I were near enough, I would give you some reasons, which I ought not to trouble you with in a letter, why I wish, in the future editions of one of your satirical pieces, you would leave out a couplet,[2] that reflects, with a roughness deserving your *revisal*, on the CZAR, in his motive to *marriage*. I have papers in my hands, which, I am sure, if you saw, would remove your mistaken ideas on that head, and throw the *noblest* and most *beautiful* colours on a circumstance, which the *malice* of some *great courts*, in *Europe*, has taken pains to *mis-represent* and to *blacken*. The shortened reign of the *lady* deprived me of great part of a *treasure*, which I see, by what came to my hands, had been *vast* and *invaluable*!—Even as it *is*, I can charge nothing upon want of *materials*, but must confess it wholly the defect of my genius, if, hereafter, I fail to give the world some *resemblance*, of a prince, who (with the fullest deduction to be made for his few foibles) has *done honour to the human species*.

Mr. *Fleetwood*—(what a *fall* is there—from *Peter Alexiowitz*!) sends me word, that the *prince* has been so just, as to insist on Mr. *Mallet*'s Tragedy, as the first to be brought on, this season. In this news he has pleased me sincerely: I adjoin my own vote, against myself, with a preference still more warm than the prince's. And, may what I *write* be never *read*, but by the *Fleetwoods* and *Luns*[3] of futurity, if I would not rather burn it, with my own hand, than oppose it to the interest of a man of genius and worth—though a *stranger*!

[1] Evidently a copy of the fifth edition of *The Northern Star*, which in its first edition had printed a Preface attacking Pope.

[2] Lines 131–2 of the first Moral Essay (To Lord Cobham) were what offended Hill. In his 'death-bed' quarto Pope revised the lines to meet Hill's objection. See EC, iii. 63 n.

[3] i.e. theatrical managers. *Lun* was a nickname for Rich, the manager at Covent Garden, due to his promotion of pantomimes.

But, to see the management of our *Theatres* reduced to such an unfathomable descent, in *profundity*, that a Tragedy, writ with the care that has been bestowed upon *Caesar*, should be driveled, humm'd, and hesitated over—should be complimented with the dull mysteriousness of apology, to cover but neglect and irresolution—is a nettling alarm to the patience of a *writer*, and, indeed, a trial, to the quick, of his vanity.

And yet (as a check to the solemn impertinence I am suffering myself to slide into) it was in this very country, and in this very age—YOU were born!—*That* reflection shall serve as a balance, and cut short all complaint in, | Dear Sir, | Your most humble, | And affectionate Servant, | A. Hill.

*POPE *to* HILL[1] 22 *January* [1738/9]

1760 (Hill)

London, Jan. 22

Your kind letter, and agreeable present of an improved edition of your poem, wandered long ere they found me; they came to Twitnam while I was at Dawley, then to Dawley when I was gone to London, then followed me again to Twitnam. I came upon receipt of it again hither, to speak to Mr. Mallet, who told me the manager's most extraordinary conduct. He had engaged to bring on his play first, and Mr. Mallet had told him it was equal to him if he preferred yours, provided his might immediately succeed it. He waited afterwards several times upon the manager, but he never gained admittance. He then told two of his principal advisers the regard to be had to your tragedy, and used (it seems) my Lord Bolingbroke's name, and mine, in a manner I had no objection against, nor his Lordship, for it is what both of us will speak in the gates, as the scripture expresses it; and to all mankind. But not a word, either by writing or message did the gentleman send him, either concerning yours or his own: till he heard he intended to postpone his, notwithstanding his promise, and that he had told the Prince (who asked about it) that one Mr. Brookes[2] had a Tragedy to come on, and that what he had said to Mr. Mallet did not extend to a promise. Upon this he obtained of Mr. Littleton to assure his Royal Highness of the contrary, who did so before Mr. F's face, and upon that Mr. Fleetwood said it should be brought on first. You see how unfairly therefore this has been represented to you, as a *Command of the Prince*. I

[1] The text is taken from Hill's *Dramatic Works* (1760), i. vi–vii. It answers Hill's letter of the 15th.

[2] Brooke's *Gustavus Vasa*, possibly already in rehearsal, was presently forbidden by the Lord Chamberlain, as was Thomson's *Edward and Eleonora* subsequently in March of this year. These were the first plays to be forbidden under the Licensing Act of 1737. In defence of Fleetwood one may note that he was offered four new tragedies in this one season. Of these only Mallet's *Mustapha* was performed.

have moreover reason to think he never made any engagement to Mr. Brooke—but that the whole truth is, he finds his house full, every night, with hearers worthy the stuff they are entertained with, and wou'd discourage any new play whatever. In the mean time, in what condition is merit! A work that wou'd excite noble sentiments in the audience, wou'd ruin our present taste, and his present profit. I am so full of this vexation, I can hardly express myself, you see it by my blots—All the ways I can do you justice, I will; and tho' I wish Mr. Mallet's play all possible success, I will say, and must, there is that in yours, which merits as much, as his, or any that I can ever hope to see. Forgive my abruptness, I must write to you again, having more to say, but wanting time.

Your most faithful obliged servant, | A. Pope.

*POPE *to* MICHAEL RACKETT[1] 22 *January* 1738/9

Ushaw College

Dear Cosen,—My Nephew Henry Racket tells me he has Sent you a full account in Detail of all the Estate in the ffamily, and acquainted you by what Losses it hath been so Impair'd Viz; by Mortgages, Law Suits, and by your Fathers Neglect, as well as by the Sums of money and Bonds he took away with him before he Dyed. I suppose he also told you, how much my Sister your Mother's affairs have been reduced, by the Several Law-Suits Endeavouring to recou'r those Losses, and by the many Demands from her Younger Children. I can assure the account is but too true.

As to the particular Estate of Hall-Grove we have the misfortune to find, (notwithstanding the Deed you formerly executed to your Mother) that the Laws here against Papists, render it Ineffectual to Secure that Estate from being taken possession of and Seized upon by Compares[2] Executors for your Debt. We also find upon Enquiry, that the said Executors have taken out an *Outlawry* against you: by which means, the Moment my Sister Dyes, they will inevitably Enter upon the Estate and Receive the Rents in your Stead, till all the Debt is pay'd. As tis now near 800l. principal and Interest you would not

[1] This letter to Mrs. Rackett's eldest son is preserved only in the hand of the attorney son, Henry, who after the subscription adds: 'The above is a true Copy of Mr Popes Letter to my Brother which I sent to him on the 29th of the above Dated Month | H. Rackett.' One suspects from the letter that Michael's debts had caused him to leave the country, and that the army was perhaps a means of securing himself, if he could purchase a commission. Since on 1 Jan. 1739/40 Pope writes Fortescue that he has had to borrow £150 for a relation, one may assume (?) that no purchaser for Hall Grove appeared and that Pope was helping his nephew into the army. The tone here seems kindly, but the legal troubles of the Racketts had been in process for over a decade, and were by no means ended. To Pope they were a continual headache, and one can see why Mrs. Rackett was incensed when in 1744 Martha Blount turned out to be Pope's residual legatee.

[2] Meaning executors who are compairs or equals?

now, receive any thing in *Twelve years*: The House will every year be worth less and less, (being in a Decaying State) and the Whole Land without it, is let but at 55l. a year: So that if my Sister lives ten years more, the Debt will increase to the *whole Value* your Father gave for the purchase.

This being the True State of the Case, I thought proper in Kindness, to tell it you my self: and then to offer you what I think the best Advise for your own Interest.

I would Advise you to joyn with my Sister to sell Hall Grove, after her Death, to a protestant; which sale will be good notwithstanding the Laws against papists; and notwithstanding your OutLawry. This way you may receive Some hundreds of pounds soon; whereas otherwise you will in all probability, never live to see any thing from it: What ever the Reversion will sell for after her Death you will thus enjoy forthwith, if we can find a purchaser. Indeed, as there seems to be some Right, after your own Death, to your next Brothers, upon whom originally it was Entaild, it would be kind in you to give them some part of the money: but the Chief Consideration is, that it would Enable you to raise more than enough for your present purpose of purchasing in the Army, (150l) and the rest might be put out to use in England, or in life Rates, or otherwise in ffrance, as you like best for your own benefit. if you Consent to this measure, I will send you word what is offer'd for it.

The truth is, your Mothers whole Income is so strait that she would not propose to pay 150l. off in some years (haveing herself and Children to support ou't of it) and I do not see how you could possibly repay it, but by this method: which will enable you to do that, and much more for your Self.

At the same time I am ready to Advance you the 150l tho' I know She cannot repay it, and therefore what I tell you is not to Excuse myself; but really, because there is no other possible way to make the Estate of any use to you, in Case She Dies.

Believe me, Dear Nephew, Glad of any occasion to serve you, and at all times very Sincerly and Affectionatly | Sir | Your Faithfull and real | Servant, | A. Pope.

Twickenham, Jan: 22d 1738.

HILL *to* POPE — *26 January 1738/9*

1753 (Hill)

Jan. 26. 1738–9.

My letter, dear Sir, had but the fate of its writer, when it laboured, and longed to *approach* you, yet, was kept distant, by mistake and ill fortune.

Yours has warmed me, with the spirit of gratitude, for a concern it expresses so kindly. But, I will give up all pursuit of my *Caesar*, since Mr. *Mallet* and Mr. *Thompson*, with the aid of such powerful assistants,[1] found it a difficulty to engage the manager into the resolution, that must have been *due* to their Tragedies. The first of the gentlemen just named, has obliged me, with uncommon delicacy, by an offer so generously made me, when his *own* Play was finished and ready. This was an act of friendship, which I could not have *deserved*, if, as soon as I knew it, I had not, from that moment, *declined* any purpose of pressing the man of the stage about *mine*. Indeed, I should hate all the little I have of the *poet*, if I could not receive as much pleasure, from another writer's success, as from my own; even were that other an *enemy* (of merit). But, since he is my friend, his success *is* my own, and, as such, I sincerely consider it.

There is only one thought that disturbs me;—the respect I would publickly pay to a great name, so known and so dear to you, is held back by this inaccessible retrenchment, that the devil of dullness has thrown up, round our *Theatres*; for, I would not trespass so far against custom, as to *dedicate*, to so chosen a *patron*, a Tragedy that had never been *acted*. I will, therefore, address (to the same lov'd name) some different subject, after having examined, which, of three or four I have long had in hand, may be found least unworthy his notice. Meanwhile, let my *Lord* know, and let Mr. *Pope* know, that I look upon the kind things, they have thought, and expressed, of my *Caesar*, as more *fame*, than a *twenty night's run*, at the Play-houses. And so, wishing Mr. *Mallet*, and Mr. *Thompson*, the success, which they are sure to *deserve*, I bid a hearty farewel to the *stage*, and only wish to be known, as, | Dear Sir, | Your most obliged Servant, | A. Hill.

WILLIAM KENT *to* THE EARL OF BURLINGTON[2]

27 *January* 1738/9

Althorp

London Jany 27, 1738/9

My Lord,—as whe have had such fine weather I was in hopes to have hear'd, of your being sett out, I had a letter from my Good Lord that designs to sup with you next tuesday nando[3] tells me you are all well,

[1] Mallet on 6 Jan. 1739 had written to Hill saying that he had informed the Patentee that Pope and Bolingbroke 'entertained the highest opinion of' *Caesar*. But at a moment when two tragedies were about to be suppressed by the Lord Chamberlain for 'Patriotism', Bolingbroke's recommendation and even Pope's might well be fatal.

[2] Kent's letter, first printed by Mr. H. Avray Tipping in *The Architectural Review*, lxiii (1928), 210, deserves a permanent niche for its spelling alone. It gives us a classic picture of Pope in his cups (Kent as well as Pope was something of a *gourmet*) and possibly helps to date the beginnings of Pope's friendship with Sarah Duchess of Marlborough.

[3] Ferdinando Fairfax.

which I am very glad to here & the Doe you sent was extreemely good the more you send the better—The oratorio's goe on well, I was there with a handsom widow fatt, which has given much diversion to the looker on & whe was in the box you us'd to have—There is a pritty concerto in the oratorio[1] there is some stops in the Harpsicord that are little bells, I thought it had been some squerrls in a cage—my Ld Lovell desirs his service to you, and this day goes to chiswick with Marchese Sacchette, my Ld told him Mich: Angello was an Ignorante in Archetr: come nostro Michll Angello—nove non ci niente che value—They say the Ds M: sent to mr P:[2] to know if he was a coming into the ministry he sent her word that he heard she was a going to be marry'd but he had not enquir'd into it—

Pope is very busy, last night came to me about eight a clock in liquor & would have More wine, which I gave him, you may tell Mr Bethell he's very sorry, so am I he's not well, but he lays it all his not takeing a cup of red—the Genll is extreemely ill and I believe cannot hold long, but is still bying bronzo's, he's ask'd a hunderd times for you, I was there last night with Mr. Pelham & the Gent; the Gent I think is not well and the old afaire makes him think worse than I hope it is thats the stones in short whe are all sickly folks.

Thuanns[3] keeps a dinner for the Antique paintings for you, & is more happy than ever they have cleand the old walls there are a hunderd more wild things that cannot be write | so hope to see you soon | I am your most sencere humble servant: | Wm: Kent

If Stephen has done I wish you would send him back he would save me a great deal of trouble & time that I am forced to do now

Endorsed (on the back): Mr. Kents to be kept.

*POPE *to* WARBURTON[4] 2 *February* 1738/9

Egerton 1946

Sir,—I cannot forbear to return you my thanks for your Animadversion on Mr Crousaz: tho' I doubt not, it was less a Regard to me, than

[1] Handel's *Saul* was first performed 16 Jan. 1738/9.

[2] Since, after this witty bit of gossip, Kent passes to talk of Pope, one may guess that the gossip (involving Sarah, Duchess of Marlborough, now 78 years old, and William Pulteney, leader of the opposition to Walpole) was passed from Pulteney to Pope, to Kent. Writing to Swift 17 May this year, Pope speaks of the duchess as making great court to him.

[3] Possibly Thuanisi's as mentioned in Kent to Burlington, 28 Nov. 1738.

[4] Warburton's (at first) anonymous defence of the *Essay on Man* began in *The History of the Works of the Learned* for Dec. 1738 (ii. 425–66). The successive letters of defence appeared in issues of the periodical for January, February, March, and May. They were published (with an additional sixth Letter) presently collected as *A Vindication of Mr. Pope's Essay on Man.* They replied to the Swiss logician's attacks found in his *Examen* (Lausanne, 1737) and

to Candor & Truth, which made you take the pains to answer so Mistaken a Man. I fear indeed he did not Attack me on quite so good a Principle: and whenever I see such a Vein of Uncharitableness & Vanity in any Work, whether it concerns me or another, I am always ready to thank God to find it accompanyd with as much Weakness. But this is what I should never have Exposed myself, because it concern'd myself: And therfore I am the more oblig'd to You for doing it.

I will not give you the unnecessary trouble of adding here to the Defence you have made of me (tho much might be said on the article of the Passions in the Second Book) Only it cannot be unpleasant to you to know, that I never in my life read a Line of Leibnitz,[1] nor understood there was such a Term as Præ-established Harmony, till I found it in Mons. Crousaz's Book.

I am, Sir, with a due Esteem for your Abilities & for your Candor, (both which I am no Stranger to, from your other Writings, as well as this) | Your most obliged & | most humble Servant, | A. Pope.

Twickenham, | Feb. 2d 1738

Address: To the Revd | Mr Warburton.

*THE EARL OF BURLINGTON *to* POPE

6 February 1738/9

Chatsworth

from one that I love and value as I do you, even rebukes are pleasant, as they must proceed from friendship. that you had not heard from me is purely owing to the agreable, and by me, much envyed life you lead. I thought that any breaking in upon it wou'd be impertinent, especially as I cou'd say nothing to you from home but what I flatter, nay assure myself that you have been long convinced of. as to my not having written of you, that lazy mortal the Signors letters from hence can prove the contrary. Bethel, who is not well, gives his service to you, and intends to set out for London, so soon as he can bear the air. I

Commentaire (1738) on the *Essay on Man*. The former of these was translated by Elizabeth Carter and published as *An Examination of Mr. Pope's Essay on Man* in Nov. 1738 (dated 1739). The *Commentary* was translated, but only in part, for Curll by Charles Forman in Nov. 1738, apparently to forestall a translation by Dr. Johnson, which appeared with 1739 (copy at Yale) or 1742 on the title-page. The excitement which the faulty French translations of Pope's poem caused on the Continent and then in England led to Warburton's defence (which made Pope a Christian) and to his friendship with Pope (which, as the King remarked to Dr. Johnson, made Warburton a bishop).

This is Pope's first letter to Warburton. The first paragraph was quoted by Ruffhead (p. 262), who omitted 'because it concerned myself'. It is fully printed by A. W. Evans, *Warburton and the Warburtonians* (1932), p. 78.

[1] For a discussion of the influence of Leibniz on Pope see Professor C. A. Moore, 'Did Leibniz Influence Pope's Essay?' in *JEGP*, xvi (1917), 84–102.

propose to set out, on friday, and my first visit you may assure yourself shall be to Twittenham. pray tell my Lord Bolingbroke that I am still so rusticated, that no one can be more his humble servant than I am. I long to see you, and am with the most sincere affection, my dear Pope | ever yours | Burlington

Londesburgh | feb: 6 1738

*POPE *to* ALLEN 6 *February* [1738/9]

Egerton 1947

My Movements are so uncertain, between the Town & this place, that if you can do me the pleasure of passing a day here as yourself & Family travel to London, I desire to have notice a post (or rather two) before. I am sometimes too at Dawley, & it is possible (without such notice) that your Letter may not reach me in time. I cannot express how impatiently I wish for this, or any Opportunities of our meeting. I never was more hurryed in my life, by Various business; tho few men ever might have lived with less than myself, had I cared for no man besides myself. I want the Comfort of an honest Friend, in these wretched Immoral times, when almost all the Tyes that bind Man to Man, are Combinations of Iniquity, or at best of mean Interest. Adieu: & let Mrs Allen know me for hers, in being | Dear Sir | Your faithful | Friend & Servant | A. Pope.

Twitnam | Feb. 6.

On second thought, I wish I had a line per next post About what time you may come? to me at Mr Lewis's in Cork street London where I shall be for near a week.

Address: To Ralph Allen Esq | at Widcomb near | Bath.
Postmark: (smudged) /FE

POPE *to* HILL[1] [14] *February* 1738/9

1751 (Hill)

London, Feb. 12. 1738–9.

I have felt an Uneasiness of Mind (occasioned by a conscious Sense, how unequally I have express'd my Anger and Contempt, at the Treatment of your *Caesar* by the Man of the Stage) ever since I last wrote to you; and a hundred Interruptions from Day to Day (for I have

[1] *Mustapha* was first acted on Tuesday the 13th. Consequently this letter was not written on the 12th: there were no Sunday performances, naturally, in Pope's day. The 14th is the probable date.

lived in the World, and a busy and idle World both, it is) have ever since hindered me from enjoying one Hour of collected Thought. Yet I am the less concerned, since, by my Delay, I can now tell you I have last Night seen Mr. *Mallet*'s Play, the fifth Act of which I had not before read, thro' those Interruptions I have mention'd. It succeeded (hitherto at least; for Yesterday was the first Day) as well as I could expect: But so vilely acted in the Womens Parts and the Mens (except two) that I wonder it could succeed. Mr. *Thomson*, after many shameful Tricks from the Manager, is determined to act his Play at the other Theatre, where the Advantage lies as to the Women, and the Success of *his* will depend upon them (I heartily wish you would follow his Example, that we might not be deprived of *Caesar*). I have yet seen but three Acts of Mr. *Thomson*'s, but I am told, and believe by what I have seen, that it excels in the Pathetic. The Dignity of Sentiment, and Grandeur of Character, will still be *Caesar*'s, as in his History, so in your Poetry, superior to any.

The Person to whom you intended so great a Compliment[1] as to address that Piece to his Name, is very sensible of your delicate Manner of Thinking: He bids me assure you, his own Knowledge of your Intention is sufficient Pleasure to him, and desires you would not think of doing him either Favour or Justice, till the World knows better how to do itself the former, in doing you the latter. He is still detained here by the Perverseness of his Affairs; and wishes, as I most heartily do also, that Fortune did not treat you so much alike. The Stage is as ungrateful to you, as his Country to him: You are both sure of Posterity, and may say in the mean time with *Scipio*, *Ingrata Patria, ne ossa quidem habeas*! Believe me most truly, | Your affectionate, angry Servant, | A. Pope.

*POPE *to* FORTESCUE [*February* 1738/9]

The Pierpont Morgan Library

Wednesday.[2]

I have been out of Town some days since I saw you, & ill others, and taken up with Dinners the rest: So as never to get a Dining Time with you. I would propose to injoy your Company for a day, or a Night, or so, in the Country; the only place of Quiet; if you could go to Twitnam on Saturday & take me with you or to Richmond. If this can't be, I must try to fix some other day in Town. On Friday I am ingaged. Adieu. I hope you find the increaseing Benefits of the Bath;

[1] Bolingbroke.

[2] The Wednesdays relevant are 7, 14, 21, 28. The first of these seems impossible since Pope was in Twickenham on the 6th. The second seems probable since Pope is evidently in town for the opening of Mallet's *Mustapha*, on Tuesday the 13th. As to later Wednesdays, we have no evidence.

A full Restoration of your Health is what no one more sincerely wishes then | Dear Sir | Your Ever affectionate | faithful Servant | A. Pope

Address: To the Honble Mr Justice | Wm Fortescue, in | Bell Yard, near | Lincolns Inne

Endorsement (by Fortescue): Mr Pope. | Feb. 1738/9

POPE *to* MALLET[1] [16 *February* 1738/9]

Sir John Murray

Friday | night.

I heartily rejoice in the Success, you so justly merit, & so fortunately have met with considering what a Stage, & what a People, you have to do with.

I hope you have secur'd a Side box on your Sixth Night for Mrs Blount, Lady Fanny,[2] &c. which I think I mentiond to you when you found it too late to get one on your Third Night.

I am faithfully & affectionately | Dear Sir Ever Yours | A. Pope

Address: To Mr Mallet, | Speed.

HILL *to* POPE 21 *February* 1738/9

1753 (Hill)

Feb. 21, 1738/9

I am oblig'd, both by your letter, and the good news it brought, of Mr. *Mallet*'s Success on the Theatre; it is what I was sure he deserv'd: And, if I had, now and then, a moments *fear*, he might miss it, it was when I reflected, how warmly I wished it him.

If Mr. *Thompson*'s new Tragedy is to depend on his women performers, he has certainly, judg'd well, in his choice of the *Covent-Garden Theatre*. There, or any where may his best expectations be answer'd! I shall, myself, have the less to complain of, when such justice is done, where I reverence it.

As for *Caesar*, it was his *fate* to be ill understood: and it was his *custom*, to forgive his *detractors*: only once when he fell into such *free-booters*'s hands, as have thought fit to restrain him at present, he broke a rule, for the sake of mankind; and got 'em *hanged*, for the *good of* the *publick*. I am glad I have none of his power; since I am afraid I should use it profusely:—'Tis a ridiculous world, that we live in; yet, in spite of contempt, one grows serious, when a *fool*, that expects to

[1] The only Friday to fall after Mallet's third night and before his sixth night (his benefit nights) is the 16th.

[2] Probably Lady Fanny Shirley.—EC. Lady Frances Shirley was the daughter of the first Earl Ferrers. Her widowed mother lived in Twickenham, as did probably Lady Fanny, who was much admired by Lord Chesterfield. In the idiom of Horace Walpole, she bestowed 'the dregs of her beauty' on religion. She was a friend of Martha Blount.

be flatter'd, is in a situation, to insult his despisers. I will not disguise my own weakness: I am nettled at the treatment, I have met with, concerning this Tragedy: But, at the same time, I confess, that I ought not to be so: For *you* have been so good, as to declare yourself touch'd, in my cause—and, in *that*, I have more than recompence.

I did not recollect, 'till you told it me, that the *Gazetteers* were printed by Mr. *Richardson*:[1] I am acquainted with none of their authors; not so much, as with any one of their names: And, as to Mr. *Richardson himself*, (among whose virtues I place it, that he knows, and considers, you, rightly) there should be nothing imputed to the *Printer*, which is impos'd *for*, not *by* him, on his *papers*, but was never impress'd, on his *mind*. I am very much mistaken in his character, or he is a plain-hearted, sensible, and good-natur'd, honest man: I believe, when there is any thing put into his *presses*, with a view to such infamous *slander*, as that which you so justly *despise*, he himself is the only man, *wounded*: For I think, there is an *openness*, in his spirit, that would even repel the *profits* of his business, when they were to be the *consequence*, of making war upon excellence.

In the mean time, give me leave to be glad, you are slander'd a little:—*Crimes* deserve to be heartily pardon'd, when they are the cause, of producing great *virtues*; and, I am sure, one such generous example of *charity*, as that which you shew, in your letter, will, by the contagious effect of its beauty, carry influence enough, to deface all the triumphs of a thousand heavy patterns of malice.

Methinks, I gather from a hint, you but drop, in your letter, that my *Silence* would be the most acceptable compliment, to a person, I will not here mention:[2] Be it so—where we wish, but to please, we *are* pleas'd even with the prohibition of our measures, of pleasing. His *worth* cannot want such a *witness*, as I am; and the respect I would pay it, is too *due* to depend on his thoughts of, | *Dear Sir*, | *Your faithful and obedient Servant*, A. Hill.[3]

*POPE *to* SLINGSBY BETHEL[4] 18 *March* [1738/9]

Sotheby's sale of 28 Nov. 1913, lot 355, item 17.

March 18.

The bearer of this is my nephew, who has been long conversant in the

[1] Samuel Richardson, friend of Hill, was the printer of *The Daily Gazetteer*, a Walpole paper, which had recently been attacking Pope violently. In spite of the essential truth of the character Hill gives Richardson, it is probable that he had a prejudice against Pope.

[2] Again, regrets for not being able to dedicate to Bolingbroke.

[3] This is the last letter in the correspondence with Hill. There is no reason to think they did not remain on friendly terms and exchange letters; but none of later date is known.

[4] The year is uncertain. Sir William Codrington (1st Baronet) had married Bethel's sister Elizabeth in 1718, had died in Dec. 1738, leaving property in Barbados. Pope's sailor nephew, John Rackett, evidently hopes to please by reporting on what he has seen.

West Indies, and used those parts as Master and Supercargo. He thinks he can acquaint you with some improvements that may be made in Sir William Codrington's Estates, etc.

*POPE *to* FORTESCUE[1] 27 *March* [1739]

Harvard University

March 27.

I thank you for yours as it gives me always Satisfaction to know you are well, and eases me of the apprehension I was under lest your late Disorders of the stomach might have return'd upon you: I have sufferd so much that way, that I pity the Life any man (much more any friend) must lead, who is Daily subject to them. I have not had any accounts to give you from hence of so satisfactory a nature; my own health is breaking more ways than one; and I begin to be so great a fool, as to be concerned for the Publick weal, which I think breaking too. I can't help wishing well to the World I am leaving, and should do the same to my Country, tho I were parting from it for ever next week. In particular I wish the Honour, the Spirit, and the Independency of this free Nation may continue when I am dust and ashes, & tho' no Child of mine (but a Poem or two) is to live after me. I never had any ambition, but this one, that what I left behind me (if it chanced to survive me) should shew its parent was no Dishonest, or Partial, Man, who owed not a sixpence to any Party, nor any sort of advantage to any Mean or mercenary Methods; and who lamented not any part of his fortune here, but that of living to see an Age, when the Virtue of his Country seem'd to be at a period.

I have a hundred times congratulated you in my own Heart, upon your being now in a Situation, where you are confined to Acts of Justice, & no thing more required of you than the strict administration of it, which is so agreable to your own mind. Your days may pass in *Peace* & *Honour*, the two most desireable things in this world; and that Health may be added to them, is all I can wish for you.

Pray keep your word, & let me know from Bath what effect the Repetition of those waters may have upon you? When do you intend to see Mrs. Shepherd again? I shall settle soon at Twitnam, & hope we shall meet, somewhere upon the banks of the Thames, with Mrs. Blount & Lady S.[2]—tho the former (I call her so in point of precedency in Friendship, tho not so in Quality & Title) is too uncertain still *Where* she shall lay her Head next Summer. The Birds of the Air & the Beasts of the Field, in this, have the advantage of her. I write

[1] During March Fortescue was holding assizes on the Oxford Circuit. He was at Hereford the 24th, at Monmouth the 29th, and at Gloucester the 31st, and thereafter at Bath. The date for the year is from the endorsement.

[2] Suffolk.

this by her side, & she will fill the rest of my paper. So adieu abruptly, but depend, constantly & continually, upon the frindship & affection of, Dear Sir, | Yours. A. Pope.

Mrs B. is just now interrupted by Company, & says she will write you a whole Letter next post, or two.[1]

Address: To the Honble Mr Justice | Wm Fortescue | in Bellyard
Endorsement: Mr Pope | Mar. 27, 1738/9

POPE *to* RICHARD NASH[2] [? *April* 1739]

1762 (Goldsmith's *Life of Nash*, pp. 122–3)

Sir,—I have received yours, and thank your partiality in my favour. You say words cannot express the gratitude you feel for the favour of his R. H. and yet you would have me express what you feel, and in a few words. I own myself unequal to the task; for even, granting it possible to express an inexpressible idea, I am the worst person you could have pitched upon for this purpose, who have received so few favours from the great myself, that I am utterly unacquainted with what kind of thanks they like best. Whether the P— most loves poetry or prose, I protest I do not know; but this I dare venture to affirm, that you can give him as much satisfaction in either as I can.

I am, | Sir, | Your affectionate Servant, | A. Pope.

LYTTELTON *to* POPE[3] [*April* 1739]

1769 (Ruffhead, p. 198)

Since my last, I have received his Royal Highness's commands to let you know that he has a mind to present you with some urns or vases for your garden, and desires you would write me word what number and size will suit you best. You may have six small ones for your Laurel Circus, or two large ones to terminate points, as you like best. He wants to have your answer soon.—Adieu, my dearest friend. | Yours most affectionately, | G. Lyttelton.

[1] This sentence is in the hand of 'Mrs. B.' herself.

[2] Because of honours conferred upon the city of Bath by the Prince of Wales in 1738, Beau Nash was erecting in Queen Square of Bath an obelisk 70 feet high in honour of the Prince. Pope here begs off, somewhat curtly, from composing an inscription. Later he relented; see Pope to Nash [15 May 1739]. This letter and that of [15 May] have formerly been placed respectively in January and February; but the neglected postmark on the second letter places it, and January seems too far from May to be plausible.

[3] Since it is apparent from letters to Swift and Allen that Pope had received and placed the urns (and some busts for his library) by the middle of May, this letter can hardly date later than early April. In EC it is wrongly dated 1740.

POPE *to* GEORGE ARBUTHNOT[1] [*April* 1739]

Elwin–Courthope, vii. 487

Twitnam. [April, 1739]

It is so long since I was able to call at your house, and I am now engaged the worst way, by a rheumatism at home, that I cannot propose seeing any of you, till I shall be again full of company here. In the interim I have asked my Lord Bolingbroke often if he had seen your uncle which I find he has not, though he always desires it,—and he now in particular bids me tell him so. He is in Dover Street only till Saturday noon,[2] when he comes hither again with another lord, and then returns to town about the middle of the week, and sets sail from London directly for France about Saturday following, or Monday. He has ordered me to acquaint your good uncle of this, that if it suits with his conveniency, he can carry him with him in the yacht.[3] I will, if able, go to town with my lord, and wait on you all, next week. In the meantime pray assure him, your sister, and self of my being at all times faithfully theirs, and, dear sir, your most affectionate, humble servant.

POPE *to* WARBURTON[4] 11 *April* [1739]

Egerton 1946

London Apr. 11th

Sir,—I have just receivd from Mr Robinson two more of your Letters.[5] It is In the greatest hurry imaginable that I write this, but I cannot help thanking you in particular for your Third Letter, which is so extremely clear, short, & full, that I think Mr Crousaz ought never to have another answerer, & deserved not so good an one. I can only say you do him too much honour, and me *too much Right*, so odd as the expression seems, for You have made my System as clear as I ought to have done & could not. It is indeed the Same System as mine, but illustrated with a Ray of your own, as they say our Natural Body is the same still, when it is Glorifyed. I am sure I like it better than I did before, & so will every man else. I know I meant just what you explain, but I did not explain my own meaning so well as you: You

[1] The relation of this letter to those immediately following and, more particularly, to the departure of Lord Bolingbroke on Saturday, 14 Apr., places it during the first week of April.

[2] Bolingbroke was visiting William Chetwynd, Esq., M.P. for Stafford, whose son was accompanying Bolingbroke to France. See *LEP*, 28 Apr. 1739. Saturday would be the 7th.

[3] Robert Arbuthnot, the banker of Rouen, was evidently on a visit to England.

[4] This letter was printed by Warburton in 1751.

[5] These would be the third and fourth of Warburton's replies to Crousaz, as printed in February and March issues of *The History of the Works of the Learned*, published by Jacob Robinson. Pope's hurry was due to the farewells to Bolingbroke—who perhaps fortunately had no time to read. If he had had time to persuade Pope to disregard the defence, literary history would have been modified.

understand me as well as I do myself, but you express me better than I could express myself. Pray accept the Sincerest Acknowledgments of Sir Your most obligd & real humble Servant | A. Pope

I cannot but wish these Letters were put together in one book, & intend (with your leave) to procure a Translation of part at least of them into French,[1] but I shall not proceed a step, without your Consent & Opinion.

Address: To the Revd Mr Warburton.

*POPE *to* THE EARL OF BURLINGTON[2] [? 12 *April* 1739]

Chatsworth

Thursday.

My dear Lord,—I am got again to Towne, where accidentally I met Lord Bolingbroke to day, who proposes to dine at Chiswick; if it prove not inconvenient to you, it will be convenient to him on Sunday next; I have taken upon me to procure your answer, and he says he will stay in London till then (which he did not design) in order to it. Believe me with the most sincere Esteem & affection, ever | My Lord | Your most obliged Servant | A. Pope

Your Directions will find | me at Lord Oxford's.[3]

Address: To the Earl of Burlington, | at Chiswick.

*POPE *to* ALLEN 17 *April* 1739

Egerton 1947

April 17. 1739.

I deferrd my Letter to send you the inclosed, & to acquaint you, if I could certainly, by this post of the State of Mr Carteret, who was

[1] They were all translated into that language by a French gentleman of condition, who is now in an eminent station in his own country.—Warburton, 1751. They were translated by Étienne de Silhouette, who had also translated the *Essay on Man* into French prose. A part of the dissension over Pope's poem in France was due to rivalry between the verse translation by du Resnel, which was the basis of Crousaz's attack, and this prose version, supposedly more faithful.

[2] If written in 1739, the only possible Thursday for this letter is the one here assigned. Bolingbroke planned to sail on a yacht from London on either Saturday the 14th or Monday the 16th. (See Pope to G. Arbuthnot in the week preceding this date.) Pope says Bolingbroke will stay for a Sunday dinner at Chiswick, 'which he did not design' to do. Evidently Lord Burlington was not available, and Bolingbroke sailed on Saturday. (See Pope to Allen, 17 Apr. 1739.) The year of this letter is probably, but not quite certainly, 1739.

[3] Lord Oxford and the Chetwynds both lived in Dover Street; hence Pope and Bolingbroke were neighbours.

given over yesterday by the Physicians,[1] but as I am here at Twitnam, I have not been able to know more: tho probably you'l have the account directly from the Office. I presumed it might occasion you a Journey back, which yet I should be very sorry for, tho' I always want fresh Opportunities of seeing you. If it be so, pray call & lye here as you come or as you go, and let me know when & where we may meet? I guess You would indulge Mrs Allen's Love of Quiet join'd to an unfashionable Taste of the Country, & not give her a Second Journey; unless another as unfashionable Taste in her, the Love of her Husband, should overcome you. You would find me still a cripple in the Rheumatic Arm, but my Heart & Spirit as ready, as my Flesh is weak. This is not a Season to hope a recovery in my case. I hope the Bath will supply the Want of Heat in other cases, & particularly in some who are now there, whose health I am concern'd for. Let Judge Fortescue know he is the first of these for whom I wish so warmly, and pray commemorate me with him rather by a Fireside, than on your delectable Mountains in this Weather.[2] It is well (pray tell him) both for him and for me, that his next journey is not to Devonshire but to London, where and at Richmond I hope to see him much oftner, in the Summer, than I could in the Winter, or the chill Northern Spring, that has followd, and more than equald it.

I am now alone, and left to myself. My Lord Bolingbroke executed his Deeds for the Sale of Dawley on Friday and set sail the next day for France from Greenwich. God knows if ever I may see again the Greatest Man I ever knew, and one of the best Friends. But this I know that no man is so well worth taking any Journey to see, to any man who truly knows what he is. I have done so these thirty years, & cannot be deceivd in this point, Whatever I may be in any other man's Character. If you and I could expect to live so long, I think we should never complain of one another. Of how few can I say the one, or think the other!

Believe me as I believe you; I don't mean so good a man, but as sincerely inclined to be so, were I able, and Esteeming every good quality I cannot equal. Upon those Principles my friendship must last, & no Friendship can last upon other Principles, not even State-Friendships or Church Friendships.

Adieu Dear Sir, | Yours always | A. Pope.

[1] Pope's news was not the latest: Edward Carteret, Esq., (one of the Commissioners for executing the office of Postmaster General, and uncle of John, Lord Carteret) had died on 15 April.—*Gent. Mag.* ix. 217.

[2] Fortescue was at Bath at this time. Prior Park was located high above Bath, delectably, but not on mountains.

SWIFT *to* POPE[1] 28 *April* 1739

1746 (Faulkner)

Dublin, April 28, 1739.

The Gentleman who will have the Honour to deliver you this, although he be one related to me,[2] which is by no Means any Sort of Recommendation; for, I am utterly void of what the World calls natural Affection, and with good Reason, because they are a numerous Race, degenerating from their Ancestors, who were of good Esteem for their Loyalty and Sufferings in the Rebellion against King Charles the First. This Cousin of mine, who is so desirous to wait on you, is named Deane Swift; because his Great Grandfather, by the Grandmother's Side, was Admiral Deane, who having been one of the Regicides, had the good Fortune to save his Neck by dying a Year or two before the Restoration.

I have a great Esteem for Mr. Deane Swift, who is much the most valuable of any in his Family: He was first a Student in this University, and finished his Studies in Oxford, where Dr. King (Principal of St. Mary Hall) assured me that Mr. Swift behaved himself with good Reputation and Credit: He hath a very good Taste for Wit, writes agreeable and entertaining Verses, and is a perfect Master equally skilled in the best Greek and Roman Authors. He hath a true Spirit for Liberty, and with all these Advantages, is extremely decent and modest. Mr. Swift is Heir to the little paternal Estate of our Family at Goodrich in Herefordshire. My Grandfather was so persecuted and plundered two and fifty Times by the Barbarity of Cromwell's Hellish Crew, (of which I found an Account in a Book called Mercurius Rusticus) that the poor old Gentleman was forced to sell the better half of his Estate to support his Family. However, three of his Sons had better Fortune; for coming over to this Kingdom, and taking to the Law, they all purchased good Estates here, of which Mr. Deane Swift hath a good Share, but with some Incumbrance.

I had a Mind that this young Gentleman should have the Honour of being known to you, which is all the Favour I ask for him; and that if he stays any time longer in London than he now intends, you will permit him to wait on you sometimes. | I am, | My Dearest Friend, | Your Most Obedient and | Most Humble Servant, | J. Swift.

[1] Faulkner printed this letter at the very end of vol. viii (1746) of Swift's *Works* with the head note: 'After we had printed the foregoing Letters in this Volume, we were favoured with the following one from London.'

[2] Deane Swift (b. 1706) was a cousin once removed of the Dean of St. Patrick's. In 1755 he published a biographical *Essay upon the Life, Writings, and Character of Swift*, which gives us important information.

*POPE *to* ALLEN[1] [5 *May* 1739]

Egerton 1947

Lincolns Inn. Saturday night.

I acknowledge your very friendly Letter, & that is all I can do from a Lawyers Chambers, just before the Post goes out. It is only to tell you, that a Young Bounce is ready for you at my Lord Oxford's:[2] the sooner you send for the Dog the better, but Care must be taken, he can but just lap milk: & I know your Humanity Extends to all the Creatures that have life. I love You for it, and am Ever | Your faithfull affectionate | Friend & Servant, | A. Pope

Address: To | Ralph Allen Esqr | at Widcomb near | Bath.

Stamped: JA

Postmark: 5/MA

SWIFT *to* POPE ?10 *May* 1739

1765 (Deane Swift)

May 10th, 1739, at a conjecture.

You are to suppose, for the little time I shall live, that my memory is entirely gone, and especially of any thing that was told me last night, or this morning. I have one favour to entreat from you. I know the high esteem and friendship you bear to your friend Mr. *Lyttelton*, whom you call the rising genius of this age. His fame, his virtue, honour, and courage, have been early spread even among us. I find he is secretary to the prince of *Wales*; and his royal highness hath been for several years chancellor of the university in *Dublin*. All this is a prelude to a request I am going to make you. There is in this city one *Alexander M'Aulay*, a lawyer of great distinction for skill and honesty, zealous for the liberty of the subject, and loyal to the house of *Hanover*; and particularly to the prince of *Wales*, for his highness's love to both kingdoms.

Mr. *M'Aulay* is now soliciting for a seat in parliament here, vacant by the death of Dr. *Coghill*, a civilian, who was one of the persons chosen for this university: And, as his royal highness continues still chancellor of it, there is no person so proper to nominate the representative as himself. If this favour can be procured, by your good-will and Mr. *Lyttelton*'s interest, it will be a particular obligation to me, and grateful to the people of *Ireland*, in giving them one of their own nation to represent this university.

[1] Written very likely from Mr. Murray's chambers.

[2] The puppy is mentioned again in the letter of 18 May. Since *Bounce to Fop* was written, the Prince of Wales and Allen have joined the distinguished circle guarded by Bounce's Berecynthian offspring. Pope's Bounce was the 'ancestor' (iv. 181) of this puppy.

There is a man in my choir, one Mr. *Lamb*;[1] he hath at present but half a vicarship: the value of it is not quite 50*l. per annum.* You writ to me in his favour some time ago; and, if I outlive any one vicar choral; Mr. *Lamb* shall certainly have a full place, because he very well deserves it: and I am obliged to you very much for recommending him.

POPE *to* RICHARD NASH[2] [*c.* 15 *May* 1739]

Harvard University

Sir,—I had sooner answerd yours but in the hope of procuring a Properer hand than mine; & then in consulting with some, whose Office about the P. might make th[em] the best Judges, What sort of Inscription to set up? Nothing can be plainer than the inclosed, tis meerly the Common sense of the thing, & I don't know how to flourish upon it. But this you would do as well, or better yourself, & I dare say may mend the Expression. I am truly | Dear Sir Your affectionate Servant | A. Pope

I think I need not tell you my name should not be mentioned.[3]

Address: To Richard Nash Esqr | at | Bath.

Postmark: [ ]5/ MA (the first digit is missing)

Endorsement: (No. 3)

POPE *to* SWIFT 17–19 *May* 1739

Add. 4806

May 17. 1739.

Dearest Sir,—Every time I see your hand, it is the greatest Satisfaction that any Writing can give me, and I am in proportion grieved to find that several of my Letters to testify it to you, miscarry; and you ask me the same Questions again which I prolixly have answer'd before. Your last which was deliverd me by Mr Swift inquires where & how is Lord Bolingbroke? who in a Paragraph in my last under his own hand gave you an account of himself, & I employd almost a whole

[1] Concerning Lamb, recommended by Pope for Lyttelton's sake, see Pope to Swift, 12 Oct. 1738.

[2] This was first printed, without date, by Goldsmith in his *Life of Nash* (1762). In EC, x. 219, it is dated '[Jany., 1739?]', but since the original letter bears the postmark here indicated, it must have been written on or about 15 or 25 May.

[3] Pope was much pestered by applications for prologues, epilogues, epitaphs, and monumental inscriptions. By this time he habitually required anonymity. His epitaphs for John Knight and Nicholas Rowe (see Ault, *New Light*, pp. 147–55) were not acknowledged as his, and there are other cases.

The inscription as printed by Goldsmith has been thought undistinguished, and it is so; but it would have been difficult to collocate the names of Prince Frederick and Beau Nash with a 'flourish' without being ridiculous.

Letter on his Affairs, afterwards. He has sold Dawley for 26000l, much to his own Satisfaction: his Plan of Life is now a very agreable one in the finest Country of France, divided between Study & Exercise, for he still reads or writes 5 or 6 hours a day, & hunts generally twice a week: he has the whole Forest of Fontainbleau at his command, with the Kings Stables, Dogs, &c. his Lady's Son-in-Law being Governour of that place. She resides most part of the Year with my Lord, at a large House they have hired; & the rest with her Daughter, who is Abbess of a Royal Convent in the neighbourhood. I never saw him in stronger Health, or in better humour with his Friends, or more Indifferent & dis-passionate as to his Enemies. He is seriously set upon writing some Parts of the History of his Times, which he has begun by a Noble Introduction, presenting a View of the whole State of Europe from the Pyrenean Treaty: He has hence deduced a Summary Sketch of the Natural & Incidental Interests of each Kingdom; & how they have varied from or approachd to, the True Politicks of each, in the several Administrations to this Time. The History itself will be Particular only on such Facts and Anecdotes, as He personally knew, or produces Vouchers for, both from home & abroad. This puts into my mind to tell you a Fear he express'd lately to me, that some Facts in your History of the Queen's last years, (which he read here with me in 1727) are not exactly stated, & that he may be obliged to vary from them, in relation I believe to the Conduct of the Earl of Oxford: of which great Care surely should be taken: And he told me that when he saw you in 1727, he made you observe them, & that you promis'd to take that care.

We very often commemorated you, during the five months we liv'd together at Twitnam; at which place, could I see You again, as I may hope to see him, I would envy no Country in the world, and think not Dublin only, but France & Italy not worth the visiting once in my Life.

The mention of Travelling introduces your old Acquaintance Mr Jervas, who went to Rome & Naples purely in search of health; an Asthma has reduced his Body, but his Spirit retains all its vigor, and he is returned, declaring Life itself not worth a Day's journey at the expence of parting from one's Friends.[1]

Mr Lewis every day remembers you, I lye at his house in Town. Dr Arbuthnot's Daughter does not degenerate from the Humour & Goodness of her Father. I love her much,[2] She is like Gay, very idle, very ingenious, and inflexibly honest. Mrs Patty Bl. is one of the most considerate & mindful Women in the world, toward others, the least

[1] Jervas died 3 Nov. 1739.

[2] She seems, from letters postdating this, to be one of Pope's closest friends in these later years.

so with regard to herself: She speaks of you constantly. I scarce know two more Women worth naming to you; the rest are Ladyes, run after Music, & play at Cards.

I always make your Complements to Lord Oxford & Lord Masham when I see them; I see J. Barber seldom, but always find him proud, of some Letter from you. I did my best with him in behalf of one of your Friends,[1] and spoke to Mr Lyttelton for the other, who was more prompt to catch, than I to give fire, and flew to the Prince that instant, who was as pleasd, to please You. You ask me how I am at Court? I keep my old Walk, and deviate from it to no Court. The Pr. shews me a distinction beyond any Merit or Pretence on my part, & I have receiv'd a Present from him, of some Marble Heads of Poets, for my library, and some Urnes for my Garden. The Ministerial Writers rail at me,[2] yet I have no quarrel with their Masters, nor think it of weight enough to complain of them. I am very well with all the Courtiers, I ever was, or would be acquainted with; at least they are Civil to me, which is all I ask from Courtiers, & all a wise man will expect from them. The Duchess of Marlborow makes great Court to me, but I am too Old for her, Mind & body.[3] Yet I cultivate some Young people's friendship, because they may be honest men, whereas the Old ones, Experience too often proves not to be so. I have droppd ten, where I have taken up one, & hope to play the better with fewer in my hand: There is a Lord Cornbury, a Lord Polwarth, a Mr Murray, & one or two more, with whom I would never fear to hold out against all the Corruption of the world.

You compliment me in vain upon retaining my Poetical Spirit. I am sinking fast into prose; & if I ever write more, it ought, (at these years, & in these Times) to be something, the Matter of which will give value to the Work, not meerly the Manner. Since my *Protest*, (for so I call the Dialogue of 1738) I have written but ten lines, which I will send you. They are an Insertion for the next[4] New Edition of the Dunciad, which generally is reprinted once in 2 years. In the second Canto, among the Authors who dive in Fleet ditch, immediately after *Arnall*. Vers. 300. add these

Next plung'd a feeble, but a desp'rate pack,
With each a sickly Brother at his back:[5]

[1] William Dunkin. See Ball, vi. 122. M'Aulay, the other friend, was recommended by Lyttelton to the Prince.

[2] Especially the authors of *The Daily Gazetteer*. In spite of Pope's indisposition to 'complain' of these men, they slide into rhyme in the next paragraph of the letter.

[3] This serves to indicate the beginning of a friendship with the duchess. She was ardent in opposition to Walpole and his government.

[4] Significantly, perhaps, Pope first wrote *for the new Edition* and then crossed out and wrote *for the next new Edition*. One doubts whether the general revision of *The Dunciad* was at this time decided upon, but possibly it was.

[5] They print one at the back of the other, to send into the Country.—Pope's marginal

Sons of a *Day*! just buoyant on the flood,
Then number'd with the Puppies in the Mud.
Ask ye their *Names*? I could as soon disclose
The names of these blind Puppies, as of those.
Fast by, like Niobë, her children gone,
Sits Mother Osborne, stupefy'd to Stone!
And ruful Paxton[1] tells the world with tears,
"These are—ah no! these were, My *Gazetteers*!"

Having nothing more to tell you of my Poetry, I come to what is now my chief care, my Health & Amusement: The first is better, as to Headakes, worse as to Weakness & Nerves, the changes of Weather affect me much, otherwise I want not Spirits, except when Indigestions prevail. The Mornings are my Life; in the evenings I am not dead indeed but sleep, and am stupid enough. I love Reading still, better than Conversation; but my Eyes fail; and at the hours when most people indulge in Company, I am tired, & find the Labour of the past day sufficient to weigh me down: So I hide my self in bed, as a Bird in his Nest, much about the same Time, & rise & chirp the earlyer the next morning. I often vary the Scene, (indeed at every Friends Call,) from London to Twitnam, or the contrary, to receive Them, or to be receivd by them: Lord Bathurst is still my constant Friend, & yours, but his Country-Seat is now always in Glostershire,[2] not in this Neighborhood. Mr Pulteney has no Country Seat, & in town I see him seldom but he always asks of you. In the Summer I generally ramble for a Month, to Lord Cobham's, the Bath, or elsewhere. In all those Rambles, my Mind is full of the Images of you and poor Gay, with whom I travell'd so delightfully two Summers.[3] Why cannot I cross the Sea? The unhappiest Malady I have to complain of, the unhappiest Accident of my whole Life, is that Weakness of the Breast which makes the Physicians of opinion that a strong Vomit would kill me: I have never taken one, nor had a natural Motion that way, in fifteen years. I went some years agoe with Lord Peterborow about

gloss in the original letter. Pope's tone echoes the satire on the *Gazetteer* that Fielding had put into his *Pasquin* (Act II), where it is implied that the *Gazetteers* were distributed gratis in the country by 'the old Woman' who wrote them. The anti-Walpole papers commonly charged that the *Gazetteers* were written by 'Mother Osborne'. They were by William Arnall (*c.* 1700–36), who signed himself as 'Francis Walsingham', or by James Pitt, who used the signature 'Fr. Osborne'—which his opponents in *The Craftsman* changed to 'Mother Osborne'.

[1] A Sollicitour who procur'd & payd these Writers.—Pope's MS. gloss. On Nicholas Paxton, Solicitor to the Treasury, see Twickenham ed. iv. 375. The lines here sent to Swift did not appear in print until 1743 (Griffith, Book 578), and Paxton's name then disappeared in favour of the line: 'And Monumental Brass this record bears.'

[2] Riskins was not far from Twickenham, but in recent years Lord Bathurst's son had lived there, and now the place was being sold to Lord Hertford.

[3] 1726 and 1727.

10 leagues at Sea,[1] purely to try if I could sail without Seasickness, and with no other view than to make yourself & Lord Bolingbroke a Visit before I dy'd. But the Experiment, tho almost all the way near the Coast, had almost ended all my Views at once. Well then, I must submit to live at the distance which Fortune has set us at, but my Memory, my Affection, my Esteem, are inseperable from you; and will (my dear Friend) be for ever | Yours.

P S. This I end at Lord Orrery's, in company with Dr King. Where-ever I can find two or three that are yours, I adhere to them naturally, & by that Title they become mine. I thank you for sending Mr Swift[2] to me: he can tell you more of me.

London. May 19.

One of my new Friends Mr Lyttelton, was to the last degree glad to have any Request from You to make to his Master The moment I shewd him yours concerning Mr Mac-Aulay, he went to him, & it was granted. He is extremely obliged for your Promotion of Lamb. I'll make you no particular Speeches from him, but You & He have a mutual Right to each other Sint tales Animæ concordes. He loves you, tho he sees you not, as all Posterity will love you, who will not see you, but reverence & admire you.

Endorsement (by Swift): Mr Pope. | Dated May 17th 1739 | To answer

*POPE *to* ALLEN 18 *May* [1739]

Egerton 1947

May 18th

I am truly obliged to you, because I know always the Principle of all your Invitations to be a Sincere Freindship for me, but I thank God the Season has almost cured my Rheumatism, and there are insuperable Reasons that would make a Journey to Bath at this time impossible to me, nay inconsistent with some offices, which You would prefer to Health itself, were you in my case. One of them is what I intend to make you Partaker in, the Sending a Man to be Saved,[3] both in this World & in the next (I hope.) He is to cost me ten pound a year, as long as he thinks fit to live regularly, & if you will let him cost you as much, we shall want few further Aids, & I believe you don't care how long our Benevolence may last, tho I think it can't many years. I told

[1] In 1734 Lord Peterborow and Pope had a pleasant day around the Isle of Wight—perhaps Pope's longest sea voyage. See Pope to Martha Blount, 11 Aug. 1734.

[2] Deane Swift, Esq.

[3] Richard Savage is the 'man to be saved'. He ultimately left London in July of this year. This is one of the few mentions of Savage in Pope's letters.

you of him last Spring, & he sets forth from this World for a better, that is from London to a Remote Country in Wales, in a fortnight; but we are to advance him nothing but by an Agent of mine in that Neighborhood quarterly, after he is setled there.

Biggs has just set up the remaining Urns in my Garden,[1] & is repairing my Portico, where the Rain overflowed the Stucco. I have exceeded the Princes Present by 2 Urns & 3 Pedestalls, for which I desire to be accountable to him or you.

I hope the Puppy[2] is by this time arrived at Widcomb, to be a Guard to your house & Companion to you in your Walks, as his Ancestor Bounce is to me. I gave full orders to my Lord Oxfords Porter, (who had it in charge) the day before Your Letter acquainted me you had commissiond the Carrier.

Mr Hook I've not seen long: by which I conclude he is hard at his Study, as my Lord Polwarth[3] has told me who sees him oftner, and I have lived almost constantly at Twitnam, when I was not obliged for a day or two to attend my businesses in London.

I have just seen Mr Justice Fortescue, who is very mindful of your kind distinction, and reckons the Notice of a Man of Worth no small one.[4] Every Man bears respect to Virtue, even a Lawyer, & a Courtier: The Wonder is, when an Honest dis-interested Man will descend to take notice of *Them*, which really nothing but Charity could make Us do.

My Sincerest thanks to Mrs Allen for continuing as good a Woman as You deserve her to be. I shall esteem her more than a Countess, and be hers, as I am (Dear Sir) Your, faithfull affec-|tionate Servant, & real Friend, | A. Pope.

Bigs will be the Bearer of this, & bring you my Last Works:[5] Pray bind them, just as I have lay'd them together, in order.

Address: To Mr Allen, at | Widcombe

Endorsements: (In Pope's hand:) With 2 Books.
(In Allen's hand:) Mr Diggle (?)
(In another hand:) Letters to Mr Allen

[1] The urns given by the Prince of Wales and evidently some that came from Allen. Were they of stone? The gardens of Mapledurham have leaden urns that supposedly came from Twickenham after Pope's bequest to Martha Blount. Biggs seems to be either permanently or frequently in Allen's employ, and will be mentioned more than once in later letters.

[2] See the letter to Allen of 5 May 1739.

[3] Son and heir of the second Earl of Marchmont, whom he succeeded as earl within a twelvemonth.

[4] The Allens had shown hospitality to Fortescue while he was at Bath in April.

[5] A made-up volume to include poems published since 1735. See Griffith, Book 514.

POPE *to* WARBURTON[1] 26 *May* 1739

Egerton 1946

The Dissipation in which I am obliged to live, thro many degrees of Civil Obligation, which ought not to rob a man of himself who passes for an Independent one, and yet make me every body's Servant more than my own: This Sir is the occasion of my Silence to you, to whom I really have more Obligation than to almost any man. By writing indeed I proposed no more than to tell you my Sense of it. As to any Corrections of your Letters, I could make none, but what resulted from inverting the Order of them, & those Expressions relating to myself which I thought exaggerated: ⌜It was truly from this, not a pretended, Modesty, & from a Respect to your own Character; because I think Any Character truly Respectable, (& above all that of a Clergyman) is lessen'd by the least appearance of too great Complaisance.[2] Therfore I request seriously that you would leave them out.⌝

I could not find a word to alter in your last Letter, which I return'd immediately to the Bookseller. ⌜He has not yet sent it me in Print, nor have I heard of him in relation to the Edition of the Whole of which I desird to see & revise the sheets, to prevent any Errors that might escape Him if printed at this distance from You. But if they are sent to your own hands, I am content.⌝

I must particularly thank you for the mention you have made of me in your Postscript[3] to the Last Edition of the Legation of Moses. I am much more pleased with a Compliment that links me to a Virtuous Man, & by the best Similitude, that of a Good Mind, (even a better & stronger Tye than the Similitude of Studies) than I could be proud of any other whatsoever. May that Independency, Charity & Competency attend you, which sets a Good Priest above a Bishop, & truly makes his Fortune, that is his Happiness, in this life as well as in another.

⌜I have nothing to add but the Assurance of my being desirous to deserve half what you think of me, & of my continuing always | Sir | Your faithfull, & | affectionate Servant | A. Pope.⌝

May 26. 1739.

Address: To the Revd Mr Warburton. | at Newark upon | Trent
Postmark: 26/MA

[1] Printed by Warburton in 1751, with omissions here placed in half-brackets.

[2] This reproof did not cure Warburton. Late in 1743, when Pope and Martha Blount were angry with the Allens and with Warburton, Pope wrote Martha, 'W. is a sneaking parson, and I told him he flattered.' This friendship was based on self-interest to a degree on both sides.

[3] He means a *Vindication of the Author of the Divine Legation*, against some papers in *The Weekly Miscellany*: in which the Editor applied to his own case those lines in the epistle to Dr. Arbuthnot,/ *Me let the tender office long engage*, *&c.*—Warburton, 1751.

*POPE *to* MARTHA BLOUNT[1] [? *June* 1739]

1930 (Lady Charnwood, *An Autograph Collection*)

FRAGMENT

I shall be extreme glad of your making any opportunity of coming hither, with Mrs. Grenvill, to whom pray make my sincere acknowledgements. I have nothing to add but that I live, and live yours A. P.

*POPE *to* FORTESCUE[2] [?26 *June* 1739]

The Huntington Library

Tuesday

Being disappointed the foregoing week of being at home, by which I missd of seeing you, I went to Lord Burlington's & asked him concerning the Lady's making her Affidavit:[3] His answer was, he had resignd that Place, & could take none, & that those who thought it Hereditary, were mistaken, for my Lord Carlton's Patent run only durante beneplacito.—This last Saturday I sent to bespeak you for Sunday, at Mrs Shepherd's, but she said you did not come this week. I am obliged to go my Journey which I have stood ingaged for, to Buckinghamshire, & to Oxfordshire directly, to morrow, from whence I cannot return (I fear) before you go on the Circuit.[4] Mrs Blount dined here on Friday, & I told her, on taking my leave of her, that you had given her your permission, if she wanted to improve her health in the Country, to use your Cottage again. This she took extreme kindly, & I believe would do, after you have left it, if you have really

[1] The fragment is placed here, quite hypothetically, because on 22 June Miss Blount dined with Pope at Twickenham (see To Fortescue [26 June 1739]) and because Mrs. Grenvill (or Grevill) is again mentioned this year in a letter to Miss Blount of 7 July.

Lady Charnwood (pp. 45–46) writes of this letter: 'It is a sheet of paper on the upper part of which is hinged an irregularly cut scrap. On the reverse—in Pope's writing—is part of a list of table-cloths and napkins in fine Irish damask; probably he is asking his correspondent to get them for him. On the side that faces outwards are the concluding words of a sentence too much mutilated to make sense.' Below Pope's fragmentary writing is the comment: 'Fragment of a letter addressed by Alexander Pope to Miss Martha Blount of Maple Durham, Oxford. With permission taken from the collection of his correspondence preserved in the Library of Maple Durham, Monday, 19 April 1824, when the collection was entrusted to me to be bound together. | Michael Jones.'

[2] Fortescue's endorsement of the date is disconcerting since normally he is careful and accurate. One must assume, however, that he here endorses the date on which he receives the letter. The first Tuesday in July was the 3rd, but the letter to Martha Blount dated 4 July indicates that Pope has been for a day or more at Stowe before writing: hence if his 'Tuesday' is accurate, he must have arrived at Stowe about the 27th—before Fortescue got his letter.

[3] The matter of the affidavit refers to difficulties of Lady Gerard mentioned in letters to Miss Blount (4 July) and George Arbuthnot (3 Aug.). See also A. L. Reade, 'Pope's "Mr. Russel" of 1739', in *Notes & Queries*, 17 June 1939.

[4] This summer the assizes for the Western Circuit, to which Fortescue was assigned, were a bit late—31 July to 1 Sept. See *LEP*, 26 June 1739.

no other Use for it. But she said she would write to you to thank you —I beg just to hear of the Continuance of your welfare, a line sent to Twitnam will be sent after me whereever I am: who am Every where Sincerely Yours | A. Pope

Address: To | the Honble Mr Justice | Fortescue: | in | Bellyard
Endorsement: Mr Pope | July 1739 (Fortescue's hand).

MRS. WHITEWAY *to* POPE[1] [*June, or later,* 1739]

Huntington Library

Sir,—I am now with the Dean of St Patrick's who has commanded me to write for Him to You. He is extremely Deaf and Giddy, which is Doubly heavy at this juncture, as it prevents Him from making You acquainted with one of the most valuable Men of this Kingdom, Mr McAulay; whose only business to England is to Pay His Duty, respects, and Most Humble thanks, to the Prince of Wales, to you Sir, and Mr Littleton. The Character which the Dean hath ordered me to give You of Councelour McAulay is this; that He is a Man of Religion without Enthusiasm or Hypocrisy, of excellent understanding Learning taste and Probity, a just defender of other men's Propertys and the Liberty of *His Prince* and Country, A most Dutiful Son, a faithful friend—

Here I stopped to put the Dean in mind that I was writing to Mr Pope, not of him; He bid me go on, finish my Sentence, and then make my remarks—A tender Husband Father and Master.

The Dean now in His turn asked me what I thought of My Precipitation? Was I still of opinion it was Mr Pope I was discribing? as we women like to own our Selves Mistaken, I insisted on my being in the right in what I said, for I could see no other difference in the Pictures, than what an able Artist might designedly have made, Where one Part was Darkly Shaded, for the imagination of the Beholder to fill up.

The Dean says, His great Loss of Memory and very bad State of health, would still be more supportable, if he were not incapacitated by it, to converse with you, who have His Heart, His Warmest Wishes, and tenderest affections. Allow me Sir, to add one wish for my Self, that I may be an Humble Attendant on You both, in that Glorious Space, Where Great Souls will I am sure from a just God, enjoy a more exalted happiness in being perpetually together. I am Sir

[1] This letter introducing McAulay (or M'Aulay) is evidently written after the Prince has promised to countenance his candidacy for Parliament: McAulay is now coming over to thank his friends in England. We are told by Ball (Swift's *Correspondence*, vi. 134 n.) that M'Aulay won the election, but by petition of his rival was denied the seat.

with the highest respect | Your most Humble and | most Obedient Servant | Martha Whiteway.

Endorsement: Mrs Whiteway to Mr Pope 1739

POPE *to* MARTHA BLOUNT 4 *July* [1739]

Mapledurham

Stowe, July 4th

The Post after I writ to you, I receivd with great pleasure one from you, and it increasd that pleasure to hope you would be a little time in the Country, which you love so well, & when the weather is so good. I hope it will not be your fate, tho it commonly prove that of others, to be deserted by *All* Your Friends at Court. I direct to your own house, supposing this will be sent after you, & having no surer way. For the same reason I have directed a Haunch of Venison to be sent Mrs Dryden,[1] in case you are out of town. It will arrive next Munday early at Lord Cobham's house in Hanover Square; but if you are in town and would have it otherwise disposed, of, you may prevent it, by sending thither overnight a new direction to the Porter. I will send you another from Hagley, if you appoint beforehand where it shall be left. Your next direction is to Sir Tho. Lyt. at Hagley near Stowerbridge, Worcestershire, where I hope to be on the Tenth, or Sooner if Mr Lyt. come: Mr Grenville[2] was here & told me he expected him in 2 or 3 days, so I think we may travel on the 8th or 9th tho' I never saw this Place in half the beauty & perfection it now has, I want to leave it to hasten my return towards You, or otherwise I could pass three months in agreable Rambles & slow Journies. I dread that to Worcester & back, for every one tells me tis perpetual Rock, & the worst of rugged roads; which really not only hurt me at present, but leave Consequences very uneasy to me. The Duke of Argyle was here yesterday, & assures me what Mr Lyt. talks of as one day's Journey must be Two, or an intolerable Fatigue. He is the Happiest Man [he] ever was in his life. This Garden is beyond all description [in] the New part of it; I am every hour in it, but dinner & night, [an]d every hour Envying myself the delight of it, because [not] partaken by You, who would *See* it better, & consequently [enj]oy it more. Lady Cobham & Mrs Speed[3] who (except two [days]) have been the Sole Inhabitants, wish you were here, as [muc]h at least as they wish'd for their Gowns, which are not [yet] all recoverd, & therfore I fear yours is not. You might [be] more at your own disposal than usually, for Every one takes [a di]fferent way, & wanders about, till we meet at Noone. [All] the

[1] Presumably a London neighbour. See also [7 July 1739].
[2] Probably George Grenville, nephew of Lord Cobham.
[3] Henrietta Jane Speed, for whom, with Lady Cobham, Gray's 'Long Story' was written.

Mornings we breakfast & dispute; after dinner & at [nig]ht, Musick & Harmony; in the Garden, Fishing; no Politicks [and] no Cards, nor much Reading. This agrees exactly with [m]e, for the Want of Cards sends us early to bed. I have no Complaints, but that I wish for you & can't have you. I will say no more—but that I think *of* & *for* you, as I ever did, & ever shall, present or absent. I can really [forge]t every thing besides.

I don't see that any thing can be done as to Mr Russel,[1] [witho]ut having the Lease carried to Mr Arbuthnot & the alterations added. He will correct the Draught, & if it be ready for Signing, so much the better: for else I fear the Lawyers will be all out of town before she[2] returns.

I desire you will write a post letter to my Man John[3] at what time you would have the Pineapples to send Lady Gerard, and whither he is to send them in Town? I have had none yet, but I bad him send you the *very first* that ripen'd, I mean for *yourself*, but if you are out of town, pray tell him to whom he shall send it? I have also orderd him, as soon as *several of them* ripen, to enquire of you where & when you would have any, which I need not say are wholly at your service.

The Post comes in crossly here, & after I have written for the most part: but I keep this to the last, in case I have any Letter to night, that I may add to it; as I sincerely shall my Thankes, whenever you oblige me by writing, but still more by thinking Me and all I say Sincere: as you *Safely* may, & *always* may.

Wensday: 12 aclock.

Adieu. I'm going into the Elyzian Fields, where I shall meet your Idæa.

The post is come without any Letters which I need answer, which is a pleasure to me except with regard to yours. I did not expect another from you, but as you said in your first that you might send one; and I thank you for the Intention. I hope the more that you are out of Towne for it, & shall rejoice the more when I have one. Pray take care of yourself. Mr Bethel is got well home.

Adieu once more. I'm going to dream of you.

9 at Night.

Address: To | Mrs M. Blount at Mrs | Blounts in Welbeck street | near | Oxford Chappel | Harley Square | London.

Frank: Frank | Cobham

Postmark: 6/IY

[1] See Pope to Fortescue [26 June 1739] and to George Arbuthnot, 3 Aug. [1739].

[2] i.e. Lady Gerard.

[3] John Searle, Pope's gardener.

POPE *to* MARTHA BLOUNT[1] [7 *July* 1739]

Mapledurham.

Stowe. | Saturday.

Dear Madam,—I think you will not complain that I don't write often enough, but as to long Letters, it is hard to say much, when one has nothing to tell you but what you should believe of course, and upon long experience. All is Repetition of only One Great Truth, which is lessened when it really is so, by too frequent Professions. And then the other things are of Places & Persons that little or not at all affect you, or interest you: You have often rebuked me for talking too much of myself & my own Motions, & it is surely more triffling & absurd to write them, than to talk them; considering too that the Clerks of the Postoffice read these Letters. But I am not at all ashamed, that They & all the world know how much I esteem You, or See that I am one who continue to live with Men out of favor at Court, with the same Regard as if they were in Power. Mrs Blounts Friend, & Lord Cobham's Friend & Mr Lytteltons Friend, does not envy Them nor their Master's best Friends; & has more Honour, & less impertinent Curiosity, than to open any of their Letters, did they fall in his way: Nor does he think they have any Secrets more worth Enquiry, than what they will find in this Letter. So I go on, to tell you that I am extremely well, as well as ever I expect to be in every thing, or desire to be, except my Constitution could be mended, or You made happier. Yet I think we have both of us the Ingredients about us to make us happy; Your natural Moderation is greater than mine, yet I have no sort of Ambition nor Vanity that costs me an Uneasy moment. Your Temper is much more chearful; and That Temper, joined with Innocence, & a Consciousness of not the least Inclination to hurt, or Disposition to envy another, is a lasting Security of that Calm of Mind which nothing can take from you, nor Sickness nor Age itself. But the *Skill* of your *Conduct* would be, to avoid & fly as far as possible from all Occasions of ruffling it, or such Vexations, which tho they can't destroy it, can & will cloud it, & render you the *more liable* to be uneasy, for being *more tender*, & *less inclind* to make or see others uneasy. *That way* they will get your very Temper into their power, & you will grow (in Appearance) the worse Woman, for being really at your heart the better. *Unkindnesses*, & *ungrateful returns* are therfore the things you should get out of the way of, and by so doing you will preserve *all* that Good will for them, which tho they don't merit; yet you would preserve, & avoid seeing what they cannot but wish you did not *see*, tho they can't help showing. It is certain both They and You would be Easier, were you quite removed from

[1] Pope's 'Saturday' and the postmark make the bracketed date certain.

them. However while you stay with them I am glad you can find any Circumstance of Satisfaction, & particularly that you like so well the Situation of the House, Fields &c. but do not be like the Swallow, & because it is pleasant in the Summer, lye still & be frozen to death in the winter; for you'l certainly find it no winter habitation, & would do well to provide a better against that Season.

I wonder you've not heard from Mr Fortescue. I writ to him just after,[1] & mentiond the same thing, and to me he has yet return'd no answer, at least John has Sent me no Letter. I think he is more to be depended on than a direct Courtier, tho' a Judge. I was disappointed in finding you not gone with Mr Schutz;[2] As a German, I think it possible he may be dull enough not to care for you; but be that as it will, as a Courtier, if his Duty to Madam V— co[mes] in the way, he must prefer it to any other Request whatsoever. I had directed the Venison beforehand just as you wish'd I see, & that was a pleasure to me. I had sent also 2 lines to Mrs Dr.[3] to tell her it came by your order. in case you had been out of town—As to the fine Pineapple, I wish I had had it myself, or that you had sent it to any better Friend, Mrs Price, or any honest body.

Mr Lyttelton is just arrived, and I set forward on Munday. On Tuesday I hope to get to his house, & if able to get to Genl Dormer's in ten days (including Journey & all)

I thank you for what you told Lord Cornbury. he writ to me very warmly, & talks of finding me wherever I am. I've given him the best account I can of the time of my Return to Genl Dormers, about the 20th I believe. I wish you would go with Mrs Grevil to Astrop, it is but 15 miles off,[4] & stay with Lady Cobham till Lady Gerard return'd from Lancashire & calld you. She & Mrs Speed wish extremely for any honest Company at present, & you would be quite easy. But this, I know, is a Dream: and almost Every thing I wish, in relation to You, is so always! Adieu. I hope you take Spaw waters tho you mention it not. God keep you, & let me hear from you.

Address: To Mrs M. Blount, at Mrs | Blounts in Welbeck street, | near Oxford Chapel, | Cavendish Square | London.

Frank: Cobham

Postmark: 9/IY

[1] On 26 June.

[2] Augustus Schutz, Esq., one of the Germans at court, whom Martha came to know through Mrs. Howard. He was Master of the Robes and Privy Purse to King George II.

[3] Mrs. Dryden again.

[4] Astrop Wells, fifteen miles from either Rousham or Cornbury, where Pope might be. Mrs. Greville is the sister of Mrs. Price; both are daughters of Lord Arthur Somerset.

*POPE *to* THE DUKE OF ARGYLE[1] 11 *July* 1739

The National Library of Scotland

I am very much ashamed to give your Grace so much more trouble than I am worth; but having a sort of title now given me to Adderbury,[2] by your Grace's allowing me a little Bed in your house, and too much self-interest to give up a place before a Place Bill passes; I send this with my thanks for what you have done, attended (as you have I believe generally found them) with a Petition for something more. It is that your Grace will spare your Chariot to Mr Lyttelton the Elder & me at our return to Edgehill on the nineteenth (Thursday) at Noone or by Ten in the morning if equally convenient, by which means we shall be able some hours the sooner (for if we meet it not we shall make it night first) to have the honor & satisfaction to pay you in person such sincere respects as we can really pay to very few great men; & which have been long owing to you, & now increas'd in him who is entirely | Your Grace's most | Obedient & faithful | Servant | A. Pope.

July the eleventh | 1739.

POPE *to* FORTESCUE 26 *July* 1739

1797 (Polwhele, i. 325)

Rousham, July 26, 1739.

I write this much out of humour, to find it impossible for me to get to London in time before your journey. I had written to my servant to send my chaise, and horses to it, about the middle of this week; and wrote to Mrs. Blount, that I hoped to see both you and her here, the moment after I received your most kind letter. I find by one from her, that you have met at last, and that you have complimented her with the shepherd's tabernacle, of which I doubt not she is very glad, and for which I thank you too. The day before I was to set out, my lord Cornbury came hither to general Dormers, and insists so urgently, that he did so, purely to get me to Cornbury for some days, (where I formerly made, and am to make some alterations) that I can't refuse it; or must take another journey expressly, which, indeed, I am not able to do, my weak frame being almost shook to pieces with this. I am within a mile of your brother Page,[3] who threatens to come hither,

[1] The text is from a late transcript, not from the original.

[2] Adderbury was at this time a residence of the Duke. It had been the home of the poet John Wilmot, Earl of Rochester. In the *Additions* to Pope's *Works* (1776), i. 24, appear Pope's 'Verses left by Mr. Pope on his lying in the same bed which . . . Rochester slept in, at Adderbury . . . July 9, 1739.' Pope has already visited his grace, but will, on his return from Hagley with Sir Thomas Lyttelton, visit again, and wishes his grace's chariot from Edgehill on the 19th.

[3] Assizes for Fortescue and his fellow-justice Sir Francis Page were to begin at Winchester on the 31st. Page's 'insolence and severity' in the trial (1727) of Richard Savage probably

and 'tis very probable I may see him at dinner to-morrow. If we were well enough acquainted, I might be tempted to go the circuit with you as far as Southampton. I fancy no coaches are so easy as the judges, and no journies more gradual; then I might be sure of reposing some days between whiles, and keeping sober and sad company. To be serious; I wish yours may contribute to your health, more than I fear it will to your entertainment. Let me hear now and then how you continue, and be assured, all the effects of an old and an experienced friendship dwell about me, and will ever wait upon you; whatever be the events of a world, I am daily weaning myself from, as I think it less and less lovely, and less worthy either remembrance or concern. Adieu! dear Sir, and think (as you truly may) he is a disinterested man who makes you this profession, and who will ever be, your most affectionate, faithful, humble servant, | A. Pope.

I beg you to send the inclosed letter to Mrs. Blount. I never received that which you mention to have written to me to Twitnam.

Address: To the Hon. Mr. Justice Fortescue, at his house in Bell-yard, near Lincoln's Inn, London.

*POPE *to* ALLEN 2 *August* [1739]

Egerton 1947

Augst 2d.

Tho you and I are past all Ceremonials, & dwell in Essentials, in the point of Friendship; yet I believe I should have given you some account of myself sooner had I not been divided among many Engagements & hurry'd about from Journey to journey. The result of which is, that I do not find myself the less yours, tho several have a part in my Regards & Motions. But in truth I find myself less able every year to pay them that proof of my affection, for the Infirmity of my Frame corresponds but ill with the Promptitude of my Spirit: and the Journies I have now made will disqualify me from making more, till I become almost a New Body. It can allow me no Thought of going this year to Southampton, but if in the End of it I could reach You, and if I could stay a full month with you, I would. I am really otherwise Sore & sick of a Journey so many days after it, that it deprives me of all the Enjoyment & Quiet I propose by it, & can only give my Friends Pain & no pleasure. Among other places I have been at Sir Tho. Lyttelton's, where your Pillar is impatiently expected, & where I have plannd three Buildings. Lord Cornbury remembers him kindly

led to Pope's satirical mentions of him in his imitation of Horace's First Satire of the Second Book and in the more recent 'Epilogue', II. 159. Page would probably be leaving for Winchester after dinner, and might (?) take Pope along *en route* to Southampton.

to you & was extremely pleas'd, not with You only, but your House, & all that is about you. I am very glad that Mr. Hook has persuaded himself to take a little Rest with you. No man living wishes better for him than I; Could I be but any way serviceable to him by those Wishes, they would content me, but as they are, they take much of my own quiet from me, by a real Anxiety for him.

It was but yesterday that I got home, from a whole Months absence,[1] and found my Pavement new layd by Biggs. he found so much more trouble in it than was expected that it cost him a weeks work, so that he had not time to amend a few things in the Urns &c, nor would I take up more of his time this year at least. Indeed I think all my Vanities of this sort are at an end; & I will excuse them to the Connoisseurs by setting over my door, in conclusion of them, *Parvum Parva decent.*[2] I must charge You for incoraging some of them, & others of my friends for incoraging others: But I have had my Share too of Discouragement & Censure from Enemies; nevertheless, upon the whole, I neither repent much, nor am very proud, but tolerably pleas'd with them. Adieu for this time dear Sir. God preserve your Happiness, secure your Quiet, & extend your Satisfactions. I am ever Yours. | A. Pope.

Address: To | Ralph Allen Esq | at Widcombe, near | Bath
Postmark: /AV
Stamped: RT (?)

POPE *to* GEORGE ARBUTHNOT — 3 *August* [1739]

The Pierpont Morgan Library

Upon my return from my Journey, I found the Enclosed, which you have had some Trouble about before, and as Lady Gerard is out of town, I beg you to send to the attorney Atwood, & settle the alterations as you have corrected it. I must give you a hint, that I hear the Landlord is to be taken care of, & guarded against, so as to bind him as close as possible, to Each article.[3] Be so kind therfore to see that the attorney insert all your Clauses, & to compare his Draught with this, which when you have seen & approved pray send me that it may be Endorsed against Lady Gerard returns to sign it. If you acquaint me Dear Sir when I may see you & your sister in town, or rather when you could both pass a few days with me at Twitnam, you would very much oblige me. Somewhere or other, I must have the pleasure of a

[1] This remark fixes the year of this letter, for this year was the only one during which Pope was away from home all July. He had been at Stowe, Adderbury, Hagley, Rousham, and Cornbury.
[2] Horace, *Epistles*, I. vii. 44.
[3] See Pope to Fortescue, 26 June, and to Martha Blount, 4 July, both of this year.

Sight of you, now I am near you again. I was this day in hopes to have been able to visit you, but am obliged to go home, where I've not yet been. Believe no man more truly loves you both, & is with greater warmth | Your real Friend | & most affectio-|nate Servant. | A. Pope

Aug. 3d

Address: To George Arburthnot Esq. | in Castle yard | Holborne

*POPE *to* LORD [BATHURST?][1] 9 *August* [1739?]

Roger W. Barrett

Twitnam. Aug. 9th

My dear Lord,—I cannot but think the kindest [th]ing I can do to your Lordship is [to] se[em] to forget you because [that] discharges you of the Remembrance of so un-Important a man, as myself, so unworthy of any place in a Mind which ought to be filled with Greater & Better Objects, as your Lordship's; which yet is so susceptible of the Tenderest Passions, that it can languish after an Old Friend, or an Old Mistress. Therfore I rarely write to you, tho' I often think of you. But another Reason is, that I doub[t] I [k]now how to write *att* you: I might as well direct a Letter to the Sun, who when I rise, is at the East, & when I lie down, at the West. In my late Peregrinations, [I he]ard of you every where, w[h]ere you *Had been*; where you *was*, no mortal cou'd tell. I found every body pleased with the vivifying Infl[ue]nce you had shed upon them in your rapid passage; but none could say, on what Regions, or what people; the future Beam was to shine? Only the D. of Argyll, like the Old General Josuah, thought [he] could make the Sun stand still, for a day or two, in the *Vale* of Cirencester.

To lay figures aside, I am very unhappy, that at the Only time [I] have been able to find your Lordship *fixed*, I could not be with yo[u], especially, when I might have seen those Two pleas'd whose Happiness I equally wish: Thinking alike; & living together; the Duke & yourself—Sint Tales Animae concordes[.]

Whenever your Travels are renew[e]d (which I presume will be tomorrow morning, with your fellow Traveller Phoebus) be so good as to imitate him so far as to shed a Compassionate ray on one of his wretched Sons, who h[a]s met with the Fate of Phaeton & by trying to take the same sort of Journy, is fairly knockd down & lyes breathless on the banks of his own Po, the Thames.

[1] Both the year and the addressee are for this letter doubtful; but Pope has before this (23 Nov. 1738) joked Bathurst concerning his mobility, and the year seems probable. Pope and the Duke of Argyle, it is implied, might have stood still for a bit at Cirencester, if Bathurst had not been away. But Pope had used his joke of writing *att* Lord Peterborow, who was (so Swift told Stella) 'the ramblingest lying rogue on earth'; he had also used it on Bathurst, and possibly the remark would better fit a lord upon whom it had not been staled.

No[thi]ng else could have hinderd me from rendring myself again from this place at your Palace; but a thousand Nothin[g]s, which all together make something insuperable, imploy [m]e here. And, so ridiculous an account as this is, it is as much as the Busiest man alive can plead in his excuse for keeping him from any rational Pleasure. Such [as] it would be to me to see you, to live with you, to dye with you. Believe me, my Lord, with a sincere Esteem, & long establish'd Love, your most oblig'd faithfull Servant | A. Pope.

POPE *to* FORTESCUE 17 *August* 1739

1817 (Warner, p. 58)

Aug. 17, 1739.

I was truly concerned, at my return from my rambles, (which was a whole week longer than I intended, or could prevent,) to hear from Mrs. Blount, how ill you had been; worse than really you had told me in your kind letter. I called at your house a day or two, but mist the ladies; but the servants told me they had heard twice from you, and that you was much better. I hope it proved so; and that as your journey advanced, your strength did the same. I wished to hear more of you; and now desire it, that I may no longer want the knowledge how you find yourself. I dined yesterday with Jervas upon a venison pasty, where we drank your health warmly, but as temperately, as to liquor, as you could yourself: for neither he nor I are well enough to drink wine; he for his asthmatic, and I for another complaint, that persecutes me much of late.[1]

Mrs. Blount is not yet at Richmond, which she is sorry for, as well as I; but I think she goes to-morrow: and she told me she would give you some account of herself, the moment she was under your roof. She expected I could have informed her of your state of health, and almost quarrelled with me that I had not writ sooner. Indeed I forget no old friend a day together; and I bear you, in particular, all the good-will and good wishes I can harbour for any one; though as to writing, I grow more and more remiss. The whole purpose of it is only to tell, now and then, one is alive; and to encourage one's friends to tell us the same, in the consciousness of loving and being loved by each other. All news, if important, spreads of itself; and, if unimportant, wastes time and paper; few things can be related as certain truths, and to hunt for pretty things belongs to fops and Frenchmen. Party stories are the business of such as serve their own interests by them, or their own passions. Neither of all these is my case, so that I confine myself to

[1] See also Pope to Fortescue, 26 July, where Pope remarks on being 'almost shook to pieces' in coaches. This summer one notes the trouble with his kidneys, which was to continue until his death.

meer howd'yes, and repeated assurances that I am concerned to know what I ask of my friends. Let me, then, sometimes be certified of your ways and welfare; mine are pretty uniform, neither much mended nor worse. But such as I ever was, I am; and I ever was, and shall be, dear Sir, | Faithfully your's, | A. Pope.

Address: To the Hon. Mr. Justice Wm. Fortescue, in Bell-Yard, near Lincoln's Inn, London.

*POPE *to* JONATHAN RICHARDSON[1] [*post August* 1739]

1791 (Boswell, *Life of Johnson*)

Enclosing Dr. Johnson's *London*

This is imitated by one Johnson who put in for a Publick-School in Shropshire, but was Disappointed. He has an Infirmity of the convulsive kind, that attacks him sometimes, so as to make Him a sad Spectacle. Mr. P. from the Merit of This Work which was all the knowledge he had of Him endeavour'd to serve Him without his own application; & wrote to my Lord gore, but he did not succeed. Mr. Johnson published afterwards another Poem in Latin with Notes the whole very Humerous call'd the Norfolk Prophecy. | P

*POPE *to* ALLEN 14 *September* [1739]

Egerton 1947

You know my Opinion as to Letter-writing, that except Business which demands it, it should only be a Memorandum at Seasonable Intervals, between Friend & Friend: to do it too often, seems to Imply a Doubt that a Friend is too forgetful of one: & is but a Repetition of a Profession which should be taken for granted from the first time that an Honest Man makes it. I will neither believe you forget me in 2 or 3 months, nor that you imagine I am alter'd in my affections. Therfore it is but at some distance of time that I write: & when I have any thing to tell you. Mr Hook is here,[2] very well, & very full

[1] This note illuminates a distinguished 'contact' of Pope with Dr. Johnson. In May 1738 Johnson's *London* appeared on the same day as Pope's *1738* (Dialogue I), and Pope's praise of *London* is well remembered. Thereafter (presumably moved by Savage, who was friend to both Pope and Johnson) Pope had urged Earl Gower to help Johnson to a post in a 'Shropshire' school. (The school seems actually to have been at Appleby in Leicestershire.) We have Gower's letter to Swift about the affair, but not Pope's letter to Gower. Since the election had to take place by 11 Sept., and since Johnson visited Lichfield and Appleby in August, that month probably dates his disappointment. How long thereafter this note was written is uncertain. See Boswell (ed. Hill–Powell), i. 132 n. and 143.

A contemporary transcript of Pope's note is preserved in the Hyde Collection.

[2] Hooke had been Allen's guest in August 1739; see letter to Allen of 2 Aug.

of your kind usage of him. He is very earnest with me to pass some time with you this coming Winter, which is making Us both a Compliment, for he shews me thereby, that he thinks You will be pleased, and knows I shall be pleased, in doing so. Among my Complaints I have one, & the most dangerous of any, that may as the Doctors tell me, be mended by drinking the Waters warm at Bristol: that would mortify me, if it is to keep me from you, so near you; But whatever happens, I will pass some weeks with you, about November, or after the Idle Part of mankind leave the Bath. If I came Sooner, one Respect or other, or one Decorum or other, would ingage me too much among them. Whereas I intend to be better imployed, in revising some Papers I have long intended to print,[1] for future times, in case of Mortality, and not to leave what I hope will be of some Benefit to mankind, to Accident or Caprice, after my Death.

I have of late had these Serious things so nearly at heart, that I've not been once from home these 5 weeks, nor seen London a day. Whenever I go thither, I'll call on Mr Vandiest.

Pray return my kindest Services to your Nearest Friend, in whose, & in Your own Happiness, (which are one & the same) I take a true Interest—My best Wishes, and most Entire Friendship will ever be Yours, Adieu. My health is tolerable at present, & my Heart belongs to Good Men, of whom there are not so many but You must have a large Share in it. Dear Sir | Yours | A. Pope.

Sept. 14th

I fancy you have prevented Biggs from bringing me his Bill, which is Insidiously done of you, for I protested against it, and I draw upon you so often for charities, that you should not encourage me in Superfluities.

Address: To | Ralph Allen Esqr | at Widcomb, near | Bath.
Postmark: 15/SE

POPE *to* WARBURTON[2] — 20 *September* 1739

Egerton 1946

Twitenham, Sept. 20th | 1739.

Sir,—I receivd with great pleasure the Paper you sent me, & yet with greater the Prospect you give me of a nearer Acquaintance with You, when you come to Towne. I shall hope what part of your Time you can afford Me, among the number of those who esteem you, will be

[1] Either the correspondence with Swift or the 'Memoirs of Martinus Scriblerus', and very likely both, are included among these 'papers' undergoing revision.

[2] This letter was printed by Warburton in 1751.

past rather in this place than in London, since it is Here only I live as I ought, Mihi et Amicis. I therfore depend on your promise; & so much as my Constitution suffers by the Winter, I yet assure you, Such an Acquisition will make the Spring much the more welcome to me, when it is to bring you hither, cum Zephyris & hirundine prima.[1]

As soon as Mr R.[2] can transmit to me an Entire Copy of your Letters, I wish he had your leave so to do, that I may put the book into the hands of a French Gentleman to translate,[3] who I hope will not subject your work to as much illgrounded Criticisme, as my French Translator[4] has subjected mine. In earnest I am extremely obliged to you, for thus espousing the Cause of a Stranger whom you judgd to be injur'd; but my own part in this Sentiment is the least: The Generosity of your Conduct deserves Esteem, your Zeal for Truth deserves Affection, from every candid Man: And as such, were I wholly out of the Case, I should esteem & love you for it. I will not therfore use you so ill, as to write in the general Stile of Complement; It is below the Dignity of the Occasion: and I can only say, (which I say with sincerity & warmth) that you have made me really | Sir Your faithfull & | affectionate Servant | A. Pope.

Address: To the Reverend Mr Warburton | at Bruton near Newark upon | Trent | Notinghamshire

Postmark: 22/SE

*POPE *to* THE EARL OF BURLINGTON[5] 15 *October* 1739

Chatsworth

Oct. 15. 1739.

My Lord,—I take the liberty to send you the Inclosed, upon presumption of the Fact mention'd in it. I hope it may be the means of making happy a very Virtuous & Deserving Man, who is one of the best Examples I know in his Profession, & for whom I have so many years had your Promise of kind Intentions. He will be quite easy with such a thing as whoever has the Benefice of Eyam will be content to part with. As for the Benefice of Eyam, I wish it were given to the best Preacher in England, who has printed the best Sermons, led the most Christian Life, never askd a favour at Court, never flatter'd one Patron,

[1] Horace, *Epistles*, I. vii. 13.

[2] Robinson, the publisher of Warburton's 'letters' that became the *Vindication of Mr. Pope's Essay on Man*.

[3] See Pope to Warburton, 11 Apr. 1739, iv. 172 and n.

[4] DuResnel,—'on whose very faulty and absurd translation Crousaz founded his only plausible objections'.—Warburton, 1751.

[5] Pope's tone is not clear. Obviously he wishes to recommend a virtuous and deserving clergyman for the place to be vacated by the candidate for Eyam. As for Eyam, it deserves perfection, but barring that impossibility, Mr. Kent might take orders. . . . See also Pope to Lady Burlington, 29 Oct. 1738.

& would be certain to give half its Income to the Poor. If such a man cannot be found, I wish I had it myself, or that Mr Kent would take Orders, for we are e'en as good Christians as most Parsons. I am with all Esteem & Affection My Lord | Your most faithfull & | most Oblig'd Servant | A. Pope.

POPE *to* THE COUNTESS OF BURLINGTON

15 *October* [1739]

[A letter dated 15 October 1738 was sold on 9–10 December 1918 at Sotheby's to G. D. Smith. It has not been traced. It seems probable that the year was wrongly affixed (by a cataloguer ?) in the knowledge that the living of Eyam fell vacant in 1738. It was again vacant in 1739. Pope's letter to Lady Burlington, 29 October 1738, does not sound as if the matter of this living had been opened by him previously, and one suspects that on 15 October 1739 he addressed a joint letter or two letters to Lord and Lady Burlington. To determine the matter, the text of the letter is necessary.]

POPE *to* SLINGSBY BETHEL 31 *October* [1739]

Arthur A. Houghton, Jr.

I have not been in London but one day these 3 months, & not one day in the City (I think) since I saw you. This day I intended to have made you a Visit at Towerhill, being to pass most of the day in the City upon business. But so it is, that the person I am ingaged to requires me to goe as far as Highgate, which prevents me. I wanted to know how your good Brother does, it being long that neither Mrs Blount nor I have heard a word of him, and a Lady tells her, that a Misfortune has happend in the family where he generally resides in Yorkshire. We are in pain for him, & his health. Another thing I had to beg of you was on Mrs B's account, who wants 3 or 4 dozen of Madera: if you can't help her she does not know where to get any Good, & she drinks almost no other wine that agrees with her. If you can send some to her in Welbeck street near Oxford Chapel, Cavendish Square (where they now live) you'l oblige both her & me. I hope Sir you enjoy your own health, which I sincerely wish you, & all other happiness. I know you wish me mine, & therfore I must tell you it is pretty good at present. I am with all truth, | Dear Sir | Your most affec-|tionate & obedient | humble Servant | A. Pope. Oct. 31st

Address: To Mr Slingsby Bethel, at | his house on | Tower-Hill, | London

Postmark: PENY POST PAYD (blurred)

Endorsement: A. Pope | October 31, 1739
14 (?)number of the letter

*POPE *to* FORTESCUE[1] [1 or 8 *November* 1739]

The Pierpont Morgan Library

Thursday.

I had dined with you this day, but have been visited slightly with the Gout (as Mr Cheselden thinks). It has put me into a wider Shooe, & till the pain is over, I dare not venture to Richmond tho to morrow I must go to the farther End of the City (if it does not continue too bad.) In such case, I will stay till I can meet you at your own house in Town at your return. I hope your own Health & Limbs are perfect. This is almost the only thing in which I would not resemble you. Adieu dear Sir | Yours Ever | A. Pope.

I hope you'l not forget speaking to Mr Cruwys.

Address: To the Hon. Mr Justice Wm | Fortescue in Bell Yard | Lincolns Inn

Postmark: PAYD [PENY P]OST

Endorsement: Mr Pope | Nov. 1739

HENRY BROOKE *to* POPE[2] [*November* 1739]

1804 *Brookiana*, ii. 9–14

I was much concerned that I had not an opportunity of taking leave of you when I came for Ireland. I earnestly wished to see you, because I feared it was for the last time, and I wanted to thank you once for all, for much good you have done me, and more particularly for revising and passing your friendly judgment upon some lines of mine that, indeed, were scarcely worth your reading;[3] keep me from the vanity of thinking you have any cordial regard for me, I should then lose the pleasure of reflecting that I esteem and most heartily love you, without an expectation of any return of the like nature, as you have done me many kindnesses, without the possibility of a recompence.

I brought over a set of your works, and as I hear you every day in them, I am tempted, perhaps impertinently, to put in my word; I always considered you as a very worthy man, but I really never knew you until now.

I remember Mr. Spence and I had a dispute about you one day in the park; he asserted you were the greatest poet that the world ever produced, but I differed from him in that respect; I told him to the

[1] Since Pope arrived in Bath the 14th or 15th of November, the first two Thursdays of the month are the only ones possible as dates; in view of his gout, perhaps the first is preferable.

[2] After the banning of his *Gustavus Vasa* Brooke had returned to Ireland. His inquiry here about Pope's beliefs is chiefly important for the reply it evoked, 1 Dec. 1739.

[3] *Universal Beauty* (1735).

purpose, that Virgil gave me equal pleasure, Homer equal warmth, Shakespeare greater rapture, and Milton more astonishment, so ungrateful was I to refuse you your due praise, when it was not unknown to me that I got friends and reputation by your saying things of me which no one would have thought I merited, had not you said them.

But I spoke without book at the time; I had not then entered into the spirit of your works, and I believe there are few who have. Far be it from my intention, and farther be it from the power of any man to compliment you; I only speak the ruder parts of my sincerity, and am little concerned how I fail in point of ceremony, since I shall never fail in my good intentions towards you.

Any one of your original writings is indisputably a more finished and perfect piece than has been wrote by any other man; there is one great and consistent genius evident through the whole of your works, but that genius seems smaller by being divided, by being looked upon only in parts, and that deception makes greatly against you; you are truly but one man through many volumes, and yet the eye can attend you but in one single view; each distinct performance is as the performance of a separate author, and no one being large enough to contain you in your full dimensions, though perfectly drawn, you appear too much in miniature; your genius is like your sense; one is too crowded for a common eye, and the other for a common reader. Shall I dare to say that I am heartily angry at it, and that I wish all the profits of Homer were sunk in the sea, provided you had never improved him, but spent your time in excelling him his own way. Is it yet too late?

I should not have presumed to express myself thus far if it had not come in my way, as I was going to speak to you upon a matter that is much nearer and dearer to me than even your fame. I have often heard it insinuated, that you had too much wit to be a man of religion, and too refined a taste to be that trifling thing called a Christian; those who spoke this, perhaps, intended it to your praise, but to me it was a cloud that intercepted the brightness of your character; I am amazed whence this could proceed, and now I feel that they little knew you. I had not read your Messiah, your Ode of the dying Christian to his Soul, and your Letters to that great and good man the Bishop of Rochester, till very lately, and that at a time when sickness indisposing me for light thoughts, gave me a true and affecting relish for them, and I am sure it is as impossible for any other than a Christian to write them, as it is for the best Christian to read and not be made better by them.

I wish you had wrote more upon divine subjects, or that you would go on to make your ethics perfect, as I am confident you would rather improve a single man to his advantage, than entertain thousands to your own fame.

I have had a tedious illness since I saw you last, but I think I am growing better with change of air and exercise; I have now better health, and much more leisure than usual, and it would be no compliment to tell you, in my present disposition, that I would rather enjoy your friendship than all that crowds or courts could give me, for barely to say that I care for neither is to speak as charitably as I can.

May you live long, Sir, to give profit to the world, and pleasure to your friends, to be the shelter of such shrubs as I am, and to know that every sentiment I have, is full of love and respect to you, and that I am, with all truth, your grateful and affectionate | H. Brooke.

*POPE *to* CHARLES BRINSDEN[1] [15 *November* 1739]

The New York Public Library (Berg)

Sir,—By not expecting You here, but at Bristol, Mr Allen's Servant deny'd me to you, as I was forc'd to order him to do to every one in general, being but just come hither, & otherwise sure to be perpetually interrupted. I desire you will not take this ill, as I could not help it, nor mention my being here, but if you can call to morrow you'l find me, or if you please to tell me where I may find you in two days time, I will wait upon you. I am | Sir | Your most obliged | humble Servant | A. Pope

Address: To the Revd Mr Brinsden
Endorsement: Nov. 15, 1739 (in Brinsden's hand?)

POPE *to* MARTHA BLOUNT[2] [? 19 *November* 1739]

Mapledurham

Bristol, Munday.

I am glad I sent you my last Letter on Saturday without expecting yours, which did not come till the day after the Post, by passing first thro Mr Allen's hands at Bath. I thank you for it, & must now give you some account of this Place. I rise at seven, drink at the Well at 8, breakfast at 9, dine at 2, go to bed at ten, or sooner. I find the Water very cold on my Stomach & have no Comfort but in the Asses Milk I drink constantly with it, according to Dr Meads order. The three

[1] Other letters following make the date of the endorsement probable. Having just arrived at Allen's on his way to Bristol, Pope was being denied to visitors, but would like to see Brinsden. Charles Brinsden was the son of Bolingbroke's secretary, John Brinsden.

[2] The bracketed date superscribed by the editor may seem strange in view of the postmark. Obviously, however, the letter to Miss Blount dated the 24th is a continuation of this letter, and one must assume that this letter did not get into the post so soon as it should have done. The year seems certainly to be 1739: Roscoe wrongly placed it in 1742.

days I was at Mr Allens I went for 2 or 3 hours to Bath two days, but saw no public place, nor any persons but the 4 or 5 I writ you word of. It grieved me to miss twice of Lady Cox in that time. I had a line from Mr Slingsby Bethel to acquaint me his Brother was well and I will write to him from hence, as soon as I can give him a Physical account of myself.

I hardly knew what I undertook when I said I would give you some Account of this place. Nothing can do it but a Picture, it is so unlike any Scene you ever saw. But I'll begin at least, & reserve the rest to my next letter. From Bath you go along the River, or its Side, the Road lying generally in sight of it, on each Bank are steep rising Hills cloathd with Wood at top, and sloping toward the stream in Green Meadows, intermixt with white Houses, Mills & Bridges, this for 7 & 8 miles, then you come in sight of Bristol, the River winding at the bottom of steeper banks to the Town where you see twenty odd Pyramids smoking over the Town (which are Glasshouses) and a vast Extent of Houses red & white. You come first to Old Walls, & over a Bridge built on both sides like London bridge, and as much crowded, with a strange mixture of Seamen, women, children, loaded Horses, Asses, & Sledges with Goods dragging along, all together, without posts to seperate them. From thence you come to a Key along the old Wall with houses on both sides, and in the middle of the street, as far as you can see, hundreds of Ships, their Masts as thick as they can stand by one another, which is the oddest & most surprising sight imaginable. This street is fuller of them, than the Thames from London Bridge to Deptford, & at certain times only, the Water rises to carry them out; so that at other times, a Long Street full of ships in the Middle & Houses on both sides looks like a Dream. Passing still along by the River you come to a Rocky way on one Side, overlooking green Hills on the other; On that rocky way rise several white Houses, and over them red rocks, and as you go further, more Rocks above rocks, mixd with green bushes, and of different colourd stone. This at a Mile's end, terminates in the House of the Hot well, whereabouts lye several pretty Lodging Houses open to the River with Walks of Trees. When you have seen the Hills seem to shut upon you & to stop any further way, you go into the House & looking out of the Back door, a vast Rock of 100 foot high, of red, white, green, blue & yellowish Marbles, all blotch'd & variegated strikes you quite in the face, & turning on the left, there opens the River at a vast depth below, winding in & out, & accompanied on both sides with a Continued Range of Rocks up to the Clouds, of a hundred Colours, one behind another, & so to the end of the Prospect quite to the Sea. But the Sea nor the Severn you do not see, the Rocks & River fill the Eye, and terminate the View, much like the broken Scenes behind one another in a Playhouse.

From the room where I write, I see the Tyde rising, and filling all the bottom between these Scenes of Rocks, on the Sides of which on one hand are Buildings, some white, some red, every where up & down like the steepest side of Richmond to the Thames, mixd with Trees & Shrubs, but much wilder, and huge Shaggy Marbles, some in Points, some in Caverns, hanging all over & under them in a thousand shapes. —I've no more room, but to give Lady Gerard my hearty Services, & to wish you'd see next summer or spring what I'm sure would charm you, & fright most other Ladies. I expect Mr Allen here in 4 or 5 days. I am always desirous to hear of you. Adieu, Remember me to Mr Lyt, Lord Cornbury, Mr Cleland.

Address: To Mrs M. Blount, at Mrs | Blounts in Welbeck street near Oxford Chappel | London.

Frank: Free | Chesterfield

Postmark: 26/NO

*POPE *to* FORTESCUE 20 *November* [1739]

The Pierpont Morgan Library

Bristol Novr 20.

Your Kindness has been a Post beforehand with me, for I intended to give you, by this, some Account of myself: but retarded it that I might say something with a little Certainty. I believe the Bristol waters at the Well, would be serviceable, if I could stay long enough, viz: six weeks or 2 months, for as they are an Alterative, & of no great Strength, they require a longer time to operate, than warmer & more impregnated Mineral-Waters, such as Bath &c. The place is so Exposed, & so inconvenient for want of Chairs, Coaches at all Easy, &c. that there is no living long here in winter; for such thin Bodies as mine: The only Convenience I now have is in the Coach of a Gentleman my Neighbor at Twitnam; but he leaves Bristol at the End of the month, or sooner. I am advised to take the same waters at Bath, mingling a little warm Bath water in 'em, not enough to be inflammatory; I have written to Dr Mead for his opinion herein. Upon the whole I am not worse for the Journey, and a little the better for the Cool Regimen I have follow'd; for Wine I have not drank six Glasses of since I came. This is all I can yet say, and it is more than I've yet said to any of my Friends I correspond with: but I know you expect it, & wish me as well as any of them. I am truly Sensible of [t]he many & long proofs I have had of your Friendship & Remembance, & hope if I live a little longer, to see you Quite at your Ease, & at leisure to attend your Health, that we may both Walk gently and inoffensively together out of this world, without any Animosity to any

Creature in it. I know this is your Disposition, & it really has ever been mine, tho the world thinks me a Satyrist. I hate no man, as a Man; but I hate Vice, in any man.—I was much Edify'd with what you said to me when we met last at Twitnam, of the *Matter* you wish'd for your Epitaph, & the *Character* you desired to leave.

I made your Sincere Compliment to Mr & [Mrs] Allen, who truly deserve what you say. Ma[ke] mine, as soon as you can, to Mrs Blount, who deserves as much as any body, & wants only that Fortune should set her on an Elevation, to show it. I desire when next you write to know, how Mrs Spooner has her health, & all your family to whom I am a Sincere Wellwisher, Friend & Servant. Mr Coleman I always remember & desire him still to remember me. And believe dear Sir, you have no man more truly & affectionately Ever Yours, than | A. Pope.

Pray send for & read Mr Warburton's Vindication of the Essay on Man, just printed.

Address: To the Honble Mr Justice Wm | Fortescue in Bellyard, by | Lincolns Inne

Postmark: PENY POST PAYD WTU

Endorsement: Mr Pope | Novr 1739/40

POPE *to* MRS. RACKETT *22 November* [1739]

Ushaw College

Bath. Novr 22. [1739]

Dear Sister,—This is only to keep my word and acquaint you that I am safe here; shall be either here, or at Bristol, for near a month more. My health is as usual, but I hope Benefit from the Bristol waters, & drink 'em daily with other medicines. I found Mr Brown here had no Thoughts of purchasing Hallgrove but for his Son, who will not, I see, resolve; tho he has been tempted to have it at one thousand pound only for his part of payment. So I hope my Cosen Henry [will find] some others to be more in ear[nest. I had][1] some hopes of a Lawyer a friend of Mr Murray's, but he promised to send to you if he went on. pray tell me if you have heard of any, or anything that you would inform me of by a Line directed to me, under cover to Ralph Allen Esq at Bath. Pray give my love to my Cos: Harry, & my Services to Mr & Mrs Cheselden. I saw her Kinsman at Bristol. Let me know how you have your Health, which is with all other happiness, sincerely wishd by | Dear Sister | Your affectionat | Brother

Address: To Mrs Racket, at Mr Eustas's | the corner of East street. | Red lion street | Bloomsbury | London.

Postmark: BATH.

[1] The signature on the verso has been cut away, causing gaps in the text here.

POPE *to* MARTHA BLOUNT[1] 24 [*November* 1739]

Mapledurham

Saturday the 24th

Dear Madam,—I have just received yours, for which I most kindly thank & love you, & You will have this a Post the sooner, by Mr Allen's Messenger coming hither—I have had a kind letter from the Judge,[2] with very friendly Mention of You, & concern that he could not see you. As he expects a particular account of myself, I inclose it to save the trouble of writing it over again to you, who I know desire as much or more to know it—and I proceed in my Description.

Upon the top of those high Rocks by the Hotwell, which I've described to you, there runs on One side a large Down, of fine Turf, for about three miles. It looks too frightful to approach the brink, & look down upon the River; but in many parts of this Down the Vallyes descend gently, & you see all along the Windings of the Stream, & the Opening of the Rocks, which turn, & close in upon you, from space to space, for several Miles, on toward the Sea. There is first near Bristol a little Village upon this Down, called Clifton, where are very pretty Lodginghouses overlooking all the woody hills, & steep cliffs, & very green Vallies: within half a mile of the wells; where in the Summer it must be delicious walking & riding, for the Plain extends one way many miles. Particularly there is a Tower, that stands close at the Edge of the highest Rock, & sees the Stream turn quite round it; & All the Banks one way are Wooded, in a gentle slope for near a mile high quite green; the other bank all inaccessible rock, of a hundred colours & odd shapes, some hundred foot perpendicular. I am told that one may ride ten miles further on an Even Turf, on a Ridge, that on one side views the River Severn & the banks steeper & steeper quite to the Open Sea, & on the other side a vast Woody Vale as far as the Eye can stretch; & all before you the Opposite Coast of Wales beyond the Severn again. But this I have not been able to see; nor would one, but in better weather: when one may dine or lye there, or cross a narrow part of the Stream to the nearest Point in Wales, where Mr Allen & Mr Hook last Summer lay some Nights in the cleanest & best Cottage in the World with excellent Provisions, under a Hill on the Margin of the Severne. Let him describe it to You, & pray tell him we are much in fear for his health, not having had a line since he left us.

The City of Bristol itself is very unpleasant, & no civilized Company in it. Only the Collector of the Customs would have brought me acquainted with Merchants, of whom I hear no great Character. The

[1] This is a continuation of the letter of [19 Nov.]. The two seem to have been posted at the same time—at least the postmarked dates are the same.

[2] Fortescue.

streets are as crowded as London but the best Image I can give you of it is, Tis as if Wapping and Southwark were ten-times as big, or all their people run into London. Nothing is fine in it but the Square, which is larger than Grosvenor-Square, & wellbuilded, with a very fine brass Statue in the middle, of K. William on Horseback: And the Key, which is full of Ships & goes round half this Square. The College Green is pretty & (like the Square) set with Trees, with a very fine Old Cross of Gothic curious work[1] in the middle, but spoild with the folly of new gilding it, that takes away all the Venerable Antiquity. There is a Cathedral very neat, & 19 Parish Churches.

Once more my Services to Lady Gerard. I write scarce to anybody, therfore pray tell any body you judge deserves it, that I enquire of, & remember myself to them. I shall be at Bath soon, & if Dr Mead approves of what I askd him of the Bath water mixd, I'll not return to Bristol: Otherwise, I fear I must. For indeed my Complaint seems only intermitted while I take larger Quantities than I used of Water, & no wine: & it must require Time to know, whether I might not just as well do so at home? Not but that I am satisfyd the Water at the Well is very different from what it is any where else; for it is full as warm as new milk from the Cow: but there is no Living at the Wells without more Conveniencies, in the Winter. Adieu. I write so much, that I've no room to tell you what my Heart holds of Esteem & affection.

Pray write to me every Thursday's post, & I shall answer on Saturday. for it comes in & goes out the same day. & I can answer no sooner what you write on Tuesday.

N. B. This bit fills up the place torn off

Address: To | Mrs Martha Blount, at Mrs Blount's, | in Welbeck street, near | Oxford Chappel | London.

Frank: Chesterfield

Postmark: 26/NO BATH

*POPE *to* HUGH BETHEL — 27 *November* 1739

Egerton 1948

Bath, Novr 27. | 1739

I had been in a great deal of concern for you, on a melancholy piece of news I accidentally heard from Lady Irwin,[2] & since on account of

[1] Since removed, and now [1886] at Stourhead.—Elwin–Courthope.

[2] Probably the wife of the 7th Lord Irwin, who was about this time Lord Lieutenant of the East Riding. She would know the state of Yorkshire officialdom. Possibly the widow of the 5th Viscount is intended. She was in 1737 married to Col. James Douglas, and was doubtfully friendly to Pope. The widow of the 3rd Viscount was also still living.

being told you were in danger of being Sheriff, when I was forced hither & to Bristol on account of a Complaint I formerly mentiond to you. I believe the Bristol waters at the Hot Well would be serviceable, could I stay long enough, for they are apparently softer & as warm as New Milk, there, & known to be excellent in all Inflammatory Cases. But the Rigor of the Season & the Want of all Conveniencies to guard against it, of Coaches, chairs, & even warm Lodging, is too great to bear without hazard of Colds &c, which would do me, ev'n in this Complaint, more harm than I could expect benefit. I have therfore after a Fortnights tryal returnd to Bath where Dr Oliver & Cheyne advise me to mix Bristol water with a small quantity of Bath at the Pump, & with some other Medicines, which Dr Mead prescribd me to add. At worst if I can obtain no remedy for this, I will try a New Spa which they all allow to be of the nature of the Gerunster, lately found here, and near Mr Allen's (at whose house I am lodged) for my old Stomach ailments, which I doubt not they will mend.

You will join to this the good hours which here I can keep, & the Leisure which I can never obtain in London, as well as the Regularity of dining & the Simplicity of the Food. But you will have no doubt remaining of my Amendment when I tell you that I have left off wine so far as to have drank but one Glass a day, & four days in six not a drop. The Town of Bath I have hardly seen. I was half a day there the first I arrivd from London, & 2 hours a day or 2 after in both which I went to Lady Cox's, but had the ill luck to miss her; the second time indeed twas partly my own fault, for I had told the Servant before, I was to go to Bristol next day as I intended, but went not till the third day.

I am just got back, & will as soon as I go to Bath find her & your Sisters. I will be very little there, & if you can write me a Line it will find me at Ralph Allen's Esq's at Widcomb, where I shall live, read, & plant away my time, leaving the Madness of the Little Town beneath me, as I've done the Madness of the Great Town behind me.

I am only sorry I could not carry a few Righteous People along with me. I wish you thought this place for your health, and I wish Mrs Blount, to whose health it certainly would conduce, would have been here, where she might find more Quiet, & better Countenances than in her own Family.

A few honest People, is all the World is worth: but you shall never find them agree to stand by one another & despise the rest; which if they would they would prevail over all the Follies, & the Influence of the World: But they comply with what is round about 'em & that being almost [Sure] to be folly or misery, they must partake of [both].[1]

I wish I knew anything worth telling you, but I thank God I

[1] Ruffhead quoted this paragraph (p. 487).

know nothing of London or its Works, Public or Private, to tell you. We are a most Profligate Nation, & if we prove a Victorious one, it is what seldome has happen'd.[1] I am faithfully | Dear Sir Ever Yours. | A. Pope

You'l put Mr Moyzer in mind of me, | & tell me when you think of coming nearer.

Address: To | Hugh Bethel Esq at Beswick | near Beverley | Yorkshire
Postmark: 1/DE

POPE *to* HENRY BROOKE 1 *December* 1739

1804 (*Brookiana*, ii. 14–16)

Bath, Dec. 1, 1739.

Your's came to me no more than two days since, having been at Bath for some time on account of ill health; it is impossible I should answer your letter any farther than by a sincere avowal that I do not deserve the tenth part of what you say of me as a writer; but as a man I will not, nay, I ought not, in gratitude to him to whom I owe whatever I am, and whatever I can confess, to his glory, I will not say I deny that you think no better of me than I deserve; I sincerely worship God, believe in his revelations, resign to his dispensations, love all his creatures, am in charity with all denominations of Christians, however violently they treat each other, and detest none so much as that profligate race who would loosen the bands of morality, either under the pretence of religion or free-thinking. I hate no man as a man, but I hate vice in any man;[2] I hate no sect, but I hate uncharitableness in any sect; this much I say, merely in compliance with your desire, that I should say something of myself.

I am truly glad of every opportunity to assist a man of your disposition, whose morals go hand in hand with their talents, and whose modesty is not spoiled by the applause that is justly given to their merit; esteem such men I must; it is no obligation on them but on me when I can serve them, and, let me add, that the esteem I bear them is inseparable from so much affection as must make me a sincere friend to you, in whom I discover as many good qualities of the heart as the head, and from my heart I wish you health and prosperity in every thing you undertake, as I am convinced your ends will always be honourable.

Your accidental mention of the ill use some infidels would be glad

[1] Great Britain had declared war against Spain on 19 Oct., and minor victories at sea were already reported when Pope wrote.

[2] This sentence to this point is verbatim from a remark made to Fortescue, 20 Nov. 1739.

to make of my writings, makes me send you a book[1] just published by a person utterly a stranger to me, though not to my meaning, in which he has perfectly explained me in a vindication of the Essay on Man, from the aspersions and mistakes of Mr. Crousaz; it shall come to you by the post, in one or two parcels, franked, and I believe will be some satisfaction to you and others upon that head.

Your's in truth and affection, | Alex. Pope.

POPE *to* LYTTELTON[2] — 12 *December* 1739

Hagley

Bath Decr 12th 1739.

I write to you soon, because I know it will please you to hear I am not Ill, nor ill at ease: Either my Lord Cornbury mistook my letter, or you him. I think that ever since I was a Poet, nay ever since I have ceas'd to be one, I have not experiencd so much Quiet as at this place. Tho I let the World alone, from my very Entrance into it, I found as much Envy & Opposition, as if my Ambition had design'd to over turn it, and since I chanc'd to succeed in my own Low Walk, as much Sollicitation & vile Flattery, as if I had Places & Preferments to bestow. I never deserved or desird Either. If I deserve any thing, it is from a Constancy to my first Philosophical Principles, a General Benevolence, & fix'd Friendships where-ever I have had the luck to know any honest or meritorious Men. I am Yours by every Tye; few have, or ought to have, so great a Share of me; if I say two or three more, I should correct myself, & say rather one or two. Were it not for a Hankering (tis a good expressive English word) after these, I could live with honest Mr Allen all my life.

Tho I enjoy deep Quiet, I can't say I have much Pleasure or even any Object that obliges me to smile, except Dr Ch.[3] who is yet so very a child in true Simplicity of Heart, that I love him; as He loves Don Quixote, for the Most Moral & Reasoning Madman in the world. For I maintain & I know it, that one may smile at Those one loves, nay esteems, & with no more Malice or Contempt, than one bears to an Amiable Schoolboy. He is, in the Scripture language, an *Israelite in whom there is no Guile*,[4] or in Shakespear's, *as foolish a good kind of Christian Creature*[5] as one shall meet with.[6]

I am told your Brother is come to Bath, & I will seek him out

[1] Warburton's *Vindication*, of course.

[2] Elwin wrongly placed this letter in 1736. Pope's own dating seems correct: in 1739 he was in Bath; in 1736 he was not.

[3] Dr. Cheyne. See Lyttelton to Pope, 4 Dec. [1736].

[4] St. John i. 47.

[5] *Merry Wives*, IV. i. 73–74.

[6] At this point in the original letter four lines are heavily overscored. Some words are possibly legible, and the overscoring is perhaps designed to blur excessive compliment to Lyttelton from the Doctor.

diligently, because I am also told that he is related to you. Adieu. I wish you all Earthly blessings, all you enjoy, or can wish; Your own Welfare & your Country's, Lord Chesterfield's Health, Lord Polwarth's Success, & every good that can befall you, in yourself or in any other

Dear Sir, Yours | A. Pope

Address: To | George Lyttelton, Esqr

*POPE *to* JOHN BRINSDEN[1] 15 *December* 1739

The Pierpont Morgan Library

Bath. Decr 15th 1739.

I am very much obligd by your kind Letter, and desire you particularly to make my Acknowledgments to the Author of the inclosed Verses, so greatly in my favor, & which I merit no otherwise than as I really Intended well that Essay of mine, & meant it to virtuous purposes. If he does me the honour to print them, I desire it may be known to whom I am indebted for them; as I think it more an honour done me, from One who is known to be so good a Poet himself. But I cannot consent to your proposal to put them into the Common Sense;[2] or any avowed Party-Paper, on either side.

I am much concern'd at the Continuance of your Complaint but will conceal it from your Family here, for the humane reason you give. I hope in a short time to see you; but now, or hereafter, if the little House I offerd you can be of any Use to you, to breathe fresher air in, pray enter & possess it freely.[3] Adieu. I am affectionatly, Dear Sir Ever yours. A. Pope.

Address: To | John Brinsden Esq. in | Rathbone Place. | near Sohoe. | London.
Postmark: 17/DE BATH
Endorsement: Alexander Pope Esqr | Decr 15th 1739

POPE *to* MALLET 17 *December* 1739

Sir John Murray

Bath. Decr. 17. 1739

I fear this Answer to yours will be too long delayd by the accident of my having been at the Bath & Bristol these many weeks. It has no

[1] A modern endorsement in pencil on this letter reads: '11 letters from | Mr Pope to | Mr B | 1 Dr Trapp | 1 Voltaire.' Only 10 letters—to John (7), to Charles (2), and to Mrs. Brinsden (1) are known to the present editor.

[2] *Common Sense* was an organ of the Opposition, patronized by Chesterfield, Lyttelton, and others of Pope's friends; but Pope wisely wished to keep the *Essay on Man* out of politics.

[3] John Brinsden lived in London, and Pope offers him his Twickenham villa during his own absence in Bath.

date, so that I am not without fears it may have lain at Twitenham a great while, or otherwise given you reason to think me less ready than I am, to comply with any demand of Yours. This morning it reachd me, but I think (and I believe you think by this time, when you have had leisure to repeat more than One Alphabet) that You have no Sort of Reason to Answer a *Fact* that *is* false in itself, & *Appears* plainly so to every Man, that reads your Mustapha & my Lord Orrery's.[1] Who was the author of the Preface you mention, I know not, but if it be the present Lord, he deserves *Some Respect* from his Rank, yet more from his Character; & *no small Compassion* for so palpable a Mistake: which I can't help fancying he has been led into by some *Affirming Critick*, who had given him an account of what he had never read.

My ill State of health carried me to Bristol, at so severe a Season, as made my Stay there impracticable. There was Mr Savage *to be* found,[2] but indeed I could not persuade myself to *find* him, thinking it would have given him some Confusion (as it would have given me,) to meet the face unawares of a Friend, with whom he had broken his Word. But I wrote to him a very sorrowful letter, which he answerd in a higher ~~strain~~ Key than I deserv'd, and a much harsher than his other Friends deserv'd: However it ended in a promise to go in a few days to Swanzey. I reply'd in sober strain, & layd hold only on That Circumstance, as the only one upon which I could fix any Good to himself. And I have renewd my orders since for prompt payment of my part of the *Subscription for his Retirement* (for so he calls it) to *his own hands* this Xmas. For he declares against all Measures, by which any of us pretend to put him into a *State of Infancy*, & the Care of another.

Pray let Mr Thomson[3] know my Sincere Wishes for his health & prosperity. I hope my own health rather mends, & in a Month at farthest to enjoy it with you sometimes.

Dear Sir adieu. | I am Your faithfull & affect: | Servant | A. Pope.

Address: To | Mr Mallet. to be left at Mr | Dodsley's at Tully's head | in Pall-Mall. | London.

Postmark: 19/DE

[1] Pope perhaps writes with some embarrassment, since he surely must know who brought out, earlier this year, an edition in two volumes of *The Dramatic Works of Roger Boyle, Earl of Orrery*. Dodsley was the publisher, and Pope's friend the 5th Earl gave copies to friends. The Preface (p. viii), in speaking of Orrery's rhymed *Mustapha*, says: '. . . a late Author has with great Sagacity taken away the Rhyme, and has made his Play (by the Help of a first Minister, and some other lucky Incidents) as fashionable now, as my Lord *Orrery's* was heretofore: The impartial Reader will distinguish the Merit of each.' Mallet evidently interpreted this as a charge of plagiarism.

[2] Savage had not gone to Swansea, as he had agreed to do, and he did not go there 'in a few days' as Pope says he promised to do.

[3] The author of *The Seasons*.

POPE *to* THE EARL OF OXFORD[1] 25 *December* [1739]

Longleat Portland Papers, xii

Mr Allen's at Bath. Decr 25. | [1739]

My Lord,—It is so long since I lived in London (where I have not stay'd a week together these seven months), & my ill Fortune in missing you, twice in thrice that I have endeavourd to wait on your Lordship, (which was every time that I was in Town) has been such; that being still detaind at Bath, I cannot but write to assure you with what True Esteem I continue, & shall continue every New Year I live, to be yours; and with what real Zeal I wish you Joy of every Year that is added to You.

I hope your Lordship will not find the Increase of them so burdensome, as I do; but more & more peaceful & enjoyable. And that every additional Comfort will yearly be growing round you, in your Family, to all whose prosperity there is not a more sincere, (tho there may be many more loud, & officious) Well wisher, than | My Lord | Your most Obliged, most Affection-|ate, faithfull Servant, | A. Pope.

Address: To the Right Honble the | Earl of Oxford, in Dover street, |London
Postmark: 26/DE BATH

POPE *to* MARTHA BLOUNT 27 *December* [1739]

Mapledurham

Decr 27th

I am sorry you are so engaged, & dissipated, as you say. If your Friends would but do as most other peoples, invite you once to dinner, & then not care if you were hang'd, it would be better. But to be all day, first dressing one's body, then dragging it abroad, then stuffing the guts, then washing them with Tea, then wagging one's tongue, & so to bedd; is the life of an Animal, that may for all that I know have Reason in it (as the Country Girl said a Fiddle had a Tune in it) but wanted somebody to fetch it out. And Ladies indeed do seldome learn to play this way, or show what's in them at all, till they meet with some clever Fellow, to wind them well up, & frett their fiddle-strings. But as next to Action is Contemplation, so Women unmarryd betake themselves wisely to Thinking; as I doubt not you do sometimes, when after the fatigues of the day, you get to bed; and then how must every Considerate Woman be struck, when she hears the Watchman every hour, telling how *Time is Past*! If you think I write a little extravagantly, you are mistaken, for this is Philosophy: I am just come from hearing Dr Cheyne, and besides I have the headake, which heats my brain, and he assures me I might be inspired if It had but one Turn

[1] The year is added in another hand. This is apparently the last letter from Pope to Lord Oxford that we have. His lordship's financial reverses had probably kept him in the country increasingly and away from London. He died in 1741.

more. I must just say a word or two in the usual form, to let you know I've been once at Bath, & dined with Mrs Arbuthnot who sends you many Services. I will not fail to speak of what you desire to Lady Peterborow. Mrs Arbuthnot tells me she is very great with Mrs Nugent, & so am I (to be) with Mrs P. but I have not seen her, & she has no Coach and can't get at me. I thank God for all his benefits. Pray tell me of any thing that pleases you, or any thing that vexes you. And give Lady Gerard my humble Service—And take care of your health, & finish the Picture when you go into the City, or to Judge Fortescues, & don't mind Mr Price.—You tell me very few of my Friends in Town remember to ask about me. You shall see how I remember Them, & how I ask about them. Pray tell my Lady Suffolk in the first place that I think of her every night constantly, as the greatest Comforter I have, under her Edder-down Quilt: I wish Mr Berkley lay as easy, who I hear (& am sorry for it) has had the Gout. Pray ask the Duchess of Queenbury, (if you can contrive to ask her without seeing her) what She means, by forgetting you are as good a Dancer as some she invites? and ask my Lady Marchmont, to carry you to see how well her Lord performs? Pray tell Mr Lyttelton to tell a Friend of his, that of all the Princes in Europe I admire the King of Prussia, because he never tells any body any thing he intends to do. Pray tell Mrs Price how kindly I take her Remembrance of me & desire her to tell my Lord Cornbury so. And those who love writing letters, and those who can write a-bed, should write, for the same reason that those who hate writing letters, & those that can't lye or sit still, should not write And tell Mr Nugent that I will sit for my Picture for him, as I once did for his Lady, and that I believe it will be a very excellent picture, because I am very much alterd for the better. Pray assure Mr Cleland that I am reading Don Quixote. And assure Lady Fanny Sh[1] that I have writ no Verses this year at Bath. I wish Lord Chesterfield knew, that a very scandalous paper is handed about in his name upon Lady Thanet,[2] which I am glad of, because he gave Copies of an incorrect Libel of mine against Pride & Covetousness.

Among the rest of my friends, I wish you had told me what is become of Moratt? is it not for him, that your Sister has cry'd out her eyes?

HENRY BROOKE *to* POPE[3] [1739–40]

1804 (*Brookiana*, ii. 16–19)

Your letter and packet gave me the greatest pleasure. I have read the notes on your essay with attention, and think the author, in doing you

[1] Lady Fanny Shirley. [2] Lady Thanet (Mary Savile) was Lady Burlington's sister.

[3] This is Brooke's reply to Pope's letter of 1 Dec. How long after receipt of that letter Brooke replied it is not possible to determine.

bare justice, has worthily served the cause of virtue, and abased the triumph of those infidels who would fondly have hailed you as their patron.

Upon reading this treatise, your system appears so connected and evident, as by no means to want an explanation, and yet to assent that I saw thus much before I read it, would be to boast an understanding of which I am not master. The world could not make your poem any other than it is in itself; if it had not been just and clear at first, if would never appear so afterwards, and yet toward your readers these annotations have all possible merit; their author not only removes those shades and mists that envy and ill-designs had interposed, but is also the Newton of your system, which he illustrates by sharpening and assisting our sight: he serves you only by enlarging our minds, he leads us on in a farther progression of thought, and not suffering us to dwell upon particular beauties, gives us the comprehension and higher relish for that beauty which results from the whole.

I own myself, among thousands, obliged to this ingenious writer, and no longer offended with Mr. Crousaz, from whose darkness such light has been educed. Indeed, through your whole life you have been particularly happy in your enemies; you shine brighter through the fire of a continued malice, than you could possibly have done from all the additional splendours of eulogium and panegyric.

If heaven has given me those talents you mention, I am truly humbled in the indifferent use I have hitherto made of them; the more my reason improves and expands itself, it gives the greatest light to see my own weakness, to see the vanity of those things with which such an idle creature is still but too much embarrassed. Such as I am, be assured you hold the warmest place in my heart, and are entitled to see all its furniture, its wealth, and also its lumber; at once it loves and detests, pursues and avoids, approves and despises the same succession of follies, empty honours, traitorous riches, unpleasing pomp, and unsatisfying pleasures, and now is grieved, and now is glad, to find that its only business in this world is to learn to leave it.

I heartily thank you for that paragraph in your letter, which contains the generous assertion of your faith and principles. I sincerely wish you every acquisition that is necessary to your happiness or possible to your fame, and only want you to know that I am more than ever, perhaps more than any man, your very affectionate servant, | H. Brooke.

1740

In Pope's correspondence this is a very full year, and hence its pattern unfolds clearly. As the year began, Pope was still at Bath on his longest visit to the Allens. He got back to London about the middle of February. In the autumn he was again eager to be with the Allens, but various causes delayed the journey (made apparently with George Arbuthnot) until almost Christmas. Throughout the year he was worried by the unceasing financial perplexities of his relatives the Racketts. During the spring he was busy refurbishing his grotto, which now begins to become a geological museum. In the spring also he sent off to Dublin, in a highly furtive fashion, the clandestine volume of Swift–Pope letters that he had had printed. From October to the end of the year this was almost the sole topic in his many letters to and from Lord Orrery and others in Ireland. The hypocritical suspicions that he readily casts upon Mrs. Whiteway and Deane Swift, her son-in-law, are painful to record. From about 22 April Warburton had spent a month in and about London, making his first acquaintance with Pope. The two men were at once so transparently aware of their serviceable potentialities to each other that the association—one hesitates to call it a friendship—became permanent. It took longer for Pope (in good King George's golden words) to make Warburton a bishop than it did for Warburton to make Pope a Christian: but such were the rewards of their connexion. A final interesting aspect of the year is Pope's attempt to spur Lord Marchmont to political activity. At this time there is little doubt of Pope's political bias.

*POPE *to* FORTESCUE[1] — 1 *January* [1739/40]

Harvard University

Bath New years day

I thank you for your Letter, & constant memory of me & my affairs. What you told me of the State of that before the Master in chancery,[2] Mr Murray hath since confirmed; that he hath had a Computation made, but that upon the whole, he thinks best to go on next Term, in order to bring them to a more reasonable Proposal. I am fully satisfied to leave the Matter to him, either to treat, or to fight, as he judges most fitting.

I am very sorry not to enjoy the Holydays with my friends, & particularly with you, when our neighbourhood might bring us often together. An attempt to improve my health, or at least palliate a very troublesome Disorder, the consequence of which may be dreadful,

[1] The year is from Fortescue's endorsement.

[2] Presumably the suit of Mrs. Rackett, or, in view of the remark at the end of the letter, that of her son.

brought me hither at this inconvenient season; and the necessity of serving my next Relation immediately, who will lose a great opportunity of making his fortune much easier if I do [not] furnish him with 150ll in less than a fortnight), will force me back, very incommodiously in this Severe weather. You will therfore See me the sooner, (if that be any pleasure to you, as it will be to me); yet it may be attended with some trouble to yourself; for, if I should be disappointed of the whole or a part of that Sum (by one of my Friend's being out of Town till the Parliament meets again), I may be obliged to borrow it of you. In that case it shall be repayd you next month. I shall be obliged if you tell me whether you can do this, by a line to Twitnam on Sunday next, unless you find me there; which (if I can any way get this crazy body thither) you will. I have good Mr Allen's Services to send you, whom I leave with regrett, & wish I could have stayed to have come together, as he intends to make the same Journey at the end of January: But I cannot be wanting to my Sister's Son on this occasion—I wish you the happyest of Men, this year, & all the year's that you shall live, being very truly | Dear Sir | Your Ever affectionate | Friend & faithful Servant | A. Pope.

Address: To | The Honble | Mr Justice William Fortescue | in Bell-Yard near | Lincolns Inne | London.

Postmark: 2/IA

Endorsement: Mr. Pope | Jan. 1. 1739/40

POPE *to* WARBURTON[1] 4 *January* 1739/40

Egerton 1946

Jan. 4th 1739

Sir,—It is a real truth, that I should have written to you oftener, if I had not a great Respect for you, & owed not a great Debt to you. But it may be no unnecessary thing to let you know that most of my Friends also pay you their thanks; and that Some of the most Knowing, as well as most Candid Judges think me as much beholden to you as I think myself. Your Letters meet from Such with the Approbation they merit, and I have been able to find but two or three very slight Inaccuracies in the whole book, which I have upon their observation alter'd, in an Exemplar, which I keep against a Second Edition.[2] My very uncertain State of health, which is shaken more & more every Winter, drove me to Bath & Bristol 2 months since, & I shall not

[1] Printed by Warburton in 1751.

[2] A second edition of the *Vindication* (so advertised, *Daily Post*, 4 Jan.) was just appearing. In the following summer Warburton added a seventh letter, and a new edition appeared in late August.

return towards London till February. But I have receivd nine or ten Letters from thence of the Success of your Book, which they are earnest to have translated. One of them is begun in France. A French Gentleman about Monsieur Cambis the Ambassadour[1] hath done the greatest part of it here, but I will retard the Impression till I have your directions, or till I can have a pleasure I earnestly wish for, to meet you in Town, where you gave me some hopes you sometimes past a part of the Spring for the best Reason I know of ever visiting it, the Conversation of a few Friends. Pray suffer me to be, what you have Made me, One of them; & let my House have its Share of You: Or if I can any way be Instrumental in accomodating you in Town during your Stay, I have Lodgings and a Library or two in my Disposall: Which I believe I need not offer to a Man to whom All Libraries ought to be open, or to One who wants them so little: but that it is possible you may be as much a Stranger to this Town, as I wish with all my heart I was.

I see by certain Squibs in the Miscellanies that you have as much of the Uncharitable Spirit pour'd out upon you, as the Author you defended from Crousaz. I only wish you gave them no other answer than that of the Sun to the Frogs, Shining out, in your Second Book, & the Completion of your argument. No man is, as he ought to be, more, or so much a Friend to your Merit & Character, as | Sir Your truly obliged & faithful Servant | A. Pope.

Address: To the Reverend | Mr Warburton. | at Mr Robinson | A Bookseller | near Hungerford Market

*POPE *to* FORTESCUE — 5 *January* 1739/40

Harvard University

Jan. 5th 1739

I write to you the moment I receive yours that you may not have the trouble of a Thought more about what I might seem to want. I thank you for your Care to help me by another's means, when it was not in your own immediate power: but as I only meant in mentioning it to you first to give You the Preference, as an Elder Friend, so I do not care to make an Obligation of this sort where I never thought of one. And indeed I never gave a Bond yet in my life; so that I am as much *Free* in that Sense as in All others, and as much an Independent as God made me. I have somewhat more than that sum owing me from two of my acquaintance in Town; but one of 'em is at his Country house, of whom else I had receivd his debt, & drawn upon

[1] Cambis died on 1 Feb. of this year. Silhouette, the only known French translator of the *Vindication*, was not officially of Cambis's entourage, but he is probably intended by Pope's remark.

the other (who sent me word he would pay it readily.) But I have taken it up of Mr Allen,[1] till I return to Town, upon my Promissory Note: So that I have only my thanks to give you for this, which has proved an Unnecessary, Trouble. I long to be at home, in spite of the Rigour of the Season but it is not really, meerly my own good that I consult; for the Reason that would principally carry me to Twitnam & London, is to attend some Friends there; and That which keeps me here yet, is principally Mr Allen's extreme Desire to detain me, till he can bring me back; and some hopes I have that I may serve him a little in laying out his Garden &c. Your Thought of seeing Mrs Blount I will let her know, for I know how kindly She will take it. I wish you would do me the good office I desird to Mrs Jervas (if you can see her) for I would not have her think me a Brute, or not sensible of my old Friend's Testimony of Kindness to me;[2] tho I did not mention it at all to her, thinking it a piece of decency not to do so. My sincerest good wishes attend on Yourself & Family, for as many New years, as you all wish your selves, or one another. The Landlord of this place desires your acceptance of his Real Services. I am always | Dear Sir | Your most faithfull | & affectionate Servant, | A. Pope.

Address: To | the Hon. Mr Justice Fortes-|cue in Bellyard, by | Lincolns Inne | London

Endorsement: Mr Pope | Jan. 5. 1739/40.

Postmark: 7/IA

POPE *to* VISCOUNT POLWARTH[3] 10 *January* 1739/40

Arthur A. Houghton, Jr.

Mr Allens, Bath. Jan. 10. 1739

My Lord,—I have at last prevailed over my Modesty to write to your Lordship. It is a truth I desired one of my Friends to tell you, that the only Reason I did not in all this time, was, that I esteem you so much, I can't tell what to say to you. I can account to myself for the Motives, near or remote, of most of the old & young men's Virtue and Publick Spirit; & I can perceive some Views or other in each: But if you have any, in any degree adequate to the Spirit you act with, I think they must be Very Great; you must be Interested in a higher view than others; and therfore I wish I knew what it is? that I may admire you less, & understand you better.

[1] Presumably this is the £150 mentioned in Pope's letter of 1 Jan., and also in his letter of 22 Jan. 1738/9 to his nephew Michael.

[2] By Jervas's will Pope, if he survived the widow, was to get £1,000.

[3] Alexander, Earl of Marchmont, died in Feb. 1739/40, and Hugh, Viscount Polwarth, to whom this letter is addressed, succeeded his father as 3rd Earl.

You cannot think, how three months of this winter have thinn'd my Correspondences; the Leaves have dropp'd off more & more every week. The world about St James's cou'd not faster forget a retired minister; but I think I can forget that World much easier than He could do. I am learning Horace's Verse, Oblitusque meorum, obliviscendus & illis,[1] but I learn it (what I think the best way) backwards.

In unambitious Silence be my lot,
Yet ne'r a Friend forgetting, till forgot!

My Lord Cornbury will not fall under this Predicament. It is I that don't write to him, for a reason not unlike that which made me silent to you. I don't pay him, because he has trusted me too deep. I am in debt too to Cleland, but tis for another sort of Coin, of a more plentiful kind than Lord Cornbury's: however pray when you see him (that I may be honest, even to farthings) give him my Receipt.

Jan. 10. 1739.

Recd of Mr Cleland the Sum of six pages, quarto, of an obliging Letter for which I hereby acknowledge myself accountable. | A. Pope

Now my Lord, to the whole business of this letter; I only wish to know, you, & all you love are well; and particularly that Lord Marchmont is as well as yourself: I wish him almost as young too, (deducting only those Years without which he could not have begot you.) I am with the sincerest respect, and warmest affection, | My Lord | Your most faithfull & oblig'd Servant, | A. Pope.

Endorsement: Mr. Pope to | Lord Polwarth | Jany 10—1739 | Bath.

*POPE *to* DR. OLIVER[2] [11 *January* 1739/40]

Harvard University

Friday, the 11th

Sir,—Since the Congelation of all my Faculties by this Frost, you will not wonder that I am not un-thawed before Eleven in a morning, or I had been with you at Ten this day. I find myself less encumberd by my Planetary Crust, than with this Atmospherical Shirt over it; however I will certainly, if I retain any Locomotive Powers, bring them both to you on Munday early, & try whether I can soften the one with Butter, & dissolve the other in Tea? I am, with Serious Respect & Obligation, | Dear Sir | Your faithfull humble Servant | A. Pope.

Address: To Dr Oliver, | at | Bath.
Endorsement: Pope.

[1] *Epistles*, I. xi. 9.

[2] It is impossible to date this innocuous note surely. The bracketed date superscribed is probable; so is Friday, 11 Dec. 1741, when also Pope was at Bath amidst congelation.

*POPE *to* DR. OLIVER[1] [? *Early* 1740]

The Hyde Collection

Saturday

Sir,—I am obliged to you for your attention to my Affairs. The Name of the Captain is Mr Francis, who is to be heard of at Mr Ruth's, in Puddinglane near the Tower.

Mrs Allen will be very glad of the Favour Mrs Bonoevrier offers her, on Monday: You must not exclude me from the Company, as I have a Respect for a Person of such a Character as Mr Glover gives me of this Lady: Otherwise you know, I leave Mr Allen a free Parlour on these occasions.

I am with all affectionate regard | Dear Sir | Your most obedient | humble Servant | A. Pope.

Address: To Dr Oliver, at | Bath.

Endorsement: Pope.

POPE *to* WARBURTON[2] 17 *January* [1739/40]

Egerton 1946

Sir,—Tho' I writ to you two posts agoe, I ought to acknowledge now a New & unexpected favour, of your Remarks on the fourth Epistle;[3] which (tho' I find by yours attending them they were sent last month) I receivd but this morning. This was occasiond by no fault of Mr Robinson,[4] but the neglect I believe of the person to whose care he consigned them. I have been full three months about Bath & Bristol, endeavouring to amend a Complaint, which more or less has troubled me all my Life: I hope the Regimen this has obliged me to, will make the remainder of it more Philosophical, & improve my Resignation to part with it at last. I am preparing to return home, & shall then revise what my French Gentleman has done, & add this to it. He is the same person who translated the Essay into Prose, which Mr Crousaz should have profited by; who, I am really afraid, when I lay the circumstances all together, was moved to his Proceeding in so very unreasonable a Way, by Some Malice, either of his own, or some

[1] This letter is perhaps impossible to place in time. It is written from Prior Park, apparently, where (first assumption) Mrs. Allen will be glad to see Mrs. Bonoevrier on Monday. Pope also will be glad to see her as a friend of 'Leonidas' Glover. Another major assumption concerns Captain Francis. If one imagines that he is a ship captain (possibly of the *Happy Couple*, which in April is to bring materials for Pope's grotto), one may assume that Pope before leaving Bath in February arranged with Oliver for shipments of stone by sea.

[2] Warburton printed this letter in 1751.

[3] Presumably an advance copy of *A Seventh Letter, Which finishes the Vindication of Mr. Pope's Essay on Man*. The letter was advertised somewhat later in the newspapers.

[4] Since the bookseller Robinson died 18 Jan., it is possible that an illness may have delayed the pamphlet.

Other's; tho' I was very willing at first to impute it to Ignorance or Prejudice.

I see nothing to be added to your Work; only some Commendatory Deviations from the Argument itself, in my favour, I ought to think might be omitted.

I must repeat my urgent desire to be previously acquainted with the precise Time of your Visit to London; that I may have the pleasure to meet a Man in the Manner I would, whom I must esteem one of the greatest of my Benefactors. I am with the most grateful and Affectionate Regard, | Sir | Your faithfull Servant | A. Pope.

Bath. | Jan. 17th

Address: To the Revd | Mr Warburton

*POPE *to* THE EARL OF BURLINGTON

19 *January* [1739/40.]

Chatsworth

Jan. 19th Bath

My Lord,—You will not wonder I have been so long no man can tell where, but how will you wonder when I tell you I have been all this while in one place? How I have constantly rememberd my Friends, I know very well; and how they have remembered me, I know also. I never was so quiet from Letters in all my life; and I now write only to tell them when I am coming to interrupt their peace again. It is high time the Town should say, *He is not dead, but Sleepeth.* As your Lordship is one of the very first I shall haunt, this notice is but necessary to you. My Lady Burlington needs not be at the trouble to keep the Gazetteers of these 3 months past for me, for I have constantly read them here, & intend at my return to plead it as great Service & Suffering, for the Government.

The truth is, my Lord, I have stayed to do myself all the Good I could, having too long neglected the Care of One, whom I take to be (as the world goes) an honest kind of man; but one, who, like other well meaning people, has been much hurt by The Wickedness of the World he has past thro', & dealt with. My Complaints are manifold, & of a sort that very much wanted the Waters of Regeneration. I can no way so decently express them as in Dr Shadwells Dialect: The Kitchen, Backside, & Yard requird Scowring, & I hope to have done it so effectually, as to present you at my Return with a most Clean Creature.

If his Majestys Principal Painter (for so I read again in My Paper, the Gazeteer)[1] would follow my example here for as many months,

[1] Early in Jan. 1740 it was announced that Kent was to succeed Jervas as His Majesty's Face Painter.

(for so many at least it will take) to cleanse his Pencil, & purify his Pallat, from all that greasy mixture & Fatt Oyl they have contracted, he would paint like a Raphael, & look like an Angelo; whereas if he proceeds in his Carnality & Carnivoracity, he must expect not to imitate Raphael in any thing but his untimely End.

It is not fit I should give my Service to Lady B. in this filthy Letter, & therefore I conclude (with the sincerest wishes for hers & your health & happiness) My Lord your Ever faithfull | humble Servant | A. Pope.

*POPE *to* FORTESCUE — 23 *January* 1739/40

Harvard University

I thought of seeing you about this time, but Mr Allen not being able to Settle his Post-Accounts so soon, & resolving to accompany me, I am kept longer, & so once more inquire of your Welfare, which no man has wishd more truly or more constantly for many years than myself.

I once more thank you for your Readiness in endeavoring to accomodate me in the Sudden Want I had of 150ll. But you mistook me in imagining my Unwillingness to enter into Bond proceeded from the Conceit that a man is *less bound* by his Note, (which every honest Man, I hope, thinks equally binding) It was only an Awkwardness, as I told you, of fancying myself the less a Free Man for *Any* sort of Bonds; to which your answer is a very just one, that Men as to these as well as other Bonds, are apt to fancy themselves Freer than they are. But Say what you will, of these or other Bonds, I will venture to affirm No man loves them, but for Interest, & I am still as loth to be bound, as many are to be blooded, the first time; because I would at least reserve it for a Greater Occasion, than a Loan of one month.

I should be sorry to be detaind longer here, as if it should thaw, tis to be feard I must, and yet I would almost rather suffer any Confinement than *hear* of the Poor perishing round me by Want & Cold. I say *hear* of it, for I *See* nothing of it in this Place; the Good Man of it suffers no misery near him; He actually employs on this occasion some hundreds, (all the neighbouring Parishes can send him) of labouring Men, & has opend a new Quarry on purpose which he has yet no sort of occasion for. Whoever is lame, or any way disabled, he gives weekly allowances to the wife or children: Besides large supplies of other kinds to other Poor. God made this Man rich, to shame the Great; and wise, to humble the learned. I envy none of you in Town the Honours you may have received at Court, or from the Higher

Powers: I have past this Christmas with the Most Noble Man of England.[1]

I thank you for mentioning what I desird to Mrs Jervas. A Scruple has risen in my mind, upon your telling me you could not with any Conveniency act as an Executor to Him; whether my having namd you in the same Circumstance (as you very kindly gave me leave to do some years since) might not, now, be less convenient to you than formerly? Our long Friendship certainly justifies all manner of freedome & unreserve. I have given you perpetual instances how much I think so, & therfore deal plainly with me in this.[2] The other person I nam'd is one not naturally very active, Mr Bethel, but I believe, mine being only personal Estate will give little trouble, for I have no Debts in the world.

This is not a place to afford news, the best is what you will think such, that I am well, & that Mr A. is so, & we are both with Sincerity of heart yours | Dear Sir, believe me | Your most faithful | affectionate Servant | A. Pope.

Jan. 23, 1739

Address: To the Honble | Mr Justice Fortescue | at his house in | Bell Yard | nr Lincolns Inne

Endorsement: Mr Pope. | Jan. 23, 1739/40

Postmark: PENY POST PAYD WSA

*HENRY LINTOT *to* POPE — 29 *January* 1739/40

Egerton 1951

London Jan. 29. 1739

Sir,—I thank you for your advice about the Odyssey and shall consult you before I reprint. You may have 25 of the 1st vol. LP. when you please and I will take Second Volumes for them.

as to the affair of Mr Osborne,[3] I exchanged all the Iliads in large

[1] Pope's glowing tribute may well remind one that Allen seemed equally worthy to Henry Fielding, and became the prototype of Squire Alworthy in *Tom Jones*. In this same month Dr. Oliver writes to his friend Borlase concerning Pope and Allen: 'They are extremely happy in each other: the one feeling great joy in the good heart and strong sense of his truly generous host; while the other, with the most pleasing attention, drinks in rivers of knowledge continually flowing from the lipps of his delightful stranger' (*The Quarterly Review*, cxxxix [1875], 380–1).

[2] Fortescue was not eventually named as executor, nor is he mentioned in Pope's later will.

[3] This letter evidently answers inquiries made by Pope concerning the astonishing outburst of advertisements during this month in which T. Osborne offers for sale copies of Pope's *Iliad*. The advertisements began: 'There being a very small Number left of Mr. Pope's Homer's Iliads, in six Volumes, Folio, in large and small Paper, as also in Quarto, large Paper. . . .' These advertisements appeared in the early months of 1740 in *The London Daily Post*, *The London Evening Post*, *The Daily Gazetteer* several times (especially in January) in each paper. Pope naturally was curious to know how quarto copies, especially, should be available, since the quarto edition of the *Iliad* was his property for distribution only among his subscribers. The confused and at times illegible notes that Pope affixed to this letter are

and small folio for other Books but not one Quarto. Upon Enquiry he has but one Set of the Subscription papers, the others that he advertises in Quarto, are the Large paper folio, cut down to a Quarto size with Ogilby's Cuts cut down likewise. when I sold the odd Volumes of the Iliad to Mr Gilliver, upon his Complaining of a hard bargain I gave him Liberty to reprint the first Volume, in Quarto, by which means he has several Sets, and in the Title it is mentioned, printed for me and sold by Gilliver &c. but the Initial Letters and Headpieces and Tail pieces are not exactly the same. I sold a large Number of the small folios, which could be worth your purchasing. I thank you for speaking to Mr Cole.[1] My Mother is very well and gives her Service to you. I hope Bath has been of service to you and am Sir your Obliged Servant | H. Lintot

Address: To Alexander Pope Esqr | at Mr Ralph Allen's at | Bath | Somersetshire

Postmark: 29/IA

[*On this cover, in Pope's hand, follows:*]

see Gillivers assignment Lords.
Silend: The dunciad, qu. of Lintot, Gillivers Property is expir'd or expires next year ~~or this~~ not to purchase it—
Tell him of the Prohibition of *any* Quartos so that what he did to Gilliver was first Breach of Covenant, to whom he sold many Quarto Iliads as I learnt by this Letter. Interrogate Gilliver—how many Sets?

Lintot here says He gave Gill. leave to print up first vols of Quarto Iliads, & he gave him copper plates to them—Contrary to articles.

This Letter of Lintots first discoverd to me that Fraud.

[*On two other independent leaves occur the following additional notes in Pope's hand:*]

The Pastorals, & Merchants Tale, being

What I printed by Mr *Tonson Senr* is included in the First Clause of the act of Q. Anne. "That all copies sold before 1710, shall remain the Property of Author or Purchaser no longer than 21 years from thence." Those 21 years expired in 1731. so that it is no man's Property, but common.

What I printed by Mr *Tonson junr* is included in the Second Clause, "that is, to revert to the author after 14 years from the Day of Publication." Sapho to Phaon was published in 1712. the first time, in Ovids Epistles; & the Wife of Bath's Prologue in Steel's Miscellany, 1714—The fourteen years of the first expir'd in 1726, of the second in 1728. & the property is therfore reverted to Me from that time, unless I covenanted to the contrary; which will appear by the writing I gave. & by which I am ready to be determined.

In the meantime, Mr Lintot is not to give the Proportion of sheets to

reprinted as significant of the difficulty attending early copyright procedure as well as of Pope's later intention to sue in chancery for his rights to *The Dunciad*.

[1] Nathaniel Cole, solicitor to the Stationers' Company.

either Mr Tonson or to Me; but to see which of us has the Right, by my agreement with Mr Tonson. which I have really forgot, but believe could only be *pro tempore*, because the Mony I receivd was a very triffling Sum, no way proportiond to a Perpetuity—and

turn over

and[2] because[1] further I never alienated, intentionally, any Copy for ever, without expressly giving a Deed in forms, to witness & that the Copy right was to subsist after the Expiration of the 14 years in Queen Ann's Act, which *then* was understood generally to be the Case, unless covenanted to the Contrary. In testimony of this, all my assignments to Mr Lintot for perpetuity, will be found expressly articled for.

2. NB. A Covenant ~~subsisted~~ as to the *Odyssey* that none should be printed in 4°. or, with the like copper ornaments, within ten years, which expird in the year 1733. on penalty of 50ll.
1. A Covenant from Lintot, Senr never to print any Books of the Iliad on the same, or any royal paper. or with *any Copper ornaments* except the 750 which he deliverd to me as my sole property.

Qu: the first Cov'nant as to the Iliad being *never* to print more why was the second Covenant as to the Odyssey limited to *ten years* except Mr L. intended to print up Odysses to make up sets of Iliads he had by him, tho not openly vended?

And Qu: why the Copper plates to the Odyssey (tho payd for by Mr Pope) were by the second covenant, to *be kept in Lintots hands*? like the first Copper plates to the Iliad which Lintot pay'd for? Of what use were the first Plates to Lintot. when he was to print no more Iliads. or the second unless he intended to have it in his power to print up such Sets tho unknown to Mr P. Wats of the Odys. Bowyer what number of Iliad above 750 were printed in 4°.

Interrogate Osborn. & Interrogate Lintot if no Odysses in 4° were sold by Lintot within the ten years.

Bought of Mr Lintot by Gilliver

Quarto's about 75 Setts all but first vols. sold by Gilliver at 15s a vol.

He payd two hundred thirty two pd for the whole Quarto's, & folios he valu'd the Quartos only of the Purchace, & accounts the folios at very little.

Quere of Lintot if he has no Setts of the Iliad 4°? all my Property.

Bowyer printed all along of the Iliad but 660, 4° in stead of 750 articled to be mine.

Watts printed of the Odysses, 750 all along, mine also.

*POPE *to* HUGH BETHEL — 18 *February* [1739/40]

Egerton 1948

London. Feb. 18.

I was about to write to you, & give you some farther account of my self, as well as enquire of you, before I left Bath. When I was made to think you would be in London before me, my Lady Codrington being gone thither, after which I concluded to have found you here. I stayed till last week, & got hither not quite starved,[1] and have been ever since in Pain for your Journey, who I know can bear Cold but ill. I am now told you fear it so much that you shall not set out till the Severity of the Weather relax, and therfore I must tell you once more how unable I am to forget you, & how desirous to be made certain of your present state of health in so trying a Season. Mrs Blount has had many Colds but no severe one, and is obliged to live more at home than can be any other way Comfortable to her but by the Warmth, which is all that's Good in her Fireside. As for her Sister, she is kept warm enough by her Passions. ⌜(Since I came to London, I am not so much in Spirits, nor in the same Quiet, as at Bath. The Irregular hours of Dining (for as to Nights, I keep the same) already have disorderd my Stomach, & bring back that Heaviness & Languor upon me after dinner, which I was almost entirely free from. Tho I still continue to make Water my ordinary drink, with as little Mixture of Wine as before. I am determind to fix my dining to Two a clock, tho I dine by myself, & comply afterwards with the Importunities & Civilities of Friends in *Attending*, not *Partaking* their Dinners.⌝[2]

The Death of the Earl of S.[3] has affected everybody very sensibly, but those who had the longest & greatest obligations to him. He has left a Testimony of his Friendship & good opinion of our Friend Cleland, by a Legacy of a hundred a year to him & his wife, or the Survivor of them. ⌜Another Testimony of the same kind has been left me, by an Old Friend, from whom I had not the least imagination of such a thing, Mr Jervas;[4] But it takes no effect, unless I out live his Widow, which is not very likely, however I think him absolutely in the right in giving nothing from her, to whom he owed almost every thing, & the sum is considerable, viz. a thousand pound It is the first Legacy I ever had, & I hope I shall never have another at the expence of any man's life, who would think so kindly of me.⌝[5]

Pray make me certain of your health, unless you see us speedily, & assure Mr Moyzer of my Services. I have something I think material to speak to you, but do not care to trust it by post. Believe dear Sir, no man is with more constant Esteem and affection, | Your faithfull & ever | mindful Servant, | A. Pope.

Address: To Hugh Bethel Esq. at | Beswick near | Beverley in | Yorkshire.
Frank: Free G Lyttelton
Postmark: 19/FE

[1] i.e. not quite frozen to death!

[2] Quoted in Ruffhead, p. 501.

[3] The Earl of Scarborough committed suicide on 29 Jan. Pope does not seem to have been among his intimates, but his close friends Cleland and Lord Chesterfield were much grieved by the circumstances of his death.

[4] Jervas had died 3 Nov. 1739. Pope did not outlive Mrs. Jervas.

[5] This part of the paragraph was quoted by Ruffhead, p. 190.

LORD AND LADY ORRERY *to* POPE[1] 23 *February* 1739/40

Harvard University

Caledon: February 23d: 1739–40.

Sir,—You may look upon this as an Epistle from the Dead: We are buried to the World, and pass our time in as much tranquility, and in as much ignorance of what is doing in the great neighbouring Island as if we were stretched at full Length in our Coffins. Some Life indeed we have still remaining, just enough to remember the happy Hours we enjoyed in England: particularly at Twick'nam: You must allow our Gratitude to break out now and then in a Letter: and must forgive an Interruption occasioned by the warmest Wishes, tho' in the coldest Climate, for your Health and Welfare during the late severe Season our Fears and Anxieties for you, have been great. The strongest Constitutions and the most robust Frames have been shatterred, and unable to withstand the Keeness of the Frost: in pity tell us then how you have escaped. a Letter directed to Caledon near Tynan in the County of Tyrone,[2] Ireland, will reach two of the faithfullest Servants you have in the World.

The Dean has lately had another Fitt of the Gout, but is now in perfect Health.[3] We hear often of him, but seldom from him. The Lady's[4] Power (one may say it without danger of hurting one part of his Reputation) encreases daily: at night her Influence ends: that is She retires to her Lodging, and the Dean to his Bed: but returning Light brings her back to her Station, which she quits not, till, as She poetically expresses it (for now She scarce deigns to call for small Beer in Prose) the Goddess Luna, whom She once worshipped as Lucina, borrows Light from her Brother Phoebus to guide her Votaries to their peacefull Home.—Of other People we know little and enquire less.—the fatal Catastrophe of the E. of Sc—[5] has reached these Greenland Territories, but the Name of the Heiress who was run away with, and the running Translator at Charing Cross, will in all likelyhood like other mysteries of State remain unknown to the Caledonians for ever. Let Mr Pope live and enjoy his Health, Let him sometimes think of us, just to say he is well, and we will sow our Potatoes, and spin our Flax with all imaginable Content, and without the least grain of Envy or Complaint of the Age we live in: for be assured, Sir, we are with the utmost Truth and Respect, | your most obliged | & most obedient humble Servants. | Orrery. | Margaret Orrery.

[1] The entire transcript, with a heading 'To Alexander Pope Esq.', is in Lord Orrery's hand.

[2] Actually Tynan is in Co. Armagh.

[3] Lord Orrery for once is not alarmist as to Swift's condition, but he still continues to denigrate Mrs. Whiteway—of whom in other letters from the Orrerys to her they seem to be fond.

[4] Mrs. Whiteway.

[5] The Earl of Scarborough.

POPE *to* DR. OLIVER 25 *February* [1739/40]

The European Magazine, xx (1791), 409

Feb. 25th [1740.]

I am obliged to you present and absent. Your enquiries after me are as kind as your offices towards me, and your constant memory of every thing that can please me, leaves me nothing to wish, but an opportunity of shewing the same attention to any thing that might be serviceable to you.

Be pleas'd to tell the lady whose love letter you enclosed that I am sorry she has plac'd her affections so unfortunately. The person who is the object of them was (as you know) in a very languid state at Bath; it's true as Mr Pierce[1] inform'd you, that he got alive to Town & shewd there the first week some new signs of life & symptoms of a Resuscitation. But he relaps'd immediately, became comotose, & a sudden paralytic took away, first his Verse, & after his Prose side. In short between seven and eight on Friday Evening he became deaf to the voice of the charmer and a few hours after upon the application of a Ladys warm hand it appear'd that the Torpor was general. In a word he dyed & some people who have read a case in Dr Cheyne affirm he did it on set purpose.

Since his Burial (at Twitnam) he has been seen some times in Mines and Caverns & been very troublesome to those who dig Marbles & Minerals: If ever he has walk'd above ground, He has been (like the Vampires in Germany) such a terror to all sober & innocent people, that many wish a stake were drove thro' him to keep him quiet in his Grave. The Lady may therefore be assur'd he is no longer a subject for any thing but an Epitaph. | I am Dear Sir with all respect, | Your faithfull obedient Servant | A. Pope.

Address: To Dr. Oliver at | Bath.

Frank: Free. | Bathurst.

POPE *to* HUGH, EARL OF MARCHMONT

29 *February* 1739/40

Arthur A. Houghton, Jr.

Feb. 29. 1740.

My Lord,—If God had not given this Nation to Perdition, He would not have removed from its Service the Men, whose Capacity & Integrity alone could have saved it. But if you despaired of it before, you should the less regret your present Situation; for I dare say, no Vanity, but the sole View of doing good, was your Motive of Action. You are

[1] Pierce was a surgeon at Bath. He seems to have accompanied Allen and Pope to London, and has now returned to Bath.

reduced to Philosophy, as Bolingbroke was before you; but you can animate, you can supply, you can better, a better Age than this, & prepare happier Scenes for the Coming Generation. I'll answer for it, the World will have you again, if ever the World grows worthy of you, and whenever Providence finds Us to merit your help, it will put you in a capacity of helping us.

I wish to see you while I may; I am afraid of Losing You, as I have lost Those whom I most wished to have lived with & for. What hour shall I meet Dr King to morrow? It is only a Modest Periphrasis for asking, what hours you can allow to one who honours you truly?

Your Lordship's ever | faithfull, obliged Servant | A. Pope.

Address: To the Rt Hon. Ld Polwarth

[1]*Endorsement*: Feby 29. 1740 | A. [Alexander] Ld Mt | had just died | but he writes to H. Ld Mt | as Ld Pth

*POPE *to* WILLIAM BORLASE[2] 9 *March* [1739/40]

Yale University

Twickenham, March 9. | 1740.

Sir,—I ought to take this Occasion of thanking you for so obliging a Testimony as you are giving me of your Inclination to assist me; And surely the warm and particular Manner in which you do me this favor, deserv'd a more ready Acknowledgment. I am as much indebted to your Letters to Dr Oliver, as to me, upon this subject; but I was willing at the same time that I thanked you, to give you an account of my receipt of the Box, & of the Choice I made of the Materials. But I find this morning, (the first day that It arrived here) that your Bounty, like that of Nature, confounds all choice. But as I would imitate rather her Variety, than make Ostentation of what we call her Riches; I shall be satisfy'd if you make your next Cargo consist more of such Ores or Sparrs as are beautiful, & not too difficult to be come at, than of the Scarce & valuable kinds. Indeed the 2 or 300 of Cubes of Mundick which you mention, might find a place luminous enough in one part of my Grotto, and are much the finest Ornaments it can receive. It will want nothing to complete it, but Your Instruction as to the Position, and the Direction of the Sparrs & Ores in the Mine, for I would be glad to make the Place resemble Nature in all her workings, & entertain a Sensible, as well as dazzle a Gazing,

[1] Alexander, Earl of Marchmont, died on 27 Feb., and though his son is at once the 3rd Earl, Pope addresses him by his courtesy title.

[2] The Rev. William Borlase, D.D. (1695–1772), was like his friend and relation, Dr. Oliver, and like Ralph Allen, a Cornishman. He was a well-known antiquarian, gardener, and collector of minerals and crystals. Through Oliver he became Pope's benefactor with regard to the grotto. See Nichols, *Lit. Anec.* v. 291–303, and *The Quarterly Review*, cxxxix (1875), 367–95, where this letter and some others are printed.

Spectator. The Stalactites are appropriated to the roof, & the Marbles (I think) of various colors to the pavement.

I extremely wish one Day to have the pleasure of seeing You Sir, in the Place which you are contributing to make so agreeable: And I hope you will take the surest way to prevent your Favours from being lost upon me; which is what we desire of Providence, that He who bestows them will direct us how to make a right Use of them. I am | Sir, | Your most obliged & | faithfull humble Servant | A. Pope.

As to your kind desire that I should acquaint you what Quantity I want, I have indeed but few, not above a Hamper or 2: from others I expect more, but none so good as these of yours.

Wm: Borlase.

*POPE *to* DR. OLIVER 10 *March* [1739/40]

Harvard University

Twitnam. March 10.

I cannot tell how to thank you for perpetual Tokens of your kind Memory of me. I receiv'd last week the Barbado's waters, & this week the Specimens of Ores &c from Dr Borlase. I have written to him, & charged Myself upon him to Your account. The day I receive what he can send me, I begin my Work, & hope it will be the best Imitation of Nature I ever made. In these sort of works we may pretend to understand her better than in her Animal, much less in her Rational Productions. I beg you Dear Sir, to continue to rank me with your Friends, & sometimes to tell me so, till I can renew the pleasures of your Conversation at Bath. I am always, | Your most faithful | & oblig'd Servant | A. Pope.

Pray desire Mrs Oliver to forgive my Endeavours to turn her out of her House.

[*On the back (outside) of the note:*] I think you have not this Edition of my things, which contains every Line that is mine.

Address: To Dr Oliver, at | Bath

DR. OLIVER *to* POPE 19 *March* 1739/40

Sotheby Sale, 5 November 1928

[An untraced letter sold in 1928 to Maggs Bros. is quoted in the sale catalogue as saying, 'I dine tomorrow upon the Hill[1] with our good Friends, where I shall see the little green Chair, shall try by all the Strength of Imagination to replace you in it.' The letter (or draft of a letter) thanks Pope for the gift of his *Works*, mentioned by Pope in his letter of 10 March, and promises minerals for the grotto.]

[1] With the Allens at Prior Park—where Pope has his own undersized chair.

*POPE *to* ALLEN 25 *March* [1740]

Egerton 1947

Twitnam. March 25.

Your first Letter gave me the Joy to hear you was safe, & in the Enjoyment again of all you hold so dear, & deserve so well. May Providence ever continue it to You, & to the Partaker of it, whose happiness & yours is the same.

Your Second shews me how much in every instance I am in your thoughts, in your hastening the shipping of the Rock-work. I know not by what accident the Bristol water is not yet arrived, which I find the want of, notwithstanding I drink the best in London. I have been confined there almost ever since you went, & lament the Difference I find between the Life I lead here, & that which I led with you. My Quiet & My Health suffer alike in so bad an Exchange.

I am but this day got home, in the hope of staying a week intire. Mr Hooke will joyn me to morrow, & here is Mr Roberts[1] as usual. The weather gives me Cold upon Cold, & I cannot attend my works in planting. I am sensible now, that your Proposal to defer Mr Omer's Coming[2] till Whitsuntide was but reasonable, for so long it will be, before I can have all my Materials ready, & the severe Northwinds would kill me, with a Damp in my Grotto as fatal as those in the Mines, if I presumd to work there now. The unwholesome Season has carried off many, & two more in the Familys of my nearest Acquaintance have dyed last week. So that half my time is spent in the House of Mourning——I've seen little Felicity, & little Enjoyment any where, since I saw Widcombe; where I hartily hope it will long be found, & daily increase. Adieu dear Sir, & let Mrs A. know no one can be more her Friend, for no one is more Yours.

Address: To Ralph Allen Esqr at | Widcomb near | Bath. | Somersetshire.
Postmark: (illegible)

POPE *to* ROBERT NUGENT[3] 26 *March* [1740]

Yale University

Twitenham, March 26.

Sir,—When you did me the Favour to acquaint me of Mrs Whiteway's Offer, I thought it not necessary to give You a Trouble, which

[1] Pope's next-door neighbour was Henry Robartes, 3rd Earl of Radnor. 'Mr. Roberts' is doubtless a relative, possibly the cousin John, who in 1741 succeeded as 4th Earl.

[2] Omer, apparently one of Allen's gardeners, will be mentioned more than once in letters following.

[3] Robert Nugent, who in 1776 was created Earl Nugent, and who married Pope's friend Mrs. Knight and assumed her maiden name of Craggs, here enters upon correspondence with Pope. Mrs. Whiteway seems to have written Nugent that she wishes to return to Pope more of his letters to Swift. The wish drags on throughout the year and is mentioned in several letters.

I imagined would be less so to my Lord Orrery. But upon reflection, I believe He is not upon the best terms with the Lady:[1] at least as She chose to propose this to your selfe, it may be better to apply by the same Person to whom she mention'd it: And for my own part, I assure you Sir, you are not the last Man I would owe a Favour to. I shall be therfore truly obliged to you, if you write as you proposed, & thank her in my name for securing those papers against all disagreable accidents; If she sends them, by some honest hand, to You, I shall know they are as safe as in my own custody.

Tho I have many Poetical Thanks[2] to pay you, I must particularize Your Ode to Lord Marchmont, both the Design & Execution of which manifest that Spirit, which once animated the Heads & Hearts of Poets, & for which your Odes, like those of Alcæus, will challenge Esteem, as well as Praise. I am | Sir, | Your most obliged | & obedient humble | Servant | A. Pope.

I may remember Mrs Nugent as one of the Companions of my younger & gayer Days, & sigh to be able to live on with them. But we are no longer Creatures of the Same Element: They are all Air & Fire, & I am Earth: however I admire their Flights, & am their Servant.

POPE *to* THE EARL OF ORRERY[3] 27 *March* 1740

The Pierpont Morgan Library

My Lord & my Lady Orrery,—So very obliging a Memorial, of your joint Goodness & Condescention, to One who honours you for those Qualities for which you love one another, ought never to be forgot, much less to be un-acknowleged. But so it happens, that I rather shall prove my retaining the Sense of it long, than my confessing it readily. Indeed I never receivd it till above a month after the date, having been myself upon a wild Winter Ramble (not unlike a Scythian Expedition) for near three months, essaying the Virtue of Waters when they were almost Ice: However between Bristol and Bath, I kept a moderate share of health & heat, during the Severe Season: And since Cold will not kill me, as it has done all our Bays, I look upon myself as an Ever-green of a stronger kind, than those which Emblematize our common Poets, & dye generally in twenty winters. I will

[1] Certainly from Orrery's letters to Pope one would gather that his lordship was not upon good terms with Mrs. Whiteway; but other letters indicate friendly relations.

[2] In 1739 Nugent had published a volume of *Odes and Epistles*, and for this volume, one judges, Pope is thanking him.

[3] Pope here answers the Orrery letter of 23 Feb. His answer should be associated with the preceding letter to Nugent. Orrery, being in Ireland, might seem a natural channel through which to recover Pope's letters from Mrs. Whiteway; but as Pope told Nugent, Orrery seemed evidently not on the best of terms with the lady. Pope was wrong in this opinion.

venture to prophecy, your Loves will as much out-last those of others, as your Myrtles in some part of Ireland out-flourish ours, & prosper in native Air & Sun, beyond any which owe their growth to Artificial Fires. It would be the most advantageous of all the Comparisons with which Poets ever flatterd themselves, if I could imagine my Laurels as durable, as bright, & as unchanging, as your Myrtles: But I am thus much better than a Vulgar Poet, that I do not flatter either others or myself, in particular neither my Lady Orrery, nor your Lordship. Yours & her Virtue & Temper will be happy, without such Aids to make you think well of your selves, as none can admit who know themselves: Even in the Down-hill-walk of Old age. These two Props will support you in Good Sense & Good Humour. God forbid that even I should live to find a Flatterer a necessary Help to Old age! But if ever I do, it shall never be a Woman, so poetically mad, so romantically impertinent, as the Lady you describe to be about a Friend of ours. The Gout itself is a better Companion, & I think I should be much less inclined to curse & swear at that, than the other.

I cannot be quite pleased that your Lordship expresses so much Pleasure in your amusements in Ireland. Surely England ought to have a Share in you; she cannot spare one honest Peer, as she is now circumstanced. I have often wished to see that Kingdome, for the sake of my dear, old Friend, Swift, & no other, till you took yourself away. My mortal Fear in visiting him, was, to be choak'd with Feasting & Poetry, and it is now certain every Dish would be serv'd up to me in Verse in his family. But with you my Lord, & with my Lady, I might hope to breathe Christian Air, & hear sober Prose; wherfore I am really now tempted strongly to wish myself with you & with Him together. Pray when you see or write to him, let him know my Constant Remembrance, Esteem, & Love of him. And believe me, my Lord, no man with more gratitude receives, or with more Joy will cultivate, every Demonstration of your Friendship, than | yours & Lady Orrery's | most faithfull & obliged Servant | A. Pope.

Twitenham March 27. 1740.

I lately saw the Duchess of B.[1] who looks upon yourself as her best friend, & spoke with great Esteem of Lady O. She has been ill of a Fever this winter, but is well recover'd.

I intend to write to the Dean, but I wish he knew that I did so from Bath 6 weeks agoe.[2] It is perfectly grievous, to have the common proofs of affection between Friends pryed into, & often stopt, by the Clerks of the Post.

[3]*Endorsement* (on p. 4 of the text): Mr Pope. March 29 | 1740.

[1] The Duchess of Buckingham. [2] Pope's letter has not come down to us.

[3] Orrery's endorsement of 29 Mar. is an error: Pope's 27 is clear.

ROBERT NUGENT *to* MRS WHITEWAY[1] 2 *April* 1740

1768 (Deane Swift)

Bath, April 2, 1740.

Madam,—I had not until very lately an opportunity of letting Mr. *Pope* know his obligations to you; of which he is very sensible, and has desired me to beg that you will remit to me, by a safe hand, whatever letters of his are now in your possession. I shall be in town next week; so that you may be pleased to direct to me, by the first convenient opportunity, at my house in *Dover-street*, *London.* I am, Madam, with great esteem, your most humble and obedient servant, | R. N.

My compliments to Mr. and Mrs. *Swift.*[2] I shall say nothing of the picture, because I am sure you remember it. I must beg that you will let Mr. *Bindon*[3] know I would have the picture no more than a head upon a three-quarter cloth, to match one which I now have of Mr. *Pope.*

POPE *to* WARBURTON[4] 16 *April* 1740

Egerton 1946

You could not give me more pleasure than by your Short Letter, which acquaints me that I may hope to see you so soon. Let us meet, like Men who have been many years acquainted with each other, & whose Friendship is not to begin, but Continue. All Forms should be past, when people know each others mind so well: I flatter my self you are a Man after my own heart, who seeks Content only from within, & says to Greatness, Tuas habeto tibi Res, egomet habebo meas. But as it is but just, your other Friends should have some part of you, I insist on my making You the first Visit, in London, & thence after a few days, to carry you to Twitenham, for as many as you can afford me.[5] If the Press be to take up any part of your time, the sheets may be brought you hourly thither by my Waterman, and you will have more leisure to attend to any thing of that sort than in Town. I believe also I have most of the Books you can want, or can easily borrow them. I earnestly desire a Line may be left at Mr Robinsons

[1] See Pope to Nugent, 26 Mar., for the occasion of this letter.

[2] Mrs. Deane Swift was Mrs. Whiteway's daughter.

[3] Francis Bindon painted at least four portraits of Swift. See Swift's *Works* (ed. T. Scott), xii. 24. In question here is the third portrait, not yet painted. About it William Dunkin later wrote his *Epistle to Robert Nugent, Esq.*

[4] Printed by Warburton in 1751.

[5] There are varying stories of the first meeting of these two, but this letter states Pope's plan, which seems to have been carried out. The meeting took place less than ten days after this writing. See Pope's *Works* (ed. Warton), ix (1797), 342 n., and J. S. Watson, *Life of Warburton* (1863), p. 183.

where, & when, I shall call upon you? which I will daily enquire for, whether I chance to be here, or in the Country. Believe me Sir with the Truest regard, & the sincerest Wish to deserve yours, | Your faithfull, & | affectionate Servant | A. Pope.

Spring Garden,[1] | April the 16th 1740.

Address: To | The Revd Mr Warburton

POPE *to* SAMUEL GERRARD[2] — 18 *April* [1740]

Arthur A. Houghton, Jr.

April the 18th

Sir,—I was sorry not to be able to wait on you when you sent me Dr Swifts Letter: I was at Dinner with my Lord Burlington, & a great deal of Company, at His Tab[le.] I could only reply, that as soon as I returned to London, I would receive the pleasure of seeing a Friend of Dean Swift's. In the meantime, Sir, I send this to my Lodging to be deliverd you which is all I can do till my Return from Windsor Forest,[3] & if you leave a line to acquaint me where you may be found, I will do myself that Satisfaction, in five or six days. I am, with all respect, | Sr Your most humble Servant | A. Pope.

*POPE *to* ALLEN[4] — 19 *April* [1740]

Egerton 1947

April 19th

Dear Sir,—

For You are always truly so to me: and I know your Goodness so well, that I need not to be put in mind of it by your Benefactions. A Man is not amiable because he is Good to Ourselves only, but the more so, the more he is good to. Therfore when We hear of Benefits, we ought to be as Sensible of them as when we feel them: Yet this is seldom the case; we Apply the Terms of Good, Benevolent, Just, &c, meerly as relative to ourselves, and are in this as unjust to Men, as Philosophers & Divines are to God, Whose Ways & Workings they magnify or disapprove according to the Effect they have on them selves only. This is

[1] Cheselden lived in Spring Garden.

[2] This is Pope's first letter to Samuel Gerrard, long a friend of Swift's, and one of whom Pope will presently make notable use.

[3] On the 16th Pope had written to Warburton that he would inquire daily at Robinson's for the date of Warburton's arrival in London. Evidently Warburton had informed Robinson of the date, and Pope felt free to visit Windsor Forest for 'five or six days'.

[4] At the end of the Allen letters in Egerton 1947 on f. 153*r* occurs, in Warburton's hand, a letter which he fabricated (but did not publish) out of three of Pope's letters—those of 19 Aug. 1738 and 17 July 1740, as well as from this present letter. From this present letter he included the first half of the first paragraph and the short paragraph about Fortescue and Dr. Cheyne. The fabrication is undated, and there seems no reason for printing it. Warburton indulged in this conflation of letters more than once.

a long preface to my Letter, whose business is to tell you that if I would forget you, I could not, from the frequency of your Benefits. One day brought me the Cyder, the next the Bristol water, the third the Stones. And for these little things, little in comparison of the other Evidences of your Good Will to me (& little in comparison to those they would be, if you sent me Diamonds) for these I say, I catch my self at the Folly of thanking you.

The Arrival of this *Happy Couple*,[1] loaded with what I am now fond of, makes me reflect on Another, constantly charg'd with All that I love & value, all whose Voyages I wish may be as prosperous! The Ship thus named ought to be your own; but whether it be or not, no man will ever hear of it without thinking of you.

I can never expect that any other Man will be so ready or Earnest as you to humour me in my Desires, & therfore I fear I shall not have the Collection I most want, of Mundicks & Minerals from Mr Borlase, time enough to finish the work this Spring. I wish Dr Oliver could forward that Favour as soon as Mr Omer's Coming at Whitson-tide.

I must intreat you to send the inclosed to Mr Nugent, who I pre-sume is at Bath: If he be gone be pleased to inclose & direct it to London.

You must assure Judge Fortescue of my Friendship & admit him to yours, (so Justice & Righteousness will meet) And as you are a sincere & honest Man, even Dr Cheyne will believe you, if you tell him I love him, and am of His Religion.

It would be almost a sin in me to conclude without a word of Mrs Allen, and yet I have been thinking of her throughout all this Letter. Is there any need of naming her just over against the *Happy Couple*? Can I forget her a Single Day, when I am always directed by her Almanack? or can I help, when I see but one Bottle on my Table, to think what a Number stood before us, at hers? But pray let her not fancy, from my mention of these, that they are All I remember her for? any more than suffer yourself to think, that when I thank you for Water, Wine, Alabaster, Spars, & Snakestones, they were the best things I ever had from you.

Mr Hook seldom comes in my way, since You (who were the Centre of Union between us) are gone. He is as much too modest, as any man can be too confident, for no man can want Merit, more than he possesses it.

Adieu. pray desire Mr Fortescue to tell me how his Daughter is? I was extremely concerned to hear of her accident. I am | Dear Sir, Wholly Yours. | A. Pope

[1] The *Happy Couple* seems to be the name of the ship that brought Pope his cargo of cider Bristol water, and stone. The name reminds him of the happiness of the Allens.

*POPE *to* WARBURTON[1] [? *Late April*, 1740]

Egerton 1946

Sir,—I was in haste to see you, but unfortunately attempted at no very proper hour to day. If you pass near me to morrow morning, I lodge at Mr Cheselden's (the Surgeons) in Spring Garden by Charing cross, & will not be abroad till after eleven, in hopes of you. I fear I cannot dine at Lord Oxford's. I am every where Dear Sir Sincerely Yours. | A. Pope.

*POPE *to* WARBURTON[2] [26 *April* 1740]

Egerton 1946

Saturday, 11 a clock

Sir,—The Desire I unfeignedly have to pass what Time I can with you would have brought me to your Lodging this morning but I thought you would mis-interpret it Ceremony, the only Use of which (as a Modern said well) is to keep People that care not for one another, at a distance. To manifest the Contrary to you, I wish you would dine to day with me at a Friend's house, a little after three. He is one I think you will like, because I have loved him on twenty years Experience: I mean my Lord Bathurst, in St James Square; where at that hour you'l find me, if it be no way inconvenient to yourself. On Munday I shall challenge you at ten in the morning for the Country.[3] Yours faithfully | A. Pope.

[1] Warburton's letters to his friend Dr. Robert Taylor (transcribed in part for the editor by Miss Edleen Begg at the University of Texas) help date his movements in April and May of this year. He wrote on 22 April: 'I came late last night to Town'; and the remark dates his arrival. Pope was eager to exhibit his champion to friends, and he seems to have shown him to Oxford, Bathurst, Lyttelton, and others. Engagements come so fast that some have to be cancelled: Pope could not go to Oxford's, but apparently Warburton did, since his letters to Dr. Taylor record conversations with Oxford during this period.

[2] This letter may possibly date in 1741, when Warburton was again in London, but it is most probably a part of the record of his first visit. To Pope he is still (as in the preceding letter), 'Sir.' He becomes 'Dear Sir' later. The first Saturday during his present visit was the 26th.

[3] One thus assumes that on 28 Apr. Pope and his guest went to Twickenham for the week. Warburton writes to Conyers Middleton a letter of 6 May that he has passed a pleasant week with Pope at Twickenham. Warton (Pope's *Works*, ix [1797], 342 n.) repeats Dodsley's story that Pope and Warburton first met 'in Lord Radnor's garden, just by Mr. Pope's at Twickenham'. Dodsley, who was present, was 'astonished at the high compliments paid him [W—] by Pope as he approached him'. Dodsley may have witnessed such a gathering, but it was not the first meeting of the two. More interesting is Pope's own record (given to Spence in Feb. 1743, and recorded in the MS. of his *Anecdotes* preserved in the Huntington Library [HM 1271, f. 440]) of their first dinner together at Twickenham. Pope as gourmet did his best, but '. . . Shall I help you to some Lobster? No, I thank you.—What, do you never eat any? I never did.—You hate it then! I can't tell.—You had as good try, how you like it. No; as I never tasted it, I don't know why I shou'd get a taste to it now. (Warburton, the first time he was at Mr Pope's table; he served him much the same, as to his Cyprus wine: "We have desires enough; why should we add to them?")' Pope was perhaps just 'philosophical' enough to be pleased with such reasoning.

I should have told you, that my Lord B. has long been desirous to be known to you, & makes this His request.

Address: To the Revd Mr Warburton, | at Mr Gyles, a Booksellers | over against Grays Inne in | Holborne

*POPE *to* THE EARL OF BURLINGTON[1] [? 30 *April* 1740]

Chatsworth

My Lord,—I attempted to wait on you in my way hither; but Mr Warburton coming in the Interim, ingaged me to go directly home. I am always cautious of bringing people to trouble you; & I know your Indulgence to me will lead you to see any of my Companions, (except Irishmen.)[2] If your Lordship shall have no other Avocation, & no Objection, shall I bring him with me as I return with him to Town? He happens to know the Learned & Admirable Mr Wood,[3] in his neighborhood, & (I find) has the true Key to admire him by. I think to go to London on Friday or Saturday; if you shall *not* be at Chiswick, I'll shew him the Place & go on till the next opportunity.

I enquird of Lady Burlington, without much satisfaction, at Piccadilly-door. I hope however she is every day mending, & will every day mend, till she becomes a New & glorified Body. I am sincerely hers & | My Lord | Your most faithfull & obligd Servant | A. Pope.

Twitnam. | Wensday morn.

Address: To the Rt. Hon. the Earl of Burlington.

*POPE *to* WARBURTON[4] [? 5 *May* 1740]

Egerton 1946

Monday.

Sir,—I was willing to leave you one day, which was Saturday, in Quiet. and yesterday from Morning to Night & all this morning I have been layd up very sick of the Headach. Mr Cheselden having removed all his family into the Country, I now lodge at Mr Lewis's

[1] The dating may well be pure guesswork, but if Pope, as he planned on the 26th, took Warburton home to Twickenham on Monday the 28th, he might well be explaining why he had not called at Chiswick for a customary Sunday dinner.

[2] Does this refer to Mr. Gerrard? See Pope to Gerrard, 18 Apr.

[3] The Rev. Thomas Wood became rector of Barrowby in 1732, and thus was not far from Brant Broughton (spelt *Bruton* by Pope), which was Warburton's parish.

[4] The letter seems to fit the hypothetical date nicely. Pope and his guest had returned to town on Friday or Saturday, as he told Lord Burlington they planned to do. This is the following Monday, and Pope has had to move to his friend Erasmus Lewis's. Meanwhile Warburton writes to Conyers Middleton (Egerton MS. 1953, f. 44) that he has passed a pleasant week with Pope at Twickenham. The mention of Gyles makes any date later than 1741 impossible. Fletcher Gyles, Warburton's bookseller, died in 1741.

in Cork street by Burlington Gardens, Piccadilly. Where you'l commonly find me before ten in a morning, and if you'l dine with us on Wensday there, pray let me know by a line to morrow. I wish you had time to call on Lord Bathurst or Mr Lyttelton about ten, any day, & send your Name in, before you. Be assured I am at all times Sincerely Your obliged & faithful | Servant | A. Pope

If Mr Gyles can conveniently | pass next Sunday at Twitnam, you & I | may go before, & receive him there.

Address: To the Revd Mr Warburton | at Mr Gyles's Bookselle[r] | over against Grays Inn. | Holborne

*POPE *to* WARBURTON[1] [7 *May* 1740]

Egerton 1946

I am quite ashamed & concerned, that after appointing to dine together to day, I find I am obliged to disappoint you & myself, being forced by necessary Business to be at the other End of the Town all day. I hope to call upon You at Mr Gyles's soon. The Underwritten I receivd last night from Mr Lyttelton by which I hope you met together. I will not fail you. | Yours | A. Pope

Mr Lyttelton begs the favour of Mr Pope to meet Dr Warburton at his House Thursday evening at eight a clock.[2]

Wensday morn.

If you do not know Mr L.'s Lodging, pray step to Lord Bathurst's where they will tell you. it is not above twenty steps off in Pallmall.

Address: To the Revd Mr | Warburton at | Mr Gyles's, over against | Grays Inn

*POPE *to* ALLEN[3] 15 *May* 1740

Egerton 1947

May 15, 1740.

You are never to imagine I forget you when I have long been silent; I never will imagine you forget me, by any silence. My good Wishes,

[1] The year might be 1741, when Warburton came to town late in May. But assuming that Pope was leading his champion about in 1740, one guesses that the date falls on the Wednesday after the first week together at Twickenham.

[2] This sentence of invitation is in Lyttelton's hand: Pope wrote his letter on the same sheet, above and below the invitation.

[3] It is strange that the letter does not mention Warburton. On the afternoon of this day (the 15th) Warburton wrote to Dr. Taylor, 'I am this afternoon come from *Twickenham*, where I have spent another Week most agreeably.' He found himself 'thrown pretty much amongst the Anti-ministerial Men', but he himself 'never was of any Party except the Love of my Country may be called a Party. . . .' He has now met the Duke of Argyle and Lord

I will venture to say, keep an equal & a Constant pace, like yours, & are always the same. No matter who writ last; I think I did, but I want to know your health is good, & to tell you mine is. I intended to acknowledge all your kind offices, & possibly nevertheless I omitted to mention half. I know you intend me all you do not, as well as prove your Goodness in all you do. I have just receivd a fine Cargo of Minerals & Spars from Penzance, & am now enabled to begin my Subterraneous work as Soon as Mr Omer comes. But I wish, if it suited him, it were the Week after Whitsun-week, & that he could stay some days. I could be glad of a few of the Bristol Diamonds, to match with the finer Cornish Diamonds of which Mr Borlase has sent me a noble Quantity, & offers more if I draw upon him. Pray desire Dr Oliver to tell him, how much I think myself oblig'd to Him In His Friend, & what a Part I take too to my Self, of both. I am only troubled I can less hope to see the Dr in my Mines, than in his Castle, where I might have some hope to find him in the Autumn, if His Imagination & my Poetry together could draw the Stones from your Quarry to the Side of his Hill. It is my firm resolution to inhabit the Room at the end of your Gallery one Fortnight at least in September, & as much longer as I can, to see your Gardens finish'd (ready for Mrs Allen's Grotto & Cascade the following year) I must inquire, next after hers & your health, after that of the Elms we planted on each Side of the Lawn? & of the little Wood-work to join one wood to the other below, which I hope you planted this Spring. I have sufferd more, in my Garden as well as in my Body, since the End of the Great Frost, than before: But what wonder? I was then in your Care, & since in my own. Yet upon the Whole, my Garden would look well, & I should be well, if the Sun would but shine on us. And let us pray, that it may do so now, both upon the Just & the Unjust; for all equally want it. Believe me Entirely, Yours & Mrs As.

Whenever Omer comes, I must have previous notice. Vandyst has made an Excellent Picture of Mr Hook, which I hope will fall to your Lott. I will sit to him too, when we meet at your house

Address: To | Ralph Allen Esqr: | at Widcombe, | Bath.
Frank: Free
Postmark: (illegible)

Cobham. He records, interestingly, that 'Mr. P. has wrote a pleasant Drole History in imitation of *Don Quixote* & Sancho to ridicule all false learning. *Scriblerus* is the Hero & his man *Crambe* puns as much as Sancho strings proverbs. We read this together. The first Vol. in a little 8vo or 4 will be published in about a Year I believe.' The text of the Warburton extracts is again kindly furnished by Miss Begg.

With Warburton back in London Pope can relax and write of his grotto.

POPE *to* HENRY LINTOT 16 *May* 1740

[Pope wrote an important but untraced letter to Lintot under this date, and from it Lintot used a postscript in his reply to Pope's chancery bill of 16 Feb. 1742/3. The reply, PRO C11 549/39 (lines 38, 39), presents the postscript as follows: 'I have a favor to desire of You that you would not part from your purchase of a Third share of the Dunciad or assign it to any Man but myself.']

MRS. WHITEWAY *to* POPE 16 *May* 1740

1768 (Deane Swift)

May 16, 1740.

Sir,—Should I make an apology for writing to you, I might be asked why I did so? If I have erred, my design at least is good, both to you and the Dean of *St. Patrick's*; for I write in relation to my friend, and I write to his friend, which I hope will plead my excuse. As I saw a letter of yours to him, wherein I had the honour to be named, I take the liberty to tell you (with grief of heart) his memory is so much impaired, that in a few hours he forgot it; nor is his judgment sound enough, had he many tracts by him, to finish or correct them, as you have desired.[1] His health is as good as can be expected, free from all the tortures of old age; and his deafness, lately returned, is all the bodily uneasiness he hath to complain of. A few years ago he burnt most of his writings unprinted, except a few loose papers, which are in my possession, and which I promise you (if I out-live him) shall never be made publick without your approbation. There is one treatise in his own keeping, called *Advice to Servants*, very unfinished and incorrect, yet what is done of it, hath so much humour, that it may appear as a posthumous work. The history of the four last years of queen *Anne*'s reign I suppose you have seen with Dr. *King*, to whom he sent it some time ago, and, if I am rightly informed, is the only piece of his (except *Gulliver*) which he ever proposed making money by, and was given to Dr. *King* with that design, if it might be printed: I mention this to you, lest the Doctor should die, and his heirs imagine they have a right to dispose of it.[2] I intreat, Sir, you will not take notice to any person of the hints I have given you in this letter; they are only designed for yourself: to the Dean's friend in *England* they can only give trouble, and to his enemies and starveling wits cause of triumph. I inclose this to

[1] Pope, it seems, has asked Swift for 'tracts' to be included in the volume of their forthcoming correspondence. Although Swift's other letters written at this period show that he was perfectly capable of sending his own replies, he was willing to let Mrs. Whiteway write instead. But it must be insisted that when Swift wrote, for example, the ironic recommendation of his drunken servant (Ball, vi. 149: letter of 9 Jan. 1740), he was not senile!

[2] This remark would not allay suspicions that Mrs. Whiteway and her son-in-law imagined that Swift's writings had a commercial value—to his heirs.

alderman *Barber*, who I am sure will deliver it safe, yet knows nothing more than it's being a paper that belongs to you.

The ceremony of answering women's letters, may perhaps make you think it necessary to answer mine; but I do not expect it, because your time either is or ought to be better employed, unless it be in my power to serve you in buying *Irish* linen, or any other command you are pleased to lay on me, which I shall execute, to the best of my capacity, with the greatest readiness, integrity, and secrecy; for whether it be my years, or a less degree of vanity in my composition than in some of my sex, I can receive such an honour from you without mentioning it. I should, for some time past, have writ to you on this subject, had I not fancied that it glanced at the ambition of being thought a person of consequence, by interfering between you and the Dean; a character of all others which I dislike.

I have several of your letters to the Dean, which I will send by the first safe hand that I can get to deliver them to yourself;[1] I believe it may be Mr. *M'Aulay*, the gentleman the Dean recommended through your friendship to the prince of *Wales*.

I believe this may be the only letter which you ever received without asking a favour, a compliment, extolling your genius, running in raptures on your poetry, or admiring your distinguishable virtue. I am, Sir, with very high respect, your most obedient and most humble servant, | Martha Whiteway.

Mr. *Swift*, who waited on you last *Summer*, is since that married to my daughter: he desires me to present you his most obedient respects and humble thanks for the particular honour conferred upon him in permitting him to spend a day with you at *Twickenham*; a favour he will always remember with gratitude.

POPE *to* SAMUEL GERRARD[2] 17 *May* 1740

The Huntington Library

May the 17th 1740

Sir,—I am obliged to you for the notice of your intended Return to Ireland, in order to what I desird, that I might charge you with a Letter to the Dean. But I had an opportunity just after I saw you, of sending him a very long & full Letter by a safe hand, which leaves me nothing to tell him more, except what I would always tell, to the Last

[1] These 'several' letters could not be separated from Mrs. Whiteway's hands before Jan. 1741—a fact used, hypocritically perhaps, by Pope to colour his expressed suspicions of Mrs. Whiteway's complicity in the publication of the Pope–Swift volume of letters.

[2] This letter is doubtless a part of Pope's scheme to get his and Swift's letters published. He here writes Gerrard that he has nothing to send to Swift, and then presently (see Lord Orrery to Pope, 6 Oct. 1740) a packet is left by an unknown hand at Gerrard's lodgings in Bath, a packet to be taken to Swift. In addition to Lord Orrery's statement that Gerrard was the envoy, we have Faulkner's statement to Thomas Birch made on 17 Aug. 1749. See note 1 to the letter immediately following.

day of my Life, & desire you Sir to tell Him & all mankind, that I Love, Esteem, & Respect him, & account it the most pleasing circumstance of my Fortune to have known him long, & experienced his Friendship thro' my life.

I am glad you found the Benefit I promisd my Self you would from Dr Cheyne's Care, to whom pray make my heartiest Services. There lives not an Honester Man, nor a Truer Philosopher. I wish you a good Journey, & am with respect | Sir, Your most obedient humble | Servant | A. Pope

Address: To | Samuel Gerrard Esqr | at Mrs Henshew's Apothecary | Cheap street | in | Bath

Frank: Cornbury ffree

Postmark: 17/MA

[POPE] *to* SWIFT[1] [? *May* 1740]

Harvard University

Sir,—The true Honour which all the honest and grateful Part of this Nation[2] must bear you, as the most publick spirited of Patriots, the best of private Men, and the greatest polite Genius of this Age, made it impossible to resist the Temptation, which has fallen in our Way, of preserving from all Accidents a Copy of the *inclosed Papers*,[3] which at once give so amiable a Picture of your own excellent Mind, and so strong a Testimony of the Love and Respect of those who nearest know, and best can judge of it.[4]

[1] The text is from Orrery's transcript of Pope's letter of 30 Dec. 1740, in which this was included. Elwin (viii. 418–19) printed it with no indication of provenance, and for no clear reason placed it in Sept. 1740. Since, in his letter to Pope of 29 July 1740, Faulkner enclosed a copy of it (so Pope informed Orrery, 30 Dec. 1740), the letter probably started towards Dublin in May or June. The present text (N.B.!) is that of a transcript (by Orrery) of a transcript (by Pope) of a transcript (by Faulkner, made in July 1740). Mrs. Whiteway sent the 'original' letter to Orrery, who, 8 Jan. 1740/1, sent it to Pope. Elrington Ball (vi. 157), reprinting Elwin, says the text came from the original 'in the possession of the Earl of Cork'. This is probably wrong. Since Orrery sent the original to Pope, one may suspect that he never got it back. The text here given seems at one point slightly better than that printed by Elwin: see below, note 4. The letter is called 'that from Bath' by Mrs. Whiteway, writing to Orrery 30 Dec.; and although neither Orrery's transcript (here printed) nor Elwin's text has any superscription indicating Bath, the clandestine volume, with this letter, was evidently known to come from Bath. Thomas Birch (BM Add. 4244, f. 38*r*) records conversation with Faulkner on 17 Aug. 1749, which, in part, is: 'Mr P[ope] sent to Ireland to Dr Swift by Mr. Gerrard, an Irish Gentleman, then at Bath, a printed Copy of their Letters, with an anonymous Letter: which occasion'd Dr Swift to give Mr. Fawkner Leave to reprint them at Dublin, tho' Mr. Pope's Edit. was publish'd First.' For Gerrard's departure from Bath, see the preceding letter of 17 May 1740 and also Pope to Allen, 27 May 1740.

[2] 'this Nation' is italicized in Elwin's text to emphasize (as other italics in the letter do) the Irish origin of the volume it accompanies. But Orrery did not underline these two words.

[3] A curious way of speaking of a printed volume. Intentionally perplexing, perhaps. See Pope's letter of 30 Dec. 1740 here iv. 317, 318.

[4] Elwin's text here somewhat illogically falls into past tenses, and says, 'who knew, and best could judge of it'.

As there is Reason to fear they would be lost to Posterity after your Death, if either of your Two great Friends[1] should be possessed of them, (*as we are informed you have directed*)[2] they are here collected and submitted to your own mature Consideration. Envy itself can find Nothing in them that either You, or They, need be ashamed of. But you, Sir, are the Person *most* concerned, and ought to be made the *only* Judge in this Case. You may be assured there is *no other Copy*[3] of this Book in any Hands but your own: So that, while you live, it will be in the Power of no other, but yourself, to bestow it on the Publick. In so doing You shall oblige all Mankind in general, and *benefit any deserving Friend* in particular. But if during your Life, you suppress it, yet after your Death it is not fit that either You should be robbed of so much of your Fame, or We of so much of your Example;—We are, | Worthy Sir, | your sincere Admirers, Obliged *Country-Men*, and | Faithful, Affectionate Servants.

*POPE *to* WARBURTON[4] [*c.* 23 *May* 1740]

Egerton 1946

Sir,—With my thanks for all your favors, I must grieve that I cannot meet you at dinner, I fear, but I will endevor to find you after dinner. I go to morrow home; & thus we must part, as all Friends have parted. But with all good Wishes, & sincere desires of meeting again: If Fortune and your Merit shall agree to bring you nearer this Part of the World. In the meantime, pray let me some times know you are well, & remember as one truly Yours, | Your faithfull Friend | & affectionate | Servant | A. Pope.

*POPE *to* FORTESCUE[5] [*May* 1740]

Harvard University

I am sorry to be as little master of my time as if I were a Judge: Twice

[1] Orrery's marginal annotation here is 'Lord Bolingbroke and Mr. Pope'.

[2] Swift had himself, in his letter of 22 Apr. 1736, informed Pope of such direction. His letters were to go to Pope.

[3] Swift's experience in the intricacies of printing would compel him to regard this statement as improbable. Pope very likely had printed a normal-sized edition.

[4] This farewell letter cannot be dated precisely as to the day. Warburton goes to Cambridge from London, and we hear from him there in a letter (printed in part by Warton, ix. 340–2) from Hon. Charles Yorke to his brother Earl Hardwicke, dated 1 June. Other excerpts from this interesting summary of the conversations of Pope and Warburton are presented in George Harris's *Life of Lord Chancellor Hardwicke*, i (1847), 477, which informs us that Warburton has been conversing with Mr. Yorke 'for three or four days'. Warburton probably left London on Saturday the 24th, and Pope (as the following letter to Fortescue *may* indicate) went to Twickenham on Saturday also.

[5] Fortescue's endorsement roughly places the letter. The day may be that of Warburton's departure, Saturday the 24th.

at Twitnam I mist you, and now I'm going again, but ingaged on Sunday. Lord Burlington has a kind of Claim to that day by long Precedent. I am glad you are tolerably well this unnaturall Season, which I may well call an Ungratefull one, if not Pestilential: It half kills me, but I will not yield to it, till I dye of it. The next time I am in town I will be glad to fix any day with you. In the meantime God keep you. | Yours | A. Pope.

I've been layd up 2 days this week.

Endorsement: Mr Pope | May 1740

POPE *to* DR. OLIVER 27 *May* [1740]

The European Magazine, xxi (1792), 6.

Twitnam May 27th.

Without any compliment every occasion I can have of assuring you of my memory and regard is and will be gladly embrac'd by me. But if I could forget you, I should meet with you in your friends and feel your obligations thro' them; they are so ready and punctual in serving me. Mr. Cooper's Cargo arrived safely, but I think there is less beauty and variety in those marbles than in those of Bristol. Mr. Borlase's present is extremely valuable to me and his manner of obliging me with the sollicitude he shows in his letters to have my work a perfect one, contributing (contrary to any practice now left in the world) not only his best advices, but his finest discoveryes and richest treasures, is such as I cannot take wholly upon myself to acknowledge, but beg you to do it first, as well and warmly as you can; that is as well and warmly as you or he serve a friend—And then and not before (for I am too much obliged to be able singly to repay him) I will thank him as much again. In taking his advice I do not make him the poorer; but I fear that in taking more of his Collections I may. And therefore shall hardly have the conscience to trouble him for another cargo how much soever I am unprovided. If he will ingage his word not to send me any that he intended to keep I would ask him for some of the metallic kind that are most common. So they do but *shine* and *glitter* it is enough and the vulgar spectator will of course think them noble. Few philosophers come here but if ever Fortune, Fate, or Providence bring Dr. Oliver Mr. Borlase and Mr. Allen hither I shall not envy the Queen's Hermitage either its natural or moral philosophers.

I have unawares scribbled out my paper. Impute the warmth of it to my heart, the nonsense of it to my haste, rather than to my head; and you will prove yourself one way more a friend to | Dear Sir | Your affectionate faithful Servant | A. Pope.

*POPE *to* ALLEN 27 *May* [1740]

Egerton 1947

Tuesday May 27.

This is written to you in great hurry, to desire Omer may come the first day he can; if he is to be in London about this time, let him come hither first, for I am to have a Meeting at Mr Murray's, with my Sisters Antagonist in order to a Reference, which we have agreed on, to Conclude our long Chancery suit next week: So that probably I must attend in London after Tuesday next. But if Omer has no other Call of Business this way, do not let him come, for I shall make shift to finish the Grotto myself, which is alredy layd out & begun.

I am a little Impatient to know whether that Pacquet I sent for Mr Gerrard reached him? in time before he went from Bath?[1] The Bristol Diamonds I send for to morrow to the Swan. I shall still want more of *Your Quarry*, the Passage taking up more than I was aware of (3 or 4 Baskets.). I hope this will find you & Mrs A. as healthy as happy! Let me know, if you are Quite recovered? Adieu. Ever Yours.

Address: To | Ralph Allen. Esq. at | Bath.
Postmark: 27/MA

*POPE *to* WILLIAM BORLASE 8 *June* 1740

The Quarterly Review, cxxxix (1875), 383–4

Twickenham, June the 8th, 1740.

Sir,—As soon as I received your very obliging present and letter, I writ to Dr. Oliver, designing him to prepare the way for my thanks, by assuring you I wanted words to express them, and by taking to himself a part of an obligation which is really above any Merit I can claim to it. I fear, by a Paper I found in the Box, that you have robb'd your own Collection to enrich me, and the same paper gave me an excellent Motto for my Grot,[2] in some part of which I must fix your name,[3] if I can contrive it, agreeably to your Modesty and Merit, in a Shade but shining. I deferr'd writing to you 'till I should form a guess how far your materials would go in the work, which is now half finished, the ruder parts entirely so; in its present condition it is quite natural, and

[1] The packet contained the printed letters of Swift and Pope, thus forwarded to Swift for publication in Dublin. Gerrard pretty certainly did not know the packet came from Pope. See Pope to Gerard, 17 May, and the Orrery letters of 6, 17, and 25 October, &c.

[2] Over the entrance to the grotto Pope carved from Horace, *Epistles*, I. xviii. 103: *Secretum iter et fallentis semita vitae*. The line may not have been the motto found in Borlase's letter.

[3] On 15 Dec. 1741 Dr. Oliver wrote Borlase: 'I suppose Sir John [? St. Aubyn] has told you that he has read your name in letters of gold in the grotto, an honour the greatest man might be ambitious of; but if it had been in black letters, made only of the common ink the little gentleman uses when he embalms his friends, it would be more likely to give you immortality.'—*Quarterly Rev.* cxxxix. 384.

can only admit of more beauties by the Glitter of more minerals, not the disposition or manner of placing them, with which I am quite satisfy'd. I have managed the Roof so as to admit of the larger as well as smaller pendulous [crystals]; the sides are strata of various, beautiful, but rude Marbles, between which run the Loads of Metal, East and West, and in the pavement also, the direction of the Grotto happening to lie so. And I have opened the whole into one Room, groin'd above from pillar to pillar (not of a regular Architecture, but like supporters left in a Quarry), by which means there is a fuller Light cast into all but the narrow passage (which is cover'd with living and long Mosse), only behind the 2 largest Pillars there is a deep recess of dark stone, where two Glasses artfully fix'd reflect the Thames, and almost deceive the Eye to that degree as to seem two arches opening to the River on each side, as there is one real in the middle. The little well is very light, ornamented with Stalactites above, and Spars and Cornish Diamonds on the Edges, with a perpetual drip of water into it from pipes above among the Icicles. I have cry'd help to some other friends, as I found my Want of materials, and have stellifyed some of the Roof with Bristol stone of a fine lustre. I am in hopes of some of the Red transparent Spar from the Lead mines, which would vastly vary the colouring. If you will be extravagant, indeed, in sending anything more, I wish it were glittering tho' not curious; as equally proper in such an Imitation of Nature, who is not so Profuse as you, tho' ever most kind to those who cultivate her. As I procure more Ores or Spars, I go on enriching the Crannies and Interstices, which, as my Marbles are in large pieces, cramp'd fast with iron to the walls, are pretty spacious and unequal, admitting Loads and Veins of 2, 3, or 4 inches broad, and running up and down thro' Roof, Sides, and Pavement. The perpendicular Fissures I generally fill with Spar. I have run into such a detail, that I had forgot to tell you this whole Grotto makes the communication between my Garden and the Thames. I hope I shall live to see you there. . . . I have neither room nor words to tell you how much you oblige your Humble Servant, | A. Pope.

*POPE *to* ALLEN — 17 *June* [1740]

Egerton 1947

Twit'nam, June 17

You had been troubled with a much longer letter, of Descriptions of the Execution of the Grotto, if Mr Omer was not the bearer; who will ease you, (not to say me) of all that Detail. I would not keep him a day longer, than his own necessary Business detain'd him; knowing of how much Use he is to you, & your works. Moreover, I am at a full stop at present, for a reason that has put many a man to a full stop, the having no more Stock to spend; For till I can procure more Materials from the Mines, & from the Quarries, my Mine Adventure (like the Adventure of the Bear & Fiddle)[1] Must End, and break off in the Middle. However it is some Satisfaction, that as far as I've gone, I am content; & that is all a Mortal Man can expect; for no man finishes any View he has, or any Scheme he projects, but by halves.

And Life itself can nothing more supply
Than just to plann our Projects, & to dye.[2]

Those men indeed, who marry & settle, undertake for more; they undertake for future ages, and Sam, & Betty, are *in* for Life, and afterwards, if they have Children. I am content to leave nothing but my Works behind me; which (whether good or evil) *will follow me*, as St. John[3] expresses it. As to my *Mines*, and my *Treasures*,[4] they must go together, to God knows Who! A Sugar-baker or a Brewer may have the House & Gardens, and a Booby that chanced to be my Heir-at law, the other, except I happen to disperse it to the Poor in my own time.

I shall see Vandiest in a day or two, & concert the best method I can for the Statues for the Library: I would not neglect seeing him, to prevent any Errors, tho I'm in the midst of my Grand-Workes in the Garden.

Pray give my Services to Dr Oliver; tell him I have lately written to Mr Borlase; & that I must Recant what I told him of the Plymouth Marbles which Mr Cooper sent me:[5] I had not then found the Means to cutt them into pieces; but since I have, I find they are very beautiful, sparry, & various-colour'd: Wherefore I should be glad of Another Load of them, the same way by Ship.

And you must not forget my Religious Respects to Dr Cheyne. I am Yours dear Sir, and Mrs Allen's Very Sincere, faithfull Servant, | A. Pope.

When you come to Newburry, Can Mrs Allen & you take a day or two's Look at my Grotto? or must I put you to Shame & come to meet you both at a Review? Methinks we should not come so near as halfway, without a Meeting.

I have ask'd Omer about a hundred questions concerning the Garden, Trees, the House, & Finishing, &c I rejoyce in the Prosperity of you all: May but Health attend you, that you may long, & without allay, *enjoy it*.

The Eleventh of July we should spend together.[6]

Endorsement: Mr Pope

[1] An allusion to the 'Argument' of the first Canto of *Hudibras*.
[2] Pope parodies ll. 3 and 4 of Epistle I of his *Essay on Man*.
[3] Revelation xiv. 13.
[4] His grotto and its 'furniture'.
[5] See Pope to Dr. Oliver, 27 May.
[6] Either Allen's birthday (see Pope to Allen, 26 July 1737) or the date of the review at Newbury.

POPE *to* MRS. WHITEWAY 18 *June* 1740

1768 (Deane Swift)

Twickenham, June 18, 1740.

Madam,—I am extremely sensible of the favour of your letter, and very well see the kindness as well as the honour which moved you to do it. I have no merit for the one, but being (like yourself) a sincere friend to the Dean, though a much less useful one; for all my friendship can only operate in wishes, yours in good works. He has had the happiness to meet with such in all the stages of his life; and I hope in God and in you, that he will not want one in the last. Never imagine, Madam, that I can do otherwise than esteem that sex, which has furnished him with the best friends.

The favour you offer me,[1] I accept with the utmost thankfulness; and I think no person more fit to convey it to my hands than Mr. *M'Aulay*, of whom I know you have so good an opinion. Indeed any one whom you think worthy your trust, I shall think deserves mine, in a point I am ever so tender of.

I wish the very small opportunity I had of shewing Mr. *Swift*, your son, my regards for him, had been greater; and I wish it now more, since he is become so near to you, for whom my respect runs hand in hand with my affection for the Dean; and I cannot wish well for the one without doing so for the other.

I turn my mind all I can from the melancholy subject of your letter. May God Almighty alleviate your concern, and his complaints, as much as possible in this state of infirmities, while he lives; and may your tenderness, Madam, prevent any thing after his death which may any way depreciate his memory. I dare say nothing of ill consequence can happen from the commission given Dr. *King.*[2]

You see, Madam, I write to you with absolute freedom, as becomes me to the friend of my friend, and to a woman of sense and spirit. I will say no more, that you may find I treat you with the same delicacy that you do me (and for which I thank you) without the least compliment: and it is none when I add, that I am, with esteem, Madam, your most obliged and most obedient servant, | A. Pope.

POPE *to* THE EARL OF MARCHMONT 22 *June* [1740]

Arthur A. Houghton, Jr.

June 22d

My Lord,—The more I wish to be rememberd by you, the less I feel my self able to deserve your regard; & the more faint will my expres-

[1] She has offered to return several additional letters by Mr. M'Aulay. See her letter of 16 May, to which this is an answer.

[2] Concerning Swift's *Four Last Years.*

sions be, as the Sense is strong of that Inability. But above all times I am at this, least disposed to speak what I feel; & still more unwilling to add to your Concern, which I know is greater, than that of any man less honest & less a lover of his Country, can possibly be, & therfore greater than almost any man's whatsoever. Yet may one miserable Comfort be derived to you, even from the Loss of Sir W. Wyndham;[1] that your own Seclusion from Public business will be mitigated by the Thought, What an Assistant you must now have wanted, had you continud in it? & that there is no man left worthy to draw with, if you consider him Entire, Head & Heart. For the same Ability without the same Spirit, Strength without Union, drawing ever so powerfully, without drawing all one way, are either to no purpose, or a bad one. The only one fit to work with you, is gone, & you must have tugg'd by yourself, where no single Force can prevail, no single Virtue animate. Two Props may support one another, but one Prop cannot stand by itself. You could only have layd down, and seen the State (if it shou'd change its Supporters) come to carry the present Minister. I don't know now whose Life or Death to wish for; I know whose death I should have wishd some years ago, to have prevented the mischiefs that are now remediless; & whose Lives, to have enjoyed better Times:[2] but in certain Situations, it is happier for honest men to dye than live, & in some times fitter that Knaves should govern, to stand charged with the Infamy of them to Posterity. God Almighty certainly knows what he does, when he removes those from us whose lives we pray for; & leaves behind those Scourges, which a mercenary People[3] deserve, tho' the Partiality of a few Virtuous or Brave men (who happen to be born among them) would save them. We do not live, my Lord, under the Jewish Dispensation, nor are to imagine the most dirty, rascally Race on Earth are the Favorite People of God.[4] You know when they were so, after they had provok'd him enough, he punishd them with an Absolute King. He has done as much to all Europe of late days, & if Britain should be the only Corner left still free; do you think it must not be more His Goodness than our Merit?

I would willingly turn to any subject from that, which not only extremely afflicts me, but those two men in the world whom I most

[1] Sir William had died at Wells on 17 June. Pope's disillusionment with the Patriot Opposition, which here finds expression, had of course been evident since 1738. In April and May Sir William, Marchmont, and William Chetwynd had visited Bolingbroke in France.—*Daily Gazetteer*, 16 May 1740.

[2] The elliptical expression opposes some whose deaths would have remedied evils to others whose lives (if continued) would have made the times better.

[3] Both in his satires and in his letters the venality of the age obsesses Pope.

[4] This racial self-denigration is the common cry of the disillusioned at this moment. Usually the contrast is with the ancient Romans. One of Fielding's men in *Amelia* (Bk. XI, c. 2) cries out to Dr. Harrison: 'Do you not know, doctor, that this is as corrupt a nation as ever existed under the sun?' Fielding also had been a Patriot.

esteem; I mean the man who Led, & the man who seconded, the great & worthy Person we have lost. In all the steps he made of late, when the true Interest & Honour of his Country became his only Passion, his Judgment was determin'd by the one, & his Action by the other: with the one, he could not have err'd, with the other he could not have cool'd, in any generous Purpose. And it is not the world, or the Party, that I condole with on this death, but Those Two, who feel for the Publick what it feels not for itself, & what Party-men but pretend to feel. If I see any man merry within a week after this death, I will affirm him no Patriot; And such I have seen, who might at least have seem'd more concern'd, since they can be hot without Principle, passionate without affection, & eloquent without sensation.

It would anger a warm or a tender heart so much, to see the Conduct of the World, on all the most important or affecting occasions, that one would be tempted to wish every such thinking or feeling man retired from it. I, who have really no other, or no equal merit to that of loving & pursuing Merit, in, & thro' others, do sincerely wish myself in Scotland or the Forest, contemplating some *One Good Mind*, preferably to the melancholy study of the world, or Reading the very worst sort of Books, men & manners. The very Gazetteer is more innocent & better bred.[1] When he abuses the Brave, or insults the Dead, he lays the fault another day upon his *Printer*: But our Great Men & Patriots cannot so much as lay their Brutalitys & ill Breeding upon their *Porters* & *Footmen*. They hate Honour openly, & pray devoutly for the Removal of all Virtue. Their prayers have been pretty well heard, & when one or two more are gone, the nation will be much of a piece. I could then be glad to travel, and I could be more glad if your Lordship would travel. You may perhaps think it less merit to travel from Scotland, than from *Twitnam*: But consider here's a Camp close by, in whose Neighborhood Minerva cannot dwell, tho no Mars be there. I am seriously desirous to run from my Country, if you'l run from yours, & study Popery & Slavery abroad a while, to reconcile ourselves to the Church & State we may find at home on our return.

Pray, my Lord, do not think I can forget you, nor on that Imagination use me as if I could, by not putting me in mind of you. Whether you take any notice of me or not, I shall never see any Good or any Evil happen to this Country, but I shall immediately ask myself the question, How will it please or displease Lord Marchmont? and I shall

[1] This remark, like Pope's line 84 in Dialogue I of the 'Epilogue to the Satires' ('No gazetteer more innocent than I'), has been taken as referring to the writer of the official *London Gazette*; but since the *Gazette* did not abuse the brave and insult the dead, the reference is doubtless to Walpole's most objectionable party paper of the moment, *The Daily Gazetteer*. This in the late thirties became the aversion of men like Pope and Fielding, both of whom replied to personal attacks in it.

sett my own Mind by that, either to be glad or sorry. May ev'ry Domestic happiness attend you! and Resignation & Expectation mend whatever is amiss, & palliate whatever is incurable, as to the Public. Believe no man more your mindful Servant than I; but Lord Chesterfield & Mr Lyttelton bid me tell you they will dispute it with me.

Endorsement: June 22.

POPE *to* WARBURTON[1] 24 *June* [1740]

Egerton 1946

Twitnam. June 24.

It is true that I am a very unpunctual Correspondent, tho no unpunctual Agent or Friend, and that in the Commerce of Words I am both poor, & lazy. Civility & Compliment generally are the Goods that Letter-writers exchange, which with honest men seems a kind of Illicite Trade, by having been for the most part carryd on, & carried furthest, by designing men. I am therfore reduced to plain Enquiries how my Friend does, or what he does? & to Repetitions, which I am afraid to tire him with, how much I love him. Your two kind Letters gave me real Satisfaction in hearing you were safe & well, & in shewing me you took kindly my unaffected Endeavors to prove my Esteem for you & Delight in your Conversation: Indeed my languid State of health, & frequent Deficiency of Spirits, together with a number of Dissipations—& aliena negotia centum,[2] all conspire to throw a Faintness & Cool Appearance over my Conduct to those I best love: which I perpetually feel, & grieve at. But in earnest no man is more deeply touchd with Merit in general, or with particular Merit toward me, in any one. You ought therfore, in both views, to hold yourself what you are to Me, in My Opinion & Affection: so high in each that I may perhaps seldom attempt to tell it you. The greatest Justice & Favour too that you can do me is to take it for granted.

Do not therfore commend my Talents but instruct me by your own. I am not really Learned enough to be a judge in Works of the nature & Depth of yours, but I travel thro your book,[3] as thro an Amazing Scene of ancient Egypt or Greece, struck with Veneration & Wonder, but at every step wanting an Instructor to tell me all I wish to know. Such you prove to me in the Walks of Antiquity & such you will prove to all Mankind: But with this additional Character, more than Any other Searcher into Antiquities, that of a Genius equal to your Pains, & of a Taste equal to your Learning.

I am obligd greatly to you, for what you have projected at Cam-

[1] Printed by Warburton, 1751.

[2] Horace, *Sermones*, II. vi. 33.

[3] *The Divine Legation of Moses*, 1738, 1741.

brige in relation to my Essay;[1] but more for the Motive which did originally, & does consequentially in a manner, animate all your goodness to me, the Opinion you entertain of my honest Intention in that Piece, & your Zeal to demonstrate Me no Irreligious Man. I was very sincere with you in what I told you of my own opinion of my own character as a Poet, & I thi[nk] I may Conscientiously say I shall dye in it. I have nothing to add, but that I hope sometimes to hear you are well, as you certainly shall now & then hear the Best I can tell you of myself.

I am, with true regard & affection, | Dear Sir | Yours. | A. Pope

*POPE *to* ALLEN 17 *July* [1740]

Egerton 1947

July the 17th

You will never wonder at the silence of a Man, who you are sure can never forget you, or express to you more of his Regard & Friendship than he has already over & over. It is Enough in this life to be sure of the Principle of any one, the Effect & Action can only appear as Occasions bring them forth: and it is but seldome (God knows) that those offer, to the Men who most desire them.

I have imployed you often this year in triffles, about furnishing my Grotto, tho such triffles cost you as much trouble as if they were more serious things, and the Zeal you have for sending me Supplies as soon as possible, (by Land rather than to make me stay for the Ships,) costs too much for a piece of Vanity, for so our Friends the Quakers would call it, unless I set a Sentence of Scripture in the Grotto, *Oh come, & see the Works of the Lord!*

I wish this Sentence might be an Exhortation to Mrs Allen & You to proceed hither from Newbury for a few days, for I cannot possibly hope to go to Bath before the End of Septr. I have been obliged for a very good reason (the Health of a Friend who was prescribd to travel for his Life) to go with him as far as Southampton,[2] where I think I have taken my last Sight of that Place, which has so long been a pleasing one to me. For I am very sure, I have not much strength left, nor much Life, all it can allow me will be to see You, & (if I can stretch it so far) One Friend more abroad.[3] In either of your Houses if I drop, I drop contented; Otherwise, Twitnam will see the last of me. I am in no pain but my Case is not curable, & must in course of time as it does not diminish, become painful first, & then fatal. And what

[1] Mr. Pope desired the editor to procure a good translation of the *Essay on Man* into Latin prose.—Warburton, 1751.

[2] The friend is unidentified. Pope's last view of Bevis Mount is what he regrets.

[3] Probably Bolingbroke.

of all this? without any Distemper at all, Life itself does so, & is itself a pain, if continued long enough. To that Providence is equal, even between what seem so wide extremes, as Health & Infirmity.

Before the End of this month, I hope to send you one or two Pine-apples, that they may not miss you on your March to Newbury. This warm Season makes them very good.

I've seen Mr Vandiest again. We are quite agreed now about Moses & St Paul; & I hope we shall be as much of one accord concerning Homer & Socrates.

Just now I hear of another Cargo of your Stone for my Grotto. I may properly be said to be *loaded* with your favours; but that they may not be *heap'd upon my head*, I have taken care to secure them by many Cramps: and as soon as I get a few more things from Cornwall, I shall finish this last of the laborious Baubles of my life.

Do not think I forget the happy Union of Mr Prynn & Mrs Cadwallador;[1] I wish them Joy, and such an Heir, as may not (like most Heirs of Great Familyes) disgrace the high Plood of the Welsh Princes: Who, I have heard, the first Syllable they utter, cry Ap-ap- to prove their Genealogy; 'tho some modern Criticks fancy they only cry for Applepye: I am Dear Sir Ever faithfully Yours. A.P.

Address: To Ralph Allen Esqr, at | Widcomb, near | Bath.
Postmark: 17/IY

POPE *to* HUGH BETHEL[2] [1740]

Egerton 1948

Twitnam. Sunday Evening

The Truth is, I have been in a low dispirited way, with a constant Pain at my side, & a difficulty of Urine: so that I've drank only milk & water, to keep cool, & scarce us'd any Motion but by Water. I wish'd much to see you agen, but fear'd running about or taking Cold, apprehending the least Inflammation. If it continues, I will send to Mr Cheselden or go to him to Chelsea & if I do, I will not fail to go on to London to pass an hour or [two] with you; in case you do not set out this morning, (which I fancy if Lord Sh—[3] comes to Town, you may not.) If you do, God bless you, and preserve you long, for a Comfort to your Friends, & Example to a World of little worth. I shall as long

[1] In Allen's will £400 is bequeathed to his clerk Samuel Prynne and £100 to his wife. They are presumably the 'Sam and Betty' who are '*in* for life' in Pope's letter of 17 June. See R. M. Peach, *Life and Times of Ralph Allen*, p. 237.

[2] The date is most uncertain. The letter was written after 1737, when Cheselden's connexion with Chelsea Hospital began, and before 1741, when Bethel went abroad for his health. It seems to fit the summer of 1740. See Pope's next to Bethel, 2 Aug.

[3] ? Lord Shelburne. See Pope to Bethel, 2 Aug.

as I live, desire to hear of you: pray let me have a line as soon as you are at your Journy's End: and believe, no man more truly loves & Esteems you, than | A. Pope.

*POPE *to* ALLEN[1] [? *August* 1740]

Harvard University

FRAGMENT

enable me) I will go with you from Newbury, or if I can venture, before I've done it. In the meantime, I'l take your advice, & go on with my Plaything, the Grotto: But I am at a full stop. The Gold-cliff which Mr Omer has taken so much pains about, altho he writ me word 3 weeks ago it was procurd, has never arrived, & I've inquird at both Carriers very often in vain. Which way it was sent, from Wales or Bristol or Bath, I know not: and desire to have timely notice when anything comes. I need no more of your Stone; and I rejoice extraordinarily that Mrs Allen has begun to imitate the Great Works of Nature, rather than those Bawbles most Ladies affect. I hope you have not impoverishd Your Rock to beautify mine.—I long for Dr Oliver's supply; He and his Friend, Mr Borlace, ought to have their Statues erected in my Cave, but I would much rather see their persons there; & I should be prouder of their approbation, if they think I have imitated nature well, than they would be of Statues, though Art had counterfeited them ever so well. I would go to Cornwall on purpose to thank them, if I were able.

Endorsement: Mr Pope

*POPE *to* HUGH BETHEL 2 *August* 1740

Egerton 1948

London, Aug. 2d. 1740.

I was much eased in my mind on the receit of your Letter, as I was in pain at hearing in how ill a State you left the Town. And I wished for a more Speedy Account of you. Indeed My Lord Shelburn's accompanying you was an Act of Friendship, and yet I hope there are more than he who would as gladly attend or assist you, as there must be more who are Sensible enough of Virtue to Esteem You, & wish

[1] This letter was offered for sale by Thomas Thorpe in his catalogue of 1833, apparently as a complete letter. It exists now as a fragment bound with other Popiana. Omer is concerned with Pope's grotto (so far as we know) only in 1740. He has been away at least three weeks, and the Allens are still planning a journey to Newbury, though that has evidently been postponed beyond the time first suggested. The phrase 'if I can venture before I have done it' may refer to the proposed treatment by Cheselden—which should precede a journey to Bath. The fragment, when printed by Carruthers (1857), p. 176, was the property of his publisher, H. G. Bohn, and was already only a fragment.

the Prolongation of your Life. Nay I think the more any Man is sensible of Virtue, the more he will wish You well, & such as you. I am heartily glad to hear the Quicksilver has the usual good effect upon your asthma, pray let me hear how it proceeds in your Cure, & if you are quite recoverd? till when I shall not be quite releas'd from my Solicitude. I am at last *resolvd* (tho perhaps *compelld* were the truer word) to submit to the Operation of Mr Cheselden; he comes to me to morrow for that End. In truth, the constant fear of being in Extremity, on every little Cold I catch, or upon any Heat by Motion, makes Life uncomfortable & precarious; and it is arrived of late to that point that I am waked five or six times in a night with a Pressure to make water, whatever Diet or Liquids I can use. You shall know how it goes with me; but it shall be upon this Bribe, that you first tell me how you do? There is unfeinedly no man, if I live, whose Life I shall more desire to be Coæval with; and no man, if I die, whose Friendship I would so soon confide in, to execute my Last Cares, & extend them to my Friends left behind. Mrs Patty Blount is in Town, in the same unpleasant State we have so long known and lamented her in: but always faithfully yours, & always remembring and regretting you. I'm sorry we are not allowed by Fate to be more constant Neighbours, & that Souls that think & feel alike must live in so disagreeing Spheres of Action, and Habit. We are equally Lovers of Quiet, but she has none at home, and I have none abroad. I hope in God you have in both. Had I Strength & health, I might travel sometimes & pass part of the Summers (which are my best days) in Yorkshire: Had she Resolution, we might both see her with more comfort, in Winter in London. Nor would it be a Sin, or shame if we lived now & then all together at Twitnam. I h[ave] nothing to tell you, but that Mr Ralph[1] is detected of [ha]ving writt at one & the same time for the Ministry, in the Free Britons, Courants, & Gazetteers, and against them in Fog & the Champion: which the Gazetteer has publishd, & he has replyd to by owning & defending it. Adieu, May all health & happiness attend you. My Services to Mr Moyzer. I am ever | Faithfully Yours | A. Pope

I kept this till another post that I might just tell you how I under go this operation. It is with a good deal of pain. the Stoppage is found by the Probe, and lies within an inch of the Os Pubis; it must be often repeated in hopes to wear the passage wider. The worst is the Pain upon every making water after it, for six or seven hours, the Salts of the Urine stimulating the Sore places; which must continue till by

[1] *The Daily Gazetteer* (e.g. 1 Aug.) was at this time attacking James Ralph (notable for being in *The Dunciad*) for his part in *The Champion*, &c. Ralph protested that he had not written a single line *for* 'his Honor' (Walpole) since he began in *The Champion*.

Use it grow more open & callous. The Remedy is (at present) worse than the Disease, for that gives me no pain, but Uneasiness.

Address: To Hugh Bethel Esq at Beswick | near Beverley | Yorkshire.
Postmark: 3/AV (possibly 8/AV)

POPE *to* ROBERT NUGENT — 14 *August* 1740

Yale University

Augst 14th 1740.

Sir,—I cannot enough acknowledge your obliging Endeavors as to what has given me so much apprehension, the affair of the Letters:[1] all which, I am now convinced, has been a mere Feint to amuse us both. For last week I receivd an account from Faukener[2] the Dublin Bookseller, "That the Dean himself has given him a Collection of Letters; of his own & mine & others, to be printed; & he civilly asks my Consent: assuring me the D. declares them genuine, & that Mr Swift, Mrs Whiteway's Son in law, will correct the press, out of his great respect to the Dean & myself." He says, they were collected by some unknown persons, & the Copy sent with a Letter, importing that "it was criminal to suppress such an amiable Picture of the Dean, & his private Character appearing in those letters, & that if he would not publish them in his life time, others would after his death."

I think I can make no Reflections upon this strange Incident, but what are truly melancholy, & humble the Pride of human Nature. That the greatest of Genius's tho Prudence may have been the Companion of Wit (which is very rare) for their whole Lives past, may have nothing left them at last but their Vanity. No Decay of Body is half so miserable! I shall write, & do, all I can upon this vexatious Incident, but I despair of stopping what is already no doubt in many hands. Can it be possible the Dean has forgot, how many years, & by how many instances, I have pressd him to secure me from this Very thing?[3] or can it be imagind Mrs W. has remonstrated against it? The moment

[1] The 'several' letters that Mrs. Whiteway has offered to return.

[2] In the letter of 29 July from Faulkner, mentioned (but not preserved) by Pope in his long narrative letter to Orrery of 30 Dec. 1740. In writing now to Nugent Pope begins his pretences of ignorance as to how the letters got to Ireland. From now on he writes to Nugent, Mrs. Whiteway, but chiefly to Orrery about the matter. If he wrote to Swift (which at this time is doubtful), the letters were not preserved. Many of his letters to Swift about preserving and publishing their letters must have been destroyed. Swift's letters about the matter Pope willingly printed.

[3] Pope pressed Swift by his own letters (most of which he did not preserve), such as those of 30 Dec. 1736, or 17 Aug. 1736, where he says significantly to Swift: 'I . . . will preserve all the memorials I can that I was of your intimacy.' Other such passages would exist in suppressed letters. He also pressed Swift vicariously through Orrery, who became his agent in Ireland for the whole matter. How completely Orrery was in Pope's confidence is not clear.

I had your Intimation that she would return them, I wrote to her, & embraced her offer with thanks: She answerd me, lately, that she would not send them to Mr Nugent, but by a certain Mr MacAulay: I presume now, that she would have sent but a few of no consequence; for the Bookseller tells me there are several of Lord Bolingbroke's &c (which must have been in the Dean's own custody; and one of which was printed twelve years ago.) I would therfore trouble you no more in this unlucky affair. I believe they had entertained a Jealousy of You, as the same persons did before of my Lord Orrery: They then prevented the Dean from complying to any purpose with my request: they then sent a few, just to save Appearances; & possibly to serve as a sort of plea to excuse them from being taxed of this Proceeding, which is now thrown upon the Dean himself.

The Mundicks[1] will arrive very seasonably: If any thing will amuse me at present, it must be playing the fool any way but by Writing; and yet you see how long this Letter is. I heartily wish you Success in bringing a little more English Spirit into Cornwall, and in routing the Gog-magog's of the present Age. I am not without hopes of meeting you at Bath, and joyning with the Waters to heat your Head to Poetry.

—Satyrarum ego, ni pudet illas,
Adjutor, gelidos veniam caligatus ad agros.[2]

I am Sir | Your most obliged & faithful Servant | A. Pope.

POPE *to* ROBERT NUGENT[3] 16 *August* 1740

Yale University

Aug. 16. 1740.

Sir,—I did not think, when I troubled you so lately with an Account, in how surprizing a Manner Your kind Negotiations in my behalf were terminated; that I should so soon again have interrupted your present, better, business. But upon reflection, that my Answer to Faukener concerning this, ought to be hasten'd, & in an Apprehension that some pretence might be taken, as if it was not received, I thought it proper to have it transmitted otherwise than by the Common Post. I beg therfore that you will send it by or thro' some hand you know,

[1] For the grotto.

[2] Juvenal, iii. 321–2.

[3] Pope's reply to Faulkner's letter of 29 July was not, apparently, preserved by Faulkner. Pope sends it for sure carriage, so he says, to Nugent, with this letter. The next we hear in the matter is Faulkner's letter to Orrery, undated, which comments on Pope's reply, received in September.

Pope answered promptly, but transmission was delayed. He sent the letter to Nugent at Bristol. An original address, 'the hot Well, in | Bristol', has been marked out, since the letter had to be sent back to London, where Nugent actually was. The second Postmark (30/AV) indicates the date at which it was returned to London.

who may deliver it personally to Faukener, after you have read it, or (if you think fit) Copy'd. Excuse this in One, who sees, & is obliged by, the Part you have taken; & wishes himself capable of proving how much he is | Sir Your most faithfull humble Servant | A. Pope.

Address: To R: Nugent, Esqr at | the Hon Mrs Nugent's, at | the hot Well in | Bristol.

Postmarks: 23/AV and 30/AV

POPE *to* SARAH, DUCHESS OF MARLBOROUGH[1]

[1740]

Blenheim

Your Grace will excuse this short Note. I was in Town from Saturday last, & must be there again (I fear) for two or three days, more, about a troublesome Business of a Relation of mine. I am not certain what day I shall be sent for, which makes me unwilling to name one; but I think I can come to Wimbledon from London some day next week, of which I will advertise your Grace. I will not go to Bath while you stay there, that I may have the more opportunities of seeing you. I send the Green book,[2] with many thanks, by the Bearer, Which I have read over three times. I wish Every body you love, may love you, & am sorry for every one that does not.

POPE *to* SARAH, DUCHESS OF MARLBOROUGH[3]

[? 1740]

Blenheim

I can say nothing to your Grace that is pretty, or in the Way of a Wit; which I thank God never was the character of me or my writing, But I honestly thank you; you are directly kind to me, & I shall love you. This is very ill-bred, but it is true, & I cannot help it.—The Papers you favord me with, shew so much Goodness, & so much

[1] As Pope remarked to Swift (30 Dec. 1736), the river of time had removed many friends; but, he adds, 'it throws weeds and sedges in their room'—a metaphor that he printed in 1741. Among these was no less a personage than Sarah, Duchess of Marlborough. Pope's acquaintance with her dated at least from early 1739, when (17 May) he mentions to Swift her 'advances'. Courthope (EC, v. 408–22) dated the first letters from Pope to Her Grace in 1741; but the late summer of 1740 seems better for this brief and informal note. It evidently would not be the first letter Pope addressed to the Duchess, but it seems to be the first that we have preserved to us. In 1740 Pope was involved in his sister's lawsuit, not in 1741. In 1740 he was doubtful as to the date of departure to Bath; in 1741 the date depended on Allen, who was to take him thither.

[2] The 'Green Book' (bound in green parchment) contained data on the career of the 1st Duke and on the difficulties between the Duchess and her daughters. It is used by Sir Winston Churchill in his *Marlborough*, vi. 641 ff.

[3] This letter seems to come early in the friendship of the Duchess for Pope, and perhaps just after he has expressed such pleasure (in the preceding letter) for 'the Green Book'. One can hardly be sure.

Frankness of Nature, that I should be sorry you ever thought of writing them better, or of suffering any other to do so. In a word your Conquest will be Complete over me, but you conquer a Cripple that would follow you, but cannot. You are the last person that shall ever see him sleep, tho he has been, some years, fast asleep to all other Great people. If your Grace dares to try next Saturday, how long he can talk at Ease in his own Chair, pray come at any hour and see. I am to be from home till then, & then indeed Mr Hooke & his Daughter are to be here: so that if your Grace likes me best alone, I will wait for this pleasure any other day after Sunday, & will then return into your own hands the very obliging Deposite[1] you intrusted me with, & which I esteem as I ought, a particular Mark of the Friendship your Grace honors me with. I am, with true Sense of it, | Madam, | Your most faithfull and obedient, humble | Servant, | A. Pope.

It is so late, & my Eyes so bad toward night, that I beg you to excuse what is hardly legible to my own, I hope in God it is more legible to yours: even at your age.

POPE *to* CHARLES BATHURST[2] — 29 *August* [1740]

The Gentleman's Magazine, xliv, N.S. (1855), 586

Twitnam, Aug. 29.

Sir,—I had many things to say to you when I sent, but there's no haste. I shall print some things more of Scriblerus, and add to what is already done; but it will be in Quarto, and the new part of the Vol. be above two-thirds of the old. I don't care to alienate the Property, but if you have any mind to treat for the impression I will give you the refusal.

I have endeavoured to serve you as to a Volume of all Dr Swift's Pieces collected, and more selected than the present. It would be for his Honour, and, when I can be in town for a day or two, I will tell you the Event of my Negotiations. I believe Dr King has mentioned it to you.—I am your very affectionate Servant | A. Pope.

Pray deliver the inclosed[3] to Mr. Lintot.

[1] Papers, presumably, in addition to the Green Book mentioned in the preceding letter.

[2] This letter was placed in 1741 by Elwin, but since it concerns the publication of *Scriblerus* in the volume of Swift's letters, it must fall in 1740, since the volume (including *Scriblerus*) appeared in Apr. 1741. Bathurst, J. & P. Knapton, and Dodsley were the publishers whose names appeared on the quarto title-page of *The Works of . . . Pope in Prose*, vol. ii, which contained the first published edition of the Swift letters. The additional things were 'Tracts' which he had wished to print with the letters of 1737. See above, iv. 68 and 240.

[3] The nature of the enclosure is unknown.

POPE *to* ROBERT NUGENT 3 *September* 1740

Yale University

Sept. 3. 1740.

Sir,—The more I read your Ode, the less I find any Necessity of making it clearer; You have sufficiently distinguish'd your Idæa of the Multitude. The very few things I could imagine alterable, I have put in; but in so modest a Character, as easily to be erased if you disapprove them. I could be willing to be of greater Service to you, but you must thank your Superior Circumstances, as a Poet no less than as a Man, that I cannot. I am however intentionally, tho not virtually, | Sir | Your most faithfull & | obedient humble Servant. | A. Pope.

I hope you have had my Letter, which I beg you to forward by some particular hand to Faukener.[1]

Mrs Nugent I know remembers me, & so do I her, always, & acknowledge her Good Temper towards me, who does not quarrel with me as other Ladies have done.

Address: To | R. Nugent, Esqr

POPE *to* BOLINGBROKE[2] 3 *September* 1740

Add. 35586

Septr 3d 1740.

My Dear Lord,—Your every word is kind to me, & all the openings of your mind amiable. Your communicating any of your Sentiments both makes me a happier & a better man. There is so true a fund of all Virtue public & Social within You, I mean so right a Sense of things as we stand related to each other by the Laws of God, and indebted to each other in conformity to those Laws, that I hope no partic: Calamity can swallow up your care & concern for the General. Indeed the loss of Sir Wm Windham must have been felt more deeply, as a particular, by You than by any other: and I see nothing so manly, nothing so edifying, as your not deserting the com: Cause of your Country at this juncture. No man has less obligation to her, no man feels a stronger than yourself. Your Resolution to return to her if She wants to be saved, & will or can be saved, is by far a more disinterested one than any of her Sons can pretend, & every one, who knows either

[1] The letter had come from Bristol 30 Aug., and Pope is probably more concerned about it than about Nugent's ode, which is unidentified. Writing to Nugent on 26 Mar. 1740 Pope had particularized the excellence of Nugent's Ode to Marchmont.

[2] This letter, hitherto printed (in the *Supplement* [1825] to Warton's ed. of Pope and in EC) from the transcript made by Thomas Birch (Sloan MS. 4291), is here printed from a transcript found among the Hardwicke Papers. Both scribes have excessively bad hands, but the present text seems slightly superior.

her Condition or your Ability, (& more than your Ability your sense of Duty & honour) must rest his chief hope upon it. Lord M.[1] does so in the ultimate Resource. he holds no other Language, as he knows to hold no language but that of his heart; and unless You animate him to act by that hope will drop all thought of action. No other has the least influence, & all his friends Entreaties have been tried in Vain to draw him from Scotland for this Winter to come. Lord Chesterfield despairs as much; but resolves to act. He & Lyttelton think alike & act the best part, that I believe ever was acted, in their conduct & Counsels to their Master.[2] But still I will say, be others as honest as they will, they cannot be so generous as You. They must, if good Counsels prevail, reap benefits You will not reap, & may expect to have those fruits, of which You can see the blossoms only. The Monks & Asceticks tell us we are not attained to perfection till we serve God for *his* sake only, not *our* own, not even for the hope of Heaven. You really would serve *men* in this manner, and men, whom You have no obligation to love, & who have done their best to ruin You, all in their Turns. It must therefore be called by it's true Name; not so much Love to your Country as to God: It is not Patriotism, but downright Piety, & instead of celebrating You as a Poet should, I would (if I were Pope) Canonize You, whatever all the Advocates for the Devil could say to the contrary.

But I hope the Time for that is not near, & that your Reward in the next life (which I am satisfied must be the sole motive of such a Conduct) will be defered at least during my own time. There is nothing at present I desire so much to hear as that your bilious fever is quite removed; the repeated Attacks of which have given me an Alarm greater I assure You than almost any other worldly Event could give Me, who daily find my self passing into that State of indifference, out of which I would wake others, whom Providence seems (by their Talents) to ordain to do more good to mankind. I have a more partic: Interest too in that Life than any other at present as a private man; for the greatest Vanity I have is to see finished that noble work, which You address to me,[3] & where my Verses, interspersed here & there, will have the same honour done them to all Posterity as those of Ennius in the Philosophic writings of Tully.

Next to patching up my Constitution, my great Business has been to patch up a Grotto (the same You have so often sate in the Sunny part of under my house,) with all the varieties of Natures works under ground—Spars Minerals & Marbles. I hope yet to live to philosophize

[1] Marchmont.

[2] The Prince of Wales, whom they tried to regard as the titular leader of the Opposition.

[3] This noble work seems not to have been executed. As here described it would seem to have involved an interpretation of the *Essay on Man*, rival to that of Warburton.

with You in this Musæum, which is now a Study for Virtuosi, & a Scene for contemplation. At least I am resolved to have it remembered that You *was* there, as You'l see from the Verses I dare to set over it.[1] Adieu; may You & Your's be happy.

Thou, who shalt stop, where Thames translucent wave
Shines a broad Mirror thro' the Shadowy Cave;
Where lingering drops from Mineral Rocks distill,
And pointed Crystalls break the sparkling Rill;
Unpolished Gems no Ray on Pride bestow,
And latent Metals innocently glow.
Approach! Great Nature studiously behold.
And Eye the Mine without a wish for Gold.
Awful as Plato's Grove or Numa's Grot
Here nobly-pensive St John sate & thought.
Here patriot Sighs from Wyndham's bosom stole,
And shot the growing Flame thro' Marchmont's Soul.
Let Such, Such only, tread this Sacred Floor,
Who dare to love their Country & be poor.

Endorsement: Copy of a letter from | Mr P. to Lord B. | Sept. 3. 1740

POPE *to* THE EARL OF ORRERY — *3 September* 1740

The Pierpont Morgan Library

My Lord,—I have many Reasons, & One (God knows) almost peculiar to me, not to trouble even my Friends, & above all, those who are most partial to me, with my Letters: Yet once a Year or thereabouts, I cannot but renew my Claim to the Memory of those by whom I should be sorry ever to be forgotten, as I am sure they think the most candidly of me; and You, my Lord, must be content to be in this Class. My Lady Orrery too has obliged me with so much Distinction, that I know no Words good enough to be grateful to her, but by obtaining of your Lordship to express to her in Your own, how sensible I am of the honour She has done me. God forgive her for endeavouring (as a Lady) to be useful to her Inferiors, & for thinking of a thing so much below her, as the Linnen for my Table.

But would to God I had nothing more to say, and that I did not now write to beg your Help, in a most disagreeable Circumstance. I remember with all Acknowledgment the kind pains your Lordship took some years since, in the Transaction with the Dean of S. Patrick's about my Letters. Give me leave to make a short Recapitulation of

[1] The verses, somewhat revised, were printed in *Gent. Mag.* xi (Jan. 1741), 45. Another version (with two additional lines) was sent to Dr. Oliver, and is printed in *The Quarterly Review*, cxxxix. 384–5.

them, and to add the Conclusion to that History, with the astonishing Catastrophe of it at this present

Upon what had happen'd to me from the famous Curll, and upon finding one or two Letters of Lord Bolingbrokes & mine to the Dean, in print,[1] which could have come out only thro' his channel, I prest him to destroy or return me the rest, if he had kept any. He answerd, "he had kept Every Scrap I had written to him, fastend in a folio Cover, and indorsed in order: that he would give his EXECUTORS strict orders in his Will to burn every Letter he left behind him, but that he was unwilling that those of Mr Pope & a few other Friends should die before him."[2] When your Lordship press'd the Matter again, it was answerd, "there was a Chasm in those Letters of several years, of which he could find no Copies; but believd they were left in some Friend's hands, when on certain occasions he secreted his papers." he "had therfore but a *few*, which he would send by your Lordship."[3] —After this, to my great surprize, the Dean writes me word, that "Every letter I ever sent him these twenty years & more, were deliverd to Mrs Whiteway, a very worthy, rational, & judicious Relation of his: All which SHE was directed to send me at his decease." But in a Post-script he corrects himself, & says, "She assures him She has them not, but that a *great Collection* of them are in *some very safe hand*."[4] This was just when your Lordships Negotiation ended;[5] and here it rested, notwithstanding any repetition of my Desire to have them restored, till the End of the last year.

Mrs Whiteway then acquainted Mr Nugent, that the Letters were found, and that she would transmit them to me.[5] He came away without them; but wrote at my request, & proposed some methods of conveying them safely, the last of which was sending them by his Mother, but she also came without them. In the mean time Mrs W. was pleas'd to write to me confirming Mr N.'s account, but chusing to send them by another hand. I answerd her with all respect, accepted her offer with all acknowledgment and remained in full expectation of the Favour.

Her Letter bore date the 3d of June last, and was followed the next month by one from Mr Faukener the Bookseller,[6] which in short acquaints me,

[1] Curll had printed (in vol. v of *Mr. Pope's Literary Correspondence* [1737]) as two letters the joint letter from Pope and Bolingbroke of [Aug. 1723]. See ii. 183–9.

[2] Pope seems to conflate remarks from Swift's letters to him of 3 Sept. 1735 and 31 May 1737.

[3] Here Pope paraphrases Lord Orrery's report in a letter to Pope of 2 June 1737 as well as Swift's letter of 31 May 1737.

[4] See Swift to Pope, 8 Aug. 1738.

[5] Pope is with deceitful intent writing here for publication. He quite omits the important detail that Orrery brought over the autograph letters to him from Dublin in July 1737, and goes on to the second lot that Mrs. Whiteway in 1740 offered to return. See the letters to and from Nugent, 26 Mar., 2 Apr., &c.

[6] Neither of these letters was printed or (apparently) preserved by Pope.

"That a Collection of Letters betwixt the Dean & me, had been sent to the Dean by some unknown persons (from London he supposes, tho they call themselves in their letter, His Countrymen, & speak of his Merits to Ireland) And that the Dean having read, & thinking them genuine, has given them to him to be printed."

I am sure I need make no Reflections on this whole Proceeding from the beginning to the end; they will be abundantly suggested to a Man of your Candor & Honour. We shall both join in One, which is to lament the Dean's Condition, & not to irritate, but pity him.

I returnd to Faukener the strongest Negation I could possibly. I could not honestly do otherwise, but I fear the Strength of my Refusal will hinder the End I propose, to get the Book out of their hands (tho I apprehend that in a Month's time or more they may have taken Copies, or at least will before they send it me) I told him I could not otherwise judge whether mine were genuine? But if to this pretence, your Lordship would add as from yourself "That if You, upon perusal of them, find no Objection, and are of the Dean's opinion, you will endeavour to obtain my Consent, provided they send me the Copy first, to *correct* & to *improve* it," (for to *Expunge* or *Omit* I fear are words not to be used to a Bookseller, tho That would be a Point worth obtaining in so vexatious a Circumstance) And I should at least know by this means, if they show it your Lordship, the Opinion of one Man of Sense, what the things are, & what Fate I am to expect?

My Lord, I think you will not deny me this favor; I think it no small one, the rather because it is a sort of Trick, a thing I am sure you would not practise, except in Extremity, and without any possible ill consequence or injury to any one.

I have nothing to add but my sincere Wishes for your own & Lady Orrery's mutual felicities, & the health & prosperity of all yours. I am with true Esteem, | My Lord | Your most Obliged & | most faithfull humble | Servant, | A. Pope.

Sept. 3d 1740.

POPE *to* SARAH, DUCHESS OF MARLBOROUGH[1]

5 *September* [1740]

Blenheim

London, Sept. 5

I have found it out of my Power to get to your Grace from hence: therfore if you please to send for me to Twitnam, on Tuesday morning,[2] or to come thither any time that day, I will be Wholly in your

[1] Dated by Courthope 1741, it seems to follow the note here placed in late August. The year 1741 is not impossible.

[2] Tuesday would be the 9th. Courthope wrongly printed 'evening' for 'morning'.

Disposal. Your Grace will find me, upon farther Acquaintance, really not worth all this Trouble. I have nothing & possess nothing, but a little Common Honesty, & Common Gratitude, for both which I have been often hated, & often hurt. But if I preserve, or obtain, the good opinion of a Few, & if your owne in particular is added to that of those Few, I shall be enough rewarded, & enough satisfied. I am | Madam | Your most obliged | & faithful Servant | A. Pope.

Address: To her Grace, the | Duchess of Marlborough.
Indorsement: Mr Pope

MARTHA BLOUNT *to* MRS. PRICE[1] 8 *September* 1740

Bowles (1806), x. 136

Sept. 8, 1740.

Dear Madam,—Considering how long I have been without writing to you, you will think I have no fair pretence to take ill your not writing to me: but the case is very different. You could give me great pleasure in telling me you had a good journey, that the waters did you good, etc. this is the chief: I could add, you do and can write agreeable Letters; you know I cannot: I can only repeat, what I have often told you, in a very dull but very sincere way, that nobody has more regard for you, nor is more interested in all that concerns your health and happiness, and wish you both with all my heart. I am told you don't come back this winter, which I grieve at, till you convince me 'tis for your advantage. I am also told Mrs. Pitt has left you much better in health, and that your liking and opinion of each other is just what I foretold. I hope my dear Miss Greville is in good health; pray assure her of my affectionate services. I have been ten days at Richmond, and confined ever since I came with a violent cold. I rejoice at Lord Cornbury's good health, and am his very faithful servant. The Princess lies in in the beginning of December. Lady Charlotte Edwine is gone to Bristol, I fear far gone in a consumption. Mrs. Greville[2] was extremely kind and obliging to me, when I was last at the Grove: I think all that country excessively fine. Miss Longs were there all the time: we played at quadrille; and every thing was so agreeable, that instead of staying as I proposed, a week, I stayed five.

I was just going to give you and Lord Cornbury an account of Mr. Pope; but he is come to see me, and will do it himself. I've also desired him to say something for me; for I can say so little for myself, that

[1] Mrs. Price, Lord Cornbury, and some of the ladies mentioned here are (or have been) at Spa.

[2] Sister of Mrs. Price and daughter of Lord Arthur Somerset.

by all I can say, you'll not believe me half so much as I sincerely am, my dear Mrs. Price, | Your most faithful and affectionate | humble servant, | M. Blount.

I can't quite forgive your writing to all your acquaintance, some of which, I think, deserved that favour less than I did, before you gave me that pleasure.

They have given over talking of the Duchess of B.[1] I don't hear her named now: I was sensible of the grief that affair gave you. Adieu. I hope your son is well.

POPE *to* MRS. PRICE[2] [8 *September* 1740]

Bowles (1806), x. 134

Pray, Madam, tell my Lord Cornbury, I am not worse than he left me, though I have endured some uneasiness since, besides that which his indisposition, when I parted, gave me. I am amply rewarded by his very kind Letter, and the good news it brought me of his amendment. I have had a correspondence with my Lord Clarendon,[3] who has in the most obliging manner imputed his journey to Spa to the encouragement I gave him to travel, and to the experience that he was abler to do so than he imagined himself. I earnestly wish his return, but not till he can bring himself whole to us, who want honest and able men too much to part from him: I hope, therefore, to see him this Sessions in full health and spirit. Madam, as to yourself, it would be some compliment in me to put any Lady in the same line with him; but as I know he likes your company, and as I know you deserve he should, I make no apology either to you or to him. *Sint tales animæ concordes!* (as you very well understand) is the best wish I can form for you both: and I leave it to his Lordship to translate, if you pretend you cannot. Sure I am you have already translated into your life and manners, if not into your language. I desired Mrs. Blount to write this sentence to you, and with it her service to Lord Cornbury, but she would not trust herself with so much Latin: I know some Ladies that would. If you don't come home, it imports you to be extremely the better for being abroad, for we shall be extremely the worse for it: so pray mend as fast as you can, the only way you can be mended. I am, Madam, | Your most faithful humble servant.

[1] Thought to be the Duchess of Beaufort. The 3rd Duke was a cousin of Mrs. Price. The Duchess was the daughter of Pope's deceased friend Viscountess Scudamore. Scandal about her was evidently active during this summer, though she was not divorced until 1744. See *Journals of the House of Lords*, xxvi. 279.

[2] Obviously sent to Spa with the preceding letter by Mrs. Blount.

[3] Cornbury's father.

*POPE *to* FORTESCUE 17 *September* 1740

The Pierpont Morgan Library

Your Letter is truly friendly, and contains in it all that I think a Friend's without Ostentation ought to contain; an Account of Your own, & an Enquiry after my health, & that of one or two others near me. All the Vanity and all the Folly of Letter-writing is out of date with me, and it is only to You & such as you, that I can sit down to put pen to paper to speak of myself. I am just as I was when I saw you, have been out of order with a difficulty of urine, & am better. I intend for Bath at the end of October.[1] Mrs Blount is at the Vineyard, where she has had a great Cold, but is out again. She has often rememberd you, & charged me to tell you so whenever I writ. I lent her some books, among the rest One by chance that was too philosophical for her, but Mrs Shepherd took it & read it all over.

Many of my Acquaintance have been ill, but I assure you there is no one for whom I am more concernd, than for yourself: The Gravel is a severe distemper, which I hoped you had not counted among yours, at least to any great degree. I wish you had Strength and Time enough to use so much Exercise as is requisite for that Complaint.

My whole Amusement this Autumn has been my Grotto, which proved a laborious Work, but is now ended, all but the pavement. I have conveyd into it three falls of water, which break very naturally over two Rocks of Cornish Diamonds & Plymouth Marbles, and murmur in a Cavern till they run out of sight. But this is an ill-timed pleasure, which may cost me a cold; unless I have the prudence & patience (two uncommon Virtues) to wait till next Summer to enjoy it. That all rational and seasonable Enjoyments may attend you & yours, is the hearty wish of | Dear Sir | Your ever faithfull | & obliged affectionate | Servant, | A. Pope.

Sept. 17. 1740.

Address: To the Honble Mr Justice For|tescue, at Fallapit near | Totness: | Devon:

Postmark: 18/SE

Endorsement: Mr Pope | Sept. 17. 1740

*POPE *to* GEORGE ARBUTHNOT 26 *September* 1740

Professor John M. Berdan

Sept. 26. 1740.

I should at all times willingly inquire after your Health during any absence from us, and had done it before now, if I had not receivd good

[1] Actually it was the middle of December before he went.

& frequent accounts of it from Mrs Arbuthnot.[1] I wish I could give you as satisfactory an account of Her health, which I have had several occasions of observing at Dr Broxholm's[2] here in my neighborhood, and indeed have seen (as well as learn'd from his own account of her Condition) to be greatly declining. A sort of low Fever, with a great Dejection of Spirits, and some unaccountable disorders about the Kidneys as She thinks, and from Indigestion as the Doctor believes, accompanied with Headakes and a Loss of appetite; all together really make me think it necessary to tell you of what I dare say She suppresses, and what I fear may be dangerous, if not taken in time. The Doctor tells me the Bath would be of service, but this she is very averse to. If you were here, to advise her, or persuade her to any thing you should find necessary, I believe it would be a Satisfaction to you as well as to herself; tho' I found (upon asking & examining at Mrs Broxholms desire whether she had told you the Whole of her Case,) that you had not been fully inform'd of it; I fancy out of an Unwillingness in her to deprive you of the Recess & Amusement you now injoy by knowing she is so ill, or of shortning it by bringing you up a little the sooner. You will, I am sure, take this officiousness of mine in good part, especially since I see your Doctor of opinion no Time should be lost. She was not at all the better for the Country, & Indeed looks ill and I think falls away. Believe me dear Sir, I shall always bear a sincere Concern for the Family and dear Children of so worthy a Father, and am, with the Esteem due to so deserving a Son, | Your faithfull affect: Servant | A. Pope

*POPE *to* HUGH BETHEL — 26 *September* [1740]

Egerton 1948

Sept. 26.

I was willing to delay my answer a while to your very kind letter, in a view of giving you the fuller account of the Effect of my progress in the Operation for the Strangury.[3] But I cannot do it in a way that will be satisfactory; for indeed the Severity of it, & the present Consequences from the Soreness of the Parts, made it too much for me to repeat often enough to obtain any effectual remedy. I find much will depend upon Diet & drink, and if that will not do to palliate I shall never be able to remove, the Complaint entirely. When one arrives to a certain Time of Life, stepping into Age, so many Maladies come upon

[1] This is George Arbuthnot's sister Anne, of whom Pope was very fond. There were two sisters, Margaret and Anne. Margaret apparently died in May of this year. See Mrs. P. S.-M. Arbuthnot, *Memories of the Arbuthnots* (1920), p. 161.

[2] Dr. Broxholm (see *DNB*) lived at Hampton when in the country.

[3] See Pope to Bethel, 2 Aug. 1740. Mention of the operation fixes the year of this letter.

us, that the only question seems to be, Which of them one had best die of? and whichsoever promises the most Easy, or threatens the least painfull death, e'en submit, to let that take its course, if we can stave off the others. So I must compound with the Piles, and Indigestion, and suffer them to get ground, in hopes to defeat the pains of the Strangury. Vegetable diet & cool liquors, with frequent purges, &c. I am tired of all this account, and pray say no more of it, when you write: but make me a pleasanter man than I can make you, in giving a better account of yourself than I can of myself. I am sorry for Col. Moyser and for you, who take so much interest in the welfare of your friends as to be sincerely (I know) afflicted for them. I am sorry for your Sisters loss in Mr Hucheson,[1] indeed ⌜he was a Man of a better sort than most of the present generation, a Man *natus melioribus annis*, when Gratitude, Honour, and the Love of our Country, were not made Objects of Ridicule. A little seeming Virtue in the Professions of Friendship, still remains; but the Misery is, no man can have a Sense of his Duty to his friend who wants it for his God or his Country, and such Professions can be depended on no farther, than they advance each other's Ends, or as long as two Knaves draw together. So that I fear Friendship is upon the wing, when Honour has taken its flight.⌝[2] The more is the death of a Man of the Manners of the Past Times, to be regretted. You give daily proof how valuable a true Friendship is, to all those who have any title to yours in any degree, & to me in particular, I should have said first to Mrs Patty B. to whom we both wish equally well, but who I fear will not be so much the better for it as I shall be. Your kind Motion as to laying out my Mony I have not yet embraced; but will if I find it necessary, and if your Brother find it as convenient, not else. in the meantime I put it into the S. Sea Annuities. I see Mrs Blount somtimes, but have been interrupted much by Accidents, & this Indisposition forces me to be very cautious of Cold-catching, or I should oftner cross the water.[3] She is as kind as she can in coming to me, and (to give her her due) will never be wanting in any Good she can do, or say, or wish, to those she thinks well of; in particular her constant Memory, and Expressions of Esteem, of and for you make her worthy of your kindness. She would write, but I have taken it on me at this time to tell you at once, how much We are both | Dear Sir. | Truly & Ever yours.

Lord Burlington is coming imediately to Landesborow, without my Lady, to stay a fortnight or 3 weeks.

[1] Possibly the 'loss' is that reported in *Gent. Mag.* x (1740), 413—the death of 'Archibald Hutchinson, Esq; near 80, Treasurer of the Middle Temple; formerly Member for Hastings, and famous for his Calculations on the public Debts'. He died 12 Aug.

[2] The passage in half-brackets was quoted by Ruffhead, p. 485.

[3] To Richmond.

THE EARL OF ORRERY *to* FAULKNER 27 *September* 1740

Elwin–Courthope, viii. 419–20

Caledon, Sept. 27, 1740.

Mr. Faulkner,—A painful fit of the gout in both my feet, and thank God only in my feet, has hindered me for some time past from telling you that I have lately had a letter from my friend, Mr. Pope,[1] who is under apprehensions that some of his letters, whether genuine or not he cannot tell, are going to be published by you on this side of the water. I should be extremely sorry that you, for whom I have a real regard, should give cause of uneasiness to a gentleman of Mr. Pope's consequence to the world in general, and to me in particular. You must give me leave therefore to interpose, and to entreat you would let me see the copy from whence you are printing, that I may endeavour to judge whether the letters are genuine or not. If I see no objection to their appearance in print I will endeavour to obtain Mr. Pope's consent for your publishing them, and you may assure yourself that my friendship for you will make me always zealous in promoting your advantage. I am, sir, your faithful servant.

My most humble service, and best wishes attend the dean. I have kept my bed fifteen days.

FAULKNER *to* THE EARL OF ORRERY[2] [*September* 1740]

Elwin–Courthope, viii. 420–1

[Sept. or Oct. 1740]

My Lord,—I had the favour of your lordship's favour of the 27th instant, and am exceedingly sorry to hear of your lordship's indisposition, of which I hope you are quite recovered. I wrote to Mr. Pope about two months ago[3] to let him know that the dean had given me a volume of letters to and from D. Swift to print, which he said were genuine. I waited more than a month for his answer, and not hearing from him I put them to the press. However, upon the receipt of his letter I put an entire stop to my impression, the sheets of which I shall show your lordship, as well as the book that was sent from London, in two or three days' time, as I propose to set out for Caledon to-morrow to have the honour of waiting on your lordship. It was the great esteem and regard I had for Mr. Pope which made me write to him,

[1] The letter of 3 Sept. 1740.

[2] Since Lord Orrery forwards this letter to Pope under date of 4 Oct., Faulkner (speaking of 'the 27th instant') must be writing about the end of September.

[3] Pope speaks of the letter (30 Dec. 1740, to Lord Orrery) as dated 29 July. Pope replied without much delay on 13 Aug., but addressed the letter under cover to Nugent at Bristol. Faulkner evidently received the letter during the first half of September, and has put an entire stop to the impression. There has been little, if any, dilatoriness in the matter.

for I could have published those letters without his knowledge; but as he had been ill-used by Curll and other booksellers, I was willing to convince him there was a bookseller in Ireland who had honour enough to forego his own advantage rather than offend or injure him, although at the hazard of losing the friendship of the dean, who has ever been my great friend and benefactor.

POPE *to* THE EARL OF MARCHMONT[1] [*October* 1740]

Arthur A. Houghton, Jr.

My Lord,—I know you as incapable of neglecting a man you think well of, as a Cause you think well of, and therfore I will always be so happy as to believe myself in your memory, while I continue in the same sentiments & Conduct which alone could ever make me deserving in any degree of your friendship. And that you can be forgot or neglected by any Honest man is as impossible as that he should renounce Virtue itself or the Cause for which he esteems you. If you knew the manner, in which every one you desire to be regarded by, expresses himself in your regard, both those who act in Publick, & those who would live with you in private life, your Lordship would not stay in Scotland a day longer than your necessary affairs require. There can be nothing where you are, to justify your Absenting yourself from them: & I will consent that you shall remain there as long, as you find the Scots more honest & more honorable than the English. I think the time of your quitting them (upon those terms) must happen a little after my Lord I—y's[2] arrival. But for God's sake, my Lord, how much soever you may despair of any Public Virtue, are you to renounce the Enjoyment of as much Private as can be had in this age? If you cannot exercise with success your Endeavors for your Country, are you to give up the only Comforts left a worthy man in that circumstance, the Presence of those of the same Heart, who if they cannot assist, will attend, will protest, will bear Testimony to Truth & Honour, and if those two are to dye in this nation, will see them decently interred, & join to weep over their graves. Is there *no Duty left*, after you have discharged the last to your Country? No Friends?

[1] This letter has hitherto been placed in August, shortly after Wyndham's death in June; but its mentions of Wyndham are merely designed as inducements to bring Marchmont back from Scotland for the opening of Parliament in November. At Hagley is preserved an autograph letter from Marchmont to Lyttelton, 24 Sept. 1740, in which Marchmont expresses his intention of staying in Scotland. 'I can be of no use', he says, and he has heard nothing to convince him to the contrary. At such a juncture the appeal of Pope's rhetoric may have been sought. Pope is stimulated by a letter from Bolingbroke, which he quotes in part to Marchmont. Pope may have preserved much of his correspondence with Bolingbroke, but his will left all MSS. to Bolingbroke, and as a result we have almost no letters for this period to or from his lordship.

[2] Ilay.

no Family? no Posterity? are there no Suppedimenta Philosophica, to sweeten the Life of a man, whose Conscience is clear, & makes (nay of its own nature must make in spite of all Clouds in the lower region) a Heaven within; and a situation preferable to all Worldly Glory, all Human admiration, or approbation? and above all which we call the Greatest? All this my Lord remains still to you. These Duties, and These Pleasures call upon you; If you enjoy & pursue them here, amid the sphere of ambition and Vice, you will render them greater, & enhance them, and invigorate them by the Opposition you will cause them to make, in some instances, and by the Example you will become of their Contraries, in all. Your Spirits cannot sink, your Talents cannot languish nor continue unexerted, while such Provocations are round you. Whereas, heaping earth over your head, and rusting into study, you will be—what shall I say—you will be—still no doubt an honest man, but no better than Lord C—.[1]

You will very much wrong the Candour that is natural to Great Genius's, if you make the least doubt of Lord B.'s[2] Professions of Friendship. He wrote to me upon this lamented Death. Multis Fortuna Vulneribus percussus, huic uni se imparem sensit. Yet it is no untruth I tell you, that more was said in his Letter of you, than of Him. I will transcribe only a paragraph or two—He no sooner mentions that loss, but he adds—"What a star has our Minister? Wyndham dead, Marchmont disabled![3] The Loss of Ma: & Wy: to our Country —I take for granted that you have a Correspondence with Lord M. I writ to him the other day; but do you write to him. I wish the event of W.'s death may not determine him to settle in Scotland? God forbid! Do not fail when you write, to tell him how much I honour his Virtue, and his Talents, & love his Person. He, and you, & I, are, by different causes, in much the same situation; Lovers of our Country, grieved at her present state, & unable to help her. I too have been ill, not yet recover'd, wounded afresh; Yet I will try to live, and renew a fund of health that may last some little time longer, and be more usefully imployed abroad than my last ten years were at home."—But after all this, he declares himself "ready to return, on the first probable occasion to do any service." Pray my Lord make this an Example. For my part, I am so elevated in my own opinion by his adding me in the Triumvirate, that I am the better in my Heart for it, tho no way else. I feel an ardent desire to be worthy to be joind to

[1] Probably Cornbury. A line in Pope's unfinished '1740' reads: 'Good C— hopes, and candidly sits still.'

[2] Bolingbroke's.

[3] That is, by moving up to the House of Lords upon the death of his father. The moment is distilled in a couplet in '1740':

Good M[arch]m[on]t's fate tore P[olwarth] from thy side,
And thy last sigh was heard when W[yndham] died.

you, tho but for an impotent Wish, not any ability, to do good. That must be my case, forever; but you & He cannot be impotent or useless if God shall please to save us. Unless it be his will to give us to destruction, you must be Instruments of our safety, & till you can be so, your example, your exhortation, will operate, with the Good, and cast shame upon the Bad: This is the least you may do; to keep Virtue & Honour alive, in the breasts of many Young Men who are to give them on to Posterity; and to dash the Forehead and shake the soul of Guilty Wretches, who else would intail their Profligacy on all future generations. Come then my Lord, to those who love and want you; appear among those who fear, who hate, and yet respect you: make the noblest of figures, Independent among slaves, and Amiable with great Talents; the Fruit & Exercise of which, if you are deprived of at present, it may make you less *Envy'd*, but cannot make you less *Esteem'd*, either by friend or enemy: It may ease you of a Pain, that of attending when you can do no service, but cannot take from you a Reputation which you have for what you have done, and for what the world will think you wou'd have done.

POPE *to* ALLEN[1] 3 *October* [1740]

Egerton 1947

Oct. 3d

I would not omit one post to answer your very kind Letter, tho a very unwelcome one to me, in finding by it that the severe Headakes still continue to afflict you. I could be willing to Endure more than I now do of that distemper, could it be taken from you; but I have commuted it for this other Ailment, which tho' less painfull, keeps me in continual apprehensions & Confinement. By fits I am not at all uneasy, tho never free from it: and upon any little Cold, or Heat, extremely ill of it. I am now better, & Mr Hooke is finely recoverd for the present. We both intend to see you as soon as we are able, but my unlucky condition has made my last Scheme unpracticable, for my Lord Chesterfield is of a sudden going to Bath, sooner than I can stir, with any safety, and 3 weeks sooner than he intended, so that I see now no prospect of my getting any part of the Way on my journey, unless I stay for the time that his Coach goes for him to Bath again: in which too I could not travel *Alone*, for the tumbling, unless I could get some other to go with me thither. ⌜My Vexation about Dr Swifts proceeding has fretted, & imployed me a great deal, in writing to Ireland, & trying all the Means possible to *retard* it; for it is put past preventing, by his having (without asking my Consent or so much as letting me see

[1] Printed in part by Ruffhead (p. 467). He begins with 'My Vexation about Dr Swift's proceeding . . .' and goes to the end of that long paragraph.

the book) printed most of it.——They at last promise me to send me the Copy, & that I may correct or Expunge what I will. This last would be of some use, but I dare not even do this, for they would Say I *revised it*. And the Bookseller writes, that he has been at great Charge. &c, however the Dean, upon all I have said & written about it, has orderd him to submit to any Expunctions I insist upon; This is all I can obtain, and I know not whether to make any Use of it or not. But as to your apprehension that any Suspicion may arise of my own being any way consenting or concernd in it, I have the pleasure to tell you, the whole thing is so Circumstanced, & so plain, that it can never be the Case. I shall be very desirous to See *what* the Letters are? at all Events. and I think That must determine my future measures, for till then I can judge nothing. The excessive Earnestness the Dean has been in for publishing them, makes me hope they are castigated in some degree: Or he must be totally deprived of his understanding.—— They now offer to send me the *Originals* (which have been so long detained) & I'll accept of them (tho they have done their Jobb) that they may not have them to produce against me, in case there be any offensive passages in 'em. If you can give me any Advice, do. I wish I could show you what the Deans People, the Women & the Bookseller, have done & writ on my sending an Absolute Negative, & on the Agency I have imployd of Some Gentlemen to Stop it, as well as Threats of Law &c. The Whole thing is too Manifest to admit of any Doubt in any man, how long this thing has been working; how many tricks have been playd with the Deans Papers; how they were Secreted from him from time to time, while they feard his not complying with such a Measure: And how, finding his Weakness increase, they have at last made *Him* the Instrument himself for their private profit; whereas I believe, before, they only intended to do this after his death.⌉

Dear Sir, I am tired, but your Concern in all that concerns me makes me say so much—I must tell you that Omers Gold Cliff was never more heard of, nor any ever Sent to the Inn. I shall get some another way. My Grotto is now finishd (I wish you could have seen it, now) tho still I could improve, had I more fine Stone: It has cost infinitely more pains & time than I could have conceivd; so true it is, that "Every little thing, to be done *Well*, requires a great deal." Adieu. Let Mrs Allen know I am truly hers. You know I am truly Yours.

I dont know but I may desire her & you soon to be of some Service at Bath to One I very much value, in a very bad way of health, Dr Arbuthnots Daughter.[1]

[1] Anne Arbuthnot .See Pope to George Arbuthnot, 26 Sept. 1740.

POPE *to* FAULKNER — 4 *October* 1740

Elwin–Courthope, viii. 422

Oct. 4, 1740.

Sir,—I think myself obliged to you for your conduct upon the refusal of my consent to the printing of my letters. Your offer of sending me the book before publication I accept with thanks, it being indeed very necessary that I should at least see what it consists of. I thank you yet more for your promise not to publish it even in Ireland, (notwithstanding the dean's own inclination,) till I shall judge proper. This is all I can expect from you. I wish very much to have the book itself, with the original letter, which was sent with it to the dean as I understand, from which I have some hopes I may find out the hand that did it, if done really in London. As to the person to send it by, Mrs. Whiteway tells me Mr. M'Aulay is to bring me the letters she has so long promised me in fear of the same fate. By him be pleased, sir, to send them to me at Twickenham, and, in the meantime, let me have what sheets you have printed, by post. I must desire you to show this to the dean, and to assure him here under my hand of my unalterable affection, esteem and gratitude. No man has loved him longer than I; no man has loved him better, and I shall continue to do it to the end of my life. I should be heartily pleased to see but just such a line or two as this under his hand. If it be not too great a task to his head it will I know be an agreeable one to his heart, and upon the least intimation from himself that a letter from me will be so to him, I shall write with all pleasure, as I am with all truth, his ever constant and ever faithful friend.

THE EARL OF ORRERY *to* POPE — 4 *October* 1740.

Elwin–Courthope, viii. 421

Caledon, Oct. 4, 1740

I enclose to you, sir, a copy of my letter to Faulkner and his answer. You will find I am to be honoured with a visit from him.[1] In the meantime I would not lose a moment in letting you see that there is a stop put to the publication of those letters here. If Faulkner brings down the copy with him from whence he printed, I will endeavour to keep it[2] till I know your further commands, and you shall certainly hear from me again, as soon as I have had an interview with Faulkner. Excuse a man in pain from ceremony and believe me most faithfully yours.

[1] See Faulkner's letter to Orrery here printed at the end of September.

[2] Pope writes to Lord Orrery (3 Sept.) that his end is to get the book of printed letters 'out of their hands'.

THE EARL OF ORRERY *to* POPE 6 *October* 1740

Elwin–Courthope, viii. 422–4

Caledon, Oct. 6, 1740.

Sir,—The great torments I was under when I writ my two last letters to you, rendered them I fear unintelligible. Whatever my hand might write I am sure my heart meant to assure you of my warmth, and most obedient friendship towards you. In compliance to your commands I lost no time, ill as I was in writing to Mr. Faulkner, who came down hither on Saturday,[1] and brought with him the printed book of letters which the dean gave him to reprint here. This book he leaves in my hands upon the terms, that if the dean, whose property the book is, requires it from me, I am then to send it to him. In the meantime the letters are safe not only from being printed, but from being seen. I have read the letters over, and can plainly see they are stolen. Faulkner has sent you the sheets he printed here, but he has laid aside all thoughts of continuing that design without your full leave and permission. Had he received your letter sooner by Mr. Nugent he would not have put any to the press. He is perfectly desirous to act in obedience to your commands, but these letters were brought from England by Mr. Gerrard, a gentleman you knew at Bath, the packet left for him there by an unknown hand, and the dean imagined they came from you.[2] It is strange the dean should have such a surmise, or be desirous to have them reprinted here, because there are some things in them which, upon a cooler consideration, I believe he would not think ought to appear, especially as they now are.[3] If they are printed in England they will soon be published there, and the dean may insist upon the copy I have. If so, it will be impossible for me to refuse to give him what is already his own. All I can do I have done, but all I fear to little purpose.

I shall not be surprised to see the dean's manuscripts of all kinds in print. To give you one instance of the careless unsuspicious manner in which they are kept, out of thirteen volumes in manuscript on one particular subject he has lost ten.[4] Poor dear man, the pain of mind I feel for him is worse than the pains of the gout.

Your humanity will be inquisitive after my health. My pain, I thank God, is over, but my feet are as yet useless to me, my heart and head still my own, and therefore you may be sure, dear sir, most devoted to you.

[1] 4 Oct.

[2] Swift understood better than his Irish friends what was going on as to the publication of the letters. He himself had more than once used ingenious methods of concealment.

[3] Political remarks may have been in Orrery's mind, but Swift's reflections upon his Irish milieu are more likely to be what raises his eyebrows.

[4] Possibly he had burnt them, as Mrs. Whiteway wrote to Pope (16 May 1740), but there is considerable evidence of carelessness on Swift's part, and one may perhaps doubt if Swift ever wrote thirteen volumes on 'one particular subject'.

MRS. WHITEWAY *to* LORD ORRERY 7 *October* 1740

Elwin–Courthope, viii. 425–6

EXTRACT

Oct. 7, 1740.

I shall now talk to you as freely on another subject. The letters to and from [Dr. Swift][1] had been printed long ago but for me. Mr. Faulkner can tell you that I opposed it publicly at the d[ean's] table, as I did often privately to himself, and with that warmth, which nothing could have excused but friendship. I got several persons to do the like, and put the book out of the way for some time,[2] and kept it till I was forced to restore it, or perjure myself. This I know was going greater lengths than honour could answer. When I saw all this was to no purpose, I insisted on Mr. Faulkner's writing to Mr. P[ope], which he did willingly. What has passed since he can acquaint you with. Yet I fear all will be to no purpose if your lordship does not engage Mr. Faulkner to refuse it absolutely, and a promise not to lay it in the d[ean's] way to command him.[3] This is *entre nous.* I would give more than I will say to talk with you one quarter of an hour, and most humbly desire, if you come to town for ever so short a time, that I may have that honour. In the meanwhile depend upon the truth of a woman in this particular, that let what will come out, or be done by a certain person,[4] it is entirely against my opinion, though all that is in my power is to show my dislike publicly to it. There is a time in life when people can hear no reason, and with a sigh, I say this is now the case with our friend. There is but one mortal in the world that I ever took notice of this to before, and he is such a friend to him as your lordship.

THE EARL OF ORRERY *to* SWIFT 8 *October* 1740

Elwin–Courthope, viii. 424–5

Caledon, Oct. 8, 1740.

I write this from the bed of pain, but when I consider your complaints, and how much greater loss your head will be to the world in general, than even my feet can be to me, I think I have no reason to murmur at my sufferings. They have been great this month past. Those cruel cramps which used to make your humanity pity me, are now turned into a settled confirmed gout, an hereditary evil, which renders my prospect of future life truly dismal. Yet for the sake of some young folk it is necessary I should live, and so God's will be done. But gouty as I am, January next will only complete me thirty-four.

[1] Presumably Mrs. W. has seen Faulkner's projected title-page: *Letters to and from Dr. J. Swift, D.S.P.D. from the Year 1714, to 1738.*

[2] The book pretty certainly did not reach Swift much before the middle of June, and Faulkner was ready to print before the end of July. Mrs. W. had not succeeded in keeping it long from Swift's attention.

[3] Swift is evidently firm in wishing publication.

[4] Swift.

When I cannot see you I am glad to see anybody who has seen you, or will see you. Mr. Faulkner will deliver you this. I have at our friend Mr. Pope's request, detained your book of letters, and could wish you would let them stay in my hands for some time till this mystery of their being in print is a little cleared up. I own, if you will forgive my impertinence, I wish they had not been printed, and now they are so I wish they may not be published. How they came into the press is, perhaps, one of those secrets which are reserved for the day of judgment, but certainly Mr. Pope had no hand in it. A private correspondence between familiar and open-hearted friends ought not to be opened to the public, since it may give pleasure to a man's enemies, and can add no reputation, nor give the least satisfaction to his friends. But I am preaching to Tillotson, I am teaching Delany to read, or mending Lord Oxford's heart. Pray forgive me, and believe all I ever have written to you, or ever shall write to you, is only meant to show the ever honoured Dean of St. Patrick's how much I am his most obedient, and obliged humble servant.

*POPE *to* DR. OLIVER[1] — 8 *October* 1740

Harvard University

Oct. 8th, 1740

Sir,—I am ashamed not to have written to you so long, ashamed not to have written to your Friends Mr Borlase & Mr Cooper, more than once, to each, when their Favors to me have been repeated, in the most valuable & most durable Presents, of Gems and Marble. But I have been studying, by what means to give them some tokens of my Reconnoissance; & you, Sir, in helping me to do this, will oblige me yet more, than in your Assistance to procure the Materials themselves, of all my present Pride, & my Pleasure. The Work is executed in a manner that I think would please them, & I only wish I may ever have an opportunity of asking their approbation upon a Sight of it. Something I wou'd send them, if you could tell me what; something that might please them but the twentieth part as much as they have pleased me. In the meantime, pray write & tell them that I am placing two Marble Inscriptions, one over the Grotto, which is Spar and Mineral, & one over the Porch, which is Marble, giving their Names to each of those Parts to which they have respectively been Contri-

[1] In a thin quarto bound in green morocco (presumably by Mr. H. G. Bohn, who in the nineteenth century owned the items) is also preserved with this letter a floor plan of the grotto described in Dr. Oliver's handwriting as 'A Sketch of Mr. Pope's Grotto drawn by himself in my Study Decemb 29—1740.' The sketch is reproduced by Carruthers (1857), p. 175. Carruthers knew that the letter was addressed to Dr. Oliver. Bohn, speaking apparently of this letter in his edition of Addison's *Works* (1856), vi. 703 n., wrongly says it is addressed to Dr. Charlett. The address is certainly to Dr. Oliver.

butors: And I design You a *Bath* (which is the Honour of a Physitian) to go by yours with a perennial *Spring*, by Mr Allen's. I have entirely finished all except the Outward Façade, which my Lord Burlington opiniatres should be of the same Materials, Plymouth Marbles & Sparrs, but here my Stores fail: I have not a Stone, nor a Diamond or Mineral left. I expect a few from Wales, but not this Autumn, & perhaps by next year I may be under the Earth, but not in my Grotto; & I protest I am so fond of it, that I should be more sorry to leave it unfinishd, than any other Work I at present can think of.

I hope, in a Month's time, or not much longer, to have the pleasure of seeing you at Bath, and of renewing my Obligations to you. Believe me, sir, | Your most affectionate, hum|ble servant, | A. Pope.

Address: To Dr | Oliver, at his | house, at | Bath.
Postmark: 9/OC.
Endorsement: Pope

THE EARL OF ORRERY *to* POPE 10 *October* 1740

Elwin–Courthope, viii. 426–7

Caledon, Oct. 10, 1740.

Sir,—I should not send the enclosed letter to any person in whom I had not the most unlimited confidence, because the first part of it contains some particulars fit for no eyes but my own,[1] but I think it so fully explains from what quarter, and in what manner these letters came, that I am resolved you shall see every syllable in her own hand, though there are some secrets of a very nice nature in it relating to me and my family. I am persuaded the first part of the epistle was written to introduce the other part, but I beg of you, if you think fit to keep it, blot out all that relates to your two faithful servants; if not, send me back the original. I shall make no comments. They will easily occur to yourself, but the particulars which I know I shall tell you. I asked F[aulkne]r in a careless manner what Mrs. W[hiteway]'s opinion was of these letters. He told me she was fully persuaded you published them in England, and sent them privately to the dean. You will find your name is mentioned but once, and there she claims the merit of making F[aulkner] write to you, nor would he leave the letters with me till I writ by him to the dean that I had detained them, etc. I took occasion

[1] Orrery herewith forwards to Pope the letter of Mrs. Whiteway (7 Oct. 1740) *entire*. What he copied into his letterbook (which Elwin saw, but which the present editor has not seen) was only the latter part of the letter: the family details are missing. This present letter from Orrery is surprising: Mrs. Whiteway, normally esteemed by him, is here concluded to be scheming for a publication of the letters apart from that by Faulkner. Orrery's suspicions play into the unscrupulous desires of Pope to conceal his own connexion with the publication, and the two men begin to join in unwarranted blame of Mrs. Whiteway.

to speak honestly, but tenderly my opinion to the dean, and entered my protest—God knows I often protest to no purpose—against their appearance in public. If the dean requires them back I will take occasion from her letter to delay sending them, but what will or can secure you if they are already printed, as I really believe they are, in England? Her son-in-law has been lately there.[1] You will see she endeavours to lay the whole blame on F[aulkner], and writes to me as soon as she knows he is come down hither. I said not one word to him of this letter from her, but by comparing his answers to my questions and her assertions, one might easily find that her fear of perjury does not hinder her from [lying]. I am impatient to hear from you, impatient that this should get safe to your hands; for your reputation, and your commands are dear and sacred to your faithful servant.

FAULKNER *to* LORD ORRERY — 14 *October* 1740

Elwin–Courthope, viii. 428

Dublin, Oct. 14, 1740.

At my return from the north I found the enclosed letter from Mr. Pope,[2] which I beg your lordship will please to return to me, as also the volume of letters that I may send them as he desires.

*POPE *to* ALLEN — 14 *October* [1740]

Egerton 1947

Oct 14.

I am many ways taken up, often wishing to hear from & write to you, & troubled to live so far asunder. But so it is, that I never know a fortnight together What I can do, or where I must be? but am imployed for others, & about others; At home I have enough to do, if I had uninterrupted Hours, and many Papers to take care of, which I should put into some Order in case of Accidents or Mortality. I've begun to do so, and would finish one little work before I leave this place, to avoid the Inconvenience of sending so far, as to you. I intend then to set forward, but would also have the Bath less populous before I come, that I may be Wholly Yours. I need not give you All the Trouble you propose of sending your Chariot, for I would chuse to come in my own little Chair, which would be highly useful to me when with you, in securing my very crazy person from Cold in the works in your Garden, Rock, &c. And I would, if I could contrive to put all my Things first here into such forwardness, as to have them

[1] By innuendo Orrery suggests that Mr. Deane Swift may have arranged in England for the publication.

[2] Presumably that of 4 Oct., in which Pope demands a sight of the clandestine volume.

carryd on while with you, & So stay with you till I may return back to Town in your Company about February. If Mr Hooke gets forward enough in his History,[1]—I should be glad he attended me in the Way best for his health, on Horseback: but at present I fear it would be injurious to Him to take him away.

You'l see many of my Friends at this time, who joyn with me in valuing You. Mr Lyttelton, Lord Cornbury, Lord Bathurst, &c—If I have no hopes of finding the last of these Gentlemen at his own house at Cirencester (as I fancy he will be little there, while others are at Bath, & the Parliament so nigh) I must be content to see him in London, and as Soon as I have just lookd at them, before they grow too Busy, and too warm, for me. (Who am only a By-stander and no Partizan, but only a Wellwisher to my Country, whoever prove its Friends) I shall leave the place where I can do no good and the People to whom I can do none, and fly to You, and think of Posterity. Adieu, don't show this letter to anybody, but keep it, as you do the Writer, for your *owne*. I am Mrs Allen's & Your faithful Servant. | A. Pope

Address: To | Ralph Allen Esqr | at Widcombe nr Bath.
Postmark: 13/OC[2]

*DR. OLIVER *to* POPE[3] 15 *October* 1740

Harvard University

Bath Octob 15. 1740

Sir,—I heartily congratulate you on your having brought your Work so near to perfection in which you seem to take so much delight; but you must pardon me if I can't believe that any Adamant will be as lasting as your Productions upon Paper. You do us too much honour by giving our Names a place in your Grotto, tho we all have such Strong Longings after Immortality that we cannot but be proud of what we are conscious we do not deserve. I think I have heard Mr Allen hint that you designed to favour the Publick with a Description of your Mine, you can't but beleive me impatient to see it, and tho' I don't doubt but that every Diamond has acquired new Lustre from it's artful Disposition, yet it will Shine much brighter in your Lines than it can do in your Grotto. I must beg of you to let me know particularly what Quantity of Marble Spar or Diamonds you want for the finishing the Façade, and I will immediately desire my Friends to

[1] The first volume of Hooke's *Roman History* appeared in 1738, the second in 1745, and the others after Hooke's death: iii in 1764, and iv in 1771.

[2] The postmark almost certainly is 13/OC. It should be 15, unless Pope misdated the letter.

[3] This letter, printed by Carruthers (1857, p. 174), is preserved in a draft written on an inside page of Pope's letter to Oliver of 8 Oct.

supply you with all Expedition. They will gladly contribute all in their power to oblige Him by whom they will think themselves and me so much obliged. But if you are resolved Still to add to the Favour already conferred, and will make me the Judge of what will please them, I must be influenced by the Pleasure I myself felt upon receiving your Works of which I know their Opinion to be | Sir[1]

You make this Month tedious by promising to see me in the next. I hope to meet you in a State of Health likely to last you many years above Ground; but whenever the World is robbd of you where can you be better reposited than in your own Grottos, for I know you have no Ambition to be laid with Kings, and lie where you will your own Works must be your everlasting Monument.

POPE *to* THE EARL OF ORRERY[2] 17 *October* [1740]

The Pierpont Morgan Library

Oct. 17th 1740

My Lord,—I can never enough thank you, for the Constancy & Continuation of your Lordships Favour & Friendship to me. Every warm Instance you give of it, awakens the Gratitude due for all the former. I am not able to express my Concern, that This Trouble should be added to you, (for I know the Generosity of your Heart has made it a serious one) at the time you had so much Pain beside, from the severe Treatment of the Gout. I heartily wish & pray for your Entire Recovery. I thought it unreasonable to write to your Lordship instantly again, which I knew would only quicken your Concern, & Labour, in endeavouring to prevent what I so much apprehended. I am quite in doubt as to this whole Transaction. It is certain they all knew how disagreeable this was to me, from all that your Lordship knows past before: and I suspect, whatever Communication might be in England, it must have begun in Ireland. The Letter of which Falkner sent me a Copy, which was (they say) sent to the Dean with the Book, is plainly of Ireland, by two or three tokens.[3] As to the Gentleman who carryd it, he was no acquaintance, as they pretend, of mine at *Bath*[4] (I only saw him at London, by the Dean's recommendation:) Nor was I then, nor have I been since at Bath tho I shall go soon. Upon the whole, I wish they would send me (or that your Lordship would take it upon you) the Book itself in some shape or other, and that Origin[a]l Letter, by which I may probably discover whether it was really done

[1] Naturally, in a draft, Oliver did not complete the subscription. He did add what follows as a postscript.

[2] The year is added to the superscription by Lord Orrery. Pope here answers Orrery's letter of 6 Oct., not having received that of the 10th.

[3] Details of these 'tokens' are given in Pope's letter of 30 Dec. 1740.

[4] Orrery had (6 Oct.) written of Gerrard as 'a gentleman you knew at Bath'.

here, or there? I can't conceive, if here, why they have made a Compliment of their Edition to Falkner, & not publishd it all this while? Certainly from many things I hear, & particularly from Two very Extraordinary Letters from Mrs Whiteway, (as well as from the account your Lordship now gives of so many of the Deans MS. Volumes being stolen) the practise appears common on your side of the Water, of clandestinely secreting his papers, & of *copying* the very Letters he sends to his friends, as well as *stopping* others, from & to Him, which that Lady mentions (but of Her I beg you to say not a word, for a reason I shall hereafter open to your Lordship more at large.) She has own'd a large Collection[1] to be in her hands, & promised Mr Nugent & me full nine months to send them. Her Son in law was writing a Preface to tell the world, These Letters were procurd by the *corrupt practises of Printers in London*; This he has owned to me; but I beggd him not, 'till I could be convincd *it was true*. I must remark, that in the two sheets Faukener sent me, are some Notes plainly Irish,[2] & (what is very observable) a whole long Letter of the Deans, which I can swear I never receiv'd.[3]——Putting this together, I must doubt the Conduct of those, about the Dean, more than any Casual stealths: But till I see the Book, I can judge little. And can any thing be more strange, & unjustifiable, after all their pretences to Civility & Regard for Me, than that in all this time they never would send it? I wish to God you would be so good to score over the passages which you find improper or indiscreet, either in the Dean's, or my Letters:[4] I fear it will be but a necessary Care, for whether this book be printed in England or Ireland, with, or without confederacy of people there, Come out it certainly will, one time or other: And I cannot but wish, for His sake as well as mine, the Expunctions were made ready forthwith, against all Events.[5] I think as I am equally concern'd in this case with the Dean, I have a Right to expect a Revisal of the book in time, nor will it otherwise be in Faukners power to do me that justice, if indeed it be printed in London: & it is ridiculous in him, first to have askd my Consent to what I had not read, then to proceed to print it before I gave him any, & since to offer me a Revisal in order to correct what is not in his power to suppress.

[1] 'Several of your letters' was her expression in her letter to Pope of 16 May 1740.

[2] Such notes had been added by Swift in the two sheets forwarded to Pope.

[3] Swift's letter of 10 Jan. 1721 (probably an actual unpublished pamphlet, which he now determined to publish) had been inserted in Faulkner's printing in sheets B and C, which he had sent to Pope. When printing this new letter in 1741La Pope added the footnote: 'This Letter Mr. Pope never received.'

[4] The Dublin texts of the letters do differ from the texts in the clandestine volume or in the other London editions, but there is no extensive revision and no evidence that Orrery took a hand in the revisions made.

[5] This remark as well as the postscript to the letter show Pope leaning towards probable publication.

He must have receivd my last letter at least in good time (tho the first was pleaded to be long retarded;) and in that I accepted his offer, & desird him to send it. Therfore your Lordship in transmitting it to me will do no more than what He promis'd himself to do.

I am sorry to tire you, & ashamed. The few lines following shall only tell my high sense of the obligation you lay upon | Your Lordships Ever oblig'd, affectiona[te] | constant Servant | A. Pope.

I beg my Lady Orrery may be assured of my sincere and respectful services. When will the time come that I may hope to see you both here?

Though I would give your lordship as little trouble to write as possible in your present condition, I beg just three lines by the next post to tell me if any of those letters of that six years' chasm (which the dean told us formerly were missing) are to be found in this book, and if any of those are there which your lordship brought over to me? These two particulars will very much aid my guess. If the book were sure to be published in London, though I could not give Faulkner my consent in form, yet, as he has the dean's, I should prefer him to another, provided your lordship would be so good as to expunge for me. But in this no time should be lost. They might be sent under your frank by post. I have had no more than the two first sheets from Faulkner,[1] though he promised to send the rest by two posts more.[2]

Endorsement (on the original letter, in Orrery's hand): Mr Pope | 1740.

THE EARL OF ORRERY *to* FAULKNER 18 *October* 1740.

Elwin–Courthope, viii. 428

Caledon, Oct. 18, 1740.

Mr. Faulkner,—I send to you by this post, in four parcels, the printed letters which were left in my hands, and I hope and believe you will forward them to Mr. Pope by the first opportunity. There was no title-page, though it ought to be sent, if you have not torn it. Enclosed is Mr. Pope's [letter]. Pray tell me if they arrive safe.

POPE *to* CHARLES BATHURST[3] 18 *October* [1740]

The Gentleman's Magazine, xliv, N.S. (1855), 587

Sir,—If you are returned to London, and will send to Mr. Cheselden's the Surgeon in Spring Garden, they will deliver you the books of

[1] These were all that Faulkner had printed—at least so he said.

[2] The text for these two postscripted paragraphs is taken from EC. viii. 434–5, where they are printed from the missing volume of Orrery's letterbooks. The paragraphs are not preserved with the original letter.

[3] Elwin placed this letter in 1741, but at that time Pope was planning to leave for Bath,

Miscellanies with my note how to rectify several mistakes for the future when you reprint[1]—pray observe them—and when I am next in town I shall be glad to meet you and settle the other matter, I believe to your satisfaction. | Yours, | A. Pope.

Twitnam, Oct. 18th.

POPE *to* CHARLES BATHURST[2] 23 *October* [1740]

The Gentleman's Magazine, xliv, N.S. (1855), 586

Twitnam, Oct. 23.

Sir,—I should be glad to see you at dinner on Sunday at this place. You'll meet nobody that I know of, except by chance Mr Knapton should call from Marshgate, where he is generally on a Sunday. I thought this would be the most convenient day to you.

I am, Sir, your humble Servant, | A. Pope.

POPE *to* THE EARL OF ORRERY 25 *October* 1740

The Pierpont Morgan Library

Oct. 25th 1740.

My Lord,—Your Letter[3] with that of Mrs W. inclosed came to my hands but this day, & in general I find great Delays by the Post to & from Ireland. I answerd your Lordships former Letter,[4] with Falkeners inclosed, the same day I received it also, and in that open'd my thought so fully to you, that I need say little here. Only you'l find that we think as much alike in this, as I hope we do in other things, or I must think very wrong. The Lady had made just the same Protestations to me, but with one or two circumstances so strong, that I was overdoz'd; As for instance, *That tho' she had secreted* the Book, she *had not once look'd into it, she disapprovd it so much*: (tho she had never read it.) She took great pains to insinuate, the *Copies of the Letters* must come from England, as well as *the Book*; which I know to be Impossible, because even in the first 2 Sheets (the only ones sent me to this day, printed by Faukner) there is a Letter of the Dean's which I never had; nor indeed is it possible they should be copied from my papers, for I

and not likely to be vaguely available for conference in London. In 1740 he was intermittently in the care of Cheselden. See also the following letter to Bathurst.

[1] The *Miscellanies* were apparently next reprinted in July 1742. Pope's interest in them, and their texts, at this time is obviously due to the fact that he was planning to include *Peri Bathous* and other items from the *Miscellanies*, of which Bathurst had the copyrights, in his quarto edition of the Swift–Pope letters.

[2] This, like the preceding letter, is here transferred from 1741 to 1740. In 1741 the Allens were Pope's guests on the 23rd, and he left for Bath with them presumably on Saturday the 24th. He would not be inviting Bathurst to dinner on Sunday the 25th—in 1741.

[3] Of 10 Oct.

[4] Of 4 Oct.

burn'd almost all long ago & particularly those your Lordship brought over,[1] (which makes me wish you could tell me if *any of those are in their book*? if so, they kept them from being sent till they were copied there[2]) and I need in such case, enquire no further *on this side* the *water* for a Plagiary. Mrs W. in two letters to me on this occasion, betrays that it "has been long the practise of the Dean & herself, to *open* each others Letters, & to *stop* some, both *to* & *from* him.["][3] But all this shall be an inviolable Secret between your Lordship & me. Perhaps the Gentleman whom they untruly told you I knew at Bath, or Mr Swift,[4] if he has been in England lately, (in which case I wonder he did not make me the Compliment of a Visit, since they both talk of it in their Letter as so great a pleasure.) perhaps some agency has been on foot with Printers here: but I will not be too censorious. I think it very *possible* to be *printed* here, but *sure* I am, the papers must be *stolen* In Ireland. And I am convinced upon the whole of the Necessity of their being revised, & Expunctions made forthwith, to be ready, whenever they publish them here.[5] I begg'd your Lordship in this to stand in my stead, & cutt out every thing you think proper, in my letters at least; & why not in the Dean's? If he be in the Condition She describes, it is the part of a Friend, to do that for him, which he wants ability or memory to do for himself. I see no harm in F.'s printing such an Edition, provided I do not revise it myself (which would be construed as tantamount to publishing it) and when it is done by F. with the known Consent of the Dean, I may suffer it here without Imputation,[6] as being really past my power to prevent. So F. will gain His point to have the first Impression; The Dean will never miss what is left out; nor should I quarrel with your Lordship tho you left out All mine entirely.

But all this while, my Lord guess in what a Situation I must be, who cannot get any sight, or account what the Things really are, that the whole World is to read as mine? I wish your Lordship did but in 2 words tell me, what your opinion of them is? & whether there be any thing offensive, (very idle I am sure there must) in my own? & what are those of Lord Bolingbroke? and of what Dates? If they are meerly familiar, without any very exceptionable passages, the Method

[1] These (if burned) were burned after the transcripts made for Lord Oxford's library were produced; i.e. the transcripts of some of the letters, now preserved at Longleat.

[2] The theory of Irish copying was essential if publication was not to be imputed to Pope himself, to whom the originals had been returned. Without copies the letters could not have been printed in Ireland.

[3] No letter from Mrs. W. preserved to us warrants any such statement as Pope here quotes. It is hard to believe that as of 1740 any such statement could truthfully be made.

[4] Mr. Deane Swift.

[5] Pope almost concedes here that the letters may well have been printed in England.

[6] It is Pope's great fear of 'Imputation' that leads him to all this chicanery—a fear difficult in our day to comprehend at all.

I have proposed will be best, & without Falkener's knowledge your Lordship may send me the sheets: If they contain any strong reflections, or are within 6 or 7 years of the Queen's death,[1] I must have nothing to say to them, & will write instantly to Lord Bolingbroke. In such case, I hope you would have no scruple to burn the book, that the Dean at least or his Guardians may not see it more: And when ever it appears, I must prosecute the Publisher.

I re-inclose the Lady's Letter.[2] All the while I've been writing my Heart was full of a desire to employ the paper in the fulness of my Gratitude, with the warmest Expressions of all your Goodness, Care, & Honour, in this affair of mine. On whatever side I turn it, I find cause to thank, to love, & to esteem you. Whatever Uneasiness I feel, in the anxious Uncertainty of this most aukward situation, & in the whole Conduct of my poor departed Friend (for so I may call the Dean) It is overpayed with the Joy I receive, in knowing by this accident that my Lady Orrery is just upon making you the most agreable Present,[3] & which most strongly cements that Union of Hearts which you alredy enjoy. May That, and every Blessing, be accumulated, upon You & Her! I must intreat your Lordship that the next Obligation you lay upon me may be the News of her happy Hour, and of the Continuance of her Welfare. I am, with all truth, | My Lord, Your faithfullest & most obliged Servant. | A. Pope.

THE EARL OF ORRERY *to* POPE — 27 *October* 1740

Elwin–Courthope, viii. 439–40

Caledon, Oct. 27, 1740.

I am entirely of your opinion, sir, that this dark affair has been transacted on this side of the water, but as I read the letters but once over, it is impossible to tell you whether there are any among them during the chasm you mention. The letters I brought over to you were delivered sealed up to me, but I hope you will have received this mysterious collection even before this reaches your hands. I sent them to Faulkner to be forwarded to you two posts ago, upon sight of a letter from you to him desiring them immediately. I write by this post to know if he has performed his promise, nor shall I be easy till I hear they are in your possession. Had the book been Faulkner's instead of the dean's I would have sent it directly. But the dean's name is constantly made use of on these occasions, and such pains taken to insinuate into him suspicions of his friend that I was obliged to obey

[1] Before Bolingbroke was pardoned, correspondence with him would be treasonable; and no letters of that period to or from Swift or Pope should exist.

[2] Mrs. Whiteway's letter of 7 Oct., of which only an extract has been preserved.

[3] On 31 Oct., according to *The Lond. Eve. Post* of 13 Nov., 'the Countess of Orrery was brought to Bed of a Daughter . . . christened Catherine Agnes'.

the summons. As to the letter delivered with the printed book I never saw it. If you will have me write to the dean for it I will obey you in that, or any other particular. I am really and heartily vexed at this whole affair. I see it is aimed to hurt you, and all the art and malice exerted that is possible. I wish, and hope you will discover it plainly. Lady Orrery is much obliged to you for your kind remembrance. We hope to see you next summer. In the meantime, wherever we are, believe us, dear sir, devotedly yours.

POPE *to* WARBURTON[1] — 27 *October* 1740

Egerton 1946

I am grown so bad a Correspondent partly thro' the weakness of my Eyes, which has much increasd of late, & partly thro other disagreable accidents (almost peculiar to me) that my Oldest, as well as best Friends, are reasonable enough to excuse me. I know you are of the number, who deserve all the Testimonies, of any sort, which I can give you of Esteem & Friendship, and I Confide in you as a man of Candour enough to know it cannot be otherwise if I am an honest One. So I will say no more on this head, but proceed to thank you for your constant Memory of whatever may be serviceable or reputable to me. The Translation[2] you are a much better Judge of than I, not only because You Understand my Work better than I do myself,[3] but as your continued familiarity with the Learned Languages makes you infinitely more a Master of them. I would only recommend, that the Translator's attention to Tullys Latinity may not preclude his usage of some *Terms*, which may be more *Precise* in Modern Philosophy than such as He could serve himself of, especially in Matters Metaphysical. I think this Specimen close enough; & clear also, as far as the Classical Phrases allow, from which yet I would rather he sometimes deviated, than sufferd the Sense to be either dubious or clouded too much. You know my mind perfectly, as to the Intent of such a Version, and I would have it accompanied with your own Remarks translated,[4] such only I mean as are General, or Explanatory of those Passages which are Concise to any degree of Obscurity, or which demand perhaps too minute an attention in the Reader.

[1] Printed by Warburton in 1751.

[2] Of his Essay on Man into Latin prose.—Warburton, 1751. It is doubtful if this translation (? commissioned at Cambridge. See Pope to Warburton, 24 June 1740) was ever published. Writing to Christopher Smart (? 18 Nov. [1743]) Pope does not mention this translation.

[3] This obvious flattery is not too serious. On 4 Jan. Pope had written to Warburton that he noted 'two or three very slight Inaccuracies' in the *Vindication*, which might be corrected in a second edition. He yielded too much to his commentator, but not so much as this absurd flattery implies.

[4] In his own editions of the *Essay* Warburton used parts of the *Vindication* in footnotes.

I have been unable to make the Journey I designd to Oxford and Lord Bathurst's, where I hopd to have made You of the party. I am going to Bath for near two months. Yet pray let nothing hinder me some times from hearing you are well. I have had that Contentment from time to time from Mr Gyles.—The Incendiary you mention attempted not mine but a Lady's house of the same name, unsuccessfully.[1]—Scriblerus will, or will not be publishd, according to the Event of some other Papers coming or not coming out, which it will be my utmost Endeavor to hinder. I will not give You the pain of acquainting you what they are.[2]—Your Simile of Bentley & his Nephew would make an excellent Epigram. But all Satire is become so ineffectual, (when the Last Step that Virtue can stand upon, Shame, is taken away) that Epigram must expect to do nothing, even in its own, little, province, and upon its own, little, Subjects. Adieu. believe I wish you nearer us; the only Power I wish is that of attracting,[3] & at the same time Supporting, such congenial Bodies as You are, to | Dear Sir | Your ever-affectionate | faithful Servant | A. Pope.

Oct. 27th 1740.

*POPE *to* JOHN BRINSDEN[4] *November* [? 1740]

Harvard University

Novr

Sir,—I beg you to forward the Inclosed by the safest hand you can. I have never been in town since we met, but intend soon to try to find you, Who am always sincerely, | Your affectionate | humble Servant, | A. Pope

There is a Man who formerly serv'd my Lord, who I think saved my Life in the Accident I had in the River at Whitton his name is Phil. Hanaus, of Brussels, he wants a footman's place & I wish you could help him to one, if you know his Character not a blameable one.

Address: To Mr Brinsden, in | Durham yard.
Endorsement: H St J L
Seal: Homer's head.

[1] In 1751 Warburton omitted this sentence from the letter. [2] The Pope–Swift letters.
[3] For 'attracting' Warburton and Elwin wrongly print 'attaching'.
[4] Brinsden had long been in the employ of Bolingbroke as secretary or business agent. From the endorsement one assumes that Pope is asking Brinsden to forward something to his lordship. The postscript concerns the footman who pulled Pope out of the river on the occasion, in Sept. 1726, when the coach overturned. See *The Harvard Library Bulletin*, ii (1948), 121–3, and here ii. 401–3.
The date of the letter is most unsure. The day and year have been torn away. Bolingbroke must be out of England; Phil Hanaus must be out of a place (i.e. Dawley has been sold). Pope does not, probably, write from Bath. Early November of 1740 is a possibility, and it seems the most probable date. The Novembers of 1735–7 are possible. Brinsden died in Mar. 1742–3.

*POPE *to* ALLEN 4 *November* [1740]

Egerton 1947

Novr 4th

Having been in Windsor forest at my Sisters house,[1] I received not Mrs Arbuthnots letter[2] till this day, at the same time with yours. I had otherwise been in great pain from her account of you, and I wish you do not soften it, and that you are as much recoverd as you say. To be as well as I wish you, is not possible, as yet, after such a disorder. Pray confirm your good news, if you continue to mend, or are really well. I am quickend in my desires to be with you, by the apprehensions I have had for you: and therfore write this, when I have scarce a minute's time left to send it by the post, only to tell you I will come to you instantly, if you have any particular Desire I shou'd; Your Chariot shall meet me when you will, at Newbury or Hungerford, & I could get thither in a day and half. On Wednesday Sennight I believe I may have the opportunity of a Coach so as to be at Bath by Friday night; but I dare not venture So much tumbling *alone*, in my present Circumstance; or I would not put you to the Trouble at all of sending. If I can get Mr Hooke, or Vandiest if he were well enough to accompany me, I will come. If not, I'll take any other Means, in less than a Week more: For my Sister's affair[3] shall not detain me longer, nor any Tolerable Ailments of my own. I will be with you, God-willing, by the 25th at farthest at all Events. Adieu. God preserve you. My hearty thanks for your good offices to Mrs Arbuthnot, who is the most honest of Women. Let Mrs Allen know they will not be the worse for each others Company; tho' a great Wit sayd, No Two Women ever were acquainted without being So. Once more adieu. Yours Entirely. | A. Pope

Direct to me in London, at the Honble Mr Murray's[4] in Lincolns Inn fields.

POPE *to* FAULKNER 4 *November* 1740

Elwin–Courthope, viii. 440–1

Nov. 4, [1740.]

Sir,—I received yours but yesterday, and opened. I have never received any letter from Ireland of late in less than a month after the date.[5]

[1] Hallgrove, which obviously has not been sold.

[2] On 26 Sept. Pope had written to George Arbuthnot about the desirability of his sister Anne's going to Bath for her health.

[3] Her interminable lawsuit.

[4] Murray was handling Mrs. Rackett's suit.

[5] Since we do not have Faulkner's letter, we do not know its date. Presumably Faulkner had suggested that Pope answered letters slowly, and Pope counters with this exaggerated

However, as I desired before, pray send what sheets you have printed by post, directed to me under cover to Ralph Allen, Esq., postmaster at Bath, but no letter with them. Whatever you write, address under cover to Lord Oxford, and send to him the original letter I desired, which the people writ to the dean, (by which I fancy I may discover something further,) as also those letters which Mrs. Whiteway intended me by Mr. M'Aulay. Whatever I determine upon sight of the book, (till when I can determine nothing,) no prejudice shall arise to you for the deference you show to, sir, your humble servant.

As soon as I have seen these letters I will give the dean my full thoughts upon them. In the meantime assure him my whole heart is his, and my sincere love shall attend him to the last moment of his, or my life. I could abide, I think, by my Lord Orrery's judgment in this, even more than by my own, if he will be at the trouble of giving it me upon his perusal of the book, and pray tell his lordship so.

FAULKNER *to* THE EARL OF ORRERY 6 *November* 1740

Elwin–Courthope, viii. 441

Dublin, Nov. 6, 1740.

My Lord,—I most heartily congratulate you on the birth of Lady Catherine, and hope that her ladyship and Lady Orrery are both in good health. When I returned from the north I immediately sent a letter to Mr. Pope[1] to let him know that I would send the letters under cover to him, or in any other manner he thought proper, and at the same time let him know that Mr. M'Aulay would not go to London this year. I mention this to your lordship because I have not received his answer. Therefore I shall be advised in any manner your lordship thinks proper to forward them to him, and I do assure your lordship that I have not made the least progress in them since I had the honour of being at Caledon. The book had no title page, of which I informed Mr. Pope. * * * I am, my lord, etc.

THE EARL OF ORRERY *to* POPE[2] 8 *November* 1740

Elwin–Courthope, viii. 441–2

Caledon, Nov. 8, 1740.

Sir,—I have of late constantly writ to you under some uneasiness either of mind or body, and it is still my doom, but I will act for you

and untrue statement as to the slowness of mails from Ireland. He had answered Lord Orrery's letter of the 6th on 17 Oct., and Orrery's of the 10th on the 25th. But the mails evidently had been slow.

[1] Faulkner returned from his visit to Lord Orrery about 9 Oct. His letter would seem to be that which Pope answered on 4 Nov.

[2] Orrery here replies to Pope's letter of 25 Oct.

in all circumstances as zealously and as faithfully as I can. By this day's post I received a letter from Faulkner. He tells me he has not sent you the letters. I will send for them directly,[1] and, unknown to him, transmit them to you. Make what alterations you think proper, and return them to me. The alterations, omissions, and additions shall, if you will have it so appear to Faulkner to be mine; or act in this matter as you think fit, and I will obey whatever commands you lay upon me. I cannot say more at present. My second son is ill of the small pox. My whole life and comfort is wrapped up in my wife and children, so that my present anxiety is as great as possible. Lady Orrery and my new born daughter are both well. Your friendship for us is infinitely obliging. I will send the letters as soon as possible. Adieu.

THE EARL OF ORRERY *to* FAULKNER 8 *November* 1740

Elwin–Courthope, viii. 442

Caledon, Nov. 8, 1740.

Mr. Faulkner,—I desire and insist you will without the least delay send me those letters you left here with me, and which I sent to you to be sent to Mr. Pope. I will be answerable for them, and endeavour to serve you, but I cannot be particular now for reasons I cannot give you.[2] I hope to receive the letters on Thursday. I am Mrs. Faulkner's, and your faithful, humble servant.

*POPE *to* ALLEN[3] 11 *November* [1740]

Egerton 1947

Novr 11th Tuesday.

I sent a Letter by the Bath Fly (as they call it) in hope it might reach you on Tuesday night, to prevent sending your Chariot to Newbury, but fear it could not, & therfore have writ by this first post to Newbury to Mrs Cary, to let your servants know I could not be there possibly, & to return home. Nothing can afflict me more. But sure my Letter was Express, that I *could not come unless* I *could procure sombody to go in Lord Chesterfields Coach.* It is impracticable (in my Condition) to bear the Jolting alone. Mr Hook, & every one else I could try, could not attend me, or I had done it, tho' excessively to my Inconveniency. I am at Mr Murrays where I have Business of much importance yet, for a fortnight at least; but I would have left all, had *you been Ill, & in any respect wanted or wish'd my* Coming. I thought I exprest that

[1] See the following letter.

[2] The concealed reason is that if Pope makes revisions, they may, if he likes, masquerade as Orrery's. See the preceding letter.

[3] As a result of Pope's letter of 4 Nov. Allen is sending his chariot to Newbury to meet Pope: but Pope cannot be there. Fear of jolting and his sister's business will prevent. Unfortunately Pope and Allen lacked the aid of the uninvented telephone!

particularly, & that unless you were so, I would take a *longer time* & be *then* met by your Chariot: For had I been able to come now in Lord C.'s Coach, I had of course wanted no Chariot. And if I mistake not, I spoke of the 25th as a probable Time, nor indeed can it be sooner, now.

No words can tell the Vexation this gives me. I cannot think how this Mistake could arise but from our great Zeal on both sides to prevent any, & to get as soon as possible together. I hoped strongly to be able, & you took my hopes for Certainties. I am quite ashamed to put my Friends to so much trouble about me. I am really grown too Infirm to be fit to undertake any thing, or to be worth any thing when I am with them. I think I'l take my Chance & get to you *as* I can, & *when* I can. For to write agen, & appoint another time for you to renew all this trouble, I cannot answer to myself. It is certain if Joseph did not attend, to ride with me in the Chariot, I could not bear it. And to take my own John away for a *week* would destroy all my Pineapples for a Whole Season. Would to God I were like any other thing they call a Man, & I could find my way to those I wish so much & so often, to pass my life with!

Pray tell Mrs Arbuthnot her Brother insists on her Stay at Bath till Christmass, & then he will come & fetch her. So that I shall (if I live, & do not directly keep my bed) be there long enough before. I'm so distracted with things here & this vexatious disappointment, that you'l scarce read What I write so confusedly. I only know, my Heart is good, and Yours. pray be more particular as to your health

Address: To | Ralph Allen Esq. at | Widcombe. | near Bath.

Postmark: 11/NO

Stamped: JA

Endorsement (in Allen's hand): coming to Bath & disappointed

THE EARL OF ORRERY *to* POPE 12 *November* 1740

Elwin–Courthope, viii. 442–4

Caledon, Nov. 12, 1740.

I have endeavoured to compose myself as much as possible under the anxiety I suffer for my son, (who, I thank God, though extremely full of a very bad kind of small pox, is as yet free from any dangerous symptoms) to answer some particulars in your letter. I must begin by saying I think the whole collection of those letters which I read are unworthy to be published. They are only private familiarities between friends, in which the public cannot be interested or engaged. The great names affixed to them raise expectations in people, and the subject matter of the epistles will not answer those expectations. If I remember right, for I read them over but once, they begin early in the year 1715, or thereabouts. In yours there is nothing imprudent, nor can you write but what must please. Yet surely they were never meant for print. In the dean's are some sharp sayings of a very high nature, and what may give room for his enemies to alarm, if not to molest him. Lord Bolingbroke's show him a tender husband, and a firm friend. I do not remember that any of his are to be objected to, except in the general objection to the whole, that they are trifling. Mr. Gay's do him no honour as a wit, but they are, as they must be, the letters of an honest man. There are great chasms in the collection which show them snatched and stolen at different times.

I cannot see how you will hinder their being published, though it is probable whilst there is negociation on foot between you and the lady they will not come out. You shall have them the moment Faulkner returns them to me, and then do with them as you think fit, and any alterations you may desire may appear to be mine, only in that case I must insist upon striking out some passages in your letters where I am mentioned too much to my honour. In short my heart, my hand, my name is at your service, well knowing that they can never be more honourably employed. I am sorry I returned them to Faulkner, but I could not avoid keeping my promise of delivering them, when either you or the dean sent for them, and I know he dare not proceed without your leave or mine. I cannot answer for my judgment in what ought, or ought not to appear, but I will answer for my secresy if you will make what alterations you think proper. Your letters are too long in coming to me. Where they stop I know not. I believe on this side, for in this kingdom no villainy is left unpractised. I can no more at present, especially as my poor child is rather worse. Believe me, dear sir, in all circumstances, and I have seldom been in a more melancholy situation, your faithful and obedient.

I send you a piece of a poem (for you have seen the whole of it in England) to which your name is now prefixed, and the letter I received with it yesterday from Faulkner.[1]

THE EARL OF ORRERY *to* POPE — 14 *November* 1740

Elwin–Courthope, viii. 445

Caledon, Friday, Nov. 14, 1740.

In nine packets you will receive the letters which are printed.[2] It is impossible, I think, to say where. This is the tenth parcel that goes

[1] In 1733 *The Life and Genuine Character of Doctor Swift* had a dedication 'To Alexander Pope, Esq;' signed by the mystifying initials 'L. M.' No Dublin edition of this poem is known in 1740, but in 1739 and 1740 Faulkner had published several Dublin editions of the similar *Verses on the Death of Doctor Swift.* Presumably one of these is being sent to Pope by Orrery. See Swift's *Poems*, ed. Williams, pp. 551–72.

[2] It is doubtful if the 'clandestine volume', as editors like to call it, was a bound volume:

directed to you under my hand and seal by this post. The printed letters were sent to me yesterday by Faulkner, and I am answerable to him for them. He knows not that I have sent them to you, and therefore do with them as you think fit. I will act wholly in this affair as you, in your better judgment, shall command me. They will certainly appear. If you can find out a method that they may appear more to your satisfaction than in their present shape, though I apprehend that whatever is done in the case must be done soon, make use of me, and my name, as I hinted in my last, in what manner you please. I have not read them a second time. I have sealed them as they came to me, looking only at the first and last page. I am in too great anxiety of mind to do anything that requires calmness or thought. I write to you in confusion, but I write to you as I always do with a sincere heart, and with an earnest desire to serve you in whatever method you shall point out. My son continues dangerously ill, and except to yourself on this occasion I could not summon up sedateness of thought enough to compose three lines. These, I fear, are scarce intelligible. Accept them, dear sir, from your faithful and obedient.

FAULKNER *to* THE EARL OF ORRERY 15 *November* 1740

Elwin–Courthope, viii. 446

Nov. 15, 1740.

My Lord,—I hope you received the letters safe that I sent by post. I got the enclosed letter from Mr. Pope by the last packet.[1] That your lordship may be convinced that I design to act with honour by that gentleman, if you will please to give yourself the trouble to direct the letters to him as he desires, I shall take it as a particular favour, because if any miscarriage should happen your lordship can justify my conduct. I asked Mrs. Whiteway for the letter which Mr. Pope desires, and she says she sent it to Caledon.[2] If your lordship ever received it, pray send it to him. I hope, my lord, you will not take these freedoms ill, as I know your friendship for that gentleman, and the great favours conferred on me.

THE EARL OF ORRERY *to* FAULKNER 15 *November* 1740

Elwin–Courthope, viii. 445–6

Caledon, Nov. 15, 1740.

Mr. Faulkner,—The parcels you sent to me arrived very safe. I am

it would seem here, at least, to be loose sheets. In writing to Pope first about it Faulkner called it 'a collection of letters' (see Pope's quotation of the remark to Nugent, 14 Aug., and to Orrery, 3 Sept.). Writing to Orrery near the end of September Faulkner calls it 'a volume of letters'.

[1] Pope's letter of 4 Nov. 1740.

[2] This proved to be a mistaken statement. See Mrs. Whiteway to Lord Orrery, 20 Dec. 1740.

answerable for them, and whatever turn this affair may take, I will endeavour to do you service in it, but at present I am not in a condition to think of anything, my son continuing dangerously ill, in a very bad kind of small pox, and till he is recovered I can neither read, write, nor sleep.

POPE *to* THE EARL OF ORRERY — 15 *November* 1740

The Pierpont Morgan Library

Nov. 15. 1740

My Lord,—You lay your Commands upon me to tell you if the Letters are at last in my possession? They are not; tho your Lordship sent them[1] two posts before the 27 of last month: and yours of that date I have but this day receivd. There has been all along so much Shuffling in this whole Conduct, that I can bear to cajoll them no longer, & shall give it quite up. Upon the whole I am monstrously used; and their Treachery and mean Flattery is more provoking than the Injury itself, great as it is. But the Satisfaction I derive from the Zeal & Friendship your Lordship has shown me on this occasion, is a Reward for all the disagreeable Treatment I undergo. My chief Concern, I protest to you, is for the poor Dean; who is abused in the Manner you have told me, and doubtless will be more abused at last, in his Fortune, as well as in his Writings.[2] I could justify myself better, but that I cannot take any step that might hurt him; And tho' I might resent his *Neglect* (which I should call by a harder name, were he not in his present Condition) in not once acquainting me before he gave these Letters out of his & my power into that of a Bookseller; Yet I am as much concern'd, that any thing which can be Improper should appear in his Name, as in my own. For my self, I can be indifferent if my Letters are no worse than dull; and free from any of those Strokes, which in the Carelessness of a familiar Correspondence, may make any honest man uneasy, who was never meant to see them. If ever I should be forced, by their publication, to expose the Proceeding of these people; Some Letters which I have of the Dean's, (which I dare believe they have not printed) & one of your Lordships in 1737, or 38, in which you gave me permission to joyn your Testimony to the Truth, will be sufficient to manifest the whole Conduct. But this I will not do without your Lordships Consent, nor unless I am quite compell'd to it.

Let me turn from this disagreeable Subject, to express my sincerest

[1] Sent them, not to Pope, but to Faulkner. They were being forwarded to Pope on or about this same day on which Pope is writing. See the preceding letter, from Faulkner to Orrery.

[2] Pope protests here with skilful finesse—and without regard for the true facts of the case.

Joy for my Lady Orrery's happy Delivery. I hope she is in the best Condition possible, & that every additional Blessing may be heapd upon you & her. Be so just to me as to tell me That, & any other Good News of a Family I so truly respect, & so heartily pray for. I am My Lord Your most obligd, faithfull, humble Servant, A. Pope.

Endorsement: Mr Pope. | Novbr. 15, 1740.

*POPE *to* ALLEN 17 *November* [1740]

Egerton 1947

Twitnam. No. 17.

I am in many Vexations occasioned by my desire to see you at Widcomb. That of the Fear I am still under of your Servants & Horses having undergone, as well as their Master, more Trouble for me than I am worth: another and a much greater, for your Health; both which a line from you would ease me of in some degree. A third Vexation, from an Irish affair,[1] which I expect the Conclusion of every day, and (had Promises been kept by such people) had ended my Suspense at least a month ago; Nor can any real Evil afflict one more, than a Suspense of that nature. And lastly, my intended Speedy Journey retarded from week to week. Now I have a promise from Mr Arbuthnot to come with me if I can stay till the beginning of next month, which indeed tempts me so to do, because it will be a means of making his Sister happy, & prolonging her Stay where she receives so much benefit: And secondly, because his Company will not only comfort me, but render every Jolt on the road less sensible to me. Indeed Mr Ches.[2] told me plainly, a Coach would be a Herse to me, if I went in one alone. (Vandiest has not been out of his Chamber till three days past) I fancy Mr Arb. & I may get by easy journies in a Chariot from hence to Newbury in 2 days, and I don't see why yours should be at 4 days pains to come & go so far again, if we can proceed on, the Same way. Or possibly we may find some Coach with one or 2 chance passengers in it, that may be going down to Bath. But you shall hear particularly from me as soon as I can fix the day of my setting out. I have this comfort, that I shall stay with you in all probability, till we return all together to London, and that by having seen before I come, most or all of those Friends here, who have any Share in me with yourself, they will have no further Demands upon me, but I may be left (as I often desire to be) | Dear Sir | Wholly Yours. | A. Pope

I want to know of Dr Oliver, the sooner the better, where to leave a

[1] The affair of his letters has been kept from most if not all of his English friends.
[2] Cheselden.

pretty large Box directed for Mr Borlase, or what orders I can give for its being transmitted to him?

I shall return to London to morrow, & be at Twitnam again on Sunday, in case you write. Pray be particular as to your Health.

My Sincere Services to Mrs Allen, Lady Peterborow Mrs Arbuthnot—Why are there any other Women? I hope *Certain others* will be gone by next Month.

THE EARL OF ORRERY *to* FAULKNER 19 *November* 1740

Elwin–Courthope, viii. 449–50

Caledon, Nov. 19, 1740.

Mr. Faulkner,—I return to you Mr. Pope's letter.[1] I am not able to write myself, but I wish you would let him know from me that the distressful situation I have been lately in (for my son has been in extreme danger), has rendered my mind and body very incapable of doing any business. I have the letters safe, and when I can compose myself sufficiently to know what I read, I shall obey his commands,[2] but it will be a work of time before I can bring back my peace of mind, and reassume my former happiness. Hammy,[3] I thank God, is now in a fair way of recovering, but, indeed, I find myself much disordered by the perpetual terrors I have been in, not having rested one night from anxiety since the 30th of October. Pray tell Mr. Pope I will write to him as soon as I can. He feels the distresses of his friends, and will be glad to know this family is now in a likelihood of recovering health and happiness again.

I never received the letter Mrs. Whiteway mentions to have sent hither.[4] The last letter I received was a very kind compliment, which I answered as well as my anxiety would then permit me. In this whole affair you have acted very justly, and much to your honour. I will always bear testimony of it. And in acting consistent to Mr. Pope's desires, you will certainly oblige your friend and servant.

POPE *to* HUGH BETHEL 28 *November* [1740]

Egerton 1948

Novr 28th

I have been long determined to take your kind advice, in passing part of this Winter at Bath, but a Series of accidents, (as well as some necessary Trials for removing my Complaint which I have not yet utterly left off the hopes of) have from week to week retarded me. I intended

[1] i.e. that of Pope to Faulkner, 4 Nov.

[2] Orrery is willing to pretend that he has not sent the letters to Pope, but plans to study them.

[3] His son, Hamilton (b. 1729).

[4] See the letters of Faulkner to Orrery, 15 Nov., and Mrs. Whiteway to Orrery, 20 Dec. 1740.

to have delayd my answer to one of the most friendly Letters I ever receivd, till I could give you both some better account of That, and some also of your Sisters at Bath. But it will be yet a fortnight before I can set out. I am much obliged to your Brother, which I impute to you, who tells me he can dispose of some of my Mony about Ladyday next, or sooner: which I therefore intend to remove out of the Stocks. I was very unlucky in three or four days attempts to meet Col. Moyser in Town: and my own crazie health drew me back again into the Country, before I could see him.

I understand you miss'd of my Lord Burlington in Yorkshire, who was sorry not to see you, & sends you his Services. Yours and my Friend Mrs Bl. is pretty well, her friend Lady Gerard is but just returnd from Flanders, which is a Circumstance very necessary to her Well-being this winter; for in her own House is no Comfort, and no peace. And really I should have been uneasy to have left her in their power, without some Friend at her Elbow.[1] I hope you will be in town, as an additional Comfort to her, before I return from Bath, which will hardly be till February. And that as your Visit to the World will be late, you will stay the longer in it. Perhaps the Country next Summer, will be less quiet, and more Embroiled many ways, than the Town; and you will prefer the Indolence here, to the Tumult there. We are like to gain something by the death of the Emperor;[2] his Opera & Singers are to come to Our Shore, and let the French have Luxemburgh if they please. Your Friend Kent I understand has sent you Zeman's[3] Picture without any alteration, for he says he cannot, or will not, mend it, but I must sit to him for another for you. Which you may be sure I shall readily do, whenever he will. I have nothing to add but that I love you entirely, and shall do so to the end of my life. Adieu, and let me know when you come nearer me; it will be one of the greatest motives to draw me back [to town.] With true affection, Ever Yours. | A. Pope.

Address: To Hugh Bethel Esq. at Beswick | near Beverley | Yorkshire.
Frank: free Burlington
Postmark: 29/NO

*POPE *to* ALLEN — 2 *December* [1740]

Egerton 1947

I begin to be in Pain, lest You should be in an ill State of health, or your Headake return'd upon you, by your Silence this Fortnight past,

[1] Lady Gerrard lived near by the Blounts in Welbeck Street. See *Notes & Queries*, 17 June 1939, p. 419.
[2] Emperor Charles VI died on 20 Oct. 1740.
[3] The painter Enoch Zeeman (or Seeman) died in 1744. Three brothers and a son also were painters, and it is not clear which artist is here intended.

when I writ to know particularly, (& beggd also to get a Direction from Dr Oliver how to send a Box to Cornwall). I have sincerely long'd to get to You, day after day. I could not (with any Safety or Comfort) travel alone, & till Mr Arbuthnot ingaged to accompany me, had no Other. I am unwilling to renew your trouble of sending again, but can find no Conveyance suitable to my Infirmities, further than to Newbury; unless I wait longer, which I will not do, if you [are] as willing to be troubled with me as before. Mr Arbuthnot can leave his Law on the 12th instant, & will that day, (being Friday Sennight) sett out from Twitnam with me, & lye that night at Redding; thence on the 13th Saturday, we shall be at Newbury by noon, & he will poise your Chariot well with me, the rest of the way, if you can spare it so far. If it be too inconvenient, pray be free with me, & I will take some other Means, the first I can find. But if you write me a positive Answer by the first post, (which I may receive at Twitnam by Tuesday or Wensday) I will not fail to be at Newbury at Mr Cary's by Saturday dinner, the 13th (if alive, or able to stir.) I hope no worse Evil will ever befall you, than the Loss of my Company for this Fortnight past. Indeed it was not in my power to help it; and if it ever be in my power to give you a satisfaction of any sort, you may make me as happy in it as any Earthly blessing could that fell on myself.

I am most truly | & affectionately Mrs Allen's | & Your faithfull | Friend & Servant | A Pope

Twitnam | Decr 2d | Tuesday[1]

pray direct yours to Twitnam. If you have receivd any Packets for me by Post,[2] pray send them by the first post hither. They may require haste.

Address: To | Ralph Allen Esq. at | Widcombe, near | Bath.
Postmark: 2/DE

POPE *to* THE EARL OF ORRERY — 3 *December* 1740

The Pierpont Morgan Library

My Lord,—Unless your Son is recoverd, and every Distress and Anxiety as far removed from you as I heartily wish it, I beg your Lordship not to read this Letter, but throw it aside, till you have leisure.

But let me acknowledge the Excess of your Humanity: I have found you have a Heart that could be in Pain for my Concerns, when

[1] The year is certain from other letters concerning the difficult journey to Bath as well as from the subscribed 'Tuesday'. In the last ten years of his life only in 1740 was 2 Dec. a Tuesday.

[2] In his letter to Faulkner of 4 Nov. Pope had directed Faulkner to send the printed letters of Swift and himself to Allen at Bath. If Orrery posted the packets on 14 Nov., they might well be already at Bath.

it was work'd with all the anxieties of a tender Husband, & a kind Father.

Your last Letter has made me capable of imitating You, in some, tho a very unequal, degree. For tho it has Eas'd me extremely in all that regarded my self, it has given me much a greater pain for what concerns You.

The Account your Lordship gives me of the Letters being meerly familiar and inoffensive, has remov'd the great apprehension I lay under these 3 months, and entirely alterd my opinion of Altering or Omitting any thing in my Letters. Let them be thought as insignificant as they will, they will be the better Evidences they were never writ to be printed: and as to the Dean's, tho I was once inclin'd to wish you could castigate any imprudences, yet after all, as it is certain, that he opiniatres to print 'em himself; & as it appears from several things in his 6 vols[1] (& even in some Notes at the bottom of these very Letters in the 2 Sheets Falkner has sent me) that he takes a pleasure in these freedoms, I believe the printing them will give him more Satisfaction than the consequences can give him any pain. He has set himself above what the world thinks prudent: So I doubt, if you omitted or changd any thing in His Letters, the Malice you tell me of those about him, would represent our Conduct to him as assuming & impertinent, to mangle arbitrarily his Works &c. and a very ill Use would be made of it, to set him at variance with You, or me, or both. Therfore I think upon the whole it will be best to let the whole matter alone. Nor would I employ the power you so obligingly give me, of using your Name or hand, where I fear it will be to none, or a bad purpose. For if there be another Edition in London *without* Falkners knowledge, our altering in *One* will be to no effect: or if it be *with* their knowledge they will not correct *the other* Edition, for that would be to *own* it theirs. I entirely agree with you, that we can not hinder their publication, either on this or your side the water, longer than while we hold up a Negotiation with the Lady.[2] They will infallibly be publishd here as soon as Falkner has printed his, or as soon as he has desisted from it. I think it probable He may be ignorant of the London Edition; they might drive a better bargain for the book with London Printers, & let him have only the privilege of the Irish one. Dr King (who has been at the Gates of death, but whom this day I have seen in a way of recovery) assured me he was well inform'd, 800ll has been given here

[1] To the four volumes of Swift's *Works*, published by Faulkner in 1735, two more were added in 1738—making the six.

[2] The remark is obscure, but the passage wishes to imply to Orrery that the Irish plotters (Mrs. Whiteway and her son-in-law presumably) were negotiating with London publishers. 'They' will drive their own bargain and leave Faulkner with rights only to the Dublin edition. 'They' are the 'others' who are deeper in the affair than Faulkner. How much of this did Orrery believe?

for several pieces of the Dean's, (which I conclude must be for his History, & others of those Manuscripts your Lordship acquaints me were stolen from his Volumes of manuscripts of late, & not only for these Letters) & that a Person has lately been over who made this bargain——all these Circumstances convince me, there are others deeper in this affair than Falkner. And if I had time to lay before you, what has been written to me by the Lady & her son-in law, from time to time, with what Mr Nugent has told me; and to joyn this with what the Deans own Letters told me formerly, concerning my Letters & his other papers, & what has happend to them from year to year; all this would set the whole (I think) in so full a light before your eyes; that as I shall have a good deal of leisure at Bath, I intend (if you incourage it) to draw up & send you the Detail of it whenever you shall tell me, you are at Ease enough at home to read it.

I think therfore upon the whole, to have nothing at all to do with them, nor the Book; but give the inclosed Answer[1] once for all to Falkner; which I would however rather your Lordship read to him, than gave the Letter; and if you judge any part of it too *yielding*, to tell him no more of it than you think proper.

One thing I have a Curiosity to know, whether Mrs Whiteway sent you the Letter which they pretend was sent to the Dean together with the Book? (and of which Falkner luckily gave me a Copy.) For he now tells me, 'She told him "She had sent it to Caledon, when he ask'd for it to send to me; and (if I mistake not a passage in yours) your Lordship tells me "You never saw it. A good deal depends upon this Letter, and much Discovery may be made by the Original, I believe, if they have not secreted it.[2]

Once more my Lord I beg you, not to think of these Triffles, nor to give me any other account at present but of your own Family; for whose welfare I wish from the bottom of a heart, which you have made, by many titles, of Honour, Affection, Esteem, & Gratitude, | My Lord | Entirely Yours. | A. Pope.

Decr 3d 1740.

On second thoughts, it will be better not to give Falkener any answer yet, till I have had the Book, & therfore I defer it Nor will I trouble you more till I hear (what I pray for) that you are restored to full tranquillity.

Endorsement (in Orrery's hand): Mr Pope. | Decbr: 3: 1740.

[1] Not finally enclosed: see the postscript.

[2] The unorthodox use of marks indicating quotation occurs more than once in Pope's writing.

*POPE *to* GEORGE ARBUTHNOT[1] [6 *December* 1740]

Arthur A. Houghton, Jr.

Saturday.

I depend on you at Twitenham on Thursday Evening, or sooner if you can. On Friday the Chariot & horses will be ready by 7 in the morning, to carry us to Redding by night. On Saturday another Chariot & 4 horses meets us at Newbury, by noon punctually, to get to Malborow at night. You see the necessity of being punctual. Pray send me a line to Lord Bathurst's, unless it find me at Mr Murrays this day. I am Ever most affectionately | Dear Sir | Yours, | A. Pope.

I go out of town on munday.

Address: To | Mr. Arbuthnot, in | Castle Yard | Holborn.

POPE *to* THE EARL OF ORRERY 10 *December* 1740

The Pierpont Morgan Library

Twit'nam, Decr 10th 1740.

My Lord,—I have had the present Satisfaction (I hope it is an Earnest of the future) to hear from Mr Salkeld[2] that one of your Sons is out of danger, & the other in no dangerous Way: God send them a full & speedy recovery! I therfore will just thank you & own the receipt of your Last, together with the Book.[3] Upon reading it, I am wholly of your Lordships Opinion, that it was as unworthy ever to be printed, as it is now impossible to be supprest. I am however much more at ease, since I find the Letters meerly trivial & familiar; & am confirm'd in the resolution not to touch or alter a line of 'em, (unless you could prevail on the Dean to omit some Names at length) but since you see he has all along put them in himself, I fear even that would be in vain. I observe some Notes that refer to *his Original papers*, which makes me think they are printed in Ireland after all. It is scarce probable the London Printers would have the complaisance to suppress their Edition in favor to the Irish ones: But there may be a plain reason otherwise why the small Edition is kept back, till the larger is published, since it would undersell it & prejudice Falkner's now in hand.

I will detain the book a while, & then comply with the obligation they have laid upon your Lordship & return it you. I would willingly (I confess) keep the first Sheets, (where are many remarkable notes, & some interlineations in the Deans hand)[4] and as they are alredy reprinted by Faukener, he cannot plead any want of them, if I return all

[1] Pope's letter to Allen, 2 Dec. [1740], seems to fix the date of this note, in which Pope assumes that Allen will surely send his chariot to take Arbuthnot and himself to Bath.

[2] The tutor to Lord Orrery's sons.—Elwin. [3] The 'book' in nine parcels. See iv. 294.

[4] This is good evidence that Swift did his share in editing and annotating the letters for Faulkner. Orrery had seen the book, and would know Swift's very characteristic hand.

that is said to be un-printed. In the mean while (to gain Time, in order to consider with my friends what to do here) I wish your Lordship would desire the Lady to send me by your hands (the same way as these came, only directed to Mr Allen Postmaster at Bath) *those Letters* which she has promised me almost a twelvemonth.[1] Be pleas'd to tell them I want to see, if any of those are in this printed book? or, if they may not be added to it?[2] (This perhaps may bring them), & particularly to know from Her, if I cannot have with them *That Original Letter* which was sent to the Dean together with this book, & which I desird so much of her & of Falkner because I verily believe it may help me to some Discovery from what hands it came? This is all I will trouble your Lordship with at present; till I hear from your self that you are as happy, and as free from greater Cares, as I wish you! I am unwilling to add to your Concern, by telling how dangerously ill Dr King is still.[3] I know what a Heart you have, (by my own Experience) which can feel for any Anxiety of another, at the same time that it is worked by all the Tenderness of a Father & a Husband. May every such Near, such Remoter Tye of Affection, be managed so gently by Providence, as to touch you with the soft, not gall you with the severe, Sensations; tho in the disposition of this System, God has been pleas'd (no doubt for good Ends, tho to us unseen) to unite them, too closely for the tender frame of *human* Happiness. Adieu my Lord; whatever *Is*, is *Right*.[4] It was the Saying of Socrates, and the firm Faith of | My Lord, | Your truely faithfull and | obliged Servant, | A. Pope.

I am told my Lady is perfectly well, yet I dare say as much afflicted for your children, as she would be for her own & yours.

Endorsement: Mr Pope. | Decbr 10th: 1740

THE EARL OF ORRERY *to* POPE 13 *December* 1740

Elwin–Courthope, viii. 457–9

Caledon, Dec. 13, 1740.

Sir,—I hasten to answer yours[5] by the return of the post. My two sons

[1] Her willingness to return the letters some time had been mentioned to Nugent as early as March of this year.

[2] Pope inserted in his quarto and folio *Works in Prose* (his first published editions of the Swift–Pope letters) seven letters that had not been in the clandestine volume. Faulkner added them to his octavo edition as a 'Supplement' (pp. 281–300).

[3] Dr. William King, Principal of St. Mary Hall, Oxford, was the friend to whom Swift had sent the MS. of his *History of the Four Last Years of the Queen*.

[4] For parallels to this famous last line of Epistle I of the *Essay on Man*, collected by Professor Maynard Mack, see Pope's *Poems* (Twickenham ed.), III–i, 51 n. If Pope knew the expression from Dryden's *Oedipus* (III. i), is it possible that he here wrote *Socrates* for *Sophocles*?

[5] Of 3 Dec., which Pope wrote before receiving the nine packets of printed letters.

are both happily through the small pox, and recovering as fast as possible. Lady Orrery, who is your faithful servant, is in perfect health, and so are my daughters. Thus is my heart entirely at ease, but in all circumstances devoted to you.

I never received the letter Mrs. Whiteway mentioned to have been sent to Caledon,[1] though all her other letters came safe both to Lady Orrery and to me. Nor in any of them is the least notice taken of that letter, or the loss of it. However you will easily perceive that it is to be lost between Dublin and Caledon. The original cannot, must not be produced, unless some faithful transcriber be found out, though upon the alarm of these letters they will scarce trust anybody, and since your late correspondence with the lady, &c., you would certainly know the hand. Thus you have my opinion of that letter, of which however I am glad you have a copy.

I wonder you had not received the whole set of letters which I sent you about a month ago. Your reasons upon that occasion are extremely convincing to me that Faulkner should not be hindered from going on, but your name ought not to appear. He knows not, neither shall he, that you have the letters. Return them to me, and I will say I have read them, and since they are already printed I cannot see how they can be stopped, and so have writ to you that, as they are trifling, I have returned them to Faulkner, with a permission to go on. This can be looked upon only as vanity in me (let their malice say the worst) as being mentioned advantageously in them; but if you will meddle, or seem concerned about them, they will reinforce their arguments to the poor dean that you are at the bottom of all, &c. They are now trumpeting that news about, and I would have you lie by till you catch them, as I dare say you will, and expose them in the manner they deserve. You have some legacies left you by the dean; *hinc illæ lacrymæ.*[2] They cannot rest till they are secure of all. A gentleman who lately came to me from Dublin gives a most melancholy account of the dean, and mentions a great knave, though a clergyman, that is now chief he-favourite.[3] Perhaps he is one of the gang. If he is not I hope they will quarrel, and that may produce some good. Thus I tell you all I know, and all I think, and remember whatever are your commands I

[1] Mrs. Whiteway explains to Lord Orrery in her letter of 20 Dec. that she still has the letter and intends to send it to Pope 'by the first opportunity that is safe'. Again, she does not act in a hurry. Admittedly, suspicions of the reliability of the post were at this time widespread.

[2] Orrery was unaware that Swift's last will, signed 3 May 1740, left Pope only a miniature. Earlier Swift had assured Pope that his papers should all go to Pope, and Pope, like Orrery, being probably unaware of the change, could the more easily suspect Mrs. Whiteway and Deane Swift of coveting the papers.

[3] Dr. Francis Wilson, a prebend of St. Patrick's, was at this time very useful to Swift. In June 1742 the friendship ended in the notorious scene of violence that marks the public beginning of Swift's senility. See Ball, vi. 179–85.

shall certainly obey them. I write to Dr. King this post. I am tired heartily of this wretched Ireland, and therefore pray lose no time in telling me how, and what to act, for I will leave it as soon as I can. Yours, &c.

THE EARL OF ORRERY *to* POPE — 20 *December* 1740

Elwin–Courthope, viii. 459–60

Caledon, Saturday, Dec. 20, 1740.

Sir,—I have this moment received yours of the 10th instant. It has come to me sooner than any letter of yours travelled to Caledon. My domestic happiness is as complete in every respect as your good heart can wish it. I am under a necessity to return the book as I received it, but I will try to get the copy from Faulkner (that is now in your hands) as soon as he has reprinted the whole. This will answer your end as well, provided I carry my point. I have anticipated your commands in relation to the Bath letter. Upon Faulkner's desiring to know if I ever had received it, I writ to the lady last post letting her know that I had not. Possibly that may draw it,[1] or the new copy of it which is to pass for the original, from her or her son-in-law. If the letters are printed in Ireland, which I own I doubt, Faulkner I dare say is not in the secret. But be that as it will his proceedings must be applauded. It will be to no purpose to attempt to obtain from the d[ean] the alteration of any one word, though I wish it as heartily as you, on account of some particulars which I know will give a friend or two of mine great uneasiness, and some characters that are not so just as good-natured.

I will write to the lady in the manner you desire. Depend upon it they are alarmed, and will act on the defensive. But by putting on an air of blindness I shall see, as I have in many other cases, more than if I seemed to have my eyes open. In short they must be caressed; *Nec lex est justior ulla*, *Quam necis artifices*,[2] &c. Still I insist your name is not to appear. I hope they cannot hurt me with my ever-honoured, ever-lamented friend. I think they will not, because I am no legatee. But I will proceed with calmness and caution till I put all your weapons into your hands, and should be glad to be able to arm you against the wounds and stabs in the dark which I am sure are preparing, and have already been aimed at you. I could almost think from these proceedings that the dean has left the perusal of his papers to you.[3] Once I talked to him long on that subject, but I then thought his deafness was very predominant, and stopped not only his hearing, but all his other senses.

[1] See Mrs. Whiteway's letter next following.

[2] Ovid, *Ars Amat.* i. 655–6.

[3] Doubtless, by this time, if Mrs. Whiteway and Deane Swift shared Orrery's thought, they felt Swift had been unwise and might better leave his papers to them.

I am so full of this vile attempt against you, which I own rouses my indignation,[1] that I not only grow tedious but ungrateful, and forget to thank you for all your kindness to me by Salkeld's means. I shall be glad to see the detail you mention when your leisure permits, and I direct this to Bath imagining that it will find you there. I propose to see you early in the next year, when the frost is gone, and the days are longer. Lady Orrery will follow me as soon as she can. We are both most heartily tired of this detestable kingdom, and I wonder how so good a woman as she really is happened to be born among so many monsters. I am, dear sir, most cordially, your true, humble servant.

Dr. King makes me send many a sighing prayer towards the Temple.[2]

MRS. WHITEWAY *to* THE EARL OF ORRERY

20 *December* 1740

Elwin–Courthope, viii. 461

Dec. 20, 1740.

Mr. Faulkner mistook me in telling your lordship that I sent you the letter that came from Bath. It is not in my power to do it, for I am under an engagement to Mr. P[ope] to remit it by the first opportunity that is safe,[3] with some other papers that I promised him I would send by Mr. M'Aulay, who intended being in London long before this, which business has prevented. This I hope will plead my excuse for not sending it to you. In the meantime I hope there is an end of the vexatious affair, if blabs will not mention it again to the dean, who has quite forgot it. Your, &c.

THE EARL OF ORRERY *to* POPE

24 *December* 1740

Elwin–Courthope, viii. 461–2

Caledon, Dec. 24, 1740.

Sir,—I enclose to you a letter I received from the lady last post. I write to her this day[4] to let her know that you would willingly have the papers come under my cover, but I question whether she will resign them. Would it not be worth your while to write to her yourself? You see it is in her power to suppress them, otherwise how can she say that there is an end of this vexatious affair, when the letters are

[1] Orrery's letters sufficiently convict him of insincerity. Even if he believed Pope greatly wronged by Mrs. Whiteway (which one must doubt), his friendly letters continuing to her show a certain double-dealing. Intentionally or not, he aided and formulated Pope's useful, pretended suspicions.

[2] Where Dr. King had chambers.—Elwin.

[3] The lady's inability to find a safe letter-carrier would begin to be amusing if it were not for the fact that it led Pope to foster in Orrery and others unjust suspicions of her.

[4] His lordship's letter, which follows this, is far less accusing than one might expect. In this letter Orrery most definitely formulates his theory (devised perhaps chiefly for Pope's consumption) as to how the letters got into print. Did he believe his own theory?

actually printed? By "blabs" she means Faulkner.[1] He was not the bookseller for whom they were intended; but the dean, much against her will, gave them to him. This I take to have been the case, for the dean has given her lately, as I am told by a discarded favourite, some papers which he had promised to another, even the discarded favourite, and which she swears F[aulkner] shall not print. By putting all these things together, I imagine the letters were printed at her, and her son-in-law's expense in England, and a copy sent from Bath, that they might sell it here, but the dean acted against their measures. This has stopped the whole affair. The letter to me discovers, I think, great guilt, and concludes with a most strained piece of flattery to a child not two months old. But I am in haste, and am ever tormenting you with letters. Believe, your, etc.

THE EARL OF ORRERY *to* MRS. WHITEWAY[2]

24 *December* 1740

Elwin–Courthope, viii. 462–3

Caledon, Dec. 24, 1740

Madam,—The same post that brought me the favour of yours, brought me a letter from Mr. Pope, in which he entreats me to write to you, and desire you will send to me the papers you intended for him by Mr. M'Aulay, and the letter that was sent from Bath. I will take care, madam, to transmit them to him very safe, and as he seems impatient for them I beg you will lose no time in forwarding them to Caledon, and the moment I receive them, you shall have my acknowledgment of the receipt. I doubt, madam, it will be impossible to stop this vexatious affair. They are already in print. Who can stop the edition from coming out? As they were printed on the other side of the water they will certainly appear there do what we can to suppress them in Ireland. And there is nothing in them, according to my apprehension, so reflecting upon anybody, as upon my honoured friend, the dean, who has let his friend's letters be stolen out of his custody.[3] That is the only point that vexes me in the whole transaction. Lord Bolingbroke, Mr. Pope, and Mr. Gay must always write in such a manner as to give pleasure to the polite world, even in their most trifling correspondence; but as they certainly never writ these letters with an intention they should be printed, I own I am concerned upon

[1] She might possibly mean Lord Orrery himself, but Faulkner would certainly be intended.

[2] With this letter went one from Lady Orrery to Mrs. W., which is now in the Huntington Library (MS. 14356). Its friendly tone and womanly preoccupation with the new-born Lady Catherine show no reserve of friendship towards one suspected of stealing and printing letters.

[3] Obviously Orrery would not be so foolish as to blame Swift if, as Elwin thinks, Swift was at this time 'in a state of irresponsible helplessness'. That state arrived more than a year later.

the dean's account that they should appear by his means. Do you suspect, madam, any person that is or has been about him for so base a piece of theft as that of stealing papers? Such a person ought to be exposed to the whole world. I dare say you will feel all the abhorrence on this occasion that is possible, and I heartily wish you could be the means of finding out, and explaining, their black and iniquitous piece of treachery. I am in pain about my own letters, but much more about any papers that belong to the dean's friends and mine. I know this collection of letters will alarm every one of the dean's correspondents, and I should be glad, now my mind is at ease, to hear very fully from you upon this subject, but not till you are free from your cold, which I hope this will find you. I am, madam, with many thanks for your late trouble, your, etc.

Forgive me, madam, for troubling you with my thankful service to Dr. Wilson.[1]

POPE *to* THE EARL OF ORRERY[2] [27 *December* 1740]

The Pierpont Morgan Library

10r: 27th: 1740

My Lord,—With the utmost Joy of heart, I receivd lately an account from Mr Salkeld of the Safety of both your Sons. May their future life amply recompense all the Anxiety their Danger has cost you, and may every good Quality that can indeare them yet more, grow & advance with them!

I may now once more thank you for the Great proof of your Goodness, & Attention to my Concerns, at so trying a Time. I cannot wish to make you any Return, for I hope So untoward an Incident will never befall you. I only wish you may never more be in Pain for a Friend, or a Relation.

I must pity the Dean; but it's necessary to give some answer to his Bookseller, & it shall be a Final one. But I think (all Circumstances considered) it will be better done in a Letter to your Lordship than immediately to him: I send it herewith, & wish not He only but Mrs Wh. saw, but not copyd it—For I fear the Very Shadow of my Pen may be made an ill use of. What I've said of Their *Preface* is but necessary, after such a Proposal as Mr Swift actually made; and it is in this principally I would accept your Lordships obliging Offer, to use your

[1] Wilson, the 'he-favourite' of Orrery's letter (13 Dec.) to Pope, was accused of stealing books from Swift. Is Orrery possibly suggesting to himself and Mrs. W. that Wilson is involved in this 'vexatious affair'?

[2] The date is Lord Orrery's entry. Pope sent on this day two letters to Lord Orrery: the following one (dated) is to be read to Mrs. Whiteway and Faulkner; this present letter is Pope's private comment on the following letter and is designed for Orrery alone.

Name, with regard to the Advertisement inclosed,[1] and desire you to Prescribe him the very Words of it, and you'l please to let him take them for your own drawing up. I should be sorry if he or they said any thing that might lead to a Suggestion so false, as Falkener told you Mrs W. had dropt (as if I had been privy to this Affair) For in that Case I should be oblig'd to clear myself, at the Expence of the Dean, or of some about him: The first I cannot bear to think of, in his present melancholy Condition; & the other I would rather avoid, as it would still, tho more remotely, reflect upon him. What they themselves represent of him, it is by no means fit I should divulge to the publick; and what they discover of themselves might be construed as a hardship to expose, (tho it would be my own fullest Vindication.) But there are Particulars that could decently be told, of their Conduct, both to Him, & to Me, and such as would be admitted as Proofs of the Fact I believe, in any Court of justice. Some of them I will lay together, & send you, in the Form of a Letter; & ask your leave (if by their future Conduct, or the Prevalence of any Mistaken opinion in others, I should be obliged to it) to make use of: The remaining Circumstances I will keep for your private View, whenever I have the pleasure again to enjoy your Return.

Of the Book itself I think just as you do, that it was not worth printing, but cannot now be supprest. It is plain, that where ever it was printed, the Collection was made in Ireland, pickd up by pieces from time to time, and begun a good while ago. For there are some Letters of an early date, which came later to their hands, & were inserted by Interpolated half sheets and quarter Sheets,[2] after the printing of the first & second Sheets; these are marked with Asterisks * to direct the Binder where to place them?[3] 2dly I find (to the best of my Memory) some of the Letters your Lordship brought over, which I burn'd just after, & therfore could not be had on this side.[4] 3dly There is one long Letter from the Dean which he never sent; but was taken out of a Pamphlet he once shewd me but never printed, writ to justify himself after the Queens death, in Ireland.[5] 4thly Here are

[1] This Advertisement was not copied by Orrery, was not used by Faulkner, so far as is known, and has not been preserved. It was doubtless chiefly remarkable for its silences concerning the clandestine volume and the provenance of the letters.

[2] For bibliographical descriptions of the clandestine volume see Maynard Mack, 'The First Printing of the Letters of Pope and Swift', *The Library*, 4 S. xix (1939), 465–85, and V. A. Dearing, 'New Light on the First Printing . . .', ibid. xxiv (1943), 74–80. Pope cannot be speaking with scientific precision concerning the first sheets that Faulkner had sent him, but he is loosely correct about the insertion of what looked like parts of sheets. The long letter inserted in the volume by Swift became Letter *V and preceded the original Letter V (without asterisk).

[3] This use of asterisks was normal procedure in all books with last-minute interpolations.

[4] They could be had in England, at least some of them, in the Harleian Library, where they had been transcribed.

[5] Swift might have shown the pamphlet to Pope in 1726 or 1727 when in England. The

some of his Letters which I returnd him; & All those to Mr Gay, which the Duke of Queensbury & I found among Mr G.'s papers & sent him over. But Care has been taken[1] in this Collection to Suppress the Letter I then wrote him, and others of mine as sollicited the Return or the Exchange of the Letters between us; which appears however by some of the Deans answers, which I have chanc'd to keep & will shew you.

My Lord I will tire you no more: Pray take your full leisure in all this. You may well be sick of it, I am heartily so. God continue & increase Yours & my Lady's happiness!

POPE *to* THE EARL OF ORRERY[2] 27 *December* 1740

The Pierpont Morgan Library

Decr 27th 1740.

My Lord,—Your Lordship will receive by this Post in five pacquets (this Letter making a sixth) the Book which they have at last allowed me a sight of. In this I comply with the Condition on which it was sent, but I have caus'd a Copy to be taken, to which surely I have a Right.[3] I can only repeat to Mr Faukener what I told him before, that I utterly dis-approve the Printing it; tho I agree with your Lordship, it is now as impossible to be supprest as it was at first unworthy to be printed. I can't say how far my Letters in it are, or are not genuine, having no Originals to compare them with, nor having yet receivd those which Mrs Wh. has so long been transmitting (I hop'd thro *your hands*, for nothing else reaches me, not even Mr F.'s printed Sheets) To what purpose does Mr Falkener offer me to alter or correct any thing? when at the same time he assures me there is Another Edition somewhere over which he hath no Influence? In a word therfore, I will have nothing to do in it; I will neither *Revise*, *alter*, *omit*, nor *touch*, a single line of it. I will as little consent that Any *Preface* shall be written, to justify me from the knowledge of it, at the Expence of what (for all that any of us know) may be an Untruth, viz: by *laying it on the corrupt Practises of Printers in London.*[4] If ever such an Impression appears in England, I know what to do, & shall do Mr

condition of the letter (*V: 10 Jan. 1721) in the clandestine volume and in the Faulkner octavo and the London folio and quarto—all of 1741—seems to make it almost certain that it was inserted by Swift and first printed by Faulkner.

1 It had indeed been taken!—and by Pope himself. Pope was the last who would at this moment wish to publicize his efforts to get his letters back—and his success.

2 This second letter of the 27th, fully dated, was sent to his lordship to read to Faulkner and Mrs. Whiteway. It was later thought advisable not to use this letter on them, as we shall see.

3 Pope had 'the right' but he also had other copies of the printed clandestine volume, and hence it was not necessary to copy or to keep copy except for the first sheets.

4 Faulkner printed no preface to his volume.

Falkener's Edition no small service, by applying to the Laws in force here to suppress or destroy this.[1] I must own I would have taken the same Course in Ireland, but thro' a Regard to his acting by the Dean's Direction. I therfore do insist, that when his Book comes out, he fairly pleads his best Title, the Consent of *One* of the three Partyes.[2] If any other *Person's name*, or any *other Circumstance* concerning the *Book* itself be mentiond, or hinted at, I shall look upon it as meant to lead to an Insinuation, (which I understand has been dropt amongst them already) as if I secretly approved, or had been some way privy to it. By this, Mr Falkener would indeed give me sufficient Umbrage; and I should certainly do my self full Justice, at his, or any one's expence, who has or shall suggest it,[3] or who has or shall take the Liberty of printing, either my *Letters*, or *any other Part of my Works*, without my Consent: And I am persuaded, Property is better guarded even by the Laws in Ireland, than the Booksellers there are aware of. My Thanks are due to Mr F. for the Delay he has made in the publication, but I must also desire him to pay them to Mrs Whiteway, who told me that it was owing to Her, that ever I had the least Information of this whole matter. I desire he will assure her on my part, that if ever I am forced to vindicate myself from having any Share in it, I will at the same time do her & Mr Swift the same justice to the whole world, that they have done themselves to me. And pray let the Dean be told, that however disagreeably this Thing may be circumstanced, there is One Reflection pleasing to me; that the strict Friendship & Affection we have so long born each other will by this means be known to all mankind. I am | My Lord | Your most faithfull, | obligd, & humble Servant | A. Pope.

Endorsement: Mr Pope. 10r: 27: 1740.

POPE *to* THE EARL OF ORRERY[4] 29 *December* [1740]

The Pierpont Morgan Library

Decr 29th | 1740

My Lord,—I wrote to you so minutely by the last post, in the Two Letters, together with the five pacquets of the printed book which I returnd by the same post; that I have not a word to add, but to acknowledge one from your Lordship which I received at Bath this day, with

[1] Clearly Pope had resolved to anticipate any reprinting of the Dublin edition by bringing out his own edition in London.

[2] Swift, Bolingbroke, and Pope, the authors of the letters.

[3] This is indeed a threat, in view of the fact that Orrery has repeatedly told him that Swift, Mrs. Whiteway, and Faulkner all say the volume was 'instigated' by Pope himself.

[4] The year date is in Lord Orrery's hand. Curiously, the letter is unsigned, but is in Pope's hand.

the Confirmation of what I so much desird to hear, the Entire Health of your family.

I have just finishd the Narration I intended you of the whole Affair of the Letters from first to last in which you'l see the great Tenderness I would preserve for the Dean, & the Careful Evasion of charging any body else with any Guilt of any kind; nor one Reflection made but pure Relation of Fact, & in their own words. Your Lordship will tell me if you have any Objection to my making known the humane & friendly part you have acted towards me, or to any particular, of any sort: as you are my only (Creditable) Witness, & my best Judge. If you had an Opportunity of reading it to the Dean, alone; (provided you found his Judgment strong, & his Memory clear enough to compare & make a good use of the Information) it might convince him how far I am from being privy to, or pleasd with, this Measure. But unless it could open his eyes to any good purpose, so as to retrieve him from the Managements of these people, I think it as well let alone.

I also leave to your judgment whether to show Falkener the Letter I wrote for that end, & inclosed in my last, or only to tell him what you propose in this, as from your self only.

My Intention is, if I see the printed book come out, either here or in Ireland, to cause any bookseller to add to it a few of the *Dean's* Letters which verify the narrative you see, (And (if you have no Objection) one or two of your own of a former date here cited[1]) and *not to say a word in my own person*, but leave those additional Letters to show the Course of the affair. Unless by their trumpeting the Falsity about, you should judge it necessary to print at the End of the book this very Narrative.[2] I am quite passive in the matter, since I find my own so Empty of Offence & Lord B.s Letters so innocent: and I doubt not, he will slight it as much as I.[3]

No News you could tell me, of any Roguery or Lying practisd against me, can give me any Vexation; when your Contempt of the people drives you from them to Us; a Pleasure which I hope oftner to injoy, & longer to preserve, than has hitherto been the fortune of Your Lordships most | faithfull Servant.

[1] The passages are quoted in the Narrative; i.e. the letter of 30 Dec.

[2] Pope never printed his 'Narrative'.

[3] Elwin assumes that Pope had never mentioned the matter of the letters to Lord Bolingbroke. Since we have none of Pope's letters sent to his lordship in France, this is one of the many things which we do not know. If Bolingbroke had been restored to his civil rights, publication of his letters might be a breach of privilege; but he was technically (as the newspapers frequently called him) 'the *late* Lord Bolingbroke'; i.e. not entitled to sit in the House of Lords or to enjoy the privileges of lordship.

POPE *to* THE EARL OF ORRERY[1] 30 *December* 1740

Harvard University

Dec. 30th—1740

My Lord,—When I promised your Lordship an Account of the whole Transaction relating to these Letters, to refresh your Memory in some Particulars, and to acquaint you of others, I little expected I should send you a Narrative instead of a Letter. But I shall shorten it as much as possible by the Omission of all such Circumstances, as are not absolutely necessary to the clearing this Affair.

Your Lordship knows, that long since, upon the unwarrantable Publication of some of my private Letters, I endeavoured to recall as many as I could from most of the Friends, with whom I had corresponded. There were None which gave me more Apprehension, than those I had writ to Doctor Swift in Ireland, whom I often desired to destroy them;[2] which not being complyed with, it was proposed, that we should return to each other such at least, of which any ill Use might be made.[3] Accordingly I sent him several, particularly after Mr Gay's Death, together with those, which the Duke of Queensbury and my self then found among his Papers.[4] But in the Year 1735 I had Reason to grow more urgent than ever about my Letters. The Dean then answered, Sepr 2d 1735,[5] "That he had never destroyed one of them; but his Executors had strict Orders in his will to burn every Letter he should leave behind him, being loth that any from me, and a few other Friends, should dye before him."—And again October 21st he told me,—"I needed not to apprehend any *Curl's* medling with my Letters: He would not destroy them, but had ordered his Executors to do that Office."—But the next Year, April 22d 1736, he spake of this as a Thing not already ordered only that—"his Resolution was, to direct his Executors to send me all my Letters." —Adding,—"they are all tyed up, indorsed, &c—No Mortal shall copy them; but you shall surely have them, when I am no more."

In the mean Time there had been handed about, first in Ireland,

[1] This 'Narrative' letter is here printed from Orrery's transcript, preserved in his letter-books, iii. 325–38. Elwin printed from a different transcript, which had Pope's autograph signature and other revisions in his hand. Elwin's source has not been available to the present editor. The text here given has been compared with Elwin's.

[2] One may doubt if Pope expressed such a desire.

[3] In the present printed edition, care has been taken to suppress those Letters of Mr Pope, wherein this Matter was press'd; but it appears from the Dean's Answers, which have been partly preserved.—Marginal note by Pope. The note was transcribed by Orrery. It is reminiscent of the remark at the end of Pope's letter to Orrery, 27 Dec. 1740 (iv. 311). The phrase 'present printed edition' refers to the clandestine volume. At some time Pope evidently intended to publish this letter, but he never did.

[4] They were sent after the transcripts (now preserved at Longleat) were made, presumably in the Harleian Library.

[5] The printed date is 3 Sept. The dates of all the other letters quoted seem to be accurately given.

and at last in England, a Joynt Letter to the Dean from the Lord Bolingbroke and me, the Copy of which, as Neither of us had any, must have been taken from the Dean's Papers.[1] This coming soon after to be printed, occasioned me to renew my Sollicitations; and your Lordship (then in Dublin) was pleased to be charged with them. You remember, my Lord, (at least I must ever remember) with what Warmth You pressed this Matter, till you obtained a Promise, that they should be returned by your Hands. But at the same Time, in a Letter of May 31st 1737, the Dean explains it, that—"Your Lordship should have *all* the Letters he *could find* of mine, which (he says) were fastned in a Folio Cover, or kept in Bundles indorsed,"—but adds,—"by reading their Dates, I find a Chasm of six Years, of which I can find no Copies, and yet I kept them with all possible Care; but I have been forced, on three or four Occasions, to send all my Papers to some Friends—however what I have are not much above *Sixty*."

The great Alteration in this from the preceding Assurances, with the News of so many Letters lost, or in Hands unknown both to him, and to me, occasioned your Lordship, by a Letter dated two Days after,[2] to express your Surprize at this;—"considering how constantly we wrote, and how carefully he kept these Letters," You "thought two Causes only could be assigned for it; that they were either stolen by People, who had Admission into his Closet, or else were not returned by those, with whom he had entrusted his Papers on some certain Occasions." The latter seemed most probable, but You feared it would be hard to recover them, since "Those, who were knavish enough not to restore them, would probably be cunning enough still to conceal them."

Your Lordship used all the Arguments, and Means you could, to no Purpose; and could only further learn from the Dean,[3] that the Chasm began in 1722. You observed, that "a Letter from me to him in 1725[4] had lately been printed without my Consent, which alarmed you, and made you apprehend they were in very improper Hands."

The month after, (vizt) July 23d 1737, the Dean once more mentioned this Chasm, and imagined he might have carried them over in one of his Journeys to England: But says, "My Lord Orrery will take with him *all the Letters I have*, which are not above *Twenty five*."—Which few were accordingly delivered to your Lordship, and most of which I burned, as absolutely trivial, within three Days of my Receipt of them.[5] Soon after I returned to the Dean all his Letters to the

[1] This letter, printed under date of Aug. 1723, was first printed by Curll in 1737. How he got it is unknown, but the publication admirably served Pope's purpose in securing the return of his letters from Swift.

[2] The letter of 2 June 1737.

[3] Orrery so reports in his letter to Pope of 14 June 1737.

[4] Orrery's error for the date of the letter of Aug. 1723.

[5] This seems a most improbable statement, made to enforce the idea that Pope had not

same Period, except a few; which when you see, your Lordship will allow I had Reason to keep. These, together with what I have had since, will give some Light, upon whom I am to charge the disagreeable measure, that has now been taken; and how little I ought to resent it of the Dean, for whom I shall retain to the Day of my Death the true Affection I have born him the best Part of my Life.—It was a whole Year, and upwards, after all this, when, to my great Surprize, he wrote to me as follows.—Augt 8th—1738. "I can faithfully assure you, that every Letter you favoured me with these Twenty Years, and more, are sealed up in Bundles, and delivered to Mrs W—, a very worthy, rational, and judicious Cousin of mine, and the only Relation whose visits I can suffer. All these Letters She is directed to send safely to you upon my Decease."—But in a Postscript to the same Letter, tho' dated Augt 24th 1738, he says,—"I must correct my Mistake; I shewed my Cousin the above Letter, and She assures me, that a great Collection of my[1]/your Letters to you/me are put up, and sealed, and in some very safe Hand."—About this Time your Lordship returned to England, and told me, by a Letter from Marston,[2] that you were perfectly convinced "the Letters were neither lost, nor burnt;" but who the Dean meant, by a safe Hand in Ireland, was beyond your Power to guess; and You feared, "whoever had them, would keep them. Mrs W— did assure you, She had not one of them; and seemed to be under great Uneasyness, lest I should imagine She had: She told your Lordship, that she stopped the Dean's Letter, which gave me that Information; but believed, he would write such another, and therefore begged of you to assure me from her, that She was totally ignorant where they were."

The next News I heard of my Letters was from Mr Nugent,[3] who had visited the Dean, and seen some of them in his Hands, towards the End of the Year 1739, when he was commissioned by the same Lady to acquaint me, that there were several which She would send me on my Order: And some Months after I had accepted this Offer, (vizt) June 3d 1740, She writ her self to me, excusing the Delay, but confirming the Promise. But while I remained in Expectation of this

time to transcribe the letters before burning—but the Irish senders of the letters had had ample time to copy them. In his clandestine volume Pope printed something like 36 letters from himself to Swift dating from 1725 to 1737. If these came back from Swift by kindness of Orrery in the summer of 1737, as they probably did, Pope could not have preserved texts and destroyed originals in three days. Five of these 36 letters were transcribed in the Harleian transcripts (now at Longleat).

[1] It is written just thus in the Original; and the collection seems to be the same that is now printed, as it contains the Letters of both.—Orrery's marginal note. (Elwin ascribes this note to Pope.)

[2] Dated 4 Oct. 1738.

[3] First mentioned in the letters preserved to us in that of Pope to Nugent, 26 Mar. [1740].

Favour, my Hopes were dashed at once by a Letter of July 29th from Mr Faulkner,[1] Bookseller in Dublin, acquainting me, "that the Dean of St Patrick's had given him to print, a Volume of Letters of his and mine, which (he said) came from London with a Letter," of which he inclosed a Copy. As your Lordship told me You never had a Sight of it, and the Original is since said to be lost, on the Road between Dublin and your House, I transcribe it as a Curiosity.[2]

Sir,—The true Honour which all the honest and grateful Part of this Nation[3] must bear you, as the most publick spirited of Patriots, the best of private Men, and the greatest polite Genius of this Age, made it impossible to resist the Temptation, which has fallen in our Way, of preserving from all Accidents a Copy of the *inclosed Papers*, which at once give so amiable a Picture of your own excellent Mind, and so strong a Testimony of the Love and Respect of those, who nearest know, and best can judge of it.

As there is Reason to fear they would be lost to Posterity after your Death, if either of your Two great Friends[4] should be possessed of them, (*as we are informed you have directed*) they are here collected, and submitted to your own mature Consideration. Envy itself can find Nothing in them, that either You, or They need be ashamed of. But you, Sir, are the Person *most* concerned, and ought to be made the *only* Judge in this Case. You may be assured there is *no other Copy* of this Book in any Hands but your own: So that, while you live, it will be in the Power of no other, but yourself, to bestow it on the Publick. In so doing, You shall oblige all Mankind in general, and *benefit any deserving Friend* in particular. But if, during your Life, you will suppress it yet after your Death it is not fit, that either You should be robbed of so much of your Fame, or We of so much of your Example;—We are, | Worthy Sir, | Your sincere Admirers, | Obliged *Country-Men*, and | Faithful, Affectionate Servants.[5]

I was indeed surprized at what Mr Faulkner writ, and cannot but yet suspend my Belief of it, that instantly upon this the Dean (without giving, or sending, me any previous Information) delivered him the Letters, to print, and publish; and Mr Swift, a Relation of the Dean's, was to correct the Press, and write a Preface.[6] I must at least think, that, to move him to this Proceeding, some other Influence must have

[1] This important letter Pope did not preserve for us.

[2] Here also printed under date of May 1740, when (or earlier) it must have been written.

[3] *This nation* (not italicized by Orrery) was a key phrase which Pope pretended was evidence for an Irish origin of the clandestine volume.

[4] Lord Bolingbroke, and Mr Pope.—Marginal note by Orrery.

[5] This subscription was obviously designed as evidence that Irish conspirators were the promoters of the edition.

[6] Possibly Faulkner's letter of 29 July conveyed this information about a Preface.

been used, than merely the Anonymous Letter above, which, tho' it might be sent from England, appears by the Passages marked in Italics to have been composed in Ireland. It mentions a Particular, which None but Persons near him could know, that of the *Directions* in his Will concerning his Papers; and speaks of *inclosed Papers*, and *an only Copy*, expressions ill agreeing with a printed Book, and implying further Circumstances than I, or perhaps Mr Faulkner, had been made acquainted with. However he concluded by assuring me, "that he would not print it without my Consent."—My Reply was, that I desired first to have a Sight of the Thing I was to consent to; that both the Dean, and Mrs W— knew, how long, and how often I had pressed him to prevent such an Event: I express'd my Surprize at the Proceeding; I put the strongest Negative I could upon it; and I declared my Resolution to prevent the publishing it in England at least, if possible, even by a Bill in Chancery.—Your Lordship will smile, when I tell you, the Answer to this was a Representation of the—"Great Expence he had already been at in printing, for not hearing sooner from me, he had concluded I consented."—[1] Nevertheless he promised, "if I would revise, and alter any Thing, it should be complyed with;" but positively told me, "another Edition was printed in London."—If it was, to what Purpose should I alter any Thing in his? And, if it was not, why should a Preface be made, to lay it upon London-Printers? This, it seems, was proposed by Mr Swift. But he reasoned better than the Bookseller upon the Refusal of my consent: "He told me, that—"not having had it sooner, he concluded it would never be obtained. But finding, on the other Hand, all Remonstrances to the Dean ineffectual, and seeing him resolved to have the Letters published, and to employ his own Printer in the Work, he represented to him, that the World would naturally think it done by our mutual Consent; and therefore obtained Leave to write a Preface, *to lay it upon the corrupt Practices of the Printers in London*." He assures me, "this was merely an Effect of Zeal to justify me, and by no means of any Forwardness to promote the Irish Edition." So as soon as he found I would not give my Consent, he dropt the Thought.—Mrs W. also wrote to acquaint me, it was "She, who insisted with the Book-seller to give me privately an Account of what was doing, for the Dean had absolutely forbid her to acquaint me. Indeed She knew little of Mr Faulkner, besides seeing him often at the Deanery; (a Place, that once a Person of his low Character in Life would not have been admitted to)[2] yet that he bore the Character of an honest, and modest Man:

[1] Pope here is summarizing a letter not preserved. He answered it on 4 Oct., so one assumes.

[2] A strangely snobbish remark! Pope certainly was pleased to entertain booksellers and printers at Twickenham, and where else would Swift see his publisher if not at the Deanery?

And, if I had any Commands to her, I might direct them more safely to the said Faulkner than to the Deanery, where they would be opened."—Nothing could be more obliging, than the Disposition She testifyed in my Regard throughout that Letter, dated Septr 18th 1740,[1] where her Disapprobation of this whole Proceeding is expressed in so strong and convincing a Manner, that I cannot deny my self the Honour, nor her the Justice, of transcribing some Part of it.—"Believe me, Sir, that I left nothing undone to prevent the Publication of those Letters, and was so chagrined about them, that I never yet would read them. I got all the Friends of the Dean, that I thought had any Weight, to persuade him against it; and only because I imagined it might be disagreeable to You. Nay I went Lengths, that Honour could not strictly answer; for I stole the Book out of his Study, and kept it, till I was forced to return it, or add a Lye to my Theft. It is impossible to make you sensible, how positive the Dean was in having it done; nor the many warm Disputes I had with him; a Liberty I never took on any other Occasion."—I returned my humble Thanks, and desired only a Sight of the Book; I writ also more than once, to beg but three Lines under the Dean's own Hand;[2] but was answered constantly by Others,—"that his Health would not permit him to write, but that he entirely loved me; that he extremely wished to see me; that he never had a Thought of doing what was displeasing to me; but wondered I could have any Objections to printing the Letters."

In this Situation I applyed once more to your Lordship.[3] I begged You to write to the Dean, which you did, but was answered in no other manner. The Bookseller, indeed, waited on your Lordship, and let fall in Conversation one very different Circumstance, that not all the Dean's Friends persuaded, or remonstrated against this Publication: One there was, who suggested to him, that the Book must probably have come from my Hands; and to print it could not but be agreeable to me. An Insinuation, which (after what the same Person wrote so expressly to the contrary to your Lordship and my Self) I think I have no Need to observe upon, but rather to laugh than be angry at.

You have had, my Lord, an Occasion for the full Exercise of your Humanity, and sufficient Cause to pity One, if not Both, of your

[1] Not preserved.

[2] Conceivably we have all of Pope's letters written to Lord Orrery concerning this matter. We do not have all of his correspondence with Faulkner and with Mrs. Whiteway. Not to Lord Orrery but to either of the other two may have gone Pope's entreaties—natural enough —for a line from Swift himself. It is most strange that no such line (so far as we know) was forthcoming, though Swift's health was obviously very bad during the summer of 1740.

[3] The narrative becomes confused hereabouts. Pope had first applied in this matter 3 Sept.; no later letter begs Orrery to write to the Dean perhaps, though such procedure is implied in letters of October to Lord Orrery. Elwin regarded the phrase 'applied once more' as referring to the letter of 3 Sept.; the earlier application being that of 1737 when Pope was straining to get his letters returned. Elwin's explanation does not cohere with all Pope's statements here.

Friends. When you find your kind Efforts to suppress their Faults ineffectual, You take up the generous Part to excuse, and extenuate them. Will your Lordship then say for me, that whatever Weakness my Enemies, upon this Display of my private Thoughts, may charge me with, it should not be with Vanity; since it will evidently appear, of my Letters, that they were never writ to be printed; and I think the same of those of my Correspondents, though there never were greater Masters than they in this, or any other, Sort of Writing. Whatever may be disagreeable in this Incident, two Circumstances however have pleased me; that the strict Affection between Doctor Swift and me is made known to the whole World; and that I have myself received so strong an Evidence of the Friendship, and warm Attention of your Lordship, for which I shall be always, with the truest Esteem and Gratitude, my Lord, | Your most Obliged, and most | Faithful, Affectionate Servant | A. Pope.

MRS. WHITEWAY *to* LORD ORRERY[1] 30 *December* 1740

The Huntington Library

Sir,—I shall not hesitate one moment to Send your Lordship Mr Pope's Letters as likewise that from Bath;[2] but how am I to convey them to you?—not by post Surely; for then I might be justly taxed with folly or breach of trust to venture them by so uncertain and dangerous a way. If your Lordship will order a faithfull Servant or a Gentleman with a line under your hand to call for them, I shall deliver them with pleasure; and this I should not do to any other person whatsoever without an immediate direction to my Self from Mr Pope, who knows I refused them to Mr Robert Nugent, from whom I had two Letters in the last[3] telling me Mr Pope desired me to send them by his Mother then going to England; and by the same Paquet and the same date I had a letter from Mr Pope who told me he would expect them by Mr McAulay, who intended long agoe to have been in London if Business had not prevented Him. I am so far from Suspecting any person of this side the water (and therefore it would be unjust to Guess) that I do not beleive they were taken here. I will tell you my reasons for it. First, I do assure your Lordship the Dean kept no Copys of Mr Popes Letters for these twelve years past to my knowledge,[4] nor to any Body

[1] Mrs. Whiteway omitted practically all punctuation in this letter. All that here appears is supplied by the editor. The MS. seems to be a copy of the letter, kept by her.

[2] The letter that came over with the clandestine volume.

[3] Possibly miswritten for 'past'. Elwin reads 'in the last [packet]'; but since Pope's request is found in his letter of 18 June, that emendation seems doubtful.

[4] Twelve years is perhaps a long period for Mrs. W. to vouch for; but she is doubtless right, and the lack of copies in Ireland makes the English origin of the printed letters indubitable.

else excepting to a Lord Lieutenant or a Bishop whom he feared might make an ill use of them; and most of those to Mr Pope I saw him write and send off immediately. This, therefore, makes me think it reasonable to suppose it is not from this quarter that Mr Pope hath been ill used, but must have been betrayed by his English Servants, who have more Cunning and a readier way of making money of them than ours have here; and I cannot imagin any person above the degree of a servant Capable of so base an action. My Lord, I beg leave to talk freely to you, and I can have no other view in it than to defend the Dean in a particular which Concerns his Honour and all those whom he thinks proper to place confidence in. You must, I beleive, have seen a book of letters Stitched togather by the Dean,[1] wherein there are a number of them from the greatest men in England both for Genius Learning and Power; Such as Lord Bollinbrook, Oxford, Ormond, Bathurst, Peterborough, and Queensborough; Parnell, Addison, Gay, Prior, Congreve, and Mr Lewis,[2] to say nothing of your Lordship (because I am writing to *you*), which are in my possession and may be Commanded when ever [you] please; for I have Lately got the Dean's leave to give them[3] even while he is a live, which he at first refused me; and were there a person vile enough in this Kingdom to be bought, why were not these sold to Curl as well as the others; for surely not to mention [yours], Sir, some of the rest might be thought as entertaining to the world as the Dean's, and as easily to be stole. Permit me, my Lord, to ask a Question or two. Do you think the Letters to and from Doctor Swift are genuine? if so, will you look over them again and explain to me this Sentence? Mr Pope, taking occation to mention Mr Wycherley, imediately after says, "Some letters of whose[4] and mine have been lately published not without the Concurrence of a noble Lord, who is a friend of yours and mine." I hope what I have said will Convince your Lordship how much I detest the base practices of those who could be capable of betraying friendship. I once more repeat my Concern that I had not power enough with the dean to prevent their being given to Mr Faulkner, and returned to Mr Pope. If you think it proper, when you send him the papers, to present him my most obedient respects and

[1] It would be interesting to know if any extant autograph letter to or from Swift shows signs of having been 'stitched'.

[2] With several bundles large enough to make a volume.—Marginal note on the original (in Mrs. W.'s hand). These bundles are probably the letters that Swift had formerly offered Faulkner for printing. See Swift's *Works*, xiv (1772: vol. i of Correspondence), where Faulkner tells how, 'above thirty years ago', Swift made him such an offer.

[3] i.e. to return them to their authors.

[4] For 'whose' Sir Walter Scott (ibid. xix [1824], 245) and Elwin (vii. 388) print 'yours'—which makes the quotation from Pope's letter to Swift of 28 Nov. 1729 far more damning than it actually was. 'Whose' represents the 'of whom' that Pope printed. Incidentally, Mrs. Whiteway asserted that she never read the clandestine volume, but here she quotes from page 106 of it!

this Letter; for I am Sure any thing of this kind from me is not worth his paying for. However, I shall Submit this and every thing else to your Lordship's Judgment. There is one particular I had like to have forgot, that one of the letters of Mr Pope's I took out of the Dean's Stitched book with his permission, and I must say I think equal to any he writ, and yet this Letter is safe and not printed, altho the book hath been lent to many of the Dean's friends.

Decr 30th 1740

1741

In February of this year Pope returned from spending the winter with Allen at Bath, and during the spring he was occupied in beautifying his grotto and his garden as well as bringing out his *Works in Prose*, vol. ii, which contained the Swift letters. At once piracies and threats of piracies followed. In May Warburton was again in Town, and the two friends journeyed to Oxford, made expectant by unofficial offers of honorary degrees—which were not forthcoming. The summer was uneventful, though coloured by depression over the political situation and, more pleasantly, by an increased friendliness on the part of Sarah, Duchess of Marlborough. In October the Allens visited Pope briefly, and took him back to Bath for another long visit. Warburton was presently persuaded to join Pope in Allen's fine house, and under Warburton's guidance Pope worked at the Fourth Book of *The Dunciad*, and possibly at the revision of the first three books.

*POPE *ET AL.* *to* THE EARL OF BURLINGTON[1] [? 1741]

Chatsworth

The Petition of
Dorothy Countess of Burlington, Dorothy & Charlot Boyle Spinsters, Charles Duke of Grafton, Geo. Lord Euston, Sir Clemt Cottrel Knt. Alexr. Pope Gent. & Chs. Brunevall Gent.
and others—
To the Right Hon. the Earl of Burlington,
Humbly Shewing

That whereas a Certain Tree lying, being, & standing in or on the Grounds of your Lordship, at or before or on one side or the other of a Certain Edifice of your Honour's called the Casino, hath possessed occupied and held, for the space of twenty or twenty one years or thereabouts, over or under, the said Ground Place and Bank, and suffered & endured all the Changes & Vicissitudes of Wind Water & Weather in the Worst of Times. And whereas a certain Upstart Terras, hath arisen & stood opposite (tho at great distance) to your Honour's said Tree, above & before mentioned & described, which said Terras hath and can suffer no molestation, Let, or hindrance from any

[1] This petition—hardly a letter perhaps—has apparently not hitherto been printed, and seems to deserve publication. It cannot date after 10 Oct. 1741, when the unfortunate Lady Dorothy Boyle became Lady Euston. The tree in question (as well as the Casino) stood in the grounds at Chiswick. The petition is entirely in Pope's hand—except, of course, the signatures.

Shadow, Root or Branch of your said Tree, which both continued faithfully fixed to the Premises, nor ever stirred, or attempted to stir, from his said place, notwithstanding which the said Terras hath, by the Instigation of Sathan, & of William Kent, his agent & Attorney, conspiring thereunto, devised and plotted, and do at this time devise plot & conspire the Destruction, Abolition, Overthrow & Total Subversion of This Your Honour's Tree the said Tree to cut down, or saw down, or root up & grub up, & ruin for ever: We, Your Honour's humble Petitioners who have many years known, accustomed & frequented the said Tree, sitten, reposed or disported under the Shade thereof yea and seen the said William Kent, the Agent & Attorney of the said Sathan, solace himself with Syllabubs, Damsels, and other Benefits of Nature, under the said Tree, Do, for ourselves & our Posterity, most earnestly, & jointly as well as Seperately, petition & pray, that the said Tree may remain, subsist, continue & flourish in his place, during his or her natural Life (not being absolutely certain of the Sex of the said Tree) to enjoy the Small Spot of Ground on which God & your Lordship's Ancestors of ever blessed memory have placed it. And Your Honours most humble Petitioners, as in Duty bound, shall ever pray &c. &c.

	D Burlington	A. Pope.	B Fairfax	Euston
	D. Boyle	Charles Bruneval	F Fairfax	
Grafton.	C Boyle	Clement Cottrell.		

*POPE *to* CHARLES BATHURST[1] [1740–1]

Sotheby's Sale, 28 Nov. 1913

FRAGMENT

Mr. Lintot has had no right to the Key to the Locke these many years, the Term expired in the year 29 or 30. But till then I presume Mr. Motte allowed it. If not, you may set against it your Right to the Small poems in the end of Mr. Lintot's third volume of my Works 8vo, to which your Right from Mr. Motte yet continues.

[1] In this sale at Sotheby's, item 23 of lot 355 included a letter (now unknown) from Bathurst to Pope. Bathurst, so the sale catalogue tells us, asks 'if he is to allow Lintot's claim to the key to The Rape of the Lock'. Pope's reply, written on the same sheet, included the fragment here printed. It is untraced beyond the sale catalogue. Bathurst, for Pope, was including the *Key to the Lock* in Pope's *Works in Prose*, vol. ii. Lintot later tried to make trouble (see Pope to Cole, 17 Mar.), but evidently did not go to law in the matter. Lintot's name does not appear on the title-page of editions of the *Key*, which was 'printed for J. Roberts', but his account books as printed by Nichols, *Lit. Anec.* viii. 300, indicate that he purchased the copy 31 [*sic*] Apr. 1715 for £10. 15*s*. Some of the 'Imitations of the English Poets' had been transferred from the *Miscellanies* of 1728 to vol. iii of Pope's octavo *Works*, published by Lintot, 1736.

THE EARL OF ORRERY *to* MRS. WHITEWAY[1]

2 [*Januar*]*y* 1740/1

The Huntington Library

[Caledon, Januar]y 2, 1740–41.

Your obliging Offer of returning my Letters, together with those designed for Mr Pope, is most gratefully accepted by Me. and therefore I send Mr Ellis, who is One of my Agents here, and whose honesty and integrity I can trust, to receive them from your own hands and to bring them down hither without the least Loss of Time. This is the most expeditious and the safest Method I could think of. The Parcel for Mr Pope I desire may be sealed up by You, but I could wish to see the Letter from Bath if you thought proper: if You enclose it to me, I will lose no time in forwarding it to Mr Pope.

Certainly, Madam, this printed Collection has been stolen by some low, mean, injudicious Person. probably some Servant, who has snatched them at various opportunities. They will do as little honour to the Writers, as any Thing can, that comes from such great and eminent Men. People's expectations will be raised by the Names prefixed to them, but those expectations will not be answered by the Letters themselves. The more I read them, the more I am convinced of the Truth of this opinion. [Not to mention some im]prudencies of a high nature, the whole consists of private, [tho'] amiable familiarities, in which the publick can no ways be interested, nor much entertained.

I should think with You, Madam, that Some of Mr Pope's Servants had stolen them, did not many Letters appear from various People to the Dean, of which Mr Pope cannot be supposed either to have seen the copies or originals, but alass! it is but a melancholy comfort to me, that this unhappy Affair is so situated, as to redeem the honour of one Friend, at the Expence of another.

The Collection begins very early: before the Dean's Freindship with you, Madam, was in it's meridian. Since that time I am in no pain about his Letters. but yet permitt me to say that there are and have been other Persons about him, who may have very different views from You; nor can your Attendance be so constant as to hinder Transactions that may give You, Me, and all the [dean's friends uneasiness, for which rea]son I shall be extremely [glad to have my own lette]rs returned; and You will please therefore to give them into Mr Ellis's Hands, who is to leave Dublin as soon as He receives them from You.

[1] Lord Orrery here answers Mrs. Whiteway's letter of 30 Dec. 1740. His reply was printed by Sir Walter Scott (Swift's *Works* [1824], xix. 248–50), and even in 1824 the letter was torn at the top. Elwin printed the letter twice (vii. 389 and viii. 492), and supplied the missing phrases differently in the two texts. Here the text is emended from Elwin's vol. viii, but the parts not in brackets come from the original letter.

I am glad the Dean is no ways afflicted by this change of weather, his Health is extremely dear to me: would to God you could persuade him to come to Caledon, where Lady Orrery would take care to make the Place as agreable as She could to him and you. She is by profession a Nurse, and performs her part excellently, but we are both much concerned that you are acting the same part to one of your Sons: the mildness of the Season will, we hope, soon remove his Complaint. I am, Madam, | Your most obedient humble | Servant. | Orrery.

THE EARL OF ORRERY *to* POPE — 8 *January* 1740/1

Elwin–Courthope, viii. 494–5

Caledon, Jan. 8, 1740–1.

Enclosed I send you the original letter, at least what Mrs. Whiteway calls so, that came to the dean from Bath, and with it a letter I received from her some posts ago, which no sooner came to my hands than I sent away a trusty messenger to Dublin to receive from her all the papers she therein promised. He brought to me last night two parcels,—one sealed up and directed to you, which contains I suppose the letters intended for you by Mr. M'Aulay, and another parcel for myself, in which were all my letters to the dean. I have now executed all your commands, and therefore shall hasten out of this kingdom as fast as I can. I propose to leave Dublin about the 20th of next month, and Lady Orrery will follow me as soon as her daughter, whom she suckles, is able to travel. We are both tired of our situation here, and are resolved to fix our tents in England.

The packet I have for you, though not a large one, is yet too big for the post, so I will have the pleasure of delivering it to you myself. I entreat you to let Mrs. Whiteway know that I have acknowledged the receipt of a packet for you, and in case this arrives time enough to stop your sending the printed volume of letters, let them remain in your hands till we meet. You may then let me know your inclinations and your commands more fully by a personal conversation than by letters. If the people, somewhere or other, but where I cannot determine, will suffer this to go to you directly, I may receive an answer to it, which I own would give me pleasure, especially if you approve of my conduct in this affair.

Lady Orrery will execute any commands you may have during my absence, and her stay. Lord Boyle comes with me, but as I leave the greatest part of my family behind, there will be an apartment ready for you in my house as soon as I come to town. I am, dear sir, etc.

I defer all my sentiments on this transaction till I see you, having plagued you sufficiently with my correspondence.

POPE *to* THE EARL OF MARCHMONT[1] 9 *January* 1740/1

Arthur A. Houghton, Jr.

Mr Allen's at Bath. Jan. 9th 1740.

My Lord,—That I am mindful of you while I live, is the greatest of truths. That I live, I desird a friend of mine to tell you. That you are well, I shall also hear, whether you write to me or not. If I do not hear, I shall be in pain, & write to you. What then I have to say? I only write now to tell you, that you are rememberd by one, whose memory you will find a Credit, & find a Comfort, to you. He says of you, that you assist your Countrys friends, et consilio, et voce, & etiam vultu.[2] May you continue to do this, till we become a People deserving your utmost Care: at present even this is more than we deserve. But pray my Lord know, there is one man who knows your heart, and honors your Virtue, besides Lord B.[3] and that is | Your faithfull Servant | A. Pope.

I am in great pain to find out Mr Hook.[4] does your Lordship or Mr Hume or Dr King know where he is?

Address: To the Right Hon. the Earl | of Marchmont, in | Savile Rowe. | Burlington Gardens | London.

Postmark: 12/IA BATH

Endorsement: Bath Jany 9 | 1740

THE EARL OF ORRERY *to* MRS. WHITEWAY 10 *January* 1740/1

Elwin–Courthope, viii. 495–6

Caledon, Jan. 10, 1740–1.

Madam,—By not receiving any letter from you either by this day's or Thursday's post, I fear you, or some of your family, are ill, and therefore am more anxious now to hear from you concerning your health than I was concerning the letters. You will relieve me I hope even before this can come to your hands, for if I hear nothing from you on Monday I shall be very uneasy.

Mr. Ellis brought me two parcels from you. That directed to myself

[1] The editor of *Marchmont Papers* (Sir G. H. Rose) erred in saying this letter is addressed to Lord Polwarth, and he also erred in placing the letter in 1740. Pope is almost regular in dating Old Style for letters written in January, February, and early March.

[2] In 1740 Pope urged Lord Marchmont to return to London for the opening of Parliament. Now his lordship, who earlier refused, has changed his mind and assists the Patriots *etiam vultu*.

[3] Lord Bolingbroke.

[4] Allen may have wished news of Hooke, but more probably Pope foresees a chance of getting Hooke employment on the papers of Sarah, Duchess of Marlborough. Mr. Hume is very likely Marchmont's brother Alexander. Dr. King of St. Mary Hall, Oxford, was a close friend of the historian Hooke.

contained the Bath letter, which I shall take care to give Mr. Pope, together with the sealed packet, directed for him. I have writ to him this moment to let him know how obligingly, and, particularly so to me, you have complied with his request. I return you many thanks, madam, for the delivery of my letters, from Curll, from God knows who. I am much obliged to the dean for permitting them to be restored to me. Upon a revisal of them I well see how dangerous a familiar, unguarded correspondence may be, not only to ourselves but to our friends, and I hope we may hear no more of this little volume which is printed, though I must fear it will come out in opposition to all our endeavours. In the mean time it remains safe in my custody,[1] nor shall I willingly deliver it up, unless by the dean's or Mr. Pope's commands. I have many letters to write, and as I am not without some thoughts of seeing you soon (this to yourself only), I will defer saying more at present, than that I am, madam, etc.

THE EARL OF ORRERY *to* POPE 12 *January* 1740/1

Elwin–Courthope, viii. 496–7

Caledon, Jan. 12, 1740–1.

Sir,—On Monday[2] the five packets due from England arrived at Caledon, by which means I received all your letters and parcels at once. Of the printed volume there came only from page 23,[3] so that unless you have kept the beginning, which you hinted to me was your wish, it is lost. I passed all Monday in the afternoon in reading over and over your letters, and your narrative, and in considering what part I was to act with Faulkner and company. In my humble opinion the best method we can pursue will be to give him back the letters, to tell him, without showing anything under your hand, that you will have nothing to do with them, and to suffer him (but not without inserting the advertisement) to go on. All this in my own name.

Your tenderness towards the dean is like yourself. I hope there will be no occasion for opening the scene plainer,—at least that his name

[1] Orrery is writing on a Saturday, and here pretends that the clandestine volume is in his possession. Possibly he is pretending that the volume has never been out of his hands. He sent it to Pope in nine packets on or about 14 Nov. 1740, and he writes to Pope on Monday, 12 Jan. 1741, that they came back to him 'Monday'. Probably 12 is a miswriting. See 12 Jan. (Orrery to Pope) and note.

[2] Something seems wrong with the dating of this letter. When Orrery wrote to Mrs. Whiteway on the 10th, he was well aware of the fact that it was Saturday. The 12th is Monday, a fact which makes this first statement obscure. The preceding Monday is too early for him to have received the packets, and on the 8th he had not received them. On the 10th he tells Mrs. Whiteway that the book is safe in his custody: in which case he did not receive it on a Monday. Possibly someone has misread 12 for 13 or 15.

[3] Pope retained the first part of Faulkner's volume in order to have a text of the letter from Swift of 10 Jan. 1721, which 'Mr. Pope never receiv'd'. It ended on page 21, of which 22 was the verso. As issued in 1741, as vol. vii of Pope's *Works* (8vo, T. Cooper), the volume has two pages numbered 23: Orrery speaks of the first of these two.

may remain sacred from the most distant reflection. You have drawn up the narrative[1] with great skill, great friendship, and great justice, but methinks the lady's letter to me,[2] which I sent you some posts ago, explains the attack against you more fully than Faulkner's conversation with me. She there lays the theft absolutely upon your servants. Perhaps I may get more from that quarter, and they will be strong proofs of the insincerity, and vile treatment you have met with from the little senate at the deanery.

The 'deserving friend' in the Bath letter, the original of which, I hope, is now in your possession, confirms me in my opinion that Faulkner was not the bookseller for whom this collection was designed. I can explain that, and other matters, further to you when I have the happiness of *your* conversation, which I will hope for as soon as I reach Duke Street. I intend to leave this place the 11th of next month, and if the wind be fair shall leave Dublin about the 22nd. In the mean time if anything new occurs that can give you any clearer light into these mysterious transactions I shall transmit it, beseeching you to excuse the tedious repetition of my correspondence, in consideration of the motive it proceeds from—a thorough desire of approving myself your ever faithful, affectionate, and obliged servant.

If you think proper to print any of my letters on this occasion you have my entire approbation.

*POPE *to* JOHN BRINSDEN [*c.* 17 *January* 1740/1]

Buffalo (N.Y.) Public Library

Many thanks for yours I have inclosed the answer to my Lord,[3] which you'l direct. I hope it will come in time.

I'm sorry for our old Friend the Alderman,[4] I'm told he charged Ward with his death. I don't hear you have ever seen Twitnam, & I regret the less my absence from thence.

Pray tell my friends, particularly Lord Cornbury & Mr Lyttelton & Lord Marchmont that 'I have left a Spy upon them in town, that (unknown to them) gives me weekly accounts of them.' Tell them I am *not dead*, but *sleep*, and believe me always | Dear Sir | Yours | A Pope.

Address: To | John Brinsden Esq. in | Rathbone Place, over | against | Soho.
Endorsement: A. Pope Esqr Jan | 17th 1740/1

[1] In Pope's letter to Orrery, 30 Dec. 1740. [2] In her letter to Orrery of 30 Dec. 1740.

[3] Bolingbroke, whose English correspondence seems to have passed through the hands of Brinsden.

[4] John Barber, formerly Lord Mayor of London, had died on 2 Jan. 1741. He left legacies to Bolingbroke, Swift, and Pope. Ward is possibly the M.P. for Hackney who was sued by the Duchess of Buckingham. More plausibly the charge might be levied at the quack doctor, Joshua Ward (1685–1761), whose celebrated pill (from which he amassed a fortune) is said to have killed as many as it cured.

POPE *to* THE EARL OF ORRERY 23 *January* 1740/1

The Pierpont Morgan Library

My Lord,—I am much obliged by your Lordship's of the 8th of this month, and for a Sight of Mrs Whiteway's, to whom I beg you to pay my Thanks[1] for sending the Pacquet of Letters to you at my request. As So many accidents have prevented my receipt of them, it will now be time enough to see them at your Return, as your Lordship proposes. I would not trouble her with an unnecessary letter, since as your Lordship will doubtless be at Dublin, I am sure my Acknowledgment will come as agreably to her thro' You. It is a Care, worthy of the Profession She was pleas'd to make, in the first Letter she favor'd me with, the Honorable Care to prevent any more such disagreable Consequences, either with regard to Letters, or any other Papers, of Our Friend; and which she declared she would never suffer to be publishd without the Approbation of such as are truly concern'd in his Reputation.

I have nothing more, now, to trouble your Lordship or Mrs W. with, about My particular, Only what I before mention'd to you, I beg to repeat, My thanks to her for having obliged the Bookseller to give me all the knowledge I had of his printing the Letters; and an assurance, that (if ever I am compelld to justify myself from any Share in it) I will at the same time do her and Mr Swift the Same justice to the whole World, that they have done Themselves to Me.[2]

Mrs W.'s Letter says a great deal to remove the Suspicion of this thing being done originally in Ireland. I can't tell whether the Letter she has favord me with which was sent to the Dean, will be of any use towards a discovery: But the Passage she questions about, (in one of these now printed to Dr Swift) tells nothing of that sort: She will find it Explained in the second & third paragraph of My own Preface to my Letters;[3] Those Letters of Mr Wycherley were deposited in my Lord Oxfords Library, & from thence permitted to be printed for the reason there given, four years before Curl layd hold of 'em.[4]

[1] Orrery's letter of 8 Jan. (which Pope here answers) had begged Pope to thank Mrs. Whiteway for sending the packet of letters to Orrery. Pope, not wishing 'to trouble her with an unnecessary letter', writes this one, to be shown to her. Hence the mild, even friendly, tone.

[2] This might well seem to all concerned an ambiguous, if not a threatening, remark, since Mrs. Whiteway and her son-in-law had openly expressed the belief that Pope was conniving at the publication. If now Pope accused them publicly, they might be quits. But in general this letter bears an olive branch.

[3] In her letter of 30 Dec. 1740 Mrs. W. had quoted to Orrery Pope's letter to Swift of 28 Nov. 1729. Pope here points out that the remark quoted concerned the publication in 1729 of vol. ii of Wycherley's *Posthumous Works*, which included the letters to and from Wycherley. The Preface to the quarto *Letters* (1737), as Pope says, alleges that the Wycherley letters were deposited in the Harleian Library, and so were not stolen by Pope's servants. The explanation is specious, but Mrs. W. had misinterpreted Pope's letter to Swift.

[4] Always Pope insists that Curll was the publisher of the editions of the letters in 1735—and even after 1737 he hardly acknowledges anything except the quarto and folios of 1737.

I write this in haste, that it may get a post forwarder without passing thro' London, or I should say more. But I long to meet you, & will not fail to know the first day of your arrival. This is the 23d of January, and yours is dated the 8th so has been 15 days on the road. I sent you all you wrote for about the end of Decembr & hope, the several pacquets, & a long Letter reach'd your hands. Had I expected so soon the happiness of your Return, I had not sent any of 'em. I am ever, with the truest wishes for yours Lady Orrery's, & all your present & future Family's prosperity (even to the *Examina Infantium, futurusq; populus*,[1] as your own Pliny has it) | My Lord | Your Faithfull, obligd, | affectionate Servant, | A. Pope.

Jan. 23. 1740/1

POPE *to* MALLET[2] — 25 *January* [1740/1]

Sir John Murray

I am always sincerely yours, & always glad to hear of you, with or without business—surely nothing can be said *to*, or I fear done *for*, this poor unhappy Man,[3] who will not suffer himself to have a Friend. But I will immediately send him another ten pound (besides my own, which is paid him) & take what money you can collect in repayment: if more, it shall be accounted for to him; if less, I'll be at the loss. I would not trouble Mr Lewis, nor you further, at present. And perhaps if you give it Dodsley, he will take Umbrage at that too. I have really taken more pains not to affront him, than if My Bread had depended on Him. He would be to be forgiven, if it was Misfortune only, & not Pride, that made him Captious. All I can say is, I wish Providence would be kind to him in our stead, but till then, he *Is* miserable

What I writ to him, you may easily imagine he has mistaken, It could only be that you was trying to collect for him, Or that I would take care it should be sent by Mr Lewis, or to that purpose.

I have written to few or none of my Friends since I have been here; but I have left a Spy in Town (unknown to you all) who gives me Accounts of those I am concern'd about. I hope Mr Lyttelton is now perfectly recoverd, pray make him remember I am his for Life. And bid him tell Mr West so, in particular. I hope to meet you all in a few weeks. Adieu till then & believe me truly | Dear Sir | Yours. | A. Pope

Bath | Jan. 25.

[1] Pliny the Younger, *Panegyricus*, ch. xxvi.

[2] Since Pope writes from Bath, the year has to be 1740 or 1741. Since in 1740 he was hoping by the end of January to return to London, 1741 is the more probable. No year earlier is possible because Savage evidently is now in the West, and Pope deals (or tries to deal) with him by letter only.

[3] Richard Savage.

POPE *to* THE EARL OF ORRERY 29 *January* 1740/1

The Pierpont Morgan Library

My Lord,—As I have had the honour of a Letter from you since my last, I will give my self the Satisfaction of thanking you once more, and Your Lordship the trouble of One more Request, which shall conclude all your troubles on this subject.

When you are at Dublin ingage Falkener to send hither a Book, the moment he publishes; and to return you the foul Copy by which he prints,[1] for the reason I before hinted. I kept the first Sheet[2] of it, (as he had gone beyond & would not need it) in which are those *Insertions*[3] I told you of, that manifest its being printed at different times.

Mrs W.'s Letter, which by her own consent you sent me, discovers much more than at first I observed; but it will be time enough to point it to you when I have the great pleasure of meeting your Lordship.

I wish you would say every thing you can think of to the Dean from me, that would please, and nothing that can afflict, him. I dare say there has been an End some years ago of all his Intentions as to Papers, Legacies, &c. so that I should not think the least Syllable of that sort ought to be nam'd to him. But be pleased to tell him I intend him a long Letter as soon as you return to England, and as soon as I hear, from you, such an Account of him as I may depend on.

I long to find you in Dukestreet, I hope never to lose you more: I shall move towards it next week, and be certainly either at Twitnam or at Mr Murray's in Lincolns inn fields, till your arrival. My faithful & respectful Services attend your Lordship and [La]dy Orrery.

My Lord I am | Yours always. | A. Pope.

Bath Jan. 29th 1740/41.

The permission you give me so frankly, of using the Authority of your Letters in case of necessity, is extreme generous. Shall I think it proceeds from a high Spirit of Justice & Honour? or shall I flatter myself it is half from Friendship to me? I will believe both.

Address: To the Rt. Honble the | Earl of Orrery, at | Caledon near | Tynan, | Ireland

Postmark: BATH

[1] Pope wanted the 'foul copy' (i.e. the clandestine volume) because he had enough copies of the same printing so that he could issue it as a volume in his small octavo works—which he did. If Faulkner kept the clandestine sheets, he would be able to recognize their identity with this later London edition (i.e. 1742 La).

[2] Pope kept the two sheets that Faulkner had printed for his Dublin octavo, needed because of the letter (10 Jan. 1721) inserted by Swift. He also kept a sheet and a half of the clandestine volume, since Orrery acknowledged receipt of the returned clandestine printing 'only from page 23'. Page 23 of the clandestine volume was signed C4.

[3] i.e. the letter of 10 Jan. 1721 and Swift's added footnotes.

*POPE *to* HENRY LINTOT[1] 31 *January* 1740/1

Public Record Office C11 549/39

Jan: 31 | 1740/1

Sir,—I Received Yours of this last post but it does not mention one that I wrote to you some time since which I Desird Mr Cole to deliver to you with a State of that Affair upon which I troubled you last summer at Mr Murrays and as to which I wonder you have given me no answer. I hope Mr Wright has returnd to you the 50 books in exchange for yours as he was directed to do some Weeks ago. When you purchasd the Shares in the Dunciad, I hope Mr Gilliver deliverd you his Title under the Hands of the Lords as well as mine to them of which I wish you would acquaint me for he told me he coud not find it, and without it yours would be (I apprehend) insufficient.[2] I am Sir Your most Humble Servant. A. Pope

pleas to direct to Twitnam tho I am at present at Bath. I will revise the new Edit. of the Dunciad or do anything that may be of service to you which is not very greatly to my own Injury.[3]

LAWTON GILLIVER *to* POPE 1 (*or* 17) *February* 1740/1

[Such a letter is mentioned by Pope in his Chancery bill against Lintot. PRO C11 549/39, line 41 of the bill. The letter is not transcribed into the bill, but may exist in the Master's files for the case—files for which searches have been unavailing. The letter would be an answer to a letter from Pope similar to that which was sent to Lintot by Pope on 31 Jan. 1740/1.]

POPE *to* CHARLES BATHURST[4] [3] *Feb.* 1740/1

The Gentleman's Magazine, xliv, N.S. (1855), 587

Feb. 1740

Sir,—I desired Mr Knapton to mention a thing to you; and I sent you a Catalogue of some additional pieces yet unprinted which might be inserted in the two or three Vols. of Miscellanies instead of Dean

[1] This letter comes from Lintot's reply to Pope's complaint in Chancery concerning the date of the termination of Lintot's rights in *The Dunciad.* Pope's complaint is dated 16 Feb. 1742/3, and Lintot's reply (including this letter) is made on 19 Apr. Lintot had purchased, against Pope's advice, the full copyright in *The Dunciad* on 15 Dec. 1740. He has announced the purchase to Pope, and this is Pope's comment.

[2] Possibly late in 1728 Pope had privately given Gilliver some sort of assignment of rights in *The Dunciad.* That assignment at some time was lost, as Pope's scribbled note on Lintot's letter of 29 Jan. 1739–40 indicates. At this time Pope is assuming that in 1742 property in *The Dunciad* reverts to himself. He will learn better later. See iv. 448.

[3] Lintot inserted the letter in his reply to Pope's bill because of this statement: so far from objecting to a reprinting of the poem, Pope will revise the edition. He must have regretted the remark.

[4] The endorsement is not given in the text in *The Gentleman's Magazine*; it comes from the catalogue of Sotheby's sale of 28 Nov. 1913, where the letter is offered as lot 355, item 4.

Swift's and those removed into my volume.[1] I have heard nothing from you about it, but shall be in town soon & willing to do as you like.

I am, Sir, your humble servant, | A. Pope

Endorsement: Delivered 3 Feb. 1740–1.

POPE *to* WARBURTON[2] 4 *February* 1740/1

Egerton 1946

Bath, Feb. 4th 1740/1

If I had not been made, by many accidents, so sick of Letter-writing, as to be almost afraid of the Shadow of my own Pen, You would be the person I should oftenest pour myself out to: Indeed for a good reason, for you have given me the strongest proofs of understanding & accepting my Meaning in the best manner, and of the Candor of your heart, as well as the Clearness of your head. My Vexations I would not trouble you with, but I must just mention the two greatest I now have. They have printed in Ireland my Letters to Dr Swift, & (which is the strangest Circumstance) by his own Consent & direction, without acquainting me till it was done.[3] The other is One that will continue with me, till some prosperous Event to your Service shall bring us nearer to each other. I am not content with those Glympses of you which a short Spring-Visit affords, & from which you carry nothing away with you but my Sighs & Wishes, without any real benefit.

I am heartily glad of the Advancement of your Second Volume,[4] & particularly of the *Digressions*, for they are *so much more of you*, and I can trust your Judgment enough, to depend upon their being Pertinent. You will I question not verify the good Proverb, that the farthest way about is the nearest way home, and much better than plunging thro thick & thin, (*more Theologorum*) and persisting in the same Old Track where so many have either broken their necks, or come off very lamely.

This leads me to thank you for that very entertaining (and I think instructive) Story of Dr W.[5] who was in this the Image of ⌜all True

[1] 'My volume' is Pope's *Works in Prose*, vol. ii, which is to include not only the Swift letters and the hitherto unpublished *Memoirs of Scriblerus* but also various prose items that Motte and Bathurst had published in the Swift–Pope *Miscellanies*. Pope (? and Knapton) are suggesting things to be inserted in the *Miscellanies* to replace items withdrawn for 'my volume'. Pope has for some time already been planning for this new volume of his prose—and the Swift correspondence.

[2] This letter was printed by Warburton in 1751.

[3] In this remark Pope pretends that the clandestine volume was printed in Ireland without his knowledge. Faulkner's reprint of it was published in April.

[4] Of *The Divine Legation*, which was published 26 May 1741.

[5] The Rev. Daniel Waterland, vicar of Twickenham, disliked Warburton greatly, and during his last illness refused to be attended by an apothecary, who from the similarity of the two names congratulated his patient on his *Divine Legation*. See R. S. Cobbett, *Memorials of Twickenham* (1872), pp. 113–20.

Divines,⌉[1] who never admit of any Remedy from a Hand they dislike: but I'm sorry he had so much of the Modern Christian Rancor; as I believe he may be convinc'd by this Time[2] that the Kingdom of Heaven is not for such.

I am just returning to London,[3] & shall the more impatiently expect your Book's appearance, as I hope you will follow it; and that I may have as happy a Month, thro' your means, as I had the last Spring. I am most truly Dear Sir | Your ever obliged & ever faithfull Servant | A. Pope.

Address: To the Reverend Mr Warbur|ton, at | Newark, | Nottinghamshire
Frank: Free | R: Allen
Postmark: 6/FE

POPE *to* SLINGSBY BETHEL — 15 *March* [1740/1]

Elwin–Courthope, ix. 158

London, March 15 [1741].

I have been so long out of town, that I apprehend you may have sent to Lord Bathurst's, and mist to know where to find me, and if you writ, no letter reaches Twitnam by the penny post, only by the general post. I hope you have sold my South Sea annuities, for I fancy they will fall rather than rise. And any day that you can execute the bond I will meet you at Lady Codrington's, which I believe will be the least trouble to you, as you go thither sometimes. A line from you will find me all this week at the Honourable Mr. Murray's, next door to Lord Talbot's, in Lincoln's Inn Fields. I am ever sincerely, dear sir, your faithfull and affectionate servant.

*POPE *to* NATHANIEL COLE[4] — 17 *March* [1740/1]

McGill University

Lincolns inn fields. March 17.

Sir,—I assure you I need no proofs of your Inclination to serve me. I

[1] Warburton in 1751 replaces this phrase tactfully with three asterisks.

[2] Waterland had died in Twickenham on 23 Dec. 1740.

[3] Pope left Bath before the 12th, when (in the past tense) Dr. George Cheyne wrote the author of *Pamela* as follows: 'Mr. Pope here charg'd me to make his warm Compliments to you as an honest good man, and to tell you that he had read Pamela with great Approbation and Pleasure, and wanted a Night's Rest in finishing it, and says it will do more good than a great many of the new Sermons. I think I have got his Promise that he will turn the Psalms into proper Poetry and Spiritual Hymns. The two first he has done at my Desire to Admiration,—when I come to London I will make you and him acquainted. He is certainly an honest ingenious man extremely easy in his Circumstances but has suffer'd much from [?] the Booksellers, but now deals only with a Printer and proposes when he has finisht the Psalms to sell them at a Shilling apeice and give the Income to some universal Charity, but that is not yet concerted & so keep this to your self.' (Transcribed by Professor A. D. McKillop from Letter XLI in the Laing MSS. iii. 356, in the library of the University of Edinburgh.)

[4] This letter concerns something by Pope, about the publication of which Lintot is

was of opinion indeed that Mr L. would not be active to seek you on this affair, as he never answerd me upon it; but would require us to be pressing with Him. But I dare say I cannot do better than trust it to your Friendship for me, to speak & bring him to what you can. Perhaps you should tell him that unless he compromises, you must file a Bill directly: Or propose to leave it to a Reference. Judge Chappel was a Witness to the Articles, & a Friend to his Father: I'll leave it to him & Judge Fortescue—or (if he consents) to Yourself to determine what shall be my Reparation. I am sincerely Dear Sir | Your affectionate & humble Servant | A. Pope.

I lye (when in Town) at Mr Murray's.
My Service to Mr Knapton.

Address: To Mr Cole, at his house | in Basinghall St | London.
Endorsement: Alex. Pope | 17 Mar.
Postmark: PENY POST PAYD.

THE EARL OF ORRERY *and* POPE *to* SWIFT

22 *March* 1740/1

The Huntington Library

Duke Street Westmr March 22d 1740/1

Your friends here are most inquisitive and anxious about your Health. If my Wishes took place, the accounts I should give them would be extremely acceptable. May the returning Spring give You new Strength, and permitt me to add a new Inclination towards this Island. Your Mistress[1] would be happy in shewing her tender regards for You by attending You to Duke Street, where we would find Room for You, and all who belong to You.

Mr Pope, since my Arrival in London, has generously bestowed some of his time upon me.[2] A strong Instance that he loves Those who he knows love You. and indeed his Tenderness, his Affection, and his Sincerity towards You, are beyond description. I defye him, with all his Power of words, to tell You What he thinks of You, or feels for You; Were it possible I am sure He would come to You; make a whole Kingdom happy and come to him;—I am interrupted by Mr

making difficulties. Since Pope had no 'articles' with Lintot concerning *The Dunciad*, that poem may be ruled out. Lintot has been reproached by Pope for his dealings in quarto *Iliads*, but to the indenture for the *Iliad*, preserved in Egerton MS. 1951, f. 3, Judge Chappel is not a witness. It seems possible that Lintot is trying to claim permanent rights to the *Key to the Lock* (1715), which Pope was including in his *Works in Prose*, vol. ii. See Pope to Charles Bathurst, placed at the beginning of this year.

The text is from a transcript kindly made by Professor Joyce Hemlow.

[1] Lady Orrery, who was presently coming to England, is here intended.

[2] In a letter to Lady Orrery (*Orrery Papers* [1903], ii. 161) his lordship writes on 12 Mar. that 'Mr. Pope is at Twitnam, he has invited me thither but I cannot go till N.E. wind changes'.

Pope himself; Let me withdraw and leave the Paper to Him: and believe me your ever obliged and ever obedient Servant Orrery.

My Dear Friend, When the Heart is full of Tenderness, it must be full of Concern at the absolute Impotency of all Words to come up to it. You are the only Man now in the world, who cost me a Sigh every day of my Life, and the Man it troubles me most, altho' I most wish, to write to. Death has not used me worse in separating from me for ever, poor Gay, Arbuthnot &c, than Disease & Distance in separating You so many years. But nothing shall make me forget you, and I am persuaded you will as little forget me; & most things in this world one may afford to forget, if we remember, & are rememberd by, our Friends. I value and enjoy more, the memory of the Pleasures & Endearing Obligations I have formerly receivd from you, than the present Possession of any other. I am less anxious every day I live for present Enjoyments of any sort, & my Temper of Mind is calmer as to Worldly disappointments & accidents except the loss of Friends by Death, the only way (I thank God) that I ever have lost any. Think it not possible that my Affection can cease but with my last breath: If I could think yours was alienated, I should grieve, but not reproach you: If I felt myself ev'n hurt by you, I should be confident you knew not the Blow you gave, but had your hand guided by another: If I never more had a kind word from you, I should feel my heart the same it has ever been towards you. I must confess a late Incident has given me some pain; but I am satisfied you were persuaded it would not have given me any: And whatever unpleasant circumstances the printing our Letters might be attended with, there was *One* that pleas'd me, that the strict Friendship we have born each other so long, is thus made known to all mankind. As far as it was Your Will, I cannot be angry, at what in all other respects I am quite uneasy under. Had you ask'd me, before you gave them away, I think I could have proposed some *better Monument* of our Friendship or at least of *better Materials*: And you must allow me to say, This was not of my erecting, but yours.[1] My Part of them is far too mean,[2] & how inferior to what you have every where in your Works set up to Me? Can I see these without Shame? when I reflect on the many beautiful, pathetic, & amiable Lines of yours,[3] which carry to Posterity the Name of a Man, who if he had every good Quality which you so kindly ascribe to him,

[1] At this moment above all, just before the letters are to appear, Pope must keep up his pretences, even if they are mere (and insincere) pretences.

[2] It is obvious that the volume of letters contains more and better letters by Swift than by Pope.

[3] Pope here is flattering Swift. The mentions of Pope by Swift are found in the *Libel on Doctor Delany* (to which Pope had objected) and in *Verses on the Death of Dr. Swift*—probably elsewhere also; but the mentions are definitely less eulogistic than Pope's commendation of Swift—for example, in the *Epistle to Augustus*, ll. 221–4, and in *The Dunciad*, i. 19–28. This is Pope's last known letter to Swift.

would be so proud of none, as the Constancy, and the Justice, of his Esteem for you. Adieu. While I can write, speak, remember, or think, I am Yours. | A. Pope.

*POPE *to* WILLIAM BOWYER, JR.[1] [? 1741]

The Historical Society of Pennsylvania

Sir,—It is impossible I should judge of what you mention, unless I see the Collections you have made. Indeed I do not much like any man should be putting out my Works or accompanying them with Notes &c, in my Life time, other than what I think fit to do my self. But as I know you Sir to be more capable in such a matter, than most of your Profession have been, of Late years: I desire to overlook them, and will give you my sincere opinion. I am | Sir, Your most humble | servant | A. Pope

I am for 2 or 3 | days at Mr Cheseldens.

Address: Mr Bowyer, Junr | in White-Fryers.

*POPE *to* HUGH BETHEL[2] 14 *April* [1741]

Egerton 1948

Twit'nam April 14.

I expected for some Time a State of your Case, drawn up (as you told me) for me to shew Dr Mead or any other Physician you should name: I was in pain not to receive any, & fear'd you was worse, till Lady Codrington to whom I went sometimes to enquire of you, assured me, (as Col. Gee had also acquainted Lord Burlington & Mr Cleland) that they believed it was your Amendment that hinderd your Sending for further Advice. I hope you consulted Dr Johnson or Wintringham,[3] whose Characters are very good in their profession. But just now I hear that you have had some new check to your Recovery tho I know not the particulars. Believe me, dear Sir, there is no One living more concern'd to know Every Particular that regards your Safety & Welfare: and pray therfore let me be informed of all that you are, and feel, which indeed I feel with you, as far as Friendship can. Do not give yourself this trouble, as your Eyes I know are

[1] A letter from the Rev. William Clarke to Bowyer, dated apparently Apr. 1741, is printed in Nichols, *Lit. Anec.* iv. 436, concerning Bowyer's project to publish 'Remarks on Mr. Pope's Poems, containing his Imitations, Parodies, &c., of Ancient and Modern Poets, Part I'. Clarke remarks, with sure insight, 'I much doubt your success with this Dutch overture' to Pope. This letter justifies his expectations.

[2] Since on this day Lord Orrery wrote to his countess, 'I am going out of Town this morning . . . with Mr. Pope and Lord Chesterfield' (*Orrery Papers*, ii [1903], 164), one assumes the letter is written late in the day.

[3] Dr. Pelham Johnston (d. 1765) was a London practitioner, who came of a Yorkshire family; Dr. Clifton Wintringham (1689–1748) practised in York.

weak (and so truly are mine, weaker & weaker) tho otherwise my health, Colds excepted, tolerable of late. Let any Hand write, only to say how you proceed; God send it may but be as well as I wish, and am fond to hope. I have no Inclination to write any thing less important to me, at this juncture: and may assure you with truth, I desire infinitely less to hear the most glorious News from Vernon,[1] than two lines from you, to tell me you were perfectly recover'd. ⌜I much better understand the Duties of Friendship & the Merits of Virtue in Private life, than those of Public: and should never love my Country if I did not love the Best men in it.⌝[2] Such having long esteemed you, I tremble at the thought of a possibility of losing you. Believe me, while I live, sincerely & affectionatly | Dear Sir, Yours. | A. Pope.

Mrs. Patty never forgets you.

Address: To Hugh Bethel Esq. at | Beswick, near | Beverley | Yorkshire.
Postmark: 16/AP

POPE *to* WARBURTON[3] 14 *April* 1741

Egerton 1946

April 14. 1741.

You are every way kind to me; in your Partiality to what is tolerable in me, & in your Freedom where you find me in an Error: Such I owne is the Instance given of ⌜Julius Cesar, in my Epistle of the Manners of Men⌝.[4] You Owe me much Friendship of this latter sort, having been too profuse of the former.

I think every day a Week till you come to Town, which Mr G⌜yles⌝ tells me will be in the beginning of the next Month, when I expect you will contrive to be as Beneficial to me as you can, by passing with me as much time as you can; every day of which, it will be my fault, if I do not make of some Use to me as well as Pleasure. This is all I have to tell you; & be assured, my Sincerest Esteem & Affection are Yours. ⌜I am Dear Sir, | Your most faithfull | & obliged Servant, | A. Pope.⌝

⌜You will find at Mr Gyles's | a simple book of Letters,[5] left for you.⌝

Address: To the Reverend Mr | Warburton

[1] This was the moment of Admiral ('Grog') Vernon's attack on Cartagena, news of which was ultimately not glorious. It is now chiefly remembered through the vivid but prejudiced accounts in *Roderick Random*, chaps. xxviii–xxxiii.

[2] Quoted by Ruffhead (who substitutes 'beauties' for 'duties'), p. 257 n.

[3] Printed by Warburton in 1751. He omitted the words placed here in half-brackets.

[4] *On the Characters of Men: to Lord Cobham*, ll. 129–32. These were now changed (from *Czar* to *Caesar*) to please Aaron Hill (see Hill to Pope, 15 Jan. 1738/9) and displease Warburton.

[5] Pope's *Works in Prose*, vol. ii, containing the Swift Letters, was advertised for sale on 16 Apr. This copy will be left with the bookseller Gyles to await Warburton's arrival.

*POPE *to* ALLEN 17 *April* 1741

Egerton 1947

Twitnam April 17th 1741.

I have desired my Lord Orrery to see your Place, and (what he esteems more) the Master of it: And I cannot make you so Suitable a Return for the Good you have done me in your Friendship, as in putting this truly Noble Man into your Way, whom You will, and must, Esteem & love. You will find in him—what I dare not tell you, since he is the Bearer of this Letter; but what you will be thoroughly sensible of, & thank me for. His Lordship will tell you that Two of my great Cares are over, one agreable, the other disagreable, as the Cares of this Life generally run mingled: my Grotto is finished, & my Letters are printed,[1] a book of which in large paper is orderd to Mr Leake from Mr Knapton to complete your own Sett, one in folio for Dr Oliver, to match his, and three or four of a common paper for any Friend you will present with them.

I heartily thank you for the distinct & full account you give me from Mr Watts:[2] and I think I need not hesitate in the least, to desire to lay out a thousand pounds in those Shares, at the price of 30ll per Share, if they can be got, or as many as I can. If your Good Offices and His can procure me as much, or what you can, under that Sum, I need not say I shall be greatly obliged & pleased. I have not been wanting, on one or two occasions, to observe Mr Watts's good Will towards me, and am his humble Servant, in the best Sense of that phrase.

Mr Vandyest is to come (if he keeps his word) to morrow to paint one or two things of a Grotesque kind, after which I believe he will be impatient to behold his own Works at Widcombe. Mr Hooke is faithfully Yours. He *Must*, for he is an honest Man.

Pray let Mrs Allen know I envy the Cock & Hen at Widcombe, and don't let Dr Oliver turn this into a Joke. I am Sincerely Yours & Hers. | A. Pope.

Address: To Ralph Allen Esqr | at Widcombe, near | Bath.

[1] *The Works of Alexander Pope, in Prose.* Vol. II (Griffith, Nos. 529–31) was to be had in large and small folio and in quarto. The publishers were J. and P. Knapton, C. Bathurst, and R. Dodsley. The *first printed* edition of the letters, of which a single copy had been sent to Swift in 1740, to be reprinted in Dublin, was in small octavo and was used later in some collected sets of Pope's *Works* of that format. See the Introduction to this present edition, pp. xii, xiii.

[2] Mr. Thomas Watts had, according to Francis Boyer Relton (*An Account of the Fire Insurance Companies*, 1893, p. 286), long been 'the ruling genius' of the Sun Fire Office. He died 18 Jan. 1742 (*Gent. Mag.*). As one of Pope's executors George Arbuthnot sent Martha Blount in a letter (preserved at Mapledurham) of 23 July 1745 a list of securities owned by Pope at his death. The list includes 31 shares in the Sun Fire Office, purchased at £1,011. 7*s.* (see Carruthers, 1857, p. 456). Pope had some trouble getting these highly desirable shares; see his letters to Allen dated 14 July, 13 Aug., 1 Oct., of 1741, and 8 Feb. 1741/2; i.e. here iv. 350, 357, 363, and 387.

POPE *to* WARBURTON[1] [? *April* 1741]

Arthur A. Houghton, Jr.

I ought to thank you for what Mr Gyles tells me, that you will not fix the Time of your Journey to Town till you know the Certainty of my being at Twitenham. My answer is, that I will not stir from Twitenham, to any Distance; farther than to be within Call at a day's warning, whenever you come. You are sure of me all the months of May and of June.

I ought also to thank you for the very great Instruction & Pleasure I have receivd from you, in the perusal of the Sheets of your Second part: particularly for the Dissertations on the Hieroglyphicks, & the Book of Job. I have no time to add more; Mr Gyles acquainting me his Pacquet stays for me. You'l read too much of me in the Letters which he will send you. I am unfeignedly & unalterably Dear Sir, | Yours. | A. Pope.

Address: To the Revd Mr Warburton[2]

POPE *to* THE EARL OF MARCHMONT[3] [? *April* 1741]

Arthur A. Houghton, Jr.

My Lord,—Since I saw you, I have an appointment from Lord Cobham to dine at Twitnam on Tuesday next. He is to ask the Duke of Argyle to meet him there: I hope that Day will be convenient to your Lordship. To add you to Any Company, enhances the Sum extremely, to | My dear Lord | Your most faith|full Servant | A. Pope.

POPE *to* LORD BATHURST[4] [28 *April* 1741]

Cirencester

Twit'nam, Tuesday

My dear Lord,—I know this is a Day when it is not to be expected you should think of any Subjects but Love & Marriage, in both which

[1] Elwin places this letter before that of 14 Apr.; but in that letter Pope is expecting Warburton so soon that the volume of letters is to await his arrival. Now, finding Warburton delays, the volume is going to him with proofs of *The Divine Legation*, vol. ii, which was on sale 26 May, in two parts. Pope has read the sheets—with delight!

[2] The informal addresses on these two April letters indicate that Gyles forwarded them to Warburton with proof-sheets.

[3] In the *Marchmont Papers* this letter is placed as if dating from Apr. 1741, and that seems as good a guess as any. Whether these anti-Walpole noblemen were gathering in Pope's 'Egerian grot' before or after the dissolution of Parliament on 25 April is undetermined.

[4] The day of writing is the day of the marriage of William, 4th Earl of Strafford (b. 1722) and Anne, second daughter of the 2nd Duke of Argyle. The young earl was allied to Bathurst through Sir Allen Apsley, Bathurst's grandfather and Strafford's great-grandfather. Bathurst will, Pope suggests, be recollecting his own bridal day, but he is to recollect also his patriotic duties in a political world. Parliament had just been dissolved.

you have succeeded so wonderfully. But notwithstanding Your youthful Image will all this day dance before you; recollect your present, cooler age, of Friendship & Philosophy: And in that recollection, remember one, who has out-lasted twenty, (or twenty thousand) of your Mistresses, in affection, attachement, & gratitude to you. If you should leave this world (I mean this corrupt & corruptible world within the Vortex of the Court & City) without One sober Visit, one Spiritual Retreat, to Twitnam and the Grotto of Friendship & Liberty; whatever you may hope to do with your Electors, you can never answer it to the Muses. I allow you any Extravagance this Day; I shall drink & rejoice in it myself; but I shoud be ten times as glad, could I hope to live to see what sort of Man a grandson of the Duke of Argyle may make, in an Age that will want Men like him.

Pray look upon me as you go. Mr Layng[1] will come with you. Lyttelton has done so,[2] & receivd my Blessing before his Expedition. I have satisfied him his Cloth is too short for his Coat, & if you'l give it to the Bearer, you will do an Act of Charity when no Election is concern'd, & cloath the Naked

I am for ever faithfully Your Lordship's. A. Pope.

*POPE *to* THOMAS EDWARDS[3] — 28 *April* [? 1741]

Sotheby Catalogue for the sale of 14 March 1912 (lot 140)

. . . If you are perfectly at leisure to call here, I think I shall be at home these two days, or if I am summoned to Town . . . look in and see the place itself.

THOMAS EDWARDS *to* POPE[4] — 29 *April* 1741

Bodleian MSS (Letterbook transcript)

Sir,—I here send you a sample of the Stone incrusted with a kind of metal, which Mr Bathurst[5] mentioned to you sometime ago; I wish

[1] Henry Layng, rector of Paulersbury, Northamptonshire, where Bathurst was born, had assisted Pope on the *Odyssey*, and had later translated parts of Tasso and other Italians. His version of Gelli's *Circe* (1744) is dedicated to Bathurst, with somewhat ecstatic recollections of the literary geniuses met at his lordship's table. See Professor A. Warren's account in *RES*, viii (1932), 77–82.

[2] Lyttelton must have returned to town later, since on 13 June he regrets to Pope that he cannot have a parting look at him.

[3] The year of this fragment is uncertain. The letter of 29 Apr. must have been written before receipt of this, and in this Pope may be inviting Edwards to call after his contributions to the grotto are in place; for example, in 1742. The letter has not been traced.

[4] Edwards's letterbooks for this season contain many mentions of Pope's desire for 'minerals' to adorn his grotto. It was later that Edwards quarrelled with Warburton over Shakespeare. The minerals, as other letters show, were shipped from Bristol by Richard Cambridge, who was not yet a resident of Twickenham Meadows.

[5] Other letters show that the reference is to Charles Bathurst, bookseller.

I could have sent it sooner, but hope it will not now be too late. If it will be of any service towards fitting up your Grotto I shall think it an honor that I can contribute to it, and will wait on You any time you will please to appoint to receive your commands about it, only I would beg if possible it might be this week because I am obliged to leave this part of the Country the beginning of the next. I am Sir

Pitshanger April 29 | 1741.

*POPE *to* ALLEN 14 *May* 1741

Egerton 1947

The Cause of the delay of this Letter, in answer to your kind one, was partly an Indisposition, which I did not care either to complain of, or to conceal from You, which I can now tell you is removed, for as long time as God shall please.

I told you my Grotto was finished, and now all that wants to the Completion of my Garden is the Frontispiece to it, of your rude Stones to build a sort of ruinous Arch at the Entry into it on the Garden side, & the Urns to the Lawne. As for the Bath-Stone, I am in no haste: having determined to let the River side remain plain, till I cover the whole Portico with Stone, hereafter.

I am sorry to hear from Mr Pulteney of the Return of Mr Watts's[1] Illness. I heartily wish him a speedy recovery, & pray thank him for his friendly Dispositions towards Me. I have the Mony lying by me, till an Opportunity offers; & all I fear is, that any Spirit either of Expence, or (to say the truth unreservedly to You) of Compassion, should lessen the Principal in the mean time.

I did not find any Reason to keep Mr Vandyst above a Day & Night, from going on with your Pictures: We could do nothing in the Grotto, & I fear'd his taking Cold there, & renewing a Fitt of the Gout. I saw what he has done since at his house, twice, and think it will suit well enough with the rest that he hath done in the Gallery.

I should be very happy, could I ramble with you & Mrs Allen next Month. But I expect Mr Warburton here at that time, and another Incident may happen that would confine me.[2] If I possibly could contrive to get to Stowe, & from thence to Lord Bathurst's, I might see you at Cirencester. But I cannot conceive it can be otherwise than

[1] See Pope to Allen, 17 Apr. 1741, and note.

[2] Pope perhaps foresees the probability of a suit in Chancery against Curll for pirating the Swift–Pope letters. The suit was entered on 4 June, Curll's answer sworn on the 14th; and the Chancellor on the 17th laid down the revolutionary decision (made for the first time in the *Pope v. Curll* suit) 'that a letter is not a gift to the receiver, and that he has no right to publish it'. See George Harris, *Life of Hardwicke* (1913), ii. 464. Since Curll's piracy is not now a really rare book, one assumes that its sale went on.

quite inconvenient to you to bring me back (as you mention) to Twicknam? Have You any thoughts of journeying this way? tell me, & if it be any way in my power, I will make my motions answer yours. —What I think is, that I must go to *Stowe*; which you have never seen, & is most worth Seeing. I could go with you from thence to Cicester, & Bath for a Short time; but how I should get back, God knows, & back I must come.——Let me know what is the Time you allot for Travelling? and how long? & if I can manage to fall in any where with You, I will. Pray assure Mrs Allen of my heartiest Services. Mr Hooke is wholly yours. Mrs Blount sends you both a hundred good & sincere Wishes. She has been like to lose her Mother, & is very unhappy in being too tender hearted—when she has never had one proof of Kindness from her Family in twenty years. I am Ever Entirely, Dear Sir, Yours.

Tho I don't write often; yet you know I wish often to know you are well: therfore don't let my Silence create yours.

I have a particular reason to desire to hear whether the Postmaster of Swanzey paid the Ten pound to Mr Savage, or Rees, or not? for I have repayd it to Mr Lewis: and if he has not accounted with you for it, he has paid Savage 10 ll more than he ought to have taken of me. once more adieu. Are You got into your New House?

May the 14th 1741.

POPE *to* ROBERT NUGENT — 21 *May* 1741

Yale University

Twit'nam, May 21.

Sir,—I hope you are return'd with as much Health, as Success from your Elections,[1] & I rejoice that your Negotiations for your self & your Friends in Cornwall have prov'd more effectual than those for Me which you kindly undertook in Ireland.[2] You have brought a great Book upon your head;[3] and to show that You can bear any Burden with patience, pray send for it to Mr Murrays in Lincolns inn fields where one has been left some time to be deliverd to any one you order. I hope soon to see you either here or in Town, who am with all regard | Sir | Your most obliged & obedi-|ent Servant | A. Pope

My old fashiond Services attend Mrs Nugent.

Address: To | R. Nugent Esq. in | Dover street | Piccadilly | London
Postmark: 2[ ]/MA

[1] Mr. Nugent had been elected M.P. for the borough of St. Mawes.

[2] He tried to aid in getting back from Mrs. Whiteway the last 'several' letters from Pope to Swift.

[3] A folio or quarto copy of Pope's *Works in Prose*, vol. ii.

POPE *to* CHARLES BATHURST[1] [? *May* 1741]

The Gentleman's Magazine, xliv (1855), 587

Arlington Street. Monday.

Sir,—I forgot to desire you to send me a line of what Corbett says to you, hither. And if he persists in his design of pirating pray watch his motions, and I'll file a Bill. 'Twill be best of all if you can find at what Press he does it.

Sir, your humble Servant, | A. Pope.

POPE *to* NATHANIEL COLE[2] [? *May* 1741]

Elwin–Courthope, x. 238

Wensday.

I would be glad to know what you did or what passed with Corbet? I believe he will not proceed, having received a letter from him of recantation, so that I believe you need not file a bill; however, I'm glad you spoke to him. If he plays cunning I shall have him watch'd and inform you farther. I hope soon to see you at Bachelor's Hall. Dear Sir, your affect. serv.

Address: To Mr. Cole in Basinghall Street.

*POPE *to* WARBURTON[3] 27 *May* [1741]

Egerton 1946

May 27.

If you come to day, You'l find me near you in the Morning at Mr Murray's in Lincolns inn fields, by 8 a clock, if not too early—You will, I hope earnestly, stay longer than you talk of. I could contrive to pass most of our Time together, or to Extend it by taking a little Journy together to Oxford or Elsewhere. Adieu till we meet | Yours Entirely | A. Pope.

Address: To | The Revd | Mr Warburton | Bp Salisbury[4]

[1] The date depends on just what work of Pope's Corbett was designing to pirate. The assumption is that it was the Pope–Swift correspondence, presently pirated by Curll. Pope is writing from the residence of Lady Codrington (Bethel's sister).

[2] The text of this untraced letter Elwin seems to say he found (as the present editor has not) in a sale catalogue of Puttick and Simpson for 29 Apr. 1859. It also appeared in a Sotheby sale on 28 Nov. 1913 (lot 355, item 13). It relates to the same trouble with Corbett as does the preceding letter. Both the year and the month, however, are uncertain..

[3] Pope, evidently an early riser, sends off this note since he knows (see the next letter) that he must leave Town during the day, and he wishes to welcome Warburton to London before leaving. Warburton had not yet arrived.

[4] The address is curiously ingenious in spacing. The mention of 'Bp Salisbury' may be meaningless writing. At this time Thomas Sherlock was bishop. He is very likely intended as the 'plunging Prelate' of *Dunciad*, ii. 323, but was evidently much valued by Warburton.

*POPE *to* FLETCHER GYLES[1] [27 *May* 1741]

Egerton 1946

Wensday

Sir,—If Mr Warburton comes to town this day, or to morrow, pray tell him I am much concernd not to be able to be in town as I promisd myself; being forced to go into Berkshire, but will return to Twitnam or London, which he pleases, on Munday, If he sends me a line to Twitnam by Saturdays post, it will find me on Sunday evening there. I am Your humble Servant | A. Pope

Address: To | Mr | Gyles Bookseller | in Holborne | at Middle row

*POPE *to* WARBURTON[2] [28 *May* 1741]

Egerton 1946

Thursday

I acquainted you by my short note yesterday, sent in haste to Mr Gyles's, how vext I was at the Accident that carries me into Berkshire to morrow: If it happens that you have nothing to do for these 3 days in London (tho it's more reasonable to think you have most to do at your first Coming) you may make this Journey no misfortune, but a pleasure to me, if you could come to night to Twitnam & accompany me to a House where is only my Lord Cobham & his Lady and on Sunday we'l return to Twitnam or London, as you like, tho I depend on your passing as much time as you can here.[3] I have nothing to add but the sincere, inviolable Esteem & good wishes that will ever attend you from Dear Sir | Yours faithfully | A. Pope

There is a Twitnam Coach sets out about 2, from the White horse Inn in Fleetstreet

Address: To | The Revd Mr Warburton | at Mr Gyles's Holbourne

*POPE *to* WARBURTON[4] [4 *or* 11 *June* 1741]

Egerton 1946

I shall lye in your Neighborhood to night, & will call upon you at Mr

[1] Having failed to evoke Warburton at 8 a.m., Pope now sends a note to Mr. Gyles, possibly before taking the 2 o'clock coach for Twickenham. See the postscript of the next letter.

[2] Warburton wrote Dr. Doddridge on this day: 'After an extremely fatiguing journey. . . . I reached Mr. Gyles's between eight and nine last night.'—Nichols, *Illust.* ii. 827.

[3] Obviously written from Twickenham.

[4] If this letter dates in 1741 rather than 1740, it should fall on one of the two Thursdays indicated. Warburton on 6 June writes to Dr. Doddridge that he returned from Twickenham on 31 May and is going thither with Pope on the day of writing. See Nichols, *Illust.* ii. 827. Before Thursday the 18th Pope and Warburton were in Oxford. See *Orrery Papers* (1903),

Gyles's to morrow morning about ten, instead of giving you the trouble of going to the Other End of the Town. I am Ever with Truth & Affection | Yours. | A. Pope

Thursday night.

Address:[1] to the Revd The Warbur

*POPE *to* ALLEN 5 *June* 1741

Egerton 1947

June 5th 1741

I thank you for Every thing, which says much in one word.——Mr Warburton is with me, & intends to go to Oxford, from whence if I should stretch to Cirencester with him he can protract his time no longer, or I would proceed to Bath. But he & I must necessarily return together to Oxford (I'll acquaint you with the reason)[2] All I write for, is, that if the Spirit of Rambling be upon you, & if Mrs Allen & you should like to meet us at Lord Bathursts, we might travel to Cornbury, Rowsham, Lord Litchfields, D. of Shrewsbury's, all which are worth seeing, and (above all) Stowe:[3] where if I pass a few days I shall have no demand again this whole year to hinder me from enjoying Widcombe for a Month, toward the End of Autumn in the planting Season. Pray let me know your disposition as soon as possible. If I am at Cirencester, it will be about the twentieth that I must be upon return for Oxford,[4] &c.

Pray tell me (what I have twice before desired to know, & is necessary for my future Conduct towards him) whether Mr Savage took the Ten pound from the Postmaster of Swanzy? Your words are, *He has not payd it*, But whether you mean he has not paid it *to Mr S.* or not pay'd it back *to You*? Adieu, Mrs A. & You are One, & I am her faithful Servant. So is Mrs Blount, to whom I made your—Compliments I will not say—but kind Remembrances, such as She herself bears, & therfore deserves.

Address: To | Ralph Allen, Esq. at | Widcombe, near | Bath.
Postmark: (illegible)

ii. 167–8. According to another Warburton letter to Doddridge (Nichols, ii. 828), they had just returned from their ramble to Oxford, &c., on 25 June. Warburton then planned to return home 'just now' by way of Cambridge.

1 Originally Pope gave the letter a 'trick' folding, which accounts in part for the present imperfect address.

2 At this time Pope and Warburton had been encouraged to expect honorary degrees from Oxford. Apparently the LL.D. was voted for Pope, but the D.D. moved for Warburton was not voted—whereupon Pope declined the honour offered him. See the later letters of this year, e.g. to Warburton, 12 Aug.

3 During the spring Pope had seen Lord Cobham more than once, but not at Stowe.

4 The visit to Cirencester was very brief.

POPE *to* JOHN BRINSDEN[1] 8 *June* 1741

Sotheby's sale, 2–3 June 1924

FRAGMENT

I am very desirous to hear of your Recovery from that unlucky accident to your Foot. Pray give the bearer a line. Whenever you are sett on your legs again and can fix our Voyage on the Thames with Faulkner,[2] I will attend you. . . .

LYTTELTON *to* POPE 13 *June* [1741]

Hagley

I am much concernd it is impossible for me to come to Twitnam either to day or to morrow, as I shou'd have much wishd to have had a parting Look of you. I am sorry to tell you too that I have not succeeded in my Negociation for Mrs Blunt, all the Lodgings at Kew that are Furnishd being already engaged for the whole Summer. You are desir'd to send the Waterman you recommended to Lord Baltimore, who will admit him into the Prince's Service upon hearing he comes from You. His Lordship is our Admiral upon the Thames, and all *Naval Preferments* are to pass through his hands. My humble Service to Mr Warburton. I am very glad he finds any thing to be Pleasd with in the Manuscript I lent him, and shall beg his Assistance in the Prosecution of the Work to make it more worthy of his Approbation. If when he is at Cambridge he shou'd find anything in the Libraries there relating to Henry the 2d or Becket that may be of use to me I will take the liberty to desire him to Communicate it. It will be two or three years before my Book is finishd,[3] so I hope he may have leizure to think a little upon the subject of it, without taking him from his own studies, or Amusements. Lord Boling: You, and He have Engrost Philosophy, Poetry, Antiquity, and Modern History, so that nothing remains for me quâ me quoque possim tollere humo, but to endeavour to draw something like History out of the Rubbish of Monkish Annals, a disagreable Task, but yet if I can execute it well there are Materials enough to make it a Work of some Instruction and Pleasure to my Countrymen, and I hope to the Prince my Master, for whose service I chiefly design it. Certain I am, that such an Archi-

[1] This bit of text comes from the Sotheby catalogue. The letter (lot 384) was sold to Francis Edwards, and appears later in his catalogues. It has not been traced.

[2] Faulkner was in London for some weeks this summer. Lord Orrery, writing to Swift 7 July 1741, mentions Faulkner as in England. The letter (printed by Ball, vi. 177–8) gives news about Pope and several of his friends.

[3] Thus early Lyttelton seems to be at work on his *History of the Life of Henry the Second*, which finally appeared in four volumes, 1767–71. See Horace Walpole's *Letters* (ed. Toynbee), vii. 122, for Walpole's comment on *Henry the Second*.

tect as You, or Mr Warburton, cou'd out of these Gothick Ruins, rude as they are, Raise a new Edifice, that wou'd be fitt to Enshrine the Greatest of our English Kings, and Last to Eternity.

There is no Design of putting anybody as yet about Prince George. I will say more to you upon that subject at our next Meeting. I am extreamly grievd that I must give up all hopes of seeing you at Hagley this year, for when you are there with Me, Gratior it Dies et Soles melius nitent.[1] But my poor Father's ill health incapacitates him from receiving Company and me from enjoying it. I hope to God by next year Retirement,[2] and a Country Life will have mended his health, and then if Lord Bathurst will Honour us with a Visit, and bring you and Mr Warburton along with him, it will highly oblige | Your most affectionate humble Servt. | G Lyttelton

June the 13th

POPE *to* CHARLES BATHURST 15 *June* [1741]

The Gentleman's Magazine, xliv, N.S. (1855), 586

June 15.

Sir,—I thank you for your care, and Mr. Edwards[3] also, in regard to the minerals. I have received them at last safe. I am gone to Lord Bathurst's, in Glocestershire, for a week or two.[4] As soon as I return I'll put the Miscellanies[5] in order for Wright, as I promised, which I am pretty sure will be of service to you, otherwise I would not trouble myself more about them; but I am sincerely, | Sir, your friend and Servant, | A. Pope.

*POPE *to* ALLEN[6] [? 14 *July* 1741]

Egerton 1947

Tuesday, June 14.

Yesterday I have sent, by the Bath Coach from Turnham Green, Two Pine apples, which I hope will be good, directed to you. Dr Oliver has been very obliging in sending me a Hogshead of Cyder, by

[1] Horace, *Carmina*, IV. v. 7–8. [2] Sir Thomas retired from public life in 1741.

[3] On Edwards and his minerals see the letters to Edwards and Bathurst of 18 and [23] July.

[4] Pope is just leaving home; he returns in about ten days.

[5] The *Miscellanies* had to be re-formed since Pope had withdrawn items to place in his *Works in Prose*. Bathurst finally brought out the *Miscellanies* in Mar. 1742.

[6] Pope's dating is impossible. Most of the events mentioned postdate 14 June, which, in 1741—the proper year certainly—was Sunday. Hastily Pope had started his dating with something other than Tuesday; he overwrote, and went on to make an error. The probable date is 14 July. His Chancery case against Curll was decided 17 June, and the injunction mentioned could not antedate 14 June. Other events postdate 14 June also. Pope and Warburton had gone to Oxford, encouraged by the prospect of honorary degrees, about 15–17 June. Pope (without Warburton) had gone on to Cirencester, whence he returned, as he says, 'in a week'.

the Mediation of his Friend Mr Cooper, as I understood first by his own Letter (which was itself as agreable as a present) & this day by a line from Mr Cooper. But the Hogshead came yesterday by a London Waterman, & has been ill treated on the Way, for about a third of it is drank out, as appears from two pegs: but as there is more left than I any way deserve, I'll be contented. I shall enquire for the Cargo you favord me with by the Claremont, this week, & set Bigs to work.

I got home in a week from Lord Bathurst, I long to inhabit my own place for a while, which is now in its highest beauty. I hope you enjoy Yours, every way that Health & a good Heart can make You. When I can encrease my own happiness by seeing yours there, I cannot be certain, but think about the beginning of Septr. Should it happen sooner, about Bartholomew Tide, my Lord Orrery would carry me to You. As for Southampton, I fear I must never more think of any distant Places but yours, & rely upon meeting that Friend[1] at Bath. It is not impossible but one whom I entirely esteem, may be forced to apply for ill health to Bristol; in which case I would try at any rate to be near; & if our old project of a Short Stay upon Clifton down, & a Voyage to Wales were practicable, I would aim at it then.

I've heard nothing yet of Mr Watts, or the Sun fire office,[2] but my Money lies ready, & I don't know what in the world to do with it, tho to say the truth I never more needed to make use of it, for I am in near 200 ll arrear to my Printer. That Rascal Curl has pyrated the Letters, which would have ruin'd half my Edition, but we have got an Injunction[3] from my Lord Chancellor to prohibit his selling them for the future, tho doubtless he'l do it clandestinly. And indeed I have done with expensive Editions for ever, which are only a Complement to a few curious people at the expence of the Publisher, & to the displeasure of the Many. I was half drawn into this, by what Motte had done formerly, & for the time to come, the World shall not pay, nor make Me pay, more for my Works than they are worth.

My sincerest Services are Mrs Allen's, and Mrs Blount desires hers may be added, with true Esteem for you both. Mr Hooke has often shown me the Gratefulness of his Mind to you: his Work goes on well. I expect him & his Daughter for a few days, he is in unfeigned Sorrow for the death of Mrs Price.[4] Let me hear from you as often as you can, & particularly of your State of health. Mine is very tolerable, I thank God.

Address: To | Ralph Allen Esqr | at Widcombe, near | Bath.
Postmark: 14/IY (possibly IV)

[1] The Southampton friend would be Lady Peterborow. See Pope to Allen, 13 Aug. 1741.
[2] See Pope to Allen, 17 Apr. 1741, and note.
[3] On 17 June.
[4] *The London Evening Post* reports the death of Mrs. Price on 16 June.

*POPE *to* ALLEN 18 *July* [1741]

Egerton 1947

I writ to you in a hurry[1] & forgot your desire I should determine you in the Choice of a fourth Head, I agree with your Inclination to have it Sir Walter Ralegh. I went yesterday to the Sculptor's & saw the Heads, that of Milton is near finishd, & the other doing. I shall take what care I can of them, and wish with all my heart I could be employed to do any thing to serve or please You, instead of tiring myself (as I do every day) in serving & scarce pleasing others, who deserve it a thousand times less. But Fortune has made me happy in your being so, & in placing you above needing my Services. I will be revenged on others by Loving you better in my heart, tho I give you fewer proofs of it.[2]

Tho' I'm not in ill health I am so weak of body that I go every night to bed weary of the day, even without any thing that you would call Fatigue. My Mind at present is as dejected as possible,[3] for I love my Country, & I love Mankind, and I see a dismal Scene Opening for our own & other Nations, which will not long be a Secret to you. God prosper your Particular, tho in General Miseries no honest Man can be Easy. I am Ever Dear Sir | Yours & Mrs A.'s true | affectionate Servant | A. Pope

July 18th

I've not heard yet of the Stones[4] &c. Where may I send to Bigs' Brother, when they are come?

Address: To Ralph Allen Esq. at | Widcombe near | Bath.
Postmark: 18/ I[Y]

THOMAS EDWARDS *to* POPE[5] 18 *July* 1741

Bodleian MSS. (Letterbook transcripts)

Sir,—I reckon it a great misfortune that I was obliged to leave Middlesex before I had completed the commission I undertook about the Minerals,[6] which I flatter my self you would sooner have received

[1] This remark may explain the misdating of the letter of 14 July.

[2] On Warburton's projected use of this paragraph in forming a letter from parts of others see Pope to Allen, 2 Nov. 1738, and note.

[3] This dejection is probably due to disillusionment with regard to the 'patriot' leadership of Carteret and Pulteney. The 'other nations' offered a depressing scene because of Frederick the Great's invasion of Silesia, which was involving England in continental military engagements.

[4] Possibly for the garden entrance to the grotto. See Pope to Allen, 14 May 1741.

[5] This letter was printed in *Gent. Mag.* xliv (1855), 586, possibly from the original as sent. If so, the letterbook copy is an improved revision.

[6] Work on the grotto continues, though Pope had told Allen (letter of 14 May 1741)

if I could have been in Town to sollicit the affair; what delay there did happen was entirely owing to my Kinsman's[1] time being very much taken up with receiving and paying visits on account of his late marriage, so that I hope your goodness will excuse it. I am glad however that they arrived safe though late; if they are not sufficient, you may freely command whatever quantity you please, by a letter to me at Mr Pond's in Queenstreet which is the shortest way I know of conveyance to me here in Buckinghamshire, or if You as is probable should want them sooner than by this round about correspondence they can be had, please to order Mr Bathurst to write for them in my name immediately. I shall look upon it as an evidence that you excuse the delay which happened before, if it does not discourage you from employing again | Your most Obedient &c.

Turrick July 18. 1741.

POPE *to* CHARLES BATHURST[2] [23] *July* 1741

The Gentleman's Magazine, xliv, N.S. (1855), 586

Twitnam, Thursday, July 19, 1741.

Sir,—I received the inclosed very obliging letter from your Friend Mr. Edwards. Pray thank him for it, and write, as he proposes, for a Hamper or two more of those minerals, which I shall make use of as soon as I can receive them.

I beg you when Mr Edwards returns to you to let me know, that we may fix a day for yourself and him to come hither and see the use I have made of his kind present.

that it was 'finished'. Edwards copied into his letterbooks (Bodley MS. 1009, pp. 177–9) an amusing appeal in a letter to Richard Cambridge (30 July 1741), which is in part as follows: 'On the 19th of this month I wrote to you at Mr. Pope's desire for another basket of your mineral, but I yesterday received an account that he has enlarged his design intending to add two rooms, which have windows into each wing of the Grotto, one to be covered with Shells, and the other with Minerals, and so can dispense with more than two baskets if they can conveniently be had: If you designed to make use of the Stone in any building of your own I shall repent that I have robbed you by my tattling, and may expect you to apply to me Fair Rosamond's speech to young Clifford

Why did you boast of my beauty
When you rode to Woodstock town?
You might have talk'd of your Hawks & Hounds
And let your Sister alone.

But if you have no immediate use for it may I not say as Prior does in his Alma, Dick, can it have a nobler Fate? It is made immortal in the Verses which I give you below, and will shine there longer than in the Grotto.' The Verses (presumably Pope's lines on the grotto, already in print) are not copied into the letterbook.

[1] Cambridge seems to be the kinsman. He married in 1741.

[2] The date assigned by the transcriber is due to an idea that Pope wrote off to Bathurst immediately on receiving Edwards's letter of the 18th. But the 18th was Saturday; hence the 19th cannot be Thursday. Pope could not receive a letter posted at Turrick by Edwards on a Saturday before Monday the 20th. Since the 23rd was a Thursday, that seems a plausible date to assign. One needs to see the original!

I wish you would resolve upon printing in the manner I mentioned your Miscellanies, for I am now perfectly at leisure, which I shall not be a month longer. I am sure it will turn out much to their advantage; and, as for mine, I have no terms to make with you, but only to serve you in the little improvements that I shall make. By putting *all* the verse into the last Vol. (as was originally intended, as you'll see by the first paragraph of Dr Swift's and my Preface) you will be enabled (if you prefer it) to leave out whatever is another's claim or Property; for, as I have cast the volumes, it will be of equal size when you have so done. I shall be here for some days constantly; I think till Sunday | Yours, | A. Pope.

*POPE *to* ALLEN 23 *July* [1741]

Egerton 1947

Twitnam. July 23.

This day I received the Cargoe of the Stone & Bristol water, containing two Urnes forty three rough Stones, & several Blocks of Bath Stone, amounting to 6 Ton.[1] And nine Hampers of Bristol water, 5 directed to Capt Long, & 4 to me: I presume those 5 should not have been sent hither, but only the 4: pray let me know whither to send them. I now want only Bigs' Brother to set him to work on the Pedestals. Pray are Collin's Urns yet shipt off?

I hope you are well. I have not heard from you since my two last Letters, but I would not omit acquainting you of my Receit of these.

Mr Hook's Son is desirous of getting into the Army, & (considering all that has past) I approve of his desire.[2] The D. of Argyle's Removal[3] has hindred me from being Serviceable to him this way; and his Fathers Modesty will not let him name Gen. Wade[4] to you. I wish you could find means to recommend the young Man to him, in any way. It will be much better than to expect any thing another way, & All my Interest in the Army is at an End.

Pray if you are well, tell me so, often. I wish you all present blessings: future, your own Virtue only can procure, & I doubt not, will. I am faithfully Ever Yours. | A. Pope

[1] For the garden entrance to his grotto.

[2] Hooke had two sons. The younger, Luke Joseph (see *DNB*), became a professor of theology in the Sorbonne and later aumonier to Marie Antoinette. Thomas, brought up by his aunt as a Protestant, did not enter the army, but in 1742 he was a student in St. Mary Hall, Oxford, and later was rector of Birkby (York) and vicar of Leek. Dr. William King, Principal of St. Mary Hall, was a close friend of Nathaniel Hooke, for whom, he says, he served as amanuensis when Hooke was translating *The Travels of Cyrus* (Nichols, *Lit. Anec.* ii. 607–10).

[3] John, 2nd Duke of Argyle, had been deprived of all his military and other posts in 1740 because of violent attacks on Walpole.

[4] General Wade (M.P. for Bath) was about the most important military man of the time; his daughter had been Allen's first wife.

I now live at Twitnam quiet, & am going to be fully imployed in Grottofying.

Tell me something of your New Abode.

The Busto's are near done, & the Sculptor[1] will write soon to you.

Address: To Ralph Allen Esq. at | Widcombe, near | Bath.
Postmark: 24/IY

*POPE *to* JOHN BRINSDEN[2] [? *August* 1741]

Parke-Bernet Sale, 13 Oct. 1938, lot 351

I am very desirous to dine with you, but if it could be as conveniently on Friday or Saturday next, It would give me a great pleasure: & it happens that next Week Workmen & Bricklayers ingage me to my sorrow & Cost. Believe me with all affection, ever | Sir | Yours. | A. Pope:

Teem has not yet been here, or sent.

Wensday.

A line by Thursdays post will reach me time enough on Friday to come to you.

Address: To | Mr Brinsden: in | Durham yard.

*POPE *to* HUGH BETHEL[3] [? 1741]

Egerton 1948

Since I return'd I find Mr W. does not leave me with his family all this week till Sunday; I hope tho it defers me from seeing you as I have not lodging, yet it will make me amends in bringing your Brother with you *that Day* when I may conclude he is never engaged by business, & at night you are both sure of Room, & an open Heart, from him who is | Dear Sir | Ever & Entirely | Yours, A. Pope.

Address: To | Mr Bethel.

[1] Evidently for the library at Prior Park, Roubiliac was doing heads of Milton, Sir Walter Ralegh, *et al.* See letters to Allen of 18 July and 28 Aug.

[2] Dating a note like this is guess-work. Other letters show that in this month Pope was wearied by bricklayers and stonemasons, and many of his letters to Brinsden date from this year. But other times are quite possible.

The text is from a transcript kindly made by Mr. James M. Osborn.

[3] No dating is possible. In 1735 and thereafter Gilbert West, poet and nephew of Lord Cobham, occasionally visited Pope with his family. Pope tells Fortescue (Mar. 1743) that the Wests have been there for a fortnight. Aug. 1741 seems a possible time for a visit—with Bethel briefly in London.

POPE *to* MARTHA BLOUNT[1] [11 *August* 1741]

Mapledurham

London. Tuesday.

I am very glad I did not defer seeing Mr Bethel. I found him last night so bad, & panting for breath, that I can scarce imagin he ever will recover. Yet this morning he is quite another Man, & so much mended that it is scarce conceivable he is the same person. So it seems it is with him, but much worse in Town than on the Road. It was impossible to get him to Twitnam, he stays but one day more, & sets out on Thursday morning. I wish to God you could borrow Lady Ann's Chariot to morrow, just to look at him in the morning & return to her to dinner. he lodges next door to Lord Shelburn's. He dos not expect this, but I think it would be a Satisfaction to your own Mind, & perhaps we shall never see him more. God's will must be obeyd, but I am excessively wounded by it. Adieu.

I shall stay till he goes.

Address: To Mrs Blount, at Mr Tho. | Reeves's in Sion Rowe, | Twickenham. | Middlesex.

Frank: Free | Boyle.

Postmark: 11/AV

*POPE *to* FORTESCUE[2] 12 *August* 1741

Wellesley College

Twitnam. Aug. 12. 1741

You were returned from the Circuit,[3] & gone to Devonshire, without my knowing the least of your Motions; which you will be so Candid a Judge (I hope) as to ascribe to my Ignorance in Law- & Justice-affairs; For I had certainly, either at the Vineyard or in London, just snatchd a Sight of you. Had you sent me a line, it should have carry'd me to any place within my reach, to have told you the Old Story, which is still a true one; that I heartily wish you & yours all health & prosperity. I hope to hear you are in perfect Ease & Tranquillity, improving your Paternal Seat, & planning agreable Groves, under whose Shadow *in otia tuta recedas*, whenever you are weary of the *Dignitas sine Otio*. Tho both are best, *Otium cum dignitate*, as you just now (for a month or 2) injoy them: and I have nothing to wish added to them but Health, and a long Continuance of it. Mrs Blount joins

[1] The date is from the postmark. In 1741 this day was a Tuesday. Elwin strangely places the letter in 1720. The letter to Allen on 13 Aug. seems to indicate that Bethel left for the Continent on that day, i.e. as here suggested, on Thursday.

[2] Printed by Professor Helen Sard Hughes in *Modern Philology*, xxviii (1930), 103.

[3] Fortescue had been assigned to the Home Circuit, and ended his duties about 22 July at Kingston-on-Thames. Pope has evidently been much occupied.

with me in this, & in her Services which she chargd me to send you. She was concerned not to have any opportunities of seeing, or being seen unto, you: Her health is not better, nor her Situation better, than usual: but she can be easyer by a good Temper than most people under them. As for my own health, it is not worse, but rather better than twenty years ago, when we first knew one another, & therfore sure I have reason to be content with it, as well as with my Fortune, which hath always been such as I never wanted any thing I had a mind to, & yet never was obliged to any man more than I had a mind to.—Adieu, & may you & I descend to the Grave content with our several Lots, thanking God as long as we live, & loving our Neighbor as much as he'l let us. I am faithfully & affectionately Dear Sir Yours. | A. Pope.

I have a small piece of Trouble to give you; that, as a Devonian, you may contribute something to my Grotto, as well as Cornwall & Wales. It is to send me (as soon as you can) a Hogshead of Scallop Shells.

Address: To the Hon. Mr Justice | Fortescue, in Bell Yard | near Lincolns Inne. | London.

Endorsement (in Fortescue's hand): Mr Pope | Augst 12. 1741

Postmark: 17/AV

POPE *to* WARBURTON[1] 12 *August* [1741]

Egerton 1946

Twitnam Aug. 12.

The General Indisposition I have to writing, unless upon a belief of the Necessity or Use of it, must plead my Excuse in not doing it to you. I know it is not (I feel it is not) needfull, to repeat Assurances of the true & constant Friendship & Esteem I bear you: honest & ingenuous Minds are sure of each other's; the Tye is mutual, & Solid. The Use of writing Letters resolves wholly into the Gratification given & received in the knowledge of each others Welfare. Unless I ever should be so fortunate (& a rare Fortune it would be) to be able to procure, & acquaint you of, some real Benefit done you by my means: But Fortune seldom suffers One dis-interested man to serve another. 'Tis too much an Insult upon her, to let two of those who most despise her favours be happy in them at the same time, & in the same Instance. I wish for nothing so much at her hands, as that she would permit some Great Person or other to remove you nearer the Banks of the Thames; tho very lately a Nobleman,[2] whom you

[1] Printed by Warburton in 1751. He omitted two phrases here placed in half-brackets.

[2] In printing Pope's letter to him dated 20 Sept. 1741, Warburton identified this nobleman as 'Lord Chesterfield'. Bowles and Elwin thought that Chesterfield was the nobleman whose unfulfilled promises of a benefice are recounted by Ruffhead, p. 488. The details of the two instances are far from identical.

esteem much more than you know, had destined ⌜you a Living you never dreamt of, in the Neighborhood where you now are; but the Incumbent was graciously preserved by Fortune⌝.

I thank you heartily for your Hints;[1] & am afraid if I had more of them, not on this only but on other Subjects, I should break my resolution, & become an author anew; nay a New Author, and a better than I yet have been; or God forbid I should go on, jingling only the same Bells!

I have receivd some Chagrin at the *Delay* ⌜(for Dr King tells me it will prove no more)⌝ of your Degree at Oxon.[2] As for mine, I will dye before I receive one, in an Art I am ignorant of, at a place where there remains any Scruple of bestowing one on you, in a Science of which you are so great a Master. In short I will be Doctor'd with you, or not at all. I am sure, where ever Honour is not conferrd on the Deserving, there can be none given to the Undeserving; no more from the hands of Priests, than of Princes. Adieu. God give you all *True Blessings*! I am faithfully Yours, | A. Pope

Address: To the Revd Mr Warburton | at Newark.
Frank: Free | Radnor
Postmark: 15/AV

*POPE *to* ALLEN 13 *August* 1741

Egerton 1947

[Sir]—I can never enough thank you, (my dear & true Friend) for every Instance of your Kindness. at present I am loaded with them, but none touch me more sensibly, than your Attempts for Mr Hooke; for I am really Happier in seeing a Worthy Man Eased of the Burden, which Fortune generally lays such Men under, as have no Talents to Serve the *Bad* & the *Ambitious*; than in any Pleasures of my own, which are but idle at best. Therfore I say nothing of the Urns, &c, no not of Your Endeavors to place out my Mony, nor your Assistance in any Sort. I take them as you mean them; Pleasures to yourself: yet at least Confirmations of my Esteem of you, since I would do the very Same for you & yours.

[1] One suspects these concerned the revision of *The Dunciad*.

[2] This relates to an accidental affair which happened this summer, in a ramble that Mr. P. and Mr. W. took together, in which Oxford fell in their way, where they parted; Mr. P. after one day's stay going westward, and Mr. W. who staid a day after him, to visit the dean of C.C. returning to London. On this day the Vice-chancellor, the Rev. Dr. L. sent him a message to his lodgings, by a person of eminence in that place, with an usual compliment, to know if a Doctor's degree in Divinity would be acceptable to him; to which such an answer was returned as so civil a message deserved. About this time, Mr. Pope had the same offer made him of a Doctor's degree in Law. And to the issue of that unasked and unsought compliment these words allude.—Warburton, 1751.

The delay which Pope regrets became in 1743 a denial.

Fortune, or shall I say Providence, seems to ordain, that I should be more & more yours: since it seperates me from some of those Duties which every honest man has contracted in the Course of his Life to more Friends than One. Mr Bethel was one of the first of that number, to whom a part of my Time was due, which might have otherwise been yours: and it has now pleasd God that his Indisposition has carry'd him out of England;[1] so that what I apprehended, of the necessity of my attending him on his Coming to Town, is at an end; and I can the longer be with you. My Lady Peterborow tells me She Shall make a Visit to these parts soon, so that I need not ramble thither. In short, I see no probability (when my affairs with my Printer are discharged) of any Tye, moral natural or political, which can hold me from you, after Michaelmass. If a little Planting be necessary in my Garden, it shall be hasten'd at the beginning of October, so as to reach you time enough [to assist] you in Yours.

You are not particular enough as to your Headakes pray how are you in that respect? I hope One Part of you at least is quite well, which I know is the tenderest part. I need not say I mean Mrs Allen —No one can be with more affection | Yours. | A. Pope.

Biggs' Brother is here, & does very well.

Aug. 13. 1741.

Gen. Wade receivd Mr H. with all possible Goodness.[2] Would you have me go & thank him for the Promise he has made to try to serve his Son?

Address: To | Ralph Allen Esq. at Widcomb | near | Bath.
Postmark: 17/AV.

POPE *to* SARAH, DUCHESS OF MARLBOROUGH

13 *August* 1741

Blenheim

Madam,—I desire to address Your Grace with all Simplicity of Heart, like a poor Indian, & prefer my Petition to you with an Offering of my best Fruits (all I am worth, for Gold & Silver I have none, tho the Indians had) Accept therfore of these Pineapples, & be so good to let me follow them to Wimbledon next Sunday, (For the day after, I am to entertain some Lawyers upon Venison,[3] if I can get it) I will trouble your Grace's Coach no farther than to fetch me, at whatever hour that Morning you like; & if you please, I will bring with me a Friend of my Lord Marchmont's, & therfore of yours & mine.[4] I

[1] On the very day of this letter Bethel, because of asthma, started for Italy.
[2] On Hooke and General Wade see Pope to Allen, 23 July 1741, and note.
[3] In 1741 pineapples were a far rarer luxury than venison, and as ranger of Windsor Park, Her Grace . . . had venison!
[4] Hooke.

have provided myself of some Horses to my own Chariot to bring me back. I could not postpone any longer this pleasure, since you gave me some hopes it was to lead to an Honour I've so often been disappointed of, the Seeing your Grace a few hours at Twickenham in my Grotto.

I am | Madam | Your most obedient | & faithful Servant | A. Pope

Augst the 13th 1741.

POPE *to* SARAH, DUCHESS OF MARLBOROUGH[1]

[15 *August* 1741]

Blenheim

Saturday.

Madam,—Your Letter is too Good for me to answer, but not to acknowledge. I confine myself to One particular of it, I don't wonder some say you are Mad, you act so contrary to the rest of the World; and it was the Madman's Argument for his own being Sober, that the Majority prevaild, & had lockd up the few that were so. Horace, (the first of that name who was no Fool) has setled this matter, and writ a whole Discourse to show, that All folks are mad, (even Poets & Kings not excepted.) he only begs one Favor, *That the Greater Madmen would spare the Lesser.*[2] Would those whom your Grace has cause to complain of, & those whom we all have cause to complain of, but do so; not only you & I, but the whole Nation might be saved.

Your Present of a Buck is indeed a proper one for an Indian; one of the true Species of Indians, (who seeks not for Gold & Silver, but only for Necessaries). But I must add to my shame I am one of that sort who at his heart loves Bawbles better, & throws away his Gold & Silver for Shells. & glittering Stones, as you will find I have done when you see (for you must see) my Grotto. What then does your Grace think of bringing me back in your Coach about five & supping there, now the Moonlight favours your Return. by which means you will be tired of what you now are pleas'd to call Good Company, & I happy for six or seven hours together? In short I will put myself into your power to bring, send, or Expell me back, as you please. I am most faithfully | Madam, | Your Graces most obliged | humble Servant. | A. Pope.

The Friend of Lord Marchmont is Yours already,[3] & clear'd of all Prepossessions: So that you can make no fresh Conquests of *him*: as you have of *Me*.

1 The date is sure from the preceding letter addressed to Her Grace on Thursday the 13th.

2 *Sermones*, II. iii. 326.

3 The friend was doubtless Hooke. It is presumed that he was already (or had been) in the employ of the Duchess, at work on her papers. Possibly Pope is mediating between the two after one of the inevitable rages.

*POPE *to* ALLEN 28 *August* 1741

Egerton 1947

I send you, as soon as I can, the inclosed, as the best I can, at first thought, & perhaps the better for being so plain.[1] It is at least more Exact than the other. But I would by no means have you put it up as yet, & whenever you do, it should be on a Marble Tablet, not in Bath stone.

Biggs is still here, with one man more, & I don't see the Work go fast. Two days more than about the Urns I have imployd him in paving the Porch of the Grotto which was but half pavd before. And two of the Pedestals I shall deduct, for Ive found a way not to want them. So that methinks a fortnight in which they have been already at work, & this week, should be sufficient Time for making 4 pedestals & setting up 4 urns, & removing Two. yet I question if they will be done. I have given him what you desired 10s per week advance.

In a Week or two, Mr Scot[2] will make you a Visit, he is going to Set up for himself in the Art of Gardening, in which he has great Experience, & particularly has a design which I think a very good one, to make Pineapples cheaper in a year or two. In the meantime he deserves Encouragement which I doubt not he will find from you. I know you'l make him welcome, & he may be of some Use to instruct & enlarge the Idæas of Isaac.

Mr Hook hath been with me some days, & we daily talk of you. I am as desirous you should see my finishd Works, as you that I should see yours. To mine you have contributed much, to yours I can contribute little. I've not seen London this month past, I will go to the Sculptor, & see Vandyst. The only misfortune I have is my Maid's Illness, a dangerous Fitt of the Stone I fear; but certainly she will live an unhealthy, if not a miserable life.

I conclude, having nothing more to do or say, than to Love you & Thank you.

Aug. 28th 1741.

I should send my Services more frequently to Dr Oliver, but I conclude he knows I owe him them. however pray now & then mention me, to him, & Dr Cheyne.

I think you agreed with Roüillac[3] for 20 ll each Head. *Bigs* has desird me to advance him 2 guineas more, which I have done.

Address: To | Ralph Allen Esqr at | Widcombe near | Bath.

Postmark: 29/AV

Endorsement (in Allen's hand): The Inscription | for the Statue

[1] Annotated in part by Allen in his subscribed endorsement.

[2] Pcssibly the protégé of Lord Burlington mentioned in Pope to Burlington, [17 Aug. 1738]. See iv. 118.

[3] Roubiliac.

POPE *to* CHARLES BATHURST 5 *September* [1741]

The Gentleman's Magazine, xliii, N.S. (1855), 261

Sir,—I have put Mr Wright[1] in a way to go on with the Miscellanies, when I shall be at Bath. In the mean time I would not trouble you for the little note of 26lb. which was due the beginning of last month,[2] if it be any way inconvenient to you. But I would desire you to pay it by small bills, which I will draw upon you to one or two tradesmen I owe money to in London. At present I wish you would pay Mr Vaughan the chairmaker 6 pounds odd, which I'l order him next week, if you write me a line. I was sorry I could not see Mr Edwards,[3] not being able to appoint any day, my servant having been at the point of death.[4]

I am, Your affect: Friend & Servant. | A. Pope.

Sept. 5.

Address: To Mr. Bathurst.

POPE *to* WARBURTON[5] 20 *September* [1741]

Egerton 1946

Sept. 20

It is not my Friendship, but the Discernment of that Nobleman[6] I mention'd, which you are to thank for his Intention to serve you. And his Judgment is so uncontroverted, that it would really be a pleasure to you to owe him any thing, instead of a Shame, which often is the Case in the Favors of Men of that rank. I am sorry I can only wish you well, & not do myself Honour in doing You any Good. but I comfort myself when I reflect, few Men could make you happyer, none more deserving than You have made yourself.

I don't know how I have been Betrayed into a Paragraph of this kind; I ask your pardon, tho it be Truth, for saying so much⌜, & come to the business of your Letter. I think in the new Edit. of your answer to Crousaz, you should not cite those discarded Verses of mine, but rather reserve them to be made a Confirmation of your Opinion in the Commentary on the Poems themselves;[7] And I think it will better

[1] John Wright was the printer employed at this time by Pope and C. Bathurst.

[2] Bathurst may have owed Pope for profits on the *Works in Prose*, vol. ii. Possibly he owed for the *Miscellanies*.

[3] On Edwards's benefactions to the grotto see the letters to Edwards and Bathurst of 18 and 23 July 1741.

[4] See Pope to Allen, 28 Aug.

[5] In printing this letter in 1751 Warburton added the year date but omitted the considerable passages here placed in half-brackets.

[6] Lord Chesterfield.—Warburton, 1751.

[7] Here first we learn of the project to make Warburton the official commentator on *all* Pope's 'verses'.

appear there, & more naturally, than to be insisted on here, especially as you are known to have written that Vindication before you had any acquaintance with me, or any Sight of those papers.

The Alteration you have made in the Position of them is certainly right, & I thank you for it.⌉

If I can prevail on myself to complete the Dunciad,[1] it will be publishd at the Same time with a General Edition of all my Verses (for Poems I will not call them) and I hope Your Friendship to me will be then as well known, as my being an Author, & go down together to Posterity; I mean to as much of posterity as poor Moderns can reach to, where the Commentator (as usual) will lend a Crutch to the weak Poet to help him to limp a little further than he could on his own Feet. We shall take our Degree together in Fame, whatever we do at the University: And I tell you once more, I will not have it, there, without you.[2]

⌈I intend about the End of October to go to Mr Allen's at Bath, & stay with him till Christmass. I hope to hear of your health, as you shall of mine, if I have any, till the next Spring restores you to me, & me to myself. Adieu, & imploy me freely, in any thing but Poetry. I am faithfully Dear Sir Yours, | A. Pope.⌉

Address: To the Revd Mr Warburton | at Newark

*POPE *to* ALLEN 24 *September* 1741

Egerton 1947

Sept. 24. 1741.

I answer you with the Speed you require. To fix my certain Day so long before hand, I cannot; but this you may depend on, that whenever you come I will return with You, after the middle of October. I can't express the Joy it will be to me to have you see all my Works, as it will for me to see all Yours. The Grotto will be compleated then, & all my Plantations setled, so as to be carried on after I go, as I hope to do yours in person, if God give me life. For every Year that is added to me, will (I dare say) increase that Friendship between us, which is founded on so Just & true Principles. I will write no more but that I am sincerely Mrs Allen's Friend & Entirely Yours. So help me God. | Adieu.

Mr Allen

Address: To Ralph Allen Esq. at | Widcomb, near | Bath.

[1] He had then communicated his intention to the Editor, of adding a fourth book to it.—Warburton, 1751.

[2] This was occasioned by the editor's requesting him not to slight the honour ready to be done him by the University: and especially, not to decline it on the editor's account, who had no reason to think the affront done him the act of that illustrious body, but the contrivance of two or three particulars.—Warburton, 1751.

*POPE *to* ALLEN 1 *October* 1741

Egerton 1947

Oct. 1. 1741.

I received yours. am greatly obliged to you for your Compliance to the Time I mentioned, & shall be happyer than I can express, in having your Company here, & all the Way. I answerd your last in so short a warning & hurry, that I could but barely tell you my Resolution to accompany you, & will be ready by the Day you propose, the 19th. But I wish you would Stay a day or two more with me here; but all shall be as you will, when we meet. I did not return you Mr Watts' Letter, but since I found the Time of purchasing any Shares[1] very uncertain & distant, I thought it best to put that Money into E. India Bonds, that it might lye dead no longer; which I bought lately, & can easily be turnd into Money when the Opportunity offers.

Mr Hooke is with all gratitude your faithfull Friend, & Mrs Allen's. I have seen him often of late, here; but in London I have not been a day these 5 weeks. I must go before you come, & then I will cast all Thoughts of it behind me, for Some Weeks at least, if not the whole Winter, as I wish I could.

Mrs Blount is in this Neighborhood, & sends her Services (which are always sincere & cordial) to your Self & Mrs Allen. I have been much alone, but much amused, which is the State I wish my friends may have a Taste of, for it generally makes them happy & independent. It is in private Life only that I hope for pleasure; for as to the Public, I see nothing but melancholy Prospects. Adieu, pray tell me once more of your health: & may your Journey contribute to it, & be prosperous. I can't pretend to say how much I am Yours, Ever. | A. Pope.

Address: To | Ralph Allen Esqr at Widcombe near | Bath.
Postmark: 1/OC

POPE *to* THE EARL OF MARCHMONT 10 *October* 1741

Arthur A. Houghton, Jr.

Twitnam Oct. 10, 1741

My Lord,—One of the great Evils of these Immoral Times, is, that our superiors bear an Enmity not only to publick but private Virtues, & discourage every Consequence & Reward of Friendship itself. The Post office cannot suffer two Friends quietly to enjoy the Testimonies of each others Love or Esteem, or to correspond upon subjects less vile or less interested than they would themselves. Surely this must have been the only Cause that could discourage us from writing. I

1 The desired shares in the Sun Fire company were later acquired. See the letters of 17 Apr. 1741 and 8 Feb. 1741/2.

have often askd Mr Hume[1] when he had an opportunity of sending by a safe hand, & found none. I will believe your Lordship has written to me & your Lordship should believe I have written to you. But I assure you, if I have no Remembrances of you but what I bear, & ever shall bear, in my own Heart, You shall at least hear of me some way or other, if not in Writing, in Print; if not in Life, in Death; if not in a Will, in something as solemn & as sacred. For I may tell you, that I am determined to publish no more in my life time, for many reasons; but principally thro' the Zeal I have to speak the *Whole Truth*, & neither to praise or dispraise by halves, or with worldly managements. I think fifty an age at which to write no longer for Amusement, but for some Use, and with design to do some good. I never had any uneasy Desire of Fame, or keen Resentment of Injuries, & now both are asleep together: Other Ambition I never had, than to be tolerably thought of by those I esteem'd, and this has been gratify'd beyond my proudest Hopes. I hate no human Creature, & the moment any can repent or reform, I love them sincerely. Public Calamities touch me; but when I read of Past Times, I am somewhat comforted as to the present, upon the Comparison: and at the worst I thank God, that I do not yet live under a Tyranny, nor an Inquisition: that I have thus long enjoyed Independency, Freedom of Body & Mind, have told the world of my Opinions, even on the highest subjects, & of the Greatest Men, pretty freely;[2] that good men have not been ashamed of me; and that my Works have not dy'd before me (which is the Case of most Authors) and if they die soon after, I shall probably not know it, or certainly not be concern'd at it, in the next world.

The greatest, & I think the most rational pleasure I could enjoy, would be in a nearer Intercourse with one or two, whom Fortune keeps at distance, from me & from their Country. To the few who deserve their Care, I apply in their absence, and find most satisfaction in seeing they know your merit & Importance, and never forget to talk of it. You would feel some Emotion, if I namd their names, & wish at least (as we all do) that your Private affairs were so well setled, as to admit your bidding a lasting adieu to Scotland. I hope your Lordship & another of my friends will fix here together: I mean him, who tho tost all his life by so many Whirls of Fortune, still possesses all in possessing himself;[3] is ever too great a mind not to be a Beneficent one; & must love his Country however she has used him. She cannot have

[1] The Hon. Alexander Hume, brother of the 3rd Earl, to whom Pope writes.

[2] At this point the editor of the *Marchmont Papers* (Sir G. H. Rose) gives in a footnote (ii. 260) a fantastic story, coming apparently from Lord Marchmont, of how a son of John Dennis sent word to Pope at Lord Bathurst's table that he was waiting for him in a lane near by with drawn sword. Lord Bathurst went out and bravely scared the son away. Is there any reason other than this anecdote to believe that Dennis ever had a son? There is reason surely to question such an anecdote.

[3] Lord Bolingbroke.—Rose.

usd him worse than she has herself, in the Choice of such servants as she has preferrd to him these twenty years. And he cannot but desire to do her the last Honours, if every Friend he loves is resolved to attend her, even to her Funeral, and will (I dare answer for him) join as sincere a Tear with them as any man.

What (after all) have I to say, my dear Lord? It is a pain to me to write what I must write if I write to you, for the same things are at both our hearts, & they are displeasing things. To tell you my real Respect is yet more painful, for this I cannot express, tho the other I can, and even to aim at expressing it, would displease your Modesty. Put it all then, I beg you, to the account of Friendship and be assurd I love as much as I esteem you. I should be happier if you came to Town before December, yet if you do not, I shall be the less unhappy, since I am to be at Bath these 2 months, or more. I will return the sooner whenever you come, but at least next spring let not the motto be in vain which I am putting over my Door at Twitnam, Libertati & Amicitiae.

Endorsements: 10 Oct. 1741 (twice).

POPE *to* MRS. RACKETT[1] [? *October* 1741]

Ushaw College

Dear Sister,—I thank you for yours kindly. I am pretty well & constantly at home for some time, expecting Mr Allen from Bath daily to stay here a week. Whenever I am in town, I see you. I've never been there since. Do not give Holms[2] any thing for the Venison: I always pay him. Pray now & then tell me how you do, & believe I am ever, & will be ever | Your affectionate Brother, | A. Pope.

My Love to my Cos. Harry.

Address: To | Mrs Racket.

*POPE *to* SLINGSBY BETHEL[3] [? 14 *October* 1741]

Arthur A. Houghton, Jr.

Wednesday, the 14.

I give you the trouble of this to desire you will pay to Mr Drummond the Banker at Charingcross the 1 small debt of Interest, to me, Mrs

[1] Elwin chose 1741 as the year for this letter. Pope doubtfully then expected Allen to stay a week, and he says nothing about returning to Bath with Allen. Possibly his sister knew all about that plan. Pope has been out of London for some weeks, and he has been getting venison (more than once?) from the Dowager Duchess of Marlborough. But almost any year after 1736 is possible for this letter.

[2] The Twickenham waterman. He presumably carried this note together with the venison.

[3] The date is doubtful, perhaps, but the 14th was a Wednesday in 1741, and at this suggested time Pope was anxious to have Miss Blount go to Bath (see Pope to G. Arbuthnot, 29 Oct. 1741). If she planned to leave for Bath on the 15th, the journey was cancelled. In other years when she did go to Bath, Pope was not in town the day before she left.

Blount being to go to Bath to morrow for some time. I hope you are in good health. I am always | Sir | Your most faith|full affectionate | Servant | A. Pope.

Address: To Mr. Slingsby Bethel | on | Towerhill. | London
Postmark: PENY POST PAYD TTH
Endorsement: A. Pope | to | hardy. [Endorsement in three (?) hands; 'hardy' is the postman's signature?]

POPE *to* SARAH, DUCHESS OF MARLBOROUGH[1]

[22 *October* 1741]

Blenheim

Thursday night.

Your Graces Remembrance is doubly kind: I am still at Twitnam, but my Friend[2] comes to morrow whom I expected yesterday, & we set out next day I believe. I shall leave this Place with true regrett; but as you said you likd it so well as to call here in my absence, I have deputed One to be ready to receive you, whose Company you own you like, & who I know likes yours, to such a degree that I doubt whether he can be Impartial enough to be your Historian? Mr Hook & his Daughter (I hope) will use my house while your Grace is at Wimbledon. You see what Artifices I use to be Remember'd by you.

POPE *to* GEORGE ARBUTHNOT[3]

[? 24 *October* 1741]

Facsimile, Maggs Bros. Cat. 480 (1926)

I write this by the first post that you may have your trouble over as soon as possible, and I have my mony as soon as possible. I must postpone answering your Sisters kind Letter till a little while hence: that I may see what she will do with this 100*l.* before I recommend or assist her in becoming Guardian to the Old Alderman's Treasure. Mr Allen & Mrs assure you of their hearty Services. I've been all day from home & have but this moment to write in. Adieu, with many thanks.

Saturday night

Your Ever faithfull & | affectionate Servant | A. Pope.

[1] The date is probable because Hooke is mentioned as Her Grace's 'historian'—and he was at work for the Duchess in 1741; and because the Thursday before Pope's departure to Bath must be the 22nd. He was in Bath by the 27th.

[2] Ralph Allen, who is to take Pope to Widcombe. See the letter following (to G. Arbuthnot).

[3] The date is fixed by the mention of Alderman Barber's bequest to Pope of £100, which came to Pope in this year, and by the fact that the Allens are at Twickenham. The original of this letter, sold by Samuel T. Freeman & Co., 23 Mar. 1936, has not been traced.

POPE *to* GEORGE ARBUTHNOT 29 *October* 1741

The Royal College of Surgeons of England

You will be so good as to accomodate matters between your Sister & me; (like a good Lawyer as you are, who would rather promote Peace than Discord). I promised to write to her, & I expect she shoud believe that my writing to you is the same thing, as what is done unto you is done unto her: & I have so true an Esteem for you both, that I care not which I show it most to. All I had to say to her was, how confident I am that she'l be glad to hear I am safe here, & not ill. And I verily believe the news is equally agreeable to you. And all I have to desire in return is the same News on both your parts.

Your Fellow Voyagers Mr & Mrs Allen send you a hundred good wishes, & theirs are such sincere ones, that few people either make or deserve such.

But what gave you the Casting weight in the balance, when I was debating to which of you I should write, was that which is generally the Casting & Prevailing Weight in all Balances, even that of Europe, Money. For I just receivd a Letter from Mrs Dufkin (Alderman Barbars Relique) that she was ready to pay me his Legacy if I would wait on her. This I can't now do, & have writ her word, that I would desire her to pay it you, & that you should give her my Receit. She lives in Queens Square where the Alderman livd, I suppose. But Mr Barber your Neighbour will direct you. I suppose what follows will be a sufficient discharge, but if not, I will send any other you shall order.

I told Mrs Arb.[1] that I would on no account print in the Miscellanies that Sermon at Edinburgh, & it may be proper you should tell Bathurst the same thing, for the reason you gave, which is a very good one. Pray let me hear from you & Mrs Arbuthnot both, & I'll write to both tho nothing I can say will tell you half the true affection I bear you both. Yours sincerely | A. Pope.

Oct. 29th 1741.

The moment you have receivd the 100*ll* give it your Sister, & let her go to Mrs Blount with it & take a Coach instantly for themselves & their Maids, & come down to Bath.

POPE *to* LYTTELTON 3 *November* 1741

Arthur A. Houghton, Jr.

Bath. Nov. 3d. 1741

I have lately receivd a Letter, in which are these words—Suffer not Mr Lyttelton to forget me.[2]—It made me reflect I am as unwilling

[1] Anne Arbuthnot, George's sister. The pamphlet, *A Sermon preached at the Mercat Cross of Edinburgh*, was reprinted in Arbuthnot's *Works* later, but not in the *Miscellanies*. See Pope to Bathurst, 15 Nov. 1741.

[2] Possibly from Lord Bolingbroke?

to be forgotten by you; tho I do not deserve so well to be rememberd, on any account, but that of an Early, a wellgrounded, and (let me add) a well-judg'd Esteem, of you. I do not ask what you are doing? I am sure it is all the Good you can do. I do not ask any thing but to know that you are well. I see no Uses to be drawn from the knowledge of any publick Events; I see most honest men melancholy, & that's enough to make me enquire no more. When I can do any thing either to assist, or not assisting to comfort them, I will; But I fear I live in vain, that is, must live only to myself. Yet I feel every day what the Puritans calld *out-goings* of my Soul, in the Concern I take for some of you; which upon my word is a warmer Sensation than any I feel in my own, and for my own, Being. Why are you a Courtier? why is Murray a lawyer? It may be well for Other people, but what is that to your own Enjoyment, to mine? I would have you both pass as *happy*, & as *Satisfied* a Life as I have done; You will both laugh at this, but I would have you know, had I been Tempted by Nature & Providence with the same Talents that he & you have, I would have done as you do. But if either of you ever become tired, or stupid, God send you my Quiet & my Resignation. I think I've nothing more to say, but to add with how full a heart I am | Dear Sir, Ever Yours. | A. Pope.

Pray let Mr West[1] know I am alive, & while I am alive, warmly His.

Address: To the Hon. George | Lyttelton Esq. in | Pall-Mall. | London.
Postmark: 4/NO
Stamped: BATH

LYTTELTON *to* POPE — *7 November* 1741

Hagley

I receiv'd your obliging Letter[2] with that pleasure, and pride I always feel in every mark of your Friendship. As much a Courtier as I am I have no higher Ambition than to Deserve your Esteem, and that of a few Honest Men more, among whom I desire you to tell Mr Allen I reckon Him, though he is so little in my way that I cannot cultivate his Friendship as I wish to do. I envy you the Quiet, and Happiness you enjoy at his House, where you are escaped from the Vice, the Folly, and the Noise of the World, almost as much as if you were Dead, and in the Region of pure and happy Spirits. What a different Scene am I forced to Act in! But I wont recall even your thoughts to

[1] Lyttelton's cousin, Gilbert (the poet).
[2] Of 3 Nov.

it: I will only tell you that I am Well, and that I have lately heard from Mr Warburton, who desires me to acquaint you that he has Dropt his Dispute with Dr Middleton as you advised him to do;[1] though he has convinced me he cou'd well have Maintaind it, if he had not loved Peace and Friendship better than Victory, which is a temper of mind so becoming in a Divine, and so rare in an Author, that I think you shou'd express your Approbation of it the first time you Write to him. If the Person, who bid you *not suffer me to Forget him* was Lord Bol: I beg you wou'd say in your Answer that I gave a Letter two months ago to Mr Brindsden to be conveyd to him, which by those words to you I shou'd apprehend he has not receiv'd: If you add that I always remember his Lordship with the highest Veneration, and kindest Regard, you will do me but Justice. I wish he was in England upon many accounts, but for nothing more than to Exhort and Animate You not to bury your excellent Talents in a Philosophical Indolence, but to Employ them, as you have so often done, in the Service of Virtue. The Corruption, and Hardness of the present Age is no Excuse; for your Writings will Last to Ages to come, and may do Good a thousand years hence, if they can't now; but I beleive they wou'd be of great Present Benefit; some sparks of Publick Virtue are yet Alive, which such a Spirit as Your's might blow into a flame, among the Young men especially; and even granting an impossibility of Reforming the Publick, your Writings may be of Use to private Society; The Moral Song may steal into our Hearts, and teach us to be as good Sons, as good Friends, as Beneficent, as Charitable as Mr Pope, and sure *That* will be Serving your Country, though you cant Raise her up such Ministers, or such Senators as you desire. In short; my dear Friend, though I am far from supposing that if you don't write, you *Live in Vain*; though the Influence of your Virtues is felt among all your Friends, and Acquaintance, and the whole circle of Society within which you Live, yet as your Writings will have a still more extensive and permanent Influence, as they will be an Honour to your Country at a time when it has hardly anything else to be proud of, and may do Good to Mankind in better Ages and Countries, if not in This, I wou'd have you Write till a Decay of your Parts, or at least Weakness of Health shall Oblige, and Authorise you to lay down your Pen. But though in my Zeal for your Glory I tell you this, I shall Love, and Esteem you just as well whether you Mind it, or not: I have long since forgot the Author in the Companion and Friend, and though I shall read whatever you Write with a great deal of pleasure, and feel a sort of pride for you in hearing it prais'd, I had

[1] Among the Hagley MSS. is a letter from Warburton to Lyttelton, 22 Oct. 1741, which confirms this. Middleton's *Life of Cicero* was the point at issue: ideas in it differed from those of *The Divine Legation*.

rather you shoud tell me, as you do, in your last Letter, that you are *Happy, and Satisfied*, than be told, you had writt the finest Thing in the World. I was last night at West's, he, and his Wife are much Your's. I wish I cou'd write to you longer, for I feel those same *Outgoings of the Soul* which you speak of very strong in me now, and shou'd like to prate to you through a page or two more; but here are people breaking in upon me, so I can only assure you I am most sincerely | Dear Sir | Your very Affectionate | Humble Servant | G Lyttelton.

London Novemr the 7th | 1741

POPE *to* WARBURTON[1] 12 *November 1741*

Egerton 1946

Bath. Nov. 12. 1741.

I am always naturally sparing of my Letters to my Friends, for a reason I think a great one; that it is needless, after Experience, to repeat Assurances of Friendship and no less irksome to be Searching for Words, to express it over & over. But I have more Calls than one for this Letter. First to express a Satisfaction at your Resolution not to keep up the Ball of dispute with Dr Middleton, tho I am satisfied you could have done it: and to tell you that Mr Lyttelton is pleased at it too, who writes me word upon this occasion that he must infinitely Esteem a *Divine* and an *Author* who loves Peace better than Victory. Secondly I am to recommend to you, as an Author, a Bookseller in the room of the honest one you have lost, Mr Gyles;[2] and I know none who is so worthy, & has so good a title in that Character to succeed him, as Mr Knapton. But my Third Motive of now troubling you is my own proper Interest and Pleasure: I am here in more Leisure than I can possibly enjoy even in my own house, *Vacare Literis*. It is at this place that Your Exhortations may be most effectual to make me resume the Studies I have almost laid aside by perpetual Avocations & Dissipations. If it were practicable for you to pass a Month or six weeks from home, it is here I could wish to be with you, and if you would attend to the continuation of your own Noble Work, or unbend to the idle Amusement of commenting upon a Poet, who has no other Merit than that of aiming by his Moral Strokes to merit some Regard from such men as advance Truth & Virtue in a more Effectual way; In either case This Place & This House would be an Inviolable Asylum to you from all you would desire to avoid in so public a Scene

[1] Printed by Warburton in 1751. He omitted the postscript and clipped some proper names to their initials.

[2] Warburton's bookseller, Fletcher Gyles, died on 8 Nov. His son had died the preceding year.

as Bath. The worthy Man who is the Master of it invites you in the strongest terms, & is one, who would treat you with Love and Veneration, rather than what the World calls Civility and Regard. He is sincerer and Plainer than almost any Man now in this world, Antiquis Moribus. If the Waters of the Bath may be Serviceable to your Complaints, (as I believe from what you have told me of them) no Opportunity can ever be better. It is just the best Season. We are told the Bishop of Salisbury[1] is expected here daily, who I know is your Friend; at least, tho a Bishop, is too much a Man of Learning to be your Enemy. You see I omit nothing to add to the Weight in the balance, in which however I will not think myself light, since I have known your Partiality. You'l want no Servant here, your Room will be next to mine, and one Man will serve us. Here is a Library, and a Gallery ninety foot long to walk in & a Coach whenever you would take the air with me.

Mr Allen tells me you might on Horseback be here in three days, it is less than 100 miles from Newark, the road thro Leicester, Stow in the Wolde in Glostershire, and Cirencester, by Lord Bathursts. I could ingage to carry you to London from hence, and I would accomodate my Time, and Journey, to your Conveniency.

Is all this a Dream? or can you make it a reality? can you give ear to me?

Audisti? an me ludit amabilis
Insania?[2]

Dear Sir adieu, and give me a line to Mr Allen's at Bath. God preserve you ever. I am | Yours faithfully | A. Pope.

Mr Allens house (where I am, & hope you may be) is less than 2 miles from Bath, but his Brother the Postmaster lives at Bath, and takes care of the Letters to me.

POPE *to* CHARLES BATHURST 15 *November* [1741]

The Gentleman's Magazine, xliv, N.S. (1855), 587

Novr. 15, Sunday.

Sir,—I write this very post because I hate to keep any one in any sort of suspense. I should be willing to serve you, but cannot in this instance. Probably Mr Gyles's Family continue the business; in which case Mr W would favor them. But otherwise he told me formerly he liked Mr Knapton[3] so well that I believe he would naturally succeed;

[1] Thomas Sherlock. See *DNB*.

[2] Horace, *Carmina*, III. iv. 5–6.

[3] Both Bathurst and Knapton had served as Pope's booksellers. It is obvious from his letter to Warburton of 12 Nov. that at this time he preferred Knapton.

and indeed I encouraged it lately by mentioning him at his request previous to yours. I know you are a reasonable man enough to think I could not do otherwise than favor Mr Knapton herein: as I would yourself in the like situation; who am, Sir, | Your affectionate humble servant, | A. Pope.

Mr Arbuthnot will not have the sermon at the Cross at Edinburgh printed in the Miscellanies,[1] intending a General Edition of all his Father's Political and Physical Works.

*POPE *to* CHARLES BRINSDEN[2] — 20 *November* 1741

Sotheby's Catalogue, 28 Nov. 1913; lot 355, item 12.

FRAGMENT

. . I find my Lord B[olingbroke] is extremely alarmed at the last account he had of your father. I would have come to see him this day, but must be satisfied to hear he is so much better (as they tell me he is), etc.

POPE *to* WILLIAM CHESELDEN[3] — 21 *November* [? 1741]

1886 (*The Autographic Mirror*, iv, 108) (Facsimile)

You know my Laconic Style. I never forget you. Are you well? I am so. How does Mrs Cheselden? Had it not been for her, you had been here. Here are three Cataracts ripened for you—Mr Pierce[4] assures me. Don't tell your Wife that.

Adieu. I don't intend to go to London. Good night, but answer me. | Yours | A. Pope.

Show this to Mr Richardson and let him take it to Himself—and to his Son—he has no Wife.[5]

Bath, Novr 21st

[1] See Pope to G. Arbuthnot, 29 Oct. 1741.

[2] The Rev. Charles Brinsden of Rathbone Place was the son of John Brinsden, Bolingbroke's long-time agent. John was during this winter very ill at Bath. Letters to Bolingbroke were forwarded to the Continent through Brinsden. The complete letter has not been traced. The date comes from the sale catalogue.

[3] Elwin suggested 1739 or 1740 for this letter, but in 1739 Pope was probably in Bristol, and in 1740 he did not arrive at Bath until December. Nov. 1741 seems to fit. In Oct. 1741 he had been in touch with Cheselden.

[4] Jeremiah Pierce had been appointed surgeon at Bath Hospital in 1740. Cheselden, of course, was the most skilful optical surgeon of his day.

[5] Jonathan Richardson, whose wife died in 1725, was not subject to a wife's dictation, as Pope implies Cheselden was.

POPE *to* WARBURTON[1] 22 *November* 1741

Egerton 1946

Nov. 22d 1741

Yours is very full, and very kind. it is a friendly and satisfactory answer, & all I can desire. Do but instantly fulfill it—only I hope this will find you before you set out, for I think (on all Considerations) your best way will be to take London in the Way. It will secure you from accidents of Weather to travel in the Coach, both thither, and from thence hither. But in particular I think you should take some care as to Mr G⌜yles⌝'s Executors. and I am of Opinion no man will be more Serviceable in setling any such accounts, than Mr Knapton, who so well knows the trade & is of so acknowledgd a Credit in it. ⌜I ought to have told you when I wrote, that He did not desire to be imployed in your Books, if Mr Gyles's children carried on the business to your satisfaction: which is a piece of Honourable Dealing, not common to all Booksellers.⌝ If you can stay but a few days there, I should be glad, tho I would not have you omit any necessary thing to your self: I wish too you would just see ⌜Lord Chesterfield, Mr Lytt. &c.⌝ tho' when you have past a month here, it will be time enough for all we have to do in town, & they will be less busy, probably, than just before the Sessions opens, to think of Men of Letters.

When you *are* in London, I beg a line from you, in which pray tell us what day you shall arrive at Bath by the Coach? that we may send to meet you & bring you hither. ⌜Be pleasd to go, when you arrive, to the Post Master's house in Bath, where you shall find a Coach: and your Chamber here ready aired &c. with all possible care.⌝ You will owe me a real Obligation by being made acquainted with the Master of this House;[2] and by sharing with me, what I think one of the chief Satisfactions of my Life, His Friendship. But whether I shall owe you any in contributing to make me a Scribler again, I know not⌜; for what I have done, I don't like. I am, with truth | Dear Sir | Yours faithfully | A. Pope⌝.

Pray bring with you (if not too burdensome) the Strictures upon my papers, which you sufferd yourself to be troubled with. They may make a winter Evenings amusement, when you have nothing better.

Address: To | The Revd Mr Warburton | in Newark
Frank: ffree R. Allen

[1] Printed in 1751 by Warburton with omissions here placed in half-brackets.
[2] A prophetic remark: Warburton made his fortune by marrying Allen's niece.

*POPE *to* [JONATHAN RICHARDSON][1] [1 *December* 1741]

Haverford College

I had not certainly been so long without Enquiring of you, but that I've been ill from day to day, & hoped still to go to see you the next. I had orderd the coach to day, but am really too much out of order. I beg to know particularly how you go on? No man sincerely more heartily wishes your full Recovery. Ive sent the continuation of the Papers, with my Services to your Son. I am | Yours Entirely | A Pope.

They begin just where he left off.

Tuesday.

Endorsement: A. Pope Esqr Decr 2. 1741.

POPE *to* DR. OLIVER [? *Late* 1741]

Sotheby's sale of 28 Nov. 1913

[A letter, untraced, was sold at Sotheby's on the date indicated. It was dated 'Sunday night', and its contents are summarized by the sale catalogue (item 19 of lot 355): 'Pope wishes he could spend more time with Oliver but his infirmities confine him too much; mentions Warburton, who has been ill.' If the three men were at the time of writing all at Bath, the letter must date from the winter of 1741–2.]

[1] One hesitates to place this letter according to its endorsement. On the date specified Pope was in Bath. Richardson may also have been there: we do not know. But it seems strange that in Bath Pope should have his MSS. to send to the younger Richardson, who before 1741 had begun to collate the MS. readings of Pope's poems. Endorsements made a year or more after receipt of a letter easily err. 'Tuesday' would be 1 Dec. 1741.

1742

Early in January of this year Pope and Warburton returned from a long winter visit to Ralph Allen, and presently plans for going back to Prior Park in the late summer were being made. Warburton went thither from London with Allen in August, but Pope's entanglements with the difficult Dowager Duchess of Marlborough and her 'prisoner', Hooke, kept him near her until some time in October, after which he went to Bath for about six weeks. The death of his Twickenham landlady stimulated vague talk of his settling at Widcombe with Allen (while Martha Blount might settle at Hampton Manor)—but all this was mere talk. Upon returning in January to London both Warburton and Pope had been plunged in legal difficulties with publishers. Lintot's attitude with regard to the *Iliad* and to the copyright of *The Dunciad* was becoming increasingly vexatious, and in October Jacob Ilive pirated the fourth book of *The Dunciad.* When Pope returned from Allen's at the end of November, he took lodgings in London in order to be more available for counsel on these publishing worries. His literary labours in 1742 concerned the final revision of *The Dunciad,* and the preparation of a definitive edition of his works, with commentary by Warburton. At times we find him depressed by the policies of Walpole's successors or exasperated by the unhappy Richard Savage. Bolingbroke returned for a month or six weeks in May and June, but only to settle his father's estate.

*POPE *to* HUGH BETHEL — 1 *January* [1741/2]

Egerton 1948

Bath, Jan. 1st

I thought it long before I heard from your Self of the State of your health, but I was much obliged to Col. Pierson who told me constantly whenever he had any account from Mrs Moyzer, & to Dr Kaye who wrote me letters when he receivd any news of you: I had also some account from your good Brother. Having past a long time at Bath, (where Mr Pierson[1] also was, & is just now gone) I have several times seen your Sisters, who are tolerably well & send you very hearty wishes. I was therfore obliged to write to Dr Mead, not being easy in re-[t]arding to enquire of what you askd, whose reply is, That considering the long Time that your Distemper has attended you it cannot be expected that you should in a very short time find all the Benefit you may hope for from the Climate you are in. He believes it will be right for you to remove to the Solfoterra, during the Extreme cold months,

[1] Possibly the Col. Richard Pierson who died at York 3 January 1742/3.—*Gent. Mag.* xiii (1743), 51.

and to be again at Naples, (that is, out of the Town, about the *Caiae*) in the Spring, and Summer. He does not think that place (Naples) will be too hot even in the Summer: and tho' he understood you proposed to stay abroad only one year, yet, if you find benefit, he would advise you to spend two in so healthfull & pleasant a Country. These are his words.

I heard from Mr Pierson that yourself & Col. Moyser had a thought of returning next Autumn by the way of Lisbon, and so to winter there. This the Doctor does not disapprove, but would not have you leave Naples, if you find it agree with you, for any other place; at least unless you added that other Winter to the full Year there. I am in pain since I receivd yours in which I had but an unsatisfactory account of your present State, tho no bad one of your past. I beg as soon as possible to be ascertained further, and I would fain hope, that when you last wrote it was too soon to conclude (as you seemd to do) that the Air of Naples was not so favorable as we hoped: You had been there but a few days, & possibly some Cold taken on the Journey before you arrived, might then show itself; for I can't imagine the Illness you felt the very day after you got to Naples could be owing to it. Travelling in general has agreed with you, & given you Strength; & I hope little Excursions to & from Naples & the Country about it, as soon as the weather is tolerable, will do the same, & increase it. I am told Mr Moyser has quite recover'd; and no News from any Part of Europe, at home or abroad, will be so welcome to me as that you have the same benefit.

I have little worth relating to send you, I have livd without any Correspondence here, except Mrs Blount's, whose Letters have spoken more about you than anything else. But you'l have heard that the New Parliament has open'd with a Change of the Minority into the Majority in three very important and hard-fought Points; they have carryd their Chairman of the Comittee of Elections against the Court, and invalidated the Westminster Election; with a strong additional Vote, against all Appearance Whatsoever of any Military Forces at any Election. Some Application, it is said, has been made on the Ministerial part to the Prince, but without effect. Both sides are too busy, to allow almost any to keep this Christmass out of town.[1] It will probably be employd much otherwise than in Devotion, tho not without great Donatives to the poor of Scotland, & the Poor in Spirit all over this poor Kingdom—Our Winter is dreadfully sharp, & the Cattle starving for want of Fodder. No Clothes are sufficient to keep me so warm, as you & I us'd to be at each side of a Fire at this Season, and I think of you every Blast I feel. God send we may meet again, in

[1] The new Parliament met on 1 Dec. 1741, and the actions here mentioned followed within three weeks. Walpole resigned 11 Feb. Pope must have regretted being away from this final fray!

as comfortable a situation as our own Country can afford us; which (had you but the health I have) were enough to content reasonable Minds. I do not think we need Envy them (as yet) either their Government, or their Learning. I even doubt if they are so good Gardeners as we. I thank you for your remembring me in that capacity, but the *Torja* you mention, I have had, & don't think so good either as a Turnip or as Brocoli: (the fate common to most that pretend to be good for more than one thing.)

One of my amusements has been writing a Poem, part of which is to abuse *Travelling*.[1] You have made me have a quarrel to it even when it was for a good Reason, & (I hope) will be attended with a good Effect; which it rarely is in the Cases I have satyrised it for. I little thought 3 months ago to have drawn the whole polite world upon me, (as I formerly did the Dunces of a lower Species) as I certainly shall whenever I publish this poem. An Army of Virtuosi, Medalists, Ciceronis, Royal Society-men, Schools, Universities, even Florists, Free thinkers, & Free masons, will incompass me with fury: It will be once more, *Concurrere Bellum atque Virum*. But a Good Conscience a bold Spirit, & Zeal for Truth, at whatsoever Expence, of whatever Pretenders to Science, or of all Imposition either Literary, Moral, or Political; these animated me, & these will Support me.[2]

You mention the Fame of my old Acquaintance Lady Mary as spread over Italy. Neither you delight in telling, nor I in hearing, the Particulars which acquire such a Reputation; yet I wish you had just told me, if the Character be more *Avaricious*, or *Amatory*? and which Passion has got the better at last?[3]

This Letter will pass thru Mrs. B.'s[4] hands, who undertook to transmit it to your Brother, as I have no better direction to you, and am at this distance from him. She bid me say all I could put into a Line or two, of her Sincere & Earnest prayers for your Wellbeing. I need not, for you cannot but know her—Poor Cleland! I shall never forgive Sir Robert.[5] Why is he always singling out my Friends to do hurt to? In my conscience if he had known 'em, he had made them more his friends than his Way of Thinking allows him to believe, and he has painted some of 'em more formidable than they were, upon the

1 *The New Dunciad*, published 20 Mar. 1741/2.

2 This whole paragraph was quoted by Ruffhead, pp. 388–9 n.

3 This paragraph is quoted by Ruffhead, pp. 315–16 n.

4 Mrs. Blount (Martha).

5 Cleland died 21 Sept. 1741. Soon thereafter Pope must have written the note appended in the quarto *Dunciad* of 1743 to the 'Letter to the Publisher' (signed by Cleland). Here Pope records Cleland's early military service in Spain, and says: 'After the Peace, he was made one of the Commissioners of the Customs in Scotland, and then of Taxes in England, in which having shewn himself twenty years diligent, punctual, and incorruptible, though without any other assistance of Fortune, he was suddenly displaced by the Minister in the sixty-eighth year of his age, and died two months after.' See the Twickenham *Dunciad* (ed. Sutherland), pp. 19–20.

supposition they were not so. Unless (what indeed in Clelands case might be more probable, as he was so much below his fearing him) he be too Credulous to Informers. For you & I certainly know, that C. had been much softned, & temperate in his Speeches as to Party, of late years. So much, that he had been suspected by the other party; & tho it was a Severe, yet it was an honorable Justification of him, to lose his bread in proof of the contrary. Since he was to dye so soon, I am glad he was thus justified; that if he was hurt by Scoundrels who wanted his place or wanted to shew their Zeal to get some other, he was raised & preserved in the Opinion of Better Men. His having a few weeks before his death received at one post three Letters, from each of his children, from different Ends almost of the Earth, with the News that two of them were upon the way to see him; is as extraordinary an Event as I ever heard of. He accordingly lived to receive his Eldest Son with great Satisfaction, & so be pretty easy as to the other two. I hear that this Son behaves himself very kindly to his Mother & is in a capacity of assisting her: I fancy she will remove to live in France.—I wish I knew what sort of News from hence would be most agreable to you, and it would be a serious pleasure to me to send you Notices of that sort. My own health is much as usual, less Headake, bad Eyes, and Flatulencies. Excessive Regularity in dining & going to Bed seems to be the only means to make the Decline of my Life easy in any degree, & I find this almost incompatible with living in London. You can't imagine how often I wish myself with you, were there a Way of travelling without stirring, and one or two people I could waft along with me thro the Air, one of which you will guess. Adieu my dear Friend. May God preserve you to us again, & restore you entirely. Let Mr Moyzer be assured I join you together in my best Wishes. And pray let not your Letters be unfrequent; I cannot see a Line from you without more Satisfaction than I can express, except it was to bring me ill news of you: and even then I should take it kindly, tho I should feel it deeply: For indeed my Esteem for you is lasting, & the affection built upon it constant, & unalterable. | Yours faithfully, | A. Pope

Address: To Mr Bethel | at Mr Allen's, Consul | at | Naples.
Endorsement: @ 13 Febr 1742

*POPE *to* ALLEN[1] [6 *January* 1741/2]

Egerton 1947

Wensday night

We are got safely to Abery thro the Snow, and hope to do so to morrow

[1] From Avebury Pope writes of the safe arrival of Warburton and himself on their winter

to Newberry. The appearance lookd a little frightful at first, but the Strength & Vigor we received from Tongue & chicken & a huge fire (tho not equal to a Widcomb Fire) has recruited us to undertake a new Expedition over the Alps of Snow. We have nothing further (yet) to add, but the assurance of our mutual Satisfaction at all the Good we have receivd at your hands these 2 months past, & the Memory of it which will be pleasing to us for some months to come. God preserve you both & so adieu.

Address: To Ralph Allen Esq. | at the Post Office in | Bath
Stamped: H J

*POPE *to* ALLEN[1] [9 *January* 1741/2]

Egerton 1947

I am happy in being able to relieve you from the Trouble which I believe the Bad weather gave you for our sakes; for I can now tell you, We are arrived perfectly safe and perfectly well, and as full as you can desire, of the Friendly Sense of all your hearty Kindness. I hope you was not long in pain for us, for I sent you a line from Avery. But the next day's Snow between that place and Marlborough was a little frightfull, with the thick fog that attended it. I go to London to morrow morning,[2] having a new Summons of haste from Mr Hooke whose Son is here Express, and leaves me scarce a Moment to write this to dispatch Joseph, who is in haste too. Pray let us soon hear of you. May you & Mrs Allen be as happy as Fortune can make you, and as Virtue can make you! is the sincere prayer of your faithfull Friends, | A. Pope, | W. Warburton

Saturday night.

Address: To | Mr Allen.

*POPE *to* WARBURTON[3] [? *January* 1741/2]

Egerton 1946

Pray let the inclosed be altred as directed, & it will do. but either the

journey back to Twickenham from Widcombe. Later letters make the 6th practically certain as the 'Wensday' of this letter.

1 Pope writes from Twickenham after the journey through this unusually cold winter weather. The reasons for venturing were possibly political excitement and possibly Warburton's troubles with Gyles's executor, Mawhood. Mr. Hooke's son also comes into the picture. Joseph the coachman (?) will take this letter back to Allen. The letter is in Pope's hand, but both travellers sign it.

2 Frequent journeys to London wearied Pope. See his letter of 19 Jan. to Sarah, Duchess of Marlborough.

3 This and the succeeding three Letters are very difficult to date. They must be written when both Pope and Warburton are in London, and when also Lord Orrery, Dr. King, Richardson, Murray, and others are there. In 1740 Lord Orrery was in Ireland, and in 1741

Verses must be set closer, or a Letter one size less made use of for the Text. I wish I had it agen to night, with this proof.[1]

Pray send me word (if you shall not be ingaged to morrow dinner about 3.) whether you like to dine then with Lord Orrery & me & I'll indeavor to day to appoint him. But let not your own business be put off on any account. Do but favor me with a line any night to Mr Murrays, & I'll be any where you please, if I can any way be of use to you.

I am most truly Dear Sir Yours.

Address: To the Revd Mr Warburton | at Mrs Johnson's in | Warwick Court.

*POPE *to* WARBURTON[2] [? *January* 1741/2]

Egerton 1946

Tuesday night

Pray dine to morrow with me and Dr King at Lord Orrery's. If you can pass an hour or 2 at Mr Murrays this Evening, I'll come home[3] by 7. pray send me word now, for I'm forc'd to go out just this moment. and can say no more

Address: To | Alexander | at the Honble

*POPE *to* WARBURTON [? *January* 1741/2]

Egerton 1946

Lord Orrery dines at 3, he lives in Dukestreet Westminster but if you please I will call on you at Dodsley the Booksellers at half an hour past 2, & go together.

If you are at leisure to breakfast at the Celebrated Mr Richardson's in Queens Square Bloomsbury, I am to be there before ten, but obligd to go thence at 11. | Yours

*POPE *to* WARBURTON [? 1741/2]

Egerton 1946

I am returned, to know the Event of your Affair,[4] without which indeed I could not sleep in peace. Pray send me word what you've

Dr. King seems to have been in Oxford during the visits of Warburton to town. In January and February of 1742 Orrery was in town, not well, but doubtless well enough to dine occasionally. He wrote to Miss Caesar from Duke Street on 25 Feb. about his ill health there for the past two months. See Orrery Letterbooks, iv. 39, at Harvard.

[1] The first paragraph perhaps refers to the projected new edition of Warburton's *Commentary* on the *Essay on Man*, which appeared in the spring of this year.

[2] Written on the back of a letter received by Pope, as the torn address shows.

[3] At the time of supposed writing, 'home' was Murray's house in Lincoln's Inn Fields.

[4] Presumably the affair is that concerning the settlement of Warburton's accounts with the Gyles estate—through the executor, Collet Mawhood.

done, by a line to Mr Murray's to night, or let me see you to morrow as early as you can. Mr Hook has a mind to meet you, if you can pass an hour or 2 to morrow afternoon, at Mr Murray's about 7. If this Messenger finds you, pray write a Line.

Tuesday 4 a clock.

Address: To Mr Warburton at | Mrs Johnson's in Warwick | Court against Chancery Lane End [in] Holborne

POPE *to* SARAH, DUCHESS OF MARLBOROUGH[1]

18 *January* [1741/2]

Blenheim

London. Jan. 18th

It has been, and still is, a thing of great Concern to me, to find your Grace still unwilling, (I would rather Say than unable) to come nearer us, & that you will not suffer me to come nearer You. Had you sent away Sir Timothy, only, to re-call another, it had been but a natural Change in a Lady (who knows her Power over her Slaves; & that how long soever she has rejected or banish'd any one, she is sure always to recover him) But to use me thus—to have won me with some difficulty, to have bow'd down all my Pride, & reduced me to take That at your hands which I never took at any other;[2] and as soon as you had done this, to slight your Conquest, & cast me away with the common Lumber of Friends in this Town—What a Girl you are?[3] —I have a mind to be reveng'd of you, and will attribute it to your own finding yourself to want those Qualities, which are necessary to keep a Conquest, when you have made one, & are only the Effects of Years & Wisdome.—Well, if you think so ill of yourself, leave me off. I could indeed have endured all your Weaknesses & Infirmities, but this. I could have been happy in contributing any way, tho but for an hour in a day, to your Amusement, and have gone to sleep all the rest; (unless Dr Stephens would have been so idle to leave his other Anatomies for my Company, now & then.)

But to be more reasonable in my demands, I beg at least, if your Grace do not speedily return,[4] to know if you intend to stay for any

[1] Elwin placed this letter in 1743, but it seems related to the next letter, that of the 19th, and so must fall in 1742. When in the epistolary mood Pope frequently writes several letters on almost successive days.

[2] The remark is perhaps needlessly puzzling. The least probable interpretation is that it refers to a present of money which Pope has taken from Her Grace. More probable is the assumption that it continues the facetious account of a submission by Pope to Her Grace that has been followed by a rebuff. In this case 'take' is a synonym of 'suffer' in the first sentence.

[3] A striking example of Pope's highly individual use of the mark of interrogation, which indicates for him vague amazement or wonder, a dissolved sort of exclamation.

[4] Return, that is, to the country. The Duchess is ill (or has been) at Marlborough House.

time? Or at all events, to be informed more satisfactorily than I can from your Porter, of the true State of your health. I shall only add, I sincerely wish it better than my own, and You younger than I, that the Tables may be turn'd, & I leave You a Legacy at my death.[1] If I had thoughts of Casting You off, I would give it you now in my Life time, and so bid you farewell: But God forbid your Grace should ever meet with such usage, from | Your faithfull Servant | A. Pope.

Endorsement: 18th Janry | Mr Popes letter to | The Dutchess of Marlbro'

POPE *to* SARAH, DUCHESS OF MARLBOROUGH

19 *January* [1741/2]

Blenheim

Twitnam. Jan. 19.

Madam,—I said nothing to your Grace of Patriots,[2] & God forbid I should. If I did, I must do as they do, & Lye: for I have seen none of 'em, not even their Great Leader,[3] nor once congratulated any one Friend or Foe, upon his Promotion, or New Reveal'd Religion, or Regeth ration,[4] call it which you will; or by the more distinct & intelligible Name, his new Place or Pension. I'm so sick of London, in her present State, that in 2 or 3 days I constantly return hither. I shall stay no longer there till you come; & then I promise you a Day or two more, whenever you demand them. I truly am concerned at the account of your Uneasy ailments. all I wish either my Friends or myself, is more Ease, not more Money; which I think, beyond a certain point, ruins all Ease. and makes people either Poor, or Mad: *Both* which I take to be the Case of the Ignoble Earl you mention.[5] I fear what your Grace has heard about him is not true; but it would be Exemplary, and a useful Lesson to the World, if it could but be litigated.

I can assure you, You are not only as well with Sir Timothy[6] as possible, but his heart is uneasy in the fear he is not so with you; nay he is almost suspicious that I am better with you; & is as jealous as the Devil, at my writing to you. His Heart is so good, and his Spirits so

[1] Pope predeceased the Duchess and any legacy that she may have intended was cancelled by a will made after his death. That in 1742 he was in her will may be the origin of the story that she gave him a thousand pounds: a story for which the inventory of his estate at the time of his death gives no warrant.

[2] In his letter of yesterday Pope said nothing of Patriots, but his remarks here sufficiently place the letter in 1742.

[3] Walpole had not yet resigned, but the 'great leader' (Pulteney) was evidently prematurely 'counting his chickens'—or at least Pope is doing it for him, ironically.

[4] So written; possibly jocosely, possibly for 'regeneration'.

[5] Just which earl the Duchess at this moment regarded as ignoble is not clear. Very likely she is thinking of Wilmington.

[6] Sir Timothy is not identified. Can the appellation be a cipher name for Hooke?

low, that he deserves double Indulgence; and I really wish you would show him, you are as Good to him as you are; for any distinction of that kind would make him happy. For my own part, I desire no greater pleasure than to meet again all together, & see your Grace well enough to enjoy the Conversation, without one Kn. or Fool to vex you, either within or without your doors.

Address: To her Grace the | D. of Marlborough

*POPE *to* ALLEN 19 *January* [1741/2]

Egerton 1947

Mr Murrays in | Lincolns Inn fields.
Jan. 19.

I have the pleasure to tell You that Mr Hook's affair[1] is setled, & nothing wanting but Signing a paper, which I hope will make him easy for Life. As to Mr Warburton's,[2] it meets with more difficulty, for notwithstanding his Generosity of offering half the Clear profits to Mr Gyles heirs for nothing (for they have actually made already, besides all charges paid, twenty per Cent; so that every shilling he gives is an absolute Present) they scruple to take it, are willing to suppose the Whole their own, & hesitate upon paying *any*, on one pretence, that one of the Daughters is not of age, & the Executor makes a doubt if he can pay *Safely* before? I have got Mr Murray to advise him in all his Steps, but I fear this troublesome matter may detain him here very greatly to his Inconveniency, if not ingage him in a Chancery Suit.

I need not tell you his Sense of your Hospitality, and Friendship shown him; Men of his Turn are always most Sensible, & the Generosity he really has in his Nature, (which I first experienced by his Espousing the Cause of a Man he was wholly a Stranger to, because he thought it a good one, & since perceive in every other Instance of his Conduct to every one he has to deal with) This I say gives me the strongest assurance that in giving you his Acquaintance, I gave you a valuable thing: Your own Worth gave You his Esteem, & your Behavior his Affection, so that I take no part of That Merit.

I have nothing to tell you of Public Affairs: I never (I think) in my life was guilty of one Letter upon those subjects, tho no man wishes

[1] Mr. Hooke's affair is his financial settlement for his labours for the Dowager Duchess of Marlborough. His *Account of the Conduct of the Dowager Duchess of Marlborough* is dated at the end, '20 Jan. 1741/2'. It was published in Mar. 1742. See also Pope to Allen, 8 Feb. 1741/2.

[2] Warburton's publisher, Fletcher Gyles, has died, and his troubles are with Mawhood the executor. They are explained more fully by Warburton in a letter published in Nichols's *Illustrations*, ii. 830–1. Pope's sudden return to town may be due to a desire to help. Possibly the executor, Collet Mawhood, was a second cousin of Pope's, but Pope indicates nowhere a relationship to this Mawhood. See *Notes & Queries*, 2 Jan. 1858.

the Public better. But I find all those that seem to design it best, better contented than ever.

Ten thousand Sincere Thanks, Wishes, & Prayers for your own & Mrs Allen's health & Felicity you always have from your faithfull Friend | A. Pope.

Address: To | Ralph Allen Esqr at | Widcomb, near | Bath.
Postmark: 19/IA
Stamped (faintly): CI

*POPE *to* JOHN BRINSDEN[1] — 21 *January* [1741/2]

The Universal Magazine, ix (1808), 31

London, Jan. 21, 1741.

It is impossible for me to tell you how warmly I wish your amendment and Recovery; and how anxious I have been, and am when I am under any Incertainty of your Condition, while it continues so doubtful. It was a Concern to me not to See you the day before I left Bath, tho I should have felt Pain in taking leave of you. I thank your Son for your Letter he sent me, which gives me more and more hopes. I beg to hear weekly at least how you advance. Every one who knows you shews great Interest in your Welfare, and solicitude for it. It will be a kindness to them all to give me the opportunity of telling them any good news of you. Dear Sir, be assured I desire nothing so much, and that no man can be more your faithful or with more esteem | Ever affectionate Servant, | A. Pope.

Address: To John Brinsden, Esq. at Mr Cle-|land's in Bath.

*POPE *to* [? WARBURTON][2] — [1742]

Arthur A. Houghton, Jr.

I shall be obliged to Mr Warburton, if he would read over the Preface & Life of Homer; and if he finds some Objections to any part (as I think he may, especially in the Life) to communicate them to me to be amended: there being a new Edition preparing, in which I would alter any Errors I can.

[1] This letter was kindly transcribed by the late Norman Ault. It is addressed to the ailing Brinsden, who is at the house of Archibald Cleland, the surgeon in Bath. See the letter to Allen of 12 June [1742].

[2] This memorandum was probably sent to Knapton to be turned over to Warburton, while he was yet in London. There was, so Professor Maynard Mack informs the editor, an edition of the *Iliad* in 1743.

*POPE *to* WARBURTON[1] [1742]

Egerton 1946

Pray give me a Line what you have done with Mawhood? by any Porter, & do so much as breakfast with Mr Arbuthnot, where I will meet you, if possible, tho I am extremely taken up all day.

Address: To Mr Warburton.

*POPE *to* WARBURTON[2] [? 1742]

Egerton 1946

I will be at Mr Arbuthnots in Castle yard to morrow by three or sooner, where I beg you will dine with me. [If] I am not come, pray walk in & ask for me. I am faithfully Yours | A. Pope

Sunday night

Address: To the Revd Mr Warburton | at Mr Bowyer a Printers | in | Whitefriers.

*POPE *to* WARBURTON [? 1742]

Egerton 1946

I shall be glad if you can come to Breakfast here.[3] and if you have any Visits to the other End of the Town, I can carry you thither. We were sorry you would not come in last night.

8 a clock

*POPE *to* WARBURTON [? 1742]

Egerton 1946

I came back, not to omit the most speedy confuting Mr. M.[4] upon your affair. I desire to see you, the sooner the better & perhaps you'l find him with me. | Yours A. Pope.

Address: To Mr Warburton at Mrs. | Johnson's | in | Warwick Court

*POPE *to* WARBURTON [? 1742]

Egerton 1946

I'm returned to Town, if I can be of any use to you. I must go early to morrow into the City, if you can do the same, let me know, &

[1] This note must have been written after the return of Pope and Warburton from Bath and before Warburton left London for Newark; that is, between *c.* 6 Jan. and 15 Feb. It concerns the troubles with Gyles's executor, Mawhood.

[2] The following group of five notes to Warburton are not clearly datable. It is here assumed that they come in the period of early 1742 when Warburton was consulting with Pope, Murray, and George Arbuthnot concerning his troubles with Gyles's executor, Mawhood.

[3] Presumably 'here' means Murray's house in Lincoln's Inn Fields. [4] Mawhood.

we'l go together to Mr Knapton's about ten. Till then I shall be here at breakfast, as usual, & glad to see you here. Goodnight. | Dear Sir.

Address: To Mr Warburton at Mrs. Johnsons in Warwick | Court.

*POPE *to* WARBURTON[1] [? 1742]

Egerton 1946

I'm sent for home in great hurry, but I will contrive to get back. just to see you on Wensday morning at Mr Murrays or at your own, God preserve you—*& me, tui amantissimum, ama.*

Sunday 10 a clock

*POPE *to* ALLEN 8 *February* 1741/2

Egerton 1947

London, Feb. 8. 1741.

I was willing to delay this Letter for a Post or two longer than my Inclination, to give you a fuller account of what I am sure you will feel a pleasure in, equal to my own, as we both agree in our Esteem of the Persons, whose Fortune it concerns. I can now tell you that Mr Hooke is some thousand pounds richer than when I left Bath, & (if the Life of the person[2] be prolonged yet a while) in good hope of further benefits to himself & Family. But of this I would not have you (as yet) take the least notice either by Letter to him, or to any other.

And Mr Warburton has at last brought things to a kind of Conclusion by an Article with the Executors of Mr Gyles, to be paid in a month; Mr Murray revised the Deed, or he had been hamper'd, for ought I know, for years to come with them. He goes from London on Thursday home. I hope then to have a week at Twitenham at last, where I have yet not lived three days since I saw you. But I thank God I have preserved myself from Colds of any consequence, & from any distempers but my chronical ones.

The Face of Publick affairs is very much changed, and this Fortnight's Vacation very busy.[3] It is a most Important Interval—but I never in my life wrote a Letter on these subjects: I content myself as

[1] The tone of this and the phrase 'just to see you' may imply that Warburton is about to depart from London. If so, this note should date as late as Sunday, 14 Feb.; but the evidence is so small that the note is left with the others to Warburton.

[2] Sarah, Dowager Duchess of Marlborough.

[3] Sir Robert Walpole's resignation, determined upon on 31 Jan. and necessitated by an adverse division in the Commons on 2 Feb., came on 11 Feb., after he was created Earl of Orford (I. S. Leadham, *History of England 1702–1760*, p. 369).

You do, with honest wishes, for honest men to govern us, without asking for any Party, or Denomination, beside. That is all the Distinction I know: and tho they call Kings the Fountains of Honour, I think them only the Bestowers of Titles; which they are generally most profuse of, to wh—s and kn—s:

I should not omit to tell you that the Sunfire Shares have been transferrd to me, & I have receivd the Dividend. I was truly sorry for Mr Watts.[1]—Mrs Vernon my Landlady is dead, and I may, (if I please & if I am rich enough), buy the perpetuity of this House & the little Land about it, with the Cottages adjoyning on each side of me; without which indeed it would not be worth making a Purchace of. But I am neither eager, nor rash, in such a resolution, and if no disagreable person bought it who might be troublesom to me, I would as willingly let it alone. I have no Views in this Life (so much of which is not left me at my years to be worth any long prospects) but to pass the rest of it under any warm roof where Quiet resides, and since I knew You, yours is as easy to me as my own.

Pray enquire, & once more let me hear what is the Fate at last of poor Mr Brinsden,[2] whose death I have not yet heard of, & am afraid to enquire. Few men deserve so well as He did, of every man who knows the Value of a Friend.

Let Mrs Allen be assured of my grateful and hearty remembrance, and desire her to remember one also, who often speaks of her tho a late acquaintance, & likes her as well, as She can for her heart herself like any new acquaintance: I mean Mrs Blount. I can never tell you how ever mindfully I am Dear Sir | Yours. | A. P.

Four of my Friends here would have me print my Widcomb Poem;[3] which if I do, it will be by the time you come to London in March.

*POPE *to* WARBURTON[4] [*February* 1741/2]

Egerton 1946

Mr Murray thinks it very necessary to alter some things to prevent your future trouble, but could not possibly write 'em down in Court; & as soon as he was at dinner you sent for it back. particularly he thinks you should by no means make it a Condition on your part

[1] Mr. Watts had died 18 Jan. 1742. See the letter to Allen of 17 Apr. 1741 and its note.

[2] Brinsden's life was supposedly saved by the surgeon A. Cleland. See the letters to Allen of 12 June [1742] and 12 Mar. [1743].

[3] The Widcombe poem must be *The New Dunciad* (i.e. Book IV), upon which Pope evidently worked at Allen's house. It was published 20 Mar. 1742.

[4] This letter concerns the agreement that Murray is drawing up between Warburton and the executor of Gyles. It was written before Warburton left London (which was about the middle of the month).

(under a penalty) to Send up *a corrected & improved Copy in a month* &c If you would send it hither now before 8 a clock, he might possibly mark it time enough before the Engrossment, & send it back in an hour. But if Mawhood does not consent to it, I shall be glad, not sorry I confess. for if you left it to me to file a Bill (with your Memorandums & the Draught of this paper for Instructions for one) I doubt not but to give you a better account than he will make up.

Address:[1] To | Alexander Pope Esqr

*GEORGE ARBUTHNOT *to* POPE[2] [*February* 1741/2]

The Royal College of Surgeons of England

I received your Letter but according to your usual Method you have been mindfull of your friend while you forgot your own affairs and only mention in your letter what I should tell my sister about your party with Mrs Bunt[3] I should be glad to know what day Mr Lintot has apointed and would regulat my affairs accordingly. I am Sir | Ever faithfully yours | Geo. Arbuthnott

Munday Morn.

Address (partly cut away): To Alex[

*POPE *to* GEORGE ARBUTHNOT[4] [*February* 1741/2]

The Royal College of Surgeons of England

Lintot has sent no answer When he does I will trouble you with timely notice. Pray send to Mr Warburton & catechize him. I wish he would leave a Letter of Attorny, & give you power to transact for him, or I really fear he will suffer shamefully.

*POPE *to* WARBURTON[5] [16 *February* 1741/2]

Egerton 1946

This Letter came to Twitenham yesterday. I got out of Town within a day after you, not so well inclined to see it again as when you were

[1] Pope has written this letter on the cover of a letter addressed to himself.

[2] This note and Pope's reply (immediately following) are written on the same side of an octavo page.

[3] So written, presumably for Blount.

[4] Warburton seems about to leave town, since a power of attorney is wished. He planned to leave on the 11th (see Pope to Allen, 8 Feb.), and was certainly gone by the 15th. Both 1 and 8 Feb. are possible Mondays. The difficulty with Lintot probably concerns the copyright in *The Dunciad*, or the new edition of Pope's *Iliad*.

[5] The postmark gives month and day; the year is deduced from the fact that only in 1742 were Pope and Warburton together in Town. Pope writes to forward a letter to Warburton.

there. But much more at quiet, since I hope you are now so, and I pray to God for your safe Return to those at your own Home, who will be equally happy. Pray just send me a line that you are well arrived. No words can tell you how much I am | Yours. | A. Pope.

Address: To the Revd Mr Warburton | At Newark | Newark
Frank: Free | Bathurst
Postmark: 16/FE

POPE *to* SARAH, DUCHESS OF MARLBOROUGH[1]

[*February* 1741/2]

Blenheim

Thursday.

I can't express to your Grace the Satisfaction the reading your Papers gave me, as they are now *Dressed*, as you call it. When the remainder is ornamented a little, in the *like* manner, they will certainly be fit to Appear any where, & (like Truth & Beauty) *conquer* where-ever they *appear*.

Thus you have My Judgment & Advice in one word, which you asked; & (which is more than you ask'd) under my hand.

I have again been forced, (for it is always Force upon me,) to be in London. I am now at Twitnam, & at your Grace's Service on Saturday. I name the first day, tho' I believe not alone, for towards Evening I expect Mr Murray, who stays & passes Sunday here. I am most faithfully your Grace's Servant. A. Pope.

Address: To the Duchess of | Marlborough.
Endorsement: A. Pope.

*POPE *to* CHARLES BRINSDEN[2] 15 *March* 1741/2

The Universal Magazine, ix (1808), 31

I should often write to enquire of your Father's and my Friend's state, but that I constantly know it from the accounts sent to your Family in town; where I diligently call myself, when in London, and send, when out of it: and your own kind Letters give me yet a more satisfactory account. The last, both from Them and from you, almost

[1] The dating of this letter is most hypothetical. One assumes from the remark about Her Grace's papers being now 'dressed' that Pope has seen, before publication on 2 Mar., a copy of Hooke's *Account of the Conduct of Sarah, Duchess of Marlborough*. The 'remainder' of her papers will occupy Hooke for the year following—but to no very satisfactory end! Pope is writing soon after Warburton has left London. Back in his villa the poet is socially available.

[2] Practically identical texts of this letter were printed in *The Universal Magazine* for Jan. 1808 (pp. 31–32) and for April 1810 (pp. 288–9). Both were kindly transcribed by Mr. Ault, whose text from 1808 is here given.

rid me of the fears I confess I could not but entertain all along: for if the *Surgeons*, after so much experience as they have had of the process of his Case, do now think him in a fairer way than ever (as you tell me) I can lay a greater stress upon their opinion than I could upon that of *any Doctor*, whose helps in such a case, are of a slower, and therefore more uncertain operation. Pray let my dear friend know, there is no man whose welfare at this time gives me half the concern that his does, and that there is no one scheme of my future life, which would be a greater joy to me, than to make that journey with him abroad, if it please God to enable him to make it. I desire him to write so to our Great Friend,[1] whose health I hear just now is not so good as I wish it, for I'm told he has had his Bileous Ague again. I have nothing to add but my thanks for yours, and my desires of your continuance of your informations especially if they continue so favourable, and so pleasing, to | Sir | Your very affectionate | humble servant | A. Pope.

March 15, | 1741.
Address: To the Rev. Mr. Ch. Brinsden | at Bath.

*POPE *to* DR. WILLIAM HOLMES[2] — 28 *March* 1742

The Wisbech Museum

Sir,—I think, and I hope, you will not be surprized, but rather pleased, that I write to intreat a thing of you which will give me a true pleasure. It is always such (I am persuaded) to yourself to do a worthy man a kindness; and I can assure you, the Person I send with this is very deserving of any; both as an Ingenious & an honest Gentleman. He is the Son of a most particular Friend of mine, Mr Hook, to whom every Learned Society is obliged for his Roman History. He is to pass some time at Oxford as a Gentleman Commoner, (tho his Studies have been long since finishd, & there are few better Scholars) with intention to take orders. Your Countenance, Acquaintance, & (if you will permit me to add) Friendship, will lay me (as well as Mr Hook, & him) under a most particular Obligation. It may not be improper to mention in such an Age as ours, that he is a man who will be offensive to no Party by any Indiscretions, and to no Individual by any

[1] Lord Bolingbroke.—*Univ. Mag.*, 1808, p. 31.

[2] The text is from a transcript made by Professor John Butt. The letter was printed in *Iris*, i (1830), 88, from which source Mr. Ault transcribed it. The addressee seems to be Dr. William Holmes, President of St. John's, who retired as Regius Professor of Modern History in June 1742. See Nichols, *Lit. Anec.* ii. 374. The Wisbech Museum has also a letter from Lord Orrery to Dr. Holmes (27 Mar. 1742) recommending Hooke. Young Hooke was of St. Mary Hall, so Orrery says.

Vices. I am, with real Regard, & sincerity | Sir | Your most obedient | & affect: humble servant | A. Pope

Twitnam | March 28th 1742.
Address: To the Reverend Dr Holmes.

POPE *to* SIR HANS SLOANE — 30 *March* 1742

Add. 4057

Twickenham | March the 30th | 1742

Sir,— I am extremely obliged to you for your Intended kindness of furnishing my Grotto with that surprizing Natural Curiosity,[1] which indeed I have ardently sought for some time. But I would much rather part with Every thing of this Sort which I have collected, than deprive your most Copious Collection of One thing that may be wanting to it. If you can spare it, I shall be doubly pleased in having it, & in owing it to You.

The further Favour You offer me, of a Review of your Curiosities deserves my acknowledgment. Could I hope, that among the Minerals & Fossiles which I have gatherd, there was any thing You could like; it would be esteem'd an Obligation (if you had time, as the Season improves,) to look upon them, & to command any. I shall take the first favourable opportunity to inquire, When it may be least inconvenient to wait on you? Which will be a true Satisfaction to | Sir | Your most obliged & | most humble Servant, | A. Pope.

Address: To | Sir Hans Sloane, Bart. | at | Chelsea.
Postmark: PENY POST PAYD GFR

*POPE *to* ALLEN[2] — [*April* 1742]

Egerton 1947

I heartily thank you for the good newes of you both. And with the Same sincerity of heart, and the Same Earnestness I tell you what I know you are concernd in, my own amendment of Health, by the Same post that I receive yours. For it missed me the last, by my being out of Towne. The Joy you express & feel in Enjoyment of your own Home makes me wish, Mine were nearer it; that I might oft[ner par]take your happiness. But I shall now w[ait till Ma]y or June to see you again, & yet almost be sorry you leave Widcomb again.— Pray forward the inclosed to the simple Man[3] it is directed to. I could

[1] See Pope's second letter to Sloan, 22 May 1742, which explains the gift as a specimen from the Giant's Causeway.

[2] The letter is torn, and bracketed words replace those torn away.

[3] On ff. 153*v*–4*r* of Egerton 1947 there is a letter fabricated by Warburton—at least in his hand—from three of Pope's letters to Allen. The third paragraph of the fabrication begins

not bring myself to write to him sooner, & it was necessary to tell him how much I disapprovd his language & conduct.—What a pleasure it had been to me had he been a better Man whom my Small Charity had been a true relief to: or were he less miserable, that I might bestow it better without abandoning him to Ruin.

Mr Hook & Mrs Blount, & Sir John St Aubin, send you their Services—They have pyrated my Poem[1]—by the foolish Delays of my Printer[2] whom I'l pay off, & imploy less for the future. It was Charity made me use him—Adieu. No man can be more Yours & Mrs Allen's.

Excuse me., I am incompast with Company
Pray how d'ye find poor Mr Brinsden?

POPE *to* RICHARD SAVAGE[3] [*c. April* 1742]

1769 (Ruffhead, pp. 505–6)

Sir, I must be sincere with you, as our correspondence is now likely to be closed. Your language is really too high, and what I am not used to from my superiors; much too extraordinary for me, at least sufficiently so, to make me obey your commands, and never more presume to advise or meddle in your affairs, but leave your own conduct entirely to your own judgment. It is with concern I find so much misconstruction joined with so much resentment, in your nature. You still injure some, whom you had known many years as friends, and for whose intentions I could take upon me to answer; but I have no weight with you, and cannot tell how soon (if you have not already) you may misconstrue all I can say or do; and as I see in that case how unforgiving you are, I desire to prevent this in time. You cannot think yet, I have injured you, or been your enemy: and I am determined to keep out of your suspicion, by not being officious any longer, or obtruding into any of your concerns further than to wish you heartily success in

with this present sentence, 'Pray forward the inclosed', and continues to the end of the paragraph—the word 'Ruin'. Appended to the phrase 'simple Man' is the following footnote—also by Warburton: '*Savage*, whom he snatched from the sink of infamy & vice in London to save & send down into Wales. He had entertained I don't know why some hopes of his reformation as appears from the following passage in a Letter to Mr Allen, but the unhappy wretch had not parts nor sense enough to make an honest man.' There follows a quotation of the passage relating to Savage in Pope's letter to Allen of 18 May 1739.

[1] About this time J. H. Hubbard had published a piracy. See Griffith, Nos. 548, 550.

[2] Probably John Wright is here blamed. Writing to Warburton (23 Apr. [1742]) Pope speaks of Bowyer as then printing for him.

[3] Elwin placed this letter in 1743, but since Savage was in prison in Jan. 1743 and thereafter, one hopes the letter dates earlier. It threatens to be Pope's last letter to Savage, but was not actually so. Ruffhead, who first printed it, thought it was enclosed to Allen in the letter here printed immediately preceding this. Ruffhead may have found it with the Allen letter.

them all, and will never pretend to serve you, but when both you and I shall agree that I should. I am, &c.

POPE *to* WARBURTON[1] 23 *April* [1742]

Egerton 1946

April 23d

My Letters are so short, partly because I could by no Length of Writings (not even by such as Lawyers write) Convey to you more than You have already, of my Heart & Esteem; & partly because I want Time; & Eyes. I can't sufficiently tell you both my pleasure & my Gratefulness, in & for your two last Letters, which shew your Zeal so strong for that Piece of my Idleness, which was literally written only to keep *me* from sleeping in a dull winter, & perhaps to make others sleep,[2] unless awakened by my Commentatour, (no uncommon Case among the Learned.) ⌜But my Expectation of hearing Justice was done you another way, (tho they do it you as much too little, as you do it me too much) is still disappointed; I mean an account of Mawhoods payment of your arrear. I have been so hurry'd of late, *alienis negotiis*, that I've not seen Mr Knapton, nor know what he has proposed about the Shakespear.[3] And⌝ I am every day in Expectation of Lord Bolingbroke's arrival, on his Fathers death:[4] with whom I shall seize all the Hours I can, for his stay (I fear by what he writes) will be very short. ⌜Yet, as I shall be near, or in London, no Commission of yours should be neglected, if you have occasion to imploy me.

⌜I shall make my profit of what you observe in a passage or two of the Essay on Man. I do not intend to set Bowyer,[5] yet, upon any thing but the *first part of* the *Dunciad*; to which if any thing occurs to you which you think a necessary Note, I know you'l tell me.⌝

I do not think it impossible, but Lord Bol. may go to Bath for a few weeks, to see (if he be then alive, as he yet is) his old servant ⌜Brinsden⌝. In that case I think to go with him; & if it should be at a Season when the Waters are beneficial (which agree particularly with Him too) would it be a possibility to meet you at Mr Allen's? whose

[1] Warburton printed this letter in 1751. His omissions are placed in half-brackets.

[2] Pope applied to himself *Dunciad*, i. 93–94:

> While pensive Poets painful vigils keep,
> Sleepless themselves, to give their readers sleep.

[3] In 1747 the Knaptons brought out Shakespeare in eight volumes edited 'By Mr. Pope and Mr. Warburton'. The edition had been announced by Warburton as early as 1740, but it was delayed by the appearance of the Hanmer edition (1744).

[4] He had died on 8 Apr.

[5] On Pope's change of printers see his letter to Allen earlier in this month. The remark about *The Dunciad* seems to indicate that the revision of the first three books is either accomplished or nearing completion.

house, you know, & heart are yours. Tho this is a mere Chance, I should not be sorry you saw so great a Genius, tho he & you were never to meet again. ⌜You never saw a *Man*, before (if I know what a Man is).⌝

Adieu. The World is not what I wish it; but I will not repent being in it, while two or three live. I am ⌜truly yours. | A. Pope⌝

Address: To the Revd Mr | Warburton at | Newark
Frank: Free | Boyle
Postmark: 27/AP

*POPE *to* GEORGE ARBUTHNOT[1] [*April or May* 1742]

Arthur A. Houghton, Jr.

Wendesday [*sic*]

The other day Mr Lintot came to me at Twitnam, & says he has found a Receit in his Father's books, which will satisfy me that I gave him a Discharge in full for all Books, remaining of my Homers. and desired I would get you to look on it. If you please to send to him any morning from Nando's,[2] (Where he tells me you come) to his Chambers, he, or his Servant will show you the Books. I wish you would. It is certain I have no Memory of having given him any such books, & I believe it can only be some Annual Receit for the Vols of that year, or a partial one. But I would not proceed in our Bill till you see what this is.[3]—I am sorry I can't see yourself or Sister, yet: and on Friday Lord Bolingbroke & I go to Twitnam for some days.[4] Pray give her this second vol. of Jos. Andrews.[5] I am ever truly yours: | A. Pope.

Address: To | Mr Arbuthnot, in | Castle Yard.

POPE *to* SARAH, DUCHESS OF MARLBOROUGH 13 *May* [1742]

Blenheim

May the 13.

I promised your Grace to acquaint you of my Comings & Goings, & all I meant was to keep my Word, and meerly to offer myself as an

[1] The mention of *Joseph Andrews* (published in Feb. 1741/2) seems to fix the year. Pope is more likely to have given a copy to Miss Arbuthnot within the year than later. The trouble over Lintot's selling quarto copies of Homer began early in 1740, and is now getting crucial since Pope is also concerned over recovering his rights in *The Dunciad*. He wants all his troubles with Lintot clarified.

[2] A coffee-house next door to Lintot's shop.

[3] Pope filed a complaint in chancery concerning *The Dunciad* on 16 Feb. 1742/3.

[4] Bolingbroke arrived in England late in April and left on 14 June.

[5] A copy of Fielding's novel inscribed by Pope to Miss Arbuthnot is the present property of an American collector. It is bound in Pope's favourite red morocco. Why is he now giving only the second volume? Perhaps he read it before giving it.

Idle Man whenever You should chance to be an Idle Woman. I find you however a very Considerate one, in your obliging Memory of my Infirmities. I wish heartily your Grace had none of your own, to put you in mind of those of others; and that it is as pure Goodness in you, now, to forgive my Weaknesses, as it was heretofore, when you forgave what you might justly have been offended at. You are the only Great Lady that might have been angry at me, and would not. So I must confess You to be Candid & Considerate, from first to last, to me. In allowing me my Liberty, you allow me all I want & ask. In that, you are willing to leave me your Equal; and all the difference is, that you *must be* Independent in a great Fortune, and I *will be* so with a moderate one: And those who would take it from me would take it from you, if they could; which God of his infinite Mercy prevent, and so ends my Prayer for your Grace. I think it will be a fortnight before I shall be in the way of troubling you: but perhaps it would be better not to do it, till You send me a day or 2's notice, which shall at any time bring from Twitnam | Your Graces unprofitable, but real | Servant | A. Pope.

*POPE *to* HUGH BETHEL — 21–23 *May* 1742

Egerton 1948

May 21st 1742

My dear Friend,—It is longer since I wrote to you, than my Heart & sincere Inclination toward you would have sufferd, had I not receivd all the Information my Letters could draw from you, from the constant kind accounts your Brother, Mr Pierson, & above all Dr Key gave me. The last shewed me yours & Mr Moyzers Letters, from time to time: but as he is now gone for Flanders, I must desire you to take the friendly pains yourself of telling me the Progress of your health; as often, & as soon, as possible. I can only say there is no man's Life I am more concernd for, as I know no man's more Exemplary & beneficent. I have been much troubled to think of Mr Moyser's leaving you, & wish earnestly your Recovery was as quick as his, to accompany him. You have many Friends who join with me in that Wish; and who thinking of you as I do, pray for you as I do; particularly Mrs Patty Blount, Dr Teissier, Mr Mildmay, Col. Hulst, & Lord Bolingbroke,[1] all ask me after you. The last has at length succeeded to his Fathers Estate, & is now in England, for a Fortnight or 3 weeks. I believe it will be the last time he will see his native Country, and I

[1] Dr. Tessier, physician-in-ordinary to His Majesty, and of Chelsea Hospital, died, according to *Gent. Mag.*, on 22 May 1742. Pope records the death here in the part of the letter written two days later. Mildmay is possibly Carew Hervey Mildmay, Esq., secretary to Lord Bolingbroke.

should be a worse man than I am, if this were not a sensible Concern to me, on many accounts, since no man I am persuaded is so capable now to serve it. The Turn of affairs[1] here has by no means made me think better of the situation of it, than before; and I have no Prospect that can please me, (who never desird any thing but its Good), left, but what must rise from the private Friendships & Virtues, of those Men whom ill Circumstances, Accidents, or ill health, have remov'd, & are removing from me. God send you back to us, and well! or I shall lose one of those Comforts, which could best atone for other Wants & Misfortunes. We have had a very unwholesome Spring, with continual North-east winds, and in France there has been as great or a greater Mortality: While I am writing this page (at the interval of two days since I wrote the last) I hear poor Teissier is suddenly dead, but not of his Asthmatic Complaint. You have doubtless heard of the melancholy End of Lord Burlingtons Daughter, marryd to the Son of the Duke of Grafton, the Lord Euston, who has been absolutely her Murderer.[2] The Sorrow of the Father is inconsolable, but he bid me send you his good wishes. I know nothing further to tell you from England, but that the whole Nation is profligate & poor: and yet I think the rest of Europe in no better a Condition, where a few Kings have wealth, & a few Nobles the rest, to the Bloodshed or Slavery of the People. So that as yet (for a year or two perhaps) this Country is preferable to others, in that one respect and I hope, as soon as ever you can, you will return to it, while it is worth returning to.

Mrs P. Blount desires to joyn in this Letter, but laments that she can say nothing, in any degree proportionable to the Warmth of her heart & Zeal of her good wishes for you. So I will leave her the next page, finding indeed the same Inability in my self. The Words do not use to fail me, they must on this subject, & always do. God bless you.

She tells me she cannot write, but prays heartily f[or you] & so I take up the pen again, to tell you what I ha[d] forgot, & what I know you never do forget; my own Health; which has been as good as usual, only every year I grow older in my limbs & nerves, tho not in my head. And ⌜to give you Ease in relation to the Event of my Poem; which, dealing much in General, not particular Satire, has stirrd up little or no Resentment. Tho it be leveld much higher than the former, yet Men not being singled out from the Herd, bear Chastisement better, (like Gally slaves for being all linkd in a String, & on the same Rank)⌝[3] If your Brother can find a way to convey it to you it will accompany

[1] That is, of political affairs.

[2] Lady Dorothy Boyle had been married on 10 Oct. 1741, and her husband thereafter lived up to a well-established reputation for brutality. His young wife died of smallpox 2 May 1742, and he was commonly regarded as in part responsible for her death.

[3] The passage in half-brackets was quoted by Ruffhead (1769), p. 393.

or soon follow this Letter. On[ce] more God preserve you and adieu. I am at all times from the bottom of my heart Dear Sir | Entirely yours. | A. Pope

POPE *to* SIR HANS SLOANE 22 *May* 1742

Add. 4057

May 22d 1742.

Sir,—I have many true thanks to pay you, for the two Joints of the Giants Cause way; which I found yesterday at my return to Twitnam, perfectly safe and entire. They will be a great Ornament to my Grotto, which consists wholly of Natural Productions, owing nothing to the Chissel, or Polish; & which it would be much my Ambition to entice you one day to look upon. I will first wait on you at Chelsea, & Embrace with great pleasure, the Satisfaction you can better than any man afford me, of so Extensive a View of Nature in her most curious Works. I am with all respect, | Sir | Your most obliged & | most | humble Servant | A. Pope

Address: To | Sir Hans Sloane Bart | at | Chelsea.

*POPE *to* THE COUNTESS OF DENBIGH[1] [? 1742]

Harvard University

I've had a Letter subscribd I. Denbigh. I think I recollect one who was so call'd formerly, at Twitenham, but whether she be a Fine Lady, or (what I should indeed like better as well as You)—God knows! I have always contented my self with worshipping the Gods of *my Country* & so the Goddesses too: That Lady Denbigh was once one of them, but is not now, having removd herself I don't know whither.

As to Mandana,[2] I suppose by her fine name she is some Romantic Creature, & therfore advise her to be Christen'd again. I can't Communicate with such people, for I return forthwith to my Golden

[1] This letter must date after Cibber's elevation to the laureateship. Our knowledge of the whereabouts of the Countess come chiefly from the account of the Denbigh MSS. in the Hist. MSS. Comm. reports. Information is lacking for the years before 1735. We know that the Denbighs had had a house in Twickenham, which was lent to the French ambassador, Chavigny, and which during his occupancy was in June 1734 completely destroyed by fire. From 1735 to 1741 the Denbighs seem to have been living in France. In Jan. 1742 they are in Hanover Square, and they remained in England during 1742 and 1743 at least. The Countess (Isabella, daughter of Peter de Jonghe of Utrecht) seems to have been a charming person, witty and amiable. She was an intimate friend of the Marquise de Villette (Lady Bolingbroke), and letters to her show a lively interest in Pope. The letter is hardly datable. Lady Denbigh was in Twickenham in 1730 (Pope to H. Bethel, 9 June 1730), but that seems too early a year for this letter.

[2] Mandana's story is told in *Artamenes; or the Grand Cyrus*, Part II, Book ii.

apartment at Twitnam: where I sit like Apollo, incompassd with my own Gilding, under four Pillars of the Doric order, on a Throne of flame-colourd Damask; where (if you are sincerely repentant,) you may come & behold me in the fulness of my Glory & Majesty, wanting nothing but the Laurel, which you may find at Cibber's.

Address: To my Lady Denbigh.
Endorsement: This is | Mr Popes letter the poet

*POPE *to* ALLEN 27 *May* [1742]

Egerton 1947

Twitnam, May 27.

I acknowledge yours by the last post with the Bill on Barbut,[1] & that of Lading, for which I need not say I thank you. Lord Bol: has had a Return of his Fever, at my house, but has once more this day put off the Fitt. His time of staying is made the more uncertain, which otherwise would be short; in all probability before you travel this way: Or I should be glad to show you to one another. As soon as you know your Time, pray acquaint me, that if he is not actually here, your self & Mrs Allen may lodge with me in your way. Mr Warburton writ me word he would contrive to meet me, if I could be with you in the Summer or Autumn either. I wonder he has not commissiond me yet to receive his money of Mawhood,[2] which was due above a month ago, & pray mention it to him when you write. I am afraid he neglects his own Interest too much, considering the Backwardness of those he has to deal with. I am of late so Easy myself, (& made so much more so by your Friendship, which assists me on every occasion) that I have no anxiety left but for others. The Public is indeed more my Concern than it used to be, as I see it in more danger. but your Reflection & Advice, in that too, ought to alleviate those Uneasy Thoughts: when to trust Providence is all I can do: & since my Sphere is Resignation, not Action. I am every day more drawn into the small Circle of Friendship, from the Great World, and tempted to place all my enjoyments in this, which we can compass. God preserve the Few Good people that are left, and Yourself in particular! I am troubled that your Headakes continue to afflict you so long together, & hoped that they would diminish annually, as mine (I thank God) have done. Mrs Blount thanks you and Mrs A. for your kind Intention, & is heartily your [Ser]vant. Mr Hooke is going for a short time abroad. [I] have nothing to add but what happend the very day I [w]rit to you last, that Bell, your virtuous acquaintance, [wa]s called before the Sec:

[1] Presumably John David Barbutt, Secretary to the Post Office.
[2] Money from Warburton's deceased publisher, Gyles.

Comm: and appeard as clean of [ha]nd & heart as the rest.[1] But if Chance protects such men, may [P]rovidence protect their Betters! Adieu. | Ever yours. A. P.

Address: To | Ralph Allen, Esqr | at Widcombe: | near | Bath.
Postmark: 28/MA

*POPE *to* JONATHAN RICHARDSON[2] [? 3 *June* 1742]

Arthur A. Houghton, Jr.

Thursday.

I am sorry for it, but cannot help putting off my Engagement to sit to you, till the End of the next Week. It is truly a Concern to me, when I am not able to express an Equal Readiness & Warmth to comply with any desire of Yours, who show so great a degree of both, in executing any of mine. But believe me with Equal Truth at least | Ever Yours. | A. Pope

Address: To Mr Richardson

POPE *to* WARBURTON[3] 5 *June* [1742]

Egerton 1946

Twit'nam June 5th

I wish that instead of writing to you once in two months, I could do you some Service as often, for I am arrived to an Age when I am as sparing of Words as most old Men are of Money, tho I daily find less occasion for any. But I live in a time when Benefits are not in the power of an honest man to bestow, nor indeed of an honest man to receive, considering on what Terms they are generally to be had. It is certain, you have a full right to any I could do you, who not only monthly but weekly of late have loaded me with Favours, of that kind which are most acceptable to veteran Authors; those Garlands which a Commentator weaves to hang about his Poet, & which are Flowers both of his own gathering & Painting too, not Blossomes springing

[1] Col. Bell, Comptroller of the Inland Office, had been called before the Committee of Secrecy investigating possible malfeasance during the Walpole régime. Col. Bell, now released, was for his irregularities in accounting for surcharges on letters removed by Act of Parliament in 1743.—Herbert Joyce, *History of the Post Office* (1893), p. 185 n., and *Gent. Mag.* xiii. 107.

[2] Since Pope sat to Richardson several times, this note is not datable; but since we learn from the letter of 10 June that he with Bolingbroke would sit on the 12th (Saturday), the letter is placed as of 3 June (Thursday).

[3] In 1751 Warburton printed this letter with no year date. He placed it, however, as if written in 1743, and Elwin gave it that date. Both the trouble with Mawhood and Lord Bolingbroke's departure to France place it certainly in 1742. Warburton's omissions are placed in half-brackets.

from the dry Author. ⌜However I will one day make a Roman Catholic Compliment to Dr Middleton, & shine out in all the Dress of the old Heathen,[1] like a modern Christian Maypole. And all this shall be layd at your door.⌝

It is very unreasonable after this to give you a Second trouble[2] in revising the Essay on Homer, but I look upon you as one sworn to suffer no Errours in me, & tho the common way with a Commentator, be to erect them into Beauties, the best office of a Critick is to correct & amend them. There being a new Edition coming of Homer,[3] I would willingly render it a little less defective, and the Bookseller will not allow me time to do so myself.

⌜ I can find no fault in your Epistle to Mr Allen:[4] but 2 or 3 single words I would expunge in favor to his Modesty, or rather, his real humility; and the last Sentence softend, or changed into something more familiar.

⌜What is become of Mawhoods arrear to you? I hope you have receivd it, or why is it delayd? I fear I shall not be in town, or near it long, unless I have your Orders soon.⌝ Lord B.[5] returns to France very speedily, & it is possible[6] I may go for 3 weeks or a month to Mr Allen's in the Summer: of which I will not fail to advertise you, if it suits your conveniency to be there, & drink the Waters more beneficially.

Forgive me scribling so hastily & so ill. My Eyes are at least as bad as my head: and it is with my Heart only that I can pretend to be to any real purpose Your ⌜faithfull affectionate Servant | A. Pope.⌝

*POPE *to* JONATHAN RICHARDSON[7] 10 *June* [1742]

Arthur A. Houghton, Jr.

You may be certain it was no common Cause that has hindered my acquainting you till now, of the Day for executing your kind Intention, of another Picture of my Great (truly Great) Friend.[8] He has been not well, & s[o] not in Town. But on Saturday about 12 he will

[1] Warburton and Middleton differed vehemently over possible pagan influence on the ceremonies of the Church. Warburton asserted a considerable influence.

[2] The first trouble is perhaps indicated in the letter here placed just after 21 Jan. of this year. See iv. 384.

[3] The Editor did revise and correct it as it now stands in the last edition.—Warburton, 1751.

[4] Warburton evidently has submitted to Pope the epistle dedicatory to Allen prefixed to Warburton's *Critical and Philosophical Commentary on Mr. Pope's Essay on Man*, published in August of this year.

[5] Bolingbroke.

[6] The possibility, as later letters show, was pushed back several times until at last Pope reached Bath in October.

[7] The year and the identification of the 'great friend' are added in another hand, presumably Richardson's. See *Richardsoniana*, p. 132 *bis*.

[8] Lord Bolingbroke.—Richardson's MS. note.

wait on you, with much affection, as will also, Dear Sir, | Your very faithful | Servant | A. Pope.

Twitnam, June 10th 1742

He returns next week to France.

Address: To Mr Richardson, in | Queens Square, | Bloomsbury.

*POPE *to* ALLEN 12 *June* [1742]

Egerton 1947

London June 12.

I am pressed by Mr Brinsden (to whom Mr Cleland[1] has certainly done the office of a careful and diligent Surgeon, as well as an able one) to desire your Vote for his being one of the Assistant Surgeons to the Hospital at Bath; as it seems Mr Pierces[2] Prentice is to be the other, I apprehend your Interest may not be given elsewhere, and it will oblige a very valuable Man to give it here. I will add no more but my own Desire to gratify Mr Brinsden, & one who has been instrumental in saving him. Adieu. Let Mrs Allen be assured I am hers & | Your most sincere Servant. | A. Pope

The Bristol waters are just come, and I expect the Stones this week. It's to no purpose to thank you for any thing, but I love you for all.

Address: To | Ralph Allen Esqr at | Widcomb | near | Bath.

Endorsement (in Allen's hand): Mr Popes Letter | with R. Allens | answer 21st June 1742 | Mr Cleland affair.

POPE *to* SLINGSBY BETHEL 16 *June* 1742

Harvard University

Twit'nam. June 16. 1742

Col. Moyser acquaints me that you are soon to send a Parcell of Goods to your Brother at Rome: I intreat you to add in it the inclosed.

I troubled you lately with a Letter to him by Post, but did not write to you, intending the next day to have waited on you at Tower-hill, & to have seen Lady Cox:[3] but was told at night she was gone for Oxford.

If you could find any occasion for taking 300 pound more of me, to make the 700 up a thousand I should think it very safe in your hands.

[1] Archibald Cleland secured this post, but because of improper conduct was dismissed in 1743. See his *Appeal to the Publick* (21 Sept. 1743). Note also the postscript to Pope's next letter to Allen (19 July 1742).

[2] Jeremiah Pierce had been Surgeon to Bath Hospital since May 1740.

[3] Bethel's sister Mary.

But let this be as is, or is not, convenient to yourself. I have nothing to add but my own hearty Services, & Mrs Patty Blount's, who charged me with them when I thought of seeing you. I am sincerely | Dear Sir | Your faithfull, affectionate Servant, | A. Pope.

If I knew any time that you would take a bed here this fine weather, I would be sure to be at home.

Mr. Bethel, Book.[1]

Address: To Mr Bethel, Merchant | on | Tower-hill | London.
Endorsement: A. Pope 22 | June 16. 1742 | To Slingsby Bethell, Esq.

*POPE *to* WARBURTON 18 *June* [1742]

Egerton 1946

This Letter, dear Sir, will be extremely Laconic. I shall stay in or about London this month, therfore send me full powers & Instructions, & I will receive & dispose of your money. If Mawhood dos not pay it so soon, I doubt not Mr Knapton will discharge this Office as well, in my absence. I hope to pass a Month with Mr Allen in Septr or the End of Augst & my chief View in it, is to sollicit you to take the full Benefit of the Waters. I gave Lord Bolingbroke your Books, tho he was no Stranger to them: he went for Calais 4 days since, with a strong purpose never to return. The Learned World will gain, by what the Political world has lost; which to you & me is a Consolatory Consideration. Adieu dear Sir, & forgive me that I repeat the only thing I have to say, that I am Wholly | Yours. | A. Pope.

June 18th.

Address: To the Revd Mr Warburton / Newark
Frank: Free Oxford
Postmark: 24/IV

*POPE *to* WARBURTON[2] [*June* 1742]

Egerton 1946

I am not sorry you withdrew the Copy of your Book from that idle & conceited Printer. I wish, when you think fit to let it appear again,

[1] These words, written at the bottom of the leaf, suggest that the enclosure was very possibly *The New Dunciad*, which had been published three months earlier. The 'fine weather' postscript is written on the cover of the letter.

[2] The month is determined by the imperfect postmark, and the year is made probable by the fact that Warburton on 31 Mar. 1742 writes to Bowyer that the new edition of his Commentary on the *Essay on Man* is to be printed by him. See Nichols, *Lit. Anec.* ii. 152 n. In the new edition (published in August) the last letter concludes with an attack on the charity and candour of Crousaz.

to see the Whole regulated according to your Last Correxion, & the Last Letter conclude with the Sermon on Charity & Candour. Perhaps if you put together some Critical Tracts; that on Shakespear, & this, might properly accompany them, or be introduced by them. I am glad to see you *divert* & *digress* even from your Greatest Scheme; your Deviations into the Walks of Criticisme are always very entertaining.

Address: To the Revd Mr Warburton | at Newark
Frank: Free | W: Chetwynd
Postmark: /IV

*POPE *to* [JOHN] BRINSDEN[1] 30 *June* 1742

Sotheby sale of 12 June 1899, lot 1368

June 30, 1742.

I have been much concerned not to have a day in my power to see you in your confinement which I am heartily sorry to find continued. But I have a whole family of Visitors[2] who do not leave me these five days yet, after which nothing shall hinder me, I attempted the only day I had in London to get to Chelsea, but could not, so as not to be in the night.

POPE *to* WARBURTON[3] 18 *July* [1742]

Egerton 1946

July 18th

You may well expect Letters from me of Thanks, but the kind Attention you show to every thing that concerns me is so manifest, & so repeated, that You cannot but tell yourself how necessarily I must pay them in my heart, which makes it almost impertinent to say so. Your alterations to the Preface & Essay[4] are just, & none more obliging to me than where you prove your Concern that my Notions in my first writings should not be repugnant to those in my last. And you will have the Charity to think, when I was then in an Error, it was not so much that I Thought wrong or perversely, as that I had not Thought sufficiently. What I could correct, in the dissipated life I am forced to lead here, I have; & some there are which still want your help to be made as they should be.

[1] The Sotheby catalogue calls this a letter to 'Mrs. Bronsden', but the same item, apparently, turns up in the sale of 14 Feb. 1930 (library of Samuel A. Boyle) as to Mr. Brinsden.
[2] Possibly the Wests again?
[3] Printed by Warburton in 1751. His omissions are placed in half-brackets. He wrongly thought the letter written in 1743, though he did not print that date, as Elwin did. Before 18 July 1743 Pope was already in Bath: in this letter he plans to go thither in September.
[4] Prefix'd to his Homer's *Iliad*.—Warburton, 1741.

⌜I have yet had no Commission as to Mawhood. I'm sorry for it, because by the End of this month or beginning of the next I believe I must go from hence for 3 weeks or a month.⌝ Mr Allen depends on you at the End of the next, or in Septr, and I will joyn him as soon as I can return from the other party,[1] (I believe not till Septr at soonest.)

⌜I have receivd a Letter from Dr Oliver some time ago written express to justify himself from all knowledge of Tillards[2] book, & all previous Consent for its being dedicated to him. On the contrary, he gave him first his Opinion against writing the Book at all; then used the strongest Arguments against printing it; & never knew the least Syllable of the Contents, either of that or the Dedication, till it was deliverd him by the Bookseller. "I was then (these are his words) really Sorry, for Him, & for Myself." I think I need not add my Opinion of that Treatise. You have made a Man angry, & there I think you should leave him.⌝ [3]You will pardon me (dear Sir) for writing to you but just like an Attorney, or Agent. I am more concerned for your Finances[4] than your Fame, because the first I fear you will never be concerned about, yourself; the Second is secure to you already, and (whether you will or not) will Follow you.

I have never said one word to you of the Public; I have known the Greater World too long, to be very Sanguine; but *Accidents & Occasions* may do what *Virtue* would not; and God send they may! Adieu. Whatever becomes of Publick Virtue, let us preserve Our own poor Share of the private. Be assured, if I have any, I am with a true Sense of your Merit & Friendship, | ⌜Dear Sir. Ever Yours. | A. Pope.⌝

*POPE *to* ALLEN — 19 *July* [1742]

Egerton 1947

July 19th

I had written by Mr Hooke but that he undertook to say every thing to you which I could say for myself, of my real Warmth of heart as well as Esteem, which are constantly yours. And likewise to tell you, tho I may ever so much desire to Dedicate myself to you, yet I cannot (for many Ties and Respects a Man of so much acquaintance as I, is obliged to) make my Time so much yours as I would. I told you (&

[1] With Lord Cobham at Stowe. (But Duchess Sarah kept Pope at Windsor Lodge. He did not get to Stowe.)

[2] John Tillard, a merchant 'with a strong tincture of literature', had attacked Warburton in a pamphlet called *Future Rewards and Punishments believed by the Antients*. Warburton made a brief but brutal reply in his next edition of vol. ii of *The Divine Legation*. See Nichols, *Lit. Anec.* v. 572, and ii. 154 n.

[3] Elwin suspected that the new sheet with which this sentence begins is not really a part of the present letter. He may be right, but since Warburton regarded it as a part of the one letter, it is wise to print it as such.

[4] His debt from the Executor of Mr. G[yles].—Warburton, 1751.

sincerely) that I hoped I might contrive to pass a month with you about the End of Augst or beginning of Septr. That was the soonest, but I fear it cannot be till the middle or End of that Month, for a Reason Mr H. has given you. I can't deny what is so much at the heart of the old Lady[1] who has made my Friend's Fortune; & she goes not into the Country till the ninth or tenth at soonest of Augst. I can't live any where so long as I've done with you & Mrs Allen; & intend at most but to be going & coming from Windsor to Twitnam, which I can do in 3 hours. Indeed long Journies I can't often bear; & I'd rather, when I do come, stay with you all the time I can this year. I therfore intreat you not to regulate your Rambles by mine, which to have the Season pleasant, you should not delay: The best of it will be over before I can go to you, but I will endeavor to have the Tail of the fine weather at least, before Winter, & so as to plant with you a month. If Mr Warburton goes in Septr & stays part of October, it will be the best Season for his drinking the Waters, which ought to make a principal Consideration with us both and if he then takes me in his way, we may travel together without putting you to any trouble: Unless you had other business to call you this way. I have moreover so many things to do, that I am almost distracted, & were *I* yet to be with you, my *Mind* would be absent, and I am very sensible you are a friend who deserves it *all*. I wish I knew that nothing unpleasing has happend in relation to the Post-officers, &c. Barbut I hear is broke,[2] but conclude you were secured a better way than by him. I can tell you nothing by Letter, I could say a great deal by word of mouth, of other Events, very strange, & very foolish too, to such as think as you and I do.—The best news I can send you is, that by the first Coach the week after this I hope to present you with two fine Pine-apples which John[3] says will then be in perfection. Adieu, & God preserve your health & happiness, which is Mrs Allens also.

Mrs Blount is your hearty Servant, & Mr Hook's.

I think of Cleland[4] just as you do, & even by Mr Br.'s[5] account, he has not in all respects deserved so highly of *Him* as he imagines. but Br. is the most candid & goodnaturd of Men: he will think himself better used, & more obliged, than he is: So I let him take this as kindly of you, as he does; tho I know your mind as to the Man. he sends you about ten thousand thanks.

[1] The Dowager Duchess of Marlborough, who was evidently to spend the summer in Windsor Lodge.

[2] John David Barbutt was removed as secretary to the Postmaster-General this month. He was bankrupt by the end of the year.

[3] Pope's gardener, Searle.

[4] Archibald Cleland, whose restoration of Brinsden's health (see Pope to Allen, 12 June 1742) now proves not to be permanent, is less favourably regarded than he was a month ago.

[5] Brinsden.

POPE *to* THE EARL OF ORRERY[1] 23 *July* [1742]

The Pierpont Morgan Library

July 23d | 1742

My Lord,—Your Humanity, which I have seen extend over all the Human Species; I doubted not descended to the Animals, his Elder Brothers in the Creation: And in particular to Dogs; the Companions, & therfore the Precursors, of Man. Yet I will not allow, you should retard the Satisfaction I was sure to receive in hearing of your own, till you could also acquaint me of Bounce's safe arrival in Somersetshire.[2] I envy you this Distance from a Town of Knaves & Politicians, with the accounts of whom, & the Compliments paid to whom, my Retirement ecchoes, tho the first Voice be not heard. It is in vain I sequester myself from the Action, when the Riot & the Ruin spread around me; & the Joy, & the Sorrows consequential of their Joy, to every honest-hearted Englishman, are every day in my ear.

Lady Orrery ought to know, her Remembrances are & must be a Pleasure & Favour to me, & any Commissions She or your Lordship can give me will be additional favours, except you requir'd of me to answer your Noble Neighbours[3] Latin, or hear his English Oratory.

I had a Visit from your Other Noble Neighbour in the Park;[4] a very wet day it was, but no other Inconvenience. She left me really concernd for her, & heartily wishing no man afflicted her peace of mind more than I would do, and that I could do her any good office; but in the nature of Things it seems impossible. She also payd me her small debt, but I could not persuade her to come into the House but sate with her in her Coach at my door. We mentiond you with honour, & I look upon whatever she may think in my favour, as wholly owing to your kind Conduct.

If I look into your house in your absence, it must be to enquire of Lord Boyle & his Brother, in regard to whom I wish I could be of any use: and in such case, I would lodge no where else: Otherwise I intend not to be in London a Night.

Cibber is printing a Letter to me, of the Expostulatory kind in prose. God knows when I shall read it, when it is publish'd;[5] & perhaps

[1] The year is added to the superscription by Lord Orrery.

[2] For some reason Pope has given his Great Dane to Lord Orrery. See Ault, *New Light*, p. 349.

[3] Lord Hervey, at St. James's Palace.

[4] The Duchess of Buckingham, at Buckingham House (now the Palace).

[5] First written, 'tho it be publish'd'. From 15 July advertisements had been appearing for Cibber's *Letter from Mr. Cibber, to Mr. Pope, Inquiring into the Motives that might induce him to be so frequently fond of Mr. Cibber's Name.* Published by Pope's early bookseller, W. Lewis, it contained Cibber's unseemly anecdote about rescuing Pope twenty years earlier in a 'house of carnal recreation'. Pictures of the episode were speedily engraved, and the whole affair was as unpleasant for Pope as anything he had to face since the early attacks of the Dunces. Cibber's outburst was doubtless due to rumours that he was soon in a revised *Dunciad* to be crowned Prince of Dullness.

I may send to ask your Account of it; your Opinion whether or not to answer it, I need not ask. He swears he will have the *Last Word* with me,[1] upon which I've seen an Epigram.

> You will have the *last Word*, after all that is past?
> And tis certain, dear Cibber, that you may *speak last*;
> But your reas'ning, God help you! is none of the strongest:
> For know, the Last Word is the Word that lasts longest.

I am ever, My dear Lord, your faithfull, obliged Servant | A. Pope.

Endorsement: Mr Pope. | July 23d 1742.

THE EARL OF ORRERY *to* POPE 27 *July* 1742

Harvard University

Marston: July 27th: 1742.

Sir,—I have received your obliging Letter, and am rejoic'd to find you felt no ill effects from your expedition into the Coach in so wet a day. Poor Lady![2] I have often been very angry with her, and I had reason for it, but when I have consider'd, or seen the unhappy situation of her mind, when I have beheld her under all the torments I may almost say of the damned, when I have recollected her former generous Friendship to me, then my Rage has immediately turned into Compassion, I have forgot my Resentment, I have laid aside my Judgement, and I have become again, as I now am, her faithfull Servant. Your benevolent heart can feel the Truth of what I say, & I am sure our Sentiments are always the same, where my thoughts lead me to any Act of humanity or pity.

The illustrious *Leake* of Bath brought me over *Colley's* Letter, a true Cibberian performance—the Epigram is excellent.[3] This leads me to put you in mind of trying to collect your Epigrams. We want a Collection of that kind, and perhaps yours might amount to a little volume. Why will you let 'em be dispers'd, like Cybele's Leaves, in Air? *Cibber* cannot be [more] properly answered than in the epigrammatical way. If he were at Dublin the whole College would be aiming at him. He is the *Betteswortb*[4] of the Stage.

I have writ three or four Lines to you by my Surveyour, who, with your leave, will take a view of your Urns, most, if not all, of which, I should be glad to imitate in my Garden. It is at present in great

[1] Pope's epigram replies to Cibber's promise in his *Letter*, p. 8, to have the last word: 'While I have Life, or am able to set Pen to Paper, I will now, Sir, have the last Word with you.'

[2] The Duchess of Buckingham. See the preceding letter.

[3] Leake was the leading bookseller in Bath. On Cibber and Pope's epigram see the preceding letter.

[4] Arthur Bettesworth, a London bookseller?

beauty, and except one day of the week, which I give up to the Squires, the Justices, and the Parsons of our neighbourhood (for, Lords we have none) there cannot be on this Side of Paradise a place of greater Tranquility. I thank God we never dream of Courts, but contented with a plain oaken cudgell, leave gold Staffs to our Friends.

Would it were possible to find out some method to tempt you hither, you should come into a warm house, see an agreable situation, and live void of noise and disturbance, with two persons who love and honour you with true devotion. believe me, dear Sir, | your &c. | Orrery.

Heading: To Alexr Pope Esq.

*POPE *to* JONATHAN RICHARDSON [30 *July* 1742]

The Pierpont Morgan Library

Twitnam, Friday. | 30 July 1742[1]

I was obstructed in my Way home, & carryd another way, so that I arrived here but last night To morrow it happens that I must entertain some Ladies at dinner, but I wish you'd come in the Twitnam Coach which sets out from London about 2 from the Whitehorse in Fleetstreet, & comes hither by 6 in the afternoon; by which time my Ladies will be gone, & leave us the peaceable Enjoyments of Philosophers in the Garden. All Sunday I may keep you; & on Munday will attend you to London, or very near it. The Weather promises so well to day, that I hope it will incourage you. Adieu. Yours ever. | AP.

This day you may secure your places for to morrow, & I hope you will.

Address: To Mr Richardson

*POPE *to* THE EARL OF BURLINGTON[2] [1742]

Chatsworth

Tuesday.

My Lord,—I will never think myself an unfortunate man, while you Think at all of me: otherwise I would call myself so, for having 5 or 6 times miss'd of you, at Chiswick & at London. If you shall be at leisure, either to see the Hunting house in Windsor forest, or to stay at a much better, your Ldships own, any day this week (Sunday

[1] The date is added in an early hand, but not Pope's.

[2] This letter can be vaguely placed by Pope's suggestion of a visit to Windsor Lodge, residence of Sarah, Duchess of Marlborough. The summer of 1742 seems the most likely time for Pope to suggest such a visit. Other times after about 1740 would be possible.

next excepted when the Arbitrary Lord Bathurst demands me) I intreat to wait on you. My faithful Services attend the Incorrigible Lady Burlington.

I am sincerely | Your Ldships real, & most obligd | humble Servant | A. Pope.

*POPE *to* COLLET MAWHOOD[1] 4 *August* 1742

Sotheby sale, 28 Nov. 1913, lot 355, item 14

FRAGMENT

I am assured by Council there is no Pretence for his (Warburton) paying your attorney's bill. I therefore desire you to think better of it, and pay it to the Bearer. . . . If not I can only acquaint Mr. W(arburton) to take any course he thinks proper.

*POPE *to* JONATHAN RICHARDSON[2] [? *August* 1742]

Arthur A. Houghton, Jr.

Munday | about July 1742

Lord Burlington very readily sends you the inclosed, & desires that when You come, he may see you. If you intend it for any other person's use, or to be Incognito yourself, go in an Afternoon; For the House & Pictures are not shewn in a Morning, as the Family live there at present. Adieu. You [sh]all see me by the End of this week. I am truly & affectionately Yours | A. Pope

Mr Richardson

Address: To Mr Richardson. | in | Queens Square.

*POPE *to* JONATHAN RICHARDSON[3] [5 *August* 1742]

The Hyde Collection

Upon second thoughts. I will go before to Chiswick & prepare your way. You may dine first, & call on me there after four or about five, or when you will, & you shall have your fill of the Pictures. So we'l

[1] Known only through this fragment from the sale catalogue.

[2] The date is added by Richardson, whose final digit is so made as to look like a 3. The serif of his 2 ends with a descending drag of the pen. It cannot be a 3 and be correct since in July 1743 Pope was in Bath.

[3] The subscribed date '5 Aug.' is in Richardson's hand. The '43' seems to have been added later, and must be wrong, since in 1743 Pope was at Bath. If related to the preceding letter, which is endorsed 'about July 1742', the year 1742 seems appropriate, and in 1742 5 August was a Thursday.

go on to Twitnam to night in your Coach, and you may return to morrow by the Stage. In haste, adieu. | Ever Yours.

Thursday morn.

5 Aug. 43

Address: To | Mr | Richardso[n in] | Queensqu[are]

*POPE *to* WARBURTON 5 *August* [1742]

Egerton 1946

As soon as I receivd yours I wrote to Mawhood to acquaint him I had your Commission & Receit, & to desire him to appoint a Time for my receiving your Money, by a Letter to Twitnam. He sent me none. I sent another Letter that I would be in town on Wensday, & as I could not stay long, that he'd call on me, or I on him. This inclosed was his answer. To which I returned the following

Aug. 3

Sir—I am very well appriz'd by Mr W. of what you call an Article yet in dispute. I am sorry, that after so disadvantageous a bargain on his part, and contrary to Articles, the payment has been so long & (I can't help saying) so shamefully delayd, and so much trouble given a Gentleman who deserves all respect. As for myself I shall take no more than to make this Demand by the Bearer, Mr Murray's Clerk, if you please to pay it him, as I hope. If not, you must excuse me if I put it in Suit according to my orders from him. I am Yours—

But Mr Murray caus'd me to omit the last, & only require his peremptory answer whether he would pay it or not.[1] At the same time I added, that I was assurd by Council you ought no way to be accountable for his Council or attornys fees.—I sent it, with your Order, indorsed by me, by Mr M.'s[2] Clerk; to whom he said he would not pay it, till the Account was fully setled, & told him you owed still for a Shakespear & some other books. Mr M. advised me not to talk more to him, but to write to know your Resolution. I think you would do well to answer him by Woodward or Knapton, & insist on your part upon his paying Interest from the time he covenanted to have made up the account & to have paid it; & get all setled, against you come yourself: unless you would chuse to put it in Suit. In any case, I will do what you will. Mr Allen will be going from my house to Bath by the End of this month, he will be here but for a day or two, & from hence carry you to Bath[.] I cannot go so soon by near a month I fear, at least not till the middle of Septr being necessarily ingagd from home most part of the time between in Berkshire. But I will be here

[1] The letter actually sent to Mawhood seems to be the one of which we have only a fragment for this edition. See 4 Aug. 1742.

[2] i.e. Mr. Murray's clerk.

for the day or 2 Mr Allen comes, & follow you & him to Bath as soon as possible.

You'l forgive the strange Carelessness with which I am forced to write to you now & always. I can't so much as tell you any thing I think, of, or for you: but I am constantly yours to all respects. There is nothing in public affairs worth relating, or what would (if related truly, & as it really past) displease any honest man, tho there are Men who mean honestly even at Court. Adieu. I want Time, Eyes, & Head, to write a line fit to be sent to a Man I value like yourself. | I am Ever Yours | A. Pope.

Aug. 5th

I keep your Receit & Articles very safe. Mr Murray goes away for the Vacation in a Week's time: but I may receive a Letter time enough from you before he goes, if necessary.

*POPE *to* ALLEN — 10 *August* [1742]

Egerton 1947

Twitnam the 10th Aug.

I was truly glad of your last Letter & the near Prospect of seeing you; be certain nothing shall hinder my being with you whatever days you can allot me, if God spares me life & health. So on the twentieth &c, you shall be sure to find me at home. I am going to the Lady,[1] Mr Hook with me, for the first time in the Country, but not to stay above 3 or 4 days: and I hope to make no other than such short Excursions; nor to *lend* my Self, much less *Sell* myself, on any consideration, to any Dependency half so strong, as that which the Tye of our Friendship obliges me in to you & a very few others. If any Accident prevents your present Intention, let me know by the first opportunity, & however you may change yours, I will conform my Movements to you. I doubt not to be a whole month at your disposal before the End of the Season. Adieu. I am Yours & Mrs Allen's faithfully. A. Pope.

Address: To | Ralph Allen Esqr at | Widcomb near | Bath
Postmark: 11/AV

*POPE *to* ALLEN[2] — [24 *August* 1742]

Egerton 1947

Twit'nam, Tuesday night.

I hoped to have returned to pass a day or two with you, before your Journey out of Town; but my Lord Chesterfield having been ill, has

[1] Here written in above the line by an old hand, not Pope's, is 'Dutchess of Marlborough'. She had not expected to be at Windsor Lodge before this time. See Pope to Allen, 19 July.

[2] The date is certain. The year is determined by the presence of Chesterfield at Pope's

lodged with me for some days, & I am still detained by him here. I hope you are as Well and Mrs Allen too, as the Waterman tells me. I can only say, God keep you, in your Going out, & your Coming in. I'll meet you at your Return, & stay till I carry you off. The Stones are come from Bath and will be in my Grotto by the End of the Week, where I have so many Memorandums of You that I shall never live there (or any where) without thinking of you. Adieu. I am truly Mrs A.'s and | Dear Sir | Yours always. | A. Pope

Pray let the Bundle of Willows | be given to Mr *Pierce*.

Address: To | Ralph Allen Esqr

POPE *to* SARAH, DUCHESS OF MARLBOROUGH[1]

[26 *August* 1742]

Blenheim

I wish your Grace were younger, and I stronger, by twenty years; and if we could not drive out Boars,[2] we might at least plant Vines, under which we & our Posterity might sit, & enjoy Liberty a few years longer. As it is, we can enjoy nothing but Friendship, (the next great blessing to Liberty) if any will last even so long as Our Lives. I really think your Grace has brought about One that will, (if not two or three) & I can assure You, Your New Lady,[3] if once fixed, is unalterable, as I have experiencd for above twenty years tho' I never once did her any real Service, only for meaning it.

I fear Sir Timothy cannot part from his Child this week,[4] (who has left all her Swadling Clothes behind her, in a Ship that is not yet arrived.) I would have made you a days Visit myself, (for I like you very well when you are alone) and return'd to Mr Allen who comes to Twitnam again this week, for 3 day[s] but it happens that a very particular Friend of mine (an Eminent Divine of the Church of England)[5] comes to Twitnam to morrow & leaves me then. But Notwithstanding my Regard to Divines, such as he, I think your Grace's

villa (see Pope to Lord Orrery, 27 Aug. 1742) and by the arrival of the Allens in London. After a short 'journey out of town' Allen is at Pope's house—as the poet writes Orrery on the 27th. The 24th is the only Tuesday in the month on which the letter could be written.

[1] The brief visits of Allen and Warburton, with the times of their arrivals and departures, make the specific Thursday of this letter certain.

[2] Here, as normally, Pope's hand is perfectly clear, but somehow Elwin printed instead of 'drive out boars', 'dine out doors'. The allusion seems to be to Psalm lxxx. 8–13, and one wonders if the aged disciple of Socrates to whom Pope was writing realized the fact. 'Driving out boars' was a common metaphor for ridding an orderly world of politicians like Walpole.

[3] Martha Blount? See Pope's letter to the Duchess in late September.

[4] It is this sort of remark that makes one think the frequent references to Sir Timothy may refer to Hooke (and here to his daughter).

[5] Warburton, who was going to Bath with the Allens.

Ghostly Father, Socrates, ought not to be changed for the best of them. Before the End of next week, or as much sooner as I can, I shall trouble Mr Dorset & all his Horses. In the meantime, let it not be a trouble to your Grace to let me know by one line, how you proceed Doctress in Divinity, in Plato.

Thursday morning.

I ought not to forget telling your Grace how extreme kindly my Friend Allen took your Order for *Bucks*; but he will extend it no further than *One*, this year. If all his Family were not with him, he would have waited on you, & paid you His Thanks.

Address: To the Duchess of | Marlborough.
Endorsement: Mr Pope
Another Endorsement: Mr Pope's letter to | The Dss of Marlbro'

POPE *to* THE EARL OF ORRERY[1] 27 *August* [1742]

The Pierpont Morgan Library

Twitnam Aug. 27. | 1742

My Lord,—I was unlucky in missing your operator at Twitnam, but I understand he thought all the Urns but two, too small for the places you allotted. Mr Allen is here, & I find he has none of the Drawings of Lord Burlington; but my Lord B. tells me one Collins has several, who executes them for him at Bath: & that will certainly be your best method of proceeding in it.

I would say a great deal, to your Lordship & Lady Orrery both, of my frequent Dreams, & Escapes of Soul toward you: for I often imagine myself with you, enjoying what I cannot here enjoy, Solitude, Study, Conversation un-interrupted, & a Mind disengaged from all but its own best Employments. You who know what they are, would incourage & assist me in 'em instead of diverting me from them, as I am here diverted every moment by ev'ry body.

There is nothing *You* will think strange, but the Publick is in great Expectations of New Promotions or more of our Friends. It is still talked, even at Court, that the K. will go abroad, & reconcile when He Commands in chief, the Pretension of Two Generals.[2] I told the D. of Argyle yesterday that I had lately heard from you, he thought you was in Ireland. Lord Chesterfield was here, & sends you his Services. Lord Gower is recoverd of an Ague & goes soon to Bath.

[1] The year is added by Lord Orrery.
[2] The rumour proved true, and King George II commanded over the rival generals (the Earl of Stair for the English and the Duke of Aremberg for the Austrians) and won the Battle of Dettingen in June 1743.

I am sorry for the Removal of the late Lord Privyseal,[1] who would much better have ended with what This has begun, the Signing a certain Patent, & the Pardon of Rob. Knight.

Address: To the Rt Hon. the | Earl of Orrery.
Endorsement (in Orrery's hand): Mr Pope. | Augt 27th 1742.

*POPE *to* HUGH BETHEL[2] [1742]

Egerton 1948

It is indeed a great trouble to me to hear a worse account of your health from your last kind Letter, than I had been made to hope from one of Dr Kay a fortnight before. If the air of the Italian Towns agrees no better with you, I cannot but wish you nearer us, as soon as you have receivd all the benefit the Waters of Viterbo can afford. The South part of France probably will be of more Service with respect both to the Asthma, & that feverish disposition. All I should regret in your leaving Italy, would be the Company & assistance of that Physician of whom you send me so amiable a character. Worthy Men are, & must be Friends, where-ever they meet with one another, in spite of all distinctions of Party or Religion. There are some in all Countries; the Wonder is to find any in any Courts; but I believe there may be more in the Courts of Unhappy, than of Prosperous Princes. In your own Country, I can assure you with sorrow, they daily decrease, or change from good to bad, which is worse: I protest I scarce can name you any, for whose sake it would be worth your while to leave your Doctor: but could I name one such in this Profession, and one in every other Profession, I should think England the New Jerusalem. The Lady you send your Remembrances to, & who constantly speaks of you, inquires of you, & wishes you every good, has one of the best, as she has one of the Sincerest & Gentlest, hearts: and it is pity her own Infirmities should have any share in increasing that Concern for others, which is enough rais'd by her own Goodness & Compassion. I can not give you so good an account as I would, either of her health or happiness, but she lives on, & suffers on, more than she ought with her Temperance & Temper.[3] I made your Compliments to Lord

[1] Lord Gower was to succeed Lord Hervey as Lord Privy Seal. Hervey, Pope thought, might fittingly sign the patent making William Pulteney Earl of Bath (14 July) and also sign the pardon of Robert Knight, who as cashier of the South Sea Company had fled to France and lived there since the days of the 'bubble'.

[2] Pope here answers a letter in which Bethel has commented on *The New Dunciad* (published late in March) as well as on the death of Lady Dorothy Boyle (Countess of Euston), who died on 2 May. If Pope sent him through his brother Slingsby (16 June) a copy of the poem, this letter might date August or September.

[3] Miss Blount's health prevented her from visiting Sarah, Duchess of Marlborough at about this time. See Pope to the Duchess, [16 Sept. 1742].

Burlington, who shows great & continued affliction for the unfortunate Lady Euston, the whole circumstance of whose Marriage & Death would be melancholy to any Barbarian but her Husband. The seeds you were so kind to send came not to his, or to my hands. I hope the New Dunciad which I sent you, had better luck. ⌜That poem has not done me, or my Quiet, the least harm; only it provokd Cibber to write a very foolish & impudent Letter, which I have no cause to be sorry for, & perhaps next Winter I shall be thought to be glad of: But I lay in my Claim to you, to Testify for me, that if he should chance to die before a New & Improved Edition of the Dunciad comes out, I have ready, actually written (before, & not after his death) all I shall ever say about him—⌝[1]

I have just now receivd from your Brother, to my great joy, a better account of your present health, that you are returnd to Viterbo, & find the Waters so useful as to determine you to stay there this Winter. God send you more & more such good reason to keep you, how much soever I could wish to embrace you again! To hear you were well must be surely a vastly greater Satisfaction, than it could be to see you not perfectly so: and whatever gives you hopes of amendment, gives me more contentment than almost any Hopes in this world. I thank God I wish nothing it can give so much as the Welfare of honest Men, & the Continuance of their Friendship: and I still do, as I ever have done, place you at the head of them. Pray continue to write to me, & think you can do it to no one living, who is more concernd for you, than | Dear Sir | Your ever affectionate | faithful Servant, | A. Pope

If I knew any news of this place that I could imagine would in the least interest you or amuse you, I would send it: & I wish you would ask me any Questions that I might satisfy you about. Adieu my dear Friend.

Address: A Monsieur | Monsieur Bethel | A Rome [Added, not in Pope's hand:] Roma.

*POPE *to* LOUIS RACINE[2] — 1 *September* 1742

Bibliothèque Nationale

Sept. 1. 1742

Sir,—Nothing had delayed my Acknowledgment for your most Obliging Letter, but the Expectation of that agreable Present with

[1] The passage in half-brackets was quoted by Ruffhead (1769), p. 390. It pretends a casual contempt for Cibber's *Letter* (published in July or early August), and is important as indicating that the revision of *The Dunciad* making Cibber hero is practically an accomplished fact.

[2] This important letter is printed from the facsimile of the original given as frontispiece to Dean Emile Audra's *Influence française dans l'œuvre de Pope* (Paris, 1931). Its history is

which you have honourd me, the Book itself. The only Allay to the pleasure it gave me in reading it, was to find that you imputed to me Principles I never was guilty of. But then again, your Declaration at the end of it, 'That you did not understand the Original, that you could not be certain whether it really contained those Principles or not, and that you had done this only because Others had thought they found them there: This Sir, I must look upon as a great & extra ordinary proof of your Candor, your Temper, & your Charity.

But I assure you Sir, a total Ignorance of our Language has not been so fatal to me, as an Imperfect Knowledge of it. And all the Beauties of Mons. de Resnel's Versification have given less advantage to my Essay, than his continued mistakes of my Doctrine & Reasoning have injured it. You will see them sufficiently exposed in the Work I send you,[1] (written by the Learned Author of the Divine Legation of Moses) and I flatter myself, that the Chevalier Ramsay, who has so warm a Zeal for Truth, will take the trouble of explaining it to your full Satisfaction: After which, I may trust to your own Justice.

Upon the whole, I have the pleasure to answer you in the manner you most desire, a Sincere Avowal that my Opinions are intirely different from those of Spinoza; or even of Leibnitz; but on the contrary conformable to those of Mons: Pascal & Mons. Fenelon: the latter of whom I would most readily imitate, in submitting all my Opinions to the Decision of the Church.

I have the honour to be, with just regard, | Sir | Your most humble & | most obedient Servant | A. Pope.

POPE *to* COLLET MAWHOOD[2] — 2 *September* [1742]

Sotheby sale, 28 Nov. 1913

FRAGMENT

Thursday, Sept. 2nd

If this should meet you in town I shall be glad to finish Mr. W.'s[3] commission this afternoon.

unravelled by M. Audra in his *Influence*, pp. 98–104. Briefly, Racine in his poem *La Religion* (1742) had attacked the *Essay on Man*. The Chevalier Ramsay had protested, and Racine had suggested that Pope might well explain his views further. This letter aims to do just that, and constitutes Pope's clearest statement as to his religious views. Racine published the letter in French. Thereupon Voltaire discredited the letter by asserting that to his knowledge Pope was incapable of writing in French. Voltaire's opinion discredited the letter until Dean Audra discovered the English original in the Bibliothèque Nationale.

[1] Warburton's *Commentary*.

[2] The letter is known only from the sale catalogue, in which it appears as item 15 of lot 355.

[3] Warburton's.

*POPE *to* ALLEN[1] [13 *September* 1742]

Egerton 1947

Munday

With great pleasure I receive the account of your being all returned in health to Widcombe. I have been but once in London since, & that only to meet Mawhood, but he disappointed me. I am now ingaged[2] again in Windsor forest unavoidably for some time; so I was forcd to send to Mr Knapton last Sunday to dine with me at Twitnam, to whom I gave the Note, & go back to morrow. He will do his utmost to get the Mony. I also mentiond the affair of Shakespear,[3] & the Proposal to Tonson [whic]h he will make to him, & Mr Warburton & He will determine accordingly. But I hope to see it setled one way or other (and I think either will be pretty well with respect to Mr W.) before he returns. I would not have written to you yet, expecting in ten days or thereabouts to be able to fix the time of our meeting, but Savage plagues me with his Misunderstandings, & Miseries together (or I should not take so much regard to the former) and I must send him an answer. You see it inclosed,[4] & I beg you to add and put into it, an order for five guineas to be paid him by the Postmaster at Bristol. I must further desire you to inquire whether he be in any particular misfortune, or in Prison? for such a Report I have heard,[5] tho he says not a word like it, only desires me to send him a Remittance to enable him to pay his Journey to London, declaring his absolute Resolution to stay no longer in the Country. I can really assist him no further, nor will it be in that case to any purpose.

Adieu. Mrs Blount is here at Petersham & sends you & Mrs Allen a thousand hearty services.

I must beg Mr Prynne to transcribe the Enclosed letter, & you to keep it.

Address: To Ralph Allen Esqr | at Widcomb near | Bath.
Postmark: 14/SE

POPE *to* RICHARD SAVAGE[6] 15 *September* 1742

1769 (Ruffhead, p. 504)

I am sorry to say there are in your letter so many misunderstandings,

[1] The date is deduced from the postmark (partly visible) and the superscribed 'Munday'.

[2] Letters following this one make it doubtful if Pope has yet waited on the aged Duchess of Marlborough. 'Ingaged' may mean 'committed to visit'. If he has already visited Her Grace, he has returned home to meet Knapton (on the 5th or 12th, both Sundays), and 'goes back' to Windsor Lodge tomorrow. But possibly it is Knapton who 'goes back' to London—in which case 'go' is a miswriting.

[3] See the letter to Warburton, 23 Apr. 1742.

[4] The enclosure is the letter immediately following this one.

[5] Savage was imprisoned for debt in Bristol on 10 January 1742/3.—*DNB.*

[6] Presumably this is the letter enclosed to Allen in Pope's letter of 13 Sept. The fact that

that I am weary of repeating what you seem determined not to take rightly.

I once more tell you, that neither I, nor any one who contributed at first to assist you in your retirements, ever desired you should stay out of London, for any other reason than that your debts prevented your staying in it.

No man desired to confine you to the country, but that the little they contributed might support you better there than in a town.

It was yourself who chose Swanzey for your place; you no sooner objected to it afterwards, (when Mr. Mendez[1] stopt his allowance, upon complaint that you had used him ill) but I endeavoured to add to it, and agreed to send remittances to any other country place you pleased. Indeed I apprehended Bristol was too great a city to suit a frugal expence; however I sent thither all I could, and now with as good a will, I add this little more at your desire, which I hope will answer your end you propose of making easy your journey to London.

I heartily wish you may find every advantage, both in profit and reputation, which you expect from your return and success; not only on the stage, but in every thing you shall commit to the press. The little I could contribute to assist you should be at your service there, could I be satisfied it would be effectually so; (though intended only while you were obliged to retire.) But the contrary opinion prevails so much with the persons I applied to, that it is more than I can obtain of them to continue it. What mortal would take your play, or your business with Lord T.[2] out of your hands, if you could come, and attend it yourself? It was only in defect of that, these offices of the two gentlemen[3] you are so angry at, were offered. What interest but trouble could they have had in it? And what was done more in relation to the Lord, but trying a method we thought more likely to serve you, than threats and injurious language? You seemed to agree with us at your parting, to send some letters, which after all were left in your own hands, to do as you pleased. Since when, neither they nor I ever saw or spoke to him, on yours or any other subject. Indeed I was shocked at your strong declarations of *vengeance* and *violent measures* against him, and am very glad you now protest you meant nothing like what those words imported.

Pope used Allen's secretary to transcribe the letter and keep the original accounts for the presence of the letter among the Warburton–Allen papers turned over to Ruffhead.

[1] Very likely the poet-broker Moses Mendez.

[2] Lord Tyrconnel was the nephew of the lady who was, so Savage alleged, Savage's mother.

[3] David Mallet and James Thomson, according to Dr. Johnson's *Life of Savage*.

POPE *to* SARAH, DUCHESS OF MARLBOROUGH

[*September* 1742]

Blenheim

Your Grace may believe me, that my Uncertainty is what I cannot help, & that I wisht firmly to have been sooner with you. But I have had some Concerns of Mr Warburton to manage in town, & others of my own, absolutely needful before my Journey: and I am so infirm (as you but see too well) that I can't do business, or pass from place to place, so easily as others. I have put off my Journey as late as possible, so that I will yet have some days with your Grace.—I am almost sorry you are so kind to me; I can be so little useful, or agreeable, from one unlucky Circumstance or other; & so imperfectly shew you, my Sense of what you do for me, that I am ashamed to be what I cannot help, the Thing that God made me. If you send on Friday, so, as we may come in the afternoon, the same day, I will not fail; nor will Mrs B. I'm sure, if possible, (for she is perfectly sensible of the distinction you honour her with) I am faithfully Your Grace's obligd, Servant. | A. Pope

That I intended to be at Windsor ev'n now, your Grace will see by some Letters which I believe are directed to me at the Lodge: but pray keep them till I come.

Address: To her Grace the Duchess | of Marlborough.
Endorsement: Mr. Pope.

POPE *to* SARAH, DUCHESS OF MARLBOROUGH[1]

[16 *September* 1742]

Blenheim

Thursday.

I am not so sorry I could not have waited on your Grace as yet, as Mrs Blount will be to be disappointed of showing you, it is to Yourself, & not for any one's Company, that she desires to come. Indeed she was very uneasy not to have done it sooner; tho' both then & now, she is in very bad health. Lord Chesterfield & I will be with your Grace by dinner, if I understood him rightly, & perhaps stay all night. As to Lodging, I care not where, I lodge, so it be under Heav'ns & your Protection. I am faithfully | Your Grace's always.

[1] The date is arrived at through surrounding letters and chiefly from a letter from Lord Chesterfield to Lord Marchmont (*Marchmont Papers*, ii. 282). On the 8th Chesterfield writes that he is going to spend a week with Nugent in Essex (at Gosfield), and he adds: 'When I return, I shall take up Pope at Twickenham the 19th, and carry him to the Duchess of Marlborough's at Windsor, in our way to Cobham's, where we are to be the 21st of this month. Should you happen to be at the Duchess of Marlborough's the 19th or 20th, it would be a pleasure. . . .' Since the 19th was Sunday, 'Thursday' would be the 16th.

I have sent your Servant to Thistleworth, in case my Lord Ch.[1] be returnd from Essex, for an answer to your question.

Address: To her Grace the | Duchess of Marlborough
Endorsement: Mr Pope's letter to | The Dss of Marlbro'

*POPE *to* ALLEN — 23 *September* [1742]

Egerton 1947

Twitnam Sept. 23.[2]

As you had my First Fruits, so you have my Last, & I hope they were as good as the first: I speak of the Pineapples, which I hope you receivd this week.

I have been so detain'd, where I could not without an Imputation of Ingratitude refuse to pass some time, that it was past my power to avail myself of Lord Chesterfields offer of carrying me halfway to you. The Lady[3] flamed upon it, & would hear of no such thing; her Coach should carry me any whither, but I must be left with her by that Lord. So I am, & not well into the bargain, nor have been fit to be from home, tho indeed it is impossible to be better attended or kinder treated. Every day it troubles me not to be with you, & especially as I fear Mr Warburton can stay no longer than it is requisite he should be with You, both for his own health from the Waters, & for your satisfaction. Otherwise could I have him from you a fortnight, I would rather take the journey when I could stay a month or more with you, whereas now I must return in much less time. I beg to know exactly of Mr W. & you, how long is his latest stay with you? and I will do my utmost to get to Widcomb, so as to be the last fortnight there. the beginning of the next month is the soonest I can possibly set out, but if he can stay till the End of Octr I would not come till the middle, & leave you when your Honors come upon you in the Mayoralty:[4] Unless you want a grave Counsellor to assist you in the Cares of the Government, in which case I should endeavor to remain with you longer into the Winter. For in truth I am so crazy, & see a Journey with so much Apprehension & so little pleasure, that were it not we are unfortunately so far asunder, I would never more go twenty miles from home. The least cold I catch takes from me all Enjoyment of my Life & all

[1] Chesterfield.

[2] In spite of the superscribed 'Twitnam' Pope obviously writes from Windsor Lodge, where the *exigeante* Duchess has detained him.

[3] The Dowager Duchess of Marlborough. See the note to Pope's letter to her [16 Sept.]. The plan had been for Pope and Lord Chesterfield to visit the Duchess briefly, go on to Stowe, and thence to Bath. Pope was thought to be at Stowe in October (see Hist. MSS. Comm., *Denbigh*, v. 171), but he seems not to have gone thither.

[4] Allen has been elected Mayor of Bath, and one judges his term would begin about 1 Nov.

comfort of Conversation, in which condition I've dragg'd my self about these 3 weeks.

My Road to you, now, must be by Newbury, by which means I shall get the sooner to my journey's end, when ever I begin it. which I am sure no man could do with a better Heart, or a more jaded Body.

Mr Hooke & Mrs. Blount are your faithful Servants I'm just going home to see the latter, & answer for her. I hope Mr Warb. pursues the point of his health, & that Mr Knapton has receivd his Mony. I am concerned for both those: Credit, affection, & Contentment he will get for himself. I am *happy* in your mutual Friendship, and *strong* in it. Decus, & Praesidium,[1] he will english it—I am Yours, His, & Mrs Allen's, Ever | A. Pope.

I must trouble you to let your answer as to Mr Warb'ns Stay, and how far you can without inconveniency send to meet me, be a Duplicate, & send one to Twitnam, one to the Duchess of Marlboroughs at the Lodge in the Great Park at Windsor. Three lines will be sufficient. I think I can certainly be at Newbury by the 5th of October.

POPE *to* SARAH, DUCHESS OF MARLBOROUGH[2]

13 *October* [1742]

Blenheim

Bath. Oct. 13th

I can tell your Grace nothing of my self so well worth your notice, or so much to my Advantage, as that which the inclosed Paper will show you; that I am as mindful of your Commands Absent as Present, and as much your faithful Servant at Bath as at Windsor. The Inscription is the very Best I can do, in this sort of Writing, which requires to be so Short & so Plain: If it can be mended, it must be by Mr Hooke; but I will venture to say any Wit would spoil it. And a Writer of plain Sense & Judgment is as rare to be met with, as a Woman of plain Sense & Judgment.

I hope you are as well as I left you. I am not, because I have left you. And I will add no Compliments, because I am truly Yours.

Endorsements: 13th October | Mr Pope's letter to | The Dutchess of Marlbro' [And in another hand]: The inscription for Mr Vernons Busto[3]

[1] Horace, *Carmina*, I. i. 2.

[2] Courthope (EC, v. 412) placed this letter in 1741, but on 13 Oct. of that year Pope was not in Bath. The only possibility seems to be 1742.

[3] Thomas Vernon, Esq., of Twickenham had died in 1726. He was a wealthy Turkey merchant—and also Pope's landlord. The bust might be thought his, but it is actually that of Admiral Vernon, hero of Porto Bello. See M. I. Webb, *Rysbrack*, p. 167.

*POPE *to the* COUNTESS OF ORRERY 14 *October* 1742

Arthur A. Houghton, Jr.

Madam,—I am sure it ought to be a Rule with the Rich, (I mean the Few of them that are good for any thing) to bestow not only where there is Want, but where there is Merit, and above all, where both are united: I take this to be your Ladyships case, and you may be certain of what you ask from Mr & Mrs Allen.[1] They would send you one of each sex immediately, but it seems the sex is not distinguishable while they are very young, and it would be to no purpose for you to have them till they are further advanced, which will be in about six weeks. Old ones you may have now. I wish with all my heart I could attend the Happy Couple to Marston, (where every Animal, rational or irrational, I am persuaded is happy). I should be glad to share with Bounce in a few chicken there; but Dogs & Birds have the better of me: they can travell where I can't.[2] It is in Reflection only that I have the advantage of them, for they are not quite so sensible of their happiness in being yours, as I am: I beg my Lord to think me but as Grateful & as Faithfull. I am with the greatest truth | Your Ladyships most | obliged & obedient | Servant, | A. Pope.

Bath. Oct. 14.

Address: To the Rt. Hon. the | Countess of Orrery.
Endorsement: Mr Pope | No. 1.

*LOUIS RACINE *to* POPE 25 *October* 1742

The Scots Magazine, xvi (1754), 232

Paris, Oct. 25. 1742.

Sir,—The mildness and humility with which you justify yourself,[3] is a convincing proof of your religion; the more so, as you have done it to one, on whom it is incumbent to make his own apology for his rash attack upon your character. Your manner of pardoning me is the more delicate, as it is done without any mixture of reproach. But though you acquit me with so much politeness, I shall not so easily forgive myself.

[1] Lady Orrery evidently wants from the Allens a pair of guinea fowl. See Pope's letter to her of 31 Oct. 1742, which explains her desire.

[2] Jolting over 'insuperable rocks' was too painful for Pope, but not for Bounce or the Happy Couple of guinea fowl. On Bounce at Marston see above, p. 406.

[3] This reply to Pope's letter to Racine of 1 Sept. was discovered by Mr. Ault, who brought it to the editor's attention. The letter was printed (in French) in Racine's *La Religion* (5th ed., 1747), if not earlier. It is most unfortunate that we do not have Pope's correspondence with the Chevalier Ramsay or with Lord Bolingbroke for this period. Audra (*Influence*, p. 104, n. 4) mentions a Canon Hasset of Saverne as corresponding with Pope concerning the *Essay on Man*.

Certain it is, a precipitance of zeal hurried me away. As I had often heard positions, said to be your's, or at least consequences resulting from your essay, cited against certain truths, which I now find you respect as much as myself, I thought it right to enter the lists with you. The passage in my preface was extorted from me by a degree of remorse, which I felt in writing against you. This remorse, Sir, was awakened in me by the consideration, that the greatest men are always the most susceptible of the truths of revelation. I was really grieved to think that Mr Pope should oppose a religion, whose enemies have ever been contemptible; and it appeared strange, that in a work which points out the road to happiness, you should furnish arms to those who are industrious to misguide us in the research.

Your letter, at the same time that it does honour to your character, must bring a blush in my face, for having entertained unjust suspicions. But, notwithstanding this, I think myself obligated to make it public. The injury which I have done you was so, the reparation should be the same. I owe this to you, I owe it to myself, I owe it to justice.

Whatever may be said in your favour in the commentary you have sent me, it is now rendered unnecessary by your own declaration. The respect you avow for the religion you profess, is a sufficient vindication of your doctrine. I will add, that, for the future, those among us who shall feel the laudable ambition of making their poetry subservient to religion, ought to take you for their model; and it should ever be remembered, that the greatest poet in England is one of the humblest sons of the church. | I am, &c.

*POPE *to the* COUNTESS OF ORRERY[1] — 31 *October* 1742

Arthur A. Houghton, Jr.

Oct. 31st. 1742

I receiv'd a Note from Mr Brinsden, which says I must not write to my Lady Orrery; but I desire Her to tell my Lord, that his Lady has sent me so fine a Present that it shall never lye on my unworthy Table, till his Lordship & She will do me the honour to use it at Twitenham; in the order to which I am improving that place all I can this winter, to make it happier than it was last year, in seeing them oft'ner. That will carry me sooner than my Inclination, from this place where I am, & repine to be so kept by insuperable Rocks from Marston, at the same time that all lies open to the Land of Perdition, London. Yet I find it natural, when one goes to the Devil oneself, to wish to draw

[1] In spite of what he says Pope seems to be writing to the Countess. The editorial guess —an extreme one—is that Lady Orrery had sent, possibly by Mr. Brinsden, a gift of fine Irish linen for Pope's table, with the injunction that he is not to write his thanks to her. Ingeniously Pope asks that she tell Lord Orrery what value he sets on the gift.

others thither, & I do earnestly wish my Lord[1] to watch the Opening of his[2] Divan this Sessions at Pandemonium; whither every one is going in the utmost hurry. As there will be all other Orders of Angels, methinks the *Virtues* should not be absent.

But if there be such an Eve in our days, as will keep her Husband in Paradise, instead of driving him out, and prefers to pick sloes and feed chickens half the winter; she is desired to send hither, in four or five days, for a sober pair of Guinea Fowl, already marry'd, & of proper years to breed, & perhaps better qualifyd to educate their children, than a young, disorderly, unexperienc'd Couple that may over-run each other with fondness, or make love to strange Poultry, thro mere Ignorance. You may please to try Both; these are now ready, & the others will not in some time. The thing I wish is, that you would be content to see the present Pair settled, then leave them to their mutual Embraces for some time, & let me accompany you to London at any time within this Month. Your time should be mine, & Mr Allen's chariot is to attend me, which should travell your pace.[3] All this I say to my Lord Orrery, and I desire he will oblige my Lady to do what we will.—I don't write to her since she commands the contrary: but sure I may say (to any body) I am hers most faithfully | A. Pope.

Endorsement: Mr Pope | No. 2

*POPE *to* WARBURTON — 1 *November* [1742]

Egerton 1946

Munday. Nov. 1.

Everybody here, have been Every day, wishing and praying for your good Journey;[4] Your Letter has cast us all down; and given us a sincere Concern and Fear. I hope in God you are in some good hand, and that you do not neglect an Accident which may be dangerous, if it be as bad as we apprehend, from your owning it a bad one. Another Fear arises, from our apprehension you may be willing to go about, during your stay in town, which is often in such a case, a hazard. We desire to be further certifyd how your leg is?[5] and what way it is in? I hope you will not hasten your departure, till you are perfectly recover'd of it. If you are detained much longer than you expected, I

[1] 'My Lord' is written above 'you', which is crossed out. Pope thus remains equivocal as to his addressee.

[2] Parliament here is the devil's 'divan'.

[3] Pope did not leave Bath until the end of November; but since a son was born to the Orrerys on 21 Nov., he probably did not have their company to town.

[4] Pope had arrived in Bath before 13 Oct. (see his letter to the Duchess of Marlborough), and a fortnight later Warburton is returning via London to Newark.

[5] *En route* to London an accident has injured Warburton's leg. This will be a matter of concern in several letters that follow within the next few weeks—all therefore placed in 1742.

would hasten my departure hence, and come to you.—Mr Allen would have written in answer to yours this day, but he was all day taken up in Mayoralty business at Bath.—I wish Mr Bowyer would send me once more the proof of the Sheet he sent last, in which is the Conclusion of the first book, before it is work'd off.[1] He may at the same time go on with the Corrections you will make in the half sheet to be cancelld at the beginning.—so that no Time will be lost.

I shall be very uneasy till I hear more of your Leg. God preserve you always! | Dear Sir Your Entirely affectionate | and oblig'd Friend & Servant | A. Pope

*POPE *to* WARBURTON [6 *November* 1742].

Egerton 1946

Saturday

I heartily wish you a perfect Recovery of that unlucky accident, & wish you asked some advice as to the Swelling. I fear you walk too much upon it, & was sorry you had been out so soon at Mr Murray's.[2] I wish He knew, that the Affidavit & the Book he mentiond, was never sent me, nor have I heard a word from Mr Cole[3] about it. Pray if you have an Opportunity, just tell him so, with the State of the thing, for certainly if Millar has had redress, I may.[4] and I know tis Mr Murrays Opinion I should prosecute—[5]

That part of the Note may well be omitted, which Bowyer tells you, & which I found was left out. But I can't tell why he has omitted the latter part of another Note at the End of Book 1. which is work'd off. It is that which mentions the Second Lye of the Abbe Tallemant on Boileau, that he had been beaten by Pradon a bad poet, & which was paralleld by what C.[6] says of Philips & me. It certainly should be

[1] Evidently the revised *Dunciad*, on which Bowyer had been working for a long time. Book I, line 298 had to be cancelled because of the death of Lord Hervey: this cancel is perhaps what Pope speaks of. The whole sheet was reprinted?

[2] The Mawhood affair would seem to have been settled, and Warburton now is consulting Murray for Pope about piracies. See the notes following.

[3] Solicitor of the Stationers' Company.

[4] Andrew Millar had secured redress 23 Oct. 1742 for a piracy of Fielding's *Joseph Andrews*. See W. L. Cross, *History of Henry Fielding*, i. 355.

[5] Pope was already contemplating one or more suits in Chancery. On 16 Feb. 1742/3 he sued Lintot concerning the copyright of *The Dunciad* (C11, 549/39), and on the same day sued Jacob Ilive for pirating *The Dunciad Book the Fourth* (C11, 837/14). Possibly he had other troubles as well.

[6] See Cibber's *Letter*, p. 65. These notes seem to have disappeared before publication. See Boileau, *Épître VI*, 60 n.; *Épître VII*, 90, in which last locus Pope found the following literary source or precedent for Cibber's brothel episode: 'L'Abbé Tallement s'attira cette fâcheuse critique par une fausse avanture qu'il débita en pleine Académie contre l'honneur de Mr. Despréaux. Il y lut une lettre, par laquelle on lui mandoit que le jour précedent Mr. Despréaux étant dans un lieu de débauche, derrière l'Hôtel de Condé, y avoit été fort maltraité. Ceux qui ont connu ce Poëte d'une manière plus intime, savent que jamais calomnie ne fut plus mal-fondé que celle-là' (Boileau, *Œuvres*, i (1716), 241).

in, & the note as it now stands refers to it, in citing the Notes on Boileaus 6th & 7th Epistles, in the former of which the Story is told. I send the leaf, & have so shortend the thing to be added that I hope it can be cancelld, & the rather as it will contain also the Alteration I desired so much of one Verse. Pray let him Send the half sheet & this leaf to me as soon as you have corrected & work'd them off. I like the Note on Proteus much—[1]

My head akes, and therfore excuse all defects. In my heart there is none, but the truest and warmest sense of a hundred proofs of your Friendship and Sollicitude for me. Mr. Allen is well, and wholly Yours, as I Sincerely am always. Adieu.

Address: To the Reverend | Mr Warburton

*POPE *to* BOWYER[2] 13 *November* [1742]

Egerton 1946

Bath: Novr 13.

Not being certain, but rather believing Mr Warb. to be gone, before this will reach you, I do not write to him. he has omitted to say how his Leg is, pray tell me in your next, how he was when he left you: and if you send soon to him, desire that he would write me a Line of his safe arrival at home. The sooner you send your Sheets hither, the better. I shall not stay long, but will acquaint you of all my motions.

I suppose Cooper has had part of your Edition in 8o of the New Dunciad & Memoirs of Scriblerus—pray tell me what number?[3] according to which We mu[st] print or retard the Fourth Book in [thi]s edition.

I've sent you another leaf to cancel by all means.

P.S. Just now I receive yours about the *Brazen* Image.[4] I would have it stand as it is, & no matter if the Criticks dispute about it.

Address: To Mr Bowyer, Printer, in | Whitefriers near the | Temple | London.

Frank: Free | Jn Jeffreys

Postmark: 15/NO

[1] Warburton's note on Proteus concerns *Dunciad*, Bk. I, l. 37.

[2] The letter cannot be later than 1742, since in 1743 Pope had before November returned from Bath. The letter fits in 1742.

[3] The edition published as *Works*, III. ii (Griffith, No. 566) must here be in question. Griffith erred (p. 462) in the opinion that Bowyer began to print for Pope in 1743.

[4] See *The Dunciad*, Bk. I, ll. 31–32. The 'Criticks' had pointed out that the images done by Cibber's father for the entrance to Bedlam were not of brass. See *The Dunciad* (ed. Sutherland), p. 296.

This postscript is incomplete, at least one line having been cut away.

*POPE *to* JONATHAN RICHARDSON[1] 14 *November* 1742

Bath Municipal Reference Library

Bath. Novr 14th | 1742

The whole purpose of this is only to tell you, that the Length of my Stay at this distance from you, has not made me unmindful of you; and that I think you have regard enough for me to be pleased to hear, I have been, & am, better than usual. In about a fortnight or three weeks I hope to find you as little older as possible at your age, than when I left you, as I am at mine. God send you all Ease, Philosophical & Physical! I am your sincerely-affectionate Friend | & Servant | A. Pope

My Services to your Son.

Address: To | Mr Richardson. in | Queen's Square.

POPE *to* WARBURTON[2] 27 *November* [1742]

Egerton 1946

Bath. Nov. 27.

This will shew you I am still with our Friend, but it is the last day; and I would rather you heard of me pleased as I yet am, than chagrin, as I shall be in a few hours. We are both pretty well. I wish you had been more explicite, if your Leg be quite well. You say no more than that you got home well: I expect a more particular account of you, when you have reposed yourself a while at your own Fireside. I shall enquire as soon as I am in London, which of my Friends have seen you? There are two or three who know how to value you: I wish I was as sure they would study to serve you: ⌜Tho the Mediocrity of your Desires, and the Turn of your Affections, may make you (as I should myself) prefer the Plain Friendship of Mr Allen to all the Honour that Men of higher Rank can do us.

⌜Mr Murray wrote me word of his receipt of the 100. It is a very small instance of the Service I would do you 5ll a year, but if in any thing of that sort I ever can be of assistance, or Ease to you, freely tell me so. I could put out a larger Sum when you will, or be glad to add to any, to make the principal even, till you had more to dispose of: In which case you ought to have my Bond at least, and I intend to send it you even for this, in case of accidents.⌝

A Project has arisen in my head to make you in some measure the Editor of this new Edit. of the Dunc.[3] if you have no scruple of owning

1 On the back of the letter are twelve lines of undeciphered notes in shorthand.

2 Printed in 1751 by Warburton, with interesting omissions here placed in half-brackets.

3 That is, of the four books complete.—Warburton, 1751.

some of the *Graver Notes* which are now added to those of ⌜Mr Cleland &⌝ Dr Arb.[1] I mean it as a kind of Prelude or Advertisement to the publick of your Commentarys on the Essays on Man, and on Criticisme, which I propose to print next in another Volume, proportiond to This.[2] ⌜I have scratched out a sort of *Avis au Lecteur*,[3] which I'l send you to this effect, which if you disapprove not, you'l make your own.⌝ I have a particular reason to make you Interest your self in Me & My Writings. It will cause both them & me to make the better figure to Posterity. a very mediocre Poet, one Drayton, is yet taken some notice of, because Selden writ a ⌜very⌝ few Notes on one of his Poems.[4]

⌜Your next will find me probably with Bowyer, who does not quite answer my Impetuosity for getting this poem[5] out of my hands. If you direct either to him or to Twitnam there will be an Equal chance of my quick receit of it.⌝ Adieu. May every Domestic Happiness make you unwilling to remove from home, and may every Friend you do that kindness for, treat you so as to make you forget you are not at home. I am ever cordially, tho not effectually, Dear Sir. Your faithfull tho not Useful Servant | A. Pope

Address: To Mr Warburton

*POPE *to* ALLEN[6] [? 1 *December* 1742]

Egerton 1947

Twitenham. Wednesday night.

I arrived here last night, weary, but well, half repenting that I left you, yet pleasd to think I had no more Winter Journeys before me. A little Cold is all I have yet to complain of, but I had it before I came, & I fear I shall increase it in London. I already meet with News

[1] Pope liked to insist that the notes in *The Dunciad* were not all by himself: here he specifies helpers. The omission of Cleland's name in 1751 may be due to the recent publication of his son's notorious novel, which brought the name under a cloud in about 1750.

[2] Warburton believed that if he had a right to omit passages, he might also add, and at this point he inserted the following (not in the original letter): 'I only doubt whether an avowal of these notes to so ludicrous a poem be suitable to a character so established as yours for more serious studies. It was a sudden thought since we parted; and I would have you treat it as no more; and tell me if it is not better to be suppress'd; freely and friendlily.' (Pope's *Works* [1751], ix. 350.) See Pope's letter to Warburton, 4 Dec. 1742, from which this matter is lifted.

[3] A working MS. of this *Avis*, much interlined and in Pope's hand, is preserved as part of Egerton 1950. In *The Dunciad* of 1743 (quarto) it is printed (pp. v–vi) and signed 'W. W.'

[4] Pope's deference to the commentator's office here contrasts with what he prints in *The Dunciad*. See, for example, Bk. IV, ll. 101 ff.

[5] *The Dunciad* in four Books.

[6] The date is from the very imperfect postmark. Pope left Widcombe either on the 27th or 28th (see Pope to Warburton, 27 Nov.), and is writing upon arrival or the day thereafter. 1 Dec. was Wednesday in 1742.

enough from thence, to wish I could stay here, & see it as seldome as You do Bath. Indeed my Heart is sick of This bad World, (as Cato said.) and I see it daily growing worse. If there were to be Another Deluge, I protest I don't know more than One Noah; and his Wife, (for he happens to have no children) whom I could expect God would save: I hope He will live forty years however, to preach in, before it comes. And considering what Posterity generally proves, It is no great matter whether he begets Sons & Daughters, or not.—I will not thank you for any thing, but love you for every thing I know of you, whether done to myself or another.

With all the observation I could possibly make, I could not perceive you had any Anxiety about you except a sort of apprehension that the Chimney of the Pine-house might smoke so as to be offensive to the new building. John[1] assures me it will not; there need be no fires all the day, & the quantity, when once the house is tight, & the Glaziers work good, so small, that it evaporates within a few yards of the place. I would fain have it succeed, for two particular reasons; one because I saw it was Mrs Allen's desire to have that fruit, & the other because it is the only piece of Service I have been able to do you, or to help you in.

I am not hastening so soon to London, as to have yet setled my Lodging there: therfore pray direct to Twitnam: for I hope you will very soon give me the pleasure to hear of yours & Mrs Allen's welfare which no one breathing wishes more warmly. A. Pope.

Address: To Ralph Allen Esqr at | Widcombe, near | Bath.
Postmark: 1/DE

*POPE *to* WARBURTON[2] — 4 *December* [1742]

Egerton 1946

London | Decr 4.

I have just receivd yours & as I have no Words to express, further than you already know, my Sincere Desires to merit your friendship: I will not Employ any. I thank you for what you so speedily have done, & shall put it to the press with all haste, the rest of the book being ready. If any thing more can be done for the Dunciad, it must be to acquaint the public that You have thought it worth your Care by bestowing some Notes upon it to make it more Important & Serious.[3] Whether the Sketch inclosed be proper for You to authorize

[1] John Searle, Pope's gardener for many years. After Pope's death Allen employed Searle.

[2] The original of this letter has been mutilated by cutting. Ruffhead (p. 392) printed the first paragraph of it, down to the words 'Important & Serious'.

[3] Pope's suggestion in his letter to Warburton of 27 Nov. has evidently brought no response in Warburton's reply: here Pope tries him again, but diffidently.

so far, I know not: but do you consider or whether with any Initial Letters, at the End, or no? I only doubt whether an Avowal of these Notes to so ludicrous a poem, be suitable to a Character so Establishd as yours for more Serious Studies?[1]

You dont give me full Satisfaction yet that your Leg is well. Adieu. be pleasd to direct your next to Bowyer for me. Mr Murray is your faithfull Servant, & I always.

Address: To the Reverd Mr Warburton, | at Newark: | Nottinghamshire Newark
Frank: free | Scott

*POPE *to* ALLEN — 8 *December* [1742]

Egerton 1947

London. Decr 8.

Yours I just received, with one inclosed from Mr Hooke, who begins to feel the effects of a Court Life, the Dependence upon the Great, who never do good, but with a View to make Slaves. They are still at Windsor; & know not when they shall remove.[2]

Your Hopes, from what I truly told you of my unpleasant Prospect of London this Year, are wellgrounded, and I shall infallibly wish to return to tranquillity in your neighborhood, or rather in your House, if Mrs Blount come at last to her Senses & fix in your neighborhood. I won't dispute *that Place*[3] with her, or else nobody should have it but myself. I just talkd to her of it, & the Situation, & Mrs Allen's Resolution as well as your own, that it should be the Lot of nobody but One, whom she & you could wish for a neighbor; She seem'd to long for such a place, & agreed that it would fit her in all its circumstances, nobody feeling more than herself, the true Contentment such a Situation would afford her way of thinking. If God but grant her Resolution, when she has once made the step of going down with you (if that can be obtained of her foolish weakness for her family) I am convinced the thing is done: & she will become as Sure and constant Friend, as well as Tenant, for years to come, as any you have. I found her (more than I could have imagin'd) satisfied of the Conveniency & Expediency, as well as Necessity, of such a Step: & I really hope it will

[1] This last sentence (at some time cut from the preceding part of the leaf) was transplanted by Warburton in 1751 when he inserted it in the letter of 27 Nov., which he printed. In the original letter (Egerton 1946, f. 66*r*) the conclusion after this point has been cut away and apparently lost. A part of the matter lost (but not all) is added by Warburton to the letter of 27 Nov. (q.v.).

[2] Hooke has been in the service of Sarah, Duchess of Marlborough, now for over a year, and while still with her at Windsor Lodge, begins to weary of the confinement.

[3] Hampton Manor in Bathampton, which Pope wished Miss Blount to take in case he should go to live with the Allens at Widcombe. Hampton is a few miles from Prior Park.

be effectual.—I have just seen Mr & Mrs Arb. who are well, & send you most sincere services. I am sorry to hear her say Mr Warburton's Leg was far from well when he left London, & that he made slight of a dropsical humor which was fallen on his ancle. I have heard from him & he says nothing. You, who are not anxious, will hope the best. I rejoice that the Smoke of the Pine-house is blown over: at least you flatter me in saying so. I should be sorry to blacken you any way; there are others of my Acquaintance who will be black whether I will or no: and you will be white, in spite of all the accidental Smokes in the world. Once more I tell you, I am sick of *this* World & the Great ones of it, tho they have been my intimate Acquaintance. Adieu. God bless you. I think he will; there are not many who will let him bless them, tho' he has given them much. | Yours faithfully, | A. P.

I have yet escaped any great Cold.

Address: To | Ralph Allen, Esqr | at Widcomb, near | Bath.
Postmark: 9/DE

*POPE *to* ALLEN [*December* 1742]

Egerton 1947

I am much pleasd with the Birds you sent me, & Mrs Blunt & I eat them who sends you all hearty Services. I am very much the happier, for your telling me Mr Warb.'s leg is quite well, for he had not told me so. I have been, & yet am, very busy in printing the Poem[1] which has cost me much more trouble than I expected, and an additional Discourse which Mr W. has sent me to prefix before it, has retarded it, very satisfactorily to myself, tho (as you know) I don't very well bear Retardments. I am going to Twitnam to pass the Holidays with Mr Murray Lord Marchmont Lord Cornbury & some others in the Neighborhood. Never were Public Affairs, & Expectations, on so odd a foot. It doubles my resolution to withdraw out of the Sound of 'em, & injoy with, or near you, more of that Quiet which best suits the Decline of Life.

I write this in haste, not being willing to omit longer (as it was several days before I receivd yours, (which came first to Twitnam, then to London & then followd me to Twitnam & back to London again.) I am vexd at this wrongheaded Fool, for troubling You, & hope You'l discourage such correspondence. pray send the Postmaster an order to pay him 5ll upon the inclosd Receit, I write the opposite side on purpose for you to send him inclosed only in a Cover to Sav.[2]

I will take a leisure hour soon to tell yourself & Mrs Allen more of

[1] *The Dunciad.*

[2] Savage, of course.

my mind, & more of my hearty wishes which are ever offerd for your prosperity. Adieu. I wish you both & Mr Chapman, & Mrs Gatty & Miss Bounce,[1] all a merry Christmass. | Yours always. | P

POPE *to* SARAH, DUCHESS OF MARLBOROUGH[2]

22 *December* [1742]

Blenheim

It is so long ago as when I was at Bath, that your Grace wrote me word, that as soon as you was well enough to let me have the pleasure to see you, you would acquaint me. At my Return to town, Mrs Blount (who had sent sometimes to inquire during your Illness at Marlborough house) gave me the satisfaction to hear you was better: which Mr Hook also confirmed. I have ever since been in hopes of a Summons from your Grace; but instead of that, you have loaded me with Presents, which make my Friends happier than myself: for without any compliment you may believe, I love you better than Venison. Mrs Arbuthnot and Mrs Blount pay you their hearty thanks: I pay you but imperfect ones, and can pay you no other, till I see you at Windsor: tho your Bounty has enabled me to make a great figure at Twickenham these Holydays, where I am to have two or three Friends. Is not that a great number? I hope they are honest Men, but that is almost presumptuous. I hope to see better Days next year, if (for a beginning) your Grace will admit your Poet to bring his Ode along with him on the first of January. I am (present, or absent) with the truest Wishes for your Ease and Welfare, always | Your Graces most | obliged & most faithfull | Servant, | A. Pope.

Decr the 22d

Endorsement: 22d Decemr | Mr Pope's letter to | The Dutchess of Marlbro

*POPE *to* ALLEN

27 *December* [1742]

Egerton 1947

Decr 27th

My last short Letter shewd you I was peevish. Savage's strange behavior made me so, & yet I was in haste to relieve him, tho I think

[1] The members of the holiday household at Prior Park are not easily identified: Mr. John Chapman (a possibility) was an alderman of Bath, mentioned in Allen's will, and a trustee of Allen's estate. Mrs. Gatty and Miss Bounce may be Allen's nieces, Gertrude Tucker (whom Warburton married in 1746) and the much younger Mary Allen (hence *Miss*), who in 1766 became the second wife of Viscount Hawarden.

[2] Courthope assigns this letter to 1741 (EC, v. 414), but Pope's first sentence makes that year impossible, since he was in 1741 at Bath. One is encouraged to place it in 1742 by Pope's account of his holiday hospitality. Writing to Allen about the same time (see the preceding letter), he names his expected guests.

nothing will relieve him. I am now free from anxiety, & as much at ease, as you like to be, and to make others: alone at Twitnam, till to morrow; when some of the Men of This World will be with me, & Envy me the Quiet which they will not give themselves. I am offerd to purchase the perpetuity of this house & Garden & the Cottages near it, the first at 20, the rest at 13 years purchace of the present rent. I am more indifferent about it, than before I saw Hamton, or knew Wydcomb, finding there are two places besides this, I could live & dye in. Yet I am willing to finish all my works here, and wish for the Rustic Stone for the 2 little Buildings, all the other Materials being ready. I think that will be the Last Sacrifice I shall make to the Nymphs of the Thames.

My coming to Town has put a Stop to the Pyraters of my book, who have surrenderd all their Copies to get free from further prosecution,[1] but had sold 5 or 600, for which they can't refund, in my wrong. The true Edition is at last completed,[2] & pray when you write tell Mr W. how much it is owing to him that it is complete, & how much I think it advantaged by his Notes & Discourse before it.—I am trying to serve that Gentleman, with a Great Man, who declares the Greatest Esteem for him, & presses much to be brought acquainted: but I never trust entirely in Great Men, tho this has much of that which generally animates them most to any thing good, Vanity; and has besides, Learning: but I would not mention this to any but you, till I see more of it—Did I thank you for the Birds?[3] Nothing could be more agreable of that sort, & in London they had a good Effect,[4] for they made me dine at home at 2 a clock; a practise I've continud since, & invite now & then a friend, to a private lodging. Mrs Blount & Mr & Mrs Arb. are to see my Housekeeping there one day next month, & I sometimes dine with them & carry my Venison &c. I've not been at a Great Table thrice, since I came from You. My health (Colds excepted) is much the better. I desire you to be particular in your account of your own, & Mrs Allen's, which no one living can wish more ardently than I. Pray let two or three of your neighbors know I am not such a Brute as to forget them, particularly Mr Moyzer, Dr Hartley, Dr Oliver, Mr Brinsden: For as I write to no body, I stand in need of some active Friend to convince them I am not indifferent to the Civility and Attention they show me. Thank Mr

[1] Jacob Ilive, in defending himself concerning the piratical publication of 1,000 copies of 'The Dunciad Book the Fourth', says that he and other offenders 'in December or January last' sent their unsold copies (400) to the chambers of Pope's counsel. Pope's bill of complaint is dated 16 Feb. 1742/3, and Ilive replied on 6 May 1743 (P.R.O. Chancery Bills C11, 837/14).

[2] This would be the edition of all four Books.

[3] He did, in the earlier letter of this month.

[4] To enable him to attend to business affairs (piracies, &c.) Pope evidently had taken lodgings in London at this time.

Moyzer for his most welcom news from Mr Bethel, & when he writes to him I beg he will say, that I *have spoken to his Brother about what he orderd me.*—Mr Hook is still a Prisoner at Windsor,[1] Daughter & all—Lord Radnor[2] at Twitnam, & has never been in the House of Lords this Session, except the first day I have seen few honest men, but Every one I have seen (one of which was Sir John St Aubin)[3] askd after You. Peace be to You, & all your house: Joy will come after it, & a Happy new year.

Endorsement (in Allen's hand): Mr Pope | Decembr 27 | 1742.

POPE *to* WARBURTON[4] — 28 *December* 1742

Egerton 1946

Decr 28th 1742.

I have always so many Things to take kindly of you, that I don't know which to begin to thank you for. I was willing to include[5] Our whole account of the Dunciad, at least, & therfore stayd till it was finished. The Encouragement you gave me to add the fourth book, first determind me to do so: & the Approbation you seemd to give it, was what singly determind me to print it. Since that, your Notes, & your Discourse in the Name of Aristarchus, have given its Last Finishings & Ornaments [ ] son, (and also not to lay any unbecoming Stress on any thing he writes), I have orderd the cancelling of a leaf or two more. In a word, I cannot bear to be thought Serious in any thing relating to him, because I am incapable of being so.

I shall forthwith give Bowyer the Essay[6] to print with your Commentary; after which the Pastorals & Essay on Crit: &c therfore I need not hasten you. I should be much more pleased you first carryd on your Great Work of the Divine Legation; above all things I wish

[1] Hooke by this time was subjected to the rages of the temperamental Duchess of Marlborough, who was now 82 years old.

[2] The 4th Earl of Radnor had succeeded to the title in 1741.

[3] Sir John St. Aubyn, M.P. for Cornwall, had been a leader against Walpole early in 1742, and was the first member chosen—by a great majority—on the Secret Committee to investigate the Walpole régime. One version of Walpole's reputed *mot* concerned Sir John: 'All these men have their price except the little Cornish baronet.'—*DNB.*

[4] The original of this letter has been mutilated by cutting away the bottom of the first leaf. The gaps resulting are indicated here by brackets. The mutilation was very likely done by Warburton himself, who in 1751 (Pope's *Works*, ix. 351–3) printed a 'cooked' letter which used the date and the first paragraph of this letter, down to 'Last Finishings and Ornaments'. To this paragraph Warburton added parts of a letter dated 15 Nov. 1743, and he concluded with a passage from the letter of 21 May 1743. The relevant folios of Egerton 1946 are 69–70 (28 Dec. 1742), 68*r* (15 Nov. 1743), and 75*r* (21 May 1743). The passages used are specified in the notes to the three letters. The 'cooked' letter is printed in EC, ix. 226–7.

[5] For 'include' Warburton printed 'conclude'.

[6] The *Essay on Man.*

to see it compleated. Shakespear[1] & I may follow at leisure, but I think Shak [ ]n only tells me, [ ] [2]any thing done in it that is in my power, you may, you must, freely imploy me.

We have a Great Minister here, who has told my Lord Bathurst he desires to be made your Acquaintance: but whether you desire to be any great Minister's, I know not. It is my Lord Cartaret. I could indeed wish you were rather *His* Bishop, (or even His Prebendary, provided I could chuse the Prebend) than *My* Commentator: But I insist on your being more My Friend, tho I can only wish I could prove myself as much Yours.

Mr Murray (who is with me at Twitnam) sends you his faithfull Services. I am, unfeignedly & inexpressibly, Dear Sir | Yours. | A. Pope.

I have just receivd notice from Mr Allen that he shall be in London the End of this week & stay in town a fortnight. I shall therfore be with him there, for that time.

P.S. Pray tell me if the inclosed Alteration satisfies your Objection in the fourth Epist. of the Essay?

Address: To the Revd | Mr Warburton at | Newark
Frank: Free | W: Murray
Postmark: 30/DE

[1] Warburton's projected edition.
[2] From this point on the letter seems not to have been printed hitherto.

1743

At the beginning of this year we find Warburton working for Pope on the commentaries for the projected quarto edition of the poet's works—working especially on the *Essay on Man* and the *Essay on Criticism*. We find Pope, in turn, still working in vain to secure for Warburton the coveted Oxford degree. The revised *Dunciad* was in print early in the year, but publication was delayed because the copyright did not revert to Pope until October. Bolingbroke made during this year two visits to England, a brief one in the spring and a longer one beginning in October. Pope's health made further winter journeys to Bath unadvisable, and instead he visited Allen in the summer. In July we find Warburton, Pope, and Martha Blount guests at Widcombe. Pope presently left to join George Arbuthnot, evidently in some annoyance because Pope had requested and had been refused one of Allen's houses in which Pope and Arbuthnot might temporarily live. When he left Prior Park and Miss Blount remained behind, something like a quarrel between the hosts and the remaining guest took place, and the rest of the year letters to Allen (and doubtless from him—not preserved) worked gradually towards a reconciliation. Warburton remained at Prior Park until September. When Bolingbroke arrived in October, Pope began spending much time away from Twickenham, either with Murray in London or with Marchmont and Bolingbroke at Battersea. Throughout the year Pope's health was increasingly bad: asthma got worse and dropsy appeared.

POPE *to* THE EARL OF ORRERY — 13 *January* 1742/3

The Pierpont Morgan Library

London | Jan. 13. 1742/3.

My Lord,—I cannot, in pure Shame, delay one post, to acknowledge both my own Omission, and your Generosity, in putting me thus kindly in mind how defective I have been, in not writing to you. I enquired at my Coming to Town of the young Gentlemen at Westminster, who were gone just then for Marston, and two days since again of Dr Johnson[1] after the Time of your Return, who said he expected it would be very soon. This stopt me from doing, what I wish I had done that post, that your Lordship might have seen I thought of you the same day that you thought of me. In truth, I had a very particular reason to have troubled you; I correct myself, for nothing of this kind ever was a Trouble, but a Joy to you. It was that we think a Way is open by which you may do an honour to a Man of the Greatest Merit, and redeem the disgrace of a whole University. You are not to

[1] James Johnson (1705–74), undermaster in Westminster School, later Bishop of Gloucester.

be now told, that the Vice Chancellor Dr Leigh & several Heads of Houses sent & offerd Mr Warburton the degree of a Dr of Divinity,[1] when he had no such Expectation, after which it was monstrously refused by the unaccountable Dissent of 2 or 3. Dr King either has, or will acquaint you of the particulars. He met me the other day, & desird it might be brought on again by your Lordship's engaging Lord Arran to send a Recommendation to that purpose, (the present Vice Chancellor being much Mr W's friend). This it seems is a customary Method, and surely nothing is more reasonable, after such a Conduct, toward a Man of his Eminence, & unblemished Character.

I am sure I need only make you an Apology for not mentioning this to you sooner.

All your Lordship tells me of your Enjoyments at Marston, truly pleases me, but with the allay, of finding it will be long before I shall be happy in yours & Lady O.'s company: and I tell you truly, I never wanted the Comfort of *Such* Company, so much, here as this Winter: indeed *All* honest Company is a rarity, but principally among Gentlemen. I think this one Sentence includes a General account of all Publick affairs. I have seen and heard, what makes me shut my Eyes, & Ears, and retire inward into my own Heart; where I find Something to comfort me, in knowing it is possible some men may have some Principles. I wish I had been no where but in my Garden; but my weak Frame will not endure it; or no where but in my Study; but my weak Eyes cannot read all the Evening. I pick up a poor Scholar or two, who can get no Employment, to sit & read to me, and I drink in return with them, especially if they are of the University, sometimes rather too much (for me I mean.) I am really glad the Gout has treated your Lordship as you deserve, that is so moderately. You have Another Companion, that will make any thing supportable, even any Pain or Misfortune, (tho God send them both far from you!) I hope She is perfectly well, & perfectly happy you will make one another. I can never sufficiently acknowledge both hers & your perpetual Favours & Remembrances shown me. I could write not a Letter but a Book of them, they are so many, and so fully imprinted on my memory. As to any thing else I shall write, it will be very little, and very faint. I have lost all Ardor and Appetite, even to Satyr, for no body has Shame enough left to be afraid of Reproach, or punish'd by it. And Cibber himself is the honestest Man I know, who has writ a book of his *Confessions*, not so much to his Credit as St Augustine's, but full as

[1] On the first 'offering' of this degree, see Pope to Warburton, 12 Aug. 1741, and note. Pope somewhat officiously now tries to revive interest in the matter. Orrery immediately (15 Jan.) wrote to the Earl of Arran (Chancellor of the University), who wrote to the new Vice-Chancellor, Dr. Walter Hodges (who unfortunately was hostile to Warburton), as did Orrery on 16 Feb. Also on the 16th Orrery wrote to Dr. King of St. Mary Hall. But all to no avail. Orrery's letters are preserved in his letterbooks (at Harvard), vol. iv, pp. 345–54.

True, & as open. Never had Impudence and Vanity so faithful a Professor. I honour him next to my Lord ——

Pray, since you do not come yet, at least let me know when you may? that I may know Some happiness I may *expect*, and hear something I may *Believe*. Adieu my dear Lord. remember Mr Warburton & (in Him) Me that I may not be ashamed of having a Degree hereafter. I am Ever Your Lordships & Lady Orrery's. | A. Pope

Endorsement (by Lord Orrery at the top of page 1): Mr Pope. | Concerning Mr Warburton. | Dr K[in]gs desire, that I would apply | to Lord Arr: in Mr Wn's favour.

POPE *to* WARBURTON[1] 18 *January* [1742/3]

Egerton 1946

Twitnam. Jan. 18

I am forced to grow every day more Laconic in my Letters, for my Eyesight grows every day shorter & dimmer. Forgive me then that I answer you summarily; I can even less bear an equal part, in a Correspondence, than in a Conversation, with you. But be assured once for all, the more I read of you, as the more I hear from you, the better I am instructed and pleased. And this Misfortune, of my own Dulness & my own Absence, only quickens my ardent Wish that some good Fortune would draw you nearer, & enable me to enjoy both, for a greater part of our Lives, in this Neighbourhood; & in such a Situation, as might make more Beneficial Friends than I, Esteem & enjoy you equally.

⌜I consulted Mr Murray on your Question as to writing to Sir T. H.[2] We agreed you should not, as it was a thing not even to be surmized, that any Man of honour could dream of. But I have enquird farther, & am assured from one who hath seen the Copy, that there are No Notes whatsoever to it, but a Removal only of one word for another, as he thinks fitting. The Heads of some houses have subscribed for

[1] Printed by Warburton (1751) with omissions here placed in half-brackets.

[2] On Warburton's quarrel with Sir Thomas Hanmer in the summer of 1742 see Nichols, *Lit. Anec.* v. 588–90, and Evans, *Warburton and the Warburtonians*, pp. 147–58. Shakespearian rivalry was the cause. The Oxford University Press was bringing out Hanmer's edition in a superior format (6 v., 1744–3) at this time, when Oxford was not being generous to Warburton's doctoral ambitions. Warburton evidently feared that Hanmer was going to publish notes of Warburtonian origin, and Pope reassures him. After Pope's death Warburton (?) in Nov. 1744 sent to 'several heads of houses, and others, a printed leaf of the *Dunciad*, book IV, with an addition of five verses and two notes, and intimation in writing that the author had directed these verses and notes to be inserted in the copies which should be unsold, as soon as Sir Th— H—r's edition of Shakespeare should be publish'd, but that since the author's death orders were given to suppress them. A very consistent method of suppressing!' See *Gent. Mag.* xiv. 611 for the letter from Oxford here quoted. The lines are *Dunciad*, Bk. IV, 114–18. They echo this present passage in Pope's letter.

100, & 50, at 3 guineas the book, which they refund by putting them off to the Gentlemen Commoners: and this way the Press is payed. One Good Consequence will attend the printing it, which is, that it will determine the Book to be no Booksellers property, if Tonson does not contest it: & the way will be open to any whom you chuse to deal with, or to yourself, if you prefer to take the whole on yourself.

⌜You might be certain I omitted not to write to Lord Orrery[1] but I retarded it, till I had spoken again to Dr King, who perhaps should hear again from you, tho I hope it is not necessary.⌝

I have again heard from Lord Ba.[2] & another hand, that the Lord I writ to you of,[3] declares an Intention to serve you. My answer (which they related to him) was, that he would be sure of your Acquaintance for life, if once he served or obliged you; but that I was certain you would never trouble him with your Expectation, tho he would never get rid of your Gratitude.

⌜I have delayed a while longer the publication of the Dunciad,[4] but shall put Bowyer directly on the Edition of the Ethic Epistles; and I think it will be a more dignify'd Method of declaring your intention of a General Commentary, before That, than before This Poem⌝.[5]

Dear Sir, adieu, and let me sometimes be certifyd of your Health. My own is as usual; and my Affection the same. Always Yours. | A. P.

Pray will the following lines[6] answer your Idea? or can you bring them to it with a little alteration?

Ask of the Learn'd the way, the Learn'd are blind,
This bids to serve, & that to shun mankind;
Some place the Bliss in Action, some in Ease,
Apathy — 1 Epicur
[1]Those call it Pleasure, and[2] Contentment these: — 2 Stoics
[1]Some sunk to Beasts, find Pleasure end in Pain;
[2]Some swelld to Gods, confess ev'n Virtue vain;
[3]Or indolent, to each extreme they fall, — 3 Sceptic
To trust in every thing, or doubt of all — Qu
One trusts the Senses, and one doubts of all.

1 See the letter of 13 Jan. 1742/3.

2 Warburton prints 'Bathurst', or in some editions uses asterisks.

3 Warburton's larger 8vo edition of 1751 carries no note; the small 8vo has the footnote 'Lord G.', and the editions of 1753 and thereafter expand this to 'Granville'—a title to which Carteret succeeded in 1744.

4 *The Dunciad* is evidently ready for publication.

5 The announcement of an edition of Pope's poems 'with Commentaries and Notes of W. Warburton, A.M.' was, however, made on the verso of the title-page of the quarto *Dunciad*, published at the end of Oct. 1743.

6 See *Essay on Man*, iv. 19–28, in Professor Mack's volume of the Twickenham ed., pp. 129–30.

Who thus define it, say they more or less,
describe
Than this, that Happiness is Happiness?
Take Nature's path, &c.
—in no Extreme they dwell &c

POPE *to* FORTESCUE[1] *February* 1742/3

1797 (Polwhele, i. 324)

Sunday evening, Feb. 1743.

I have been disappointed much to-day, in not being able to wait on you: and as I apprehend you sit every other day, so that you are not at leisure in the afternoon, and I dare not be abroad at night, I beg to know if I may dine with you to-morrow? No man is with more respect or affection, dear Sir, yours, always, | A. P.

POPE *to* THE EARL OF ORRERY 9 *February* 1742/3

The Pierpont Morgan Library

My Lord,—I dare say your Humanity & Generous Spirit is offended, as well as mine, at such a Demonstration of the Malignity of Dulness, which is never so rancorous as under the Robe of Learning,[2] One would think the Clergy were sworn to hate each other, instead of to love each other. But we have done our best, & must acquiesce under such *Heads* as God is pleasd to put over us, that the Weak ones of this world may confound the Strong. Mr W. shall know his Obligations to your Lordship & to Lord Arran, whose letter I return you.

I am extremely mortifyd at your Retirement, & the more, as I fear the Taste of passing a whole Winter better than almost any Nobleman can, or ought, may influence you for the future, & I shall lose both you & my Lady for the few Winters I have to live, & in which I expect yearly less & less Comfort. I instantly obeyed you as to the Subscribing for the Book, which I impowerd Dodsley to do: but he seems hardly to know whether it goes on or not. If it was Lady O.'s command,[3] I would not only subscribe to, but cry up, any Poet, of any Kingdom; or any King's Poet or Historiographer, (the two greatest Lyers in Literature.) Our poor Friend in the Park is extremely ill,[4] both corporeally & mentally; & I fear her Poet will soon shed real Tears for her, as he will be of no use to any other Princess or Potentate

[1] The date is doubtless from Fortescue's endorsement. On whichever Sunday Pope wrote the meeting seems not to have taken place. See the next letter to Fortescue, in March.

[2] Possibly, after all, learned Dunces were Pope's extremest aversion. On the cause of this outburst (Warburton's Oxford degree) see the letter of 13 Jan. 1742/3.

[3] Apparently her *request* has led him to subscribe to some work.

[4] The Duchess of Buckingham. She was buried in the Abbey on 8 Apr. 1743.

whatsoever: Her Fate has been hard upon her, but not so hard as herself, for her Passions have overturn'd Mind & Body.

If ever I can form a possible hope of seeing you at Marston, it must be in the Summer; and I think there is a probability of my being about Bath next July or August. But sure, my Lord, you will just come & look at Jericho once more, before it falls at the Sound of the *Third* Trumpet. Two have called aloud upon her, & shook her Walls alredy.

I would give you an account of *Some* of your acquaintance, but I *dare* not: of *others*, but I *will* not. And I have nothing left, but to cry out (with the Christian Congregation) *Let us Pray*!

I am not publishing any new thing, but whatever I publish, (past, vamp'd, future, old or revived) it shall surely be sent you the moment the press has it. I write at Tw. the same day your Lordships letter reach'd me, (which past thro' Mr Sollicitors hands[2] & was by him forwarded hither) or I should perhaps recollect something more. But Tw. is the place of Forgetfulness, of all but such as I love, & those [now][1] are few. Believe me, while I have a being, | Your Lordships ever faithfully, | A. Pope.

Feb. 9th 1742/3.

Address: To | the Rt Hon. the Earl of Orrery. | at Marston, near | Froome, | Somersetshire

Postmark: 10/FE

Endorsement: Mr Pope. | Feb: 9. 1742/3.

*POPE *to* GEORGE ARBUTHNOT 12 *February* [1742/3]

Harvard University

Twitnam. Feb. 12

This short note is just to ask you how you both do? and to tell you that when the Term is expird if you care to see the Country this wholsome cold weather I shall be glad to attend you. As for your Sister she is too chill a creature to be of that society, as yet, except she has Mr. Murray to warm her with a Dispute.

If you have any more Screens, pray let me have two of them, for the assistance of a Lawyer or two, whose Lucubrations are of Importance. I am | Dear Sir | Ever yours, | A. Pope

Let the black wax make amends for the red wafer.

Address: To | Mr Arbuthnott, in | Castle Yard

1 These brackets are Pope's own.

3 Murray became Solicitor-General, 18 Nov. 1742.

THE EARL OF ORRERY *to* POPE — 16 *February* 1742/3

Harvard University

Marston Feb: 16: 1742–43.

Sir,—Enclosed[1] I send you my last efforts for our learned, our too learned, Friend. whatever success my Letter may have I am joyfull in an opportunity in shewing my regards to You and to Mr Warburton.

The Thoughts of seeing You here gives me true pleasure. I hope You will find our Roads less uneasy than they are represented. Consider, they are the Roads to Peace, to Solitude, and to Friendship. When you are here, altho' you may have jumbled over some Stones, and waded through some mire, you will find our Situation good, our Air wholesome, and the House, its Master, and his Territories all your own.

Since my Arrival from Bath I received very melancholy accounts of our Friend in the Park,[2] in confirmation of the hints you gave me. her Situation is deplorable. Death only can give relief to Passions of that soart. but I observe that People in her disposition of mind live generally to a great Age. "The days of Women are threescore years and ten, and if they be so strong to attain to fourscore years, yet is their Strength then but Madness or Folly."

I think so little of the great World, and am so pleased with my retirement that unless to see you I know nothing could make me wish myself a Single day from Marston, where every mortal is, as I am, Dear Sir, | your very faithfull | and obedient Servant | Orrery.

Heading: To Alexdr: Pope Esq;.

*POPE *to* GEORGE ARBUTHNOT[3] — [1742/3]

Harvard University

Tuesday night

I was in great hope you'd have come on Munday. Tuesday is gone over too, & the unlucky Time of the Watermans going will make it too late to ask it I fear to morrow, being Wensday. Let it then be Thursday, but as I expected you to pass 2 or 3 days at least with me, I have put off Lord Bolingbroke & Lord Marchmont (who are to lye & stay some days here) till Friday, & will till Saturday. As to Mr Murray, if he come a day sooner, I have room for you both. But if you will not

[1] Orrery apparently encloses copies of his letters to Dr. Hodges and Dr. King—of the same date. They occur in his letterbooks, vol. iv.

[2] The Duchess of Buckingham.

[3] Dealers have regarded this as a letter to Dr. Arbuthnot, but the address and the mention of Murray place it in the period after the doctor's death. It must fall within the visit of Lord Bolingbroke from France, and presumably refers not to his lordship's first visit to Twickenham during this sojourn from March to May. It cannot be placed with precision.

stay now & perhaps can nex[t] week, let the Party be put off till then; & I'll ingage the Lords the sooner, so that they'l be gone, by the time you can come. Mrs Blount writes me word, she'l accomodate herself wholly to you. But I insist on your being left here for what time you can. I am your Sisters faithfully, & Dear Sir, that does not hinder me from being Entirely Yours. | A Pope.

Address: To Mr Arbuthnot.

*POPE *to* ALLEN 12 *March* [1742/3]

Egerton 1947

March 12

I don't care to be always complaining, but so it is, that my Eyes grow so weak it is almost a pain to me to write a common letter. I often wish to say much to you as if we were conversing, & principally to tell you my Sentiments of Men and Things, but this difficulty becomes insuperable. I shall the sooner be obliged to live more with, or near you. Mr & Mrs Arb: seem very happy in the prospect of next Vacation, & I believe that will be the time that will best suit Mrs Blount, they may travel all together, & all your Engagements & Business will be over, so as to leave Yourself & Mrs Allen at fuller Liberty. I made your Compliment fully to Lord Oxford,[1] & am surprized at the others Carelessness, but I am less surprized, since his head has been so busy with a sort of Cares, that generally men of this world prefer to those of Friendship. One of my Tribulations was, that you had not the Bottles so soon as the Italian promised, but I sent them the moment he had them. Our Rusticks have fallen short, & I am unwilling to give you more trouble, but, I could dispose of as many more as the last Cargo, if they would cutt them off from the large block, so as to lessen the expense of the Carriage. I hope you have been as free from the headake as I, of late: pray always, when you are well, give me the pleasure to say so, & to tell me Mrs Allen is as happy too as I wish you both.—The death of poor Brinsden has really grieved me:[2] he was the most faithfull Friend as well as Servant to his Lord, in the most trying Times, & has withstood all Temptations, as manfully as he supported all Pains. Those we call the Great seldome can boast of any degree of Virtue like this.—I have not writ to Mr Warburton of late, tho I've heard much more about that very worthy & goodnatured Lord[3] who takes so much pains to obtain him a dignity at Oxford which you

[1] The 3rd Earl of Oxford, cousin of Pope's friend the 2nd Earl, succeeded to the title in 1741.

[2] The burial of Mr. John Brinsden (spelled *Brimsdon* in the register) is recorded as of 3 Mar. 1742/3.

[3] Lord Orrery.

& I set no high value on. I would not give our Excellent & Respectable Friend any uneasiness about what deserves not his Thought, but I am told at last it will be given him. I would much rather tell him what both you & I wish performed by another Lord[1] (in whose Word however I do not put the Trust you do.)

The Weather has been so sharp, that happening to be taken in it at Twitnam, I have been kept there lockd up these 8 days, & made great progress in my Grotto, which yet will not be quite finishd till Easter. I hope whenever Mrs Allen begins her works of that sort, they will be sooner brought to perfection, & I will attend them as diligently as my own, in the Autumn, before it is too cold. I heartily wish you & her all the injoyments of the approaching Spring which I long for impatiently. I am Ever Yours. | A. P.

*LORD MARCHMONT *and* POPE *to* SARAH, DUCHESS OF MARLBOROUGH 13 *March* 1742/3

Blenheim

Madam,—Having shew'd Mr Pope the Letter I had the honour to receive from your Grace,[2] as he is equally concerned with me in it, & in every thing that affects you, I am from this line forward to hold the pen in both our names.

We cannot but approve, & increase our esteem of your Grace, for the justice you do yourself to be satisfied with your own Company, tho' it be some injustice to ourselves, wholly to be deprived of it. you might at least have suffer'd us now & then to have consulted you as an Oracle in the Woods; your prophecys have proved so true in regard to some Men, of our acquaintance, who will have nothing to do with the woods, as long as they can stick to any post in Court, Having taken the same resolution with regard to the Country, as you have done with regard to the Town. But since like an Errant Sibyl as you are, you give your answers in writing, rather than by word of mouth, We have nothing to do but to explain your words, as people always did those of other Oracles, in the sense that most flatter'd themselves. So Mr Pope & I in spite of you resolve to be happy. Now as to your health & situa-

[1] ? Carteret.

[2] In the *Marchmont Papers*, ii. 265–72 are printed both the Duchess's letter to Marchmont and her reply to this present letter. She wrote Lord Marchmont on 3 Mar., and replied to this letter on the 15th. In her letter of the 3rd she says she is too much afflicted with gout to enjoy visitors, but in an interesting passage about death and immortality (at 82 even a duchess thinks of these things) she begs Marchmont, 'if you talk to Mr. Pope of me, endeavor to keep him my friend'. She seems to doubt Pope's respect for her 'philosophy'. In replying on the 15th, she says: 'If I could receive letters from you and Mr. Pope, as you had leisure, I would never come to town as long as I live.' And again: 'I shall always be pleased to see your Lordship and Mr. Pope, when you will be so bountiful as to give me any part of your time.' The original of this present letter is in Lord Marchmont's hand.

tion Madam, seeing that your Mind is so free from What affects your body, as appears by your Letter, We cannot help flattering ourselves, that we may be admitted to converse with a Soul that is certainly immortal if any Soul be so; & that the body out of which it talks at this rate is yet in tennantable repair, & fitt to enjoy any reasonable conversation. As your friend Socrates gave a stronger proof of the immortality of his Soul by his unconcern for all the pains of his body, than by all his arguments in his last dialogue; We are very desirous of being Eyewitnesses, of that same kind of proof from you Madam, which will establish us all in that belief we jointly entertain, tho' We imagine we are all equally ignorant what Soul is. And for this reason We persuade ourselves that your Grace as the head of our School of philosophy, will not fail to send for us, to give us this legacy before your death. And if we then find you not fully satisfied, We'll desire Hook to be ready with a priest in the next room, As we are not only your most Submissive scholars, but with all truth | Your Graces | most faithfull & most | obedient Servants | Marchmont | A. Pope.

Battersea 13th March | 1742/3

*POPE *to* HUGH BETHEL[1] 20 *March* 1742/3

Egerton 1948

March 20. 1743.

My dear Friend,—Since the first Letter I sent you in fulness of Heart for the Joy you gave me in so sudden an alteration of your health, and which consisted but of few words, (as indeed none could express the Satisfaction) I have delayd writing any account of my own health which I knew would occasion as much uneasiness to you, as yours had given comfort to me. For I have these 3 months or more, been advancing to an Asthmatic Complaint, (from one Cold to another, as I believe, for I saw no further Cause for it.) It is now at such a height, that I can scarce walk, or go up a pair of Stairs, or move much in my bed, without quite losing breath; And it is attended with a difficulty of urine, which makes me fear a Dropsy (the quantity I make is daily so much diminished), & a pain in the Breast is joynd to it, which I would willingly impute to Wind.[2] I may now, without much Merit, think of you every day; but I assure you, it was no more than I did, before I had any such reason to reflect on what you suffer'd.

I thank you twice for your Present of Seeds, for those I did not

[1] When the year gets towards 25 Mar., Pope occasionally (as here) dates in modern style. Normally he would date this 1742. Parts of this letter (about his villa chiefly) were printed by Warburton in Pope's *Works* (1751), iv. 94 n., and were used by Ruffhead, pp. 407–8 n.

[2] Pope gives Bethel a more serious account of his health than he gives others at this time, but it was a dropsical asthma that was to cause his death fourteen months after this letter was written.

receive, & for these I did, with which I have enrichd not my own Garden only, but some of my Friends. My Landlady Mrs Vernon being dead,[1] this Garden & House are offerd me in sale, & I believe, (together with the Cottages on each side my Grassplot next the Thames), will come at about 1000 pounds. If I thought any very particular Friend would be pleased to live in it after my death (for as it is, it serves all my purposes as well during life) I would purchace it; & more particularly could I hope two things; that the Friend who should like it, was so much younger, and healthier than myself as to have a prospect of its continuing his, some years longer than I can of its continuing mine. But most of those I love, are travelling out of the world, not into it; and unless I had such a view given me, I have no Vanity nor pleasure that does not stop short of the Grave. The Duchess of Buckingham has thought otherwise, who orderd all manner of Vanities for her own funeral,[2] & a Sum of Money to be squanderd on it, which is but necessary to preserve from starving many poor people to whom she is indebted. I doubt not Mrs Pratt[3] is as much astonishd as you or I, at her leaving Sir Robert Walpole her Trustee, & Lord Hervey her Executor, with a Marriage Settlement on his Daughter, that will take place of all the Prior debts she has in the world. All her private Papers & those of her Correspondents are left in the hands of Lord Hervey, so that it is not impossible another Vol. of my Letters may come out:[4] I am sure they make no part of her Treasonable Correspondence, (which they say she has Expressly left to him) but sure this is Infamous Conduct towards any common acquaintance. And yet this Woman seem'd once, a Woman of great honour & many generous Principles. I know you are one of those that will burn every Scrap I write to you, at my desire, or I really should be præcluded from performing the most common offices of Friendship, or even writing that I esteem & love any man.[5]

There never passes a Week but Mrs Blount & I talk of you, think of you, & pray for you. The Repetitions from several hands of your continuing to amend have been much the most welcome news I have had these 2 years. Every thing & every body here grow worse, God send You better & better! When do you think of drawing nigher to us? I shall soon see Mr Moyzer & be some time in his neighborhood at Bath, if I can get off this Complaint at my breast, &c. and then [I ho]pe to have the most frequent & particular accounts of you. I could

[1] She had died sometime before this, possibly in February of 1740 (*Gent. Mag.* x. 92, Feb. 1740), but the settling of the estate dragged on. See also Pope to Allen, 8 Feb. 1741/2.

[2] She died 13 Mar. and the burial in the Abbey took place on 8 Apr. On some amazing aspects of her post-mortem vanity see L. E. Tanner and I. L. Nevison, 'On some Later Funeral Effigies in Westminster Abbey' in *Archaeologia*, lxxv (1936), 180–3.

[3] See Pope to Bethel, 16 June [1736].

[4] These letters have not been uncovered.

[5] Most of this second paragraph is quoted by Ruffhead, pp. 407–8 and 469.

be very glad, methinks, if after a Friendship of so many years, in the whole Course of which no one Mistake, no one Passion, no one Interest has arisen, to interrupt our constant, Easy, & open Comerce; if it were yet reserved for us to pass a year or two together in a gentle Walk down the Hill, before we lye down to rest: The Evening of our days is generally the calmest, & the most enjoyable, of them.[1] In that hope, I would fain believe you have been preserv'd, & that I may be preserved: For besides the mutual Communication of wellmeaning Hearts, I know nothing at our Age worth living for. I am tender of giving your Eyes too much trouble in writing, but let the lines be ever so few, if they confirm the assurance of your Recovery, 'tis all I wish, who am with the greatest truth and cordial affection | Dear Sir, Entirely yours. | A. Pope.

Address: A Monsieur | Monsieur Bethel | Chez Mons. Belloni | Banquier | à Rome
Postmark: [Illegible]

*POPE *to* SLINGSBY BETHEL — 22 *March* 1742/3

Arthur A. Houghton, Jr.

March 22. 1742/3.

Not knowing if your Brothers Direction continue still the same, I trouble you to superscribe this.[2] and if the Bearer finds you, you may do me the favor to pay him the little you owe me, which I find was due the second of this month, and have inclosed this receit. If he misses you, it may be kept by you till we meet, or paid Mrs Blunt next month when hers is due, which is the same thing, my times of being in town being renderd uncertain, thro' a very bad cold & fevrish complaint. Believe me Ever Yours. A. Pope

March 25. 1743. Receivd of Mr Slingsby Bethel a years Interest on 700ll in full to the second day of this March, one thousand seven hundred & forty three.[3] | A. Pope.

Address: To | Mr Slingsby B[ethel]

POPE *to* WARBURTON[4] — 24 *March* [1742/3]

Egerton 1946

Twitenham Mrch 24

I write to you, among the very Few I now desire to have my Friends, merely, *Si* valeas, valeo. Tis in effect all I say, but it is very literally

[1] This sentence is quoted by Ruffhead, p. 473.
[2] Pope asks that his letter to Hugh Bethel dated 20 Mar. 1742/3 be safely addressed by Hugh's brother.
[3] In letters to Slingsby Bethel dated 16 June 1742 and 8 Feb. 1743/4 Pope asks Bethel to let him add £300 to this £700. In 1744 it was done.
[4] Printed by Warburton (1751) with omissions here placed in half-brackets.

true, for I place all that makes my Life desirable in Their welfare. I may truly affirm that Vanity or Interest have not the least share in any Friendship I have, or cause me now to cultivate that of any one Man by any one Letter. But if any Motive should draw me to flatter a Great Man, it would be to save the Friend I would have him serve, from doing it. Rather than lay a deserving person under the necessity of it, I would hazard my own Character, & keep His in Dignity. Tho' in truth I live in a time when no Measures of Conduct influence the Success of one's applications, & the best thing to trust to is *Chance & Opportunity*.

I only meant to tell you, I am wholly yours, how few words soever I make of it. A greater pleasure to me is, ⌜the Thought⌝ that I *chanced* to make Mr Allen so, who is not only worth more than[1] ⌜half the greatest men in the kingdom,⌝ intrinsically, but I foresee will be effectually more a Comfort & Glory to you every year you live.[2] My Confidence in any Man, less truly great than an Honest one, is but small: ⌜& it has been long that I have preachd to all my worthyest acquaintance of such men Blessed is he who expects nothing, for he shall never be disappointed.⌝

I have lived much by myself of late, partly thro ill health & partly to amuse myself with little Improvements in my Garden & house, to which possibly I shall (if I live) be soon more confined. ⌜Bowyer is going on with the Quarto Edit: of the Essay.⌝[3] When the Dunciad may be publishd I know not⌜, there being some Contest about the Expiration of Lintots date,[4] nor am I much concernd at the delay⌝. I am more desirous of carrying on the *best*, that is *your* Edition of the *Epistles* & *Essay on Crit.* &c. I know it is there I shall be seen most to advantage; but I insist on one Condition, that you never think of this, when you can imploy yourself in finishing that Noble work of the Divine Legation, (which is what above all, iterum iterumque monebo[5]) or any other useful Scheme of your own.

It would be a Satisfaction to me at present, only to hear that you have supported your health among these Epidemical disorders, which tho not mortal to any of my friends, have afflicted almost every one.

⌜Adieu, & know me for Yours. | A. Pope⌝

⌜You guess right as to the Verses sent that silly fellow,[6] It was done

[1] Warburton here substitutes a dash for the words omitted.

[2] Allen's influence was great, and in 1746 Warburton secured it by marriage to Allen's favourite niece, Gertrude Tucker—an alliance that added glory to his career but perhaps less than comfort to his domestic life.

[3] The *Essay on Criticism*.

[4] On this 'contest' in Chancery see Pope to Lintot, 31 Jan. 1740/1 and notes.

[5] *Aeneid*, iii. 436.

[6] On 10 Jan. 1748 Cibber told Spence (see *Anecdotes*, p. 348) that 'The false leaf of the *Dunciad* sent to Cibber, as stolen from the printer's by a friend, mentions the story about Mr.

by a friend of mine, who had your opinion of his Impenetrability, & judg'd more truly of him than I confess I did. I begin to be more scrupulous of hurting him, & wish him more Conscientiously impudent.⌉

Address: To the Revd Mr Warburton | at | Newark

*POPE *to* ALLEN 24 *March* [1742/3]

Egerton 1947

March 24th

I write this Letter the sooner, to prevent your sending Isaac too soon. Whatever particularity Mr Scot may have in removing his Pines so early, my Gardiner & all others hereabouts will not venture till the Season is better established & advanced. It will therfore do Isaac no harm to stay a little longer before he comes, and it will do Joseph[1] no harm to stay a little longer before he marries.

As to the Rusticks, (which tho they would finish all my Front with perfect beauty, I am half unwilling to trouble you further for) the same Quantity of *six Tun weight* as I last had, will accomplish all; provided they cutt off the Thick & useless part of the Stones, it's no matter of what sizes, (for we can piece them as well, if not very small) but John says those Stones are best that come from the side of the hill, not from the Top, which are too rude & large.

The Illness of my Lord Orrery gives me much concern. I beg you will sometimes see him:[2] he is a very esteemable Man, & zealous beyond Example in this age, in serving any worthy person. I desire you to tell him how earnestly I wish to hear of his recovery, & pray acquaint me how you find him. I have at last yielded to the distemper which has seized almost every body here, & am layd up at Twitnam these 7 days, with all the troublesome Symptoms about me. The worst is an excessive shortness of breath & pain in the breast, but I'm tired of tiring my friends with Complaining. I find, even at home, the Want of such a Nurse as Mrs Allen is, not to you only, but to me. I assure you all ones great Friends & great Philosophers put together, are not half so great a Comfort, as one good Woman, in these circumstances; & so tell Dr Cheyne, & Dr Hartly[3] too if you please, for I think

Pope in Cibber's letter, and insinuates that Gay was of the party, and that Cibber, breaking in upon Mr. Gay's privacy, found him in company with his own daughter, and therefore pulled him away.'

[1] Joseph, probably Allen's servant, is mentioned also in Pope to Allen, 9 Jan. 1741/2. Isaac is mentioned in Pope to Allen, [30 Mar. 1743].

[2] Orrery's health had brought him to Bath at this time.

[3] Dr. George Cheyne, authority on hypochondria, died 13 Apr. 1743. Dr. David Hartley, famous as having furnished Coleridge a Christian name for his son, had settled at Bath in 1742, and died there in 1757. First mentioned in Pope's letter to Allen, 27 Dec. 1742, he is frequently mentioned in later letters of 1743. For both these doctors see *DNB*.

neither of 'em will be angry at this; tho many Doctors would, who have the Vanity to think themselves Better as well as wiser than Women. I conclude in the sincerest assurance of my Esteem & Love for you both, hers, & your faithfull Friend & Servant. | A. Pope.

Pray remember me to Mr Moyser.

Address: To Ralph Allen Esq at | Widcombe | near | Bath.

Postmark: 24/MR

Endorsement (in Allen's hand):[1] Sir Thos White | The Stone Cutter | The Free School.

*POPE *to* ALLEN [*c.* 30 *March* 1743]

Egerton 1947

I know you'l be content with a few words, when they can tell you what you most desire to hear, the Welfare of a Friend. I have had a fever, as well as all the forms of this prevailing distemper, but by Dr Broxolms help, who of his own accord made me Visits, I am cured: so much, that this day I go to London, to comfort another (if I can) who really every way wants it, Mrs Blount, whose Mother I believe is dying.[2] What she will resolve or not resolve upon, in that case, God knows! I am sure she should not ingage her Life or Fortune with her Sister, & yet I apprehend she will scarce out of Compassion leave her, just upon it. I received the 2 chairs & think them very Easy—I have since from Mrs Allen the Oysters, & such Oysters (for ill as I was, I could not help tasting 'em) as neither the Oisters of Tenby, nor of all Wales put together, no nor the Oysters so admird by the Romans, from our Rutupian shores,[3] nor—in short nothing that bore the name of Oysters ever could equall.

A Praise as high as this has been given Your Rusticks, by the Greatest Judge Mr Kent, who prefers them to all he ever saw artificial in the world:

Since the opinion of the doctors concerning the Time of Isaac's consulting the Oracle of the Pineapples, is so various, I think you should determine it by your own Conveniency, or as you see by the Letters you sent, the Merits on both sides.[4]

[1] Allen's endorsement may have to do with Pope's desire to have his rustic stone cut to his liking. It is not to be interpreted surely.

[2] Carruthers, 1857, p. 427, tells us Mrs. Blount died 31 Mar. 1743. In Pope's next letter to Allen (12 April) he says she died 'last week'.

[3] Rutupian shores are those of Richborough (Kent). See Juvenal, iv. 140–2. The editor has to thank Professor Mason Hammond for this annotation—as well as for other details of classical lore.

[4] The letter is possibly incomplete. No second leaf is preserved.

POPE *to* FORTESCUE[1] *March* 1743

1797 (Polwhele, i. 325)

Monday, 7 o'clock, March, 1743.

It is indeed very long since we have met, but I do not forget you, nor do I think you forget me, since you were so kind as to call yesterday. I did not expect you while lord Bolingbroke was with me, (tho' I saw any friend alone). Since he left me I have been in Kent for some time,[2] and had Mr. West's family here a fortnight; have never been two days in town, nor one Sunday at home, without being confined to company. This is the truth, and I had written as much to you, but for the hope every week of seeing you the next. If this find you, dear Sir, at Richmond, I will take boat instantly: I truly am, and ever shall be, as I ever have been, your most obliged and faithful humble servant, | A. Pope.

POPE *to* MALLET[3] [? 1743]

Facsimile of item 561 of the Catalogue of the Bordoni Collection

Tuesday night

I was quite grievd to hear your self & Mrs Mallet[4] were at my door yesterday, tho I fear it was but your first flight after your Illness. Mr Brown[5] had sent his Chariot to desire me to go in it to Apscourt & return early, (he having been, & still being extremely ill) I am my self in no respect better than when I saw you; but it would have been a great pleasure to me, to have detaind You Two just for a dining-time, and a just Excuse to him. I expect Lord Bolingbroke this week, but am not certain his day will be so soon as to morrow, as he intends to stay five or six days. If you can dine with him without hurting you, I'll send you word what day? My humble Services are Mrs Mallet's, & all my true Affections are Yours. | A Pope

[1] The date probably derives from an endorsement, and normally Fortescue's endorsements must be viewed with very great respect. But Lord Bolingbroke seems to have been in England for some weeks, and his arrival is mentioned in *The Daily Post* of 13 Apr. as having occurred 'a few days since'. Conceivably the *Post* was behindhand in its reporting; but March is an early and almost impossible date for the letter. The last Monday in March was the 28th.

[2] Gilbert West lived at Wickham in Kent, and the family may have returned to Twickenham with Pope.

[3] The date is most unsure, but April or May of this year seems plausible. Mallet's illness, if it could be dated, would settle the matter.

[4] Mallet's first wife had died in Jan. 1742, and he had married the charming second Mrs. Mallet in October of that year.

[5] The manor of 'delightful Apscourt' had been sold to Jeremiah Brown, Esq., and he was still there, apparently, in 1744. See Manning and Bray, *History of Surrey* (1809), ii. 766–7. John Searle in his *Plan of Mr. Pope's Garden* (1745), p. 8, enumerates among the ornaments of the Grotto 'several Humming Birds and their Nests, from Antony Brown, Esq; of Abbs-Court'. The two Browns were doubtless related.

*POPE *to* ALLEN 12 *April* [1743]

Egerton 1947

Apr. 12. Tuesday.

Your Letters give me the truest pleasure as they constantly tell me your own satisfactions, & make me witness to those Blessings you injoy, which are the Desert & the Reward of Virtue. May you possess them always, & diffuse them on all round you. Your Resolution of increasing Mr Warb.'s happiness, by securing him in Independency, is as high a joy to me (to say all in one word) as it is to yourself, & will be to Him; who I see by a Letter Ive just receivd is making himself happy with one kindness you have done him, while you are preparing another he knows not of.

Fielding has sent the Books you subscribd for[1] to the Hand I imployd in conveying the 20 ll to him. In one Chapter of the Second vol. he has payd you a pretty Compliment upon your House.

I find by Lord Burlington that you must have your Fawns taken away soon after they fall from the Dam, or they can't be catchd when once they are able to run, in so small a Park (he says) without danger of killing. About June he thinks is the best time, when you should have them fed by hand with Cows Milk till they are strong enough to be carryd in Panniers on horseback, for any waggon will shake them to pieces.

You must accept of these Bottles of Eau sans pareille; when you would have more you shall pay for them.

You will see Mrs Blount much sooner than you or I imagin'd; if her Ill health, both of Body & Mind, (which God forbid) do not prevent, very speedily. For it has pleas'd him to take away her Mother last week; and the Melancholy which both that and some Circumstances in regard to her Sister affect her with, make her instant Removal from the Scene & the Danger of the highest Importance to her. All her Friends press her to take the Opportunity, which her Friend Lady Gerard offers her; who was this week going to Bath by advice of Physicians, and would fain have her with her. An unaccountable Tenderness she has for her Sister who is practising upon her every way, and a Dejection of Spirits, have thrown her into so weak a condition, that I dread the Consequence, if she be left but a few days longer here; and this weakness is made an Argument against her Journy: She is in Terrors at every thing. The Lady I find has not securd a

[1] Fielding's *Miscellanies* (3 vols.) were published 7 Apr. 1743. Allen's name is not printed among the subscribers, and very likely, since he loved to 'do good by stealth', he had concealed the source of the £20 that he had sent by means of Pope and another. The pretty compliment occurs in Chapter V of 'A Journey from this World to the Next', where Fielding remarks that 'a certain house near Bath' is almost the only palace on the 'Road to Goodness', whereas many are to be found on the 'Road to Greatness' (*Miscellanies*, ii [1743], 42).

Lodging for her in the same house at Bath, so possibly she may be distressd, & she will be obligd to leave her own Maid to help her Sister for a week or ten days, in removing her Goods, &c. Therfore against all Events I know you'l receive her at first (till you can get her well accomodated) at your own house, in case she comes; which if she does, it will be on Saturday next. I beg you also to ingage Dr Hartleys Particular Care of her at her first Coming, for I am alarmed at the Apprehension of the Distemper, which is more & more fatal, & fear she may suffer on the road by Cold, &c. But every thing is to be ventured rather than leave her here. And this is the first Step toward a happier Life than ever Fortune has given her an opportunity hitherto to make. It will be very reasonable she should pass some time with Lady G. who deserves well of her, & is a very honest Woman, & it will be of use to herself to drink the Waters some weeks; after which she may make her Visit to you, & Mrs Allen; & Mr Warburton & I will come when you will, & Mr & Mrs Arb. follow after. So Hampton will be inhabited, by me if not by her, & some way or other you'l have enough of me. All my present Care, is for this poor, foolishly-tender, but exceedingly honest, Woman who I hope in God may be prevaild on to set out on Thursday, & get thro the journey safe; for indeed *Many Dangers compass her round*, at this time. I know no hands, or hearts, to whom I could commit one whom I value so much with any confidence so absolute, as I can to yours & Mrs. Allen's. I would go with her myself, if she would let me, and the sollicitude I shall be under, till you inform me of her safety, You may guess, who know what it is to feel and fear for a Friend. Adieu I will tell her, as soon as she comes, to send to your Brother's.

POPE *to* MALLET[1] [? 1743 or 1744]

Sir John Murray

Tuesday

This day I intended to pay you a Visit, But am still too weak, nor is the Shortness of my breath at all mended. If you are as well as I heartily wish, will you & Mr Thomson come by 2, and dine? or after dinner & lye here. To morrow my Lord Bol. is expected by dinner, but he & his Retinue fill my house, however you'l dine with him &c. Next day he is ingaged abroad at dinner. Believe me cordially | Dear Sir | yours. | A. Pope.

Mrs Mallet has my Services.

[1] It is most uncertain whether this letter belongs in the period of Bolingbroke's brief visit to England in 1743, when Pope's health is obviously poor, or whether it belongs early in 1744, when his health is desperately bad. The remark (EC x. 96) that the letter is written 'in a very tremulous hand' exaggerates: the hand is not unusually weak.

POPE *to* FORTESCUE[1] [*April* 1743]

Arthur A. Houghton, Jr.

Wednesday | Twitnam

I thank you for your kind Invitation to dine with you, but I have not dined this long while, so as to be fit for any mans table, or Food. I am not yet free from a fever, & yet must be carryd in a Coach to morrow to London, to be nearer the Doctor. If you could as well take the air this way, I would get you a Chicken & enjoy here what I wish I could there an hour or two of your Company. The Waterman gives me but an imperfect account of the state of your Health, which I am sure no man desires with more sincerity than | Dear Sir | Your most affectionate & | ever faithful Servant | A. Pope.

Address: To the Rt Hon. the | Master of the Rolles.
Endorsement (by Fortescue): Mr Pope | Apr. 1743

*POPE *to* ALLEN 14 *April* [1743]

Egerton 1947

Apr. the 14. | Thursday.

I am sorry to tell you theres an end of Mrs Blounts journey. Lady Gerard brings this Letter without her, but she says she will positively follow in a fortnight or 3 weeks. I must desire you to pay Lady Gerard three Bills, as she shall happen to have occasion to send them to you, two of twenty each & one of forty pounds. She has payd me the Mony, & if you draw upon me for eighty pound as soon as you please I will pay it to Mr Haslem or any body. I can only add my Constant Love to you, & I desire to hear from you soon.

Yours ever faithfully | A. Pope.

Address: To Ralph Allen Esqr at | Widcombe, near | Bath
Postmark: 13/AP
Notes (in Allen's hand): 3 Bundles | 3 Lettrs & News | 1 Voucher | Jacob went away | at 3/4 after 9 in | the morning

POPE *to* WARBURTON[2] [? 3 *May* 1743]

Egerton 1946

FRAGMENT

the great Edition they can all be am[ ]

I write, you know, very Laconica[lly. I have] but one Formula,

[1] Fortescue's endorsement places this letter (and the preceding one to Mallet) in 1743. In these letters the poet's health is extremely bad; in some others there is a perplexing lack of signs of ill health. Fortescue became Master of the Rolls in Nov. 1741.

[2] This fragment of a letter (the date of which is doubtfully created from the imperfect

which says every thin[g to a friend,] 'I am Yours, & beg you to continue m[ine.' Let me] not be ignorant, (you can prevent [my being so] of *any thing*, but first & principally) [of your health] & *well-being*; and depend on my S[ense of all] the *Kindness*, over and above all [the *Justice*] you shall ever do me. | Dear Sir

Address: [The Re]vd Mr. Warburton | [Ne]wark | Lincolnshire
Postmark: 3/M[ ]
[*Frank*:] Murray

POPE *to* WARBURTON[1] 21 *May* [1743]

Egerton 1946

London. May 21.

I have scarce time enough to snatch the hour of the Post, to tell you I have receivd the first three sheets of your Comment on the Ess. on Crit. the two first of which I feard had been lost, that inclosed to Mr Murray only coming to my hands till this afternoon. I am afraid Bowyer writ about it & alarmd you.

My Lord Bol. has been with me, or I with him, these 5 weeks. he leaves Engl. next Wensday,[2] and I shall be wholly at our Friend Mr Allen's Services by the middle of June, or thereabouts. He promises me, You will come this way, & about that Time.

I never read a thing with more pleasure than an Additional Sheet to Jervas's preface to Don Quixot[3] Before I got over 2 paragraphs I cryd out, Aut Erasmus, aut Diabolus! I knew you as certainly as the Ancients did the Gods, by the first Pace, & the very Gait. I've not a moment to express myself in, but could not omit this, which delighted me so greatly.

My Law-suit with Lintot is at an end,[4] & the Edition in Quarto of

postmark) was, omitting the first line, used by Warburton in the 'cooked' letter that he printed (Pope's *Works* [1751], ix. 351–3) under date of 28 Dec. 1742. It there became the third paragraph of the letter. After printing, the right margin of the fragment was cut away, and the words inserted here to fill out the lines are taken from Warburton's printed text. The address, &c., on the verso of the leaf are injured by cutting. Pope errs as to the county.

[1] The first two paragraphs of this letter seem not to have been printed. The last two were printed by Warburton (1751), and later editors, as part of the letter 'cooked' by Warburton and published by him under the impossible date of 28 Dec. 1742. The date 1743 is certain because of the notice of the decision in his Chancery suit against Lintot.

[2] That is, on 25 May.

[3] On the origine of the books of Chivalry.—Warburton, 1751. Jervas's *Don Quixote*, published in Apr. 1742, had difficulty in competing with the cheaper editions of the Motteux–Ozell version. Evidently to aid sales, Warburton wrote his 'dissertation' on the books of chivalry, which was printed on sheet *b, a post-publication insert in the first editions. Professor R. M. Baine kindly explored the bibliography of these early editions for the editor.

[4] Pope's bill of complaint against Lintot was filed in Feb. 1743, and Lintot's answer is dated in April. Hence the obvious negligence in printing the statement here made (as Warburton and others have printed it) under the date of 28 Dec. 1742.

the Dunciad is half printed. Adieu. Believe, no Man can be more Yours, call me by any Title you will, but a Doctor at Oxford. Sit tibi cura mei, sit tibi cura tui.

BOLINGBROKE *to* MARCHMONT[1] [21 *May* 1743]

1831 (*Marchmont Papers*, ii. 279)

Rathbone place,[2] Saturday Morning.

My dear Lord,—I am going to dine at Chiswick, and from thence to lie at Twickenham. Can you dine with us to-morrow, and carry me to Battersea in the evening? If this be convenient to you, I shall have Monday and Tuesday clear to pass them with you, and shall embark at Greenwich on Wednesday about one o'clock: thus I shall leave our country with the more regret; but thus too I shall carry with me the best impressions of it.

I am most faithfully your Lordship's | Obedient humble servant, | H. St. J. B.

POPE *to* FORTESCUE[3] [4] *June* 1743

1797 (Polwhele, i. 325)

Saturday night, June, 1743.

I have twice had the ill fortune to miss you, when I went to the rolls; the last time Mr. Solicitor[4] and I were together. And now that he and I are at Twitenham, (for one day only) my lord Bolingbroke happens to be so, which hinders us from seeing you. I shall be in town again in two or three days, and hope then to dine and sup with you. I am really troubled to meet you so rarely, as I preserve the memory of so many hours and days formerly passed together: and am, with that sort of truth, which was to be found in old-fashioned friendships, dear Sir, your faithful, and ever most affectionate servant, | A. Pope.

Address: To the Right Hon. the *Master of the Rolls*, Richmond.

[1] This letter is printed because it concerns the time of Bolingbroke's departure from England. The specific date is fixed by Pope's letter to Warburton of the same day; it is contradicted by the endorsement of Fortescue on a letter here placed as [4] June. It is supported by a letter from Bolingbroke to his half-brother printed by John G. Taylor, *Our Lady of Batersey* (1925), p. 91, in which (dated 24 May) Bolingbroke says, 'I embark to-morrow'.

[2] The residence of the Rev. Charles Brinsden and of his late father. Bolingbroke's presence there bears out possibly an hypothesis that his hasty visit to England at this time concerned the papers of Brinsden's father, John, who had been Bolingbroke's agent in England.

[3] The date here is most perplexing. One hates to dispute the endorsements of Fortescue, but the preceding letters of 21 May indicate that Bolingbroke embarked on 25 May. Either the sailing was delayed considerably, or Fortescue is wrong, or somehow Polwhele has made a slip. Bolingbroke writes Marchmont from Argeville on 19 June (*Marchmont Papers*, ii. 292), and if he is dating in New Style, he could hardly have been in England on 4 June, since his journey back to Argeville involved so'ourns in Calais and in Paris.

[4] Murray.

POPE *to* SARAH, DUCHESS OF MARLBOROUGH[1]

Blenheim [*May or June* 1743]

I found myself sorry to have left you, the moment I grew into better health, as I did this afternoon. Mrs Blount happend to owne her desire to wait on you to Lady Fanny Shirley, who immediately proposed to carry her on Friday & lye a night: But as She (Mrs B.) meant to stay longer, & was not certain whether two together would be quite so convenient to your Grace, she has put it off, & I am glad of it, because we may come together next week, when I intend to stay out all my Time with you, & I am sure she will have the same desire. I say I am sure of it, because she tells me so, & she never says a word that is untrue. I think I can be certain of waiting on your Grace on Tuesday, but I'll write in time.

Address (in trick folding of the note): To | her | Grace | the Duchess | of | Marlborough.

Endorsement: Mr Pope to The | Dutchess of Marlbro

POPE *to* SARAH, DUCHESS OF MARLBOROUGH

[? *June* 1743]

Blenheim

Twitnam, Saturday.

Madam,—I hopd to have seen your Grace once more, before my Journey to Bath; which I find since, must be so soon as to morrow Evening or Munday morning. I hate to take leave, & so I should were I to go out of the world, otherwise than by a written Will, in which I commit my Soul to God & my Friends, at parting. Both your Grace & Mr Allen have done for me more than I am worth: he has come a hundred miles to fetch me, & I think in Gratitude I should stay with him forever, had I not an equal Obligation to come back to Your Grace. I feel most sensibly not only Kindnesses done me, but intended me: & I owe you more than I dare say you remember. First I owe you my House & Gardens at Twitnam, for you would have purchas'd them for me when you thought me fond of them. Secondly, I owe you a Coach & Horses, notwithstanding I fought you down to an Arm-Chair. And the other day I but named a House in Town, and I saw with what Attention you listend to it, & what you meant by that Attention. But alas! that Project is blasted, tho' a little one, & disappointed by its being tho so little, too good for me. For upon Enquiry, it cannot be bought for less than double What I was told; and I believe I shall sit down in another, (in which I am deter-

[1] The hypothesis for dating this and the following letter is that they are written after the departure of Bolingbroke and before the time in late June (?) when Pope went to Bath.

mined to sleep as well, tho not half the price:) a House not unlike myself, pretty old, & very crazy, yet possible enough to outlast me with a little Repair, & no bad bargain for my Heirs; so cheap, I may buy it with no Imputation on my Prudence; It will be laying out my Mony well. So that, let your Grace mean me whatever Good you will, at present I only desire you to send me a new order for Janette Mowat, who will want a House & Home more than I. You were pleasd to give my Friend Allen an Order last year for two Bucks, which I think were to be claimd ~~annually~~ this year again as you worded it. pray tell me, if that was your Intention, or not?

What can I say to your Grace? You think the same things, read the same Books, like the same people, that I do: I can only wish a thing I cannot doubt, that you will continue to do so. Be but so good to like me a little, & be assur'd I shall love you extremely.—I won't subscribe my Name, that I may not be thought a very impudent arrogant fellow. But if you forgive me, pray write to tell me as much, and I will declare my self to all the world for | Your devoted Servant.

PS. Just as I am writing, I receive the Billet for Janett Mowat, which God is to repay you for, and I to thank you.

Endorsement: Mr Pope's | letter to The Dss | of Marlborough

POPE *to* THE EARL OF MARCHMONT[1] [*July* 1743]

Arthur A. Houghton, Jr.

So it is, and so it always is with me, that I write last to those I love most; and now by this rule, you are the man I love the very best. The truth is, I have nothing to tell them, but what they (I flatter myself) know beyond all others, my real sensibility toward them, & my knowledge of their amiable Qualities: One must necessarily tell them the same things, if one continues the same affection & esteem: therfore I turn from that honest Tautology to some foreign subject. And what more foreign from you than a worthless man of Quality? whose death has filled me with Philosophy & Contempt of Riches. Three hundred thousand pound the sum total of his life! without one worthy Deed, public or private! he had just sence enough to *see* the bad measures we were ingag'd in, without the heart to *feel* for his Country or spirit to oppose what he condemn'd; as long as a Title, or a Riband, or a little lucrative employment, could be got, by his tame submission, & Concurrence. He lov'd no body, for (they say) he has not left a Legacy, not ev'n to his flatterers: he had no ambition, with a vast deal of Pride, and no Dignity, with great Stateliness. His Titles only must be his

[1] This letter was written from Bath on an obviously early day in July 1743, either Tuesday the 5th or Tuesday the 12th.

Epitaph; & there can be nothing on his monument remarkable, except his nose, which I hope the Statuary will do justice to.[1]

I should doubly congratulate our Victory over the French,[2] if the War would occasion you & me the Recovery of our friend[3] to England for ever. Pray how will that matter stand in his regard. I should be glad either that your Lordship was but half Master of Battersea, or I of Twitenham. I was upon the point of writing to him, but will there be a free passage for Letters at present? He is a Great man, but will never be worth three hundred thousand pounds; yet I would rather re-gain him, & live with him, three hundred thousand times. My Lord Chesterfield is here & sends you his services: there is not one man at Bath besides whom I know. He has made me dine with him *en malade*, tho my Physician prescribes me garlick; which I chuse to take in sauces rather than electuaries. He tells me your Lordship is got a-head of all the Gardening Lords, that you have distanc'd Lord Burlington & Lord Cobham in the true scientific part; but he is studying after you, & has here lying before him those Thesaurus's from which he affirms you draw all your knowledge, Millers Dictionaryes.[4] But I informd him better, & told him your chief lights were from Joannes Serlius;[5] whose Books he is now enquiring for, of Leake the Bookseller, who has writ for them to his Correspondents. I never was more at ease in my life than in this place, & yet I wish myself with you every other day at least.

There are many hours I could be glad to talk to (or rather to hear) the Duchess of Marlborough: so many Incidents happen, beside what Providence seems to have any regard to, in the Lives & Deaths of Great Men, that the world appears to me to be made for the Instruction of the Lesser only, & those great ones for our Laughter: only I must except, that I hear very good things of the Earl of Bath, which justly entitle him to Admiration. I could listen to her with the same Veneration, & Belief in all her doctrines, as the Disciples of Socrates gave to the words of their Master, or he himself to his Dæmon (for I think she too has a Devil, whom in civility we will call a Genius.) I will judge of nothing till I see her.

Believe me, my dear Lord, | Your Ever obliged, ever | affectionate Servant. | A. Pope.

Bath. | Tuesday night.

Address: To the Right Hon: | the Earl of Marchmont.

1 Spencer Compton, Earl of Wilmington, and ineffectual successor to Walpole as First Lord of the Treasury, had died on 2 July 1743.

2 The battle of Dettingen was won on 27 June.

3 Lord Bolingbroke.

4 Philip Miller (1691–1771) published in 1724 *The Gardener's and Florist's Dictionary*, and later 'Dictionaries' had followed.

5 John Searle, Pope's own gardener, had as yet published nothing: Pope writes jocosely.

POPE *to* COL. JAMES MOYSER[1] 11 *July* 1743

Egerton 1948

I am always glad to hear of you, & where I can, I always Enquire of you. But why have you omitted to tell me one word of your own health? The account of our Friend's[2] is truly melancholy, added to the Circumstance of his being detained (I fear without much hope) in a foreign Country, from the comfort of seeing (what a Good Man most desires, & best deserves, to see to the last hour) his Friends about him. The Publick News indeed gives every Englishman a reasonable Joy,[3] & I truly feel it with you, as a National Joy, not a Party-one; nay as a General Joy to all Nations, where Bloodshed & Misery must have been introduced, had the Ambition & Perfidy of France[4] prevailed.

I come now to answer your Friend's Question. The Whole of what he has heard[5] of my writing the Character of the old Duke[6] of Buckingham, is untrue. I do not remember ever to have seen it in Manuscript. Nor have I ever seen the Pedigree he mentions, otherwise than after the Duchess had printed it with the Will, & sent one to me, as I suppose she did to all her acquaintance. I do not wonder it should be reported I writ that Character, after a story which I will tell you in your ear, to yourself only, There was another Character written, of her Grace by herself, (with what help I know not) but she shewed it me in her Blotts, & press'd me, by all the adjurations of Friendship, to give her my Sincere Opinion of it. I acted honestly, & did so.[7] She seem'd to take it patiently, & upon many Exceptions which I made, ingaged me to take the whole, & to select out of it just as much as I judg'd might stand, & return her the Copy. I did so. Immediately she pickd a Quarrel with me, & we never saw each other in five or six years.[8] In the meantime, she shewed this character (as much as was extracted of it in my handwriting) as a Composition of my own, in her praise. And very probably, it is now in the hands of Lord Hervey.[9]

[1] First printed by Warburton in 1751 (Pope's *Works*, viii. 251).

[2] Col. Moyser, as a Yorkshire friend of Hugh Bethel who had accompanied Bethel to Italy in the summer of 1741, might be interested and well informed as to Bethel's present condition. Bethel, in spite of Pope's fears, was not detained much longer on the Continent—whether by his health or by the embattled condition of Europe. He was back in England before the end of Aug. 1743.

[3] The victory at Dettingen.—Warburton, 1751.

[4] Warburton omitted this word and printed simply a dash.

[5] Pope here denies authorship of *A Character of John Sheffield, late Duke of Buckinghamshire* (1729), which, with a pedigree and the Duke's will, made a pamphlet of 48 pages.

[6] He says *the old Duke*, because he wrote a very fine Epitaph for the Son.—Warburton, 1751.

[7] Warburton printed this Character in Pope's *Works* (1751), viii. 246–50, and it is in EC, v. 441–4. It first was published in 1746 (Griffith, Book 617).

[8] The quarrel came late in 1729.

[9] The Duchess's executor.

—Dear Sir, I sincerely wish you, & your whole Family, (whose welfare is so closely connected) the best health, and truest happiness; and am (as is also the Master of this place) | Your most affectio-|nate & faithfull | Servant | A. Pope.

Bath: July 11th 1743.

Address (in Allen's hand): To The Honble Col Moyser | at Beverley | Yorkshire

Frank: ffree Allen

Postmark (imperfect): 11/IY

POPE *to* GEORGE ARBUTHNOT 23 *July* 1743

The Royal College of Surgeons of England

I thank you for yours and am better than when I first came hither, of that Asthmatical Complaint, but still unable to move much about, especially to go up stairs or up-hill. I have let blood, & I take Medicines from Prescriptions of Dr Mead. It will be a great pleasure to me to see you, & it is a real Satisfaction to me to have found you could be willing to pass some time with me in a Family way of Joint-House-keeping, according to the Scheme I had so set my heart upon. But I find Mr Allen will not permit us, after all, to live any where hereabout but in his own house, with any patience. I have spoken of it (as you know) for months past, & he seemd to give into it. But since I have endeavord, in earnest, to get a bed or 2 set up there, & to lay in some things; he absolutely declares you shall be his guest at his own house, & that neither you nor Mr Warburton shall go. I told him both you & I should be Easyer at the other house; that you & I would stay twice as long there; & that we would come, after we had past a month there, & pass some weeks with him: but all to no purpose. I suspect that he has an apprehension in his head, that if he Lends that House to us, Others hereabouts may try to borrow it, which would be disagreeable to him, he making it a kind of Villa, to change to, & pass now & then a Day at it in private.

I told him, I believd you would not Come down, but in the view of our living together there & not of filling up his own house: To which he answerd, that you would come, if I sayd nothing of it, to the contrary; & charged me not to do so; for if once you were here, he would oblige you to stay with him. Nevertheless I did not think it right to conceal this from you. That you are most heartily wishd for, is certain; but whether you will care to stay so long at his house, as you would at the other, I doubt: I owne I should not. And we shall not have occasion of sending in Wine or Cyder &c, as the matter stands.—But I must beg you to come or he will take it very ill that I have acquainted you with this. Let me know your time & I will manage mine accordingly. Mr Warburton intends to go in about a month. and he & I are to make a short Visit to Lord Bathurst at Cirencester, which I'd contrive before you come: unless you should like to travel that way with us, & then I'd postpone it. Adieu My hearty Service to your Sister of whom I am always glad to hear, or to see a line of her handwriting. No man more earnestly wishes the Prosperity of you both, than | Dear Sir | Yours faithfully, | A. Pope.

July 23d 1743.

pray write me a Line as soon as you can.

MARTHA BLOUNT *to* POPE[1] [28 *July or* 4 *August* 1743]

Mapledurham

I hope you are well. I am not. My spirits are quite down, tho they should not. for these people deserve so much to be dispised, one should do nothing but Laugh. I packed up all my things yesterday, the servants knew it, Mr & Mrs Allen, never said a word, nor so much as asked me how I went or where, or when. in short from every one of them much greater inhumanity than I could conceive any body could shew. Mr Warburton takes no notice of me. tis most wonderfull. they have not one of 'em named your name, nor drank your health since you went. they talk to one another without putting me at all in the conversation. Lord Archibald is come to Lincombe,[2] I was to have gone this morning, in his coach, but unluckily he keeps it here. I shall go and contrive something with 'em to day. for I do really think, these people would shove me out, if I did not go, soon. I would run all inconveniences, & drink the waters, if I thought they would do me good. my present state is deplorable. I'll get out of it, as soon, and as well as I can. | adieu my compliments | to Mr At:[3] thursday morn | 8 o clock

Address: To Mr Pope to be | left with Mr pyne the | post master. | Bristoll

[1] Both Pope and Miss Blount had been guests of the Allens. When Arbuthnot arrived, he refused (as Pope had surmised he would) to impose on the hospitality of the Allens. So he and Pope went to Bristol, leaving Miss Blount at Widcombe. What happened thereafter is obscure, but evidently she was made to feel herself completely unwelcome. Estrangement between Pope and Allen resulted, but was somewhat, if not entirely, removed before the following Easter, when Allen visited Pope at Twickenham.

[2] Lord Archibald Hamilton, friendly perhaps through the family connexion with Lady Gerard.

[3] Arbuthnot. In EC the abbreviated name is made 'Br.' The capital A is peculiar, but is found elsewhere in the letter: it is not a B.

POPE *to* MARTHA BLOUNT[1] [*Early August* 1743]

Mapledurham

So strange a disappointment as I met with, the extreme Sensibility which I know is in your nature of such monstrous Treatment, & the bitter Reflection that I was wholly the unhappy cause of it, did really so distract me while with you, that I could neither speak, nor move, nor act, nor think. I was like a Man stunn'd, or stabbd, where he expected an Embrace. And I was dejected to death, seeing I could do or say nothing to comfort, but ev'ry thing rather to hurt you. But for Gods sake know, that I understand it was Goodness & Generosity you showed me under the appearance of Anger itself; When you bid me first go to Lord B.'s[2] from them, & then hasten hither, I was sensible it was in resentment of their Conduct to me, & to remove me from such Treatment, tho You stayed alone to suffer it yourself. But I depended you would not have been a *Day* longer in the House, after I left you last; and of all I have endur'd, nothing gave me so much pain of heart, as to find by your Letters you were still under their roof. I dread their provoking you to Any Expression unworthy of you. Even *Laughter* would be taking too much notice. but I more dread your Spirits, & falling under such a dejection as renders you incapable of resolving on the Means of getting out of all this. You frighten yourself more, than were you in any other house, you would be sensible you need do. If you would go directly to London, you may without the least danger, go in a Coach, & Six of Kings Horses, (with a [serv]ant on horseback, as far as Marlborow, writing to John to meet you there) for 6 or 7 ll as safe no doubt as in any Nobleman or Gentlemans Coach.—If you would stay a few days at Lady Cox's, you might, as many do, be carryd in a Chair to Lincomb,[3] & be all day among people who either love you, or have Civility & Humanity. Or if you cared to pass that time at Holt, where Lady Cox & Lady Bp. are, and as soon as the Duchess of Qu: comes, you may depend upon it if you write she'l send her Coach for you thither. Lady Archibald (I cannot doubt) would lend you her Coach to go, if they have not sent back their horses, which I don't suppose from your Letter.—Another easy way

[1] Written from Bristol. Early in August Pope had left Allen's house, had spent five days at Cirencester with Lord Bathurst, and had gone thence to Bristol with George Arbuthnot. During the five days or more Miss Blount had remained at Widcombe with the Allens. Pope here takes the blame of the resulting misunderstandings upon himself, and evidently they had arisen before he left—perhaps because of Allen's unwillingness to lend a house to Pope and Arbuthnot. Miss Blount has perhaps been blamed too much. The 'quarrel' has largely been presented by historians through the eyes of Ruffhead (see pp. 547–8 n.), who was prejudiced in favour of Warburton and the Allens. Though believing that Ruffhead 'knew nothing about Pope and nothing about poetry', Dr. Johnson unhappily follows him, and seriously misrepresents the two mentions of Allen in Pope's will. See Johnson, *Life of Pope* (ed. Hill), iii. 195. This letter probably postdates that here printed on p. 465.

[2] Bathurst's.

[3] To Lord Archibald Hamilton's.

of going to Amesbury is to Sandy Lane, in a morning, to which place the Duchess can easily send, & you'l be there before night.—Or lastly Mr Arbuthnot & I will come in a very good Coach from hence any day you name, take you up at Lincomb or Lady Cox's by nine in the morning, & carry you & your Maid safe either to London or Amesbury. He has a Friend who lives by Salisbury, with whom he and I would gladly pass a day or two, (Sir Edw Deboovery)[1] & then carry you on to London from Amesbury, which is within 6 miles of him.

All I beg is, that you'l not stay a moment at the only place in England (I am satisfyd) where you can be so used; & where, for your sake & for my own too, I never will set foot more—however well I might wish the Man, the Woman is a Minx, & an impertinent one, & he will do what She would have him—I don't wonder they don't speak a word of me but some words I have spoke to him, I shall not write till I get home, if then. but show my Resentment without lessning myself. For Gods sake do the same. Leave them, without a word, & send for your things But I hope you have, I am sure you have, surely you must have, done this already. In any other house, you'l breathe, & recover your self. The Bethels are good: The Ladies are wellbred, & you'l be in a State both of body & mind, not to intimidate your poor Soul to death, but consult on the easiest means either to stay or go. All I insist upon is, that you do not go directly to London without a Servant, who may come back to give an account how you got that part of the way, and that John may be with you the rest: unless (which I think best, if you don't except to it) you write to him to come quite to you. I've drawn up an Order, which you may fill up as you like, to either purpose, and date, & fix the day & place.

Pray make me easy with the news that you have left their house. I fully hoped it, when I writ to you last post. (for your Letter I did not receive till night, by the Postmasters great care, who instead of letting it lye at the Posthouse where we orderd our letters to be left, had found out our Lodgings, & sent them while we were abroad thither.) I hope you had a little Box, with some Wine: & that Lord Chest.[2] did as he promisd me as to Franks. Sir John Swinburn & his Lady, & Mr Southwell askd much of you. I've not been at the Long room or Wells, & seen no Company more, so I can't say any thing about the Venison, but I doubt not they had it, & will have the other. I think it best still to inclose to Mr. Edwyn. I should not wonder if Listeners at doors should open Letters. W.[3] is a sneaking Parson, & I told him he flatterd.

Address: To | Mrs Blount.

[1] Pope probably mistakes the second baronet, Sir Edward (who died in 1736), for his brother and successor in the title, Sir Jacob. Sir Jacob is mentioned in Pope's letter to Allen, 13 Sept. [1743].

[2] Chesterfield, who is now at Bath.

[3] Warburton!

POPE *to* SARAH, DUCHESS OF MARLBOROUGH[1]

6 *August* 1743

Blenheim

Bath. Aug. 6. 1743

Madam,—Your Grace will look upon my Letters as you do upon my Visits; whenever I have a Clear day or am less dull than ordinary, I have an Impulse that carries me to you, Mind or Body; I do not go, or write, so much to speak to You, as to make You speak to me. If I am awake, you enliven me, and if I nod, you indulge me. I hope what I said about writing no more under Mr Allen's Cover (where I think yours was opend)[2] will not prevent your favoring me under Lord Chesterfields. I am return'd again to Bath, & find he has not heard from your Grace: but I hear you live, & I hope with all that Spirit with which you make Life supportable, both to yourself & those about you. You will neither live nor die like W—n[3] who wanted the heart to pity either his Country, or his Servants, and had equally no Sense of the Publick or Private Obligations. God help him (if he will) that helpd no body! Much less had he learnt the trick some people have contrived, of making Legacies in his Life time. The Scripture has a fine expression upon Charity. He that gives to the Needy, *Lends to the Lord*; and one may say of Friendship, He that gives to the Worthy, has a Mortgage upon Merit, on the best of all *Worldly* Security.

I shall soon be upon the Wing for London, I wish indeed it could be on the wing literally, for every Earthly Carriage is too rough for me: & a Butterfly, tho as weak as a Grasshopper, has the better of him by having wings. I have been trying the Post chaise, to get the sooner home, but it is worse than a Waggon for jolting, and would send my Soul a longer Journey than I care for taking, as long as two or three people remain in their bodies. When I can arrive in London I will endeavor to set up my Rest there against Winter, and constantly keep my *Hive*, tho not an *Assembly*, for I hate a *Buzz* and I will drive out *Drones*. I don't call those that sleep, so, but those that go droning about, & do nothing, no sort of good at least, tho they look bigger than the rest of their Species, and only plunder the Flowers without making Honey, and rob others who can make it. But I'l say no more of these *Great Ones*. God hates them, & you hate them, that's sufficient.

I am | Your Grace's most obligd Servant. | A.P.

[1] Pope has evidently left the Allens, has presumably spent four or five days at Cirencester, and may now be addressed at Bath in care of Chesterfield, but he wishes the venison sent to Bristol, to which place one imagines he is now going with George Arbuthnot. He is, by this guess-work, just passing through Bath—unaware that Martha Blount is still at Widcombe. He has received a letter from her but not the one here found on p. 462, which she sent to Bristol.

[2] The remark shows Pope's new animus against the Allens.

[3] Wilmington.

As you seldom receive any Letters, that do not, first or last, beg something of you, I beg you will order your Keeper at Blenheim to send a Buck to Bristol, directed to the Honorable Mr Murray at the Hotwell: Not the Mr Murray who is so like Tully as to plead now & then in a bad Cause, but a Brother of my Lord Ellibank. And your Petitioner shall ever pray, &c.

Address: To her Grace the Duchess of Marlborough.

Endorsement: Alex. Pope.

POPE *to* THE EARL OF ORRERY 12 *August* [1743]

The Pierpont Morgan Library

Bristol. Augst 12th

My Lord,—I have been summon'd from Mr Allens to Lord Bathurst, where I past 5 days, & then return'd; not without hopes your Enemy the Gout had been repulsed, & that you would give me a challenge to meet you on Horseback, & ride toward Marston. But not seeing nor hearing from you gives me great fear you are still confined. And I was writing to inquire; when Mr Arbuthnot came from London, & insisted on my going with him, as I had ingaged, either to a House Mr Allen had promised to lend him, or to Bristol. The house was deny'd us, & he did not care to stay longer than 4 or 5 days; so we are both at Bristol, whither I came by water, thro the most Romantic Scene I could desire, to other Scenes here of still higher beauty, I can not now have any hopes of seeing Marston as the utmost Limit of our Time draws nigh. But I cannot live with any Ease under the Disappointment of that, and under the Apprehension of your continuing ill. All the purpose therfore of this Letter is to beg to know by a line, (to be left with Mr Pyne the Postmaster of Bristol) the true State of your Lordships health.

I just hear of the death of Lord Hervey.[1] Requiescat in pace! Will it not oblige you to return to London somewhat the sooner? If so, I hope I shall know the first day, & find Part of the Kingdom a much better Situation than this, for Friendship to thrive in, & for Friends to injoy Life. I cannot say with how much Truth, Esteem, & affection I am | My Lord | Your Ever obligd Servant | A. Pope.

Nor can you say too much | from me, to Lady Orrery.

Address: To the Right Honble the Earl | of Orrery, at Marston near | Froome | Somersetshire.

Endorsement: Mr Pope. Bristol. | Aug: 12: 1743

[1] He died 5 Aug. 1743. Since both Hervey and Orrery were executors of the late Duchess of Buckingham, whose estate doubtless was still being settled, Orrery might now have to return to London.

*POPE *to* HUGH BETHEL 16 *August* 1743

Egerton 1948

Bristol. Aug. 16. 1743.

My dear Friend,—I heartily rejoyce & welcome you to your native Country & your Friends, but am the most unfortunate of them, if I cannot reach London soon enough to see you. I have been in Every thing unfortunate this year, that I hoped for with regard to those I love. But I am glad first, of your being the better for your Journey, & then, that Mrs Blount will see you,[1] who has not been the better at all for hers, neither am I for mine. Would to God we were all together, somewhere, for most of our life, to come: Since if there be any Comfort in Life, it is to find honest people together, assisting one another to bear it. I have been travelling like you (would to God your Travels & Complaints were as supportable as mine!) with an Asthmatic Ailment on my breast, which I cannot remove yet. I fancyd change of air might help it, together with Dr Meads medcines; I left Bath & came to Bristol, & thence went over the channel to Wales, by which means I receivd not your kind Letter till yesterday on my return hither. I will hasten the best I can to Town; I am forced to travel very slow, by the Piles, in a Coach in rough way, & I can't ride or walk up hill for shortness of breath. pray tell me by one line the first post you can, how long or short is your stay in London? If you could not protract it, I would make the best of my way instantly. If you think Scarborow waters proper, I believe the Physicians would recommend those of Cheltenham preferably, if you enquired, and if you went thither, I would meet you & stay with you there, where also Lady Codrington is. At all Events, I must see you. I find the gradual approaches of Decay many ways, and whatever I wish to do, I wish were done, for any of those I would benefit. I wish we consulted together about Mrs B. who deserves all we can do, if ever a good Heart deserved well. It would be very convenient to me in the distribution of my affairs to grant her an Annuity of 100 ll a year, & take 1000 ll. with which I would purchase the House at Twickenham, which I am convinced would be a wise bargain for me, & my heirs. They had hung off since my offer some months; but since, Sir Charles Vernon has been bringing it on again, I believe they will come into it, and in that case I'll make use of what you gave me leave for the Advantage of having all the mony ready to clap up the bargain. At present, if the Duchess of Bucks annuity & another from Lord Bathurst be paid me regularly, as I think they will, I shall need less Annual Income than I did when I bought them & can therfore give the annuity to Mrs B. which I mentiond, at that price, which another would not easily be found to do, and settle a Security to her of 2000 ll for it.

[1] She has evidently reached London.

What you said in yours concerning her, leads me to tell you this. You will talk it over with her, and whatever else you can, to make her future life easier & more comfortable than the past. God preserve you & restore you! I am for ever faithfully & entirely Yours | A. Pope.

Pray direct to me to be left at Mr Pyne the Postmaster at Bristol. I will set out as soon as I receive it.

Address missing except for the words: near Grantham.

POPE *to* THE EARL OF ORRERY[1] [18 *August* 1743]

The Pierpont Morgan Library

My Lord,—It was beyond Expression kind in you to give me this Assurance of your Better State of health; & the knowledge that you are upon your legs again, actively setting out on Adventures. I shall do the same, on the same day, Saturday, as I believe: & proceed with Mr Arbuthnot homeward, with sure & certain hope of meeting you at London & at Twitnam, in either of which places I shall be at your devotion. I had a strong Instinct to have gone by Lord Bathurst's (as he can tell you) to Sir Clement Cottrell's, but by a Letter from him I find he is yet in London, & the Method of my Coming at him very precarious, if (after all) he should have room to lodge me: of which he speaks doubtfully, and be it as it will, this will prevent me, (for I cannot part from my Fellow Traveller.) Mr Warburton is still with Mr Allen, & I do not know certainly the time of his return to London, but I think at the beginning of next month. I shall not see Mr Allen's again this year. I am constantly obliged to Lady Orrery, & I promise if ever I drag my bones again so far, I will get to Marston from Salisbury, instead of vainly wishing it from Bath, and make that the first & ultimate End of my Journey. My health is not bad, but the inward Complaint of my Breast continues: I heartily wish that your Lordships Journies may accomplish what I never expect from mine, & Restore you perfectly. My sincerest Respects attend you both, & my prayers for the prosperity of this, & the next Generation that is to be yours, & which I hope your eyes will see when I am dust & ashes. I write nonsence, but it is quite night, & I asleep. I expect that James will call for this before I shall open my eyes to morrow to blush at what I've written: But I add one line with confidence, for never was a truer Word said, or one I can be prouder of, than that I am entirely, & by all obligations, | Your Lordship's ever. | A. Pope.

Bristol. Aug. 18. | 1743.

Endorsement: Mr Pope. | Augt 18. | 1743.

[1] The date subscribed is not surely in Pope's hand. The endorsement and perhaps part of the subscription are Orrery's.

*POPE *to* DR. OLIVER 18 *August* [1743]

The Folger Shakespeare Library

Aug. 18. Thursday.

Many thanks to you for a repetition of kind *Offices* & *Favours*: I will put them all upon a better foot; of *Inclinations* and *Affections*, shewn me on all occasions. We find in the Course of our Engagements, (which now draw us as strongly towards London, as mine have formerly drawn me from it) that we must make the best of our way, & cannot stop at Lilliput:[1] But we will stay a Night at Bath, on purpose to pass it with You & the Master of Lilliput: (but keep this Secret to yourself, or Mr Allen will take it ill.) On Sunday Evening we will be with you, about seven or eight, in order to go on for Sandy-lane early the next morning. Believe me, dear Sir, there are few, or none, in any part of this world, to whom I feel a warmer, or a more pleasing, Sense of Distinction, (I will once more say of Affection) shewn me, than from Yourself; or that have a juster Title to any Demonstrations I could be so happy as to give, of the truth & sincere zeal with which I am, | Dear Sir, | Your most faithfull | & most humble Servant: | A. Pope.

Mr Arbuthnot is heartily yours and begs you would send to Wicksted the Seal Cutter for a Seal of his, that he may take it with him from your house.

Address: To Dr Oliver, in Westgate | Street. | Bath.
Endorsement: Mr Pope

*POPE *to* DR. OLIVER[2] [? 19 *August* 1743]

Robert H. Taylor

Friday after-|noon

A new Scheme has superven'd, & we shall see you to morrow Evening, and not on Sunday; for on Sunday we shall be no more to be seen in your Hemisphære. A sudden Call to London[3] hastens us a day sooner, & we have not one to spare.—I must beg you to hire an Easy Coach of King, or any who has 4 good Horses, to be ready on Sunday, morning by six, to carry us on to Sandylane or Marlborow. Let us meet Mr Pierce with you. Adieu & forgive all the Trouble my Infirmity's &

[1] Lilliput Castle was the name given to the somewhat fantastic house built for Jerry Pierce, surgeon in Bath Hospital and friend of Dr. Oliver.

[2] Printed by R. N. C. Hunt in his *Unpublished Letters from the Collection of John Wild* (1930).

[3] The 'call' was the hope of seeing Hugh Bethel. Pope's letter to Bethel of 5 Oct. indicates that Bethel had left London before Pope and Arbuthnot arrived.

uncertaintys cause you. I am truly in the utmost hurry. Dear Sir | Yours. | A. Pope.

Address: To Dr. Oliver, at his | house in | Westgate St., | Bath To be delivered as soon | as possible to night.

POPE *to* DR. OLIVER — 28 *August* 1743

New York Public Library

Munday, Aug. 28, 1743

I ought to give you some account of two people you show'd yourself so much interested about, as Mr Arbuthnot & myself. But to me, & my Welfare, You have a double Title, as it employed the greater part of your Care and Concern. The Medicine you gave me cannot relieve my breast & stomach more, than the Medicina Animae, administred in your Conversation, did my Spirits: It cannot displease you to hear, that is what I now want the most; for I found myself mend upon travelling. The Air & Exercise about Bristol certainly did me good, and I had no sooner put myself into the Postchaise, than I felt an increase of spirit that carryd me quite to Redding the first day; & I found no ill consequence of lying four or five nights in London, from whence I am but now got home. It was a very melancholy Call to that place which hastened me so much, the last sight, (I fear) of a most valuable dying friend, Mr Bethel, who is gone to Scarborough, I don't see with what hope, but to lie down among his Friends in Yorkshire. I wish you & Dr Hartley would let Mr Allen know the Impracticability of my Calling upon him the only half-afternoon that I was at Bath, (after my first Intention of coming 2 days later, was alterd, which you know to be true, & which I had reason not to doubt Mr Pyne had told you of.) Pray make my Compliments to Dr Hartley, as I shall yours to Dr Mead. I have had such obligations to the best of your faculty, during my whole life, that I wish all others, both my Friends and my Enemies, were their Patients; in which I show that I wish well to my Friends, and not ill to my Enemies. That every Physical & moral Evil may be far from you, is the philosophical Prayer of, | Dear Sir, | Your very obliged and very affectionate | servant, | A. Pope.

Address: To Dr. Oliver, at | Bath.
Endorsement: Mr Pope | 43

[1] Pope's haste in leaving Bath was due to embarrassment in not wishing to see Allen there. He did not arrive in London in time to see Bethel, though he is willing to allow Oliver to believe that seeing Bethel rather than not seeing Allen was his objective. He exaggerates Bethel's illness. Bethel died in Feb. 1747/8.

*POPE *to* WARBURTON [4 *September* 1743]

Egerton 1946

Twitnam: Sunday.

I heartily thank you for yours. I did mention you as I thought, in both of my letters to Mr Allen,[1] but I am sure I did in my last; but he had not receivd it (I believe) so soon as the 30 of Aug. when yours is dated. I there beggd you to give me the first notice when you came this way, and you have done so (as indeed you always prevent my wishes, in doing the thing I desire, even before I desire it.) I have here Mr & Mrs Arbuthnot, & Mr Rollinson,[2] with a heap of Engagements incidental to this place, at this time of year. But I will leave them for a day or 2, & be in town to morrow night, with Mr Arbuthnot, & lye at his house, where I'l send to Bowyer's as soon as I arrive. You may be assured that no man is more zealously yours, or will be more sincere with you than Dear Sir Your faithfull & affect: Servant | A. Pope.

*POPE *to* ALLEN 13 *September* [1743]

Egerton 1947

Twitnam. Sept. 13.

I thank you for yours, tho in it you said nothing of your health, which gave me some fears, having been told the day before that you had been ill of a very bad Fit of the headake: till Mr Warburton satisfyd me it was some time ago, & that he left you well. I was glad to see him look better (I think) than ever I had seen him: We dined together every day that he stayed, & he gave me a promise that much pleasd me, to pass some part of next Winter in Town.

I braggd to you of my Amendment a little too soon, for since my return I have sufferd a good deal from the Complaint of my breath: and if it be so in this fine Weather, what must I expect in the Winter?

Mr W. gave me an account that truly concern'd me, that Dr Hartley had a Fit of the Stone, which he thought was occasiond by his Journey from Bristol, when he walk'd four or five miles to avoid jumbling by Coach. I beg to know how he is? as he is One I have a Sincere Esteem for.

[I] receivd a week or more ago four Hampers of Bristol water from Mr Haslem, for which I thank you & am in your debt. But the rough Stone is not come yet which you orderd away above a month since. It

[1] Reconciliation is beginning: Pope has written Allen twice, and is now arranging to see his commentator, who has evidently arrived in London. If Pope is answering Warburton's letter of 30 Aug., he is probably writing on the first Sunday thereafter, that is, on 4 Sept.

[2] William Rollinson was a retired wine merchant and a friend of both Pope and Bolingbroke. Pope left him £5 in his will for a ring.

will now I fear be too late to make use of this Season, & I am going for 2 or 3 weeks to Amesbury, & Salisbury with Mr Arbuthnot to his Friend Sir Jacob Debouverie's, whom I hindred him from visiting in his way from Bristol, by my Haste to see poor Mr Bethel in London. I shall be there or thereabouts, & if you favor me with a line, direct it to Sir Jacob's. I wish you All health, & joyn Mr Hook in the Wish. Sincerely Yours. | A. Pope.

Address: To Ralph Allen Esqr | at Widcomb | near | Bath.
Postmark: 13/SE
Stamped: WP

POPE *to* THE EARL OF ORRERY — 30 *September* 1743

The Pierpont Morgan Library

Sept. 30. 1743.

My Lord,—You are too good in making Enquirys after a Man not worth giving you any Account of. He can go any where but where he has most mind to go, to Marston; He was at home but a fortnight, before he was seduced into Oxfordshire, in my Lord Cornburys Coach; whence he was carried to Rousham by Sir Clement Cottrel's, stayd two days, & went to Oxford in full assurance of finding Dr King, but he was gone the day before to London; however I took possession of his lodging, & got away the next morning, un-doctor'd, the third time:[1] Sic me servavit Apollo. The Doctor has had an Escape, & so have I. Thence I made a Visit to the Duchess of Queensberry, & so returnd to Twitnam yesterday: where, notwithstanding the finest Autumn in the world, I am wishing for Winter, & November weather to bring you to Town. Lady Orrery & yourself will never rest, till you make me imagine, by so many warm Invitations, that it is my duty to convince you I am a very troublesome fellow, by passing as many days with you in St James' park,[2] as I wish'd to do at Marston. As to your Executorship, I wish no body may be more troublesome to your Lordship than I shall be in my demands: for if I can but plead Poverty, I am sure to be welcome to whatever you & Lady Orrery can help me to. I do not want Money so much as Health & Strength; of which I have scarce enough to live upon; & what vexes me more, scarce enough to speak, write, or behave toward those I most esteem & love, with Spirit and alacrity sufficient to show them, in what degree I love & esteem them: I can only protest (as I do very honestly) that I care for nothing else in this world, than the Society & good opinion of the Few like yourself, & am invariably theirs & yours of necessity.

[1] That is, this was his third visit to Oxford since the affair of the degree was broached.

[2] The Duchess had bequeathed Buckingham House to Lord Hervey: Pope seems to think that Orrery, succeeding (perhaps) Hervey as executor, may succeed to the house. Orrery continued to live in Duke Street.

So adieu my dear Lord, & recommend me to my Lady, who will take your word, for | Your ever obligd, | A. Pope.

Endorsement: Mr Pope. | Sepr 30, 1743.

*POPE *to* HUGH BETHEL 5 *October* 1743

Egerton 1948

Oct. 5. 1743.

Tho the kind account that Dr Kay gives me of the Effect of your Medicine affords me true Satisfaction, yet it is not complete, while any of your Complaint subsists; and whether I may hope or no, I'm sure I may wish, & pray, for a perfect Recovery, which it is not yet. My Satisfaction too is uncomplete, in being absent from you, & not having so much as seen you,[1] by the unfortunate distance I was at. I would willingly take the same or a greater journey, at as short a warning, and follow you to Yorkshire, if I thought It could be of any Use, or but any great degree of pleasure to you. I am told by Dr Kay that the Nostrum of Dr Robari did wonderfully, upon your last trial; but certainly You should add all the helps you can, by Riding, Diet, &c. Mrs Blount understood by you, that you wanted a good Servant, and knowing how very necessary that is to you at this time, made it her business to inquire. She verily thinks she has found one every way capable, & thoroughly honest by all accounts. He servd General Tyrrel many years & was next his person when he was in a declining way. He also attended Admiral Candish in his Illness, & Mrs Candish & Mistress Carteret give him an excellent Character. Mr Arundel on his knowledge of the Man's Merit, has kept him till he shall be provided elsewhere, and in all probability he will be very fit for you. This she causd me to write to you some weeks ago: but the Letter being directed to Scarborow has certainly mist you: We suppose he is yet out of Service, but if you like it, she desires to know, & will do any thing you desire in it.

I am sorry you have any reason to imagine your Illness has at all impaired your Memory. It is a Faculty (I know by experience) that rises & falls, with better or worse Spirits. I often think the same of my own. But what you mention as a defect in yours, that you forgot before to say, as to my Mention of an Annuity for our Friend: is no proof of it. For I did not propose it absolutely as a thing I chose to do myself, but only that it was absolutely right for her to do, & the joint Opinion of others of her Friends, that she should endeavor to purchace one. Lady Codrington in particular try'd with two of her acquaintance who had proposed lately to sell an annuity, and they failing, I meant only to

[1] This remark shows that Pope did not arrive in London in time to see Bethel there.

say, that if no other could be found, I would myself as a *dernier Resort*, which I could contrive with less inconveniency than it would have been formerly to me. I should really think 100 a year might fairly be given for a Life like hers for 1000 ll. Nor should I think it a bad bargain; tho of all mankind I should least like to deal in that way with a Friend.

Pray return hearty Compliments to Col. Moyser, whose uncertain State of health I am very sorry for. I am glad you are together once more, & hope you will both remain a mutual comfort to each other some years to come. Pray let me hear (if it be too troublesome to your-Self, by some other hand, Dr Kay's or Mr M.'s) from time to time, how you proceed. I assure you, few, very few things in this world, give me so much Concern who am with invariable affection & Esteem | Dear Sir | Your most faithfull | humble Servant. | A. Pope

Pray tell Dr Kay my Urns are not worth the Carriage to Yorkshire, & are but Leaden ones. I would send him one or 2 of Bathstone, if I knew how to have them carved, & of what Size, & how to convey them from Bristol, which he would oblige me in accepting of.

The Complaint of my Shortness of breath continues; I have some-times a Pain there, and often in my side; but the latter is manifestly Wind only, & goes off in Eructations, which makes me think the former is occasiond by Wind too. The least stirring puts me quite out of breath, but I have no Cough and generally sleep well. I find no change by any remedy. I have taken but few, Gum pills, moderate cooling purges, Rob of Elder, Pennyroyal & Linseed Tea.

POPE *to* WARBURTON[1] — 7 *October* [1743]

Egerton 1946

Oct. 7.

I heartily thank you for yours, from which I learnd your safe Arrival; & that you found all yours in health was a kind Addition to the Account, as I truly am interested in whatever is, and deserves, to be dear to you, & to make a part of your happiness. I have many reasons & experiences to convince me how much you wish Health to me, as well as long Life to my Writings; Could you make as much a Better Man of me, as you can make a Better Author, I were secure of Immortality both here & hearafter, by your means. ⌜I have given Bowyer the Comment on the Essay on Criticism this week, & he shall lose no time in the rest.⌝ The Dunciad I've orderd to be advertized to be publishd ⌜the last of October⌝ in 4°,[2] Pray order ⌜him to send

[1] Printed by Warburton (1751), whose omissions are here placed in half-brackets.

[2] *The Daily Gazetteer*, 11 Oct. 1743, advertises: 'On the 29th Instant will be publish'd, In a beautiful Royal Quarto Volume, Price 7s. 6d. sew'd in Marble Paper, The Dunciad:

You⌝ as many of them as you will; and know that whatever is mine is yours.⌜I went to Cornbury with the Lord of that place, & lay one night at Oxford. I lookd in at the Printing house. all I could see was one Sheet,[1] in the Margins of which were no various readings or marks for any references of any sort, but a fine well-printed Text that coverd a multitude of Faults, for it was in the worst of his Plays, the Love's Labor lost. Adieu. I am Yours faithfully. | A. Pope⌝

⌜Mr Arbuthnot is with me & sends you his very particular Services, with his Desire, that if, in his Way, he can be ever of any Service to you, You will freely make use of him.⌝

Address: To the Revd Mr Warburton at Newark | Nottinghamshire
Frank: Free | Radnor
Postmark: 8/OC

POPE *to* SLINGSBY BETHEL[2] 28 *October* [1743]

Elwin–Courthope, ix. 160

Twickenham, Oct. 28.

I am very lately returned home after two or three long journeys. I writ to your brother about a servant which he seemed to want, but have not in three weeks heard a word. I fear he is ill, and beg to know what you know of him. I am to send him this parcel, but know not how. I wish you could forward it, either to him or Colonel Moyser. I would give you still another trouble, to get for Mrs. Blount three dozen of Madeira of Colonel Tomlinson, or the best hand you can, fit for present drinking, and send it directed to Holmes, the Twickenham waterman, at the "Globe," at Hungerford Stairs. I should be glad to have any opportunity sometimes of meeting you for an hour or two in town (whither I think soon of removing), or here, if you had a day and night at any time to spare, and let me know, I would be in your way with pleasure. Believe me, sir, I wish you all prosperity, and am sincerely your affectionate and ever obliged servant.

*POPE *to* HUGH BETHEL 29 *October* [1743]

Egerton 1948

Twit'nam: Oct 29th

It is a trouble to me, & gives me great fears of your ticklish State of

Illustrated with a new Hero, the whole four Books corrected throughout, with several Additions to the Poem, never before printed. To which are also now first added, The Hypercritics of Aristarchus, and his Dissertation on the said New Hero. Printed for M. Cooper in Pater-noster Row.'

1 One sheet of Hanmer's Shakespeare.

2 The year is made fairly certain by Pope's letter to S. Bethel of 23 Nov. 1743.

health, that I have not heard of you since my last, where I prest it so warmly, by any hand you could imploy, only in three lines to acquaint me how you proceeded. The temperate weather favours me in my new Complaint, and I would fain hope it does the same in your old one, as they are somewhat a-kin. But more particularly I expected to hear in answer to mine, whether you thought of the Servant I writ you the character of, from Mrs Blount, in which she is very much confirmed, & she has reason to think he would be a very serviceable & useful One to you. There is another desires to have him, but she hopes he will not be gone, if you determine speedily. I send this Letter by your direction you gave me last, tho the former went the same way: Another which I sent to Scarborow certainly miscarryed. I have caused a Book, which I've just republishd with considerable Improvements,[1] to be forwarded to you the best way I can, with your Brothers help; & if that fails to reach you, pray let me know to what hand, in York, or elsewhere, I may consign it? It is a pretty large Quarto. Pray, is there any thought of your Return to London the next Spring? If you and I were together, I should think the Winter shorter, & if I might expect you in Spring, I should find it less melancholy, tho I have Encrease of ailments every winter. And it is no idle Compliment to assure you, could our being together contribute in any degree to help or palliate what your Infirmities make you suffer, I would not make my own any Excuse from going to you, any whither within this Kingdom (and beyond it, I think you have now no Thoughts). Our Friend Mrs B. has all the warm wishes in the world for you, & whatever she may want, in her present Circumstances, to make her happy & easy, nothing I am persuaded would make her more so, nor does she wish any thing above your welfare, the Restoration of your health, & Continuance of your Friendship. As for mine, God knows, half the Effects of it are renderd impracticable or disagreable to her, by malicious Insinuations, & I cannot be of the use I wish to be to her.[2] Adieu, & God preserve you, dear Friend! Remember me to Mr Moyser. I am most faithfully & | constantly | Yours. | A. Pope.

Address: To | Hugh Bethel Esq. at Beswick | near | Beverley | Yorkshire.
Postmark: 29/OC

*POPE *to* ALLEN — 30 *October* [1743]

Egerton 1947

London. Oct. 30th

I was beginning to fear you a little unkind, in not giving me a line in so long a time as since my Letter: But I check'd that thought, & enter-

[1] *The Dunciad in Four Books*, published the day Pope writes.
[2] The sentence is quoted in adapted form by Ruffhead, p. 404n.

taind another Apprehension, that you might be ill, or relaps'd into that Indisposition which Mr Hook had told me attackd you while he was with you, but of which he assurd me you was recoverd when he left you. Last post I received the Account from Mr Warburton, that you have been extremely ill of an Inflammatory Fever, of which he had but Just heard from your clark that you are got quite out of danger, but still very weak. He made no doubt I had heard it, but says, he hopes I did not, till the danger was over; knowing the Pain it would have given me. Indeed he judges very truely, and I ought to thank all those about you for saving me from that Pain, tho' if they are so ignorant of my Concern for you, as to think it more necessary to give any man else an account of you, rather than me; I am not much obliged to them. I will venture to say my Esteem & affection for you are so very well known to all the world besides, by my constant & warm Declarations of them, that every Acquaintance I had at Bath must have concluded I knew of your Condition, or would infallibly have writ me word of it. I will answer for Dr Hartley, Dr Oliver, Mr Pearse, Lord Bathurst & several others, that this was their thought, or I had not been (till two days since) perfectly easy on your account. I now thank God, sincerely & from my heart, for the Removal of your Danger, and I hope for the Continuance of a Life so important to those who depend on your Charity, & to him who values your Friendship. I desire to have a more particular & Satisfactory account how you proceed, than is due to any one that loves you less: if it be a trouble to yourself, pray let any other hand afford it me; or I shall apply to some of those I have named above, for an account, without which I cannot really be content. May God have you in his Protection, now & for ever! & pray believe you have not a Friend who is more faithfully Yours. | A. Pope

Address: To | Ralph Allen Esqr | at | Bath.
Postmark: 1/NO

POPE *to* BOWYER 3 *November* [1743]

Add. 12113

Nov. 3d

Sir,—I am for a few days at Battersea at Lord Marchmonts, whither I've left orders for the Waterman to bring me any thing from you. I doubt not you'l be upon the Watch or set any other, in case of any Pyracy of the Dunciad: to inform me, who shall be ready to prosecute —As to the *little Edition*:[1] they have still not separated it right. The

[1] The small octavo edition of *The Dunciad* was in two volumes, called *Works*, vol. iii, part i and part ii. Part i contained Books I–III of the poem as published by Lintot, 1742. Part ii contained Book IV and the *Memoirs*, &c., as published by Dodsley and Cooper, 1742. Some

Second Vol. must (as the Title you'l see implies) contain the *Fourth book* as well as the *Memoirs, & Index.* Then it will be right.

Pray close the account with Mrs Cooper of the *Octavo's Second vol.*[1] (no more of which should, I think, now be sold) and make all that remain correspond with the present Edition, ready to be re-publishd as we shall find occasion, the 2 together.

And let me know when you have vended 500 of the Quarto?[2]

I thank you for all your Care & shall be ever | Your affect: humble Servant | A. Pope.

Address: To | Mr Bowyer, Printer, in | Whitefryers, near | Fleetstreet | London

Endorsement: Batse

*CHRISTOPHER SMART *to* POPE[3] 6 *November* 1743

1797 (J. Holliday, *Life of . . . Mansfield*, p. 25)

Pem. Hall, Cambridge, the 6th of Nov. 1743

Sir,—Mr. Murray having told me that it would, he thought, be agreable to you to see a good Latin version of your Essay on Man, and advised me to undertake it, though I know myself vastly unfit for such a task, I will attempt to render any number of lines that you shall be pleased to select from any part of the work, and as you approve, or dislike them, will pursue or drop the undertaking.

I am, Sir, with the utmost respect, yours, | C. Smart.

To | Alexander Pope, Esq.

I should not have presumed to have given you this trouble had not Mr Murray assured me that I might safely venture. I have made bold likewise to send you a specimen of a translation of your Essay on Criticism, verse the 339th.

copies are extant in which Book IV has been gathered into the same volume with the unrevised text of Books I–III, and against this procedure, probably, Pope is here protesting. The matter is obscure.

[1] *The New Dunciad* (i.e. Book IV) in octavo had been advertised 1 Mar. 1742/3 as on sale by M. Cooper. The title-page (vol. iii, part ii of Pope's *Works*) is dated 1742 and the imprint has the name of T. Cooper. Thomas Cooper died on 9 Feb. 1742/3 (*Lond. Eve. Post*, 10 Feb.), and his wife Mary carried on the trade thereafter. The imprint indicates presumably an early date of printing.

[2] *The Dunciad in Four Books* (Griffith 578) is 'the quarto'.

[3] Earlier this year, according to Sir John Hawkins (*Life of Johnson*, 1787, p. 14 n.), Pope had expressed to the publisher Newbery his pleasure in the Latin translation of his Ode on St. Cecilia's Day, which was made by Christopher Smart, then a brilliant undergraduate at Cambridge. Encouraged by Murray, the young man now plans further translation of Pope's work. Pope replied to this letter on 18 Nov.

*POPE *to* ALLEN[1] 8 *November* [1743]

Egerton 1947

Novr 8th

I thank you for Mr Pryn's Letter.[2] Indeed I was extremely alarmed at hearing so late of your Condition, & joining together what Mr Hook had told me a month ago, with what Mr Warburton told me now, I apprehend was the truth, that you had a *Relapse*, which is always dangerous. I do not yet know (what I wish to do) what was the Nature of the distemper? Its Continuing still so bad as to be watch'd in the night, and what Mr Hook said of the Manner in which you were first seized (with a great Straitness & Oppression of Breath) makes me fear, the Fever threw itself on the Lungs, & was (tho' in a higher degree) of the Same Nature as mine, which after it left me in May last, has to this day continued upon my Lungs & breast, by intervals worse or better, but I see no prospect of being quite free from the Shortness of breath. I hope your Doctors have that Consequence in their eye, as well as taking off the fever. Pray do not give yourself the trouble of writing to me till you are as well as I wish you: Let Mr Pryn, or any one else do it; But let it (I beg you) be done, that I may have, as soon as possible, that news of you that I hope earnestly for. I am sorry I am so far from you, tho I know no Service I could render You, and tho you have better and nearer Comforters. I thank God for every Blessing & Comfort You have; & pray sincerely for your Health, that you may relish & enjoy them all. I doubt not you have had great Affliction in the unhappy Fate of Sir Erasmus Philips,[3] whom I knew you esteemd, & whom I believe to have been a very Worthy Man, or you would not have Esteem'd him. I have known Accidents of that melancholy kind, disorder your health: but All Events of this life must be submitted to Providence, which possibly does a worthy Man a Favor when it Shortens this life. And indeed No true Judgment can be made, here, of any Man or any Thing, with certainty; further, than that we *think* another man means well, and that we *know* we ourselves mean well. It is in this Situation that every honest man stands with respect to another, and upon which all well-principled Friendships depend. Such I hope will yours & mine always be, & always last, till that Hour in which it shall please God to seperate us from all that we now love, & give us (I trust) something better than the best we now enjoy. Adieu dear Sir & believe me Yours. | A. Pope

1 The month date is written over a blurred 'Octr'.

2 Evidently in Allen's illness his secretary, Mr. Prynne, has written for him.

3 Sir Erasmus Philips 'drowned by a fall off his horse in the Avon near Bath' on 15 October 1743.—*Gent. Mag.* xiii. 554.

POPE *to* [? DR. OLIVER][1] 15 *November* [1743]

Sotheby Sale of 28 Nov. 1913

[This untraced letter is catalogued as item 21 of lot 355 in the following fashion: 'A.L.s. 3 pp., 4to, *Twick'nham, Nov.* 15, inquiring about Ralph Allen of Bath (the original of Fielding's Squire Allworthy), about whom he has been unable to obtain any information except that he was seriously ill, and detailing the remedies he has adopted for his own complaints, *unpublished*.']

*POPE *to* WARBURTON[2] [15 *November* 1743]

Egerton 1946

Your Partiality to me is every way so great, that I am not surprized to find you take it for granted, that I observe more Method, & write more correctly, than I do. Indeed in one of your Conjectures you are right, as I see by casting my eye on the Original Copy; but in the other, no such matter, the Emendation is wholly your own. (except that I find in the margin *How-ere*, instead of *Well then*, but cross'd over.) Upon the whole I will follow your Method, & therfore return the paper that you may accordingly refer the notes. [The mark N which I've put upon the margin is only to direct the Printer to such Notes as are in the Copies already printed.] and the beginnings of verses crost over again, only to shew you how they once did stand.] As for the other part, concerning the Extravagant Motives of Avarice, I meant to show those which were Real were yet as mad or madder than those which are Imaginary [vid. vers.

For tho' Such Motives Folly you may call,
The folly's greater to have none at all.[3]

So I would let that remain as it is.—I am glad you proceed upon these Epistles first, as they will best joyn with the Essay on Man, of which & of the Essay on Crit. I will publish a small number,[4] however, very soon, to try the Taste of the Town: and then give (as soon as you can conveniently) the Notes on the Epistles all together, in one volume with the Essay on Man already printed off, (leaving the Pastorals, Rape of the Lock &c. to the last, to join with the Essay on Criticisme.)

I am glad you'l refresh the *memory* of such Readers, as have no other faculty to be Readers, especially of such Works as the Divine Legation.

[1] The addressee is probably Oliver. See Pope to Allen, 17 Nov., where he speaks of writing to Oliver about Allen's health on 'Tuesday night last'. The 15th was Tuesday.

[2] The date is from the postmark, the year being inferred from the fact that Warburton is now commenting on the Moral Essays. In the text the brackets, all inconsistent as they are, are Pope's own.

[3] Epistle III, To Lord Bathurst, ll. 157–8.

[4] Advertised 19 Jan. 1743/4 (*Daily Gazetteer*) as to be published in a few days.

But I hope you will not take too much notice of another & duller sort, those who become writers thro Malice, & must die whenever you please to shine out, in the Completion of the Work; which I wish were now your only answer to any of them: Except you'l make use of that short & excellent one, you give me, in the Story of the Reading-Glass.

The World here grows very busy. About what time is it, you think of being among us? My health I fear will confine me, whether in town or here, so that I may expect more of your Company, as one Good resulting out of Evil.[1] Adieu, dear Sir. Yours | A. Pope

Address: To the Revd Mr Warburton | at Newark
Frank: Free | Radnor
Postmark: 15/NO

*POPE *to* ALLEN 17 *November* [1743]

Egerton 1947

Twitnam Novr 17th

I have often found that Impatience, which my natural Anxiety for my Friends occasions, make me act unluckily. It was That, which carryd me two days sooner from Bristol to London, than was consistent with my seeing you at Bath (as I had proposed) in order to find Mr Bethel before he left London. And it is that, which (not hearing in two posts, the particulars I so earnestly enquir'd[2] of your Illness) made me, on Tuesday night last write to Dr Oliver;[3] who, by yours which I received that Wensday morning, I find was not employd as your Physician. What made me conclude him so, was, that I had just receivd a Letter from Dr Hartley without saying a word of you, which I wonder'd at. It was a very kind Letter to me with a Prescription, for which I beg you to thank him.—I give you many thanks for the account you send; I wish it were better, but am somewhat comforted to find there's no danger of any Asthma or Oppression on the breast, which I feel too much of, not to dread for another: I hope yours tho a very [p]ainful disorder, will leave no ill Remains behind it, of any sort. I'm surprized Mr Hook should tell me, as he did when first I saw him, that your Illness was in a manner over; nor since inform me You were worse. I never heard of it till Mr Warburton informd me, and that you still continued ill, & imployed Mr Prynne to give him accounts of you from *Time* to *Time*. Pray do but the same to me, (who (I am very sure) wish you Health, Ease, & happiness as much,) and

[1] These last two paragraphs were inserted in the letter fabricated by Warburton, and printed by him and by later editors under date of 28 Dec. 1742.

[2] 'Enquir'd' is written over a visible 'desir'd'.

[3] See the entry here bracketed as to Oliver, 15 Nov. See also with regard to Oliver, Pope to Allen, 8 Dec. 1743.

for any thing else, you need not take any pains to write yourself. Health is now your business: may God increase it daily, and bless all about you! There lies your Happiness; and I would not interrupt that, or your Quiet, for a moment. But you should know, there is not a man living, who from his concern for both, deserves better to be informed of your Enjoyment of them, than Dear Sir Your Affectionate real Servant | A. Pope.

Mrs Allen has my good wishes; and I dare say, the thing that both she and I most wish at this time, is the same.

Address: To Ralph Allen Esqr at | Widcombe, near | Bath.
Postmark: 17/NO
Notes by Allen: Novr 1 letter | 1 parcell and | news | half an | hour after 7

POPE *to* THE EARL OF ORRERY 17 *November* [1743]

The Pierpont Morgan Library

My Lord,—Your every Letter is a fresh proof of your Goodness to me, as it is unprovoked, & comes Voluntary. The truth is, I have such frequent reason to be ashamed that I never am: (like others of my Cotemporaries) Otherwise, there is not a Friend I have, but I should be asham'd ever to write to, having not done that duty so long. But what shall I say? I have a Heart, but I have no Eyes. I have the Spirit strong, but the Flesh is weak. I have nothing to do, & therfore want Time: This last is no paradox, but a common case. I know it is otherwise with you, & therfore I don't wonder you find no time to attend your Publick: Lady O. deserves more Attention than Great Britain. But what Absolute necessity to attend Mr & Mrs Ph—?[1] Do but send, or cause to be sent, me, an order for my Arrear,[2] and e'en stay from them, when My Jobb is done: Just the same Liberty, my Lord, would be given you by a Greater Man. But He desires nothing from you but Money, whereas in truth I desire it much less (let me want it ever so much more) than I do your Company. Therfore, (to be serious) if you must come after Christmass, let it alone and if you can contrive, instead of getting my whole Year pay'd (which expird last Midsummer) to cause them to pay up the Year & half at Christmas, it will be better on this particular account; that for the future the Year may be paid rather in Winter than Summer, as all the Trustees are more likely to be in town at that season.

I have just seen Lord Bathurst who gives me a very Satisfactory

[1] Constantine Phipps was the grandson of the Duchess of Buckingham and her first husband, the Earl of Anglesey. Phipps (cr. Baron Mulgrave in 1767) married in June 1743 Lepell Hervey, who had a marriage settlement from the late Duchess. See iv. 446.

[2] Pope still had his annuity of £100 on the estate of the Duchess.

account of you. I have made your Compliments to Lord Bolingbroke,[1] in whose company your Letter found me, and with whom I pass most of my time, & shall, while you continue absent. I believe you will see him when you come, for he proposes to stay a month or two. He is in very good health, busy about inclosing a Common, & improving his Estate here, about Battersea & Norwood. Would to God your Lordship's Estate was as near!

I am very ready to subscribe to the Print, but do'nt know where? or to whom? Is this all I can do at your request? I would subscribe to the *making a new Giants Causeway*, to get at you, over that Serbonian Bog in Somersetshire. I shall hardly live in Dukestreet,[2] till you come: It would at present be like shutting me up in a Monument, a place that would only put me in mind of what I have lost.

I am sorry to hear of the Dean.[3] My Letter must end, or it will grow melancholy. Pray my Lord, relieve me, and tell me as soon as you can, every thing that you can, which may please me; above all, that my Lady O. & yourself are in perfect health, & perfect happiness. If the first be not wanting, I will answer for the second.

I am ever | My Lord | Yours (in one word) | A. Pope.

Twitenham | Novr 17. 1743.

Address: To | the Right Hon. the | Earl of Orrery, at | Marston near Froom | Somersetshire

Endorsement: Mr Pope. | Nov: 17. | 1743.

Postmark: 19/NO

POPE *to* CHRISTOPHER SMART[4] 18 *November* [1743]

Add. 6911 (transcript)

Twitnam Novbr 18th

Sir,—I thank you for the favour of yours I would not give you the trouble of translating the whole Essay you mention; the two first Epistles are already well done, & if you try, I could wish it were on the last, which is less abstracted, & more easily falls into Poetry & Commonplace. A few lines, at the beginning & the Conclusion will be sufficient for a Trial, whether you yourself can like the task, or not: I believe the Essay on Criticism will in general be the more agreable,

[1] His lordship had arrived in England about the middle of October. He remained until after Pope's death.

[2] Evidently the house of his lordship in Duke Street had been offered to Pope, who planned to settle in London for the winter.

[3] Swift had been adjudged of unsound mind in the summer of 1742, and Orrery has evidently had further distressing news of his state.

[4] This letter, of which Smart was so proud that he had it included in a portrait of himself painted by Reynolds, has long been lost. The present text is from an early transcript, presented to the British Museum in 1826.

both to a young writer, & to the Majority of Readers. What made me wish the other well done, was the want of a right Understanding of the Subject, which appears in the foreign Versions[1] in 2 Italian 2 French & 1 German. There is one indeed in Latin Verse printed at Wirtembergh, very faithful, but inelegant, & another in French prose; but in these the Spirit of Poetry is as much lost, as the Sense & System itself in the others. I ought to take this Opportunity of acknowledging the Latin Translation of my Ode which you sent me, & in which I could see little or Nothing to alter, it is so exact. Believe me Sir, equally desirous of doing you any Service, & afraid of engaging you in an Art so little profitable, tho' so well deserving, as good Poetry. I am | Your most oblig'd | & Sincere humble Servant | A. Pope.

POPE *to* JONATHAN RICHARDSON[2] 21 *November* [1743]

The New York Public Library (Berg)

Nov. 21st

Every thing was welcom to me in your kind Letter, except the Occasion of it, the Confinement you are under. I'm glad you count the days when I do not see you, but it was but half an one that I was in Town, upon business with Dr Mead, & return'd to render an account of it. I shall in the Course of the Winter probably be an Evening Visitant to you if you sit at home, tho I hope it will not be by Compulsion or Lameness. We may take a Cup of Sack together, & chatter like two Parrots, which are (at least) more reputable & manlike Animals than the Grasshoppers, to which Homer likens old men.

I am glad you Sleep better. I sleep in company, & wake at night:[3] which is vexatious. If you did so, you, at your Age, wou'd make Verses —as to my health, it will never mend, but I will complain less of it when I find it incorrigible.

But for your News of my quitting Twitnam for Bath, inquire into my Years, if they are past the bounds of Dotage? ask my Eyes, if they can See, & my nostrils if they can smell? To prefer Rocks & Dirt, to flowry Meads & silver Thames, & Brimstone & Fogs to Roses & Sunshine? When I arrive at these Sensations, I may settle at Bath;[4] of which I never yet dreamt, further, than to live just out of the Sulphurous Pit & at the Edge of the Fogs, at Mr Allen's for a month or

[1] Identifiable among these versions are those of Petrarchi (Naples, 1742), Silhouette (in French prose, 1736), Du Resnel (French verse, 1737), B. H. Brockes (Hamburg, 1740), and the Latin version of Jo. Joach. Gottlob Am-Ende, advertised in London in May of 1743. The key translation (from which several others in different languages were made) is that of Du Resnel.

[2] In EC this letter is dated 1739, but the last sentence about living at Battersea (with Marchmont and Bolingbroke) makes 1739 impossible. Lord St. John (Bolingbroke's father) did not die until 1742, and Battersea was his residence.

[3] An echo of line 13 of Pope's *First Satire of the Second Book of Horace Imitated* (to Fortescue).

[4] These remarks help place the letter in 1743.

so. I like the place so little, that Health itself should not draw me thither, tho Friendship has, twice or thrice.

Having answerd your Questions, I desire to know if you have any Commands? If the first be *to come to you*, It's probable I shall, before you can send 'em so round about as to Twitnam, for I've lived of late at Battersea. Adieu. Yours Ever. | A. Pope.

Address: To Mr Richardson in | Queens Square, | Bloomsbury. | London.
Postmark: PAYD PENY POST.

POPE *to* SLINGSBY BETHEL[1] 23 *November* 1743

Elwin–Courthope, ix. 161

Nov. 23rd, 1743.

I ought to have acknowledged the receipt of your hamper of Madeira which came very safe, and I caused to be delivered, as directed, to Mrs. Blount. You will please to charge it to her account when you send to her next. She is now at Lady Gerard's house (within three doors of that in which she formerly lived) in Welbeck Street, Oxford Chappel. I heard last post but two from your brother, who is not so well as before. God send him better! I hope soon to find some opportunity of meeting you, who am always, dear sir, your obliged and affectionate servant.

*POPE *to* ALLEN 23 *November* [1743]

Egerton 1947

Battersea. Nov. 23d

I write this in the utmost hurry; being ingaged in the most agreable Conversation I know, & the most instructive, (I think you'l guess *Whose* I mean)[2] but I would not let the Post go, without thanking you for yours, and assuring you, You are not in the wrong, to imagine I would preserve (not only the *Form*, but) the *Strictness* and *Essence* of our Friendship. I hope every day will improve upon the other, in increasing your health, and augmenting your happiness. I am truly sorry, Mrs Allen's Illness should follow yours; and it is with all the sincerity in the world, that I say, I wish her as well as your Self in that respect, and am really as much Concern'd for her Recovery, on which I know how much of your Welfare depends. Pray let me hear she is well again, if It be as I hope, that the nature of that distemper you mention is short & transitory, tho violent for the time it takes place. And at your leisure, acquaint me as usual with any thing that

[1] This letter is to be associated with that of Pope to Bethel, 28 Oct. [1743].

[2] Pope seems to have spent most of this month at Battersea, listening with unabated admiration to the conversation of Bolingbroke. Bolingbroke had lent the house to Lord Marchmont.

pleases you, as One who takes part in that pleasure; and any thing that concerns you, as One who takes part in the Concern. I am truly Dear Sir | Your faithfull & affec|tionate Servant | A. Pope.

The inclosed I think I should not (in the Openness of Friendship) conceal from You. It was the answer he sent to my Enquiry after your Health (in which I supposed him your Physician, because Dr H. had said nothing of it) Your own Judgment will tell you, what Use, or whether you would make *any* use of it? I know you are unwilling to use any man hardly, if this be true. Or if it be only wrong headed in him, you'd probably set him right—I have no Correspondence with him, and will either take notice of it, or not, as you direct. Adieu.

Address: To | Ralph Allen Esqr at | Widcombe, near | Bath.

Postmark: 24/NO PENY POST PAYD THS

Endorsement (in Allen's hand): From Mr Pope | Novemr 23d | 1743 | Dr Oliver.

*POPE *to* ALLEN 8 *December* [1743]

Egerton 1947

I heartily thank you for acquainting me of Mrs Allens recovery, which I was anxious to know, & for the Confirmation of your owne, which no Friend you have can desire with more ardor.

I was no further concernd at what Dr Oliver said, than to conclude he had no Real Reason, & therfore sent you his letter, of which you will make What use you judge proper. I was sure you would not wrong, or even do the Shadow of a Wrong, to him or any one else, unless it were upon some Mis-information, or Mistake;[1] & then it would soon be set right, upon a few plain words, spoken (as I dare say yours always will be) with Truth and Openness. I do verily think he would not do or say any thing ill in your regard, he is certainly an ingenious, and (I think) a Charitable & friendly man, notwithstanding some little things, which you & I may wish mended, but few can mend, & all must overlook in one another.——Your Letter of Novr 29. came not to me till Decr 6th I have lived so much at Battersea, & to & fro, from thence to London, that I am seldome or never of late at Twitnam, nor I believe shall, while my Lord Bolingbroke stays in England. I have nothing to do but to remove from one warm Fireside to another, at this smaller distance, & from one Friends Side to another. My Asthmatic Complaint necessitates me to this Confinement, for I can neither bear Cold nor Motion. Mr Warburton speaks of passing some time this Winter in Town. I wish for it, & upon asking him when? he tells

[1] Now that the breach with the Allens is healed, is Pope perhaps reading Allen a moral lesson slightly tinged with irony?

me he is willing it should be when You come hither. Pray have you fix'd your Time? that I may accomodate mine to it as much as possible. Whenever it is, I hope you'l take Twitnam in your Way, as usual, and be assured I am to you, & shall think you are to me, as we have been, in every regard: | Dear Sir, | Your faithfull & affectionate Servant | A. Pope.

Decr 8th

Address: To | Ralph Allen, Esq. at | Widcomb, nr | Bath.
Postmark: 8/DE
Endorsement (in Allen's hand): Decemr 8th | from Mr Pope, | to R A. 1743

*POPE *to* JONATHAN RICHARDSON[1] [1743/4]

The William Andrews Clark Library

You are the first Man I shall see when I am able to get to Town. I am in a very ticklish State, dreading any Cold, from the Asthmatic Complaint; which follows me close, or I had been sooner there. No Thanks are equal to your noble, & (what yet Ennobles it more) friendly Present. Believe I am indebted to you, not in part, but Whole, & All Yours. | A. Pope.

Twitnam. | Tuesday.

Address: To Mr Richardson

*POPE *to* JONATHAN RICHARDSON[2]

20 *December* [1743] *or* 3 *January* 1743[4]

Bodleian Library

Pray tell Dr Mead, nothing but Illness had prevented my waiting on him for some days past. The first morning (to morrow, if I can get up so soon) I will see you both. | A. Pope.

Address: To | Mr Richardson
Endorsements: Jan. 3. 1743 | Decbr the 20th.

[1] This undatable letter is placed at the end of 1743 because the health of both men concerned seems to fit that period.

A negligible endorsement on the outside of the letter says, 'Note from Alexander Pope to Richardson author of Sir Charles Grandison—sent me by Rich in 1732 | Robert Gilmore.' This is obviously not a contemporary comment. Pope did not correspond with the novelist Richardson, who would not have welcomed a visit from Pope. *Sir Charles Grandison*, one may recall, appeared twenty years after 1732.

[2] Neither date is in Pope's hand. At the top of the recto of the leaf a modern hand has written in the January date, which can hardly refer to 1742/3 since Pope was then not in bad health. The date in the older hand is preferable. The note seems to have been written on the cover of a letter and folded in, and so it may originally have been part of a longer letter. But one doubts if it was a part of the letter, now lost, that did date 3 Jan. 1743/4 (q.v.).

1744

The last five months of Pope's life are naturally confused so far as his correspondence is concerned. He did not realize the seriousness of his condition, and he was perpetually planning visits to London, to Battersea (where were Lords Marchmont and Bolingbroke), and to Chelsea Hospital for treatments by his friend Cheselden. How many of these plans he executed it is impossible to determine. After about the middle of February, when fears of invasion by the French revived the proclamation against Catholics coming within ten miles of the capital, Pope seems to have gone no nearer than Chelsea. There is of course the story told by Ruffhead (*Life*, p. 219) for Warburton to the effect that 'A few days before Mr. Pope's death, he would be carried to London, to dine with Mr. Murray in Lincoln's-Inn Fields', and that there a quarrel between Warburton and Bolingbroke took place. It would seem from the letters that long after he was confined in Twickenham Pope was trying to arrange a first meeting of his two intellectual friends. When or if the meeting took place is uncertain. Friendship and the edition of his works, with Warburton's commentary, were his final preoccupations. During his very last days many friends visited him—either out of curiosity or, as one prefers to believe, out of genuine affection.

POPE *to* SLINGSBY BETHEL[1] [1743/4]

Arthur A. Houghton, Jr.

I must repeat the Enquiry after your Brother, & beg, that whenever you have any further account, you will communicate it to me or Mrs Blount at Lady Gerard's in Marlborow street. No people can be more truly concern'd in his Health, which that God may preserve is the sincere prayer of | Sir | Your most [affec-] | tionate faithful | Servant | A Pope

Wednesday.

Address: To Mr Slingsby Bethel | on Tower Hill | London.

Endorsement: A. Pope.

Postmark: PENY POST PAYD WWE

[1] Obviously undatable, the letter is placed here because during his last weeks Pope was repeatedly solicitous concerning Hugh Bethel's health. But since Lady G. moved from Marlborough to Welbeck Street in 1739, the letter is probably misplaced. See *Notes & Queries*, 17 June 1939, pp. 418–21. Possibly 'Marlborow' was miswritten for Welbeck.

POPE *to* JONATHAN RICHARDSON[1] 3 *January* 1743/4

1833 (Thomas Thorpe)

Jan. 3. 1743

['Complains of the increase of his Asthma, and was then laid up at Mr. Solicitor General's; was desirous that Richardson should come and see him there, "but cannot shew so much less tenderness to you, than to myself: for I fear your own complaint of the same kind may press as heavy upon you. God preserve you, and be assured I am always mindful of you, with wishes (such as a friend should form) for your happy year, or years to come." ']

*POPE *to* ALLEN 3 *January* [1743/4]

The Historical Society of Pennsylvania

Jan. 3d London.

It perfectly agrees with my Opinion of the Conduct you would hold, & the Justice of your Nature, what you tell me you did, & what you wrote, in regard to Dr Oliver.[2] You might truly say it was with a Friendly View I gave you notice of his Discontent, as it really concerned me in respect to both. He has not written again to me, nor I to him, but sure he cannot mistake my Motive in communicating his Letter to yourself.—I have been extremely worse of that Asthmatic Complaint which I had at Widcomb & ever since, within these 3 weeks; so ill, that I don't care to give you the trouble I think it would occasion, unless it please God soon to mend it which I will not fail to acquaint you of— You say no more, if the Inflammatory Indisposition you suffer'd so much from, be totally removed, & no Effects remaining. I thank you for telling me that Mrs Allen's Recovery is complete, for I am truly concernd for you both. I am a little sorry you come to Town so late as March, for I wishd Mr Warburton here sooner, tho my Wishes may prove unsuccessfull, but warm & sincere they are. But for my own sake I could wish you came later, when the North East winds are over, & my Breath & Spirits better, & fitter to enjoy my Friends, as well as when the Journey itself would be pleasanter, Twitnam finer, and I capable, perhaps, of taking a little Ramble with you, from thence.

I wish you could tell me if you've lately heard of Lord Orrery, Whether he comes to London or not? For I postpone till then a Claim (which is necessary for me to make) of an Arrear due to me from the

[1] The notable catalogue of Autographs issued by Thos. Thorpe in 1833 describes this untraced letter in the words here bracketed. The date 1743 seems to be for 1744—Pope's usual practice is dating Old Style. Moving from one warm fireside to another in these his last months, Pope is at this moment confined to Mr. Solicitor-General Murray's house in Lincoln's Inn Fields.

[2] On the difficulty with Dr. Oliver (? because he was not asked to attend Allen during a recent illness) see Pope to Allen, 8 Dec. 1743.

Duchess of Bucks[1] of a hundred & fifty pounds and if he dos not come, I ought to take some other method of procuring the payment.

I congratulate you on the great Advancement & Honours conferrd on Gen: Wade,[2] but I hear from several of his Friends he receives them with the utmost Modesty & Temper; not so only, but with real Reluctance. It is one proof, among many others, of his Merit, Sense, & Probity.

Dear Sir, adieu, & let me hear at all times what ever happens agreable to you. be assurd, it will ever be a true satisfaction to | Yours faithfully, | A. Pope.

Address: To | Ralph Allen Esq; at | Widcombe, near | Bath.
Postmark: 3/IA
Endorsement (in Allen's hand): From Mr Pope | Janry 3d 1743

*POPE *to* THE EARL OF BURLINGTON[3]

[? *January* 1743/4]

Chatsworth

If my Lord Burlington goes to Chiswick on Saturday or Sunday, & cares to be troubled with me, I will, upon his sending a warm Chariot (for I dare not go in a Chaise) put my self into his power, like a small Bird half starved, in this miserable weather. | A. Pope.

Friday night, from Twickenham.
Address: To the Earl of Burlington.

POPE *to* LORDS MARCHMONT *and* BOLINGBROKE[4]

[*January* 1743/4]

Arthur A. Houghton, Jr.

Sunday night | Twitnam

My dear Lords,—Yes, I would see you as long as I can see you, & then shut my eyes upon the world, as a thing worth seeing no longer. If your charity would take up a small Bird that is half dead of the frost, and set it a chirping for half an hour, I'll jump into my Cage, & put myself into your hands to morrow, at any hour you send. Two horses

1 Orrery was one of the Duchess's executors.

2 Late in 1743 General Wade had been made Field-Marshal.

3 Obviously undatable, this letter is placed here only because the figure of the small bird 'half-starved' with the cold is used in the letter to Marchmont and Bolingbroke immediately following. Pope went to Chiswick to dine on 30 Mar. (see his letter to Lord Orrery of that date), but since the 30th was a Friday and this letter is dated Friday *night*, this projected visit to Burlington cannot be that of 30 Mar.

4 Placed hypothetically. Pope has returned from a stay with Murray in town, and is eager to be with his admired friends at Battersea. He writes Warburton on 12 Jan. that he has passed most of his time recently with them.

will be enough to draw me, (& so would two Dogs if you had them) but even the fly upon the chariot wheel required some bigger animal than itself, to set it a going. *Quadrigis petimus benè vivere*,[1] is literally true when one cannot get into good Company without Horses, & such is my case. I am faithfully, to you both, a most Cordial, Entire Servant. | A P.

Endorsement: Earl | of | Marchmont

POPE *to* WARBURTON[2] 12 *January* [1743/4]

Egerton 1946

Jan. 12th

An Unwillingness to write Nothing to you, whom I respect; & worse than nothing, what would afflict you, to one who wishes me so well, has hitherto kept me silent. Of the Public I can tell you nothing worthy the reflection of a reasonable man; & of myself only an Account that would give you pain; for my Asthma has increasd every week since you last heard from me, to the degree of confining me totally to a Fire side; so that I've hardly seen any of my Friends but Two,[3] who happen to be divided from the World as much as myself, & are constantly retired at Battersea. There I have past most of my Time, & often wishd you of the Company, as the best I know to make me not regrett the Loss of all others, & to prepare me for a nobler Scene than any Mortal Greatness can open to us. I fear by the account you gave me of the Time you design to come this way, One of them, (whom I much wish you had a Glympse of, ⌜as a Being paullo minus ab angelis⌝) will be gone again, unless you pass some weeks in London before Mr Allen arrives there in March. My present Indisposition takes up almost all my hours, to render a Very few of them supportable: yet I go on softly to prepare the Great Edition of my things with your Notes, & as fast as I receive any from you, I add others in order⌜, determining to finish the Epistles to Dr Arb. & 2 or 3 of the best of Horace, particularly that to Augustus, first, which will all fall into the same vol. with the Essay on Man. I determind to have published a small number of That Essay, and of the other on Criticism, e're now, as a Sample of the rest; but Bowyer advised to delay; tho I now see I was not in the wrong⌝.—I am told, the Laureate is going to publish a very abusive pamphlet:[4] that is all I can desire; it is enough if it be *abusive*, & if it be *his*. He threatens You; but I think you will not fear, or love, him so much as to answer him, tho you have answerd one or two as dull.

[1] Horace, *Epistles*, I. xi. 29.

[2] Printed by Warburton (1751). His omissions are placed in half-brackets.

[3] Bolingbroke and Marchmont.

[4] Very shortly Cibber published *Another Occasional Letter from Mr. Cibber to Mr. Pope*, a pamphlet of 56 pages, not so effective as Cibber's first attack.

He will be more to me than a dose of Hartshorn; and as a Stink revives one who has been oppressd with Perfumes, his Railing will cure me of a Course of Flatteries.

I am much more concernd to hear, that some of your clergy are offended at a Verse or two of mine,[1] because I have a respect for your Clergy (tho the Verses are harder upon ours) But if they do not blame *You* for defending those verses, I will wrap myself up in the Layman's Cloak, & sleep under Your Shield.

⌜Have you forgot, as I did in my 2 last Letters, the Debt I owed you ever since Novr was twelvemonth? and some little matter you undertook to pay for a Saddle & Pothecaries bill, when I left you at Bath? pray send me word, if I shall pay the whole or the Interest, to any person before you come to Town?⌝

I am sorry to find, by a Letter 2 posts since from Mr Allen, that he is not quite recoverd yet of all Remains of his Indisposition, nor Mrs Allen quite well. Don't be discourag'd from telling me how you are? for no man is more Yours, than | A. Pope.

WARBURTON *to* POPE[2] [1743/4]

1788 (Hurd)

I have known this Gentleman about twenty years. I have been greatly and in the most generous manner obliged to him. So I am very capable, and you will readily believe, very much disposed to apologize for him. Yet for all that, if I did not really believe him to be an honest man, I would not venture to excuse him to you. Nothing is more notorious than the great character he had acquired in the faithful and able discharge of a long embassy at Constantinople, both in the public part, and the private one of the merchants affairs. The first reflexion on his character was that unhappy affair of the Charitable-corporation. I read carefully all the reports of the committee concerning it: And as I knew Sir Robert Sutton's temper and character so well, I was better able than most to judge of the nature of his conduct in it. And I do in my conscience believe that he had no more suspicion of any fraud, carrying on by some in the direction, than I had. That he was guilty of neglect and negligence, as a Director, is certain: but it was only the natural effect of his temper (where he has no suspicion) which is exceedingly indolent. And he suffered sufficiently for it, not only in his censure, but by the loss of near £20,000. And at this very juncture

[1] Ver. 355 to 358, second book of the Dunciad.—Warburton, 1751.

[2] This fragment of a letter concerning Sir Robert Sutton was printed by Bishop Hurd in his edition of Warburton's *Works* (1788), i. 143, as an appendix to the prefatory life of Warburton. Since Pope seems to reply agreeing to take Sutton's name out of the Epistle to Bathurst (l. 105) and the Epilogue to the Satires (Dialogue, i, l. 16) in his letter of 27 Jan. [1744], Warburton probably wrote the letter not long before Pope's reply.

he lost a considerable sum of money (through his negligence) by the villainy of a land-steward, who broke and run away. Dr. Arbuthnot knew him well; and I am fully persuaded, though I never heard so, that he had the same opinion of him in this affair that I have. But parties ran high, and this became a party matter. And the violence of parties no one knows more of than yourself. And his virtue and integrity have been since fully manifested. Another prejudice against him, with those who did not know him personally, was the character of his brother, the General, as worthless a man, without question, as ever was created. But you will ask, why should a man in his station be engaged in any affair with such dirty people? 'Tis a reasonable question; but you, who know human nature so well, will think this a sufficient answer. He was born to no fortune, but advanced to that station in the Levant, by the interest of his cousin Lord Lexington; besides the straitness of his circumstances, the usual and constant business of that embassy gave him, of course, a mercantile turn. He had seen in almost every country, where he had been, societies of this kind, subsisting profitably to themselves, and beneficially to the public. For not to think he came amongst them with a view to his own profit principally, would indeed be absurd. Yet I am sure with a view of an honest profit. For he is very far from an avaricious man. He lives up to his fortune, without being guilty of any vice or luxury. He is an extreme good and faithful husband, and with reason indeed, for it is to one of the finest women in England. He is a tender and indulgent father to very hopeful children; a kind master, and one of the best landlords to his tenants. I speak all this of my own knowledge. He has a good estate in this place. My parishioners are good people. The times (till very lately) for this last fifteen years have been extreme bad for the grasiers; I got of him, for them, two abatements, in their rents, at two several times. I will only beg leave to give you one more instance that relates to myself, and is not equivocal in his character. I chanced to know him, when I was very young, by means of my neighbourhood to Lord Lexington (whom I never knew) where he oft came. And, without any consideration to party or election-interest, he seemed to have entertained an early esteem for me. He had two good livings, on estates he had lately bought: and without the least intimation or solicitation he told me I should have the first that fell. He was as good as his word. But this was not all. As soon as I became possessed of the living, he told me, that (from what he had been informed by my predecessor, who at his death was going to commence a suit for his just dues) the living was much injured by a low and illegal composition. That he thought I ought to right myself, and he would join with me against the other freeholders (for his estate is something more than one half of the parish). I replied, that as he paid all the tithes for his tenants, the greatest loss, in my breaking the composition, would fall upon himself, who must pay me half as much more as he then did. He said, he did not regard that; I was his friend, and it was my due. I answered, that, however, I could not do it yet, for that the world would never conceive it to be done with his consent, but would say that I had no sooner got his living, than I had quarel'd with him. But, when I came to my parish, I found them so good a sort of people, that I had as little an inclination to fall out with them. So (though to my great injury) I have deferred the matter to this day. Though the thing in the opinion of Sir R. Raymond, who gave it on the case, as drawn up by the parishioners themselves, is clear and indisputable; yet they won't give it up without a law-suit. In a word, there is nothing I am more convinced of than the innocence of Sir R. S. in the case of the Charitable Corporation, as to any fraud, or connivance at fraud. You, who always follow your judgement, free from prejudice, will do so here. I have discharged my duty of friendship both to you and him.

POPE *to* ALLEN[1] 20 *January* [1743/4]

Egerton 1947

Jan. 20.

I ought sooner to have acknowledgd yours ⌜(especially as it contain'd a Bill,[2] (in which You are, as in every thing, so remarkably punctuall, as to do always more than I thought of)⌝ But I have been severely handled by my asthma, & at the same time hurry'd by business that gave an Encrease to it by catching Cold. ⌜Lord Orrery has answerd my Enquiry by coming unexpectedly to Town last week,[3] tho the Affair I want him to facilitate will still be delayd, but I believe I am very safe of receiving my Arrear, tho not soon.⌝—I am truly sorry to find that neither Yours, nor Mrs Allens disorder, is totally removed; but God forbid your Pain should still continue to return ev'ry day, which is worse by much than I expected to hear. I hope your next will give me a better account. Poor Mr Bethel too is very ill in Yorkshire, and I do assure you there are no two Men I wish better to. I have known & Esteemd him for every Moral Virtue these twenty years & more. He has all the Charity without any of the Weakness, of ⌜his Sister⌝:[4] and I firmly believe, never said a thing he did not think, nor did a thing he could not tell. I am concernd he is in so cold & remote a place as in the Wolds of Yorkshire at a Hunting Seat. If he lives till Spring,

[1] Printed by Warburton (1751) with considerable omissions that seem to be first printed here. They are placed in half-brackets.

[2] That is, a bank bill or order to pay.

[3] A letter from Lady Orrery to Mrs. Whiteway (Huntington Library MS. 14357) indicates that Orrery returned to Marston just after Easter (25 Mar.).

[4] Since Lady Cox (Bethel's sister Mary) had a house in Bath, she is possibly intended. Warburton replaced the two words with a dash.

he talks of returning to London, & if I possibly can, I would get him to lye out of it at Twitnam, tho we went backward & forward every day in a warm Coach, which would be the properest Exercise for both of us, since he is become so weak as to be deprived of Riding a Horse.

⌜Mr Hook keeps pretty well, & goes on prosperously with his History.⌝ Lord Bol. stays a month yet, and I hope Mr Warburton will come to town before he goes: they will both be pleasd to meet each other: & nothing, in all my life, has been so great a pleasure to my Nature, as to bring deserving & knowing Men together. It is the greatest favor that can be done, either to Great Genius's, or Useful Men. I wish too he were a while in town, if it were only to lie a little in the way of some proud & powerful persons, to see if they have any of the Best sort of Pride left, Namely to serve Learning & Merit, & by that means distinguish themselves from their Predecessors.

⌜Adieu. I've no more room but for a Receipt, & pray tell me in your next if I shall also indorse one on the bond?* I am Sincerely Yours.⌝—

⌜*I conclude it is receivd by this time, tho I am not certain, being at Battersea⌝.[1]

Address: To | Ralph Allen Esqr | at Widcombe | near | Bath.

*POPE *to* WARBURTON — 27 *January* [1743/4]

Egerton 1946

Twitenham Jan. 27.

This Letter will be very Laconic, it will be as Shortbreathd as I am. It is purely to give your friendly heart a little more Ease about me: I am in no pain, but Oppress'd; and I sleep better here in the Country than in Town; which has made me return home, & confine myself for the most part here. I have gone over all your Papers on the 2 Epistles, to my Satisfaction, and I agree with you to make shorter work with those to the Lady, & to Lord Burlington (tho I have replaced most of the omitted lines[2] in the former) I wish next for your Remarks, on that to Dr Arbuthnot, (which will hold, I believe, of something between a Commentary & Notes, something of the General Conduct of the piece, the Transitions &c, & something more as to particular & separate passages.) These I propose to print next together. I will omit the Person's Name to whom you shew favour,[3] in this

[1] Since the lower half of the last leaf of the correspondence folder was cut away, one may assume that it contained a receipt.

[2] On the first printing of these 'omitted' lines (including the characters of Atossa, Cloe, &c.) see V. A. Dearing, 'The Prince of Wales's Set of Pope's *Works*', in *The Harvard Library Bulletin*, iv (1950), 320–38. The crucial lines were all printed for this private edition in about the year 1738, but they were not published until after Pope's death.

[3] Sir Robert Sutton. See Warburton's letter to Pope, here placed earlier in this month of January.

Edition: I am glad to have any occasion to do any thing that may be half so agreable to You, as a hundred things you have done have been to me. Believe me, in short, but in full, cordially & entirely. Dear Sir, | Yours. | A. Pope

Address: To | the Revd Mr Warburton | at | Newark
Frank: free | Radnor
Postmark: 28/IA

POPE *to* SLINGSBY BETHEL[1] [1743/4]

Harvard University

Pray tell me by a line per Bearer, whether it will be any way inconvenient if I draw upon you for 500 ll on your Brother's account in ten days time, or a fortnight?

Believe me always | Dear Sir | Your obligd & | affectionate | Servant | A. Pope

Twitnam: | Saturday.

Address: To Mr Bethel, on | Tower-hill.

*POPE *to* SLINGSBY BETHEL[2] 6 *February* [1743/4]

Harvard University

Feb. 6th.

I have been in hopes to find a day to see you, or at least to have met you at Lady Codrington's: but now I hear she does not come to Town at all; and your good Brother mentions no Time for his Coming this way, but only in general, if he grows better. I am in your debt for some Wine, but what I now write to you upon, is that I could very much wish you could take 300*l* more of mine, to make the 700 an even thousand, if it be not too inconvenient to your self. I am adjusting several of my little affairs, & am payd in a good deal of Mony which I do not know what to do with. I must also speedily determine upon a purchase with your Brother, which according as I can, or cannot, imploy the Money, I would settle as soon as possible, both his health & mine being very precarious. For within these 4 months I am fallen into an Asthma almost as bad as his, and hardly able to stir

[1] This letter and that immediately following are placed here together as indicating that Pope wishes money either to buy a house in town (see his letter to Hugh Bethel of 19 Mar.) or to buy the annuity for Martha Blount, concerning which he has recently approached Hugh Bethel.

[2] In the date the digit indicating the day is ambiguous: it may be an 8, but in view of the following letter the preferred interpretation is 6. Pope is perhaps assembling funds for some purchase. Notable is his identical request to Bethel, 16 June 1742.

abroad. I lye at present at the Earl of Orrery's in Westminster, Duke street, whither a line will find me these 3 or 4 days, and be a particular favour to | Dear Sir | Your faithfull & obliged | humble Servant, | A. Pope.

Address: To | Mr Slingsby Bethel | at his house on | Towerhill, | London.
Endorsement: A. Pope Feb. 6. 1743
Postmark: PENY POST PAYD.

*POPE *to* SLINGSBY BETHEL[1] 8 *February* 1743/4

Arthur A. Houghton, Jr.

Feb. 8th. 1743/4.

Nothing can be more obliging than your Ready Complyance with my desire. I send you three hundred pounds in one note on Mr Sam: Child of 142*l* 10*s* & another on Mr And. Drummond of 157:10. You'l please execute the Bond, & let the Bearer be a Witness to it. If he misses you, it will keep cool till you & I meet, either at Lord Orrery's in Dukestreet Westminster, where I lodge for some days, or at Lady Codrington's, when she comes. I dare not name your own house, not daring to venture so far during the continuance of my asthmatic complaint. I hope you are free from all ailments, & nobody is with more truth | Dear Sir | Your affectionate | faithfull Servant | A. Pope.

Address: To Mr Slingsby Bethel | on Tower hill.
Endorsement: Alex Pope Feb 8. 1743

POPE *to* SARAH, DUCHESS OF MARLBOROUGH

Blenheim [*February* 1743/4]

Your Grace might almost think I *told* you *the Thing which was not*, and which the very Horses in Gullivers Travels disdain to do. But the Truth is, the day after I sent to your Grace when Lord Marchmont was with you, I was taken so ill of my Asthma, that I went to Chelsea, to be let blood by my Friend Cheselden, by which I had found[2] more

[1] Bethel evidently replied favourably to the letter preceding this, and now Pope is making his deposit with Bethel as banker. Child and Drummond were also both prominent bankers. The bond was executed on 27 Mar. (Carruthers, p. 456), and was turned over to Murray, Pope's executor, shortly before Pope's death. On 8 Feb. Pope and Lord Orrery spent much of the day dining with Lord Burlington in Burlington House: the next day both were ill. See *Orrery Papers* (1903), ii. 183.

[2] The tense here suggests that the visit to Chelsea on about 25 Feb. was not the first letting of blood. Nor was that at Battersea about the 15th. See Pope to Bethel, 20 Feb. [1743/4]. After the visit to Chelsea Pope had (as he here tells us) gone to Town, where Her Grace seems to be; but he is now back home in Twickenham.

good than by any other practise, in four months. But at my return to Town, I was worse & worse for the 2 or 3 days I stayed there, & still unable to venture out, to you, even so little a way as from Lord Orrery's. I was unwilling to inform you how bad I was, and am unwilling to inform you how bad I am still. Indeed so bad, that I can scarce breathe, or sleep, tho I've again let blood, & take a hundred Med'cines. I am become the whole Business, now, of my two Servants, & have not, and yet cannot, stir from my Bed & Fireside. All this I meant to have hid from you, by my little Note yesterday: For I really think you feel too much Concern for those you think your Friends: and I would rather die quietly, & slink out of the world, than give any Good Heart much trouble for me, living or dead. The first 2 or 3 days, that I feel any Life return, I will pass a part of it at your Bedside; in the meantime I beg God to make Our Condition supportable to us both.

BOLINGBROKE *to* MARCHMONT[1] [14 *February* 1743/4]

1831 (*Marchmont Papers*, ii. 327–8)

London, Tuesday morning.

Pope desires me to carry him to Battersea to-morrow. Let me have your chariot to-morrow before ten. The French are in Flemish Road, Sir John Norris by this time in the Downs,[2] or very near. Adieu, my dear Lord. I make my bow to Lady Marchmont, and am much a servant to Mr. Carre, and to our *malade*, *qui se porte bien.*

I shall drink your health to-day with Lord Stair.

*POPE *to* HUGH BETHEL 20 *February* [1743/4]

Egerton 1948

Twitnam, Feb. 20.

My dear Sir,—As often as I think of you I sigh, and look upon myself: Methinks our Fates grow more alike, & we go down the Hill arm in arm. For every month this winter I have been lower & lower; & yet I fear when you are at best, you are worse than I; yet if I live on, I shall certainly overtake you. It is three weeks since I heard from you, &

[1] The date may be questioned, but we know that about this time Pope was in Duke Street with Lord Orrery, and the 14th seems to be the only Tuesday in February on which such a plan of going to Battersea could be suggested. One would assume that (in view of the threatened invasion and the legal banishment of Catholics from London consequent on it) that this might be Pope's final appearance in London; but from Ruffhead (i.e. Warburton), p. 219, we get the famous story of how Pope 'a few days before his death' went to dine with Murray in Lincoln's Inn Fields—at which dinner the quarrel between Bolingbroke and Warburton over the moral attributes of the Deity broke forth. Warburton came to London in March; hence, if we accept Ruffhead's story, the dinner must have taken place later than the time of this letter.

[2] Admiral of the Fleet Sir John Norris had in this month put to sea, and an engagement with the French off Dungeness on the 24th was prevented only by a gale.

you should not have been unanswerd so long, had I not been trying every way by Medcines to give you a better account of myself than till the other day I could have done. As soon as I received yours, I went & conferrd 2 whole hours with Dr Burton:[1] he opiniatred the Continuance of his Pills which you mention: they are the same with Dr Meads, only made more quick & strong; no Quicksilver, and a draught of garlick & gas of Sulphur after them I persisted first & last in this Course 3 months, with no Effects, but at a full stop at best: till a week ago, I was seizd with a violent fit, & totally stopt from Expectorating & almost from breathing. The Case was pressing & Mr Cheselden came to me to Battersea,[2] where it happend & let me blood. The Relief was instant; & (which is more than I expected) I have now for 2 days been infinitely better, not only than before but than I have been in three months, if it will hold. I breath, sleep, & expectorate, without the Pills, yet they will have me take them on 6 in a day, they are hot, & take away all appetite, consisting of the Common gums, with assa foetid. Arum, Diagraedion, Sulph. Ammoniac, Bals. Peru. & Soap. I am inclind to repeat bleeding, which Cheselden is confident I may, often & securely. What do you think or know of that practise? As to Quicksilver, Burton is against it in my Case. Catching Cold above all things hurts me, & I am grown so tender as not to be able to feel the air, or get out of a multitude of Wastcotes. I live like an Insect, in hope of reviving with the Spring, and above all, my favorite Project would be to keep my self alive till you could come this way, & try if we can get up the hill together, instead of going down. But I am sincerely of the mind (and I believe you are) that it is hardly worth while to do so, unless we can enjoy this world better, or unless this world were better. At least unless Friends could make each other happier, or see each other made happier, by better health & better Times. ⌜I have lived long enough, when I have lived to despise & lament the Worthlessness, Perfidiousness, & Meanness of half my Acquaintance, & to see the Dirtyness & Dishonesty of those we thought best of. I dare say you feel the same Shock, & that neither of us would chuse to stay an hour more on the Earth for their sakes or Company. It is a Comfort to me, that my old & long experienced Friend Lord Bol: is here, in case this should be my last Winter,⌝[3] and it will be another, if You dear Sir come up

[1] Pope's physician, Dr. Simon Burton of Savile Row, died twelve days after Pope did. He was in some sense superseded presently by Dr. Thompson (called a quack), whose treatment is said not to have delayed Pope's death.

[2] ? Possibly on the 15th or 16th. Pope presently goes to stay briefly with Cheselden at Chelsea Hospital. Pope's 'week ago' as date for the violent attack cannot be taken too precisely.

[3] Quoted by Ruffhead, p. 520. The outburst is probably due to the intense excitement over politics and the war with the French. Evidently Pope does not anticipate the ultimate perfidy of his 'old & long experienced Friend' Bolingbroke over the *Idea of a Patriot King* (1749).

hither, in case this should be my last Spring. He will soon be going, may you be well enough to come soon! in the meantime be assurd no man is more in my heart than yourself.

I ought not to finish this Letter without acknowledging the Recceit (just now) of your Picture, which I do in the kindest manner. It is excellently painted, for it is exactly like you, and is well painted beside, I don['t] know by whom or where? but it shall be before my eyes, in my Bedchamber, where I now pass much of my time. I don't know whether Mrs P. Blount would no[t] have quarreld with me for it, had she seen it in Town, but I sent instantly for it, cased carefully up. She is much affected too by Colds, & in general a Sufferer by a delicate Constitution; tho she will sometim[es] neglect herself with great Courage, in which consists the Magnanimity of a Lady. I wish that were the only Instance of her neglect of herself, & that her Sister were out of the Question; who hinders her Quiet all she can, tho it will no way contribute to her own. For Quiet is not of such Souls as her Sisters: God bestows it better, only upon virtuous & good minds.

Adieu once more. I am truly | Yours. | A. Pope.

If Kent will still put off my picture, will you have a Copy of Vanloo's?

POPE *to* WARBURTON[1] — 21 *February* 1743/4

Egerton 1946

⌜Feb. 21st 1743⌝

If I was not ashamed to be so behind hand with you, that I can never pretend to fetch it up, (any more than I could in my present State, to overtake you in a Race) I would particularize which of your Letters I should have answerd first? It must suffice to say I have received them All; & whatever very little respites I have had from the daily Care of my Malady have been employd in revising the papers on the Use of Riches, which I would have ready for your last Revise against you come to Town that they may be begun with ⌜by Bowyer⌝ while you are here.—⌜I would also defer till then the publication of the Two Essays with your Notes in Quarto,[2] that (if you thought it would be taken well) you might make the Compliment to any of your Friends (& particularly of the Great ones, or of those whom I find most so) of sending them as Presents from yourself.—For what I writ of your forwarding the Satires & Imitations, which I agree with you to add to the Epistles;⌝ I own the late Encroachments upon my Constitution

[1] Printed by Warburton (1751) with omissions here placed in half-brackets.

[2] Pope is changing his mind too late. During his bad week of asthma advertisements have appeared announcing the publication of the quarto edition of 'the two Essays' (on Criticism and on Man). See *The Daily Gazetteer*, 18 Feb. and thereafter frequently.

make me willing to see the End of all further Care about *Me* or my *Works.* I would rest, for the one, in a full Resignation of my Being to be disposd of by the Father of all Mercy; & for the other (tho indeed a Triffle, yet a Triffle may be some Example) I would commit them to the Candor of a sensible & reflecting Judge, rather than to the Malice of every shortsighted, & malevolent Critic or inadvertent & censorious reader; And no hand can set them in so good a Light, or so well turn their best side to the day, as your own. This obliges me to confess, I have for some months thought myself going,[1] and that not slowly, down the hill; the rather, as every Attempt of the Physicians, & still the last Medcines more forcible in their nature, have utterly faild to serve me. I was at last, about 7 days ago, taken with so violent a Fit at Battersea, that my Friends Lord Bolingbroke & Lord Marchmont[2] sent for present help to the Surgeon[3] [wh]ose bleeding me I am persuaded saved my life, by the instantaneous Effect it had; and which has continu'd so much to amend me, that I have past 5 days without oppression, & recover'd what I have 3 months wanted, some degree of Expectoration, & some hours together of Sleep. I am now got to Twitnam, to try if the Air will not take some part in reviving me, if I can avoid Colds; & between that place & Battersea with my Lord Bol.[4] I will pass what I have of Life, while he stays, (which I can tell you to my great Satisfaction will be this fortnight or 3 weeks yet.) What if you came before Mr Allen, & stayd till then, instead of postponing your Journey longer? Pray, if you write, just tell him how ill I have been or I had wrote again to him, But that I will do, the first day I find myself alone with pen, ink, & paper, which I can hardly be even here,[5] or in any Spirits yet to hold a pen. You see I say nothing, & yet this writing is Labour to me. I am ⌜most faithfully Yours. | A. Pope⌝

POPE *to* BOWYER — 23 *February* [1743/4]

Add. 12113

Thursday. Feb 23

Sir,—I hope you have Enterd the Essay on Man & the Essay on Criticism with the Commentary and Notes of W. Warburton, Printed for Wm Bowyer in the Hall book[6]—I desire you to remember exactly,

[1] He had made his will (establishing Warburton as his official commentator) on 12 Dec. 1743.

[2] Warburton printed 'my friends Lord M. and Lord B.'

[3] Cheselden.

[4] Warburton printed 'Lord B.'

[5] From the account of Pope's last weeks at Twickenham recorded by Spence one gathers that friends rather constantly hovered over him. Among them were Anne Arbuthnot and Martha Blount (this last lady unmentioned by Spence) as well as Lord Bolingbroke, Hooke, and possibly Spence himself.

[6] The newly published quarto edition of these poems should be registered in Stationers' Hall. Lintot had some claim on the copy of the *Essay on Criticism*, which was included in his

& minute down what Mr Lintot has said to you of printing any thing of mine, &c. There may be Occasion for it, if ever he ventures at it, and I must beg you to be particularly watchful; if it can be found done at his Press, I would have you write him word, & keep a Copy of the Letter, that "you have publishd but *so many*[1] books to try the Tast of the Town: that the Proportion of Sheets belonging to Him, being the whole Text of the Essay on Crit. makes 4 sheets a 6th part of the book; that you inclose him a Bill of the Costs of paper & print of *so many* books as you have publishd, and have them ready to be deliverd him, on payment. Or if he would pay no money, to deduct it out of the Number, without asking him Ever to allow for any Books more than as they shall sell: "but that he may either take his proportion, whenever Mrs Cooper takes a number from time to time, or I will allow it to him & account with him for it as they are sold, without ever charging him for the remainder."

Let Wright[2] immediatly send you in what he has done, gathered, of the *little* Essay on Man. As I remember one or two Sheets at the beginning were first done by you, so that you must put them & his together. he has finishd it, but possibly a Title leaf may be wanting to the whole which pray Supply, & have it ready gatherd. Pray write to Mr Warburton to send you a List of as many persons in Town as he would send the Essays to, as Compliments from himself: tell him the more, the better. Lord Chesterfield, Lord Bathurst, Lord Carteret, Mr Murray, &c put him in mind of from me. Adieu.

I thank you, & | am Yours.

Address: To Mr Bowyer | Printer in White friers.

*POPE *to* ALLEN — 25 *February* [1743/4]

Egerton 1947

Chelsea,[3] Feb. 25th

Dear Sir,[4]—You may think it longer than ordinary since you heard of me; but I (who know no difference in my Memory of you, nor in my

small octavo editions of Pope's *Works* (1736, 1739, 1743), vol. i. Pope's bibliographical details are inaccurate. In the quarto edition the *Essay on Criticism* ran to eight sheets (B–I) and in the octavo *Works* it occupied parts of three (G3–I3). He may be trying to differentiate between text (Lintot's right) and commentary, to which Lintot had no right.

1 Between the lines here Pope inserted 'No.'—meaning that he wished to know the exact number of books.

2 John Wright was evidently the printer of the small *Essay on Man*.

3 Pope was at Chelsea Hospital, doubtless as guest of Cheselden, who was surgeon there. Again in his letter of 7 May Pope writes from 'Chelsea College', as the place was still called from the earlier foundation on the same site.

4 Below the 'Dear Sir' is written in an early hand, 'to Mr Allen a little before his [Pope's] death'.

Good Opinion of you) know, that neither this, or any other seeming Omission proceeds from the least Want of any thing but Health, & Spirit to tell you what I've so often assured you of; & you ought to believe, from a Man, whom you will find (in the future progress of his life) wholly disinterested, & upon generous Principles Your Friend. But the truth is, I have been almost dying with a violent attack of the Asthma, which at last resisted all Med'cines, & compelld me to the only Recourse, of letting blood for present Breath. It has succeeded, not only then, but I have mended so much upon it within three days, that I can truly say, it has given me more Ease in that space than all the Med'cines besides in as many months. I will suppose, you take the same part in wishing me, well, that I feel in wishing you So: and therfore the moment I grow better, I acquaint you of it. I hope tis what you would do, in your own regard to me, & that, if you [ar]e quite restored to your own health, you wou'd not [d]eprive me of the news of it. Pray let me know, some time before you set out for these parts, (which I now begin to form a prospect of) that I may contrive to see as much of you as you can; to meet, I hope, at Twitnam, in your way hither, as well as at your Return; I will make it so Easy to you to continue my friend, that you must think very meanly of me, if you don't: & so as I am sure You never, of yourself, can think, nor will ever find One Man who knows me, that can. In a word, you shall always find me, as much as I desire to find You, for Life, a Faithful & Sincere Servant. A. Pope.

Address: To | Ralph Allen, Esqr at | Widcombe, near | Bath.
Postmark: 25/FE

BOLINGBROKE *to* MARCHMONT[1] [1743/4]

1831 (*Marchmont Papers*, ii. 326)

Sunday.

My dear Lord,—I have but a moment, in which to thank you for yours, and to tell you, that I desire to go to-morrow to see Pope, at the same time as you go, for which purpose I will be at Battersea by nine or ten o'clock. If you employ your coach otherwise, let me know it, and I will come with four horses to you. We may dine at Battersea at our return, and I hope to lie there.

Adieu, ever your most faithful, | B.

I shall be able to tell you some news to-morrow, and, I fear, bad.

[1] The Monday of the projected visit would be difficult to determine. The bad news probably concerns the war.

POPE *to* BOWYER[1] 3 *March* 1743/4

Add. 12113

Mr Bowyer,—On Second thoughts, let the Proof of the Epistle to Lord Cobham, I, be done in the *Quarto*, not the *Octavo*, size: contrive the Capitals & evry thing exactly to correspond with that Edition. The first proof send me, the Number of the whole but *1000*, & the Royal *over* & above. | Yours | A. Pope.

March 3d | 1743

Address: To Mr Bowyer | in White frye[rs] | F[leet street] | L[ondon]

POPE *to* ALLEN[2] 6 *March* [1743/4]

Egerton 1947

Twitenham. March 6th

I thank you very kindly for yours. I am sure we shall meet with the same hearts we ever met, & I could wish it were at Twitnam, tho only to see you & Mrs Allen twice there, instead of once. But as Matters have turned out, a decent Obedience to the Government has since obligd me to reside here, ten miles out of the Capital,[3] & therfore I must see you here or nowhere. Let that be an additional reason for your coming, & staying what Time you can.

The utmost I can do, I will venture to tell you in your Ear. I may slide along the Surrey side (where no Middlesex Justice can pretend any Cognizance) to Battersea, & thence cross the Water for an hour or two, in a close Chair, to dine with you, or so. But to be in Town, I fear, will be imprudent & thought insolent, at least hitherto, all comply with the Proclamation[4] I write thus early, that you may let me know if your day continues & have every room in my house as warm for you, as the Owner always would be. It may possibly be, that I shall be taking the secret Flight I speak of, to Battersea before you

[1] The letter records the printing of the first of the 'Ethic Epistles', which (according to Spence, p. 318) Pope sent out 'as presents about three weeks before we lost him'. Pope's executors, out of respect for the Duchess of Marlborough who, they feared, might take the character of Atossa (Epistle II, ll. 115–50) as her own, suppressed the edition. After Pope's death (and that of the Duchess) the executors evidently sold unmarketed copies of Pope's works to Warburton, who in 1748 issued the suppressed copies with the title-page 'Four Ethic Epistles by Alexander Pope, Esq. With the Commentary and Notes of Mr. Warburton. London, Printed for J. and P. Knapton in Ludgate-street. MDCCXLVIII.' Copies with this title are identical (except for the title) with the volume (lacking title) thought to be issued by Pope before his death and now catalogued in the British Museum as C.59.e.1 (2).

[2] Printed by Warburton in 1751.

[3] The Act forbidding Catholics to reside within ten miles of London, passed first about the time of Pope's birth, was now invoked by proclamation of King George II in February 1744 because of the threatened Jacobite invasion from France. In some letters Pope takes this Proclamation less seriously than here.

[4] On the Invasion, at that time threatened from France and the Pretender.—Warburton.

come, with Mr Warburton; whom I have promised to make known to the Only Great Man in Europe[1] who knows as much as He. And from thence we may return the 16th or any day hither, & meet you, without fail, if you fix your day.

I would not make ill health come into the Scale, as to keeping me here, (tho in truth it now bears very hard upon me again, & the least Accident of Cold, or Motion almost, throws me into a very dangerous and Suffering Condition.) God send you long life, & an Easier Enjoyment of your breath than I now can expect, I fear.

*POPE *to* [? BOWYER][2] [*March* 1743/4]

Egerton 1946

If Mr Warburton come to Town before the 17th I could wish he came to Twitnam as soon as he can for Mr Allen comes that day.

I shall be in town on Tuesday, I believe & Wensday. at Mr Murray's.[3] pray call there in the morning—

Address: To | Mr Pope at Twickenham[4]

POPE *to* WARBURTON[5] [*March* 1743/4]

Egerton 1946

I am sorry to meet you with so bad an account of myself, who should otherwise with Joy have flown to the Interview.[6] I am too ill to be in town, and within this week so much worse, as to make my Journy thither at present impracticable, even if there were no Proclamation in my way.[7] I left the Town, in a decent Compliance to that; but this Additional Prohibition,[8] from the Highest of all Powers, I must bow to without murmuring. I wish to see you here. Mr Allen comes not till the 16th & you'l probably chuse to be in Town chiefly, while he is there. I receivd yours just now, & I write to hinder Bowyer[9] from

[1] Bolingbroke.

[2] A very difficult letter to place. At the beginning of March Pope was in 1744 repeatedly anxious to see Warburton before Allen arrived. If the letter belongs in Mar. 1744, it must be written about Sunday the 4th, and the Proclamation is 'forgotten'. In 1744 only in March were Allen and Warburton in London at the same time.

[3] Presumably Pope was not able to make this journey to Town since on 26 Mar. he writes Richardson that he has not been out of the house for a month.

[4] The address means that Pope is writing on the cover of an old letter addressed to himself. The addressee is most likely Bowyer, but that of course is also uncertain.

[5] Printed by Warburton, 1751. He prints as date 'April 1744'; but the text indicates that it is written before the 16th of March when Allen is expected. It is the last letter from Pope printed by Warburton, and he ends with the footnote: 'He died May 30. following.'

[6] Warburton has just arrived in London, evidently.

[7] The Proclamation, because of the expected invasion, ordered Catholics to stay ten miles from London.

[8] The additional prohibition of ill health.

[9] For 'Bowyer' Warburton printed merely a dash.

printing the Comment on the Use of Riches too hastily, since what you write me, intending to have forwarded it otherwise, that you might revise it during your stay. Indeed my present weakness will make me less & less capable of any thing. I hope at least, to now at first,[1] see you for a day or two, here at Twitnam, and concert measures, how to injoy, for the future,[2] what I can of your Friendship. I am with Sincerity | Dear Sir Affectionately Yours. | A Pope.

*POPE *to* WARBURTON[3] [8 *March* 1743/4]

Egerton 1946

I hope by what Mr Hooke says, that you are tolerable well. If it be not dangerous or ill conveniant any way, I wish you was here before Mr Allen comes. Something has happend which make[s] me wish we could Settle a poynt relating to the Commentary forthwith. The Twickenham Coach sets out from the White Horse Inn in Fleet Street at two in the afternone. I am faithfully Yours, and better then I was, but being in bed Imploy another hand.[4] | A. Pope

Thursday Six a Clock

*POPE *to* WARBURTON[5] [*c.* 12 *March* 1743/4]

Egerton 1946

Munday

I hoped to see you on Friday, but receivd a Letter from Bath within 3 hours of dinner time to tell me our Friend had been ill. and could not set out as he intended. It was too late to acquaint you, but perhaps you had the same Information, or else (which I should be more glad of) have been ingaged by Lord Bathurst to Lord Carteret This is just to tell you Mr Allen comes next Thursday. I am most Faithfully | Yours. | A. Pope

Lord Bolingbroke dines here to morrow, if you can meet him do & stay till Thursday.

[1] Pope added 'now at first' in the right-hand margin. Warburton corrected the text to 'I hope at least, now at first, to see you'. Originally Pope wrote, 'I hope to see you'.

[2] Again Pope adds in the margin 'for the future'.

[3] Pope writes on a Thursday before the 16th, when he expected Allen. This could be either the 8th or the 15th, but there is another note to Warburton written, apparently, early in the following week, that makes this one seem to fall on the 8th.

[4] Normally during these weeks Pope did not need an amanuensis: the note is doubtless written in haste after he is in bed, and hence dictated.

[5] This follows the note dated [8 March]. Pope had hoped to see Warburton on Friday the 9th, but ill health (?) prevented Warburton from coming. Pope now writes early in the following week to announce the postponement of Allen's arrival, and to express the hope that Warburton will come 'tomorrow' and dine at Twickenham with Bolingbroke.

*POPE *to* FORTESCUE[1] 15 *March* [1743/4]

The Pierpont Morgan Library

Having been very ill my self, & confined to my Chamber at Twitnam for these last 3 weeks, with Doctors, Surgeons & Apothecarys for an inveterate Asthma; I was never able to see you, nor had Spirits, to send to trouble any Friend to come to me in that Condition. It is but within 3 days I have been at all better, & therfore I sent yesterday to you, when my Waterman brings word of your Loss of your Sister[2] which I am heartily sorry for, never having heard she was in a worse State than when last I saw you, which tho bad, I did not apprehend to be mortal. God knows whether it is not better, for people of any tenderness of heart, to lead the way themselves, than to see all they love go before them. It's a thought that I've often had within this year or two, & makes me Easier as to my own ill health, every day.

God give you the best Comfort under this, which I know you enough to know must be more an Affliction to you than to any Ordinary Relation how near soever, in this world of ours. If you are or shall be at Richmond pray call upon me, I shall be here I think, tho Dr Burton would have me to his own house: Nor dare I remove while this cold Weather lasts. On Thursday[3] I shall see Mr Allen in his way from Bath. Any other Friend comes only by chance, & to most I shall if possible, be denyed. Dear Sir, be as resignd as you can, and may you live as long as Life is a blessing! I am faithfully Yours, while I live, but God forbid it should be too long! | A. Pope.

Twitnam. March 15.

Endorsement (by Fortescue): Mr Pope | Mar. 15. 1743/4

THE COUNTESS *to* THE EARL OF ORRERY[4] 19 *March* 1743/4

Harvard University

EXCERPT

An ugly accident has happened, poor Bounc is bit by a Mad Dog: Fly they tell me tho' she was in the Court at the same time has

1 Lacking an address, this letter has been thought to be to Charles Ford, but there can be no doubt that it is to Fortescue. The endorsement is characteristically his, and the mention of his sister's death confirms such a direction.

2 In Nichols, *Illust.*, iv. 394, is printed a letter of Sir John Willes that says: 'The Master of the Rolls [Fortescue] has lost his sister Grace, who was an exceeding good woman; and he is very much afflicted.' The letter is dated 20 Mar. 1743[4].

3 That is, on the 22nd.

4 The question of Pope's dogs has been treated by Mr. Ault (*New Light*, pp. 337–50), and this excerpt indicates the fate of the last Bounce. (Lady Orrery in more than one letter economizes on the final letter of the dog's name.) The Bounce of *Bounce to Fop* was, as Mr. Ault was aware, a bitch. This present Bounce is of the opposite sex. He had been sent to

escaped, I have had them both drenched by Doctor Tallow, Bounc is tied up, and till you arrive or pass some sentance upon him I shall keep him Confined: it was Yesterday morning the thing happened, all the other Dogs were locked up by good fortune, for I heard the Mad Dog about the house all the Night. he has bit Farmer Hitchcocks Dog, and one more at the Pound, where he was killed. he met Will Lewis, grouled at him, but as the Welshman had the prudence to step out of the Path, he escaped the invenomed bite. Pray get from Bale the true Receipey of Dr Mead, least any mischief should proceed, either from this Dog, or those he has bitten which may be God knows how great a Number.

*POPE *to* HUGH BETHEL

19 *March* [1743/4]

Egerton 1948

I am very Sollicitous to know how you proceed in your health, & these inveterate North Easterly Winds give me much apprehension for yours, as they very greatly affect mine. Within these 3 weeks I have been excessive ill. The Asthma in every Symptom increasd, with a Swelling in my legs & a low fever. I have been so long & yet am confind to my chamber at Twitnam & the whole business of my two Servants night & day to attend me. Dr Burton is very watchful over me, he changd the warm Pills into a cooler regimen. I drink no wine, & take scarce any meat. Asses milk twice a day. My only Medcines are Millepedes & Garlick, & Horehound Tea. He is against crude Quicksilver till he is sure there is no fever, but prescribes Alkalizd Mercury in 5 pills a day: & proposes an Issue, which I fear may drain & waste me too much, it can't be imagind how weak I am, & how unable to move, or walk, or use any Exercise, but going in a Coach, for which the Weather is yet too cold. These are all discouraging things, to cure me of buying Houses, so I've determind not to purchace this, which will cost me 1200 ll & instead of it to lay out 3 upon a cheap one in London, seated in an airy high place.[1] If I live but 5 months I shall never be able to live about, as I us'd, in other peoples houses, but quite at Ease, to keep my own hours, & with my own Servants: and if I don't live there, it will do for a Friend, which Twitnam would not suit at all.

Marston in July 1742, and in a letter of Lady Orrery's to her husband (23 May 1743: preserved at Harvard), she remarks that 'Lion . . . and Brother Bounc draw the Boy [Edmund, her son, b. Nov. 1742] all round the Gardens, and he looks like a little Bacchus drawn by his Tigars'. For Pope's comment on the fate of this last Bounce, see his letter to Lord Orrery, 10 Apr. 1744.

[1] Pope was purchasing the lease on the house in Berkeley Row (or Street), 'the last house on the end next Berkeley Square', but had not completed the purchase before he died. It was completed by Martha Blount, his residuary legatee, who lived there from about this time until her death in 1763. See Carruthers (1857), pp. 402, 458, 464.

Give me leave therfore to pay in to your Brother what I don't want of the sum I drew upon him by your kind order.—I told you in my last how very welcome was your kind present of your Picture which he transmitted very safe. The last thing I did before I was confind, was to sit the first time to Mr Kent, for you: It wants but one sitting more, & pray tell me, where, or with whom it shall be left for you?

Now I have said a great deal, all I could, of my own State, pray be as particular as to yours. I every morning & night see you in my Bed-chamber & think of you: nothing can be more resembling, but I wish your Complexion be in reality as healthy. Dear Sir, if you are not worse, do not let me wait long for the Comfort of knowing it, tho you imploy any hand, & spare your own Eyes. Above all, what is your Scheme, as to Coming to London, & when? Me you cannot miss; and we may truly say of each other, that we shall be Friends to the last Breath. Pray remember me to Mr Moyser. | Ever yours | A. Pope

Twitnam | March 19th

I must desire you to say nothing of what I tell you concerning my purchase of the House in town, which is done in anothers name.

*POPE *to* ALLEN[1] [21 *March* 1743/4]

Egerton 1947

I am very sorry to learn from Mr Hook how ill Mrs Allen has been; and I fear is, if What he also tells me be true, that she will not be persuaded to let blood. I don't know a more Vexatious and painful Anxiety, than when those we love are obstinate against their own Good, & we so tender of them, as not to be able to insist with them to consult it. I feel with you on this Circumstance; pray tell Her so, & bid her not let me think her, an unreasonable Woman. I heartily hope however She'l escape well, & come & insult over us at Twitnam at the end of the week. Pray are you not the worse for your Journey? God bless you in all your Ways. | Yours | A. Pope

A Line this days post will come to me by nine to morrow.

Address: To Ralph Allen Esqr at | Mrs Van Elson's in | Henrietta Street | Covent garden | London.

Postmark: (illegible)

[1] The date is doubtfully based upon a blurred postmark, which is taken as 22 MR. The 22 is clear; the MR is so blurred as to resemble NO or perhaps something else. On 22 and 23 Mar. (Good Friday), so Pope wrote to Martha Blount on Easter Sunday, the Allens visited Pope at Twickenham. A letter postmarked 22 MR would hardly reach Allen before his arrival at Pope's house, but it is not necessary perhaps that this letter should reach Allen before he started.

POPE *to* MARTHA BLOUNT[1] [25 *March* 1744]

Mapledurham

Dear Madam,—Writing is become very painful to me, if I would write a Letter of any Length. In Bed, or sitting, it hurts my breast, & in the afternoon I can do nothing, still less by Candlelight. I would else tell you evry thing that past between Mr Allen & me. He proposd to have stayd only to dinner, but recollecting the next day was Good friday, he said he would take a bed here & fast with me. The next morning I desird him to come into my room before I rose, & opend myself very freely upon the Subject, requiring the same Unreserve on his part. I told him what I thought of Mrs A.'s conduct to me before you came, & both hers and his after: He did pretty much what you expected, utterly denyd any Unkindness or Coolness, & protested his utmost desire, and answerd for hers, to have pleasd you. layd it all upon the *mutual dissatisfaction* between you & her, & hopd I would not be alterd toward him by any *misrepresentation* you might make, not that he bileived you would tell an untruth, but that you saw things in a mistaken light. I very strongly told him you never made any such, nor if he considerd, was it possible, since all that had past I saw with my own Eyes, & heard with my own Ears. I told him I did not impute the Unkindness shown me in behaving so coldly, to Him originally but to Mrs A. & fairly told I suspected it to have proceeded from some Jealousy she had, of some designs we had upon his House at Hampton, & confirmd it by the Reports I had heard of it from several hands. But he denyd this utterly too. I prest then that She must have had some very unjust & bad thing suggested to her against you; but he assurd me it all rested upon a *mutual Misunderstanding* between you two, which appear'd in 2 or 3 days, & which he spoke to his wife about but found he could not make her at all Easy in; & that he never in his whole life was so sorry at any disappointment. I said much more, being opener than I intended at first; but finding him own nothing, but stick to this; I turnd to make slighter of it, & told him he should not see my Behavior alterd to Mrs A. so much as hers had been to me, (which he declard he did not see) and that I could answer for it, Mrs Blount was never likely to take any notice of the whole so far from misrepresenting any particular.

There were some other particulars which I may recollect, or tell

[1] The date comes from the subscription of 'Easter Day'. The letter is both physically and psychologically difficult for Pope. He has gone much farther towards reconciliation with the Allens than he finds it diplomatic to confess to Martha. Whether the difficulty arose over Allen's refusal to lend the manor-house at Bathampton to Pope and George Arbuthnot or from Allen's disinclination to send the mayor's coach (with Miss Blount) to the 'mass house', the heat of the quarrel seems to have affected the ladies more than it did Pope and Allen—though evidently they had been estranged.

when we meet—I thought her Behavior a little shy, but in mine, I did my very best to show I was quite unconcernd what it was. He parted, inviting himself to come again at his return in a fortnight. He has been very ill, & looks so. I don't intend to see them in town. But God knows whether I shall see any body there, for Cheselden is going to Bath next Munday, with whom at Chelsea I thought to lodge, & so get to you in a morning.

My own Condition is much at one, & to save writing to you the particulars, which I know you desire to be apprizd of, I inclose my Letter to the Doctor.

I assure you I don't think half so much what will become of me, as of You; and when I grow worst, I find the anxiety for you doubled. Would to God you would Quicken your haste to settle, by reflecting what a pleasure it would be to me, just to see it, and to see you at ease; & then I could contentedly leave you to the Providence of God, in this Life, & resign my Self to it in the other! I have little to say to you when we meet. but I love you upon unalterable Principles, which makes me feel my heart the same to you as if I saw you every hour. adieu

Easter day.

pray give my Services to Lady Gerard, & pray get me some answer to Dr King, or it will cost me a Letter of Excuse to have delayd it so long.

I do not understand, by your note nor by Mrs Arb.'s[1] whether you think of coming hither to morrow? or when. Mr Murray's depends on his recovery which is uncertain, & Lord Bolingb. the End of the Week

HUGH BETHEL *to* POPE 25 *March* 1744.

Elwin–Courthope, ix. 161

Beswick, the 25 March, 1744.

I hope I need not tell you it gave me no small pleasure the account I received of your amendment, which I pray God continue, and I am glad you did not write to me sooner. I have heard of several instances where bleeding has given immediate relief, and it did so to me once or twice formerly; but of late it has failed me. Dr. Cheyne was of Mr. Cheselden's opinion, that it might be frequently repeated with safety, for he advised me to take four or five ounces every full moon. Looking over some papers I met with the prescription of Dr. Burton's pills, which upon comparing I find to be the same with the pills of squills of the Edinburgh Dispensatory, which Cheyne advised me to, but they have not Assafœtid., Arum, Diagred. and Sulph, as they have ordered

[1] Anne Arbuthnot's.

them for you, and are not therefore so healing, and if you told them of it, they probably would make some alteration in that respect. As they are so earnest with you to go on with them, and have great experience, I would persevere a little longer, though, to speak truth, three months is a fair trial. I found formerly good by a spoonful of gas of sulphur in a glass of water. I think you ventured to Twitnam too soon, where you must be lonely, and that it would have been more comfortable to have been in town nearer your friends and advice. Every one that lives in the world any time will meet with some of the disagreeablenesses you mention, and the best way not to be disappointed is to expect little: but that is thinking ill of mankind, and those that mean well are apt still to go on in being deceived. I am sorry you are likely to lose Lord Bo. so soon, I was in hopes he had been come to stay. When I have a good day I travel fast towards you, at other times I know not how I shall compass it. I have been but indifferent since my last, but am now better again. Like you, catching the least cold throws me quite down.

The picture I ordered to be sent you was done by a painter at Rome, who was reckoned to hit a likeness the best of any body there. I remembered your having your friend Mr. Digby drawn after his death, and as I had then little reason to expect to return to England, I thought I would save you that trouble if you should be so minded. I have got a copy here of that I like best of those I have seen of you—Sir God. Kneller's. Vanloe's I never saw, but I much question if I should like it better. I saw Colonel Moyser yesterday, who enquired after you, and desired his compliments to you, as does Mr. Key, who is now with me. I am sorry to hear Mrs. P. Blount has had such bad colds. Pray tell her from me nothing will answer the neglect of her health. My compliments to her and Lord Bo. Thus far I had writ when I received the disagreeable account of your relapse. Bleeding gave you a very short respite. You are too thin and weak for an issue, and it would be very painfull to you. Lord Shel.,[1] who has more flesh than you, was obliged to dry them up, upon that account, and, I believe, by Dr. Mead's advice. I had one formerly, but found no good by it. Asses' milk is good if it do not increase phlegm. Alkalized mercury is only crude quicksilver with crabs' eyes and in case of a fever I should think the same objection is ******[2] But last night I slept well, which has recruited me, and I am much better this morning. If I am able I would go to town about May or June, but as yet I am confined to my room. Living or dying believe me, yours affectionately.

I have heard of a great cure one Dr. Thompson[3] has made upon Sir John Eyles, who had a violent asthma.

[1] Shelburne (almost certainly). [2] The page was torn away at this point.—Elwin.

[3] Presently Pope sought the advice and regimen of Dr. Thompson, who is thought not to have been helpful.

POPE *to* JONATHAN RICHARDSON[1] 26 *March* 1744

The St. James's Chronicle, 13 July 1776

You had seen me had I been well; ill News I did not care to tell you, and I have not been abroad this Month, not out of my Chamber, nor able to see any but Nurses. My Asthma seems immoveable, but I am something easier. God preserve you.

Yours ever, | A. Pope.

POPE *to* SLINGSBY BETHEL 26 *March* 1744

Sotheby's Archbishop Tennison Sale, 1 July 1861, lot 122

[A letter sending £200, asking for his account and speaking of his (no doubt last) illness in these terms: 'If anything brings you near Richmond [Pope was then at Twickenham] I beg you will call upon me, who shall be confined at home yet a while longer, I fear.']

POPE *to* LORDS MARCHMONT *and* BOLINGBROKE [26 *March* 1744]

Arthur A. Houghton, Jr.

Easter Munday

My dear Lords,—When I see a finer Day, or feel a livelyer hour, I find my thoughts carried to you, with whom & for whom chiefly I desire to live. I am a little revived to day, & hope to be more so by the end of the week, since I think that was the Time you gave me hopes you would pass a day or 2 here. Mr Murray by that time, or sooner if he can, will meet you. I hope Lord Bolingbroke has settled that with him in Town.

Mr Warburton is very desirous to wait on you both. If he comes to Battersea in a morning, pray furnish him with my chaise to come on hither, and let the chaise be left here, of whose earthly part I shall make use in my garden, tho not of its aquatic. My faithful services wait on Lady Marchmont.

Address:[2] To | The Right Honle the Earle | of Marchmount | Baterse

POPE *to* THE EARL OF ORRERY 30 *March* 1744

The Pierpont Morgan Library

March 30. 1744

My dear Lord,—Nothing could be kinder than your early thought of me, at a time when, your Mind was full (I am sure) of the Joy of

[1] Roscoe (1824), i. 549, prints from the original, but modernizes the text in typography. Verbally, the *Chronicle* text is identical with Roscoe's.

[2] Although the letter is written in a steady rapid hand, it is unsigned, and the address was written by someone other than Pope.

escaping from London to my Lady & Marston. I should be sorry even your affection for me should give you a thought, that might lessen or cloud, tho but for a moment, your perfect Enjoyments there. And it is with an addition to my happiness, that I can tell you News that will please you of my self: that I am less languid, & breathe something easier than when I saw you. I have taken the air twice, & can bear a chariot very well. I am going this minuit to chiswick, not to lye abroad, which I dare not, but to dine by myself before their hour & return before Evening. I shall there & every where, proclaim Your great Goodness to me, which I shall feel while I live. My Entire Services to Lady Or. Know me for ever Yours | A. Pope

Address: To the Right Hon: the | Earl of Orrery, at Marston, | near | Froome | Somersetshire

Endorsement (in Orrery's hand): Mr Pope. | March 30. | 1744.

*POPE *to* BOWYER[1] [*March or April*, 1744]

Egerton 1946

Mr Bowyer, I had this sheet sent before, as if it were printed off, but these Corrections of Mr Warburton's were not in it. I therfore return it you.

Pray tell Mr W. he will find Lord B. here, I believe, on Sunday, or Munday.

POPE *to* HUGH BETHEL[2] [*April* 1744]

Roscoe, ix (1824), 267–8

My Dear Friend,—I continue ill, and have been the worse for the same northerly winds that have affected you so much. This day they are getting into another quarter, and I hope will continue out of the bad one. I have had the bishop's book[3] as a present, and have read it with a good deal of pleasure; but my own doctors having disagreed with your Yorkshire Dr. Thomson, on the use of waters in a dropsical asthma, I am at present confined only to gum ammoniac, sal volatile, and sena, in small quantities, and to take comfortable things, rather than much physic. I have severely suffered, but am obliged to your

[1] The letter is obviously written after Warburton's arrival in London in early March and before his hostile encounter with Bolingbroke, who is 'Lord B.'

[2] Roscoe notes that 'In this letter Pope has been obliged to have recourse to the pen of a friend'.

[3] Bishop Berkeley's *Philosophical Reflections and Enquiries concerning the Virtues of Tar-water* was published early in April and became immediately the talk of all readers. Possibly Pope as an old friend received an advance copy.

brother for the wine, which was very good. I long to see you, whenever you can come. I am utterly unable to come to you. I am now so weak that I can hardly read or write at present, but shall as soon as I can. I feel all my friendship for all my friends as strongly as ever, and for you as much as any. Heaven preserve you! | A. Pope.

*POPE *to* WARBURTON[1] [? 5 *or* 12 *April* 1744]

Egerton 1946

Thursday.

I am excessive concernd at your Illness, pray give me a speedy account how you are? Surely it would be very wrong-judgd to go out of Town in a month at soonest, while the Circle of your acquaintance might be enlargd, & more of your Wellwishers of course would arise, to form a party on your side. So reasonable a Man as Mr Allen, sure would never, (if this were suggested by you to him as the Opinion of your Friends) desire to sacrifice all other Considerations to his own particular pleasure, in enjoying your Company to himself: which might be as well indulg'd him a month or two hence. Pray tell him this from me, & I am very certain he will be the first to forward & persuade your Stay.

I am something better, & if I can possibly, will get to Chiselden's & Battersea for 2 nights, having an Operation to go thro under him, within these 3 days. It's quite a Grief to me that I can['t] go to Town to see Mr Allen. Adieu. Pray send me the Epistle on Women in Manuscript &c.

Address:[2] To the Revd Mr Warburton | at ~~Mr Bowyer's~~ Mr Van Elson's in Henrietta Street | Covent Garden | The Sheet not come back.

*POPE *to* WARBURTON [? *April* 1744]

Egerton 1946

Twitnam, | Saturday Evening.

I hope you are quite well again, I am much as when we parted. Lord Bolingbroke I saw yesterday. He will be glad to see you to morrow at Battersea as early as you will; but on Munday he goes upon business to London. On Wednesday he comes hither, & stays some days with

[1] The two Thursdays bracketed as date are those on which Allen would still be in London. Evidently Warburton is considering an early departure from London with Allen, and Pope here tries to deter him from it.

[2] Pope addressed the letter to Bowyer's place of business (sent by his own waterman, one judges), and Bowyer crossed out the address, and sent the letter on, not to Warburton's usual lodging but to the house where the Allens were lodged. See the address on Pope to Allen [21 Mar. 1743/4].

me; pray therfore come to us on Wednesday or Thursday. I have a Bed for you, as long as you will use it. Mr Hook is here & has been very ill some days. On Tuesday I am ingaged. I have no thoughts of being able to go near London or Chelsea, till the End of next week: so intreat you to give us what Time you can in the Country. Dear Sir pray assure Mr Murray of my true affections, & how kindly I take the Love he shows my Friends.

I am Ever Yours. | A. Pope

PS. I have just run over the Second Epistle from Bowyer. I wish you could add a Note at the very End of it, to observe the authors Tenderness in using no *living Examples* or *real Names* of any one of the softer Sex, tho so free with those of his own in all his other satyrs.

and

a Note on —half your Parents simple Prayr,
gave *Beauty* but refused *Wealth.*

if you think it worth one)[1]

Address: To | the Revd Mr Warburton | at Mrs Johnson's in | Warwick Court.

*POPE *to* FORTESCUE[2] [? 7 *or* 14 *April* 1744]

The Pierpont Morgan Library

It happens that I must be abroad all to morrow, & Munday, lye at Mr Cheseldens, for an Experiment he is to try upon me. But my House & Garden you may be sure [are] at yours & Mr Harries[3] Service. I shall return on Tuesday, God willing, & hope to find you. Mr Sollicitor sends you his Services, & is better: I am rather so than otherwise, & in all States | Sincerely Yours | A. Pope

Address: To the Master of the Rolls.[4]

[1] In the quarto edition presently to be suppressed by Pope's executors no such notes appear. Pope's request perhaps came too late. In Warburton's 1751 edition of the *Works* he added notes saying that in the first edition of the poem Pope 'said, that *no one character in it was drawn from the life*. The Public believed him on his word, and expressed little curiosity about a Satire in which there was nothing personal' (*Works*, iii. 193 n.). At the end of the poem Warburton commented in such a way as to stress the fact that the complimentary portrait there was not to be 'mistaken for any of his acquaintance'. Thus Warburton evened scores with Miss Blount, to whom of course it was addressed.

[2] Hypothetically placed after the 'Thursday' letter to Warburton. This seems to be written on a Saturday. Murray (Mr. Sollicitor) has been ill, but is now (?) at Twickenham.

[3] The name is obscurely written: it may be a spelling for 'Harris's' or (since the initial capital warrants it) for 'Norris's'. The mention of the garden being at their service suggests the possibility of the engraver John Harris coming to make sketches.

[4] Fortescue became Master of the Rolls 5 Nov. 1741.

*POPE *to* ALLEN[1] [? 9 *April* 1744]

Egerton 1947

Munday, | morning

It is with reall Concern I send to tell you that I am not Master of my House to day; Nor able (as I intended tho I did not tell You so) to come & meet & dine with Yourself & Mrs Allen on the road. I am so truly Yours, that I shall seldom repeat that Truth: You are always to know it. and She has my Constant best Wishes, & Esteem, Let me hear when you are safe at home, happy there you will always be, I doubt not. God grant You both, health. & remember me affectionatly to Mr Hooke | Adieu

POPE *to* THE EARL OF ORRERY[2] 10 *April* [1744]

The Pierpont Morgan Library

Twitenham Apr. 10. | 1744

My Lord,—Your Letters are things that deserve a better name than Letters; they are Emanations of the best Mind, & the kindest Heart in nature, and lessen the Force of all Illness or Pain, which is not so great an Evil, as the knowledge of so True & warm a Friend is a Good, infinitely superior to it. Lord Boyle[3] was the bearer, but (what gave me a great disappointment, & was the Only one I ever receivd from any of your Family) He would not stay to come in. But the first day I can get to Town, I will be revengd upon him by going & dining with him.

I dread to enquire into the particulars of the Fate of Bounce, Perhaps you conceald them, as Heav'n often does Unhappy Events, in pity to the Survivors, or not to hasten on my End by Sorrow. I doubt not how much Bounce was lamented: They might say as the Athenians did to Arcite, in Chaucer.

Ah Arcite! gentle Knight! why would'st thou die,
When thou had'st Gold enough, and Emilye?[4]

Ah Bounce! ah gentle Beast! why wouldst thou dye,
When thou hadst Meat enough, and Orrery?

For what in nature could Bounce want, at Marston? What shoud any one, Man or Beast, want there, but to live always under the benigne

[1] The date is hypothetical. After Allen's Good Friday visit to Pope, the poet on a Thursday (here dated 5 or 12 Apr.) in a letter to Warburton regrets that he cannot go to London to see the Allens. At the time of this letter the Allens seem to be starting for Widcombe, and Pope had hoped to meet them 'on the road' for a farewell dinner. He cannot have them at Twickenham. Presumably this Monday would be 9 or 16 Apr. In his Easter letter to Martha Blount Pope says of Allen's Good Friday visit, 'He parted, inviting himself to come again at his return in a fortnight.' So Monday, 9 Apr., seems a plausible date for this letter.

[2] The year in the superscription is added by Lord Orrery.

[3] Charles, son and heir of Lord Orrery, at this time fifteen years old.

[4] Pope quotes from a faulty memory Chaucer's *Knight's Tale*, ll. 2835–6. The first line is practically his own: it is not Dryden's adaptation.

Influence of Lady Orrery? I could dye more resign'd any where else: I should not be so patient to suffer there, as among those people here, who are less hurt by anothers Suffering, & before whom therfore I make no conscience to complain, nay to roar, or be as peevish as the devil.[1] But I thank God my days are more supportable something, than when I saw your Lordship for my Nights are better. Tho the grand Cause of all, the Shortness, & sometimes almost Stoppage of breath, continue without any alteration from the first, notwithstanding the heap of Medicines so constantly taken. And the Effect of my Confinement & utter Inability to use Exercise, make me so excessive weak of Limb & Nerve, that my Legs swell, & I have convulsive Catchings all over my body. All I can do is to ride an hour or two in a chariot, in very warm days, of which I have had but few.—Pray tell me in return for this sad Story, the Joys you & Lady Orrery are partakers of; which let them be ever so many I am sure I heartily wish doubled upon Yourselves, and continued to all your Posterity. I am, My dear Lord, | Entirely Yours: A. Pope

Address: To the Earl of Orrery, | at Marston, | near Froom. | Somersetshire
Postmark: 10/AP
Endorsement (by Orrery): Mr Pope, | April 10. | 1744.

*POPE *to* WARBURTON [11 *or* 18 *April* 1744]

Egerton 1946

Lord Bolingbroke is not well, & sent me word just now when I expected him before dinner, that he must go to advise with some Physicians to London, till after which he could not venture hither. I send you the first notice. You know how glad I am of all your Time, yet how desirous you should spend it better in your own Service. To act friendlily to Me, is to act so to yourself. do but write me a line from Bowyer's, & Ill send for it to morrow: Or if you call on Lord Bolingbroke in the Evening at Mr Chetwynds in Dover street, *sending in your Name* before You, or before ten in the morning, you'l find his Lordship there. I have not yet heard (to my Anxiety) of Mr Allen's safe Return home. Pray tell me if you have? I am Ever Yours. | A. Pope.

Wensday.

Address: To the Revd Mr War|burton at Mrs Johnsons | in Warwick Court | Holborne.

[1] Pope's picture of himself as an invalid may be put alongside the letter of Lord Orrery to Mallet (21 Apr. 1744), of which Elwin prints the following excerpt (viii. 519): 'Lady Orrery goes on with her usual spirits and good humour. We are never melancholy but when we think of poor Mr. Pope, whose pains and sufferings, excessive as they were, have been borne with surprising constancy and evenness of mind. I own I am in great fears for him. Release me from them if possible.'

*POPE *to* ALLEN[1] 20 *April* [1744]

Egerton 1947

Twick'nham | Apr: 20.

I heartily rejoice in your Safe Return & that the Wett Weather had no ill Effect on your Colds. As to my State, I escapd not so well, that Change having brought me rather worse than when we parted: so much that I have not yet been able to enjoy the benefit of any Air or Exercise, which weakens me fast. You shall hear of any material Alteration in me, the little Circumstances could only trouble not satisfy you: But this be assurd no Alterations of any other kind will ever befall me in respect to you, who have been, & shall ever be, Just to your Merit & Friendship. Let Mrs Allen know this, & that every day which adds to your joint happiness will alleviate the worst of my own days.

Dear Sir Yours Ever | faithfully | A. Pope

I expect Mr Warburton to night.

Address: To Ralph Allen Esq | at Widcomb: | Bath.

Postmark: 20/AP

Endorsement (in Allen's hand): From Mr Pope [erasure] | April 2d | 1744.

Notes: No [blot] | 3 letters with | the newes and | a parcell. | Will went away at | ½ a hour after 8 a clock

BOLINGBROKE *to* MARCHMONT[2] [1744]

1831 (*Marchmont Papers*, ii. 327)

Friday

My dear Lord,—I thank you for yours, which I have communicated to my solicitor, and expect his answer. In all events, I will be at Twickenham on Sunday morning; and, I confess, I should be for letting Ward[3] see Pope, and prescribe to him. Grevenkop will tell you what news and rumors are about. The crisis is terrible—much to be feared—little to be hoped. God help us!

1 Allen endorses the letter as of 2 Apr.; but both Pope and the postmark clearly register '20'.

2 As printed heretofore this letter has been placed early in the year; but the 'crisis' (fear of invasion) developed in February, and Pope's need of Ward may indicate a condition approaching desperation.

3 Pope mentions Dr. Joshua Ward in his Imitation of Horace, Book I, Epistle vi (line 56), and in the Imitation of the First Epistle of the Second Book, line 182. To the latter mention he appended the note: 'A famous Empirick, whose Pill and Drop had several surprizing effects, and were one of the principal subjects of Writing and Conversation at this time.'—1737. Pope's mentions were not caustic, but there is no evidence that Ward was called in on Pope's case. See *DNB*.

*POPE *to* WARBURTON[1] [*April* 1744]

Egerton 1946

Sunday afternoon | Twitenham

My Lord B.[2] is now come hither for 2 or 3 days. he wishes much for your meeting, & indeed I am sorry you could take no opportunity in all this time. I think he may leave me about Thursday, perhaps Wensday, therfore the sooner we see you, the better. There is the Hampton Coach at Charing cross, which sets out at 8 a clock every morning. which had I known, I had told you. It does not omit to come, ev'n on Sundays, it seems. I hope you are perfectly well. I have been kept in constant purging these 3 days, & I think the better for it, tho a little the weaker. Writing becomes difficult to me, & indeed what matter? when a few words are enough to Express all Truth, & all we know. I know your Merit, & I am most cordially | Your faithful Friend & | hearty Servant | A. Pope

Pray receive for me | ten-pds odd, | of Mr Bowyer.

Address: To the Revd Mr Warburton | at Mrs Johnsons in[3]

*POPE *to* WARBURTON[4] [*April* 1744]

Egerton 1946

Wensday | Night

If the Weather prove inviting enough, I wish I had yours, as my Doctors Company, here to morrow or on Friday. For I have gotten a

[1] The letter is not to be definitely placed. It precedes any meeting of Warburton and Bolingbroke, apparently, and should precede his departure to Bath.

[2] Bolingbroke. It is clear that up to the very last Pope wished to have all his friends about him. *The Quarterly Review*, cxxxix (1875), 385, prints part of a letter from Pope's Cornish friend, Sir John St. Aubyn, to Dr. Borlase, which reads: 'I doubt your friend Mr. Pope can't last long. He sent to desire Lord Oxford and myself to dine with him t'other day, and I thought he would have dy'd then; he has a dropsie which has almost drowned him.'

[3] The rest of the address has been cut away.

[4] On several counts this, though authentic, is an 'improbable' letter. Only in 1744 were Warburton and Bolingbroke possible guests together. In other years they were not in Town at the same time. In 1744 the lesser evil of rheumatism would hardly compete with a terrific asthma in depriving Pope of sleep. In 1744, one surmises, Pope could hardly suppose Warburton would be seeing much of Mrs. Blount, to whom he had been unforgivably discourteous at Prior Park in the preceding summer. We do not know that he had an acquaintance with Bethel's sister, Lady Codrington; but since her ladyship had a house in Bath, that is possible.

If the editor had not long since (before reaching 1744) strained hypothesis to the limit, he might suggest that in the days when Ruffhead had the Allen, Bethel, and Warburton correspondences at his disposal in writing Pope's life, the biographer mixed the letters, and that this really is an earlier letter addressed, possibly in Apr. 1739, to Bethel—who might naturally be asked to give Pope's services to these two ladies. As it stands, one has to place the letter in 1744 at some period when the indomitable urge to go to Town led Pope to suggest dining there with Warburton. But much other evidence of the correspondence indicates that after Warburton reached London in March Pope was obeying the Proclamation against Catholics and staying away—at least as far as Chelsea.

violent Rheumatic pain in my arm & shoulder, which hinders my Rest by night, & much of my Ease by day. I was very much inclind to have venturd to See you &c, to Town, yesterday or to day; but really was afraid of any Encrease to this Pain, which would be more than I could bear. Lord Bol. left me this day, & went alone; he comes agen on Saturday, but that need not hasten you from me by no means. God preserve you sound & well, of Body I mean, for of Mind you will always be so. Adieu. My Services to Lady Codrington & to Mrs Blount.

Believe no man is more | Dear Sir, Yours.

POPE *to* THE EARL OF ORRERY [*c.* 5 *May* 1744]

The Pierpont Morgan Library

My Lord,—I am not so well as I cou'd wish, or as you cou'd wish; but I am well enough yet, with pleasure to enjoy all the good wishes I know you bear me. I have indeed a new Physician;[1] who tells me I shall be grateful to all my friends, & mend apace. He has chang'd the nature of my disease, from an Asthma into a Dropsy; & certain it is, he has drawn from me a great quantity of pure water by stool: & after these evacuations, I am more spirited than I usd to be. I had been under one of them when Lord Boyle was here last. I go abroad almost every day in a chariot; but am very lethargick; yet I remember my Lord & Lady Orrery every day; & shall, dum spiritus hos regit artus.[2] | A. Pope.

Address: To, | The Right Honble | The Earl of Orrery; | at Marston, near Froome; | in | Somersetshire.

Postmark: 5/MA

Endorsement (by Orrery): Mr Pope's Letter not | writ by his own hand: | signed by himself: not | dated received at Marston | May 5th 1744. | No 37. | Ult.[3]

[1] In recent letters to Hugh Bethel Pope mentioned Dr. Thompson. This is the first and only indication that he is Pope's 'new physician'. His excessive addiction to purgation in Pope's case seems to have exhausted what little vigour the poet had left.

[2] *Æneid*, iv. 336.

[3] On a separate leaf Orrery has listed the last letters received from Pope and comments as follows concerning this very last one: 'No 37. Mr Pope's last Letter, signed, but not written, by himself: received at Marston: May 5. 1744. his account of his new Physician Dr Tomson:—(who is said to have hastened his death.). he complains of his being lethargic. concludes with professions of great kindness.—but notwithstanding all the many and high assurances of friendship, gratitude, and affection in these Letters, *he forgot me in his will. Mens curva in corpore curvo.*' Gentlefolk in this century were passionate about being mentioned in the wills of friends. The application of the phrase to Pope's character is of course a commonplace. Folk-lore had long fixed the vulgar error that, according to the proverb, *Distortum vultum sequitur distortio morum*, and the remark is due to folk-lore as much as to Pope's behaviour.

*POPE *to* ALLEN[1] 7 *May* [1744]

Egerton 1947

Chelsea College[2] 7 May 1744

Sir,—I am now not able to express a great part of my good sentiments for you, much less to write, my weakness has encreas'd every day, yet in order to get rid of my disease, I am forc'd to purge; I am following Sir Jno Isles[3] with as much Vigour as my constitution will admit of, and I have the Comfort to find Dr Burton, and Mr Cheselden, do not disaprove, allowing my Asthma to be Hydropical. I communicated Dr Hartleys Prescription, to the Drs Mead, and Burton, but was too ill to go, pray give him my thanks for his kind prescription and likewise to Dr Oliver for another, which I gave to Dr Mead before; there is no end of my kind treatment from the Facultie they are in general the most Amiable Companions, and the best friends as well as the most learned men I know I hope both you and I shall preserve the frienship of all we know. My true Services to You all, & Mrs Allen, and Mr Warburton.[4] I must just set my hand to my heart.

Yours | A. Pope

Endorsement (in Allen's hand): Mr Pope's | Last Letter to | R. Allen | May 7th 1744

THE EARL OF ORRERY *to* MALLET[5] 19 *May* 1744

Elwin–Courthope, viii. 520

Marston, May 19, 1744.

EXCERPT

I will write to you only a few lines, for the subject of my letter is grief and anxiety. What is become of our dear and matchless friend Mr. Pope? My accounts of him have been so various and have alarmed me so much, that I have not a moment's ease when I think of him; and to banish him from my mind is beyond my power or inclination. Pray send me, as speedily as you can, all particulars relating to his state.

MALLET *to* THE EARL OF ORRERY 19 *May* 1744

Elwin–Courthope, viii. 520–2

Strand [near Brentford], May 19, [1744.]

My Lord,—I never was at a loss in what manner to address your

[1] This letter was dictated to an amanuensis, but signed by Pope.

[2] Pope is at Chelsea College (or more properly by its newer name of Hospital), probably for his last treatment there by Cheselden, who was surgeon to the Hospital.

[3] Sir John Eyles (who had been patron to the Abbé Prevost earlier) had been wonderfully helped by Dr. Thompson, as Hugh Bethel told Pope in his letter of 25 Mar.

[4] Warburton has apparently followed the Allens to Prior Park. He returned for Pope's funeral (5 June).

[5] Elwin printed from the original, which the present editor has not seen. Obviously the letter from Mallet that follows cannot be a reply, written on the same day, to this letter from Somerset.

lordship till now. I had flattered myself with the hope of making my sincerest acknowledgments for the very particular kindness of your last letter still more acceptable by an account of our friend Mr. Pope's recovery. Instead of that I now find that I shall only afflict your lordship by what I have to say to him. He still breathes, but cannot be said to live, for he has not the smallest enjoyment of his life, hardly of his reason. I have watched the progress of his distemper with much and anxious attention. After having been treated several months for an asthma by some eminent physicians without the least abatement of that supposed distemper, there comes at last Dr. Thompson, who asserts that his illness is a dropsy of the breast, and that the asthmatic complaint is only a consequence of it. He says too that he can cure him, weak and attenuated as he is. For this end he ordered Mr. Pope several doses of physic, with what judgment I will not say, but they have evacuated him into absolute inanition. His strength, as well as his senses, is, I think, irrecoverably impaired. I staid with him all Friday evening and Saturday without being able to understand a word of what he would have said to me, till towards noon that I had him carried into the garden. There he recovered into some coherence of thought, talked intelligibly and rationally for above an hour, but grew weary, would return into the house, where I left him, without the satisfaction of taking a last farewell of him. I beg pardon, my lord, for this melancholy detail, but it is the overflowing of a heart that long loved and esteemed him as a good man, no less than an excellent writer.

This, perhaps, should not be communicated particularly to Lady Orrery, from whom, in her present condition, all things disagreeable should be kept far. My wife, with her best thanks to her ladyship for the favour lately indulged to her, bids me offer again her real good wishes that she may speedily and safely make your lordship a happy father once more.

Were I writing to a person indifferent to the subject of this letter, I would make an apology for the confused incorrectness of it, but your lordship, I know, will feel and approve what comes from the heart, however rude and disordered. Give me leave to assure your lordship that in every situation of mine I shall be, with truth and attachment, my lord, your most faithful and obedient servant.

MALLET *to* THE EARL OF ORRERY — 1 *June* 1744

Harvard University

At last, my Lord, we have lost that excellent Man! His Person I loved, his Worth I knew, & shall ever cherish his Memory with all the Regard of Esteem, with all the Tenderness of Friendship. In the midst of his extreme Weakness he remembered your Lordship, and charged me with his last good Wishes for your Health and Happiness; that You may long live, and be what you now are. This Commission he delivered to me with so much Earnestness, and Warmth of Affection, that I am sure it will have the same Effect on your Lordship, it has now on me: It brings the Tears afresh into my Eyes.

On Monday last I took my everlasting Farewell of him. He was enough himself to know me, to enquire after Mrs Mallet's Health, and anxiously to hasten his Servant in getting ready my Dinner, because I came late. The same social Kindness, the same friendly Concern for those he loved, even in the minutest Instances, that had distinguished his Heart through Life, were uppermost in his Thoughts to the last.

He dyed on Wednesday,[1] about the Middle of the Night, without a Pang, or a Convulsion, unperceived of those that watched him, who imagined he was only in a sounder Sleep than ordinary.—But I cannot go on. After the Loss of such a Friend, what can I think of but those very few I have left? As the Foremost of that Number, I am importunate with your Lordship to be very careful of what is so valuable to your Family and Country, your Health and Spirits. The uninterrupted Possession of which no Man can wish more sincerely than, | My Lord, | Your most Faithful, and | Obedient Servant | D. Mallet.

Strand. | June 1st—1744.

I had the Honour of both your Lordship's Letters. What Accounts I receive of our Friend's Will, You may expect to know by the first Opportunity.

[1] 30 May.

POSTSCRIPT

From Huntington Library MS. 1271, ff. 518–26: An early and unpublished draft of some of Spence's *Anecdotes* concerning Pope's last days.

Chelsea, May 10–17, 1744.

I am like Socrates, distributing my Morality[1] among my friends, just as I am dying.—(I really had that thought, when I was last at Twit'nam; & look'd upon myself like Phaedo:) Ay, but I can say very little that's wise to you now. Mr. Pope.

One of the things that I have always most wonder'd at is; that there shou'd be any such thing as Human Vanity. I had enough to mortify mine a few days ago; for I lost my mind for a whole day [The Sunday before; May 6.].[2] Ditto.—It was between that & the 10th he had the odd Phaenomenon he complain'd of having; of seeing every thing in the room as thro' a curtain.—(On the 14th) he complain'd of seeing false colours on objects.—(on the 15th) Here am I dying of a Hundred good Symptoms. (To mr L[yttelto]n after Dr Thomson had been saying that his Pulse was very good; &c, &c.)—Ditto. (Like a fine ring of Bells, jangled out of tune. Quoted by Chis[elde]n, from Shakespear.)—The thing that I suffer most by, is that I find that I cant think.—I never was hippish in my whole life.—They are very innocent Loves; like those of Adam & Eve, in Milton: I wonder how a man of so infected a mind as the Regent [of France] cou'd have any taste for such a Book. Ditto. (Of Longus; whom I had brought in my pocket, to read while he was dosing.)

* * * * *

May 19–29, 1744.

The greatest Hero is nothing under a certain State of the Nerves. Ld. Bolingbroke.

There is so much trouble in coming into the World, & so much in going out of it, that tis hardly worth while to be here at all. Ditto.—(His Lp has been in the Vapours himself this last month, tho' he always us'd to laugh at it before; & 'tis that which made him talk in this stile. Hooke.

—His melancholy attitude that morning, the 21st, leaning against Mr Pope's chair, & crying for a quarter of an hour like a child.)

There is no hopes for him here; our only hopes for him must be—Chiselden.—Ld Bolingbroke: Pshaw!

We can only reason from what is: we can reason on actualities, but not on Possibilities. Ld Bolingbroke.

O Great God! What is Man? Ld Bol: (looking on Mr Pope, & repeating it several times, interrupted with Sobs.)

(When I was telling his Lp that Mr Pope on every catching &

[1] The 'death-bed' edition of his four 'Ethic Epistles'.

[2] The phrases in brackets are, throughout, Spence's own annotation.

recovering of his Mind was always saying something kindly of his present and absent friends; & that this in some cases was so surprizing, that His Humanity seem'd to me to have outlasted his Understanding; his Lp said, "It has so!"—& then added,) "I never knew a man, that had a tenderer heart for his particular friends; or a more general friendship, for mankind." Ld Bolingbroke.

I have known him these 30 Years: & value myself more, for that man's Love & Friendship; than—Ditto, (sinking his head, & losing his voice in tears.)

I am so certain of the truth of the Soul's being immortal, that I seem to feel it within me, as it were by Intuition. Mr Pope.

(When Mr Hooke ask'd him, Whether he wou'd not dye as his Father & Mother had done; & whether he shou'd send for a Priest? He said,) "He did not suppose that was essential; but it will look right: & I heartily thank you for putting me in mind of it." Ditto.

The morning that the Priest[1] had given him the Last Sacraments as they call them, he said; "There is nothing that is meritorious, but Virtue, & Friendship, and Friendship indeed is only a part of Virtue." (to Mr Hooke) Ditto.—(When Mr Hooke told this very low to Ld Bolingbroke at Dinner, *he* answer'd aloud, Why to be sure that is the whole Duty of Man!)

The 27th, on speaking of his having so little to leave, he quoted two of his own verses very properly; on his whole life having been divided between Carelessness & Care.[2] (from Mr Hooke).

What's that? pointing up in the air, with a very steddy regard; & then looking down on me, he said with a smile of pleasure, & with the greatest sweetness & complacency: "Twas a Vision."

"Ld have mercy upon us! This is quite an Egyptian Feast!" Miss Arbuthnot (aside to me, on his being brought to the table, when we thought he was dying.)

"Sure Providence does this, to mortify the whole Human Species!" Ld Bolingbroke, (on the same occasion.)

Mr Pope died on the 30th of May, after 11 at Night; but they did not know the exact time; for his Death was so easy, that it was imperceptible to the standers by. May our End be like his!

[1] Huntington Library MS. 1211, in the hand of Edward Bedingfield, the correspondent of Gray and Mason and a member of the Catholic family some of whom were Pope's intimates, is a memorandum that has been found and transcribed for the editor by Professor A. D. McKillop. It reads as follows:

'Edward Pigott, of the order of S. Benedict, Son to Counsellor Pigott, (whose Epitaph Pope composed) gave Pope all the last Sacraments; and said he had Pope's Directions to declare to every body, that Pope was very sorry for every thing he had said or wrote, that was against the Catholick Faith.

'Mr Fleetwood, who informed me of this, had it from Mr Piggott himself.—Edw: Bedingfeld.'

[2] See line 291 of Pope's Imitation of the Second Epistle of the Second Book of Horace.

PRINTED IN
GREAT BRITAIN
AT THE
UNIVERSITY PRESS
OXFORD
BY
CHARLES BATEY
PRINTER
TO THE
UNIVERSITY